Harden's

Best UK 2016 Restaurants

"The UK's most helpful and informative guide"
The Sunday Times

SURVEY DRIVEN REVIEWS OF OVER 2,800 RESTAURANTS

Follow Harden's on Twitter – @hardensbites

ISBN 978-0-9929408-7-4

British Library Cataloguing-in-Publication data: a catalogue record for this book is available from the British Library.

Printed in Britain by Polestar

Research and editorial assistants: Sarah Ashpole, Jamie Cairns, Wayne Tuckfield, Saffy Ellison
Client Relations Manager: Clare Burnage
Assistant editor: Karen Moss
Designers: (text) Paul Smith, (cover) Calverts Coop

Harden's Limited
The Brew, Victoria House, 64 Paul Street, London, EC2A 4NA

Would restaurateurs (and PRs) please address communications to 'Editorial' at the above address, or ideally by email to: editorial@hardens.com The contents of this book are believed correct at the time of printing. Nevertheless, the publisher can accept no responsibility for errors or changes in or omissions from the details given.

THE SUNDAY TIMES

The UK's 100 Best Restaurants

1 Restaurant Sat Bains, Nottingham
2 Midsummer House, Cambridge
3 L'Enclume, Cartmel
4 Casamia, Bristol
5 Restaurant Martin Wishart, Edinburgh
6 Gidleigh Park, Chagford
7 Le Manoir aux Quat' Saisons, Great Milton
8 The Ledbury, London W11
9 The Araki, London W1
10 Harry's Place, Great Gonerby
11 Restaurant Nathan Outlaw, Port Isaac
12 Andrew Fairlie, Gleneagles Hotel, Auchterarder
13 One-O-One, Sheraton Park Tower, London SW1
14 Story, London SE1
15 Waterside Inn, Bray
16 Bubbledogs, Kitchen Table, London W1
17 Raby Hunt, Summerhouse
18 Le Gavroche, London W1
19 Marianne, London W2
20 L'Ortolan, Shinfield
21 Yorke Arms, Ramsgill-in-Nidderdale
22 Fraiche, Oxton
23 21212, Edinburgh
24 Hedone, London W4
25 Hambleton Hall, Hambleton

1
2
MIDSUMMER HOUSE
DANIEL CLIFFORD
3
4

THE SUNDAY TIMES

The UK's 100 Best Restaurants

26 The Peat Inn, Cupar
27 Winteringham Fields, Winteringham
28 Black Swan, Oldstead
29 Llangoed Hall, Llyswen
30 The French Restaurant, Midland Hotel, Manchester
31 The Fat Duck, Bray
32 Hibiscus, London W1
33 The Clove Club, London EC1
34 The Kitchin, Edinburgh
35 Drakes, Ripley
36 Pied à Terre, London W1
37 The Pass Restaurant, South Lodge Hotel, Horsham
38 Mr Underhill's, Ludlow
39 Amberley Castle, Amberley
40 Texture, London W1
41 The Three Chimneys, Dunvegan
42 The Square, London W1
43 The Five Fields, London SW3
44 Fera at Claridge's, Claridge's Hotel, London W1
45 The Dining Room, Whatley Manor, Easton Grey
46 Rasoi, London SW3
47 Yashin, London W8
48 The Harrow at Little Bedwyn, Marlborough
49 Bohemia, The Club Hotel & Spa, Jersey
50 The Boat House, Bangor

THE SUNDAY TIMES

The UK's 100 Best Restaurants

51 André Garrett At Cliveden, Cliveden House, Taplow

52 Fischers at Baslow Hall, Baslow

53 Pétrus, London SW1

54 Purnells, Birmingham

55 The Greenhouse, London W1

56 The Box Tree, Ilkley

57 Gordon Ramsay, London SW3

58 The Latymer, Pennyhill Park Hotel, Bagshot

59 Ametsa with Arzak Instruction, Halkin Hotel, London SW1

60 The Neptune, Old Hunstanton

61 Roux at Parliament Square, RICS, London SW1

62 Typing Room, Town Hall Hotel, London E2

63 Northcote, Langho

64 Stovell's, Chobham

65 Menu Gordon Jones, Bath

66 Simon Radley, The Chester Grosvenor, Chester

67 Sushi Tetsu, London EC1

68 Koffmann's, The Berkeley, London SW1

69 Hakkasan, London W1

70 Cotto, Cambridge

71 Sketch, Lecture Room, London W1

72 Summer Lodge, Evershot

73 Artichoke, Amersham

74 The River Café, London W6

75 Applecross Inn, Applecross

The UK's 100 Best Restaurants

76 Zuma, London SW7
77 Hunan, London SW1
78 James Martin, Manchester
79 Roger Hickman's, Norwich
80 Yauatcha, London W1
81 HKK, London EC2
82 Chez Bruce, London SW17
83 Dinner, Mandarin Oriental, London SW1
84 Kai Mayfair, London W1
85 Roka, London W1
86 Great House, Lavenham
87 Seven Park Place, London SW1
88 Amaya, London SW1
89 Wiltons, London SW1
90 Adam's , Birmingham
91 L'Atelier de Joel Robuchon, London WC2
92 Lords of the Manor, Upper Slaughter
93 Verveine Fishmarket Restaurant, Milford-on-Sea
94 Dinings, London W1
95 The Walnut Tree, Llandewi Skirrid
96 Wedgwood, Edinburgh
97 Lickfold Inn, Lickfold
98 Marcus, The Berkeley, London SW1
99 Bentley's, London W1
100 Benares, London W1

We Brits are dining out more than ever before – eating an incredible eight billion meals out.Alongside our passion for food we've developed a thirst for knowledge, about where our food is from and how it's been produced, so that we can enjoy our meal safe in the knowledge that it isn't at the expense of others.

It's easy to make those choices when shopping for food for home; just look for the labels. You can ensure your basket only contains free-range eggs and Fairtrade coffee. But it's not quite so simple when you go out to eat and quizzing the waiter doesn't make for a relaxing night out...

Food Made Good is here to help all food lovers indulge their passion for dining out without having to check their principles in at the cloakroom. So, whether you're planning a special occasion at one of Harden's Top 100 UK restaurants or want to find the best fish and chips in town, just look for our gold stars on menus, windows and websites. It's the simple and easy way to be reassured that wherever you choose to eat sources its food fabulously, watches its environmental footprint and cares about its local community.

All of the restaurants in the guide with Food Made Good stars have completed the sustainability rating in the last 12 months. Food Made Good is run by the Sustainable Restaurant Association to give people the chance to turn their passion for food into action.

One Star - Good Sustainability
Two Stars - Excellent Sustainability
Three Stars - Exceptional Sustainability

Among the Sustainable Restaurant Awards winners 2015 were:

Daylesford and Captain's Galley – Joint Sustainable Restaurant of the Year.

The Truscott Arms – Sustainable Pub of the Year.

Lussmanns – Sustainable Small Group of the Year.

Arbor, The Green House – Award for Environment.

River Cottage and ODE-dining – Award for Sourcing.

To find out more visit **www.foodmadegood.org**.

CONTENTS

Ratings & prices 12

From the Editors 13

How this book is organised & researched 14

London

Survey results & restaurant scene 16

Directory 34

Indexes 156

Maps 216

UK

Survey results and top scorers 236

Directory 246

Maps 374

Alphabetical index 398

RATINGS & PRICES

Ratings

Our rating system does not tell you – as most guides do – that expensive restaurants are often better than cheap ones! What we do is compare each restaurant's performance – as judged by the average ratings awarded by reporters in the survey – with other similarly-priced restaurants.

This approach has the advantage that it helps you find – whatever your budget for any particular meal – where you will get the best 'bang for your buck'.

The following qualities are assessed:

F — Food
S — Service
A — Ambience

The rating indicates that, ***in comparison with other restaurants in the same price-bracket***, performance is…

5 — Exceptional
4 — Very good
3 — Good
2 — Average
1 — Poor

In the **UK section**, some restaurants are worth a mention but, for some reason (typically low feedback) we do not think a rating is appropriate. These are indicated as follows:

T — Tip

Prices

The price shown for each restaurant is the cost for one (1) person of an average threecourse dinner with half a bottle of house wine and coffee, any cover charge, service and VAT. Lunch is often cheaper. With BYO restaurants, we have assumed that two people share a £7 bottle of off-licence wine.

Telephone number – *all numbers are '020' numbers.*

Map reference – *shown immediately after the telephone number.*

Full postcodes – *for non-group restaurants, the first entry in the 'small print' at the end of each listing, so you can set your sat-nav.*

Website and Twitter – *shown in the small print, where applicable.*

Last orders time – *listed after the website (if applicable); Sunday may be up to 90 minutes earlier.*

Opening hours – *unless otherwise stated, restaurants are open for lunch and dinner seven days a week.*

Credit and debit cards – *unless otherwise stated, Mastercard, Visa, Amex and Maestro are accepted.*

Dress – *where appropriate, the management's preferences concerning patrons' dress are given.*

Special menus – *if we know of a particularly good value set menu we note this (e.g. "set weekday L"), together with its formula price (FP), calculated exactly as in 'Prices' above. Details change, so always check ahead.*

'Rated on Editors' visit' – *indicates ratings have been determined by the Editors personally, based on their visit, rather than derived from the survey.*

SRA Star Rating – *the sustainability index, as calculated by the Sustainable Restaurant Association –* *see page 8 for more information.*

FROM THE EDITORS

Welcome to our 25th anniversary edition of what you users and diners have helped to make the UK's most authoritative restaurant guide.

As ever, Harden's is written 'from the bottom up' based on the results of the survey conducted in late spring 2015. It is completely rewritten each year, with the selection of restaurants based on that unique annual poll of thousands of restaurant-goers, in which you are most welcome to take part. (Further details of this are given overleaf.)

Unlike any other national UK restaurant guide – certainly of a print variety – reviews and ratings in the book are primarily statistically derived and driven from our user-survey. This is a much more direct, and we believe democratic use of user feedback than the processes of some competing publications, particularly those who solicit reader feedback, but where the linkage between such feedback and the reviews and ratings in the guide is much less clear-cut.

The survey methodology is also a very different kettle of fish from the modus operandi of user-review sites such as TripAdvisor. The latter has been put under the spotlight as never before this year with questions raised over the veracity of a huge number of reviews. With the Harden's survey however, because we don't publish the raw reviews supplied by the dining public, but only a summary based on the careful curation of those raw reviews, it is a much harder ballot to stuff. Of course, restaurants do still try to stuff the ballot in their favour – or less often to disadvantage their competitors – but the presence of so many diners who have participated in the survey for many years provides a good sanity check on the veracity of reviews from more recent sign-ups.

This guide includes the full content of our separately-published London guide, as well as coverage of cities, towns and villages across the whole of the UK. We recognise that the result is a guide somewhat skewed to London. We urge readers, though, to think of this extensive London coverage as a bonus rather than a defect. After all, our out-of-London coverage alone exceeds the headline number of reviews in the whole of *The Good Food Guide* including London. Add in our London coverage and there are more than double the number of entries than the rival publication.

It is certainly no longer true, as one could have said as recently as five years ago, that large areas of the UK are pretty much restaurant deserts, devoid of almost anything of interest to the discerning visitor. This ongoing transformation is perhaps most obvious in the great regional centres – even Manchester, a 'second city' which has been a laggard until very recently, seems finally to be getting its act together!

We urge all our readers to help us do even better justice to the restaurant scene outside the capital. If you think your area is under-represented, the answer is largely in your own hands – take part in our annual survey, and make sure your friends do too!

We are very grateful to each of our thousands of reporters, without whose input this guide could not have been written. Many reporters express views about a number of restaurants at some length, knowing full well that – given the concise format of the guide – we can seemingly never 'do justice' to their observations. We must assume that they do so in the confidence that the short – and we hope snappy – summaries we produce are as fair and well-informed as possible.

You, the reader, must judge – restaurant guides are not works of literature, and should be assessed on the basis of utility. This is a case where the proof of the pudding really is in the eating.

Our relationship with the Sunday Times continues to develop. For the sixth year, we are pleased to record, in the front section of the guide, the list we prepare for them of the Top 100 restaurants in the UK. As the years roll on, the risers and fallers – and the 'stayers' – in this tabulation are taking on an interest all of their own.

All restaurant guides are the subject of continual revision, and the more input we have, the more accurate and comprehensive future editions will be. If you are not already signed up, please do join the www.hardens.com mailing list – we will then ensure that you are invited to take part in future surveys.

Harden's, Shoreditch, November 2015

HOW THIS BOOK IS ORGANISED

The guide begins in London, and contains the full text of the guide already published as *London Restaurants 2016*. Thereafter, the guide is organised strictly alphabetically by location, without regard to national divisions – Beaumaris, Belfast and Birmingham appear together under 'B'.

For *cities and larger towns*, you should therefore be able to turn straight to the relevant section. In addition to the entries for the restaurants themselves, cities which have significant numbers of restaurants also have a brief introductory overview.

In *less densely populated areas*, you will generally find it easiest to start with the relevant map at the back of the book, which will guide you to the appropriate place names.

If you are looking for a specific restaurant, the alphabetical index at the very back of the book lists all of the restaurants – London and UK – in this guide.

YOUR CONTRIBUTION

This book is the result of a research effort involving thousands of 'reporters'. As a group, you are 'ordinary' members of the public who share with us summary reviews of the best and the worst of your annual dining experiences. This year, over 6,700 of you gave us some 63,000 reviews in total.

The density of the feedback on London (where many of the top places attract several hundred reviews each) is such that the ratings for the restaurants in the capital are almost exclusively statistical in derivation. (We have, as it happens, visited almost all the restaurants in the London section, anonymously, and at our own expense, but we use our personal experiences only to inform the standpoint from which to interpret the consensus opinion.)

In the case of the more commented-upon restaurants away from the capital, we have adopted an essentially statistical approach very similar to London. In the case of less visited provincial establishments, however, the interpretation of survey results owes as much to art as it does to science.

In our experience, smaller establishments are – for better or worse – generally quite consistent, and we have therefore felt able to place a relatively high level of confidence in a lower level of commentary. Conservatism on our part, however, may have led to some smaller places being under-rated compared to their more-visited peers.

LONDON INTRODUCTION & SURVEY RESULTS

SURVEY MOST MENTIONED

RANKED BY THE NUMBER OF REPORTERS' VOTES

These are the restaurants which were most frequently mentioned by reporters. (Last year's position is given in brackets.) An asterisk* indicates the first appearance in the list of a recently-opened restaurant.

1 J Sheekey (1)
2 Clos Maggiore (4)
3 Le Gavroche (3)
4 The Ledbury (5)
5 Chez Bruce (7)
6 Scott's (2)
7 Gymkhana (12)
8 The Delaunay (6)
9 Fera at Claridge's (-)
10 The Wolseley (10)

11 11 Brasserie Zédel (11)
12 Dinner (9)
13 The Cinnamon Club (13)
14 Pollen Street Social (8)
15 Galvin La Chapelle (14)
16 La Trompette (19)
17 The Square (15)
18 The River Café (17)
19 La Poule au Pot (22)
20= Gordon Ramsay (33)

20= The Chiltern Firehouse (-)
22 Gauthier Soho (28)
23 Le Caprice (30)
24 The Palomar (-)
25 Pied à Terre (20)
26= Benares (24)
26= Galvin Bistrot de Luxe (26)
28 Medlar (21)
29 Amaya (40)
30 Zuma (32)

31 Bleeding Heart Restaurant (16)
32 Marcus (22)
33 Andrew Edmunds (35)
34 City Social (-)
35= Moro (-)
35= Bar Boulud (-)
37 Grain Store (30)
38 Spring (-)
39 Terroirs (38)
40 Zucca (27)

J Sheekey

The Cinnamon Club

Pied à Terre

Bleeding Heart Restaurant

Top gastronomic experience

1. Le Gavroche (2)
2. The Ledbury (1)
3. Chez Bruce (4)
4. Fera at Claridge's (-)
5. Dinner (3)
6. Gordon Ramsay (7)
7. Pied à Terre (6)
8. Pollen Street Social (5)
9. Story (-)
10. Hedone (-)

Favourite

1. Chez Bruce (1)
2. Clos Maggiore (3)
3. The Wolseley (10)
4. Le Gavroche (5)
5. J Sheekey (2)
6. Gauthier Soho (-)
7. Le Caprice (8)
8. La Trompette (-)
9. The Ledbury (4)
10. Moro (-)

Best for business

1. The Wolseley (1)
2. The Delaunay (2)
3. The Square (3)
4. City Social (-)
5. Galvin La Chapelle (4)
6. L'Anima (9)
7. Coq d'Argent (7)
8. The Don (6)
9. Scott's (8)
10. Bleeding Heart Restaurant (5)

Best for romance

1. Clos Maggiore (1)
2. La Poule au Pot (2)
3. Andrew Edmunds (3)
4. Bleeding Heart Restaurant (4)
5. Chez Bruce (6)
6. Le Gavroche (5)
7. Galvin La Chapelle (8)
8. Fera at Claridge's (-)
9. Le Caprice (-)
10. Gauthier Soho (10))

Best breakfast/brunch

1. The Wolseley (1)
2. The Delaunay (2)
3. Duck & Waffle (3)
4. Riding House Café (4)
5. Roast (5)
6. The Grazing Goat (-)
7. Cecconi's (7)
8. Colbert (6)
9. Dean Street Townhouse (-)
10. Balthazar (10)

Best bar/pub food

1. The Anchor & Hope (1)
2. Harwood Arms (3)
3. Bull & Last (2)
4. The Ladbroke Arms (7)
5. The Jugged Hare (4)
6. The Truscott Arms (9)
7. Princess Victoria (-)
8. Pig & Butcher (8)
9. The Camberwell Arms (-)
10. The Eagle (-)

Most disappointing cooking

1. The Chiltern Firehouse (-)
2. Oxo Tower (Rest') (2)
3. Pollen Street Social (-)
4. Colbert (3)
5. Grain Store (-)
6. Dinner (2)
7. Gordon Ramsay (5)
8. Alain Ducasse at The Dorchester (9)
9. Dabbous (10)
10. The Ivy (4)

Most overpriced restaurant

1. The River Café (1)
2. Oxo Tower (Rest') (2)
3. The Chiltern Firehouse (-)
4. Dinner (3)
5. Gordon Ramsay (4)
6. Marcus (5)
7. Alain Ducasse at The Dorchester (6)
8. Pollen Street Social (10)
9. The Ivy (-)
10. Le Gavroche (7)

SURVEY HIGHEST RATINGS

FOOD

£95+

1 The Ledbury
2 Story
3 One-O-One
4 Pied à Terre
5 Le Gavroche

£70-£94

1 The Five Fields
2 Yashin
3 HKK
4 Ametsa
5 Hunan

£54-£69

1 Sushi Tetsu
2 Dinings
3 Chez Bruce
4 Gauthier Soho
5 Trinity

£40-£54

1 Sushi-Say
2 Babur
3 José
4 Jin Kichi
5 Honey & Co

£39 or less

1 Bao
2 Silk Road
3 Ragam
4 Santa Maria
5 A Wong

SERVICE

£95+

1 Pied à Terre
2 Le Gavroche
3 Marianne
4 The Ledbury
5 Fera at Claridge's

£70-£94

1 The Five Fields
2 The Goring Hotel
3 Alyn Williams
4 Koffmann's
5 L'Autre Pied

£54-£69

1 Sushi Tetsu
2 Chez Bruce
3 Trinity
4 Bellamy's
5 Gauthier Soho

£40-£54

1 Caraffini
2 Quantus
3 Il Portico
4 Yming
5 Roots at N1

£39 or less

1 Paradise Hampstead
2 Carob Tree
3 Andina
4 Meza SW17
5 Golden Hind

AMBIENCE

1 Sketch (Lecture Rm)
2 The Ritz Restaurant
3 The Ledbury
4 Le Gavroche
5 The Greenhouse

1 Min Jiang
2 The Goring Hotel
3 Galvin La Chapelle
4 City Social
5 Sushisamba

1 Clos Maggiore
2 La Poule au Pot
3 Wallace
4 Bob Bob Ricard
5 The Grazing Goat

1 Andrew Edmunds
2 Brasserie Zédel
3 Tate Britain (Rex Whistler)
4 José
5 Shampers

1 Churchill Arms
2 Andina
3 The Eagle
4 Blanchette
5 Princi

OVERALL

1 The Ledbury
2 Le Gavroche
3 Marianne
4 Pied à Terre
5 Kitchen Table at Bubbledogs

1 The Five Fields
2 The Goring Hotel
3 J Sheekey
4 Scott's
5 Launceston Place

1 Sushi Tetsu
2 Chez Bruce
3 Clos Maggiore
4 Trinity
5 The Grazing Goat

1 José
2 Babur
3 Andrew Edmunds
4 Roots at N1
5 Il Portico

1 Andina
2 Carob Tree
3 Paradise Hampstead
4 Blanchette
5 Bao

SURVEY BEST BY CUISINE

These are the restaurants which received the best average food ratings (excluding establishments with a small or notably local following).

Where the most common types of cuisine are concerned, we present the results in two price-brackets. For less common cuisines, we list the top three, regardless of price.

For further information about restaurants which are particularly notable for their food, see the cuisine lists starting on page 164. These indicate, using an asterisk*, restaurants which offer exceptional or very good food.

British, Modern

£55 and over

1 The Ledbury
2 The Five Fields
3 Story
4 Marianne
5 The Clove Club

Under £55

1 The Dairy
2 Rabbit
3 Shoe Shop
4 Lamberts
5 The Ladbroke Arms

French

£55 and over

1 Le Gavroche
2 Pied à Terre
3 Hibiscus
4 Gauthier Soho
5 Koffmann's

Under £55

1 Brawn
2 Casse-Croute
3 Blanchette
4 Charlotte's W4
5 Cigalon

Italian/Mediterranean

£55 and over

1 Bocca di Lupo
2 L'Anima
3 The River Café
4 Zucca
5 Enoteca Turi

Under £55

1 L'Amorosa
2 Querce
3 Pentolina
4 Bibo
5 Café Murano

Indian & Pakistani

£55 and over

1 Amaya
2 Gymkhana
3 Rasoi
4 Trishna
5 Cinnamon Kitchen

Under £55

1 Babur
2 Ragam
3 Roots at N1
4 Tayyabs
5 Ganapati

Chinese

£55 and over

1 HKK
2 Yauatcha W1
3 Hunan
4 Hakkasan W1
5 Min Jiang

Under £55

1 Silk Road
2 A Wong
3 Pearl Liang
4 Barshu
5 Taiwan Village

Japanese

£55 and over

1 The Araki
2 Sushi Tetsu
3 Dinings
4 Yashin
5 Zuma

Under £55

1 Sushi-Say
2 Kanada-Ya
3 Tsunami
4 Pham Sushi
5 Jin Kichi

British, Traditional

1 St John
2 Scott's
3 St John Bread & Wine

Vegetarian

1 Gate W6
2 Vanilla Black
3 Ethos

Burgers, etc

1 Patty & Bun
2 Honest Burgers
3 Bleecker St Burger

Pizza

1 Homeslice
2 Franco Manca
3 Oak W11

Fish & Chips

1 Nautilus
2 Golden Hind
3 Toff's

Thai

1 Sukho Fine Thai Cuisine
2 Addie's Thai Café
3 Isarn

Steaks & Grills

1 Rib Room
2 Goodman
3 Flat Iron

Fish & Seafood

1 One-O-One
2 J Sheekey
3 Bentley's

Fusion

1 Bubbledogs (Kitchen Table)
2 E&O
3 Eight Over Eight

Spanish

1 José
2 Ametsa
3 Moro

Turkish

1 Fez Mangal
2 Mangal 1
3 Best Mangal

Lebanese

1 Meza Trinity Road
2 Chez Abir
3 Fairuz

TOP SPECIAL DEALS

The following menus allow you to eat in the restaurants concerned at a significant discount when compared to their evening à la carte prices.

The prices used are calculated in accordance with our usual formula (i.e. three courses with house wine, coffee and tip).

Special menus are by their nature susceptible to change – please check that they are still available.

Weekday lunch

£85+ Alain Ducasse at The Dorchester
Le Gavroche

£80+ Gordon Ramsay
The Ledbury
Marcus

£70+ Hedone

£65+ Fera at Claridge's
Pétrus
Rib Room
Roux at the Landau
Sketch (Lecture Rm)
The Square

£60+ The Clove Club
Dorchester Grill
Pied à Terre
Pollen Street Social
Story

£55+ Alyn Williams
L'Atelier de Joel Robuchon
Dabbous
Galvin at Windows
Hibiscus
Hunan
Launceston Place
Massimo
Murano
Nobu
Nobu Berkeley
Novikov (Asian restaurant)
One-O-One
Oxo Tower (Rest')
Rasoi
Savoy Grill
Seven Park Place
Theo Randall

£50+ Babbo
China Tang
Gilbert Scott
The Glasshouse
Koffmann's
Medlar
Orrery
Outlaw's Seafood and Grill
Oxo Tower (Brass')
Quilon
J Sheekey
J Sheekey Oyster Bar
Skylon
Social Eating House
Sotheby's Café
Twist At Crawford
Village East
The White Onion

£30+ The Anchor & Hope
Bistrò by Shot
The Brackenbury
Chapters
Eelbrook
Hereford Road
Joe Allen
Linnea
Market
Mazi
Mele e Pere
Mon Plaisir
Suksan
The Tommy Tucker

£25+ Alquimia
La Bodega Negra
Cornish Tiger
Ishtar
Lemonia
The Lucky Pig Fulham
The Orange Tree
Trangallan
The Wet Fish Café

£20+ Cellar Gascon
Gem
Le Sacré-Coeur
Yming

£15+ Kolossi Grill
Olympus Fish
Sichuan Folk
Two Brothers

Pre/post theatre (and early evening)

£60+ Pied à Terre

£55+ L'Atelier de Joel Robuchon
The Goring Hotel
The Northall
Savoy Grill
Skylon

£50+ Asia de Cuba
Bentley's
Gilbert Scott
Koffmann's
Oxo Tower (Brass')
Spring

£45+ Green's
The Ivy
Yashin Ocean House

£40+ Boulestin
Chiswell Street Dining Rooms
Christopher's
The Keeper's House
Kitchen W8
Kopapa
The Swan at the Globe
Le Vacherin

£35+ Bistro Aix
Dean Street Townhouse
Gay Hussar
One Canada Square
Quo Vadis
Red Fort
Tredwell's
Trishna

£30+ Mon Plaisir

£20+ Yming

Sunday lunch

£70+ Dorchester Grill
Galvin at Windows

£65+ The Goring Hotel

£60+ Launceston Place
Roast

£55+ Bibendum
Medlar
Orrery
Petersham Hotel
Skylon
Trinity

£50+ Galvin La Chapelle
The Glasshouse
Kitchen W8
Le Pont de la Tour
Tate Britain
La Trompette
Veeraswamy
Wild Honey

£45+ Dean Street Townhouse

£40+ Brawn
Café Bohème
Charlotte's Place
Merchants Tavern
Sonny's Kitchen
Le Vacherin

£35+ Bradley's
Brasserie Gustave

£30+ Grumbles

THE RESTAURANT SCENE

Off-the-charts good

This year we list a record 179 newcomers – the largest ever in the 25-year history of the guide, easily overtaking the precrash level of 158 seen in 2008.

Closings – up a tad on last year – remain relatively low at 56: a very similar level to that seen for the last three years.

Combining the two factors, the level of net openings this year (openings minus closings) has again set a new peak: at 123, the figure comfortably exceeds last year's total – itself a record – of 101.

It is tempting to think that this is the 'new normal'. But the ratio of openings to closings remains at incredibly strong, 'bull market' levels – at 3.2:1, only one year (1996) has been higher since we started keeping this score, and only five of the last 25 years have exceeded a rate of 2.4:1.

It is tempting to prognosticate a downwards turning point based on these figures. For how much longer can London continue to boom?. But with the continued, seemingly unstoppable growth of the capital unsurprisingly comes the demand for more grub!

We are also, by the year, very aware of the much greater ease of collecting this information. Until recent times, this guide might be the only media coverage many outlying neighbourhood restaurants would receive in a year. But now every detail of every eatery is recorded in such micro-detail by review sites, blogs, social media (not to mention the big data vendors tracking mobile phone movements), that almost certainly to some degree the guide is noting more restaurants than once it did simply because it is so much easier to "clock" them as they arrive.

Still, it is hard to escape the feeling that the London restaurant scene is on the most massive roll, akin to some new form of life created by a mad (or inspired!) out-of-control scientist in a SciFi B movie. Every day the email inbox brings news of some new hybrid cuisine, some new specialist, or the rapid roll out of an existing concept.

With such vitality, however, comes a dilemma. Restaurants which once would have seemed outstanding nowadays seem commonplace. The bar is higher and higher, the challenge to stand out from the crowd tougher and tougher.

Every year, we choose what to us seem to be the most significant openings of the year. This year, our selection is as follows:

The Araki	Bao
Bonhams	Duck & Rice
Ivy Chelsea Garden	Kitty Fisher's
Paradise Garage	Portland
Smith & Wollenskys	Smoking Goat

Turning Japanese?

If there has been one constant trend in the last 25 years, it has been the enduring popularity of Italian cuisine. And it is rather uninteresting to report that this trend continues uninterrupted this year, accounting for about 10% of newcomers.

More eye-catching is the continuing rise-and-rise of Japanese cuisine, which was the classification for practically as many newcomers as Italians this year. It's a phenomenon that's easily overlooked, perhaps because of the quiet cultural style of Nipponese imports.

Americanisation is another significant trend, but its significance may be over-stated because US-inspired brands and imports generally shout so loud about what they have to offer! No doubting, however, that the US-style craze for steaks, BBQs and other meatylicious fare continues unabated. Millennials, it seems, prefer munching burgers to saving the planet...

The other most popular cuisines this year were Spanish concepts, and 'fusion' – our catch-all for a multitude of novel ideas.

London's restaurant compass continues to shift, drawn by the new magnetic poles of Shoreditch, Hackney and Haggerston. Although central London is still where we record most new openings, it is now closely followed by East London, and then South London, in terms of popularity for new sites. West London accounted for exactly half the openings out East this year, transforming the situation that prevailed when we started the guide (in which we recorded just six restaurants in an "E" postcode).

West London activity still exceeds that of North London however, which – despite the odd sign of life – still maintains a surprisingly tame restaurant scene.

If London is following Tokyo's path at all, it is perhaps evident in two areas. One (incredibly welcome) trend is restaurant-goers' increasing focus on the quality of ingredients. Another is the focus on restaurants pursuing a single activity or dish. So this year, we've seen newcomers focussed solely on egg dishes, porridge, cheese toasties... even now just chips!

Prices

The average price of dinner for one at establishments listed in this guide is £50.51 (compared to £49.46 last year). Prices have risen by 2.1% in the past 12 months: a lower rate than in the preceding 12 months. While this continues a downward trend also evident last year, this rate significantly exceeds the current very low rate of inflation (effectively zero). Thus this year's real level of restaurant price rises is higher than last year's (which broadly tracked inflation).

OPENINGS AND CLOSURES

Openings (179)

Amaru
Anima e Cuore
The Araki
Babaji Pide
Bad Egg
Balls & Company
Bandol
Bao
Bar Termini
Barbecoa W1
Barrafina WC2
Beer and Buns
Bellanger
Berber & Q
Bird N7
Bistrò by Shot
Blacklock
Bleecker Street Burger
Blixen
Bó Drake
Bone Daddies W8, EC1
Bonhams Restaurant
Boom Burger SW9
Botanist EC2
Bouillabaisse
Café Murano WC2
Carousel
Casa Cruz
Cau SE3, SW19, E1
The Cavendish
Ceru
Ceviche Old St
Charlotte's W5
Chez Antoinette
Chick 'n' Sours
Chicken Town
Chifafa
Chiswick Smokehouse
Counter
Craft London
Crosstown Doughnuts
The Culpepper
Darwin Brasserie
Delancey & Co.
DF/Mexico W1
Dip & Flip SW19
The Duck & Rice
Dumplings' Legend
Ellory
Engawa
Enoteca Rabezzana
Ethos
Fields
Flat Iron WC2
Flat Three
Flotsam and Jetsam
Foxlow N16
45 Jermyn St
Friends of Ours
Gatti's EC2
German Gymnasium
Gourmets des Ternes SW1
The Greek Larder
The Green Room
Gremio de Brixton
Habanera
Hood
Hoppers
Homeslice W1
House of Ho W1
House Restaurant
Hungry Donkey
Iddu
Ippudo London E14
The Italian Job
The Ivy Café
The Ivy Chelsea Garden
The Ivy Kensington Brasserie
The Ivy Market Grill
Jago
Jar Kitchen
Jinjuu
John Doe
Joint Marylebone W1
Jones & Sons
José Pizarro
K10 EC3
Kanada-Ya SW1
Kateh Knightsbridge SW1
Kitchen
Kitty Fisher's
Kricket
Kurobuta Harvey Nics SW1

Smith & Wollensky

Lantana Café NW1
Lardo Bebè E8
The Lucky Pig Fulham
Luppolo
M Restaurant Victoria Street
Mamma Dough SE23, SW9
The Marksman
Masala Grill
Max's Sandwich Shop
Mayfair Pizza Company
maze Grill SW10
The Melt Room
Meza SW17
Mission
Modern Pantry EC2
MOMMI
Morada Brindisa Asador
Morden & Lea
Morelli's Gelato
Murakami
Naughty Piglets
Oka
Old Tom & English
Oldroyd
On The Bab W1, WC2
One Sixty Smokehouse E1
Les 110 de Taillevent
Paradise Garage
Patron
Pedler
Pennethorne's Cafe Bar
Percy & Founders
The Petite Coree
Piquet
Portland
Pulia
Queenswood
The Refinery
Resident of Paradise Row
Restaurant de Paul EC2
The Richmond
Ristorante Frescobaldi
Rox Burger
Sackville's
Salmontini
The Salon
Le Salon Privé
Salt & Honey
Salvation In Noodles N4
Señor Ceviche
Sesame
Sexy Fish
Shackfuyu
Shake Shack WC1, E20
Shikumen
Shoe Shop
Shotgun
Smith & Wollensky
Smoking Goat
Snaps & Rye
Social Wine & Tapas
Som Saa
Sosharu
Taberna Do Mercado
Tem Tép
The Tommy Tucker
Tonic & Remedy
Tonkotsu E8
The Truscott Cellar
Tulse Hill Hotel
Twist At Crawford
Verdi's
Vico
Villa Di Geggiano
Vintage Salt EC2
West Thirty Six
The White Onion
Wimsey's
The Woodstock
Workshop Coffee W1, EC1
Wormwood
Yama Momo
Yasmeen
Yauatcha City

Closures (56)

Alloro
Assaggi
Bam-Bou
Bistrot Bruno Loubet
Bouchée
Brula
Cadogan Arms
Café Anglais
Café des Amis
Cantina Vinopolis
Chabrot Bistrot d'Amis
Criterion
Deuxième
Entrée
Ergon
Eriki
Fino
Fitou's Thai Restaurant
Food for Thought
Fountain
Foxtrot Oscar
GB Pizza
Gilak
Green Man & French Horn
Hole in the Wall
Juniper Dining
Kentish Canteen
Koya
Lawn Bistro
LMNT
Marani
Made in Italy W1
New Angel
New Tom's
Noodle House
One Kensington
Orchard
Ozer
Pavilion
Penkul & Banks
Portal
Racine
Sakura
Sam's Brasserie
1701
64 Degrees
Shiori
Shrimpy's
Solly's
T.E.D
Trois Garçons
21 Bateman Street
Union Café
Upstairs
Whits
Wishbone

25 YEARS – WHAT'S CHANGED?

Most industries change a fair amount in 25 years, and pundits talk up the "step changes" they observe. But even the most ardent cynic would agree that the restaurant industry today has risen to new heights in the last quarter-century.

In the early '90s, the joke went that in heaven, the lovers were Italian, the chefs French, the mechanics German, and the police British. In hell, the police were Italian, the mechanics French, the lovers German, and guess which nationality the chefs were...

Twenty five years ago:

- it was taken as read that the UK was in the culinary Dark Ages, especially by visiting Americans.
- the idea that our TV chefs would be household names in France and the US would have been hilarious.
- the experience of half-decent food in a pub was a rarity, and pretty disgusting fare the norm.
- an interest in eating out, food and wine was seen as middle-aged and fuddy-duddy.
- MasterChef (first episode July 2, 1990) was scarcely a year old, and the idea that kids would take interest in Junior MasterChef would have seemed pie-in-the-sky.

So what changed?

The new rock 'n' roll

When we started our guide in 1991, one of the biggest objections to a new title from bookshop buyers was that eating out was too highbrow ("only for posh bastards").

The chef oft-cited with changing all that, Marco Pierre White, featured in our first guide as head chef at Harvey's in Wandsworth. His cookbook, White Heat, had just been published, and – on its re-release this year to celebrate its 25th anniversary – was described in a recent Caterer & Hotelkeeper as "the book that showed, warts and all, that the kitchen was a cool place to be".

It was MPW's PR man of that time, Alan Crompton-Batt, who is sometimes credited with having observed that cooking was "the new rock 'n' roll". Perhaps he should have known, as he was an ex-music-promoter himself (for the late '70s band, The Pyschedelic Furs). With another of his clients, Nico Ladenis (then with three Michelin stars) the cultivation of the 'bad boy' chef had begun (although we had to wait a few more years for all the effing).

The launch of other new restaurants, however, played just as significant a role in popularising the idea that eating out is for all. In early 1993, Sir Terence Conran moved into restaurants bringing all the money and expertise he'd acquired in running his huge retail empire, Storehouse plc.

With the opening of Quaglino's, with its Q-shaped ashtrays and cigarette girl (now there's something else you wouldn't see nowadays) Sir Tel spun a compelling narrative of bringing the fraternité of Parisian brasseries to London.

More-or-less simultaneously, Planet Hollywood launched scarcely five minutes' walk away, with Arnold Schwarzenegger, Sylvester Stallone and Bruce Willis at the opening. The two debuts in short succession channelled a previously unknown amount of professionalism, capital and hype to catalyse a major shift towards democratising the idea of eating out, particularly in the London media.

Chefs trade 'the stainless steel box' for TV

By the late '90s, the Harden's office started to field fairly regular calls from TV production companies. It wasn't us they wanted to make famous, unfortunately. The question they wanted answered: "Do you know any chefs who you think would make good TV? To be honest it doesn't really matter if they can cook – what we need is a big personality: somebody who looks good on camera."

With Gordon Ramsay, the first London restaurant chef to become a global TV personality, the producers sure got that (and also someone who could cook). The rise of the Ramsay phenomenon globally was a terrific emblem of the newly discovered, insatiable desire for food-led programming.

All the glamour transformed middle-class attitudes to the kitchen. Tom Jaine, editor of the Good Food Guide 25 years ago, commented in a November 2014 interview for Radio 4's Food Programme that, in those days "respectable was owning not doing." He went on to draw the contrast with today, where many recipients of an expensive education from the country's top schools are drawn to a vocational path that a generation ago was on no-one's radar.

A proper food culture

Hand-in-hand with a growing interest in chefs has come a growing interest in, and respect for, ingredients and cooking The now-ubiquitous (then largely unknown) interest in local sourcing is part of a much foodier interest in food, that has helped spawn many more creative eating formats. Twenty five years ago, the 2-course or 3-course meal was the staple of the trade. Nowadays, the expectation has shifted completely, and it is de rigeur that anywhere with ambition will focus on tapas, sharing plates and tasting menus.

From glam to gastropubs

Away from the glamour of the TV studios, some more prosaic changes were about to transform eating out.

In 1989, the Secretary of State for Trade and Industry passed The Beer Orders. In terms of succeeding in their aims – which was to drive down the price of beer – the legislation was an abject flop. But by restricting the number of tied pubs, a new tidal wave of entrepreneurialism flourished in the pub industry which continues to this day.

Other factors have also significantly changed access by the trade to prime sites. Twenty five years ago, the City of London and top landlords thought restaurants were non-U and prevented them opening. Nowadays, any new development works hard to secure a name chef to PR.

25 YEARS – WHAT'S CHANGED?

Demographics of dining out

Five years prior to the launch of this guide, in 1987, London hit its lowest population level in the 20th Century at 6.8m. Fast forward to this year, and London's population hit a new peak, breaking through its previous 1939 high of 8.6m. That's growth of a quarter in just over a quarter of a century, and all those people need feeding.

But it's not just more people who have inspired more restaurants. The people themselves are going out more. In part that's because the London is richer than it was 25 years ago, but also it's because its residents have changed.

Mass immigration has driven down the average age of Londoners, and provided lots of willing customers (as well as motivated, skilled manpower for restaurants).

And then there's the change in our nesting habits over the last quarter century. When we started our guide, the average age of UK women when they gave birth was under 27. Nowadays it's over 30, and in London older still. In parallel, the average age for purchasing a first home for 'Generation Rent' has gone up from mid-20s to early-30s. All that energy and disposable income that would have been soaked up by nesting in an earlier generation, nowadays is available for gadding about the town for a few years more.

Private what?

The shake-up of gastropubs detailed above was largely driven by a growing industry with a new name at that time unknown to most people outside of the City: Private Equity.

The Punch Taverns deal – part of the sell-off by the brewers of the pubs – was one of the first to start to whet the appetite of the investment trade for the restaurant business.

For a trade that historically has generally been funded from savings, friends-and-family and business 'angels', the arrival of serious money on the scene nowadays provides the prospect of a bonanza exit for anyone with a hot idea apt for a 'roll out'. This promise is reflected today in the never-ending stream of new ventures – from pop-ups to proto-chains – with slick graphic design and a lucrative end in mind.

Tweet, tweet, tweet… pop!

Restaurateurs are natural self-promoters, and have taken to social media like a duck to water.

And for first-time restaurateurs, the arrival of Twitter and Facebook has helped overcome one of the biggest hurdles to them entering the business – premises. With the ability to advertise a stall, a house party, or a residency in some crumbling quarter of the East End, this prime barrier to entry has been significantly lowered.

The explosion of the technology has further boosted the emergence of younger diners at the heart of the most fashionable eating out trends. Twenty and 30-somethings by and large own the street food phenomenon further overturning all the old stereotypes about discernment about food being a fogey-ish concern.

And then there was one...

As well as changes in the restaurant trade, the lifetime of this guide has also seen more change in the publishing industry than in most of its 500-year history.

The rise of digital has been particularly disruptive to publishers of local information, and restaurant guides are no exception. Although there is some satisfaction in being the 'last man still standing', it is sobering (for us anyway!) that this publication is now the only annual guide dedicated exclusively to London restaurants still widely sold in bookshops, when in recent memory our competitors included *Time Out*, *Zagat*, and *Rough Guides* (and going further back, *Nicholson* and *The Evening Standard*).

Google, Yelp! and TripAdvisor have all targeted the local listings business, and, when it comes to "share of eyeballs", dominate the market nowadays. User Generated Reviews are now a common currency of the internet, and have revolutionised the way consumers learn about even the most humble of products, not just restaurants.

However, we like to think – and our readers and website users seem to agree – that Harden's has long been part of that progress, and there is still a lot of value in the carefully curated user feedback that has always been at the heart of the Harden's survey.

Anyone can contribute a review to the survey, and feed it into the mix. We look carefully for cheats, and we throw out many bogus reports. We follow restaurants carefully year-on-year and watch for patterns. We know the market in depth, and provide a critical overview and summary, rather than a lucky dip of random commentary. Supporters still find the system produces a handy, pithy, objective perspective to help them get the best bang for their buck.

Please help us in our endeavours by signing up to, and participating in, the survey at www.hardens.com. With your help, perhaps we can report to you all the changes that we see take place over the next 25 years...

Brasserie Blanc

Blackfoot
Fenchurch
The Ivy

LONDON DIRECTORY

A Cena TW1 £50 444

418 Richmond Rd 8288 0108 1–4A

St Margaret's locals are mightily satisfied with this neighbourhood Italian, just south of Richmond Bridge – "the interesting food is of high quality", the wine is "very good", and staff are "absolutely charming". / TW1 2EB; www.acena.co.uk; @acenarestaurant; 10 pm; closed Mon L & Sun D; booking: max 6, Fri & Sat.

A Wong SW1 £35 543

70-71 Wilton Rd 7828 8931 2–4B

"Beats Chinatown any day!"; "stunningly good" cooking (not least "fabulous dim sum") and "helpful, non-hassling" service have helped win a huge fan club for this canteen-style Chinese two-year-old – "part of Pimlico's improving food scene". / SW1 1DE; www.awong.co.uk; @awongSW1; 10.15 pm; closed Mon L & Sun.

Abbeville Kitchen SW4 £52 333

47 Abbeville Rd 8772 1110 10–2D

"It never disappoints", say local fans of this "noisy and bustling" Clapham "gem"; its "interesting" menu incorporates "great sharing plates" – "nothing earthshaking but sound and consistent cooking". / SW4 9JX; www.abbevillekitchen.com; @abbevillek; 10.30 pm, Sun 9.30 pm; Mon-Thu D only, Fri-Sun open L & D.

Abeno £42 341

47 Museum St, WC1 7405 3211 2–1C

17-18 Great Newport St, WC2 7379 1160 4–3B

Okonomi-yaki (fancy Japanese omelettes "cooked in front of you") is "good fun", and "done well" at these "comfy" but rather "tired-looking" fixtures. / www.abeno.co.uk; 10 pm - 11 pm; no Amex; WC2 no booking.

Abi Ruchi N16 £28 442

42 Stoke Newington Church St 7923 4564 1–1C

Even on Stoke Newington's Church Street, an area not short of choice for good Indian cuisine, this family-run Keralan shines thanks to "warm and friendly staff", "authentic thalis" and "great prices" – "it deserves to be much better known". / N16 0LU; www.abiruchi.com; 11 pm, Fri & Sat 11.30 pm, Sun 10 pm.

The Abingdon W8 £63 344

54 Abingdon Rd 7937 3339 5–2A

"Top end gastropub" in the chichi backstreets of Kensington, which combines "a well-run bar" with a comfy, "buzzing" dining room (the best seats are in booths); it's "a bit pricey" but has been a "dependable local" for over 20 years. / W8 6AP; www.theabingdon.co.uk; 10.30 pm, Fri & Sat 11 pm, Sun 10 pm; set weekday L £42 (FP).

About Thyme SW1 £51 344

82 Wilton Rd 7821 7504 2–4B

"Delighting locals and those from further afield" – a stalwart local in west Pimlico, lauded for its "unusual cuisine" ("Spanish with a twist") and in particular for staff who are "polite, solicitous, but not over-bearing"; if there's a quibble it's that the odd dish "lacks oomph". / SW1V 1DL; www.aboutthyme.co.uk; 10.30 pm; closed Sun.

L'Absinthe NW1 £46 233

40 Chalcot Rd 7483 4848 8–3B

"The owner JC makes the place!" – even if "better food can be found elsewhere", his "warmth of welcome at all times" ensures this Primrose Hill corner bistro is "always crowded". / NW1 8LS; www.labsinthe.co.uk; @absinthe07jc; 10 pm; closed Mon, Tue L, Wed L & Thu L.

Abu Zaad W12 £23 332

29 Uxbridge Rd 8749 5107 7–1C

Near the top of Shepherd's Bush Market, a "hospitable" Syrian café, serving "appealing and filling" mezze and kebabs at "fantastic" prices; no alcohol, but "lovely fresh juices" and "nice complimentary extras like tea and baklava". / W12 8LH; www.abuzaad.co.uk; @abuzaaduk; 11 pm; no Amex.

Adam Handling at Caxton Caxton Grill SW1 £74 332

2 Caxton St 7227 7773 2–4C

Is it "a bad case of MasterChef-itis"? – some "tortured" or "pretentious" dishes disappoint quite a few reporters at Adam Handling's "very hotel-like" dining room, tucked away in Westminster. A majority, though, say his ambitious cuisine can be "really outstanding", service is "eager" and – in this thin area – it's still "a good addition". / SW1H 0QW; www.caxtongrill.co.uk/caxton/adam-handling; @AH_Caxton; 10.30 pm.

Adams Café W12 £32 353

77 Askew Rd 8743 0572 7–1B

"A stunning little traditional Shepherd's Bush caff that turns North African at night"; "friendly management" create "a really local feel" and its "great tagines" make it a firm cheap 'n' cheerful favourite. Licensed nowadays, but you can still BYO (wine only), at £4 corkage. / W12 9AH; www.adamscafe.co.uk; 10 pm; closed Sun.

Addie's Thai Café SW5 £34 442

121 Earl's Court Rd 7259 2620 5–2A

"Dishes taste as if they were fresh off the streets of Bangkok", at this "fantastic, cheap 'n' cheerful" café, which is "worth a detour" to the "insalubrious environs, at the top of Earl's Court Road". / SW5 9RL; www.addiesthai.co.uk; 11 pm, Sun 10.30 pm; no Amex.

The Admiral Codrington SW3 £50 224
17 Mossop St 7581 0005 5–2C
Long one of Chelsea's more popular watering holes – an animated backstreet boozer that "still feels like a pub", and serves "decent" nosh in its sizeable dining room (with a roof that retracts in summer). / SW3 2LY; www.theadmiralcodrington.co.uk; @TheAdCod; 10 pm, Thu-Sat 11 pm, Sun 9.30 pm.

Afghan Kitchen N1 £27 421
35 Islington Grn 7359 8019 8–3D
"Delicious dishes" can be chosen from a small menu at this tiny, "spartan" café of decades' standing, by Islington Green; it's "a bit of a tight squeeze", to put it mildly. / N1 8DU; 11 pm; closed Mon & Sun; no credit cards.

Aglio e Olio SW10 £43 332
194 Fulham Rd 7351 0070 5–3B
"Go early – the noise level rises over the evening", at this "chaotic, cramped but fun Italian", near the Chelsea & Westminster Hospital – a "cheap 'n' cheerful" classic for "authentic and fresh-tasting mainstream dishes" (notably pasta). / SW10 9PN; 11.30 pm.

Al Duca SW1 £46 332
4-5 Duke of York St 7839 3090 3–3D
"I thought it would be incredibly expensive given its looks and location!" – but this low-key St James's Italian "gives good value in an area bereft of such options", and, in particular, "for a central working lunch", it's ideal. / SW1Y 6LA; www.alduca-restaurant.co.uk; 11 pm; closed Sun.

Al Forno £34 244
349 Upper Richmond Rd, SW15 8878 7522 10–2A
2a King's Rd, SW19 8540 5710 10–2B
"They cater to all-comers, at these bustling, fun and down-to-earth" local Italians; the "solid" food is "very acceptable" ("huge pizzas" in particular), but it's the "smiling service" and "hugely welcoming family friendliness" that stand out. / 10 pm - 11 pm.

Alain Ducasse at The Dorchester W1 £126 222
53 Park Ln 7629 8866 3–3A
"Never a three-star!" – the Gallic über-chef's foodie temple in Mayfair is just "not up to par"; OK, a minority of fans are duly wowed, but for a sizeable majority its "Michelin-by-numbers" cuisine, "characterless" style and ferocious prices create a "distinctly average" experience. / W1K 1QA; www.alainducasse-dorchester.com; @Chefalainducasse; 9.30 pm; closed Mon, Sat L & Sun; jacket required; set weekday L £87 (FP).

Albertine W12 £36 234
1 Wood Ln 8743 9593 7–1C
"How different from Westfield just across the street" – a "genuine, worn, old wine bar", with a "charming" and "reassuring" atmosphere and "a long and varied wine list"; the simple fare may avoid fireworks, but is "light and appetising". / W12 7DP; www.albertinewinebar.co.uk; @AlbertineWine; 10.30 pm; closed Sat L & Sun; no Amex.

Albion £50 122
NEO Bankside, Holland St, SE1 3764 5550 9–3B
2-4 Boundary St, E2 7729 1051 12–1B
Whether you need "a weekend breakfast fill-up before a walk around trendy Shoreditch", or a stop-off "handy for Tate Modern", Sir Terence Conran's café duo can serve a purpose, although nothing about them excels, and the food in particular is "very average". / www.albioncaff.com; 11 pm.

The Albion N1 £45 213
10 Thornhill Rd 7607 7450 8–3D
"Atmospheric", tucked-away old inn, with a "great outside space" that's long been "an Islington institution"; however despite "decent pub grub", it's too often "totally let down by its lacklustre service" – maybe "go for a drink, but not to eat". / N1 1HW; www.the-albion.co.uk; @thealbionpub; 10 pm, Sun 9 pm.

Ali Baba NW1 £23 323
32 Ivor Pl 7723 5805 2–1A
"The ambience of a genuine Egyptian café" permeates this "basic" BYO (behind a Marylebone take-away), where you eat in a living room, complete with TV (typically on, with the sound turned down), and enjoy "home-cooked" fare at very "modest" prices. / NW1 6DA; www.alibabarestaurant.co.uk; midnight; no credit cards.

The Almeida N1 £62 222
30 Almeida St 7354 4777 8–3D
There's been an air of "transition" at this "spacious" D&D London fixture, opposite the eponymous Islington Theatre, which has ditched its charcuterie trolley, and modernised the cuisine; there's a sense of 'plus ça change' though with accusations that it's still "rather ordinary all round". / N1 1AD; www.almeida-restaurant.co.uk; @Almeida_N1; 10.30 pm; closed Mon L & Sun D.

Alounak £33 323
10 Russell Gdns, W14 7603 1130 7–1D
44 Westbourne Grove, W2 7229 0416 6–1B
"Incredibly cheap, good, authentic and reliable Persian BYO cafés" in Bayswater and Olympia, attracting "a great mix of diners"; service is "rushed but pleasant". / 11.30 pm; no Amex.

Alquimia SW15 **£50** 3 4 2

30 Brewhouse Ln 8785 0508 10–2B

"It's lovely to sit outdoors close to the Thames in fine weather", at this tapas-joint in the (otherwise "rather soulless") Putney Wharf development, where service is "friendly and efficient", and the food's of high quality. / SW15 2JX; www.alquimiarestaurant.co.uk; @AlquimiaRestUK; 11.30 pm, Sun 10.30 pm; set weekday L £28 (FP).

Alyn Williams Westbury Hotel W1 **£82** 4 5 3

37 Conduit St 7183 6426 3–2C

Alyn Williams's "stunning" cuisine, along with notably "solicitous" service helps create a mightily "civilised" experience at this sleek – if slightly "muted" – hotel dining room, just off Bond Street. Top Menu Tip – "very good-value set lunch menu". / W1S 2YF; www.alynwilliams.com; @Alyn_Williams; 10.30 pm; closed Mon & Sun; jacket required; set weekday L £58 (FP).

Amaru Ivory House E1 NEW **£37**

St Katherine Docks, East Smithfield 7702 4765 9–3D

New Japanese-Peruvian fusion outlet that's dropped anchor in St Katharine Docks, with backing from the owners of Spanish tapas joint Bravas; survey feedback was limited (hence no rating), but encouraging. / E1W 1AT; www.amaru.london; @Amaru_SKD; 9 pm.

Amaya SW1 **£78** 5 3 4

Halkin Arc, 19 Motcomb St 7823 1166 5–1D

"Mind-blowing"... "mouth-watering"... "memorable" – the Indian 'tapas' cooked on-view in the open kitchen of this sleek Belgravian, make it arguably London's best 'nouvelle Indian'; any quibbles? – service can be "inconsistent". / SW1X 8JT; www.amaya.biz; 11.30 pm, Sun 10.30 pm; set weekday L £43 (FP).

Ametsa with Arzak Instruction Halkin Hotel SW1 **£86** 4 4 2

5 Halkin St 7333 1234 2–3A

"We'd heard bad things, but it was stunningly good!" – star Spanish chef, Juan Mari Arzak's "stark" Belgravian can still seem "underwhelming" to some, but (after some rocky early years) it won much more consistent adulation this year for its "passionate" service, and "fascinating, semi-molecular Basque cuisine". / SW1X 7DJ; www.comohotels.com/thehalkin/dining/ametsa; @AmetsaArzak; 10 pm; closed Mon L & Sun.

Amico Bio **£38** 2 3 2

43 New Oxford St, WC1 7836 7509 4–1C

43-44 Cloth Fair, EC1 7600 7778 9–2B

An "interesting Italian–vegetarian concept" in Bloomsbury and Smithfield – fans extol its "delicious, and ethically-minded" fare, but to critics "it's a great idea, but the realisation is pretty average". / www.amicobio.co.uk; EC1 10.30 pm; EC1 closed Sat L & Sun; no booking.

L'Amorosa W6 **£43** 5 4 3

278 King St 8563 0300 7–2B

"A great addition to west London" – Andy Needham is "showing his Zafferano pedigree" at his "small" and "friendly" neighbourhood yearling near Ravenscourt Park; the cooking is "the real deal" ("sublime" pasta in particular) and there's "interesting and manageably priced wine". / W6 0SP; www.lamorosa.co.uk; @LamorosaLondon; 9.30 pm, Fri & Sat 10 pm; closed Mon & Sun D; set always available £33 (FP).

Anarkali W6 **£36** 3 4 2

303-305 King St 8748 1760 7–2B

Veteran Hammersmith Indian which "is always very welcoming" and "highly recommended" for its "freshly cooked" fare; even those who say it's "nothing spectacular" note "I always end up meeting friends there for a curry". / W6 9NH; www.anarkalifinedining.com; @AnarkaliDining; midnight; closed Mon L & Sun L; no Amex.

The Anchor & Hope SE1 **£50** 4 3 3

36 The Cut 7928 9898 9–4A

"London's best gastropub" (for the 10th year running) – this "rammed" but "engaging" South Bank fixture is "still an exciting and exhilarating food experience" which "incorporates unusual ingredients (including game and offal) much superior to the norm". "I just wish you could book" (though you can for Sunday lunch). / SE1 8LP; www.anchorandhopepub.co.uk; @AnchorHopeCut; 10.30 pm; closed Mon L & Sun D; no Amex; no booking; set weekday L £31 (FP).

Andina E2 **£35** 3 4 4

1 Redchurch St 7920 6499 12–1B

"Not only is the atmosphere buzzing" – the "fabulous ceviche packs a punch", as do the other "fresh and delicate" dishes, at this trendy Shoreditch Peruvian yearling. / E2 7DJ; www.andinalondon.com; 11 pm; SRA-3.*

The Andover Arms W6 **£46** 3 4 4
57 Aldensey Rd 8748 2155 7–1B
"Everything you could want from a local" – this "cosy" backstreet Brackenbury Village boozer is a "rare" unspoilt pub, "energetically managed", with "proper pub grub"; (that's not why it's perpetually "jammed" however – "that TripAdvisor made it their No. 3 restaurant in London is a case study of all the flaws of its system"). / W6 0DL; www.andoverarms.com; @theandoverarms; 11.30 pm; no Amex.

Andrew Edmunds W1 **£46** 4 4 5
46 Lexington St 7437 5708 3–2D
"For the perfect first date", this "magical" (if "cramped"), candle-lit Soho townhouse is second to none – a "shabby-chic treasure" that's "barely changed in three decades" (although actually, behind the scenes, they put in a big new kitchen this year). The "simple, daily changing fare" is unfailingly good value, but the star turn is the "incredible wines at stunning prices". / W1F 0LW; www.andrewedmunds.com; 10.45 pm, Sun 10.30 pm; no Amex; booking: max 6.

Angels & Gypsies Church Street Hotel SE5 **£45** 3 3 3
29-33 Camberwell Church St 7703 5984 1–3C
It's not quite 'on the map' as once it was, but this casual bar in Camberwell still wins praise for its "unusual and amazing tapas". / SE5 8TR; www.angelsandgypsies.com; @angelsngypsies; 10.30 pm, Fri & Sat 11 pm.

Angelus W2 **£70** 3 5 3
4 Bathurst St 7402 0083 6–2D
"Sommelier-turned-restaurateur Thierry Tomassin offers a stunning, heavily French-accented wine list" and superb, "cosseting" service at his "romantic" converted pub, near Lancaster Gate; fans applaud its "high-class" Gallic cuisine too, although in comparison with the vino it can seem "nice, but a bit 'so what?'" / W2 2SD; www.angelusrestaurant.co.uk; 11 pm, Sun 10 pm.

Angler South Place Hotel EC2 **£77** 4 4 4
3 South Pl 3215 1260 12–2A
"A surprise find in the City, especially on top of a hotel" – the D&D London's rooftop venture is a superb all-rounder, complete with "great views" and an outside terrace; the fish-heavy menu is "elegantly realised", and the set-up is "super for business – calm, smart and efficient". / EC2M 2AF; www.anglerrestaurant.com; @southplacehotel; 10 pm; closed Sat L; booking: max 14.

The Anglesea Arms W6 **£50** 3 3 4
35 Wingate Rd 8749 1291 7–1B
"It's back, thank goodness!", say fans of this "true gastropub" near Ravenscourt Park (which re-opened in new hands last year) – a "lovely", if plain, old inn, long known as one of London's very best, with "way-above-average" seasonal cooking; not absolutely everyone's still smitten though – refuseniks say it's "good that it's returned, but it's lacking something nowadays". / W6 0UR; www.angleseaarmspub.co.uk; @_AngleseaArmsW6; 10 pm, Sun 9 pm; closed weekday L.

L'Anima EC2 **£70** 3 3 3
1 Snowden St 7422 7000 12–2B
"It's a bit of a noisy goldfish bowl, ambience-wise", but the "buzz of City high-flyers" continues to attest to the business-friendly appeal of this "pricey-but-worth-it" Italian; founding chef Francesco Mazzei moved on in March 2015 – fingers crossed Antonio Favuzzi maintains an even keel. / EC2A 2DQ; www.lanima.co.uk; 11 pm, Sat 11.30 pm; closed Sat L & Sun.

L'Anima Café EC2 **£46** 4 4 4
10 Appold St 7422 7080 12–2B
The "less formal (and more keenly priced) sister restaurant of L'Anima" occupies "spacious and inviting" premises around the corner from its sibling, and serves "highly authentic" Italian grub, including pizza. / EC2A 2AP; www.lanimacafe.co.uk; @LAnimacafe; 10 pm; closed Sun.

Anima e Cuore NW1 NEW **£44** 4 3 2
129 Kentish Town Rd 7267 2410 8–2B
Forget the "unprepossessing frontage" – this "tiny" and "low key" Kentish Town newcomer is a "lovely and quirky" trattoria, with "personal, if erratic" service, and an ever-changing menu of "divine pasta" and homemade gelato. / NW1 8PB; 9 pm, Sun 2.30 pm.

Annie's **£46** 2 3 5
162 Thames Rd, W4 8994 9080 1–3A
36-38 White Hart Ln, SW13 8878 2020 10–1A
"Beautiful Boho décor" ("mismatched chairs, rickety tables") and "delightful staff" create "a lovely vibe" at these "romantic" neighbourhood favourites, in Barnes and Strand-on-the-Green; the food's not amazing, but it's "consistent", and brunch is a big hit. / www.anniesrestaurant.co.uk; 10 pm, Sat 10.30 pm, Sun 9.30 pm.

The Anthologist EC2 £45 223
58 Gresham St 0845 468 0101 9–2C
"A vast space, but always a very busy one" – this bar/restaurant, near the Guildhall, is hardly a foodie hotspot, and can be "too noisy", but makes a very versatile City rendezvous. / EC2V 7BB; www.theanthologistbar.co.uk; @theanthologist; 11 pm, Thu & Fri 1 am; closed Sat & Sun; SRA-3.*

L' Antica Pizzeria NW3 £37 433
66 Heath St 7431 8516 8–1A
"Amazing pizza, with an unusually soft and fluffy base" is the product of the "proper, red-hot, wood-fired oven" in use at this "bustling", brick-walled, "café-style" outfit – "a cosy and welcoming little slice of Naples" in central Hampstead. / NW3 1DN; www.anticapizzeria.co.uk; 10.30 pm; Mon-Thu D only, Fri-Sun open L & D.

Antico SE1 £47 343
214 Bermondsey St 7407 4682 9–4D
"It's not as trendy as some nearby rivals", but this three-year-old Bermondsey Italian is still "a favourite haunt of many locals" providing "good, authentic" flavours, and a "lively" ("noisy at peak times") atmosphere. / SE1 3TQ; www.antico-london.co.uk; @AnticoLondon; 10.30 pm; closed Mon.

Antidote W1 £62 433
12a Newburgh St 7287 8488 3–2C
"Tucked away off Carnaby Street", this "wine bar gem" – with "a lovely, small upstairs dining room" – serves some "truly superb" dishes alongside a "fantastic biodynamic wine list". (However, if you seek it out mindful of the kitchen's connection to Hedone's Mikael Jonsson, aside from the marvellous bread, you may leave "a bit disappointed"). / W1F 7RR; www.antidotewinebar.com; @AntidoteWineBar; 10.30 pm; closed Sun; booking: max 8.

Apollo Banana Leaf SW17 £20 421
190 Tooting High St 8696 1423 10–2C
"Ignore the décor and occasionally rushed service" if you visit this "unprepossessing little BYO" ("an old travel agent's shop" in Tooting); "who cares" when the South Indian/Sri Lankan dishes are "fantastic" and "unbelievably cheap"? / SW17 0SF; www.apollobananaleaf.com; 10.30 pm; no Amex.

Applebee's Café SE1 £45 443
5 Stoney St 7407 5777 9–4C
"What could be better?" – "fresh fish straight off the ice" and "simply cooked" is served at this "enjoyably busy" Borough Market café (attached to a fishmongers) and at "sensible prices" too; in a hurry? – grab "a freshly grilled seafood wrap". / SE1 9AA; www.applebeesfish.com; @applebeesfish; 10 pm, Fri 10.30 pm; closed Sun; no Amex.

Apulia EC1 £39 332
50 Long Ln 7600 8107 9–2B
"Informal Italian standby" whose "authentic short menu" makes it "a good bet for a quick bite or working lunch near the Barbican". / EC1A 9EJ; www.apuliarestaurant.co.uk; 10 pm, Sun 3.30 pm; closed Sun D.

aqua kyoto W1 £75 223
240 Regent St (entrance 30 Argyll St) 7478 0540 3–2C
"Great views over rooftops onto Regent Street" are a highpoint of this "noisy and dark" nightclub-esque operation, six floors above the West End; but although its cocktails and Asian-inspired food is well-rated, even fans can find it "very expensive". / W1B 3BR; www.aqua-london.com; @aqualondon; 10.30 pm; closed Sun D; booking: max 6.

aqua nueva W1 £66 334
240 Regent St (entrance 30 Argyll St) 7478 0540 3–2C
Serving northern Spanish food in opulent rooftop surroundings, this nightclubby venue near Oxford Circus provides a restaurant, terrace, Cava bar and two private dining rooms no less! – it was much more consistently highly rated this year. / W1B 3BR; www.aqua-london.com; @aqualondon; 10.30 pm; closed Sun.

Aqua Shard SE1 £85 114
Level 31, 31 St Thomas St 3011 1256 9–4C
"The views and the loos are amazing... the rest's not worth it" – that's the often-damning verdict on the "wondrously designed" but shamelessly "overpriced" vantage point on the Shard's 31st-floor. / SE1 9RY; www.aquashard.co.uk; @aquashard; 10.30 pm.

Arabica Bar and Kitchen SE1 £49 323
3 Rochester Walk 3011 5151 9–4C
Fans of this "casual" (unusually stylish) Borough Market Lebanese acclaim its "fabulous food at reasonable prices"; sceptics however feel it's "fine but nothing special" – "pretty standard, and while pleasant, no more than that". / SE1 9AF; www.arabicabarandkitchen.com; @ArabicaLondon; 10.30 pm, Thu 11 pm, Fri & Sat 11.30 pm, S; closed Sun D.

The Araki W1 NEW £366 544
Unit 4 12 New Burlington St 7287 2481 3–3D
"The sushi is out-of-this-universe, but the prices are too" at this tiny Mayfair newcomer – by quite a margin the UK's most expensive dining experience – where "as one of only 9 customers, the skill of Mitsuhiro Araki is fully on display for your personal benefit"; is it worth the mind-boggling cost? – to most of our reporters the answer is yes! / W1S 3BH; www.the-araki.com; 8.30 pm; D only, closed Mon.

Arbutus W1 £54 3 3 2

63-64 Frith St 7734 4545 4–2A
"Seasonal" cuisine (from "an interesting menu, with lots of unusual cuts and offal") twinned with "excellent and affordable" wine (by the glass and carafe) have won foodie renown for this "unpretentious" ("cramped") Soho spot; of late, however, its performance has been more "middle-of-the-road". / W1D 3JW; www.arbutusrestaurant.co.uk; @arbutus; 10.45 pm, Fri & Sat 11.15 pm, Sun 10.30 pm.

Archduke Wine Bar SE1 £52 2 2 2

153 Concert Hall Approach, South Bank 7928 9370 2–3D
These characterful railway arches "have offered food for decades in various guises" (currently, as an outpost of the 'Black & Blue' chain); "for a quick bite pre-Festival Hall" it's mightily convenient, but otherwise "you wouldn't rush back". / SE1 8XU; www.blackandbluerestaurants.com; 10.30 pm, Sun 10 pm.

Ariana II NW6 £30 4 3 2

241 Kilburn High Rd 3490 6709 1–2B
"Small and basic, but it's the food you come for" – that's the trade-off at this "busy local Afghan BYO" in Kilburn, serving "excellent" scoff ("impeccable stews") at "throwaway prices". / NW6 7JN; www.ariana2restaurant.co.uk; @Ariana2kilburn; midnight.

Ark Fish E18 £43 4 4 2

142 Hermon Hill 8989 5345 1–1D
"Efficient" staff who "look like they're enjoying themselves" add to the appeal of this South Woodford fish 'n' chip restaurant, hailed by some as "the best in East London". / E18 1QH; www.arkfishrestaurant.co.uk; 9.45 pm, Fri & Sat 10.15 pm, Sun 8.45 pm; closed Mon; no Amex.

Artigiano NW3 £48 3 3 3

12a Belsize Ter 7794 4288 8–2A
"For what it is, where it is, excellent!" – a "very decent" and "friendly" Italian in the "quietish backwater" of Belsize Park, whose harshest critic says "it's middle of the road, but there's certainly no reason to complain". / NW3 4AX; www.etruscarestaurants.com; @artigianoesp; 10 pm; closed Mon L.

L'Artista NW11 £34 2 4 4

917 Finchley Rd 8731 7501 1–1B
Archetypal "cheap 'n' cheerful Italian family spot" that's long inhabited the railway arches near Golders Green tube; aside from the "huge pizzas", the food's only "tolerable", but its "friendly waiters" and buoyant atmosphere carry the day, and it's "always busy". / NW11 7PE; www.lartistapizzeria.com; 11.30 pm.

L'Artiste Musclé W1 £49 2 2 4

1 Shepherd Mkt 7493 6150 3–4B
"You feel like you're in France", at this cute, "cramped", little corner-bistro in Shepherd Market, where even fans admit that the "straightforward" fare is "not really the point". / W1J 7PA; @lartistemuscle; 10 pm, Fri-Sun 10.30 pm.

Artusi SE15 £46 4 3 2

161 Bellenden Rd 3302 8200 1–4D
The "simple confidence of the Italian cooking" helps inspire rave reviews for this neighbourhood yearling, hailed by fans as "a perfect culinary experience"; the odd critic though – while acknowledging "it's fairly decent" – feels "the trendy Peckham effect means prices are drifting up". / SE15 4DH; www.artusi.co.uk; @artusipeckham; 10 pm.

Asakusa NW1 £36 5 3 2

265 Eversholt St 7388 8533 8–3C
"Extraordinary value given its top quality and rock-bottom prices" – this "rare Japanese", near Mornington Crescent, serves a wide menu majoring in "amazing sushi", and its "friendly" service softens the "very cramped, mock Tudor interior". / NW1 1BA; 11.30 pm, Sat 11 pm; D only, closed Sun.

Asia de Cuba St Martin's Lane Hotel WC2 £89 2 2 2

45 St Martin's Ln 7300 5588 4–4C
Glossily glam' (and "so, so loud") boutique-hotel hang out, where accusations of style over substance are deafening nowadays; even fans concede its "massive" sharing plates are "very, very, very expensive" and to doubters it's just "a disaster". / WC2N 4HX; www.morganshotelgroup.com; @asiadecuba; midnight, Thu-Sat 12.30 am, Sun 10.30 pm; set pre theatre £51 (FP).

Assunta Madre W1 £104 3 3 2

9-10 Blenheim St 3230 3032 3–2B
With fish flown in fresh from Italy every day this Mayfair spin-off from a Roman original gets a thumbs-up for its seafood; most diners however feel the yearling's "excellent" food is overshadowed by "exorbitant prices" – the plonk is particularly expensive. / W1S 1LJ; www.assuntamadre.com; @assuntamadre; midnight.

Atari-Ya £30 5 3 2

20 James St, W1 7491 1178 3–1A
7 Station Pde, W3 8896 1552 1–2A
1 Station Pde, W5 8896 3175 1–3A
595 High Rd, N12 8446 6669 8–1B
31 Vivian Ave, NW4 8202 2789 1–1B
75 Fairfax Road, NW6 7328 5338 8–2A
"The best sushi" – "the quality of the fish is second to none" – rewards a visit to these "un-glamorous" caffs (run by Japanese food importers); there are only a few tables ("always heaving with folks from Japan"). / www.atariya.co.uk; W1 8 pm, NW4 & NW6 9.30 pm, W9 9 pm; NW4, NW6 closed Mon.

L'Atelier de Joel Robuchon WC2 £95 333
13-15 West St 7010 8600 4–2B
"Exquisite presentation" and "stratospheric" prices are long-running talking points at the Parisian über-chef's "dark and sexy" Covent Garden outpost (where "the top seats are at the chef's counter in the ground-floor dining room"). For most reporters it's still "simply out-of-this-world", but sliding ratings support those who say "the wow-factor has decreased compared to previous years". Swish penthouse bar, with roof terrace. / WC2H 9NE; www.joelrobuchon.co.uk; @latelierlondon; midnight, Sun 10 pm; no trainers; set weekday L & pre-theatre £59 (FP).

Athenaeum, Athenaeum Hotel W1 £67 333
116 Piccadilly 7499 3464 3–4B
"It aspires to no great heights", but this "pleasant" and well-located dining room (facing Green Park) wins consistent praise for its "lovely afternoon teas" ("the sandwiches kept coming...") and "good value set lunches". / W1J 7BJ; www.athenaeumhotel.com; @TheAthenaeum; 11 pm.

The Atlas SW6 £45 444
16 Seagrave Rd 7385 9129 5–3A
In the backstreets, near Earl's Court 2 (currently being demolished), a characterful hostelry that's very much "still a pub", but with a kitchen that "goes well above-and-beyond expectations", serving "often creative", "Italian-influenced" fare; cute side patio. / SW6 1RX; www.theatlaspub.co.uk; @theatlasfulham; 10 pm.

Augustine Kitchen SW11 £46 341
63 Battersea Bridge Rd 7978 7085 5–4C
"It suffers from a dreadful location", but this bistro yearling in Battersea is establishing itself on the back of its "interesting selection of dishes from Savoie", all at a very "bon prix" ("better value than you'd get north of the river"). / SW11 3AU; www.augustine-kitchen.co.uk; @augustinekitchen; 10.30 pm; closed Mon & Sun D.

Aurora W1 £52 345
49 Lexington St 7494 0514 3–2D
"A fantastic little find" in Soho (rather eclipsed by Andrew Edmunds across the road); staff are "very friendly and helpful", it has a "charming" vibe, the "regularly changing, seasonal cooking" is "dependably good", and "its cute courtyard is lovely in warm weather". / W1F 9AP; www.aurorasoho.co.uk; 10 pm, Wed-Sat 10.30 pm, Sun 9 pm.

L'Autre Pied W1 £81 443
5-7 Blandford St 7486 9696 2–1A
"Tremendous", "high-quality" cuisine (including "bargain tasting menus with excellent wine flights") ensures that Pied à Terre's "first-class" Marylebone spin-off continues to "punch above the weight" of its small ("slightly dull and cafe-like") premises. / W1U 3DB; www.lautrepied.co.uk; 10 pm; closed Sun D.

L'Aventure NW8 £60 455
3 Blenheim Ter 7624 6232 8–3A
Catherine Parisot's "little piece of France" is a treasured St John's Wood "institution", and its "gorgeous" style has "survived its recent revamp" unscathed; service is "fantastically kind" (except when La Patronne is having an off day) and its "old-school" cuisine bourgeoise is "superb" (if from a rather "unchanging" menu). / NW8 0EH; 11 pm; closed Sat L & Sun.

The Avenue SW1 £56 233
7-9 St James's St 7321 2111 3–4D
It's "a good venue for a business lunch or dinner", but this large, echoey, rather '90s St James's brasserie – nowadays with an American spin to its menu – "needs a tweak" food-wise to become more of a destination. / SW1A 1EE; www.avenue-restaurant.co.uk; @avenuestjames; 10.30 pm; closed Sat L & Sun.

Awesome Thai SW13 £28 342
68 Church Rd 8563 7027 10–1A
According to Barnes locals, this long-running Thai is "as the name says", but "what really sets it apart is the family atmosphere, with very attentive service", plus "reasonable prices". / SW13 0DQ; www.awesomethai.co.uk; @AwesomeThai1; 10.30 pm, Sun 10 pm; Mon-Thu D only, Fri-Sun open L & D.

Azou W6 £44 333
375 King St 8563 7266 7–2B
"For something a bit different" up Hammersmith way, fans tip this sweet North African café on the main drag, and its "tasty" tagines; others though feel it's "overrated". / W6 9NJ; www.azou.co.uk; @azourestaurant; 11 pm.

Babaji Pide W1 NEW £39 343
73 Shaftesbury Ave 3327 3888 4–3A
"Queues are already forming", at Alan Yau's ambitious new Turkish concept, in the heart of the West End; tables may be "cramped", but there's a "bustling atmosphere" around the open kitchen, and the pizza (pide)-based scoff is, on early feedback, well-rated. / W1D 6EX; www.babaji.com.tr; 11 pm, Fri & Sat 11.30 pm, Sun 10 pm.

Babbo W1 £80 333

39 Albermarle St 3205 1099 3–3C
Near The Ritz, fans hail this "romantic" Mayfair Italian as "a truly delightful operation" with "really lovely food"; to its least enthusiastic followers it's "all right, but nothing special". / W1S 4JQ; www.babborestaurant.co.uk; @BabboRestaurant; 11 pm, Sun 10.30 pm; closed Sat L & Sun L; set weekday L £51 (FP).

Babur SE23 £52 554

119 Brockley Rise 8291 2400 1–4D
"Long live Babur!" – this "stand-out" stalwart remains one of SE London's most notable stars, with an "ever-evolving" menu of "cracking Indian fusion dishes" served by "lovely, friendly and personal" staff in an "understated" and "lively" setting. / SE23 1JP; www.babur.info; @BaburRestaurant; 11.30 pm.

Babylon Kensington Roof Gardens W8 £72 234

99 Kensington High St 7368 3993 5–1A
"You are transported to a far-away place, and yet you are in the centre of Kensington", when you visit this "spectacular" venue, overlooking the famous, lush rooftop gardens below ("arrive early and take a stroll around"); at the price "the cooking lacks a little polish" (so look out for lunch deals). / W8 5SA; www.virgin.com/roofgardens; 10.30 pm; closed Sun D; SRA-3.*

Bacco TW9 £49 343

39 Kew Rd 8332 0348 1–4A
"So much better than the chains!" – this "lovely, easy-going Italian", with its "thoughtful" staff, is well-located opposite Richmond station (and "very handy for either the Orange Tree or Richmond Theatres"); menu-wise "the fresh pasta's always a good choice". / TW9 2NQ; www.bacco-restaurant.co.uk; @BaccoRichmond; 11 pm; closed Sun D.

Il Bacio £36 333

61 Stoke Newington Church St, N16
7249 3833 1–1C
178-184 Blackstock Rd, N5 7226 3339 8–1D
"Always my first choice for a cheap, reliably good local" – these Stoke Newington and Highbury "stalwarts" are a safe bet for "excellent pizza and pasta". / www.ilbaciohighbury.co.uk; 10 pm - 11 pm; no Amex.

Bad Egg City Point EC2 NEW £40 433

Unit 1b, 1 Ropemaker St 3006 6222 12–2A
The moniker gives it away – Neil Rankin's (of Smokehouse Islington) new Moorgate diner is all about "cheeky, naughty and delicious" yolky dishes, that early reports say are "great value". Top Menu Tip: £32 per person boozy brunch which offers unlimited drinks refills. / EC2Y 9AW; www.badegg.london; @badoeuf; Mon-Fri 10 pm, Sat 8 pm, Sun 6 pm; closed Sun D.

Bageriet WC2 £14 444

24 Rose St 7240 0000 4–3C
"Tiny (only 8 seats), but not to be missed" – this bakery and coffee shop is an "authentic corner of Sweden in Covent Garden", with "excellent coffee and divinely decadent cakes"; superb Scandi sarnies too. / WC2E 9EA; www.bageriet.co.uk; @BagerietLondon; 7 pm; closed Sun.

Balans £48 233

60-62 Old Compton St, W1 7439 2183 4–2A
Westfield, Ariel Way, W12 8600 3320 7–1C
214 Chiswick High Rd, W4 8742 1435 7–2A
187 Kensington High St, W8 7376 0115 5–1A
Westfield Stratford, E20 8555 5478 1–1D
The Soho original has all the "charm", but other branches of this late-night chain are "capable" and "well located", and remain a "go-to choice" for breakfast served with a little "vibe and edge", plus "the guaranty of interesting fellow diners at the shared tables". / www.balans.co.uk; midnight-2 am; 34 Old Compton St 24 hrs, E20 11pm; some booking restrictions apply.

The Balcon, Sofitel St James SW1 £59 232

8 Pall Mall 7968 2900 2–3C
"A perfect location for people coming from different areas" and "pretty consistent" cooking can make this "pleasant" hotel brasserie, off Trafalgar Square, an "ideal venue" for business or pre-theatre; on the downside, it can seem rather "empty". / SW1Y 5NG; www.thebalconlondon.com; 10.45 pm, Sun 9.45 pm.

Bald Faced Stag N2 £48 333

69 High Rd 8442 1201 1–1B
"Great name... even better food!" – an East Finchley gastropub that makes a "fantastic local" thanks to its "consistently good" cooking. / N2 8AB; www.thebaldfacedstagn2.co.uk; @thebaldfacestagn2; 10.30 pm, Sun 9.30 pm.

Balls & Company W1 NEW £37

58 Greek St 7851 6688 4–2A
The first restaurant from Aussie 'MasterChef: The Professionals' finalist, Bonny Porter, opened in the heart of Soho just as our survey closed this year, so a pronouncement on her 'meatballs with an elegant twist' will have to wait. / W1D 3DY; www.ballsandcompany.london; @BallsandCompany; 11 pm; closed Sun.

Balthazar WC2 £63 223

4-6 Russell St 3301 1155 4–3D
NYC supremo, Keith McNally's "pricey and flash" Grand Café in Covent Garden is "a disappointing replica" of the Manhattan original; still, even some who concede it's "a definite case of style over substance" say "the buzzy ambience is compensation", or tip it "for a girlie brunch". / WC2E 7BN; www.balthazarlondon.com; @balthazarlondon; 11.30 pm, Fri & Sat 11.45 pm, Sun 10.30 pm.

Baltic SE1 £53 333

74 Blackfriars Rd 7928 1111 9–4A
"There's more hiding behind the facade than you'd expect", at this warehouse-conversion in Borough – a "light and airy" (slightly "cavernous") space; the eastern European fodder can be "surprisingly good", but it's the "amazing list of vodkas" which ensures a visit's "loads of fun". / SE1 8HA; www.balticrestaurant.co.uk; @BalticLondon; 11.15 pm, Sun 10.30 pm; closed Mon L.

The Banana Tree Canteen £35 222

103 Wardour St, W1 7437 1351 3–2D
21-23 Westbourne Grove, W2 7221 4085 6–1C
166 Randolph Ave, W9 7286 3869 8–3A
237-239 West End Ln, NW6 7431 7808 1–1B
75-79 Battersea Rise, SW11 7228 2828 10–2C
412-416 St John St, EC1 7278 7565 8–3D
For "good-value fast food", these Asian-fusion canteens provide an "interesting" selection of dishes, and some "delicious cocktails" too; they're "uncomfortable" though, and strike sceptics as "inauthentic" and "underwhelming". / @bananatree247; Sun-Tue 10.30 pm, Wed-Sat 11 pm; booking: min 6.

Bandol SW10 NEW

6 Hollywood Rd awaiting tel 5–3B
From the owners of Earl's Court yearling, Margaux, a new, more ambitious Gallic venture in Chelsea, set to open in Autumn 2015, dishing up sharing plates of Provençal and Niçoise cuisine. / SW10 9HY; @margaux_bandol.

Bangkok SW7 £42 332

9 Bute St 7584 8529 5–2B
To its (largely silver-haired) devotees, this "old school" South Kensington Thai is "always a winner", even after over 40 years in business; its cooking style is, though, arguably a tad "monolithic". / SW7 3EY; www.thebankokrestaurant.co.uk; 10.45 pm; no Amex.

Bank Westminster St James Court Hotel SW1 £62 222

45 Buckingham Gate 7630 6644 2–4B
A "lovely conservatory" is an undisputed highlight of this "very professional brasserie", near Buckingham Palace; other aspects are mixed – what is a "good business restaurant" to fans, is to foes "overpriced, with standards equivalent to Garfunkel's or Café Rouge". / SW1E 6BS; www.bankrestaurants.com; @bank_westmin; 11 pm; closed Sat L & Sun.

Banners N8 £42 345

21 Park Rd 8348 2930 1–1C
"Make sure you're hungry" if you visit this "beloved" Crouch End stalwart, where the Caribbean-influenced scran comes in "huge portions"; brunch is a massive deal here – "you won't get a table unless you're early". / N8 8TE; www.bannersrestaurant.com; 11.30 pm, Fri & Sat midnight, Sun 11 pm; no Amex.

Bao W1 NEW £28 542

53 Lexington St no tel 3–2D
"A Soho legend in the making!"; this Taiwanese phenomenon has (with backing from the Sethi family, of Gymkhana fame) "successfully made the transition from Hackney street stall to tiny restaurant"; the pay-off for the legendary queues? – "heavenly soft buns filled with tasty, slow-cooked meat", and "the best, crunchy fried chicken in London". / W1F 9AS; www.baolondon.com; @bao_london; 10 pm; closed Sun.

Baozi Inn WC2 £24 432

25 Newport Ct 7287 6877 4–3B
"I don't mind the lack of space (even the lack of a place to put my coat)" – this Chinatown caff "isn't cheerful, but it is cheap and very good", serving "top Sichuan street food" ("succulent baozi buns... delicious noodles..."). / WC2H 7JS; www.baoziinnlondon.com; 10 pm, Fri & Sat 10.30 pm; no credit cards; no booking.

Bar Boulud, Mandarin Oriental SW1 £70 333

66 Knightsbridge 7201 3899 5–1D
"How can you not love their burgers?" – they're "the best in town" according to the armies of fans of this NYC super-chef's "stylish" and "always buzzing" brasserie in the basement of a grand Knightsbridge hotel; its ratings are slipping though, perhaps because it's just "not cheap". / SW1X 7LA; www.barboulud.com; @barbouludlondon; 10.45 pm, Sun 9.45 pm.

Bar Esteban N8 £39 534
29 Park Rd 8340 3090 1–1C
Crouch End locals "can't recommend this place heartily enough" – from the "almost perfect" tapas to the "bustling" atmosphere – a "wonderful" neighbourhood restaurant. / N8 8TE; www.baresteban.com; Mon-Sat 10.30 pm, Sun 9 pm; closed weekday L.

Bar Italia W1 £28 345
22 Frith St 7437 4520 4–2A
"Bringing a little bit of Italia to our streets since time immemorial" – a tiny Soho legend serving up "the best coffee in London and great people-watching", 24/7. / W1D 4RT; www.baritaliasoho.co.uk; @TheBaristas; open 24 hours, Sun 4 am; no Amex; no booking.

Bar Termini W1 NEW £35 444
7 Old Compton St awaiting tel 4–2B
"Small, cosy, and perfect for pre- or post-dinner drinks", Tony Conigliaro's (of Zetter Townhouse fame) new Soho cicchetti and cocktail bar attracts nothing but raves – from the "faultless" service to the "unbeatable" Italian coffee. / W1D 5JE; www.bar-termini.com; @Bar_Termini; Mon-Thu 11.30 pm, Fri & Sat midnight, Sun 10.30 pm.

Barbecoa £65 121
194-196 Piccadilly, W1 awaiting tel 3–3D NEW
20 New Change Pas, EC4 3005 8555 9–2B
"Stunning views over the roof top of St Paul's Cathedral" at the City original is the "saving grace" at Jamie O's temple for meat-lovers, where prices are "shocking" for what's basically a BBQ – "I've had better on street markets". A massive 300-cover new Piccadilly sibling is set to open in December 2015. / www.barbecoa.com; @Barbecoa_london.

La Barca SE1 £73 232
80-81 Lower Marsh 7928 2226 9–4A
"In the gastronomic desert of Waterloo", it's worth knowing of this "definitely old-style, but popular" Italian "time-warp"; its prices are a little "through the roof", but "you end up getting drawn back" by its "tasty" cooking and "excellent" service. / SE1 7AB; www.labarca-ristorante.com; @labarca1976; 11.30 pm; closed Sat L & Sun.

Il Baretto W1 £63 322
43 Blandford St 7486 7340 2–1A
"Expensive but easy-going Italian, in a very noisy Marylebone basement"; fans love its "fun" and "always buzzing" style and "quality" pizza and pasta – to critics "the food's good, but not good value, and it's not the most relaxed place". / W1U 7HF; www.ilbaretto.co.uk; @IlBarettoLondon; 10.15 pm, Sun 9.45 pm.

Barnyard W1 £44 222
18 Charlotte St 7580 3842 2–1C
"More thought to making the food good, rather than the look trendy" would go down well at Ollie Dabbous's conscientiously "casual", and rather "gimmicky" Fitzrovia diner ("decked out to look like the inside of a barn"); it's at its best for "a lively brunch". / W1T 2LZ; www.barnyard-london.com; Mon-Wed 10 pm, Thu-Sat 10.30 pm, Sun 8.30 pm.

Barrafina £42 555
54 Frith St, W1 7813 8016 4–2A
10 Adelaide St, WC2 7440 1456 4–4C
43 Drury Ln, WC2 7440 1456 4–2D NEW
"I'm never happier than perched on a stool here, watching the incredible food being prepared!" – The Hart Bros have fully captured the zeitgeist with their "thrilling" small foodie meccas in Soho and Covent Garden – "truly exciting, vibrant London experiences" founded in "some of the best tapas outside Barcelona" (and in particular "peerlessly fresh fish"), "fabulous" wines and sherries, and "empathetic" service. "You wait over an hour for a seat, but it really is THAT good!" Incredibly, the second branch is rated just as highly as the Frith Street original, and to sound in-the-know, remark on how the Josper Oven makes the fish taste even better at Adelaide Street. Can they pull it off again with Branch No. 3? / www.barrafina.co.uk; 11 pm, Sun 10 pm; no booking.

Barrica W1 £45 333
62 Goodge St 7436 9448 2–1B
"Like being transported to Madrid" – a "surprisingly genuine" Fitzrovia tapas bar, well-acclaimed for its "substantial, scrumptious plates", "fab wine list" and "decent value". / W1T 4NE; www.barrica.co.uk; 10.30 pm; closed Sun.

Barshu W1 £54 412
28 Frith St 7287 8822 4–3A
It's "not for the faint-hearted", but for a "fragrant chilli fix", the "uncompromisingly" fiery Sichuan cuisine at this Soho café makes it "one of the best Chinese options in town"; you don't go for the ambience however, and service is "curt". / W1D 5LF; www.barshurestaurant.co.uk; @BarshuLondon; 10.30 pm, Fri & Sat 11 pm.

Basilico £39 441
Branches throughout London
"The champions of pizza delivery" – this small chain provides "top quality, with fantastic ingredients", if you're prepared to "splash out a bit" price-wise. / www.basilico.co.uk; @basilicopizzas; 11 pm; no booking.

Bea's Of Bloomsbury WC1 £39 433
44 Theobalds Rd 7242 8330 2–1D
"An absolute must if you're in the area at tea-time" – a "very cosy café near the Holborn Library", serving "great coffee and the best cupcakes this side of the Atlantic"; (there are also small spin-offs near St Paul's and near Farringdon Station). / WC1X 8NW; www.beasofbloomsbury.com; @beas_bloomsbury; 7 pm; L only.

Beach Blanket Babylon £65 113
45 Ledbury Rd, W11 7229 2907 6–1B
19-23 Bethnal Green Rd, E1 7749 3540 12–1C
Atmospheric Gaudi-esque decor underpins the surprisingly enduring appeal of these hip haunts, in Notting Hill and Shoreditch – it sure ain't the clueless service, nor the inept and pricey food. / www.beachblanket.co.uk; 10.30 pm; W11 booking advisable Fri-Sat.

Beagle E2 £47 433
397-399 7613 2967 12–1B
Occupying two Hoxton railway arches, a big, "cool but approachable" brasserie with open kitchen from a former Rochelle's Canteen chef that's typically "packed and buzzing" (and can be very noisy), and serves "reasonably priced" fare. / E2 8HZ; www.beaglelondon.co.uk; @beaglelondon; 10.30 pm, Sun 5 pm; closed Sun D.

Beast W1 £113 222
3 Chapel Pl 7495 1816 3–1B
"Theatrics far outweigh the food", at this "utterly mad" Goodman-group yearling, where "huge" quantities of top-quality surf 'n' turf is served in a low-lit communal space, "evoking the spirit of a medieval banquet"; to converts its "obscenely delicious", but to those appalled by the "US-style portion excess" and "maniac pricing", "it's just gross". / W1G 0BG; www.beastrestaurant.co.uk; @beastrestaurant; 10 pm; closed Mon & Sun.

Beer and Buns EC2 NEW £36
3 Appold St 7539 9209 12–2B
Billing itself as the Square Mile's only pop-up (although now in permanent residence above K10 Appold Street) this newcomer offering Japanese beers, buns and "hot-n-spicy" wings pleases a few early days reporters, albeit in "a noisy environment". / EC2A 2AF; www.beerandbuns.co.uk; Mon-Fri 11 pm.

The Begging Bowl SE15 £37 333
168 Bellenden Rd 7635 2627 1–4D
"A real Thai", say fans of this "tiny" and "tightly packed" no-bookings Peckham hotspot, extolling its "superb", authentic flavours; doubters though say it's "by numbers for the middle class locals slumming it... oooh such adventure!" / SE15 4BW; www.thebeggingbowl.co.uk; @thebeggingbowl; Mon-Sat 9.45 pm, Sun 9.15 pm.

Bel Canto Corus Hotel Hyde Park W2 £52 244
1 Lancaster Gate 7262 1678 6–2C
An entertaining night out; considering you go to have your dinner punctuated by professionally-sung operatic arias, the food at this fun Bayswater basement dining room can be rather better than you might expect. / W2 3LG; www.belcantolondon.co.uk; 9.15 pm; D only, closed Mon & Sun.

Belgo £42 222
29-31 Old Compton St, W1 7437 7284 4–2A NEW
50 Earlham St, WC2 7813 2233 4–2C
67 Kingsway, WC2 7242 7469 2–2D
72 Chalk Farm Rd, NW1 7267 0718 8–2B
"Cavernous" Belgian moules-frites halls complete with waiters dressed as monks; critics say they've "lost their novelty", but the opening of the first new branch in years – in Soho – shows there's plenty of life in the old dog yet? Top Tips – the "brilliant Continental beer selection", and early evening 'Beat the Clock' deal. / www.belgo-restaurants.co.uk; 10 pm - 11 pm, WC2 Thu midnight, Fri & Sat 1 am.

Bellamy's W1 £60 344
18-18a Bruton Pl 7491 2727 3–2B
"A refined atmosphere not found in many restaurants" helps make Gavin Rankin's "clubby" and "luxurious" brasserie – tucked away in a tranquil Mayfair mews – a particular "winner for a business lunch"; its straightforward, often "rich" cuisine is "expensive but worth it". / W1J 6LY; www.bellamysrestaurant.co.uk; 10.30 pm; closed Sat L & Sun.

Bellanger N1 NEW
9 Islington Grn awaiting tel 8–3D
Corbin & King head outside of the West End as they take over the site some still recall as Browns (long RIP), near Islington Green; the naming strategy for the duo's latest European grand café continues the vintage car riff of the Wolseley and Delaunay – this time the marque was Bellanger Frères (1912–1925). / N1 2XH; www.bellanger.co.uk; 10.30pm, Sun 10 pm.

Bellevue Rendez-Vous SW17 £46 333
218 Trinity Rd 8767 5810 10–2C
"Old school French menu" and "very solid cooking" in a "lovely local" near Wandsworth Common; it was good under its previous owners, but fans say both "venue and service has improved" since the Gazette group took it over. / SW17 7HP; www.bellevuerendezvous.com; 10.30 pm; closed Mon L; no Amex.

Belvedere W8 £68 224
Holland Pk, off Abbotsbury Rd 7602 1238 7–1D
"A delightful walk through the park" sets the scene at this "elegant" Art Deco feature in Holland Park (and when it's warm, you can sit on the terrace); its pricey and "unadventurous" cooking has never been a highlight, but seemed even more "disappointing" this year. / W8 6LU; www.belvedererestaurant.co.uk; 10.30 pm; closed Sun D; set always available £43 (FP).

Benares W1 £95 322
12a Berkeley Square Hs, Berkeley Sq 7629 8886 3–3B
"Beautifully thought out" and "adventurous" 'nouvelle Indian' cuisine continues to make Atul Kochar's slick-looking (but "windowless") Mayfair operation one of the Capital's best-known dining destinations; slipping ratings, though, accompany fears that it risks becoming for "expense accounters only". / W1J 6BS; www.benaresrestaurant.co.uk; @benaresofficial; 10.45 pm; closed Sun L.

Bengal Clipper SE1 £42 322
Shad Thames 7357 9001 9–4D
"Solid, upmarket Indian" near Butler's Wharf, sometimes let down by "variable service", though "the food is usually to a high standard". / SE1 2YR; www.bengalclipper.co.uk; @bengalclipper; 11.30 pm, Sun 11 pm.

Bentley's W1 £82 443
11-15 Swallow St 7734 4756 3–3D
"Always fun, especially in the downstairs oyster bar" – Richard Corrigan's "classy" fish veteran, near Piccadilly Circus, won vigorous praise this year for its "amazing" oysters and other "bang-on" fish and seafood; there's a "pleasingly traditional" upstairs restaurant too. / W1B 4DG; www.bentleys.org; @bentleys_london; 10.30 pm; no jeans; booking: max 8; set pre theatre £52 (FP).

Berber & Q E8 NEW £42 434
Arch 338 Acton Mews no tel 1–2D
If you can hack the "thumping house music" at this "über-hip Haggerston railway arch renovation" you'll be dealt metal trays of "smoky, sticky, melt-in-the-mouth BBQ'd meats", surprisingly "sublime veg dishes" and "excellent" cocktails; be prepared to queue though (no ressies – natch!). / E8 4EA; www.berberandq.com; @BerberAndQ; 10.30 pm, Sun 9.30 pm; D only, closed Mon; no booking.

The Berners Tavern, London EDITION W1 £72 224
10 Berners St 7908 7979 3–1D
"You feel like a movie star" in this "opulent" and "dramatic" room – one of London's "most gorgeous" – which offers the scope for "fabulous people watching"; prices are "inflated" however, and the food (under Jason Atherton no less) is no better than "competent". / W1T 3NP; www.bernerstavern.com; 11.45 pm, Sun 10.15 pm.

Best Mangal £36 432
619 Fulham Rd, SW6 7610 0009 5–4A
104 North End Rd, W14 7610 1050 7–2D
66 North End Rd, W14 7602 0212 7–2D
"Fantastic grilled meats", "all cooked over a mammoth charcoal grill", are supplemented by "super-fresh salads" at these "cheerful and cheap" Turks, in west London. / www.bestmangal.com; midnight, Sat 1 am; no Amex.

Bianco43 £43 322
7 Northumberland Ave, WC2 7321 2915 2–3C
43 Greenwich Church St, SE10 8858 2668 1–3D
1-3 Lee Rd, SE3 8318 2700 1–4D
"Excellent pizzas" (from a Neapolitan wood-fired oven), plus other well-rated fare, win praise for this Italian trio, which have expanded from their original bases in Greenwich and Blackheath, with a recent opening near Trafalgar Square. / www.bianco43.com.

Bibendum SW3 £75 233
81 Fulham Rd 7581 5817 5–2C
"On a fine day, one of the loveliest rooms in London" – this "civilised" stalwart in the old Michelin Building is a landmark of Brompton Cross; its "stonking" wine list is nowadays a more reliable attraction than its "variable" cuisine however, and "you'll need deep pockets to enjoy it". / SW3 6RD; www.bibendum.co.uk; 11 pm, Sun 10.30 pm; booking: max 10; set Sun L £55 (FP).

Bibendum Oyster Bar SW3 £52 242
81 Fulham Rd 7589 1480 5–2C
A cute spot for a luxurious light bite – the chic café off the foyer of Chelsea's Conran Shop is "great for shellfish" ("and has been serving hot food for a few years now" too). / SW3 6RD; www.bibendum.co.uk; @bibendumrestaurant; 10 pm; no booking.

Bibimbap Soho £29 322
10 Charlotte St, W1 7323 6890 2–1C
11 Greek St, W1 7287 3434 4–2A
39 Leadenhall Mkt, EC3 7283 9165 9–2D
"The Korean experience is intensified by the K-Pop posters and Polaroids of happy punters" at these "fast, fun and creative" outfits in Soho, Fitzrovia and Leadenhall Market, whose signature dish – "basically a big stone bowl filled with rice, veg, and meat or seafood" – is "excellent value". /

Bibo SW15 £50 443
146 Upper Richmond Rd 8780 0592 10–2B
The interior is "simple and quite stark", but this Putney sibling to Barnes's Sonny's wins an all-round thumbs up for its "casual" style, "knowledgeable and professional" service, and "superb and authentic" modern Italian cooking. / SW15 2SW; www.biborestaurant.com; @biborestaurant; 10.45 pm.

Big Easy £50 223
12 Maiden Ln, WC2 3728 4888 4–3D
332-334 King's Rd, SW3 7352 4071 5–3C
Crossrail Pl, E14 awaiting tel 11–1C
"Chaotic" service can add to the "buzzy" sense of "mania" at these fun (and kid-friendly) crab shacks, where the lobster, shrimp and other fare come in "massive portions"; there's quite a feeling, though, that the less established Covent Garden branch "isn't a patch on Chelsea". / www.bigeasy.co.uk; @bigeasytweet; Mon-Thu 11 pm, Fri-Sat 11.30, Sun 10.30 pm.

Bilbao Berria SW1 £52 223
2 Regent St 7930 8408 3–3D
There are plusses and minuses at this Theatreland spot (with restaurant below); positives include "plush" decor and "unusual, delicious" tapas – negatives "Fawlty Towers service" and stiff prices. / SW1Y 4LR; www.bilbaoberria.co.uk; Mon-Wed 10.30 pm, Thu-Sat 11 pm; closed Sun.

Bill's £39 123
Branches throughout London
Explosive growth has "lost the identity and special character" of this easygoing chain, whose cooking is too often "barely average" nowadays; the rustic interiors are "still fun and appealing" however, and – for family-friendliness and "a large variety of breakfast options" it still wins many nominations. / most branches 11 pm; no booking.

The Bingham TW10 £65 324
61-63 Petersham Rd 8940 0902 1–4A
"A picturesque setting, with wonderful views over the Thames" makes this "romantic" Richmond boutique hotel dining room "an ideal spot for a long summer lunch", even if "the food can vary from lovely to blah". Top Tip – "the phenomenal value market lunch menu". / TW10 6UT; www.thebingham.co.uk; @thebingham; 10 pm; closed Sun D; no trainers; set weekday L £41 (FP).

Bird £38 332
81 Holloway Rd, N7 3195 8788 8–2D
42-44 Kingsland Rd, E2 7613 5168 12–1B
You can choose anything, so long as it's fried chicken, if you visit this hip, year-old Shoreditch canteen – on most accounts a "simple and brilliant" formula. /

Bird in Hand W14 £46 333
Brook Green 7371 2721 7–1C
"The pizzas are the best" at this "good local hangout" – an attractively converted ex-pub in Brook Green; the rest of the menu is now modern tapas, which some locals judge "less impressive". / W14 0LR; www.thebirdinhandlondon.com; @TBIHLondon; 10 pm, Sun 9.15 pm.

Bird of Smithfield EC1 £63 223
26 Smithfield St 7559 5100 9–2B
Fans of this five-story old Georgian townhouse in Smithfield (with summer roof terrace) love its "classy, tranquil and smooth" style, and "funky" cooking; its ratings are dragged down though by refuseniks who say "it's not as good as expected, and too expensive". / EC1A 9LB; www.birdofsmithfield.com; @BirdoSmithfield; 10 pm; closed Sun; cancellation charge for larger bookings; set always available £36 (FP).

Bistro 1 £28 232
27 Frith St, W1 7734 6204 4–3A
33 Southampton St, WC2 7379 7585 4–3D
"Excellent prices for central london" found the appeal of these popular budget West End bistros; are they getting a bit complacent though? – "I go about 15 times a year, and while it's still great value, quality is slipping". / www.bistro1.co.uk; @bistro1_london; midnight.

Bistro Aix N8 £53 442
54 Topsfield Pde, Tottenham Ln 8340 6346 8–1C
"They say it's in Crouch End, but it feels like rural France" – so say fans of this "small", "closely packed" and rather "romantic" fixture, which serves "traditional" bistro fare that's "well-executed and presented". / N8 8PT; www.bistroaix.co.uk; @bistroaixlondon; 10 pm, Fri & Sat 11 pm; Mon-Thu D only, Fri-Sun open L & D; no Amex; set weekday L & pre-theatre £39 (FP).

Bistrò by Shot SW6 NEW £48 343

28 Parsons Green Ln 7371 7533 10–1B

A "cosy", all-day, café-cum-bistro near Parsons Green, with an evening menu featuring 'proper' cooking; initial reports suggest it's a cut-above (and that goes for the coffee too). / SW6 4HS; www.bistrobyshot.com; @Bistrobyshot; 10 pm, Sun 6 pm; closed Sun D; set weekday L £31 (FP).

Bistro Union SW4 £46 343

40 Abbeville Rd 7042 6400 10–2D

"Great quality and great value" inspire most who report on Adam (Trinity) Byatt's "bustly" Clapham bistro; no denying the few critics, though, for whom it "doesn't quite make it", "sacrificing taste and quality for trendiness and novelty factor". / SW4 9NG; www.bistrounion.co.uk; @BistroUnion; 10 pm, Sun 8 pm.

Blackfoot Bar & Backroom Dining EC1 £45 333

46 Exmouth Mkt 7837 4384 9–1A

"Pork in all forms of delicious-ness" and the "genuine character" of its setting (a reclaimed pie 'n' mash shop) wins consistent (if not quite universal) praise for Allegra McEvedy's Farringdon yearling. / EC1R 4QL; www.blackfootrestaurant.co.uk; @blackfootEC1; 10.15 pm; closed Sun.

Blacklock W1 NEW £35 443

25 Great Windmill St 3441 6996 3–2D

"Chops, chops and more chops" is the promise at this "buzzy", new "industrial-style" Soho basement; it certainly does "exactly what it says on the tin", and "it's hard to go wrong with large piles of meat at a decent price". / W1D 7LH; www.theblacklock.com; @blacklocksoho; 11.30 pm; closed Sun.

Blanchette W1 £39 345

9 D'Arblay St 7439 8100 3–1D

"What a find!"; this "lovely and romantic" (if "cramped") Soho yearling is "a gem" – superb "buzzy" atmosphere, "knowledgeable" service, and "delightful" Gallic take on 'tapas' too. / W1F 8DS; www.blanchettesoho.co.uk; @blanchettesoho; 11 pm, Sun 9 pm.

Bleecker Street Burger E1 NEW £16 432

Unit B Pavilion Building, Spitalfields Mkt 0 7712 5405 01 12–2B

"Patties cooked to perfection with drooling cheese" is the promise of New Yorker, Zan Kaufman's popular pop-up, whose permanent Spitalfields Market perch is starting to supplant her roving matt-black van. / E1 6AA; www.bleeckerburger.co.uk; @bleeckerburger; 9 pm.

Bleeding Heart Restaurant EC1 £63 335

Bleeding Heart Yd, Greville St 7242 8238 9–2A

"Tucked away in a quiet corner of Hatton Garden", this "old-fashioned" warren – comprising a restaurant, tavern and bistro – is equally superb for "business bonding", or "seductive romance". The Gallic cuisine is "a safe bet", but it's the "epic" wine list and marvellously "cosy and intimate" style that are the real clinchers. / EC1N 8SJ; www.bleedingheart.co.uk; @bleedingheartyd; 10.30 pm; closed Sat & Sun.

Blixen E1 NEW £51 323

65a Brushfield St 7101 0093 12–2B

"Filling a gap in the market near Spitalfields" – this "light and airy" new brasserie is a "good all-dayer" occupying an attractively converted former bank (and with a "beautiful outside terrace"); service, however, is not always "up to speed". / E1 6AA; www.blixen.co.uk; @BlixenLondon; 11 pm, Sun 8 pm.

Blue Elephant SW6 £54 223

The Boulevard 7751 3111 10–1B

On the plus-side this "out-on-a-limb" Imperial Wharf Thai has "romantic" lush jungle décor, and nice waterside views; there are significant negatives too though – "it's not a patch on the old one in Fulham Broadway", and prices are OTT ("you could find better value in Mayfair without trekking to Chelsea Harbour!)" / SW6 2UB; www.blueelephant.com; @BlueElephantLon; 10.30 pm, Fri & Sat 11.30 pm; closed weekday L.

Bluebird SW3 £63 123

350 King's Rd 7559 1000 5–3C

Airy, potentially stylish bar/restaurant, on the first floor of the well-known Chelsea landmark, which shows "no great love for guests or cooking" and is "so expensive"; come on D&D London, it's time to sort this one out... / SW3 5UU; www.bluebird-restaurant.co.uk; @bluebirdchelsea; 10.30 pm, Sun 9.30 pm; set always available £32 (FP).

Blueprint Café, Design Museum SE1 £48 235

28 Shad Thames, Butler's Wharf 7378 7031 9–4D

"If you can't get romantic with the amazing views of the Thames and Tower Bridge here, best settle down to the single life!"; predictably though "it's the venue that impresses" – even fans say the food "won't blow your socks off", and to critics it's plain "lazy". / SE1 2YD; www.blueprintcafe.co.uk; @BlueprintCafe; 10.30 pm.

Bó Drake W1 NEW £44 2 2 3

6 Greek St no tel 4–2A

A "very cool, young vibe" infuses this "small and stylish" new addition to Soho, whose combination of East Asian cuisine and BBQ (plus cocktails) "is in high demand"; not everyone is wowed though, with a couple of reports of "a totally underwhelming experience". / W1D 4DE; www.bodrake.co.uk; @bodrakesoho; 10.30 pm; closed Sun.

Bob Bob Ricard W1 £65 3 4 5

1 Upper James St 3145 1000 3–2D

"Love the 'press for champagne' button on every table!" – this "wacky" Soho diner is "perfect for an intimate meal" or "girl's lunch" thanks to its fun, boothed seating, "OTT" decor and "charming" service; on the downside, the cooking is no more than "high-end comfort food" and "prices are silly for what you get". Top Menu Tip – "excellent beef Wellington". / W1F 9DF; www.bobbobricard.com; @BobBobRicard; Sun-Fri 11.15 pm, Sat midnight; closed Sat L; jacket required.

The Bobbin SW4 £46 3 4 3

1-3 Lillieshall Rd 7738 8953 10–1D

"A cosy little gem in a side street off the Pavement in Clapham", with "an airy conservatory and adorable garden out back", providing "excellent" service, and "a great range" of pub grub. / SW4 0LN; www.thebobbinclapham.com; @bobbinsw4; 10 pm, Sun 9 pm.

Bobo Social W1 £45 4 4 3

95 Charlotte St 7636 9310 2–1C

"Outstanding" rare-breed burgers are improbably served on "chintzy crockery" at this "tiny", "simple town-house, front room conversion" at the northerly end of Fitzrovia's restaurant row; it's all "a welcome departure from the typical ranch-style approach" – nice cocktails too. / W1T 4PZ; www.bobosocial.com; @BoboSocial; 10.30 pm; closed Sun.

BOCCA DI LUPO W1 £58 5 4 4

12 Archer St 7734 2223 3–2D

"Phenomenal" Italian tapas – "really unusual" dishes from all over the country, including lots of game and offal – help inspire mass adulation for Jacob Kennedy and Victor Hugo's "wildly popular" venture, near Piccadilly Circus. It has a "wonderful", "casual" atmosphere too – if an "incredibly noisy" one – with many reports tipping the bar-side perches as the best seats in the house. Desserts are "particularly original" too (or "skip pud, and go to Gelupo, their 'sister' ice cream shop opposite"). See also Vico. / W1D 7BB; www.boccadilupo.com; @boccadilupo; 11 pm, Sun 9.30 pm; booking: max 10.

Al Boccon di'vino TW9 £67 4 4 5

14 Red Lion St 8940 9060 1–4A

"Holy moly!"; "a mind-boggling parade of Italian dishes" from a "never-ending, no-choice tasting menu" rewards the trip to this "mad one-off" in central Richmond; "you never know quite what you're going to get", and "it's a little overwhelming, but certainly an experience!" / TW9 1RW; www.nonsolovinoltd.co.uk; 8 pm; closed Mon, Tue L & Wed L.

Bodean's £44 2 2 3

10 Poland St, W1 7287 7575 3–1D
4 Broadway Chambers, SW6 7610 0440 5–4A
169 Clapham High St, SW4 7622 4248 10–2D
201 City Rd, EC1 7608 7230 12–1A NEW
16 Byward St, EC3 7488 3883 9–3D

These "very casual" US-style BBQ haunts "have some real competition" nowadays, and – though "reliable" – their meaty-licious mix of ribs, pulled pork, steaks, burgers and dogs needs to "up its game" to stand out as once it did. / www.bodeansbbq.com; 11 pm, Sun 10.30 pm; booking: min 8.

La Bodega Negra W1 £50 2 2 4

16 Moor St 7758 4100 4–2B

Fans say there's a "fun" (if "so noisy") time to be had at this dim-lit Mexican basement in Soho – the food's "quite good" too ("if overpriced for what it is") but the service can be "appalling". / W1D 5NH; www.labodeganegra.com; 1 am, Sun midnight; set weekday L £28 (FP).

Boisdale SW1 £63 2 2 3

13-15 Eccleston St 7730 6922 2–4B

"Plush jock-inese decor"... "spectacular cigar terrace and whisky selection"... "amazing wine list"... "traditional, meaty Scottish fare"... live jazz – this Belgravia bastion is well-known as a "clubbable" redoubt of male revelry; its ratings were hit this year though by some reports of "terrible" service and "unexciting" meals. / SW1W 9LX; www.boisdale.co.uk; @boisdale; midnight; closed Sat L & Sun.

Boisdale of Bishopsgate EC2 £66 2 2 2

202 Bishopsgate, Swedeland Ct 7283 1763 9–2D

"A Dickensian alley" leads to this City offshoot of the Victoria original "with an old world club-like feel to it"; fans applaud its meaty Caledonian fare and appeal as a business venue – critics though find the cooking merely "acceptable". / EC2M 4NR; www.boisdale.co.uk; @Boisdale; 11 pm, Sat midnight; closed Sat L & Sun.

Boisdale of Canary Wharf E14 £63 333

Cabot Pl 7715 5818 11–1C
Canary Wharf spin-off from the famous Belgravia Caledonian that's "a little on the expensive side", but often tipped especially for business, thanks to its "excellent" steaks and seafood bar, "great range of drinks" and "spacious" interior; "cigars outside a bonus" (if you like that sort of thing). / E14 4QT; www.boisdale.co.uk; @boisdaleCW; 11 pm; closed Sun D.

Bombay Brasserie SW7 £59 333

Courtfield Close, Gloucester Rd 7370 4040 5–2B
This "posh" South Kensington stalwart wins praise for its "refined" cooking and "elegant" décor (particularly in the conservatory); even fans can find it "pricey" however, and its ratings slipped a tad this year – perhaps the challenges caused by its ongoing refurbishment programme. / SW7 4QH; www.bombaybrasserielondon.com; @bbsw7; 11.30 pm, Sun 10.30 pm; closed Mon L.

Bombay Palace W2 £49 542

50 Connaught St 7723 8855 6–1D
"All the ambience of Terminal 3, but quality is sky high!" – this grand but "drab" Bayswater Indian is "not the most exciting venue", but "that does nothing to disguise the fabulous flavours" of its "exemplary" cooking, which has been "consistent over many years"; it closed unexpectedly in summer 2015, but was set to re-open in mid-Autumn. / W2 2AA; www.bombay-palace.co.uk; @bombaypalacew2; 11 pm.

Bone Daddies £34 444

30-31 Peter St, W1 7287 8581 3–2D
Whole Foods, Kensington High St, W8 7287 8581 5–1A NEW
The Bower, Baldwin St, EC1 7439 9299 12–1A NEW
"Go early to avoid the crazy queues, and being rammed next to loads of self-adoring 20-somethings", if you grab a bite at this "rock 'n' roll ramen house" in Soho, which doesn't only offer "silky, rich noodle dishes", but lots of other "enormously tasty" snacks. (Top Menu Tips include the "incredible miso aubergine" and "ever-so nice green tea ice cream".) It has an OK spin off over Kensington's Whole Foods too, and – coming soon – a branch in its spiritual home – Shoreditch (and see also Shackfuyu). /

Bonhams Restaurant, Bonhams Auction House W1 NEW £68 433

101 New Bond St 7468 5868 3–2B
Especially for a business lunch, it's worth considering this smart new dining room, set at the back of the famous Mayfair auction house (but also with its own entrance) – the cooking's very "accomplished", and "there are some genuine bargains lurking within the wine list". / W1S 1SR; www.bonhams.com/locations/RES; 8.30 pm; closed Sat & Sun.

Bonnie Gull W1 £58 443

21a Foley St 7436 0921 2–1B
"Like a weekend to the Cornish coast without the traffic!" – this "cute" Fitzrovia "seafood shack" may be "cramped" and "noisy" but it has won a wide reputation with its "simply prepared and beautifully cooked fish". See also Bonnie Gull Seafood Bar in Exmouth Market. / W1W 6DS; www.bonniegull.com; @BonnieGull; 9.45 pm, Sun 8.45 pm.

Bonnie Gull Seafood Bar EC1 £55 332

55-57 Exmouth Mkt 3122 0047 9–1A
"Little portions of deliciousness" from a menu of "simple", but "different" fishy small plates mostly win a very good rep for this Exmouth Market café, although there is also a school of thought that it's "fine but not outstanding". / EC1R 4QE; www.bonniegullseafoodbar.com; @BonnieGull; 9.30 pm; closed Sun.

The Booking Office, St Pancras Renaissance Hotel NW1 £66 224

Euston Rd 7841 3566 8–3C
All agree the "unique" setting – the conversion of St Pancras's old ticket office – is "glorious" and "very atmospheric" at what's nowadays an adjunct to a swish hotel; too often of late however, it's been "a shame" about its "poor cooking", and "prices are very salty". / NW1 2AR; www.bookingofficerestaurant.com; 11 pm.

Boom Burger £20 332

272 Portobello Rd, W10 8960 3533 6–1A
1 Brixton Station Rd, SW9 awaiting tel 10–2D NEW
"Jamaican patties are all the rage at this different Portobello venue" (which now has a new Brixton spin off). / www.boomburger.co.uk; @BOOMburgerLDN.

Boopshis W1 £40 333

31 Windmill St 3205 0072 2–1C

"The owners found their Austrian grandmother's recipe book and copied well!" – a "cheap 'n' cheerful" corner café in Fitzrovia, majoring in "excellent schnitzels"; a downside? – "it can get a bit boring after a few visits!" / W1T 2JN; www.boopshis.com; @boopshis; 10 pm; closed Sun.

Boqueria SW2 £34 344

192 Acre Ln 7733 4408 10–2D

"It's easy to over-order" at this "vibrant" and extremely popular little outfit, between Clapham and Brixton – the "terrific tapas" is "inexpensive", and there's "a really warm welcome" too. / SW2 5UL; www.boqueriatapas.com; @BoqueriaTapas; 11 pm, Fri & Sat midnight, Sun 10 pm; closed weekday L.

Il Bordello E1 £50 354

81 Wapping High St 7481 9950 11–1A

"Exemplary service" – "full of Italian warmth" – helps win this "closely packed" and "noisy" Wapping local "gem" a hugely devoted following, and it's atmosphere's "terrific"; as for the "proper, homely Italian cooking", portions are "enormous" (with "brilliant pizza" a highlight). / E1W 2YN; www.ilbordello.com; 11 pm, Sun 10.30 pm; closed Sat L.

Boro Bistro SE1 £42 333

Montague Cl, 6-10 Borough High St 7378 0788 9–3C

Limited feedback this year on this small bistro (with outside terrace), cutely nestled against picturesque Southwark Cathedral – it's well-rated though, and praised for its good value tapas-y fare. / SE1 9QQ; www.borobistro.co.uk; @borobistro; 10.30 pm; closed Mon & Sun.

La Bota N8 £35 334

31 Broadway Pde 8340 3082 1–1C

"Wonderful cooking at hard-to-beat prices" ensures that this long-established Crouch End tapas haunt is "always busy". / N8 9DB; www.labota.co.uk; 11 pm, Sun 10.30 pm; closed Mon L; no Amex.

The Botanist £63 223

7 Sloane Sq, SW1 7730 0077 5–2D

Broadgate Circle, EC2 awaiting tel 12–2B NEW

The hugely convenient location of this "very buzzy" Sloane Square rendezvous, "probably explains why it's overpriced"; it has a new Broadgate sibling, which is "good for a quick business lunch", but likewise only "averagely good" in most respects. / www.thebotanistlondon.com.

Boudin Blanc W1 £58 224

5 Trebeck St 7499 3292 3–4B

"A beautiful Mayfair setting" (with many al fresco tables) and "festive" atmosphere ensures this Shepherd Market bistro remains "absolutely packed"; its menu of Gallic staples is "not cheap" though, and sceptics feel it's now "trading on its location". / W1J 7LT; www.boudinblanc.co.uk; 11 pm.

Bouillabaisse W1 NEW £84

4 Mill St 3794 8448 3–2C

Kurt Zdesar's seafood specialist on the former site of Alvin Leung's Bo London (RIP) in Mayfair opened in June 2015, too late for our survey; at £60 a portion, let's hope they do a good job with the signature dish. / W1S 2AX; www.bouillabaisse.co.uk; @BouillabaisseW1; 10.30 pm.

Boulestin SW1 £70 232

5 St James's St 7930 2030 3–4D

"Reviving the name of the very famous Boulestin", Joel Kissin's ambitious yearling occupies "elegant" premises "tucked away in St James's", and is "brilliant in warm weather" thanks to its "delightful private courtyard"; it's "not cheap" though, and while the food is "trying hard", critics feel it's "lost its way". / SW1A 1EF; www.boulestin.co.uk; @BoulestinLondon; 10.30 pm; closed Sun; set pre theatre £42 (FP).

The Boundary E2 £63 335

2-4 Boundary St 7729 1051 12–1B

The "stunning rooftop terrace", and "impressive basement dining room" both win praise for Sir Terence Conran's "chilled" Shoreditch operation; its "professional" cuisine is well-rated too, although "tiny" portions are a bugbear. / E2 7DD; www.theboundary.co.uk; @BoundaryLDN; 10.30 pm; D only, ex Sun L only.

The Brackenbury W6 £52 343

129-131 Brackenbury Rd 8741 4928 7–1C

"It's so nice to have this neighbourhood pearl back in business"; Ossie Gray's year-old regime at this convivial, if higgledy-piggledy, Hammersmith favourite is working well, and "you have to admire doing proper cooking in a small backstreet spot";"strong wine list too". / W6 0BQ; www.brackenburyrestaurant.co.uk; @BrackenburyRest; 10 pm; closed Mon; set weekday L £33 (FP).

Bradley's NW3 £59 332

25 Winchester Rd 7722 3457 8–2A

"Close by Hampstead Theatre" – this Swiss Cottage backstreet fixture is "always full before a show"; for other occasions, it inspires limited feedback, but it's quite a classy spot in an "area that's not well-endowed" – "fish is particularly reliable". / NW3 3NR; www.bradleysnw3.co.uk; 10 pm; closed Sun D; set Sun L £37 (FP).

Brady's SW18 **£34** 3 3 3
Dolphin Hs, Smugglers Way 8877 9599 10–2B
"Upmarket", "quirky" fish 'n' chip restaurant, run by the Brady family, whose longstanding success allowed it to expand to a Battersea riverside site a year ago; one or two regulars feel it has "no ambience" now, but ratings support those who say it's "still an excellent, unpretentious local". / SW18 1DG; www.bradysfish.co.uk; @Bradyfish; 10 pm; closed Mon, Tue L, Wed L, Thu L & Sun; no Amex; no booking.

La Brasserie SW3 **£55** 2 2 4
272 Brompton Rd 7581 3089 5–2C
"Truly French in feel" – this "slick and buzzy" old-favourite is, say fans, "always a safe bet" particularly for a languid breakfast with the papers; it's not cheap however, and harsher critics jibe that its "Chelsea clientele is obviously easily pleased..." / SW3 2AW; www.labrasserielondon.co.uk; @labrasserie; Mon-Sat 11.30 pm, Sun 11 pm; no booking, S & Sun L; set always available £35 (FP).

Brasserie Blanc **£51** 2 2 2
Branches throughout London
Raymond B's brasserie chain "looks more attractive than most" (especially its wonderfully situated Covent Garden branch above the piazza); even many fans describe its performance as "nothing outstanding" though, and some reports were "terrible" this year ("Maman Blanc would be appalled...") / www.brasserieblanc.com; most branches close between 10 pm & 11 pm; SE1 closed Sun D, most City branches closed Sat & Sun.

Brasserie Chavot W1 **£71** 3 4 4
41 Conduit St 7183 6425 3–2C
Eric Chavot's "classy and delightful" Mayfair chamber "just gets better and better", winning very solid praise this year for its "spacious" setting, "consistently excellent" service and for its "high quality", "upmarket brasserie fare". / W1S 2YQ; www.brasseriechavot.com; @brasseriechavot; 10.30 pm, Sun 9 pm.

Brasserie Gustave SW3 **£49** 4 5 3
4 Sydney St 7352 1712 5–2C
A charming host of the "bon-bibeur variety", along with "definitively French" cooking have made a big hit of this brasserie yearling, on the Chelsea site that was formerly MPW's Sydney Street Grill (RIP); named for Gustave Eiffel (designer of a Parisian landmark) – it's amiably clichéd style is "one of dated reminisces through-and-through". / SW3 6PP; www.brasserie-gustave.com; @brassergustave; 10.30 pm, Fri & Sat 11 pm; closed Mon & Tue L; set Sun L £39 (FP).

Brasserie Toulouse-Lautrec SE11 **£45** 3 3 3
140 Newington Butts 7582 6800 1–3C
"A good bolt hole" in the unlovely environs of Elephant & Castle, this Gallic venture provides "dependable bistro-ish food in large portions, plus friendly service, all at a decent price". / SE11 4RN; www.btlrestaurant.co.uk; @btlrestaurant; 10.30 pm, Sat & Sun 11 pm.

BRASSERIE ZÉDEL W1 **£40** 2 4 5
20 Sherwood St 7734 4888 3–2D
"Sumptuous and gilded", Corbin & King's "amazing" (listed) Art Deco basement is reminiscent of the grandest Parisian brasseries, and in three short years has become a West End landmark. OK, the realisation of the huge Gallic menu is extremely "pedestrian", but compensation is provided by the "really efficient" service and – mindful of all the grandeur – prices that are "astonishing value" for somewhere a stone's throw from Piccadilly Circus. / W1F 7ED; www.brasseriezedel.com; @brasseriezedel; 11.45 pm; set always available £29 (FP).

Bravas E1 **£44** 3 3 3
St Katharine Docks 7481 1464 9–3D
"A nice surprise in lovely St Katherine Docks" – this "buzzy" yearling provides an "attractive" vantage-point from which to envy the marina's yacht-owners, and "genuine" tapas that's "slightly out-of-the-ordinary". / E1W 1AT; www.bravastapas.co.uk; @Bravas_Tapas; 10 pm.

Brawn E2 **£50** 5 4 4
49 Columbia Rd 7729 5692 12–1C
"Quirky" but "outstanding" dishes from Ed Wilson, twinned with "adventurous wines, with advice from passionate staff" make for a "fascinating foodie experience", at this "rustic" East End bistro, which remains Caves de Pyrène's top property. / E2 7RG; www.brawn.co; @brawn49; 11 pm; closed Mon L & Sun D; no Amex; set Sun L £41 (FP).

Bread Street Kitchen EC4 **£67** 1 1 1
10 Bread St 3030 4050 9–2B
As a business option, Gordon Ramsay's "enormous" venue in a City shopping mall does have a few fans; for non-expense-accounters though, it's "a Kitchen Nightmare", given its "thoroughly impersonal" style, "thinly stretched" service, and food that's very "run-of-the-mill". / EC4M 9AJ; www.breadstreetkitchen.com; @breadstkitchen; 11 pm, Sun 8 pm.

Brew £38 223

45 Northcote Rd, SW11 7585 2198 10–2C n
Lower Richmond Rd, SW15 8789 8287 10–2A
342 Old York Rd, SW18 8871 0713 10–2B
21 High St, SW19 8947 4034 10–2B

"A great brunch range" and "top quality coffee" help win praise for these "easygoing" hang outs in Clapham, Putney, Wandsworth and Wimbledon; they often miss their mark too though – even many who say the food is "fine" say it's "extortionately pricey for what it is", and service-wise can evoke the spirit of "compu'er says no"! / www.brew-cafe.com.

Briciole W1 £40 343

20 Homer St 7723 0040 6–1D

Fans of Latium's "buzzy" little brother in the backwoods of Marylebone say it "continues to delight" with its "very attentive" service and "simple, high quality deli food" from an open kitchen; "don't go when it's busy though", when it can seem more "average". / W1H 4NA; www.briciole.co.uk; @briciolelondon; 10.15 pm.

Brick Lane Beigel Bake E1 £6 421

159 Brick Ln 7729 0616 12–1C

"Unbeatable for fending off the munchies 24/7!"; a treasured "defiantly no frills" East Ender, serving "the best take-away salt beef beigel in London" – "how long can it hold out against gentrification?" / E1 6SB; open 24 hours; no credit cards; no booking.

Brigade The Fire Station SE1 £54 233

139 Tooley St 0844 346 1225 9–4D

Former fire station, near London bridge – nowadays a bistro providing employment for the homeless; most (if not quite all) reporters are satisfied by the provisions, and all agree it's "a worthwhile social enterprise". / SE1 2HZ; www.thebrigade.co.uk; @brigadeSE1; 10 pm; closed Sun.

The Bright Courtyard W1 £59 434

43-45 Baker St 7486 6998 2–1A

There's "major competition nearby" (from the Royal Chinas), but this "upmarket Chinese" is – for its smaller following – "by far the best", with "modern and superior surroundings" (indeed with a bright courtyard), and dim sum that's "excellent" and "sophisticated". / W1U 8EW; www.lifefashiongroup.com; @BrightCourtyard; 10.45 pm, Thu-Sat 11.15 pm.

Brilliant UB2 £38 443

72-76 Western Rd 8574 1928 1–3A

"The name says it all!", say fans of this Southall legend, lost in a tangle of suburban streets – "it's busy and vaguely chaotic" but serves "authentic Punjabi food" that's "excellent value". / UB2 5DZ; www.brilliantrestaurant.com; @BrilliantRST; 11 pm, Fri & Sat 11.30 pm; closed Mon, Sat L & Sun L.

Brinkley's SW10 £54 224

47 Hollywood Rd 7351 1683 5–3B

"A really fun, local haunt" for the (older) Chelsea set – John Brinkley's buzzy bar/restaurant is an "old favourite" hereabouts, although its "fantastic value wines" are the big draw, not its "very average food"; (sadly its lovely garden is now an extension to the main restaurant). / SW10 9HX; www.brinkleys.com; @BrinkleysR ; 11 pm, Sun 10.30 pm; closed weekday L.

The Brown Cow SW6 £43 333

676 Fulham Rd 7384 9559 10–1B

"Nearly as good as its sibling the Sand's End" – a heart-of-Fulham gastropub (on the site that was Manson, RIP) with quality cooking and an atmosphere that's "part pub, part French brasserie". / SW6 5SA; www.thebrowncowpub.co.uk; @TheBrownCowPub; 10 pm.

The Brown Dog SW13 £50 334

28 Cross St 8392 2200 10–1A

"A perfect country-style pub, tucked away in a super-cute terraced Barnes backstreet, and a great oasis for a quiet, relaxing meal from the short menu of simple, fresh dishes"; "being able to take the dog along is a bonus". / SW13 0AP; www.thebrowndog.co.uk; @browndogbarnes; 10 pm, Sun 9 pm.

(Hix at Albemarle) Brown's Hotel W1 £73 222

Albemarle St 7518 4004 3–3C

Fans of this "discreet and quiet" Mayfair "oasis" approve of its "classy", business-friendly grandeur, including for a "civilised breakfast"; "despite being well-appointed, it feels somewhat soulless" however, and even with Mark Hix's involvement the cooking is "very mainstream" and "very expensive". / W1S 4BP; www.thealbemarlerestaurant.com; @HIXMayfair; 11 pm, Sun 10.30 pm.

Brunswick House Café SW8 £48 225

30 Wandsworth Rd 7720 2926 10–1D

The "surreal" set up – "an eccentric but charming dining room full of reclaimed objects from the adjacent architectural salvage operation" – is the special draw to this vast Georgian house, at Vauxhall Cross; on the downside, service can be "shoddy", and "you pay a lot" nowadays for food that arguably "tries too hard". / SW8 2LG; www.brunswickhousecafe.co.uk; 10 pm; closed Sun D.

Bubbledogs W1 £30 1 2 3
70 Charlotte St 7637 7770 2–1C
"A glass of fizz and a huge variety of hot dogs... great!", so say fans of this Fitzrovia two-year-old, for whom it's "delightfully fun"; "once is enough" for many reporters though, who either find the concept no more than "faintly amusing", or who "just don't get it". / W1T 4QG; www.bubbledogs.co.uk; @bubbledogsUK; 9 pm; closed Sun.

(Kitchen Table) Bubbledogs W1 £102 4 4 4
70 Charlotte St 7637 7770 2–1C
"What a concept!" – you discover this "haven of gastronomy arranged around an open chef's table" by walking through a curtain from the adjoining hot dog place; it's a "unique" and "fascinating" experience – "great fun talking to the chef", with cuisine that's "imaginative, well-balanced, amusing, exciting... absolutely superb". / W1T 4QG; www.kitchentablelondon.co.uk; @bubbledogsKT; 9.30 pm (6 pm & 7.30 pm seatings only); D only, closed Mon & Sun.

Buddha-Bar London SW1 £69 3 3 3
145 Knightsbridge 3667 5222 5–1D
"Lacking the caché of its international counterparts", this nightclubby operation generates little feedback for a large haunt in the heart of Knightsbridge; still, even if it's "not cheap", its Pan-Asian fare is worth a try. / SW1X 7PA; www.buddhabarlondon.com; @BuddhaBarLondon; 10 pm.

Buen Ayre E8 £52 5 3 3
50 Broadway Mkt 7275 9900 1–2D
A carnivore's delight, this "bare" and "noisy" Argentine 'parrilla' in Hackney provides a "fantastic informal atmosphere" – "tremendous steak (cooked just the way it should be)" and "a great choice of Malbec" help make it "impossible to get a table". / E8 4QJ; www.buenayre.co.uk; 10.30 pm; no Amex.

Buenos Aires Cafe £51 3 4 3
86 Royal Hill, SE10 8488 6764 1–3D
17 Royal Pde, SE3 8318 5333 1–4D
"Excellent steaks, pizza and decent wine" are highlights of this popular Blackheath Argentinian (run by a retired tango dancer!); no feedback this year on its café-like Greenwich offshoot. / www.buenosairesltd.com; SE3 10.30 pm, SE10 7 pm, Sat & Sun 6 pm; no Amex.

The Builders Arms SW3 £48 2 3 4
13 Britten St 7349 9040 5–2C
Some feel "it rests on its lovely location", but this modernised backstreet boozer is nevertheless one of Chelsea's better watering holes, with an "excellent" ambience and reasonable scran. / SW3 3TY; www.geronimo-inns.co.uk; @BuildersChelsea; 10 pm, Thu-Sat 11 pm, Sun 9 pm; no booking.

The Bull N6 £46 2 3 4
13 North Hill 8341 0510 1–1C
"A real gem" that's "widely popular among Highgate residents" – a "most comfortable" pub with its own microbrewery, serving "a fantastic selection of beers and ales", plus food that's "successful enough". / N6 4AB; thebullhighgate.co.uk; @Bull_Highgate; 10 pm.

The Bull & Gate NW5 £49 3 2 3
389 Kentish Town Rd 3437 0905 8–2B
It took Young's two years to restore this old Kentish Town boozer, but by all accounts its a huge improvement – "great food, so different from how it was". / NW5 2TJ; www.bullandgatenw5.co.uk; @BullandGateNW5; 10 pm, Sun 9 pm.

Bull & Last NW5 £60 4 3 3
168 Highgate Rd 7267 3641 8–1B
"Just what a gastropub should be" – North London's top boozer is an "always enjoyable" Kentish Town destination, with "hearty food that gives a nice nod to the seasons". / NW5 1QS; www.thebullandlast.co.uk; @thebullandlast; 10 pm, Sun 9 pm.

Bumpkin £52 2 2 2
119 Sydney St, SW3 3730 9344 5–2B
102 Old Brompton Rd, SW7 7341 0802 5–2B
209 Westbourne Park Rd, W11 7243 9818 6–1B
Westfield Stratford City, The Street, E20 8221 9900 1–1D
"The success is mystifying" of these "casual" faux-rustic diners, that make much of their local sourcing and seasonality; aside from being "patient with kids", service can be "atrocious" and the food "distinctly average". / www.bumpkinuk.com; 11 pm; closed Mon.

Bunnychow W1 £11 3 2 2
74 Wardour St 3697 7762 3–2D
South African former street-food pop-up that now has a permanent Soho base, serving "cheap, bountiful and tasty" scoff; in case you're wondering, a bunnychow is a stuffed loaf. / W1F 0TE; www.bunnychow.com; @thebunnychow.

Buona Sera £40 3 3 3
289a King's Rd, SW3 7352 8827 5–3C
22 Northcote Rd, SW11 7228 9925 10–2C
"I've been going for 26 years: same staff, same menu, same ambience – what's not to like?"; the "happy but loud" Battersea original of this Italian duo is perpetually "crammed with yelling locals of all ages" drawn by its "cheap, simple and tasty" pizza and pasta; (no-one much mentions SW3, with its funny double-decker seating). / midnight; SW3 11.30 pm, Sun 10 pm; SW3 closed Mon L.

Burger & Lobster £45 323
29 Clarges St, W1 7409 1699 3–4B
36 Dean St, W1 7432 4800 4–2A
6 Little Portland St, W1 7907 7760 3–1C
40 St John St, EC1 7490 9230 9–1B
Bow Bells Hs, 1 Bread St, EC4 7248 1789 9–2B
"For a simple, no-nonsense meal" with "a real buzz", armies of fans still heartily recommend these "relaxed" surf 'n' turf diners, lauding the "succulent lobsters" and "amazing" burgers. Ratings continue to slide south however, and for a few cynics it's turning into "McDonalds, but with better lighting". / www.burgerandlobster.com; @Londonlobster; 10.30 pm; Clarges St closed Sun D, Bread St & St John St closed Sun.

Busaba Eathai £39 224
Branches throughout London
"Just that bit more interesting than Wagamama" (same founder) – these highly popular, communal Thai canteens make a "dependable" option, even if their stylish interiors "have greater wow factor than the food"; "favourite dish? – the calamari". / www.busaba.co.uk; 11 pm, Fri & Sat 11.30 pm, Sun 10 pm; W1 no booking; WC1 booking: min 10.

Bush Dining Hall W12 £45 222
304 Uxbridge Rd 8749 0731 7–1B
For a "homely brunch" or "simple" bite, fans recommend this Boho café next to the music venue; the menu is "limited" however, and critics see its distressed, vintage style as a case of "Shepherd's Bush mutton dressed as Chiswick lamb!" / W12 7LJ; www.bushhalldining.co.uk; @BushHallDining; 10.30 pm, Fri & Sat 10 pm; closed Sun D.

Butcher & Grill SW11 £42 223
39-41 Parkgate Rd 7924 3999 5–4C
Battersea restaurant, deli and attached butcher shop; for a steak or brunch it has its fans, but service is "not always up to scratch", and "the food has a way to go to be more than average". Top Menu Tip – on 'Happy Mondays' get 50% off steaks. / SW11 4NP; www.thebutcherandgrill.com; @ButcherGrill; 11 pm, Sun 4 pm; closed Sun D.

The Butcher's Hook SW6 £48 343
477 Fulham Rd 7385 4654 5–4A
"It's brilliant!", say fans of this attractive boozer, just down the road from Stamford Bridge, applauded for its "always great cooking and friendly staff". / SW6 1HL; www.thebutchershook.co.uk; @thebutchershook; 10.30 pm; no Amex.

Butlers Wharf Chop House SE1 £59 233
36e Shad Thames 7403 3403 9–4D
The main reason to seek out this Thames-side business-standby is for "great views of Tower Bridge" – the food can be hit-and-miss ("better to eat that which hasn't been cooked") and the place feels "in need of a refurb". / SE1 2YE; www.chophouse-restaurant.co.uk; @BWChophouse; 11 pm, Sun 10 pm.

La Buvette TW9 £42 334
6 Church Walk 8940 6264 1–4A
"Tucked away" in "a lovely old courtyard beside a church", right in the heart of Richmond, this "sweet and secluded" bistro feels rather "special", and serves "dependable" and "good value", traditional French cuisine (if from a "limited" menu). / TW9 1SN; www.labuvette.co.uk; @labuvettebistro; 10 pm.

Byron £38 233
Branches throughout London
"In spite of the Five Guys and Shake Shacks of the world, this takes some beating!"; its attractive, "individually designed" branches "come in all shapes and sizes", staff are "very cheery and efficient" and "you always get a delicious burger". / www.byronhamburgers.com; -most branches 11 pm.

C London W1 £100 123
25 Davies St 7399 0500 3–2B
"Full of wannabes!"; this "extortionately expensive" Mayfair eurotrash-magnet too often provides "amateur" service and "terrible" Italian food – "thank god we were taken!" / W1K 3DE; www.crestaurant.co.uk; 11.45 pm.

C&R Cafe £35 422
3-4 Rupert Ct, W1 7434 1128 4–3A
52 Westbourne Grove, W2 7221 7979 6–1B
"A stand-out in Chinatown" – the original West End branch of this Malaysian duo, serving "excellent", "cheap" food that's "a great approximation of the real thing" (high marks for the lesser known Bayswater outlet too). Top Menu Tip – "the best Laksa in the UK!" / www.cnrrestaurant.com; 10.30pm; W2 closed Tue.

Caboose, The Old Truman Brewery E1 £31
Ely's Yd, Brick Ln 07437 209 275 12–2C
For a "small get-together with family and friends", this custom-built railway cabin outside Brick Lane's Old Truman Brewery is an "amazing" place, according to its tiny fan club (too few reports for a rating); complementing the keenly priced private hire experience is a street food offering of slow smoked meats and burgers. / E1 6QR; www.wearecaboose.com; @WeAreCaboose; 11 pm.

Café 209 SW6 £26 2 3 3

209 Munster Rd 7385 3625 10–1B

"Joy is hilarious" – long may she reign over her tiny BYO caff in deepest Fulham, where "cheap" Thai chow is part of a visit that's "very good fun". / SW6 6BX; 10.30 pm; D only, closed Sun, closed Dec; no Amex.

Café Below EC2 £40 3 3 4

St Mary-le-Bow, Cheapside 7329 0789 9–2B

"Hard to believe such a quiet haven exists just off Cheapside" as this "atmospheric crypt" under Bow Bells church, where service is "friendly and fast", and the "simple", "distinctive", "daily-changing" cooking is "delicious" and "decently priced". Top Menu Tip – "the set, 3-course Friday dinner is a bargain". / EC2 6AU; www.cafebelow.co.uk; @cafebelow ; 9 pm; closed Mon D, Tue D, Sat & Sun.

Café Bohème W1 £48 2 4 4

13 Old Compton St 7734 0623 4–2A

"Perennially jam-packed", all-hours French-style bar/café/restaurant in the heart of Soho, where everyone loves the "lively" vibe; it "can deliver some very good dishes" too, but some non-drinkers find it "so crowded you don't really want to eat". / W1 5JQ; www.cafeboheme.co.uk; @CafeBoheme1; 2.45 am, Sun midnight; no booking; set Sun L £41 (FP).

Café del Parc N19 £43 5 4 3

167 Junction Road 7281 5684 8–1C

"There's no menu" – you eat the chef's selection of "magical", "Moorish-influenced" tapas at this "terrific", if "tiny" neighbourhood "sparkler" in Tuffnell Park, and service is "brilliant" too. / N19 5PZ; www.delparc.com; @delParc; 10.30 pm; open D only, Wed-Sun; no Amex.

Café du Marché EC1 £55 3 3 4

22 Charterhouse Sq 7608 1609 9–1B

"Well hidden down an alleyway in Smithfield", this "delightfully tucked-away" stalwart imports the ambience of a rustic French farmhouse to EC1, serving a "solidly Gallic" menu of "classic bistro fare". By day it's a business lunch favourite, at night live jazz adds to its "cosy, candlelit and romantic" appeal. / EC1M 6DX; www.cafedumarche.co.uk; @lecafedumarche; 10 pm; closed Sat L & Sun.

Café East SE16 £23 4 2 2

100 Redriff Rd 7252 1212 11–2B

"Tremendous value at negligible cost" is provided by this "fast-paced", "basic" and "noisy" canteen in Bermondsey, "which sticks faithfully to its Vietnamese roots" (in particular the "satisfying and delicious pho"). / SE16 7LH; www.cafeeast.foodkingdom.com; @cafeeastpho; 10.30 pm, Sun 10 pm; closed Tue.

Cafe Football, Westfield Stratford E20 NEW £46 2 3 3

The St 8702 2590 1–1D

Themed around 'the beautiful game', this large and glossy Stratford venue doesn't aim for foodie fireworks, but is "great for kids, or to watch a game with the lads". / E20 1EN; www.cafe-football.com; @cafefootballuk; 11.30 pm.

Café in the Crypt, St Martin's in the Fields WC2 £33 2 2 3

Duncannon St 7766 1158 2–2C

"If you want a quick bite" near Trafalgar Square, St Martin-in-the-Field's "bustling" self-service crypt is just the job – the food (soup, sarnies, a few hot dishes) is only "average", but the characterful setting is "delightful", portions are "generous", and prices low. / WC2N 4JJ; stmartin-in-the-fields.org/cafe-in-the-crypt; 8 pm, Thu-Sat 9 pm, Sun 6 pm; no Amex; no booking.

Café Murano £53 4 4 4

33 St James's St, SW1 3371 5559 3–3C
34-36 Tavistock St, WC2 3371 5559 4–3D NEW

"Satisfying on every level" – Angela Hartnett's "cosmopolitan and delightful" year-old spin off in St James's has shot to fame thanks to its "disciplined" service and "well-pitched", "reasonably priced" Italian fare; post-survey, a 140-cover Covent Garden sibling opened in late June 2015. / www.cafemurano.co.uk.

Café Pistou EC1 £46 3 2 3

8-10 Exmouth Mkt 7278 5333 9–1A

"Bustling and characterful little bistro" that on most accounts is a welcome addition to Exmouth Market; the small plates are possibly a bit "too small" though, and loud music contributes to a "noisy" atmosphere. / EC1R 4QA; www.cafepistou.co.uk; @CafePistou; 10.30 pm.

Café Spice Namaste E1 £56 4 4 3

16 Prescot St 7488 9242 11–1A

Cyrus Todiwala's "vibrantly decorated" Indian is a longstanding bright spark in the "culinary desert" south of Whitechapel; service is "jolly" and his "original" and "delicate" Parsi cooking remains a distinct "cut above" ("the specials are always worth a try"). / E1 8AZ; www.cafespice.co.uk; @cafespicenamast; 10.30 pm; closed Sat L & Sun.

Caffè Caldesi W1 £60 3 4 3

118 Marylebone Ln 7487 0754 2–1A

A "comfortable" and "pleasant all-rounder" that's long been a fixture of Marylebone; the "robust, regional food is utterly reliable" and "served with friendliness and care". / W1U 2QF; www.caldesi.com; 10.30 pm, Sun 9.30 pm.

Caffé Vergnano £39 2 2 3

Staple Inn, 337-338 High Holborn, WC1 7242 7119 9–2A
62 Charing Cross Rd, WC2 7240 3512 4–3B
Royal Festival Hall, SE1 7921 9339 2–3D
2 New Street Sq, EC4 7936 3404 9–2A

Smaller outlets can still be "a delightful sanctuary with excellent coffee", but the best-known and biggest SE1 branch ("convenient for the Festival Hall", and serving light Italian dishes) put in a mixed showing this year, with too many reports of cooking that was "tired" and "tasteless". / www.caffevergnano1882.co.uk; EC4 11 pm, SE1 midnight; WC2 8 pm, Fri & Sat midnight; EC4 Sat & Sun; no Amex.

La Cage Imaginaire NW3 £49 3 4 4

16 Flask Walk 7794 6674 8–1A

"A smashing little French restaurant in a cute corner of Hampstead Village", this "hidden gem" is "very cosy" indeed; however, food-wise it's "variable (you suspect when the chef is off, they're not as clued up)". / NW3 1HE; www.la-cage-imaginaire.co.uk; @CageImaginaire; 11 pm.

Cah-Chi £37 3 3 2

394 Garratt Ln, SW18 8946 8811 10–2B
34 Durham Rd, SW20 8947 1081 10–2B

"Numerous well-dressed Korean diners is testament to the freshness and quality of the cooking" (some of it BBQ at the table) at these "simple" venues, in Earlsfield and Raynes Park; BYO. / www.cahchi.com; SW20 11 pm; SW18 11 pm, Sat & Sun 11.30 pm; SW20 closed Mon; cash only.

The Camberwell Arms SE5 £55 4 3 3

65 Camberwell Church St 7358 4364 1–3C

"Unusual and utterly delicious" British fare – "strong cooking geared towards offal" – helps make this "confident" yearling "a great addition to SE5"; it's from the same stable as Anchor & Hope – "at least the wait here is shorter". / SE5 8TR; www.thecamberwellarms.co.uk; @camberwellarms; closed Mon L & Sun D.

Cambio de Tercio SW5 £69 3 3 3

161-163 Old Brompton Rd 7244 8970 5–2B

"Expert" cooking (in particular "innovative" tapas) and a "spectacular selection of Spanish wines" has carved a major culinary reputation for Abel Lusa's "colourful" Earl's Court Spaniard; one or two "average" experiences, however, dented ratings this year. / SW5 0LJ; www.cambiodetercio.co.uk; @CambiodTercio; 11.15 pm, Sun 11 pm.

Camino £47 3 3 3

3 Varnishers Yd, Regent Quarter, N1 7841 7331 8–3C
The Blue Fin Building, 5 Canvey St, SE1 3617 3169 9–4A NEW
15 Mincing Ln, EC3 7841 7335 9–3D
33 Blackfriars Ln, EC4 7125 0930 9–2A

The "buzzy" King's Cross original of this emerging chain, now has a popular (if "terribly noisy") spin off, near the Old Bailey, and a new outlet in Bankside too; all win praise for "helpful" service and "tasty" tapas. / www.camino.uk.com; EC3 & EC4 closed Sat & Sun.

(Hotel du Vin) Cannizaro House SW19 £60 2 3 3

West Side, Wimbledon Common 0871 943 0345 10–2A

"Delightfully positioned" by Wimbledon Common, this "romantic" small property is nowadays part of the Hotel du Vin group; you can eat in either the 'bistro' or garden-side Orangerie – reports are few, but suggest that since it changed hands the food is somewhat "improved". / SW19 4UE; www.hotelduvin.com/locations/wimbledon/; @HotelduVinBrand; 10 pm.

Canta Napoli £37 3 3 2

9 Devonshire Rd, W4 8994 5225 7–2A
136 High St, TW11 8977 3344 1–4A

"Terrific, half-metre pizzas" and service that "tries to please" are highlights of these Chiswick and Teddington Italians. / 10.30 pm; no Amex.

Canteen £42 2 2 1

Royal Festival Hall, SE1 0845 686 1122 2–3D
Park Pavilion, 40 Canada Sq, E14 0845 686 1122 11–1C
Crispin Pl, Old Spitalf'ds Mkt, E1 0845 686 1122 12–2B

The promise is of British "comfort food" efficiently delivered at these spartan canteens (whose handily located South Bank branch can be "great for a business lunch"); its ratings are perennially hamstrung though by incidents of "sloppy" service, and "the worst cooking ever". / www.canteen.co.uk; 11 pm, E14 & W1 Sun 7 pm; no booking weekend L.

Cantina Laredo WC2 £52 4 4 4

10 Upper St Martin's Ln 7420 0630 4–3C

"It's great how they make the guacamole at the table" – that's just part of the array of "fresh", "clean-flavoured" Mexican food at this "polished" and "buzzy" Covent Garden operation. / WC2H 9FB; www.cantinalaredo.co.uk; @CantinaLaredoUK; 11.30 pm, Fri & Sat midnight, Sun 10.30 pm.

Canton Arms SW8 £48 3 2 4
177 South Lambeth Rd 7582 8710 10–1D
"In a drab bit of Stockwell", this well-reputed Anchor & Hope sibling is extolled by its fans for its "unfussy, brilliant dishes with huge flavours and no messing about"; it's rated lower than its stablemate though, and sceptics – experiencing average meals – say "it gets good reviews, but we've been unlucky". / SW8 1XP; www.cantonarms.com; 10.30 pm; closed Mon L & Sun D; no Amex; no booking.

Canvas SW1 £70
1 Wilbraham Pl 7823 4463 5–2D
It's all change at this ambitious venture, which in 2014 relocated to Chelsea (to the home of Le Cercle, RIP), and in spring 2015 lost both chef Michael Riemenschneider, and his 'design-your-own-menu' concept; feedback is limited and divided (hence the ongoing lack of a rating) – to fans its "a wondrous experience", but to critics has "no redeeming features". / SW1X 9AE; www.canvaschelsea.com; @CanvasbyMR; 9.30 pm, Fri & Sat 10 pm; D only, closed Mon.

Capote Y Toros SW5 £49 3 4 4
157 Old Brompton Rd 7373 0567 5–2B
"Straight out of Andalucía" – Cambio de Tercio's neighbouring bar "isn't a cheap night out", but is, on most accounts, "a real gem", with "extremely good tapas", plus a quaffable selection of wines, sherries and gins. / SW5 0LJ; www.cambiodetercio.co.uk; @CambiodTercio; 11.30 pm; D only, closed Mon & Sun.

LE CAPRICE SW1 £74 3 4 4
Arlington Hs, Arlington St 7629 2239 3–4C
"Sooooo smooth, soooo suave" – this "effortless" '80s brasserie tucked away behind the Ritz has always "eschewed culinary heights", and even if its "classy comfort food" is a tad less excellent under Richard Caring's ownership it's "the front of house staff and overall buzz which make it so special". / SW1A 1RJ; www.le-caprice.co.uk; @CapriceHoldings; 11.30 pm Mon-Sat, Sun 10.30 pm.

Caraffini SW1 £53 3 5 4
61-63 Lower Sloane St 7259 0235 5–2D
"There's always a wonderful, sincere welcome" at this "traditional" Chelsea stalwart, near Sloane Square, whose "white haired clientele" would find it "a sad day if anything changed"; prices are "fair" for the "always dependable" Italian fare. / SW1W 8DH; www.caraffini.co.uk; Mon-Fri 11.30 pm, Sat 11 pm; closed Sun.

Caravaggio EC3 £62 3 3 2
107-112 Leadenhall St 7626 6206 9–2D
To impress a business associate, this "busy" City Italian provides "spacious tables" and "very responsive service", plus cooking that's consistently well rated. / EC3A 4DP; www.etruscarestaurants.com; 10 pm; closed Sat & Sun.

Caravan £45 3 2 3
1 Granary Sq, N1 7101 7661 8–3C
11-13 Exmouth Mkt, EC1 7833 8115 9–1A
"Big on bizarre sounding breakfast dishes" – and with "top expertise in the art of coffee-making" – these "hip and trendy" fusion-haunts get "very busy", particularly as major brunch destinations; nowadays the "cavernous, coolly industrial" King's Cross branch overshadows the Exmouth Market original. / www.caravanonexmouth.co.uk; EC1 10.30 pm, Sun 4 pm; closed Sun.

Carob Tree NW5 £35 4 5 4
15 Highgate Rd 7267 9880 8–1B
"The manager gives the best service ever" at this "always bustling" ("loud") Dartmouth Park favourite; the menu is "mainly Greek", and the big draw is the fish – "a top selection, simply and beautifully cooked". / NW5 1QX; 10.30 pm, Sun 9 pm; closed Mon; no Amex.

Carom at Meza W1 £35 2 3 3
100 Wardour St 7314 4002 3–2D
Closed by fire in May 2015, D&D London's "buzzy" ("loud") Soho Indian has been popping up all over London ahead of a 2016 relaunch; the food takes a back seat, but the cavernous room, complete with bar and DJ, is "great for socialising" and "appeals to any kind of party". / W1F 0TN; www.meza-soho.co.uk; @CaromSoho; 11 pm; closed Sat L & Sun.

Carousel W1 NEW £53 4 3 3
71 Blandford St 7487 5564 3–1A
"I can't stop going back!" – the "inspired rotating chef programme" creates "a wonderful diversity of menus", at this Marylebone merry-go-round, which hosts an ever-changing roster of guest chefs; it's a bit of a Russian Roulette job though – the odd meal turns out "too experimental". / W1U 8AB; www.carousel-london.com; @Carousel_LDN; 11.30 pm.

The Carpenter's Arms W6 £46 3 3 3
91 Black Lion Ln 8741 8386 7–2B
A tucked-away Hammersmith location helps set up a "relaxed" atmosphere at this backstreet pub, praised for its "great value" cooking; cute garden too. / W6 9BG; www.carpentersarmsw6.co.uk; 10 pm, Sun 9 pm.

Casa Brindisa SW7 £46 2 3 2
7-9 Exhibition Rd 7590 0008 5–2C
Fans may "love everything" about this "hugger mugger" Brindisa-outpost near South Kensington tube (best on the "chilled" terrace), but tapas-wise, "it's not cutting edge", in fact arguably "a bit formulaic". / SW7 2HE; www.casabrindisa.com; @TapasKitchens; 11 pm, Sun 10 pm.

Casa Cruz W11 NEW **£48**
123 Clarendon Rd 3321 5400 6–2A
A luxurious new addition to the borders of Notting Hill and Holland Park, from South American restaurateur Juan Santa Cruz, set over two floors, and complete with first-floor roof terrace; early days press reports have focused more on the steep pricing than the Argentinian-inspired European food. / W11 4JG; www.casacruz.london/; @CasaCruzrest; 12.30 am, Sun 5 pm; closed Mon.

Casa Malevo W2 **£56** 3 2 3
23 Connaught St 7402 1988 6–1D
"Great steaks" and "other delicious Latino delicacies" are the pay-off for truffling out this "cosy", "dimly-lit" Argentinian, in a "slightly out-of-the-way" corner of Bayswater. / W2 2AY; www.casamalevo.com; @casamalevo; 10.30 pm, Sun 10 pm.

Casse-Croute SE1 **£45** 4 4 4
109 Bermondsey St 7407 2140 9–4D
"Take all the best bits of a tiny Parisian bistro, put it in SE1, et voilà" – this "bustling, chaotic and cramped" little two-year-old is a stroke of "genius", serving "the classic bistro fare you rarely find in France nowadays" in "fun", if "basic" conditions. / SE1 3XB; www.cassecroute.co.uk; @CasseCroute109; 10 pm, Sun 4 pm; closed Sun D.

Cau **£49** 4 3 3
10-12 Royal Pde, SE3 8318 4200 1–4D NEW
33 High St, SW19 8318 4200 10–2B NEW
Commodity Quay, E1 7702 0341 9–3D NEW
"A good addition to Wimbledon" – this new Argentinean offers "an eclectic mix of original small and large plates", "smiley" service, and "stylish" surroundings, all "without devastating your wallet!". There are branches in Blackheath and St Katharine Docks too. /

The Cavendish W1 NEW **£75** 3 4 4
35 New Cavendish St 7487 3030 2–1A
There's a "gentleman's club" vibe to the design of this ambitious, all-day Marylebone newcomer, which has inspired promising early reports on its straightforward but comprehensive selection of dishes (incorporating a raw bar, with an array of ceviches, and caviars). / W1G 9TR; 35newcavendish.co.uk; @35newcavendish; 10.30 pm, Sun 6 pm; set weekday L £45 (FP).

Cây Tre **£36** 3 2 3
42-43 Dean St, W1 7317 9118 4–2A
301 Old St, EC1 7729 8662 12–1B
"Some of the best pho ever" is a highlight of the "honestly priced, simple, tasty fare" at this "busy and buzzy" (if totally "unpretentious") Vietnamese duo, in Soho and Shoreditch. / www.vietnamesekitchen.co.uk; 11 pm, Fri & Sat 11.30 pm, Sun 10.30 pm; booking: min 8.

Cecconi's W1 **£77** 3 3 5
5a Burlington Gdns 7434 1500 3–3C
"The central bar is a great focal point" at this "slick" and "sophisticated" brasserie, whose long opening hours (from breakfast on) and flexible Italian tapas menu help make it "a great Mayfair meeting place" (although it can feel a bit like "Hedge Fund Central"). / W1S 3EP; www.cecconis.co.uk; @SohoHouse; 11.30 pm, Sun 10.30 pm; set weekday L £35 (FP).

Cellar Gascon EC1 **£33** 3 3 3
59 West Smithfield Rd 7600 7561 9–2B
"Tasty and innovative" little appetisers and "interesting" wines by the glass make for a gastronomic treat at this small wine bar spin-off, from Smithfield's Club Gascon (next door). / EC1A 9DS; www.clubgascon.com; midnight; closed Sat & Sun; set always available £17 (FP), set weekday L £20 (FP).

Ceru EC4 NEW **£36** 3 3 3
135 Cannon St 3195 3001 9–4D
A "little gem" – this pop-up looking for a permanent home is currently rooted in the City; as one would expect from restaurateur Barry Hilton (Yalla Yalla) it wins praise for its "fresh tastes of the Levant". / EC4N 5BP; www.cerurestaurants.com; @cerulondon; 10 pm.

Ceviche **£46** 3 4 4
17 Frith St, W1 7292 2040 4–2A
Alexandra Trust, Baldwin St, EC1 3327 9463 12–1A NEW
"Intriguing" Peruvian fare – in particular "fantastic ceviche" washed down with "wonderful" Pisco Sours – still wins praise for this atmospheric Soho South American, whose "bustling" new EC1 sibling is also off to a good start; "pushy" service and "noisy" conditions can grate though. / www.cevicheuk.com; @cevicheuk; SRA-3.*

Chakra W11 **£55** 3 1 2
157-159 Notting Hill Gate 7229 2115 6–2B
"Brilliant" food can be found at this "posh", but slightly "weird" ("white leather and chandeliers") Notting Hill Indian, but the overall effect is too often spoiled by "shambolic service" and top end prices – "we had to ask three times for our rather substantial bill!" / W11 3LF; www.chakralondon.com; @ChakraLondon; 11 pm, Sun 10.30 pm.

Chamberlain's EC3 **£63** 3 4 3
23-25 Leadenhall Mkt 7648 8690 9–2D
"In the fascinating heart of Leadenhall Market", this well-established fish restaurant majors in "mainstream" favourites (grilled Dover sole, lobster, and so on); lunch prices can seem "forbidding", but "for the well-off who like their fish" it's well-rated. / EC3V 1LR; www.chamberlains.org; @chamberlainsldn; 9.30 pm, Sun 4 pm; closed Sat & Sun D.

Champor-Champor SE1 £51 334
62 Weston St 7403 4600 9–4C
Hidden away in Borough, this "quirky" Thai-Malay fusion outfit is just as known for its "unique" décor as it is for its "flavoursome" food – a "varied and lively crowd" provides a further boost to the atmosphere too. / SE1 3QJ; www.champor-champor.com; @ChamporChampor; 10 pm; D only.

The Chancery EC4 £66 443
9 Cursitor St 7831 4000 9–2A
Graham Long's "thoughtful" and "beautifully executed" cuisine wins high praise for this "smart and fairly formal" 10-year-old, near Chancery Lane, not only recommended as a "very professional" business option, but also as a foodie destination in its own right. / EC4A 1LL; www.thechancery.co.uk; @chancerylondon; 10.30 pm; closed Sat L & Sun.

Chapters SE3 £50 332
43-45 Montpelier Vale 8333 2666 1–4D
"The best all-rounder in Blackheath" (by the Common) – open all day, with "always friendly service", and "reliable brasserie fare"; however, while of a "perfectly creditable standard, it's not very individual". / SE3 0TJ; www.chaptersrestaurants.com; @chaptersvillage; 11 pm, Sun 9 pm; set weekday L £30 (FP), set dinner £33 (FP).

Charlotte's £51 344
6 Turnham Green Ter, W4 8742 3590 7–2A
Dickens Yard, The Old Stable Block, Longfield Ave, W5 awaiting tel 1–3A NEW
"Staff give just the right amount of attention" at this ("slightly cramped and noisy") "neighbourhood gem" in Chiswick, where an evening often kicks off in the tiny bar, with its "enticing selection of wonderful gins". In Autumn 2015 it is to get this new Ealing sibling in addition to the existing grander W5 operation (see also). / www.charlottes.co.uk.

Charlotte's Place W5 £52 343
16 St Matthew's Rd 8567 7541 1–3A
"It's great to have quality cooking in W5!" – this "homely" neighbourhood favourite, on the Common, delivers "well-presented, seasonal food" in a "warm and friendly manner". / W5 3JT; www.charlottes.co.uk; @Charlottes1984; 10.30 pm, Fri & Sat 11 pm, Sun 9 pm; set Sun L £43 (FP).

Chettinad W1 £38 433
16 Percy St 3556 1229 2–1C
"Delicious and authentic South Indian food" (from the state of Tamil Nadu), with "consistently superior spicing" wins very high praise for this café-style Fitzrovian. Top Tip – "amazing value lunchtime thalis". / W1T 1DT; www.chettinadrestaurant.com; @chettinadlondon; 11 pm, Sun 10 pm; no Amex.

Cheyne Walk Brasserie SW3 £70 333
50 Cheyne Walk 7376 8787 5–3C
"Full of beautiful people", a stylish Gallic brasserie near the Thames in Chelsea; the "straightforward" menu is "pricey", but on most accounts "the quality of the food is matched by the scents and theatre of the central wood-grill" (where most of the cooking takes place). / SW3 5LR; www.cheynewalkbrasserie.com; 10.30 pm, Sun 9.30 pm; closed Mon L; set always available £55 (FP).

Chez Abir W14 £38 432
34 Blythe Rd 7603 3241 7–1D
Previously known as Chez Marcelle (till she retired), this "little gem" in the backstreets behind Olympia may be only "modest and functional", but "remains an excellent source of authentic Lebanese food". / W14 0HA; 11 pm; closed Mon.

Chez Antoinette WC2 NEW £44
Unit 30 The Market Building 7240 9072 4–3D
Forget on-trend pizzas and burgers; this cute, new 'Tartinerie' in the heart of Covent Garden Market is giving the one-dish restaurant craze a touch of Gallic class, with a menu devoted to the classic French tartine. / WC2E 8RD; www.chezantoinette.co.uk; 7 pm, Fri & Sat 11 pm, Sun 8 pm.

CHEZ BRUCE SW17 £66 554
2 Bellevue Rd 8672 0114 10–2C
"Still at the top of its game after all these years" – Bruce Poole's "unpretentious" yet "consistently excellent" neighbourhood restaurant is yet again the survey No. 1 favourite, and "well worth the schlep to Wandsworth Common". "There are no fads – just classic, interesting, perfectly executed cooking", matched with service that "while impeccable, is completely devoid of airs and graces". All this plus "stellar" wine and a "cheeseboard probably visible from space". And price-wise, it's "so reasonable for something so good!" / SW17 7EG; www.chezbruce.co.uk; @ChezBruce; 10 pm, Fri & Sat 10.30 pm, Sun 9 pm.

Chez Patrick W8 £50 353
7 Stratford Rd 7937 6388 5–2A
"A side-order of French cheekiness" is the order of the day at this stalwart spot in a Kensington backwater, where "charming owner" Patrick, "seems to be on first name terms with all his customers"; fish and seafood are the highlight of the "simple", "well-prepared" Gallic fare. / W8 6RF; www.chez-patrick.co.uk; 10.30 pm; closed Sun D.

Chick 'n' Sours E8 NEW **£32** 424

390 Kingsland Rd 3620 8728 1–1D

On Dalston's main drag, a "fun and buzzy" little fried chicken specialist from pop-up maestro Carl Clarke, where poultry is given an oriental twist and accompanied by sour cocktails – it's an "excellent" combo. / E8 2AA; www.chicknsours.co.uk; @chicknsours; 10 pm, Fri & Sat 10.30 pm, Sun 09.30 pm.

Chicken Shop **£32** 344

199-206 High Holborn, WC1 7661 3040 2–1D NEW
79 Highgate Rd, NW5 3310 2020 8–1B
Soho House, Chestnut Grove, SW12 8102 9300 10–2C NEW
141 Tooting High St, SW17 8767 5200 10–2B
27a Mile End Rd, E1 3310 2010 12–2D

"They do one thing and do it well" at these "posh Nandos" – "succulent free range chicken cooked on a spit, great chips, salad and little else apart from some puds" (notably "delicious apple pie"); they look "quirky" and "fun" too, "if only you could book..." / www.chickenshop.com; Mon - Sun 10.30 pm ;WC1V closed Sun.

Chicken Shop & Dirty Burger E1 332

27a Mile End Rd 3310 2010 12–2D

"It's greasy, it's dirty, but it tastes so good" – a Whitechapel two-in-one, where you can opt for either of Soho House's casual, "comfort food" brands. / E1 4TP; www.chickenshop.com; @chickenshop; 11 pm, Sun 10 pm; closed weekday L.

Chicken Town N15 NEW

Tottenham Grn 3310 2020 1–1C

A new, healthy – part crowd-funded – twist on London's ubiquitous chicken shop was slated to open in the badlands of Tottenham as this guide went to press, founded by Create and supported by the Mayor, no less. / N15 4JA; @Chickentown; 11 pm, Sun 10 pm.

Chifafa EC1 NEW **£11** 433

45-47 Clerkenwell Rd no tel 9–1A

'To save the reputation of the kebab' is the bold mission statement of this posh, new, little Clerkenwell pit stop; for once the marketing doesn't lie, with high marks for its healthy nosh ('no doners, no chips, no foam, no neon'), and "speedy service". / EC1M 5RS; www.chifafa.com; @chifafakebabs; 11.30 pm, Sat 9 pm.

Chilango **£16** 332

76 Chancery Ln, WC2 7430 1323 2–1D
27 Upper St, N1 7704 2123 8–3D
32 Brushfield St, E1 3246 0086 12–2B
64 London Wall, EC2 7628 7663 9–2C
142 Fleet St, EC4 7353 6761 9–2A

"You can't go wrong with a big burrito" from these US imports, and you get a "fast turnaround" too; they've not made the same waves here as they have Stateside however. / www.chilango.co.uk; @Chilango_uk; EC4, EC2, EC1 9 pm, N1 10 pm, Fri & Sat midnight; EC4, EC2, E1 closed Sat & Sun; no booking.

Chilli Cool WC1 **£33** 311

15 Leigh St 7383 3135 2–1D

"The really interesting, Sichuan 'nose to tail' food will take your breath away (literally!)", at this Bloomsbury dive, and "makes it worth enduring the very offhand service"; ("order less than you think, as portions are huge"!) / WC1H 9EW; www.chillicool.com; 10.15 pm; no Amex.

The Chiltern Firehouse W1 **£82** 124

1 Chiltern St 7073 7676 2–1A

"Full of Z-listers, models and wannabe movers-and-shakers", this achingly hip Marylebone yearling is "so overhyped" it's hilarious. It's undoubtedly a "gorgeous-looking" place and "fun" too (especially if you like people-watching), but you pay "silly money" for service that's "confused" (going on "obnoxious"), and food for which "mediocre would be a flattering description". / W1U 7PA; www.chilternfirehouse.com; 10.30 pm.

China Tang Dorchester Hotel W1 **£72** 213

53 Park Ln 7629 9988 3–3A

"Bog standard" Chinese fare ("no better than Chinatown but double the cost") is served by "indifferent" staff at Sir David Tang's "opulent and buzzy" Mayfair basement (whose top feature is its gorgeous, '30s-Shanghai-style cocktail bar). / W1K 1QA; www.chinatanglondon.co.uk; @ChinaTangLondon; 11.45 pm; booking: max 14; set weekday L £50 (FP).

Chinese Cricket Club EC4 **£63** 431

19 New Bridge St 7438 8051 9–3A

Shame about the "cold and formulaic" atmosphere at this hotel dining room, near Blackfriars Bridge – even those who say it "lacks heart" and is "unjustifiably pricey" concede the food is "good and ambitious". / EC4V 6DB; www.chinesecricketclub.com; @chinesecclub; 10 pm; closed Sat & Sun L.

Ceviche

The Refinery

Claude's Kitchen Amuse Bouche

Chisou £51 4 4 2

4 Princes St, W1 7629 3931 3–1C
31 Beauchamp Pl, SW3 3155 0005 5–2D

"Always-outstanding sashimi and sushi" and "some unusual izakaya-style dishes" are washed down with a "mind-blowing sake selection" at the low-key Mayfair original of this small group; SW3 is little-known but also well-rated, but the W4 branch is no more. / www.chisourestaurant.com; Mon-Sat 10.30 pm, Sun 9.30 pm.

Chiswell Street Dining Rooms EC1 £62 2 2 2

56 Chiswell St 7614 0177 12–2A

Near the Barbican, this "slightly faceless, but perfectly decent" operation serves a need for its City clientele – it's "pricey" but "a good venue for a business lunch", and loosens up a little in the evenings. / EC1Y 4SA; www.chiswellstreetdining.com; @chiswelldining; 11 pm; closed Sat & Sun; set pre theatre £41 (FP).

Chor Bizarre W1 £63 3 2 3

16 Albemarle St 7629 9802 3–3C

Trinkets and ornaments festoon this antique-laden Mayfair Indian (named for one of Mumbai's biggest flea markets); despite the odd gripe that it's "pricey", most reporters applaud its cooking. / W1S 4HW; www.chorbizarre.com; @ChorBizarreUK; 11.30 pm, Sun 10.30 pm.

Chotto Matte W1 £55 4 3 4

11-13 Frith St 7042 7171 4–2A

"Loving this Peruvian/Japanese fusion!" – this "large and absolutely buzzing" Soho yearling "ticks all the boxes" with its "wild" cooking and "really cool" atmosphere. / W1D 4RB; www.chotto-matte.com; @ChottoMatteSoho; Mon-Sat 1 am, Sun 11 pm.

Chriskitch N10 £27 4 4 2

7 Tetherdown 8411 0051 1–1C

"Muswell Hill locals queue around the block" for this "brave but wonderful venture", in "a converted front room with awkward seating"; "there's no menu – it's whatever the chef cooks on the day", but its salads, cakes and so on have "brilliant flavours", and "the mismatched furniture and rickety tables add to the charm". / N10 1ND; www.chriskitch.com; @chriskitch_; Mon-Fri 6 pm, Sat & Sun 5 pm.

Christopher's WC2 £72 2 2 3

18 Wellington St 7240 4222 4–3D

A "beautiful" interior is the only surefire plus-point of this well-established, grand American restaurant in a spacious Covent Garden townhouse; "they seem to be trying hard", and it's a favourite for a number of reporters, but standards are inconsistent and its surf 'n' turf cuisine can appear "dull and overpriced". / WC2E 7DD; www.christophersgrill.com; @christopherswc2; 11.30 pm, Sun 10.30 pm; booking: max 12; set pre theatre £40 (FP).

Churchill Arms W8 £36 3 4 5

119 Kensington Church St 7792 1246 6–2B

"The brilliant jungle atmosphere" is "something else" at this slightly "bonkers" pub, off Notting Hill Gate, where Thai food is served in a conservatory filled with "dried butterflies and hanging flowers"; the scoff's "always delicious" too and "super cheap" – "eat yourself to a standstill for little more than a tenner!" / W8 7LN; www.churchillarmskensington.co.uk; @ChurchilArmsW8; 10 pm, Sun 9.30 pm.

Chutney Mary SW1 £58 4 4 4

73 St James's St 7351 3113 3–4D

Moved this year from its long-standing Chelsea home to a "wonderfully decorated" new site in St James's, this renowned Indian seems to have transported well – the new location is "lovely", as is the "superb, fragrant and subtle" cooking, and all-in-all it's "expensive but worth it". / SW1A 1PH; www.chutneymary.com; @RealindianFood; 10.30 pm; closed Sat L & Sun.

Chutneys NW1 £31 2 2 2

124 Drummond St 7388 0604 8–4C

"I've been going for over 20 years and it never disappoints"; a mainstay of Euston's 'Little India' scene, this "friendly" Keralan won't "blow you away", but the lunchtime and Sunday evening buffet is "ridiculously good value"; BYO too. / NW1 2PA; www.chutneyseuston.co.uk; 11 pm; no Amex; need 5+ to book.

Ciao Bella WC1 £42 2 4 4

86-90 Lamb's Conduit St 7242 4119 2–1D

"Pictures of the golden age of Italian cinema lining the walls and a white piano" set the tone at this "buzzing" trattoria veteran (a favourite of Boris Johnson, apparently); the "classic cheap 'n' cheerful scran is lifted by the ambiente" – it's "so friendly, so happy, (and ideal with kids too)". / WC1N 3LZ; www.ciaobellarestaurant.co.uk; 11.30 pm, Sun 10.30 pm.

Cibo W14 £54 4 5 4

3 Russell Gdns 7371 6271 7–1D

Lost in a side-street on the Kensington/Olympia border, Michael Winner's favourite Italian (or it was) is rather forgotten nowadays, but fans still cross town for its "delightful" approach, not least "simple, flavoursome and unfussy" cooking that's "always fantastic". Top Menu Tip – "very successful" fish and seafood dishes. / W14 8EZ; www.ciborestaurant.net; 10.30 pm; closed Sat L & Sun D.

Cigala WC1 £50 2|2|2
54 Lamb's Conduit St 7405 1717 2–1D
"Homely" Bloomsbury Hispanic long known as "a charming" neighbourhood "gem", with "simple and tasty" tapas; quite a number of reporters found it "most unremarkable" this year however, citing "mediocre" cooking and a "pretty poor" ambience. / WC1N 3LW; www.cigala.co.uk; 10.45 pm, Sun 9.45 pm.

Cigalon WC2 £52 3|3|2
115 Chancery Ln 7242 8373 2–2D
The "beautiful" and "airy" room (in days of yore, an auctioneers' premises) is the "special", feature of this Club Gascon sibling ("very handily located for legal types"), but its Provençal cooking is "usually excellent" too. / WC2A 1PP; www.cigalon.co.uk; @Cigalon_London; 10 pm; closed Sat & Sun.

THE CINNAMON CLUB SW1 £72 3|3|4
Old Westminster Library, Great Smith St 7222 2555 2–4C
London's most "impressive"-looking Indian occupies Westminster's "soaring" former library, near the Abbey (and looks even more dashing after its recent £1m refit). Nearly fifteen years old, it's still one of the capital's most noteworthy culinary destinations, thanks not least to Vivek Singh's "seriously brilliantly spiced" (if "expensive") cuisine. / SW1P 3BU; www.cinnamonclub.com; @CinnamonClub; 10.30 pm; closed Sun; no trainers; set always available £47 (FP); SRA-3.*

Cinnamon Kitchen EC2 £58 4|2|2
9 Devonshire Sq 7626 5000 9–2D
"Delicious food with superb flavours" makes this Indian-fusion venture in the City a worthy cousin to the Cinnamon Club; however – aside from the "beautiful terrace" within an impressive atrium – the setting can seem "bland" and "noisy", and service can be "muddled". / EC2M 4YL; www.cinnamon-kitchen.com; @cinnamonkitchen; 11 pm; closed Sat L & Sun; set always available £26 (FP).

Cinnamon Soho W1 £45 4|2|2
5 Kingly St 7437 1664 3–2D
"The less well-known, more basic sibling of the Cinnamon Club family" lives just off Regent Street; "it's not a big place", the ambience is "about average" and service can falter, but its "wonderful Indian-fusion fare" is "superior" and "good value". / W1B 5PE; www.cinnamon-kitchen.com/soho-home; @cinnamonsoho; 11 pm, Sun 4.30 pm; closed Sun D.

City Barge W4 £47 3|3|3
27 Strand-on-the-Green 8994 2148 1–3A
"It's high time Strand-on-the-Green had a decent pub!" – this refurbished boozer enjoys "a great setting by the Thames" and cooking that's "very promising". / W4 3PH; www.citybargechiswick.com; @citybargew4; Mon-Thu 11 pm, Fri & Sat midnight, Sun 10.30 pm.

City Càphê EC2 £18 5|2|2
17 Ironmonger St no tel 9–2C
"Closest to the streets of Ho Chi Minh I've tasted in London!" – an "astonishingly good" Vietnamese café, near Bank, with "wonderful" salads, báhn mi and pho; "be prepared to brave a queue down the street". / EC2V 8EY; www.citycaphe.com; 3 pm; L only, closed Sat & Sun.

City Miyama EC4 £52 3|4|2
17 Godliman St 7489 1937 9–3B
"A typical, old-style Japanese near St Paul's that hasn't changed in 30 years"; there's a character-free basement, but "it's best eating at the ground floor sushi counter... delicious!" / EC4B 5BD; www.miyama-restaurant.co.uk; 10 pm; closed Sat & Sun.

City Social EC2 £76 3|3|5
Tower 42 25 Old Broad St 7877 7703 9–2C
"Stunning views" help create a "fabulous" and business-friendly setting for Jason Atherton's year-old City eyrie, on the 24th floor of Tower 42; but – after its magnificent debut – ratings slipped this year, and though fans still say its cuisine is "superb", critics say it "lacks x-factor". / EC2N 1HQ; www.citysociallondon.com; 9 pm; closed Sat & Sun.

Clarke's W8 £69 4|4|3
124 Kensington Church St 7221 9225 6–2B
Sally Clarke's "fabulous", "honest", "incredibly fresh", seasonal cuisine is "re-establishing itself" after a few rocky years at her long-serving Kensington HQ; service is "charming and sensitive", and the refurb and expansion a year or two ago has "enhanced the ambience". / W8 4BH; www.sallyclarke.com; @SallyClarkeLtd; 10 pm; closed Sun; booking: max 14.

Claude's Kitchen, Amuse Bouche SW6 £50 4|4|4
51 Parsons Green Ln 7371 8517 10–1B
"Lucky Parson's Green locals" to have this "special little marvel" opposite the tube, with a ground floor bar and cosy upstairs dining room – its "interesting small menu" is "always a treat". / SW6 4JA; www.claudeskitchen.co.uk; @AmuseBoucheLDN; 10 pm; closed weekday L.

Clockjack Oven W1 £32 333
14 Denman St 7287 5111 3–3D
"Fun and funky" rotisserie yearling in Soho, whose "great chicken and amazing chicken bites" make for "reliable, cheap, cheerful, tasty" central nosh. / W1D 7HJ; www.clockjackoven.com; @ClockjackOven; 10 pm, Fri & Sat 11 pm, Sun 9 pm.

CLOS MAGGIORE WC2 £65 455
33 King St 7379 9696 4–3C
"A girl knows she's being spoilt" at this Covent Garden "haven" – the survey's No. 1 romantic choice – where for full effect you must sit in the "magical back conservatory, which is second-to-none for a date". Service is "charming and courteous" and the cooking "delicious", if arguably eclipsed by the "massive tome" of a wine list. / WC2E 8JD; www.closmaggiore.com; @ClosMaggioreWC2; 11 pm, Sun 10 pm; booking: max 7.

The Clove Club EC1 £95 433
Shoreditch Town Hall, 380 Old St 7729 6496 12–1B
"Deserving its many awards" – this groovy pop-up-turned-permanent in Shoreditch's fine old town hall wins kudos for its "incredibly interesting" cuisine, "perfectly matched" wines and "casual" approach. The setting can seem "Spartan" though, service is a little "earnest" and to some diners "the new ticketing system for reservations smacks of hubris". / EC1V 9LT; www.thecloveclub.com; @thecloveclub; 9.30 pm; closed Mon L & Sun; set weekday L £60 (FP).

Club Gascon EC1 £75 333
57 West Smithfield 7600 6144 9–2B
"Brilliantly executed flavour combinations from SW France" – featuring "foie gras in every imaginable form" – and "a wine list with some unusual gems" have won a huge following for this Gallic, City-fringe business stalwart; but has its performance been slightly "tired" of late? / EC1A 9DS; www.clubgascon.com; @club_gascon; 10 pm, Fri & Sat 10.30 pm; closed Sat L & Sun.

Coco Di Mama EC4 £12 342
90/91 Fleet St 7583 9277 9–2A
"Truly Italian coffee" – "the best in the city" – plus "excellent" pastries and some good pasta win praise for this small Square Mile chain. / EC4Y 1DH; www.cocodimama.co.uk; 5 pm; L only.

Cocochan W1 £50 333
38-40 James St 7486 1000 3–1A
"An imaginative fusion of Eastern cuisines", helps win consistent praise for this café-style St James's venture; "tables are quite close together, but that makes for interesting conversations with your neighbours!" / W1U 1EU; www.cocochan.co.uk.

Colbert SW1 £58 123
51 Sloane Sq 7730 2804 5–2D
"How did Corbin and King get things so wrong?" – this "buzzing" Sloane Square two-year-old looks "elegant", but service can be "appalling" and the brasserie fare is "seriously underwhelming" – "it's like an expensive Café Rouge!" / SW1W 8AX; www.colbertchelsea.com; @ColbertChelsea; Sun 10.30 pm, Mon-Thu 11 pm, Fri & Sat 11.30 pm; booking: max 6.

La Collina NW1 £56 322
17 Princess Rd 7483 0192 8–3B
At its best in summer when you can sit in its "attractive garden", this "small" Primrose Hill local impresses (nearly) all its (older) fanclub with its "interesting" Piedmontese cooking "subtlety prepared from fresh ingredients". / NW1 8JR; www.lacollinarestaurant.co.uk; @LacollinaR; 10.15 pm, Sun & Mon 9.15 pm; closed Mon L.

Le Colombier SW3 £60 334
145 Dovehouse St 7351 1155 5–2C
"A little bit of France in Chelsea" – Didier Garnier's "delightful", "old-fashioned" stalwart is a treasured (if rather pricey) backstreet favourite, especially for an older Francophile crowd; it's "not known for its originality" – expect "classic" dishes delivered to a "consistent" standard. / SW3 6LB; www.le-colombier-restaurant.co.uk; 10.30 pm, Sun 10 pm.

Colony Grill Room, Beaumont Hotel W1 £59 322
Brown Hart Gdns 7499 1001 3–2A
"A new favourite" for many reporters; Corbin & King have made a strong debut with this "club-like" Mayfair yearling – a "beautiful" (if "noisy") room that "feels like it's been here for years"; true to their DNA, the American-inspired menu is "good but a bit too much on the side of comfort food". / W1K 6TF; www.thebeaumont.com; @ColonyGrillRoom; midnight, Sun 11 pm.

Como Lario SW1 £48 244
18-22 Holbein Pl 7730 2954 5–2D
"A huge regular following of well-heeled locals" sustains this "old-school" Italian, "tucked away in a side street close to Sloane Square"; "the cooking's a little variable, but if you know the right dishes it's great". / SW1W 8NL; www.comolario.co.uk; 11.30 pm, Sun 10 pm.

Compagnie des Vins Surnaturels WC2 £52 334
8-10 Neals Yd 7344 7737 4–2C
"Try to guess the mystery wine!" – one of an "intriguing selection by the glass", served at this Covent Garden yearling – a "great place" for a drink, and with "good" small plates too. / WC2H 9DP; www.cvssevendials.com; @CVS7Dials; midnight.

Comptoir Gascon EC1 £45 333
63 Charterhouse St 7608 0851 9–1A
"Splendidly earthy dishes from SW France" – "the deluxe duck burger is a treat" – and "esoteric" wines to match are "knowledgeably" served at this "cute" Club Gascon spin-off, near Smithfield; it can seem "expensive for what it is" though, especially given the "wee portions". / EC1M 6HJ; www.comptoirgascon.com; @ComptoirGascon; 10 pm, Thu & Fri 10.30 pm; closed Mon & Sun.

Comptoir Libanais £34 443
Branches throughout London
A "cleverly conceived" Lebanese chain, with "characterful" branches; critics say their food is "nothing special", but most reports praise its "really lovely soft drinks" and "value for money mezze". / www.lecomptoir.co.uk; W12 9 pm, Thu & Fri 10 pm, Sun 6 pm; W1 9.30 pm; W12 closed Sun D; no bookings.

Il Convivio SW1 £58 333
143 Ebury St 7730 4099 2–4A
With its "smooth" service, and "spacious" interior, this "stylish" Belgravian "old favourite" is, say fans, always "under-rated"; there is the occasional report of "uninspiring" cooking, but on most accounts it's "beautifully judged". / SW1W 9QN; www.ilconvivio.co.uk; 10.45 pm; closed Sun; set weekday L £39 (FP).

Coopers Restaurant & Bar WC2 £50 223
49a, Lincoln's Inn Fields 7831 6211 2–2D
A Lincolns Inn Fields "staple" – "very popular amongst the Bar and the Judiciary, but that's not necessarily a recommendation for the food!"; fans do applaud its "informal" style and solid value, but other "struggle to find something appealing on the menu". / WC2A 3PF; www.coopers-restaurant.com; @coopers_bistro; 11 pm; closed Sat & Sun.

Copita Del Mercado E1 £39 432
60 Wentworth St 7426 0218 12–2C
"A beacon in the culinary wasteland around Petticoat Lane Market" (from the team behind Soho's Copita) serving "fresh, tasty and innovative tapas" that's "in a different league to its nearest rivals"; on the downside, it's "a bit soulless". / E1 7TF; www.copitadelmercado.com; @copitamercado; 10.30 pm.

Le Coq N1 £42 232
292-294 St Paul's Rd 7359 5055 8–2D
Fans hail "a winning formula" for this Islington yearling, offering "tasty rôtisserie chicken, with a good selection of sides" (from a limited set menu incorporating two starters and desserts); it also has its critics though, who judge it "disappointing". / N1 2LH; www.le-coq.co.uk; @LeCOQrestaurant; 10.15 pm.

Coq d'Argent EC2 £74 233
1 Poultry 7395 5000 9–2C
With its "stunning rooftop garden", this well-known D&D London venue is "perfect for business entertaining" and – especially in summer – something of "a City boy power-lunch extravaganza"; the food is "acceptable but dull" – "if they really sorted it out, it would be one of London's top spots". / EC2R 8EJ; www.coqdargent.co.uk; 9.45 pm; closed Sun D.

Cork & Bottle WC2 £48 235
44-46 Cranbourn St 7734 7807 4–3B
"Somehow sheltered from the worst ravages of the tourist hell that is Leicester Square", this "proper, independent wine bar" is a treasured "haven in the West End"; "you don't go for the food, but it's perfectly tolerable to accompany the exceptional wine list, and lovely, old-school cellar ambience". / WC2H 7AN; www.thecorkandbottle.co.uk; @corkbottle1971; 11.30 pm, Sun 10.30 pm; no booking at D.

Corner Room E2 £48 344
Patriot Sq 7871 0461 1–2D
"Hidden away at the back of the hotel", this "tiny", "sparse" chamber shares a kitchen with the better-known Typing Room; for fans, it's "a wonderful fashionista inside secret" and a "splendid gastronomic delight", but for sceptics "the food doesn't taste quite as good as hoped". / E2 9NF; www.viajante.co.uk/corner-room/; @townhallhotel; 10.30 pm.

Cornish Tiger SW11 £51 333
1 Battersea Rise 7223 7719 10–1C
All agree this ambitious modern British yearling is "a lovely variation to the normal Battersea Rise opening"; but while some acclaim its "affordable, most interesting and piquant seasonal cuisine", others feel "it's not bad but a bit ordinary". / SW11 1GH; www.cornishtiger.com; @cornishtiger; 11 pm, Sun 6 pm; closed Mon; set weekday L £25 (FP).

Corrigan's Mayfair W1 £90 344
28 Upper Grosvenor St 7499 9943 3–3A
Richard Corrigan's "spacious" and dignified Mayfair dining room has long been a business favourite, and – although it's undeniably pricey – won very solid praise this year for its "top quality" cuisine and service that's "attentive yet unobtrusive". / W1K 7EH; www.corrigansmayfair.com; @CorriganMayfair; 10.45 pm, Sun 9.30 pm; closed Sat L; booking: max 10.

Côte £44 222
Branches throughout London
"A step up from Café Rouge" – these useful "modern, all-day French brasseries" are nowadays the survey's most talked-about chain; the cooking will "never win awards" but is "solid", "affordable" and "pleasant enough". / www.cote-restaurants.co.uk; 11 pm.

Counter SW8 NEW £48 222
Arch 50, 7-11 South Lambeth Pl 3693 9600 10–1D
"A much needed addition to Vauxhall", say fans of this "unlikely debut in the railway arches" praised for its brasserie fare (including an "excellent value brunch"); it's pricey though, the space can feel "confined", and service in particular is a "work in progress". (NB – if you do go, "just make sure go into the right arch and not one of the fetish clubs by mistake!") / SW8 1SP; www.counterrestaurants.com; @eatatcounter; 12.30 am, Fri & Sat 1.30 am.

The Cow W2 £54 444
89 Westbourne Park Rd 7221 0021 6–1B
"Fab fresh shellfish" makes the packed bar of Tom Conran's Irish boozer in Bayswater "heaven" for lovers of Guinness and oysters, and other seafood treats; more limited, but positive feedback too on its quirky, first floor dining room. / W2 5QH; www.thecowlondon.co.uk; 10 pm, Sun 10 pm; no Amex.

Coya W1 £76 323
118 Piccadilly 7042 7118 3–4B
"Sexy and dark" Peruvian haunt in Mayfair extolled by fans for its "incredibly buzzy" (ie "very noisy") vibe, and its "zingy" fare (not least "wonderful ceviche"); it's arguably "too expensive" though, and to some reporters the whole set-up is "just the wrong side of euro-trashy". / W1J 7NW; www.coyarestaurant.com; @coyarestaurant; Sun-Wed 10.30 pm, Thu-Sat 11 pm; booking: max 12.

Craft London SE10 NEW £64 224
Peninsula Sq 8465 5910 1–3D
"Great to have a proper restaurant at the Dome!" – underserved locals laud the arrival of foodie luvvie Stevie Parle at this "spacious", 3-floor venue, with "fantastic" river views from the rooftop bar; but his 6-course meals in the dining room are "very expensive" (maybe grab pizza in the café), and service "needs to up its game". / SE10 0SQ; www.craft-london.co.uk; @CraftLDN; Café 6 pm, Rest 10.30 pm, Sun 4 pm.

Crazy Bear W1 £64 334
26-28 Whitfield St 7631 0088 2–1C
A "quirky hidden gem", "tucked away off Tottenham Court Road", with a glam, if slightly faded cellar bar ("very unusual WCs"), and stylish, ground floor dining room; it's not the destination it once was, but still "great fun" and with "good Thai food" too. / W1T 2RG; www.crazybeargroup.co.uk; @CrazyBearGroup; 10.30 pm; closed Mon L & Sun; no shorts.

Crocker's Folly NW8 £55 223
23-24 Aberdeen Pl 7289 9898 8–4A
Praise for this monumental, St John's Wood, gin palace – "lavishly restored" by the Lebanese Maroush group, but with a British menu – is primarily aimed at its "extraordinarily beautiful" Victorian setting; the food is "unexciting" though and service "needs to improve" – perhaps the curse of Crocker strikes again? (Frank Crocker went bust in 1898 when he built this as a railway hotel... but they moved the station). / NW8 8JR; www.crockersfolly.com; @Crockers_Folly; 10.30 pm.

The Crooked Well SE5 £49 344
16 Grove Ln 7252 7798 1–3C
This sizeable, stylish Camberwell gastropub is "simple" in its aims – a "pleasant neighbourhood place" with good all-round standards. / SE5 8SY; www.thecrookedwell.com; @crookedwell; 10.30 pm; closed Mon L; no Amex.

The Cross Keys SW3 £54 334
1 Lawrence St 7351 0686 5–3C
"Back with a bang!"; it's not a hotspot for culinary fireworks, but Chelsea's oldest boozer (recently re-opened) has a brilliant atmosphere, and generally wins the thumbs up for its "friendly and attentive" service and "honest" pub tucker. / SW3 5NB; www.thexkeys.co.uk; @CrossKeys_PH; midnight.

Crosstown Doughnuts W1 NEW £5 342
4 Broadwick St 7734 8873 3–2D
First permanent site for this purveyor of designer doughnuts – "the best 'nuts in town", with great fillings. / W1F 8HJ; www.crosstowndoughnuts.com; @CrosstownDough; 10 pm.

The Culpepper E1 NEW £43 434
40 Commercial St 7247 5371 12–2C
"A superb new addition to Spitalfields" – this old gin-palace underwent a "cool and comfy refurb" this year, and combines a busy bar with a more "chilled upstairs dining room"; prices are not bargain basement, but the best dishes from its "inventive" menu are "exceptional". / E1 6LP; www.theculpepper.com; @TheCulpeper; Mon-Thu midnight, Fri & Sat 2 am, Sun 11 pm.

Cumberland Arms W14 £44 443
29 North End Rd 7371 6806 7–2D
An unexpected find, in the still un-lovely area at the top of the North End Road, near Olympia – an "unpretentious" but "wonderful" pub, with "delicious" food, "well-kept beers" and "lots of affordable wines". / W14 8SZ; www.thecumberlandarmspub.co.uk; @thecumberland; 10 pm, Sun 9.30 pm.

Cut, 45 Park Lane W1 **£117** 2 2 2
45 Park Ln 7493 4545 3–4A
What is it about Americans and their pricing strategies? – US über-chef Wolfgang Puck's "strangely proportioned" Mayfair dining room offers "steaks of the highest quality", and yet it is "insanely overpriced". / W1K 1PN; www.45parklane.com; @the_cut_bar; 10.30 pm.

Da Mario SW7 **£42** 2 3 3
15 Gloucester Rd 7584 9078 5–1B
"Still thriving" – a "long-time favourite Italian", near the Royal Albert Hall, where "excellent pizza" is a highlight; "it's a bit cramped but always lively", and very "family friendly". / SW7 4PP; www.damario.co.uk; 11.30 pm.

Da Mario WC2 **£42** 3 4 4
63 Endell St 7240 3632 4–1C
"To be treasured amongst all the chains of Covent Garden" – a "small and noisy" traditional Italian, "packed with regulars" drawn by its "reliable" fare at "fair prices". / WC2H 9AJ; www.da-mario.co.uk; 11.15 pm; closed Sun.

Dabbous W1 **£82** 3 3 2
39 Whitfield St 7323 1544 2–1C
Aficionados of Ollie Dabbous's foodie legend still extol the "inventive and refreshing" cuisine at his "chilled" Fitzrovia HQ. However, ever-more sceptics "don't understand the hype", given the grungy, "industrial" decor and food that increasingly seems "strange", "gimmicky" and "none-too-thrilling". / W1T 2SF; www.dabbous.co.uk; @dabbous; 9.30 pm (bar open until 11.30 pm); closed Sun; set weekday L £57 (FP).

Daddy Donkey EC1 **£15** 4 3 2
100 Leather Ln 0 7950 4484 48 9–2A
"Truly the daddy!"; punters still flock to this legendary Clerkenwell food truck to experience its "amazing burritos" – "even when there's a queue, the anticipation just makes you want it more!" / EC1N 7TE; www.daddydonkey.co.uk; @daddydonkey; Mon-Fri 4 pm; L only, closed Sat & Sun.

The Dairy SW4 **£40** 5 4 3
15 The Pavement 7622 4165 10–2D
"Well worth the trip to Clapham!" – this notable "Brooklyn-vibe" two-year-old provides an "endlessly interesting" selection of "unbelievable" tapas-style dishes "explained in detail by the waiting team". Top Tip – "one of London's best-value tasting menus". / SW4 0HY; www.the-dairy.co.uk; 9.45 pm; closed Mon, Tue L & Sun D; SRA-2.*

Dalchini SW19 **£36** 3 4 2
147 Arthur Rd 8947 5966 10–2B
"Interesting Indo-Chinese cooking" helps win a regular following for this well-established 'Hakka' haunt, opposite Wimbledon Park tube. / SW19 8AB; www.dalchini.co.uk; 10.30 pm, Fri & Sat 11 pm, Sun 10 pm; no Amex; set always available £24 (FP).

Daphne's SW3 **£72** 2 3 2
112 Draycott Ave 7589 4257 5–2C
This "very, very Chelsea" haunt – once famously Princess Di's fave – is "taking time to settle in after a major makeover" in 2014; some fans – "not crazy about the new decor" – still applaud its "classic" Italian cuisine, but others feel it's become "a little disappointing". / SW3 3AE; www.daphnes-restaurant.co.uk; @CapriceHoldings; 11 pm, Sun 10 pm; set weekday L £47 (FP).

Daquise SW7 **£49** 2 2 2
20 Thurloe St 7589 6117 5–2C
Advocates of this South Ken survivor (est 1947) say it "deserves better ratings" for its "semi-Polish" fodder (more contemporary nowadays than in times past); it's sometimes accused, though, of "tired" results. / SW7 2LT; www.daquise.co.uk; @GesslerDaquise; 11 pm; no Amex.

The Dartmouth Castle W6 **£47** 3 4 4
26 Glenthorne Rd 8748 3614 7–2C
Whether it's as "a perfect spot for a business lunch in Hammersmith", or "a great place for an evening pint", this "buzzy" little gastropub is "always reliable and good value". / W6 0LS; www.thedartmouthcastle.co.uk; @DartmouthCastle; 10 pm, Sun 9.30 pm; closed Sat L.

Darwin Brasserie, Sky Garden EC3 NEW **£64** 2 2 3
20 Fenchurch St 033 3772 0020 9–3D
Inevitably, "the magnificence of the view over the Thames and Tower of London isn't matched by the food" at this new "barn of a place" at the top of the Walkie Talkie, plus it's "absurdly overpriced", and service "needs work"; even so, by the standards of such places "it's fine". / EC3M 3BY; www.skygarden.london/darwin; @SG_Darwin; 10.30 pm, Sun 8.30 pm.

Daylesford Organic £42 213

44b Pimlico Rd, SW1 7881 8060 5–2D
Selfridges & Co, 400 Oxford St, W1
0800 123 400 3–1A
6-8 Blandford St, W1 3696 6500 2–1A NEW
208-212 Westbourne Grove, W11
7313 8050 6–1B

Lady Bamford's painstakingly stylish organic cafés – now also in Marylebone – are most often tipped for brunch; more generally they are "decent enough but too expensive for what they are", and service "lacks focus". / www.daylesfordorganic.com; SW1 & W11 7 pm, Sun 4 pm – W1 9 pm, Sun 6.15 pm; W11 no booking L.

Dean Street Townhouse W1 £56 234

69-71 Dean St 7434 1775 4–2A

"Spillover from the bar helps fuel the really buzzing atmosphere" at the Soho House-group's clubby Soho brasserie, which is "a little noisy but great fun"; its "comfort food" cooking is best for brunch – otherwise "there's not much actively bad about it, it's just a bit 'meh'!" / W1D 3SE; www.deanstreettownhouse.com; @deanstreettownhouse; 11.30 pm, Fri & Sat midnight, Sun 10.30 pm; set Sun L £0 (FP), set pre-theatre £38 (FP).

Defune W1 £67 432

34 George St 7935 8311 3–1A

"Like Tokyo... but you might be able to fly there for these prices!" – so "bring a fat wallet" if you visit this long-established Marylebone Japanese, where there's "no atmosphere" but "outstanding teppanyaki" and top sushi. / W1U 7DP; www.defune.com; 10.45 pm, Sun 10.30 pm.

Dehesa W1 £50 334

25 Ganton St 7494 4170 3–2C

For a "casual" occasion, this "busy and buzzing" corner-site, just off Carnaby Street, is an "intimate and very friendly" choice (if a "cramped" one); its "interesting" Italian/Spanish tapas can be "excellent" too, but doesn't excel as once it did. / W1F 9BP; www.dehesa.co.uk; @SaltYardGroup; 10.45 pm; SRA-2.*

Delancey & Co. W1 NEW £15 433

34 Goodge St 7637 8070 3–1D

"I can't tear myself away from the salt beef!" – this new, NYC-style 'Grab n' Go & Grab n' sit Deli' delivers a slice of the Lower East Side to Fitzrovia. / W1T 2PR; www.delanceyandco.co.uk; @DelanceyandCo; 9 pm.

THE DELAUNAY WC2 £58 345

55 Aldwych 7499 8558 2–2D

"Less hectic than the Wolseley but with all the good bits" – Corbin & King's "so-very-civilised" three-year-old, on the fringe of Covent Garden, is a less showy, more "luxurious" alternative to its bigger stablemate (and likewise "pitch perfect" for business). The mitteleuropean cooking "isn't really the point", but it's usually highly "satisfactory" (in particular the "utterly fab" breakfasts and "most delicious afternoon teas"). / WC2B 4BB; www.thedelaunay.com; @TheDelaunayRest; midnight, Sun 11 pm.

Delfino W1 £49 322

121a Mount St 7499 1256 3–3B

"Surprisingly good pizza, in the middle of Mayfair, at reasonable prices" – that's the USP at this straightforward spot, by the Connaught. / W1K 3NW; www.finos.co.uk; 10.45 pm; closed Sun.

Delhi Grill N1 £35 443

21 Chapel Mkt 7278 8100 8–3D

Styling itself an Indian 'dhabas' (an informal canteen), this "delightful" curry shop on Chapel Market provides "terrific", "fresh" street food "that's much more interesting than usual", all at "very cheap prices". / N1 9EZ; www.delhigrill.com; 10.30 pm; no credit cards.

La Delizia Limbara SW3 £40 323

63-65 Chelsea Manor St 7376 4111 5–3C

"Proper", "no-frills" pizza – amongst "the best in town" – justifies the discovery of this "cheerful" and crowded "hole in the wall", in a quiet backstreet, off the King's Road. / SW3 5RZ; www.ladelizia.org.uk; @ladelizia; 11 pm, Sun 10.30 pm; no Amex.

Department of Coffee EC1 £15 445

14-16 Leather Ln 7419 6906 9–2A

"Faultless coffee" helps this City hang out live up to its name, but it has "friendly" service and consistently well-rated snacks too. / EC1N 7SU; www.departmentofcoffee.co.uk; 6 pm, Sat & Sun 4 pm; L only.

The Depot SW14 £44 225

Tideway Yd, Mortlake High St 8878 9462
10–1A

"If you're lucky enough to nab a window table, it's magical gazing over the Thames" at this long-established spot, near Barnes Bridge; "food and service have never matched the location", but are "good enough", and it's "really recommended for a multi-generation lunch". / SW14 8SN; www.depotbrasserie.co.uk; @TheDepotBarnes; 10 pm, Sun 9.30 pm; set always available £32 (FP).

Les Deux Salons WC2 £54

40-42 William IV St 7420 2050 4–4C

New owner Sir Terence Conran has taken on this big, two-floor site, just off Trafalgar Square, and given a re-tread to its faux-Parisian brasserie style; it re-opened in June 2015, too late for survey feedback – early press reports suggest it's now more the handy theatreland amenity it was originally meant to be. / WC2N 4DD; www.lesdeuxsalons.co.uk; @lesdeuxsalons; 10.45 pm, Sun 5.45 pm; closed Sun D; set always available £37 (FP).

DF Mexico £31 433

28-29 Tottenham Court Rd, W1 no tel 2–1C NEW

Old Truman Brewery, 15 Hanbury St, E1 3617 6639 12–2C

"Fabulous Mexican street food" wins high praise for this year-old diner in Brick Lane's Old Truman Brewery, from the founders of Wahaca – "a great concept, which should be all over London". A new branch opened on Tottenham Court Road in September 2015. / www.dfmexico.co.uk.

Diner £34 233

Branches throughout London

Though one or two critics do write them off, these "hip" (perhaps "slightly cheesy") US-style diners also garner a fair amount of praise too for "some of the most calorific shakes ever", "burgers to die for" and "real, kosher style hot-dogs just like back home in NYC!" / www.goodlifediner.com; most branches 11 or 11.30 pmMidnight Fri - Sat; booking: max 10.

Dinings W1 £56 541

22 Harcourt St 7723 0666 8–4A

"The best sushi this side of Tokyo Fish Market" is to be had at Tomonari Chiba's "worn out looking" den in Marylebone (either sit at the ground-floor counter or in the "bizarre" basement); take care though – "you can really blow a big hole in your wallet here!" / W1H 4HH; www.dinings.co.uk; @diningslondon; 10.30 pm; closed Sun.

DINNER, MANDARIN ORIENTAL SW1 £100 333

66 Knightsbridge 7201 3833 5–1D

"I love a bit of history with my meal!" – Heston's "self-consciously creative" menu of rediscovered Olde Worlde English dishes is "pure foodie heaven" for fans of this park-side chamber ("lovely views if you get a window table"). Esteem for the place continues to wane year-on-year, however, and to a growing band of refuseniks "what first seemed novel and exciting now seems boring" and "oh-so overpriced". Top Menu Tips for first-timers – the Meat Fruit ("to die for") and Tipsy Cake ("divine"). / SW1X 7LA; www.mandarinoriental.com; 10.30 pm.

Dip & Flip £25 422

87 Battersea Rise, SW11 no tel 10–2C

62 The Broadway, SW19 no tel 10–2B NEW

"Awesome burger 'n' chips, made even better with a rich succulent gravy!" – that's the deal at this Battersea joint where "no knives and forks, just a roll of kitchen roll" makes a visit "a great big, messy, indulgence"; now also in Wimbledon too. / www.dipandflip.co.uk.

Dirty Burger £14 322

78 Highgate Rd, NW5 3310 2010 8–2B

Arch 54, 6 South Lambeth Rd, SW8 7074 1444 2–4D

13 Bethnal Green Rd, E1 7749 4525 12–1C

"A dirty indulgence after a late night" – these self-consciously "rustic" shacks make a "handy pitstop" for their "heavenly", "sticky, gooey fistfuls of flavour", "amazing fries" and "fabulous shakes". / www.eatdirtyburger.com; Mon-Thu 11 pm - midnight, Fri & Sat 1 am - 2 am, Sun 8 pm - 11 pm.

Dishoom £40 434

Kingly St, W1 awaiting tel 3–2D NEW

12 Upper St Martins Ln, WC2 7420 9320 4–3B

Stable St, Granary Sq, N1 7420 9321 8–3C

7 Boundary St, E2 7420 9324 12–1B

A "brilliant vibe" has been captured by this "energetic" and impressively executed concept – a growing chain of Mumbai-inspired Parsi cafés; "vibrant street-food" (including a great "brunch Bombay-style") is served in its "stunningly designed" outlets; "shame you can't book". In Autumn 2015, a new branch is slated to open off Carnaby Street. / www.dishoom.com; @Dishoom; 11 pm, Sun 10 pm.

Diwana Bhel-Poori House NW1 £26 321

121-123 Drummond St 7387 5556 8–4C

"Forget service, forget ambience!"; it's the grub – in particular the "delicious and incredible value lunchtime buffet" – that makes this "scruffy" canteen both a Little India institution, and "a vegetarian's dream"; "I've been enjoying deluxe dosas here for 30 years and they haven't changed... in a good way"; BYO. / NW1 2HL; www.diwanabhelpoori.com; 11.45 pm, Sun 11 pm; no Amex; need 10+ to book.

The Dock Kitchen, Portobello Dock W10 £60 345

342-344 Ladbroke Grove, Portobello Dock 8962 1610 1–2B

"The magical canal-side setting at night" is a huge plus-point at Stevie Parle's "designer-style" venture, in deepest Notting Hill; its "unique, ever-changing menu pays homage to all four corners of the globe" – fans applaud its "mastery, in spite of its breadth", but to sceptics it's "a little bit too eclectic at times". / W10 5BU; www.dockkitchen.co.uk; @TheDockKitchen; 9.30 pm; closed Sun D.

The Don EC4 £65 3 3 3
20 St Swithin's Ln 7626 2606 9–3C
This well-established venue near Bank combines a "civilised" ground floor, with a more atmospheric cellar bistro; critics feel its cooking has become more "complacent" in recent times, but it remains a top City entertaining spot. / EC4N 8AD; www.thedonrestaurant.com; @thedonlondon; 10 pm; closed Sat & Sun; no shorts.

Donna Margherita SW11 £44 4 3 3
183 Lavender Hill 7228 2660 10–2C
For a "friendly Italian meal" in south London this "always busy" Battersea Neapolitan exudes an "excited buzz", and its pizza and other fare is generally a safe bet. / SW11 5TE; www.donna-margherita.com; @DMargheritaUK; 10.30 pm, Fri & Sat 11 pm; Mon-Thu D only, Fri-Sun open L & D.

Donostia W1 £49 5 4 4
10 Seymour Pl 3620 1845 2–2A
"Simply amazing" and "authentic" Basque tapa/pintxos are dished up by "really helpful" and "knowledgeable" staff at this "stylish yet informal" fixture, "in a quiet corner north of Marble Arch". See also Lurra. / W1H 7ND; www.donostia.co.uk; @DonostiaW1; 11 pm; closed Mon L.

Dorchester Grill, Dorchester Hotel W1 £102 2 3 2
53 Park Ln 7629 8888 3–3A
"New décor's a big improvement", as this famous chamber has at long last ditched its vile, faux-Scottish theme; ratings remain lacklustre across the board though – the whole operation still needs a major kick up the backside to avoid being just-another-overpriced-Mayfair-dining-room. / W1K 1QA; www.thedorchester.com; @TheDorchester; 10.15 pm, Sat 10.45 pm, Sun 10.15 pm; no trainers; set weekday L £64 (FP), set Sun L £74 (FP).

Dotori N4 £28 4 3 2
3a Stroud Green Rd 7263 3562 8–1D
"The secret of this excellent-value, tiny, cramped Korean near Finsbury Park station is well-and-truly out, and you have to book well in advance, even mid week"; "if you don't know what to order, staff will talk you through it". / N4 2DQ; www.dotorirestaurant.wix.com/dotorirestaurant; 10.30 pm; closed Mon; no Amex.

The Dove W6 £46 2 2 5
19 Upper Mall 8748 5405 7–2B
A "quintessential", small 18th-century pub, "beautifully located" on the Thames in Hammersmith, which is supremely "cosy in winter", and has "a sunny terrace in summer" – just the job for a Sunday roast. / W6 9TA; www.fullers.co.uk; 11 pm; closed Sun D; no booking.

Dragon Castle SE17 £36 3 3 2
100 Walworth Rd 7277 3388 1–3C
"In the most unlikely of locations", near Elephant & Castle, this "cavernous" Cantonese is "worth a trip"; it may look a little "tired", but its dim sum is "amazing value, and comes in great abundance". / SE17 1JL; www.dragon-castle.com; @Dragoncastle100; Mon-Sat 11 pm, Sun 10 pm.

Drakes Tabanco W1 £49 3 2 3
3 Windmill St 7637 9388 2–1C
"An educational selection of wonderful sherries on tap" beefs up the attractions of this "authentic" Andalucían-inspired Fitzrovian ("off the hustle and bustle of Charlotte Street"), but its "yummy" tapas is also "very well done". / W1T 2HY; www.drakestabanco.com; 10 pm.

The Drapers Arms N1 £50 2 2 3
44 Barnsbury St 7619 0348 8–3D
"Sociable" Islington gastropub, which remains a bit hit locally; service is "inconsistent" however, and the food can turn out "mediocre" – "go for the excellent, knowledgeably-selected wines". / N1 1ER; www.thedrapersarms.com; @DrapersArms; 10.30 pm; no Amex.

Dub Jam WC2 £24 4 4 3
20 Bedford St 7836 5876 4–3C
"Come for the potent rum punch, stay for the awesome Caribbean BBQ" – so say fans of this "laid-back, cheap 'n' cheerful" shack, in Covent Garden. / WC2E 9HP; www.dubjam.co.uk; @dubjambbq; 11.30 pm, Fri & Sat midnight, Sun 10.30 pm.

The Duck & Rice W1 NEW £58 2 3 5
90 Berwick St 3327 7888 3–2D
There's real "whoa factor" to the "striking" fit-out and "great-vibe" of Wagamama-creator, Alan Yau's much-anticipated "Chinese gastropub concept", in the heart of sleazy Soho (formerly, The Endurance, RIP). No surprise that some find it "over-hyped" considering food that's arguably only "good-to-average", but beer and dim sum in the downstairs bar is a particularly "winning combination". / W1F 0QB; www.theduckandrice.com; @theduckandrice; Mon -11.30 pm, midnight, Sun 10.30 pm .

Duck & Waffle EC2 £68 2 2 5
110 Bishopsgate, Heron Tower 3640 7310 9–2D
"Go mainly for the extraordinary views" to this 24/7, 40th-floor hang out; "the signature dish (confit duck with a fried egg, waffle and syrup) is better than it sounds", but opinions are mixed on the "mainly meaty, high cholesterol" fare and you pay "City boys' drinks prices". Maybe try breakfast or coffee. / EC2N 4AY; www.duckandwaffle.com; @DuckandWaffle; open 24 hours.

Ducksoup W1 £54 [3][4][4]
41 Dean St 7287 4599 4–2A
"A dark, intimate, welcoming den in Soho"; the "beautiful" Mediterranean small plates are "creative" and "served with real charm". / W1D 4PY; www.ducksoupsoho.co.uk; @ducksoup; 10.30 pm; closed Sun D; need 6+ to book at certain times.

Duke of Sussex W4 £46 [3][3][4]
75 South Pde 8742 8801 7–1A
A "dramatic" interior, and "lovely rear dining room and garden" score points for this traditional Victorian tavern by Acton Green Common, as does its very dependable "Spanish-inspired" tapas, and more substantial fare. / W4 5LF; www.metropolitanpubcompany.com; @thedukew4; 10.30 pm, Sun 9.30 pm.

Duke's Brew & Que N1 £54 [3][2][3]
33 Downham Rd 3006 0795 1–2D
"Hipster heaven" is to be found at this "laid back" US-style Dalston hang-out in the form of "proper, Texan-style BBQ (ribs to die for)" and "brilliant" home-brewed beer; even fans however can find it "massively too expensive". / N1 5AA; www.dukesbrewandque.com; @DukesJoint; 10.30 pm, Sun 9.30 pm.

Dumplings' Legend W1 NEW £35 [4][2][3]
16 Gerrard St 7494 1200 4–3A
"Don't let the modern, white exterior fool you" – this Chinatown newcomer's dim sum is "of very high quality"; as is often the case in these parts though, service "can be a bit off-hand". / W1D 6JE; www.dumplingslegend.com; midnight, Fri & Sat 3 am, Sun 11 pm.

Durum Ocakbasi N3 £30 [3][2][2]
119 Ballards Ln 8346 8977 1–1B
"Good, marinated meaty kebabs" at "cheap prices", plus "fast service" means there's "always a queue" at this "consistently reliable" Finchley Turk. / N3 1LJ; durumrestaurant.co.uk; midnight.

The Dysart Petersham TW10 £69 [4][4][3]
135 Petersham Rd 8940 8005 1–4A
Kenneth Culhane's "super" cooking can come as a "real surprise" at this leafily located pub – a large Arts & Crafts house overlooking Richmond Common; despite its "leaded windows, log fires, and twinkly lights in the trees outside", at lunch it can "lack atmosphere". / TW10 7AA; www.thedysartarms.co.uk; @dysartpetersham; 9.30 pm; closed Sun D; set weekday L £42 (FP).

E&O W11 £60 [3][3][4]
14 Blenheim Cr 7229 5454 6–1A
"Still exciting and vibrant" – this "intimate and buzzing" (if slightly "arrogant") Notting Hill hang-out is "not quite as outstanding as it was half a dozen years ago", but "still the place to go" for many, thanks to its "amazing Pan-Asian tapas and cocktails". / W11 1NN; www.rickerrestaurants.com; 11 pm, Sun 10.30 pm; booking: max 6.

The Eagle EC1 £34 [4][3][5]
159 Farringdon Rd 7837 1353 9–1A
Even after all these years, there's still "rarely a false note" at "the original and best gastropub" – an engagingly "grungy" and "low key" hang-out, near Exmouth Market; the "rustic" Mediterranean cooking is "reasonably priced", and "there's always something new and interesting on the menu". / EC1R 3AL; www.theeaglefarringdon.co.uk; @eaglefarringdon; 10.30 pm; closed Sun D; no Amex; no booking.

Ealing Park Tavern W5 £44 [3][3][4]
222 South Ealing Rd 8758 1879 1–3A
South Ealing locals are divided on the new regime at this "huge" neighbourhood gastropub; but while some are disappointed, most say it's "much improved", with "smarter" décor and "thoroughly enjoyable" cooking. / W5 4RL; www.ealingparktavern.com; @ealingtavern; 10 pm, Sun 9 pm.

Earl Spencer SW18 £45 [4][2][3]
260-262 Merton Rd 8870 9244 10–2B
Despite its trafficky Wandsworth location, this sizeable road house is "a wonderful local" with cooking that's "consistently a cut-above on the pub food scale"; "the beer's always excellent too :-)". / SW18 5JL; www.theearlspencer.co.uk; @TheEarlSpencer; 11 pm; Mon-Thu D only, Fri-Sun open L & D; no booking, Sun.

Eat 17 £39 [3][4][2]
28-30 Orford Rd, E17 8521 5279 1–1D
64-66 Brooksbys Walk, E9 8986 6242 1–1D
"A real find!" in Walthamstow – a "fun and friendly" spot with "interesting" food that's "very well priced"; also with an offshoot in Hackney. / www.eat17.co.uk.

Eat Tokyo £24 [4][2][2]
50 Red Lion St, WC1 7242 3490 2–1D
15 Whitcomb St, WC2 7930 6117 4–4B
169 King St, W6 8741 7916 7–2B
18 Hillgate St, W8 7792 9313 6–2B
14 North End Rd, NW11 8209 0079 1–1B
"High end it isn't", but for "authentic" Japanese fare that "doesn't cost the earth" – "amazingly fresh sushi" and "very good bento boxes" – these "deservedly busy" staples are just the job. / Mon - Sat 11.30pm, Sun 11 pm.

Ebury Restaurant & Wine Bar SW1 **£53** 2 3 3
139 Ebury St 7730 5447 2–4A
A great, "old-school" wine bar, not far from Victoria; the cooking is only "standard", but the atmosphere is "charming" and there's an "excellent wine list". / SW1W 9QU; www.eburyrestaurant.co.uk; 10.15 pm.

Eco SW4 **£36** 2 2 4
162 Clapham High St 7978 1108 10–2D
Owned by one of the co-founders of Franco Manca, this perennially "lively" Clapham institution (now 20 years old) has long been the home of some "great pizza". / SW4 7UG; www.ecorestaurants.com; @ecopizzaLDN; 11 pm, Fri & Sat 11.30 pm.

Edera W11 **£61** 3 5 3
148 Holland Park Ave 7221 6090 6–2A
"A little pricey" but "very solid and reliable" – that's the universal view on this low-key, quite "stylish" Holland Park Sardinian (also "a dependable spot for business"). Top Menu Tip – "truffles a speciality". / W11 4UE; www.atozrestaurants.com; 11 pm, Sun 10 pm.

Edwins SE1 **£48** 3 3 3
202-206 Borough High St 7403 9913 9–4B
"At a safe distance from the City expense-accounters and Borough Market crowds", this year-old bistro above a pub is well-rated all-round (especially for its "good value" set menu). / SE1 1JX; www.edwinsborough.co.uk; @edwinsborough; 11.30 pm, Sat midnight, Sun 4 pm; closed Sun D.

Eelbrook SW6 **£56** 3 4 3
Eel Brook Common, New King's Rd 3417 0287 10–1B
"A relaxing park-side location" adds to the appeal of this year-old venture, by Fulham's Eel Brook Common; weekend brunch is a highlight, but the menu of small plates is well-rated generally. / SW6 4SE; @EelbrookTweets; 10.30 pm, Sun 5.30 pm ; set weekday L £32 (FP).

8 Hoxton Square N1 **£49** 4 4 3
8-9 Hoxton Sq 7729 4232 12–1B
"Ticking all the boxes for a relaxing evening with friends" – a "lovely and intimate" spin-off from 10 Greek Street that "would be good, even without its secret weapon of a wine list"; the cooking's "low key, but accomplished, and extremely well-prepared". / N1 6NU; www.8hoxtonsquare.com; @8HoxtonSquare; 10 pm; closed Sun D.

Eight Over Eight SW3 **£56** 3 2 4
392 King's Rd 7349 9934 5–3B
"It looks a bit like an '90s nightclub", but Will Ricker's "very popular" Chelsea haunt makes "a good poor man's Nobu" – the Pan-Asian tapas is "consistently high quality", and it's still quite the "buzzing scene". / SW3 5UZ; www.rickerrestaurants.com; 11 pm, Sun 10.30 pm.

Electric Diner W11 **£44** 2 4 4
191 Portobello Rd 7908 9696 6–1A
"Busy and bustling" diner, where you battle with Notting Hill's trustafarians for a "fun" brunch, featuring "top burgers", or "a welcome twist on a Full English"; however even some who think it's great concede that "you don't go for the pretty average food". / W11 2ED; www.electricdiner.com; @ElectricDiner; 11 pm, Sun 10 pm.

Elena's L'Etoile W1 **£52** 1 1 1
30 Charlotte St 7636 7189 2–1C
"What was once a shining star, is now just very tired..." – this ancient Gallic Fitzrovian (est 1896) "used to be remarkable when it was presided over by Elena", but "continues its lurch downwards", and is nowadays well "past its sell-by". / W1T 2NG; www.elenasletoile.co.uk; @elenasletoile; 10.30 pm; closed Sat L & Sun.

Elliot's Café SE1 **£50** 2 2 3
12 Stoney St 7403 7436 9–4C
An "ever-changing" menu ("mainly small plates") and interesting wines inspire devotees of Brett Redman's "buzzy" bare-brick café, in Borough Market; "standards seem to have dropped this year" though – staff can be "uninterested" and a few meals were "a great disappointment" – the pressure of opening The Richmond E8? / SE1 9AD; www.elliotscafe.com; @elliotscafe; 9.30 pm; closed Sun; booking: max 8.

Ellory, Netil House E8 NEW
Westgate St awaiting tel 1–2D
A collaboration between ex-Mayfields chef, Matthew Young and sommelier, Jack Lewens (Spring and River Café) that's got foodies excited; it's expected to open in Hackney's über-hip Netil House in September 2015. / E8 3RL.

Ember Yard W1 **£49** 3 3 3
60 Berwick St 7439 8057 3–1D
"I love the use of charcoal!" – this Salt Yard group yearling serves "deep-flavoured" tapas from its char grill, which can be "wonderful"; it's a stylish spot too, although it can get "too squashed", and one or two doubters feel the food is "OK, but could be better". / W1F 8SU; www.emberyard.co.uk; @SaltYardGroup; midnight; SRA-2.*

Emile's SW15 **£48** 3 4 2
96-98 Felsham Rd 8789 3323 10–2B
"Emile adds that personal touch" to his longstanding Putney backstreet "stalwart", where the "well-priced, French bistro-esque" cooking and "well-selected" wines "continue to offer good value". / SW15 1DQ; www.emilesrestaurant.co.uk; 11 pm; D only, closed Sun; no Amex.

The Empress E9 £45 444
130 Lauriston Rd 8533 5123 1–2D
"A favourite stop-off after a bracing walk in Victoria Park" – this popular East End gastropub "always hits the mark" with its "different" cooking, "spot-on" service, and "great vibes". / E9 7LH; www.empresse9.co.uk; @elliottlidstone; 10 pm, Sun 9.30 pm; closed Mon L; no Amex.

Engawa W1 NEW £86 343
2 Ham Yd 7287 5724 3–2D
Just off Shaftesbury Avenue, a small and "tightly packed" new temple to Japan's outrageously expensive Kobe and Wagyu beef (plus sake bar); many reporters do laud "exquisite food" and "stunning presentation", but – at the vertiginous prices – even some fans "expected better quality cuts of the meat". / W1D 7DT; www.engawa.uk; 11.15 pm .

Enoteca Rabezzana EC1 NEW £48 223
62-63 Long Ln 7600 0266 9–2B
The Italian grub is not the star attraction at this "fun" if "chaotic" new City wine bar – it's the massive selection of wines by the glass ("over 100 of them") that make it worth seeking out. / EC1A 9EJ; www.rabezzana.co.uk; @RabezzanaLondon; midnight, Sat 1 am.

Enoteca Turi SW15 £61 443
28 Putney High St 8785 4449 10–2B
"Don't be put off by the slightly off-piste location, near Putney Bridge!" – Giuseppe and Pamela Turi's "personal" yet "efficient" stalwart offers "a truly memorable" combination of "beautifully cooked, regional Italian cuisine" and one of London's top Italian wine lists ("about the size of the Encyclopaedia Britannica"). "Worryingly, it's under threat from its landlord – long may it survive!" / SW15 1SQ; www.enotecaturi.com; @enoteca_turi; 10.30 pm, Fri & Sat 11 pm; closed Sun.

The Enterprise SW3 £58 233
35 Walton St 7584 3148 5–2C
In a chichi Chelsea enclave, this corner-bar/restaurant is a real "local's hang out"; "you don't go for the food" (though it's not bad), but the "friendly" service and "fun" ambience. / SW3 2HU; www.theenterprise.co.uk; 10 pm, Sat 10.30 pm; no booking, except weekday L; set weekday L £38 (FP).

Esarn Kheaw W12 £34 441
314 Uxbridge Rd 8743 8930 7–1B
Rather forgotten nowadays, but this stalwart Shepherd's Bush café still wins praise for its "personable service, and very delicious and highly authentic" north Thai cooking; "the shabby mint decor is all part of the charm". / W12 7LJ; www.esarnkheaw.co.uk; @esarn_kheaw; 11 pm; closed Sat L & Sun L; no Amex.

L'Escargot W1 £60 333
48 Greek St 7439 7474 4–2A
Brian Clivaz's datedly glamourous old-timer provides a "cosseting" and "romantic" refuge from Soho, and its slightly "formal and traditional" style would also suit a business occasion; under new owners for a year now, the Gallic cuisine is proving "reliable". / W1D 4EF; lescargotrestaurant.co.uk; @EscargotLondon; midnight; closed Sun D.

Essenza W11 £60 323
210 Kensington Park Rd 7792 1066 6–1A
Notting Hill offers up a "good local Italian" with a "very high standard of Roman-inspired food"; expect to receive "a warm welcome, very generous helpings of well-prepared dishes and a lively atmosphere". / W11 1NR; www.essenza.co.uk; @Essenza_LND; 11.30 pm; set weekday L £38 (FP).

Ethos W1 NEW £38 423
48 Eastcastle St 3581 1538 3–1C
"Bonus points for an interesting concept" – a new, self-service veggie, where you "load up as much as you like and pay-by-weight"; "prices add up pretty quickly", but there's an "excellent selection" of "perky", health-conscious dishes (and "you don't need a hair shirt to enjoy them"). / W1W 8DX; www.ethosfoods.com; @ethosfoods; 10 pm, Sun 5 pm .

L'Etranger SW7 £72 342
36 Gloucester Rd 7584 1118 5–1B
"The wine list's amazing", the "interesting" Asian/French fusion cuisine can be "exceptional", and service is "very professional" too at this lesser-known spot near the Royal Albert Hall; it's "expensive" though, and – "being unpredictably quiet or busy" – the "ambience is patchy". / SW7 4QT; www.etranger.co.uk; 11 pm; set weekday L £44 (FP).

Everest Inn SE3 £35 453
41 Montpelier Vale 8852 7872 1–4D
"Fresh-tasting Gurkha curries" and other "unusual Nepali dishes", together with "smiling and efficient" service win consistent praise for this local Blackheath favourite. / SE3 0TJ; www.everestinnblackheath.co.uk; midnight, Sun 11 pm.

Eyre Brothers EC2 £64 533
70 Leonard St 7613 5346 12–1B
"Terrific Iberian tapas, made with care from well-sourced produce, and a strong wine list" inspire fervent praise for this low-key, but quite swish haunt, near Silicon Roundabout, whose "quiet ambience and big tables" have long established it as a business favourite. / EC2A 4QX; www.eyrebrothers.co.uk; 10 pm; closed Sat L & Sun.

Faanoos £27 223
472 Chiswick High Rd, W4 8994 4217 7–2A
11 Bond St, W5 8810 0505 1–3A
481 Richmond Road, SW14 8878 5738 1–4A
"Simple but tasty Persian fare at very reasonable prices" – that's the formula that wins fans for this "cheap and cheerful" locals in Chiswick and Ealing, where the oven-baked flatbread is a "pleasure"; now with a site in East Sheen too. / SW14 11 pm; W4 11 pm; Fri & Sat midnight.

Fabrizio EC1 £50 442
30 Saint Cross St 7430 1503 9–1A
"Fabrizio is a wonderful host" and injects life into his "basic" Hatton Garden premises, where the "simple and fresh" Sicilian dishes are "authentic", and offer "very good value for money". / EC1N 8UH; www.fabriziorestaurant.co.uk; 10 pm; closed Sat L & Sun.

Fabrizio N19 £35 242
34 Highgate Hill 7561 9073 8–1C
"Ideal for a family outing" – this Highgate Hill trattoria is "a consistent neighbourhood Italian, serving fresh pasta and pizza choices of the day". / N19 5NL; www.fabriziolondon.co.uk; 10 pm; no Amex.

Fairuz W1 £48 343
3 Blandford St 7486 8108 2–1A
"A very consistent performer" – this Lebanese "longstanding favourite", in Marylebone, serves "excellent mezze", and its staff are extremely hospitable too. / W1H 3DA; www.fairuz.uk.com; 11 pm, Sun 10.30 pm.

La Famiglia SW10 £52 222
7 Langton St 7351 0761 5–3B
A '60s, "old-school, family-run Italian" in the heart of Chelsea that's still a "characterful" classic for its loyal fan club, especially for a family occasion (and with "a lovely garden in summer"); even some fans might however concede that to some extent it's "living on its past, and very expensive". / SW10 0JL; www.lafamiglia.co.uk; 11 pm.

FERA AT CLARIDGE'S CLARIDGE'S HOTEL W1 £144 344
55 Brook St 7107 8888 3–2B
After a dazzling debut, Simon Rogan's second year in this "stunning" Art Deco chamber still inspires adulation for his "wizard" tasting menus and "astonishingly good wine matches". Prices, however, are "breathtaking", and ratings slipped perceptibly across the board this year, with growing gripes about "an absence of fireworks". / W1K 4HR; www.claridges.co.uk/fera; 10 pm; set weekday L £65 (FP); SRA-2.*

Fernandez & Wells £32 224
16a St Anne's Ct, W1 7494 4242 3–1D
43 Lexington St, W1 7734 1546 3–2D
73 Beak St, W1 7287 8124 3–2D
Somerset Hs, Strand, WC2 7420 9408 2–2D
"Consistently terrific coffee", and "wonderful sarnies, pastries and cakes" distinguish these "quirky, if not comfy" cafés; Somerset House is its most striking outlet, and the tiny Soho ones are good too – South Ken seems more of a "rip off", with staff who are "too cool to care". / www.fernandezandwells.com; Lexington St & St Anne's court 10 pm, Beak St 6 pm, Somerset House 11 pm; St Anne's Court closed Sun.

Fez Mangal W11 £26 543
104 Ladbroke Grove 7229 3010 6–1A
"Hectic, as it's often jammed with customers" – an "inexpensive Turkish BBQ" in Notting Hill, whose "freshly prepared" food is "first rate"; "BYO too!" / W11 1PY; www.fezmangal.co.uk; @FezMangal; 11.30 pm; no Amex.

Ffiona's W8 £56 344
51 Kensington Church St 7937 4152 5–1A
"Ffiona has become a personal friend" to regulars at her "unique and very intimate" Kensington venue, whom she makes feel "welcome and special"; food-wise it's a case of "well-cooked staples, plus a few more international dishes", and there's a popular weekend brunch. / W8 4BA; www.ffionas.com; @ffionasnotes; 11 pm, Sun 10 pm; closed Mon; no Amex.

Fields SW4 NEW £30
2 Rookery Rd 7838 1082 10–2C
The owners of Balham's achingly hip coffee shop Milk bring a second location to SW London with this brunch-tastic revamp of a modest park café in Clapham Common. / SW4 9DD; www.fieldscafe.com; @The5Fields; 5 pm.

Fifteen N1 £60 122
15 Westland Pl 3375 1515 12–1A
"What is all the fuss about?"; Jamie Oliver's Hoxton Italian continues – as it always has done – to provide "a totally overrated experience with terrible food", and at prices that are plain "rude". / N1 7LP; www.fifteen.net; @JamiesFifteen; 10 pm; booking: max 12.

The Fifth Floor, Restaurant Harvey Nichols SW1 £62 333
109-125 Knightsbridge 7235 5250 5–1D
Few reports nowadays on this forgotten-about landmark atop the famous Knightsbridge department store – a "light and airy space, with a top-lit glass ceiling and simple but appropriate decor"; for a "classy" lunch though, fans say it's "first rate". / SW1X 7RJ; www.harveynichols.com; 11 pm; closed Sun D; SRA-2.*

Fire & Stone £42 2 2 2
31-32 Maiden Ln, WC2 7632 2084 4–3D
Westfield, Ariel Way, W12 7763 2085 7–1C
The cavernous Covent Garden original is the mainstay of this modern pizza chain; but while fans like its trademark weird and wonderful array of toppings, sceptics say they're "odd and don't work", or rail at general "chain-style dreariness". / www.fireandstone.com; WC2 11 pm; W12 11.15 pm; E1 11pm, Sun 8 pm.

Fischer's W1 £58 3 4 4
50 Marylebone High St 7466 5501 2–1A
Whether it's "another star in the Corbin & King stable" or merely "a useful addition to Marylebone", this "fun pastiche of old Vienna" earnt higher ratings this year; the slightly "kitsch Austrian" interior is "gemütlich", and the mitteleuropean victuals – mainly wurst and schnitzels – is "good but pricey". / W1U 5HN; www.fischers.co.uk; @fischers; 11 pm, Sun 10 pm.

Fish Central EC1 £32 3 3 2
149-155 Central St 7253 4970 12–1A
For "very crisp" fish 'n' chips at "unbeatable prices" this family-run Clerkenwell chippy is a hit with cabbies and Barbican-goers alike; take a punt on one of the specials – "be it lobster, halibut or Dover Sole, it's some of the best". / EC1V 8AP; www.fishcentral.co.uk; 10.30 pm, Fri & Sat 11 pm; closed Sun.

Fish Club £40 4 2 2
189 St John's Hill, SW11 7978 7115 10–2C
57 Clapham High St, SW4 7720 5853 10–2D
"Amazing fish 'n' chips" – using "the best range of fresh fish", and with "unbeatable" roast root and sweet potato accompaniments – mean these "slightly cramped" south London chippies are "well worth a few extra quid over the average". / www.thefishclub.com; 10 pm; closed Mon L; no bookings.

Fish in a Tie SW11 £36 2 4 3
105 Falcon Rd 7924 1913 10–1C
"Good food in generous portions at unbeatable prices", summarises the appeal of this "most reliable (if predictable)" Clapham Junction bistro, whose menu is "diverse, Italian in feel, with an ever changing list of specials". / SW11 2PF; www.fishinatie.co.uk; midnight, Sun 11 pm; no Amex.

Fish Market EC2 £49 3 3 3
16B New St 3503 0790 9–2D
"An attractive heated courtyard with umbrellas" frames the entrance to this "bright and airy" converted warhouse (a D&D London operation), a stone's throw from the crowds on Bishopsgate; it's somewhat under-the-radar, despite serving dependable "fresh fish, simply cooked". / EC2M 4TR; www.fishmarket-restaurant.co.uk; @FishMarketNS; 10.30 pm; closed Sun.

fish! SE1 £56 3 2 2
Cathedral St 7407 3803 9–4C
It's "rather crowded" and "a little expensive", but this glazed shed, by Borough Market, serves a decent array of dishes, including "surprisingly good fish 'n' chips", "excellent mixed grill" and "great fish finger sarnies". / SE1 9AL; www.fishkitchen.com; @fishborough; 10.45 pm, Sun 10.30 pm.

Fishworks £51 3 2 2
7-9 Swallow St, W1 7734 5813 3–3D
89 Marylebone High St, W1 7935 9796 2–1A
"Walking through the fish shop to get to the restaurant sets the scene" at these straightforward bistros in Mayfair and Marylebone; "there's a wide range" and results are "consistently good", but the overall experience is a bit "functional". / www.fishworks.co.uk; 10.30 pm.

The Five Fields SW3 £76 5 5 5
8-9 Blacklands Ter 7838 1082 5–2D
"It just gets better and better!" – Taylor Bonnyman's "grown up" and "romantic" two-year-old in the heart of Chelsea is one of London's most deeply impressive all-rounders – service is "impeccable", and the "exciting" cuisine provides "a beautiful blend of original flavours". / SW3 2SP; www.fivefieldsrestaurant.com; @The5Fields; 10 pm; D only, closed Mon & Sun.

Five Guys £13 2 2 2
1-3 Long Acre, WC2 7240 2657 4–3C
71 Upper St, N1 7226 7577 8–3D NEW
"An upgrade on McDonald's which hits the spot", say fans of this US-import-chain who dig the "proper dirty burgers", "good salty fries" and "really nice mix of free toppings"; not everyone's wowed though – "you get McD quality at GBK prices!" / www.fiveguys.co.uk.

500 N19 £48 3 4 2
782 Holloway Rd 7272 3406 8–1C
"An unpromising-looking bit of Holloway hides this Italian treasure which is almost always packed"; the interior is "quite minimal", but it serves "well thought out", "seasonal" Sicilian fare, from a "small but unusual menu" (albeit one that "could do with rotating a little more"). / N19 3JH; www.500restaurant.co.uk; @500restaurant; 10.30 pm, Sun 9.30 pm; Mon-Thu D only, Fri-Sun open L & D.

Flat Iron £22 444

17 Beak St, W1 no tel 3–2D
17 Henrietta St, WC2 no tel 4–4C NEW
9 Denmark St, WC2 no tel 4–1A
"Steak and salad for a tenner – WOW!"; these "simple", "hipster" hang outs in Soho and by Centrepoint "do what they do very well indeed"; "arrive early, but it's always worth the wait". A second Covent Garden site is set to open in Henrietta Street in October 2015. / www.flatironsteak.co.uk.

Flat Three W11 NEW £75 233

120-122 Holland Park Ave 7792 8987 6–2A
With its "experimental fusion of Asian and Scandi' inspirations", this "cool", new, Holland Park basement (born of a supper club collaboration) sure is "bringing something new to the 'hood"; but while fans say it's "exciting", or sense "great potential", sceptics say "the menu is incomprehensible", and results plain "poor". / W11 4UA; www.flatthree.london; @FlatThree; Tue-Sat 9.30 pm.

Flesh and Buns WC2 £50 333

41 Earlham St 7632 9500 4–2C
"Nice buns..."; this "funky" Soho basement (sibling to Bone Daddies) serves "mouthwatering, meat-filled steam buns" and other "unusual Japanese-influenced dishes" to a "hip" crowd, some of it on communal tables; it's "too loud" though. / WC2H 9LX; www.bonedaddies.com; @FleshandBuns; Mon & Tue 10.30 pm, Wed-Sat 9.30 pm, Sun 9.30 pm.

Flotsam and Jetsam SW17 NEW £14 434

4 Bellevue Parade 8672 7639 10–2C
"An inviting, new Antipodean-style indie coffee shop and café", by Wandsworth Common; "instantly and deservedly popular", it offers "awesome" brunches, "lovely light lunches" and "top coffee" in a "crowded but fun" setting. / SW17 7EQ; www.flotsamandjetsamcafe.co.uk; 5 pm.

FM Mangal SE5 £28 322

54 Camberwell Church St 7701 6677 1–4D
With its "hefty grills" and "smoky flatbreads", this "totally unpretentious" Camberwell Turkish grill "never disappoints" – "don't forget the totally addictive charred, marinaded onions". / SE5 8QZ; midnight.

(1707) Fortnum & Mason W1 £54 223

181 Piccadilly 7734 8040 3–3D
Below the famous food halls, a bar with "reliable" snacks, but which "is really all about the wine" – "a great range of flights", plus the chance to "drink anything from their impressive adjacent wine shop" (with £15 corkage). "Service has dropped off" this year however, and prices seem increasingly "astronomical". / W1A 1ER; www.fortnumandmason.co.uk; @fortnumandmason; 7.45 pm, Sun 5 pm; closed Sun D.

(The Diamond Jubilee Tea Salon) Fortnum & Mason W1 £66 333

181 Piccadilly 7734 8040 3–3D
"I didn't think posh afternoon tea would be my thing, but I was bowled over!" – Fortnum's "light" and "elegant" third-floor salon is a relatively new addition to the store, with cake trollies and "light and fluffy scones" à gogo; it's pricey though, and critics say "the big hotels do it better". / W1A 1ER; www.fortnumandmason.com; @fortnumandmason; 7 pm, Sun 6 pm; cancellation charge for larger bookings.

(45 Jermyn St) Fortnum & Mason W1 NEW

181 Piccadilly 7437 3278 3–3D
In autumn 2015, HM's grocer announced that its hallowed (if slightly crusty and expensive) old buttery, The Fountain, would close, to be replaced by an all-day operation with a midnight closing time; 10/10 to F&M for moving with the times, but if they'd run the old one better would they need to revamp? / W1A 1ER; www.fortnumandmason.com.

40 Maltby Street SE1 £45 434

40 Maltby St 7237 9247 9–4D
"30% bistro, 70% wine warehouse under the London Bridge station Arches"; the "very unusual" wine selection is "sensational" and "in the tiny open kitchen Steve Williams and team produce amazing dishes with the freshest seasonal ingredients". / SE1 3PA; www.40maltbystreet.com; @40maltbystreet; 9.30 pm; closed Mon, Tue, Wed L, Thu L, Sat D & Sun; no Amex; no booking.

The Four Seasons £34 411

12 Gerrard St, W1 7494 0870 4–3A
23 Wardour St, W1 7287 9995 4–3A
84 Queensway, W2 7229 4320 6–2C
"Still the benchmark for roast duck" ("it's the best ever") – the claim to fame of this duo of "run down" looking Chinese diners in Bayswater and Chinatown; "don't expect 5-star service though!" – it can be "terrible"! / www.fs-restaurants.co.uk; Queensway 11 pm, Sun 10h45 pm; Gerrard St 1 am; Wardour St 1am, Fri-Sat 3.30 am.

Fox & Grapes SW19 £55 222

9 Camp Rd 8619 1300 10–2A

Right by Wimbledon Common, this "upmarket" gastropub is "ideally located to walk off any over indulgence"; but while fans say its "traditional food with a twist" is "always excellent", for a disgruntled minority it's "shamefully overpriced", and "overall not a great experience". / SW19 4UN; www.foxandgrapeswimbledon.co.uk; @thefoxandgrapes; 9.30 pm, Sun 8.15 pm; no Amex.

The Fox & Hounds SW11 £47 444

66 Latchmere Rd 7924 5483 10–1C

"If only all pubs were like this Battersea gastroboozer" (sibling to Earl's Court's Atlas) – "cracking med-inspired food from an open kitchen", "great beer festivals and brewery-led events alongside good wines", and with "a lovely garden". / SW11 2JU; www.thefoxandhoundspub.co.uk; @thefoxbattersea; 10 pm; Mon-Thu D only, Fri-Sun open L & D.

The Fox and Anchor EC1 £49 334

115 Charterhouse St 7250 1300 9–1B

"Stunning" sausage rolls, "excellent pork pies" – not to mention, of course, notorious "blow out breakfasts" ("all washed down with a pint of Guinness") – are the orders of the day at this famous, "very olde worlde" Smithfield tavern. / EC1M 6AA; www.foxandanchor.com; @foxanchor; Mon-Sat 9.30 pm, Sun 6 pm.

Foxlow £50 333

71-73 Stoke Newington Ch' St, N16 7014 8070 1–1C NEW

St John St, EC1 7014 8070 9–2A

"First class" steaks and "cool" styling win fans for these Hawksmoor-lite spin-offs, which now have a Stoke Newington branch as well as the Clerkenwell original; "prices add up quickly" however, results can be "unspectacular", and – while "edgy" – the decor is a tad "functional". / www.foxlow.co.uk.

Franco Manca £20 433

Branches throughout London

"Even my Italian girlfriend rates it!"; "amazingly yummy", sourdough-based pizza ("how do they make it fluffy and crisp simultaneously?") at "very keen" prices wins a ginormous fan club for this fast-expanding, "energetic" ("crowded and noisy") chain; no bookings – "you queue out of the door most days". / www.francomanca.co.uk; SW9 10.30, Mon 5 pm; W4 11 pm; E20 9 pm, Thu-Sat 10 pm, Sun 6 pm; no bookings.

Franco's SW1 £74 343

61 Jermyn St 7499 2211 3–3C

"Attentive" staff know how to treat expense accounters at this St James's Italian, whose dependable cooking and "absence of riff raff" appeal to local pinstripes (including for a working breakfast); it can also seem a tad "boring" and pricey however, and "all those hedgies make a lot of noise". / SW1Y 6LX; www.francoslondon.com; @francoslondon; 10.30 pm; closed Sun.

Franklins SE22 £50 434

157 Lordship Ln 8299 9598 1–4D

"Wonderful seasonal creations at reasonable (Dulwich) prices", wins the highest praise for this "really friendly local", which nowadays boasts a neighbouring farm shop on the other side of the road. / SE22 8HX; www.franklinsrestaurant.com; @franklinsse22; 10.30 pm; no Amex.

Frantoio SW10 £56 233

397 King's Rd 7352 4146 5–3B

Expect much "bonhomie" ("you 'll be made to feel like a long lost brother!") from the owner of this World's End Italian; the cooking is generally reliable, but primarily it's "always fun" (and "excellent for families"). / SW10 0LR; 11.15 pm, Sun 10.15 pm.

Frederick's N1 £62 224

106 Islington High St 7359 2888 8–3D

"It's been around forever" – this "beautiful" favourite "in the heart of Islington", with its "lovely" and "spacious" interior (especially the conservatory); critics say its pricey, "grown up" food is "coasting on its longevity" – but it's been like this for as long as we can remember! / N1 8EG; www.fredericks.co.uk; @fredericks_n1; 11 pm; closed Sun; set weekday L £36 (FP).

Friends of Ours N1 NEW £19 442

61 Pitfield St 7686 5525 12–1B

"In the slightly less fashionable bit of Hoxton", this small, sparse new indie café is "a real find"; it dishes up "an interesting range of brunch-type options" and "coffee made with real care". / N1 6BU; www.facebook.com/TheFriendsofOurs; @friends_ofours; 5 pm.

La Fromagerie Café W1 £39 323

2-6 Moxon St 7935 0341 3–1A

"Cheesy heaven on a plate" (along with other "great nibbles") is served in this "buzzing" Marylebone café, adjacent to the famous cheese shop; "perfectly matched" beers and wines too. / W1U 4EW; www.lafromagerie.co.uk; @lafromagerieuk; 6.30 pm, Sat 6 pm, Sun 5 pm; L only; no booking.

The Frontline Club W2 £52 333

13 Norfolk Pl 7479 8960 6–1D

"There always seems to be a journo' or two", at this comfy dining room (part of a club for war reporters), which is particularly "handy for Paddington"; the food's "good value" and eye-catching reportage photography on the walls make for a slightly "different" ambience. / W2 1QJ; www.frontlineclub.com; @frontlineclub; 10.30 pm; closed Sat L & Sun; set always available £33 (FP).

Fulham Wine Rooms SW6 £55 334

871-873 Fulham Rd 7042 9440 10–1B

Bustling Fulham wine bar, where the food offers few pyrotechnics, but is still "a good standard and price in this location" – quality plonk is of course its prime raison d'être, and there's a "great selection by the glass". / SW6 5HP; www.greatwinesbytheglass.com; @winerooms; midnight; closed weekday L.

Gaby's WC2 £29 333

30 Charing Cross Rd 7836 4233 4–3B

"Viva Gaby!"; this small '60s caff by Leicester Square tube (Jeremy Corbyn's favourite!) continues to see off the developers "despite the fact that everything around it is being replaced by faceless chains"; true, service is "perfunctory" and the interior "scruffy", but everyone cherishes its "genuine" style, not to mention "the best falafel" and salt beef. / WC2H 0DE; no web; midnight, Sun 10 pm; no Amex.

Gail's Bread £27 322

Branches throughout London

"Even though it's a chain", these "favourite" bakeries score well for their "amazing cakes", "interesting sarnies", "great coffee" and "excellent bread"; "unless you like being surrounded by yummy mummies and their offspring however, you might want to take-out". / www.gailsbread.co.uk; W11 & WC1 7 pm; NW3 & NW6 8 pm, W1 10 pm, SW7 9 pm, Sun 8 pm; no booking.

Gallery Mess, Saatchi Gallery SW3 £52 223

Duke of Yorks HQ, Kings Rd 7730 8135 5–2D

As "a haunt for ladies-who-lunch" or "a lovely place to meet on business", this "attractive" annex to the galleries housing Charles Saatchi's art-collection has its fans, but the "unexciting" cooking is often "underwhelming". / SW3 4RY; www.saatchigallery.com/gallerymess; @gallerymess; 9.30 pm, Sun 6 pm; closed Sun D; set always available £32 (FP).

Gallipoli £35 343

102 Upper St, N1 7359 0630 8–3D

107 Upper St, N1 7226 5333 8–3D

120 Upper St, N1 7226 8099 8–3D

"Buzzy and friendly" (if "cramped and noisy") Turkish bistros – a micro empire with three nearby sites in Islington; their mezze-biased menu includes "all the favourites" at easygoing prices. / www.cafegallipoli.com; 11 pm, Fri & Sat midnight.

Galvin at Windows, Park Lane London Hilton Hotel W1 £100 224

22 Park Ln 7208 4021 3–4A

"For a spectacular business lunch" (or date), this 28th floor perch – with a "perfect vista" over Buck House and Hyde Park – still has many fans. It has seemed more "machine-like and touristy" of late however, and – at the sky high prices – can too often seem "decidedly average" nowadays. (Top Tip – skip your meal: head over the hall to the bar, where the view is actually better!) / W1K 1BE; www.galvinatwindows.com; @Galvin_Brothers; 10 pm, Sat & Sun 10.30 pm; closed Sat L & Sun D; no shorts; set weekday L £55 (FP), set Sun L £72 (FP).

Galvin Bistrot de Luxe W1 £67 444

66 Baker St 7935 4007 2–1A

The "bustling" cradle of the Galvin brothers' empire – this "very grown up", slightly "formal" Marylebone bistro is celebrating its tenth birthday, and remains one of the best-liked all-rounders in town, serving a "staunchly Gallic" menu which provides "no pyrotechnics – just solid excellent cooking". / W1U 7DJ; www.galvinrestaurants.com; @galvin_brothers; Mon-Wed 10.30 pm, Thu-Sat 10.45 pm, Sun 9.30 pm; set weekday L £40 (FP), set dinner £42 (FP).

GALVIN LA CHAPELLE E1 £80 445

35 Spital Sq 7299 0400 12–2B

"To impress a client or date", you can't beat the "gorgeous" and "dramatic" setting of the Galvin brothers Spitalfields venture ("like eating in a minor cathedral"); it's a "very slick operation" all round, with "classic, not overly fussy" Gallic cuisine and "top notch" service. / E1 6DY; www.galvinrestaurants.com; @Galvin_Brothers; 10.30 pm, Sun 9.30 pm; set Sun L £53 (FP).

Ganapati SE15 £43 544

38 Holly Grove 7277 2928 1–4C

"The most authentic South Indian outside of Kerala" (well nearly) – this "crowded" but "lovely", tiny "breath-of-fresh-air" makes a "marvellous find" in deepest Peckham; "genial" staff provide "a limited menu" of "crisp dosas" and other "herb-filled, fresh-tasting" fare. / SE15 5DF; www.ganapatirestaurant.com; 10.30 pm, Sun 10 pm; closed Mon; no Amex.

Garnier SW5 £54 4 4 1
314 Earl's Court Rd 7370 4536 5–2A
"Really like the good honest French cooking that goes on here... I just wish they could inject something to make it look less, well, dull"; that's the dilemma at Eric & Didier Garnier's calm "slice of Paris", which makes a surprise find in an "unprepossessing" corner of Earl's Court, with "very sound" traditional cuisine, "keenly priced" wine and notably "excellent and charming" service. / SW5 9BQ; www.garnierestaurant.com; Mon-Sat 10.30 pm, Sun 10 pm; set weekday L £40 (FP).

Le Garrick WC2 £49 2 3 3
10-12 Garrick St 7240 7649 4–3C
This Covent Garden "bolt hole" is a good "safe bet" in this touristy locale; "it's a standard, very French bistro, with no wow factor, but you'll probably go again". / WC2E 9BH; www.frenchrestaurantlondon.co.uk; @le_garrick; 10.30 pm; closed Sun.

The Garrison SE1 £51 3 3 3
99-101 Bermondsey St 7089 9355 9–4D
"The yuppification of Bermondsey" can be partially blamed on this "boisterous" and "cramped", but "very enjoyable, buzzy and busy ex-pub", near the antiques market; all reports found it "worth the trek" this year – hopefully that sentiment will survive its sale in June 2015. / SE1 3XB; www.thegarrison.co.uk; @TheGarrisonSE1; 10 pm, Fri & Sat 10.30 pm, Sun 9.30 pm.

The Gate £43 4 2 3
51 Queen Caroline St, W6 8748 6932 7–2C
370 St John St, EC1 7278 5483 8–3D
"Who needs meat?" – some of London's best vegetarian cooking is to be found at this quite "stylish" duo; the Hammersmith original occupies a "bright" and "airy" hall near the Broadway (recently refurbished), while its "noisy" newer EC1 sibling is "handy for Sadler's Wells". / www.thegaterestaurants.com; @gaterestaurant; EC1 10.30 pm, W6 10.30, Sat 11 pm.

Gatti's £62 3 4 3
1 Finsbury Ave, EC2 7247 1051 12–2B
1 Ropemaker St, EC2 7247 1051 12–2A NEW
A duo of "discreet and efficient" Italianos recommended – especially for business – by all who comment on them; the 20-year-old original is one of Broadgate's oldest denizens, and there's also a larger spin-off near Moorgate. / www.gattisrestaurant.co.uk; closed Sat & Sun.

Gaucho £70 2 2 2
Branches throughout London
"The steaks are great... but value for money it ain't!"; this "plush and glitzy" chain does still win fans for its "succulent" imported Argentinean meat, "excellent" south American wines, and "dramatic" decor, but it has many critics nowadays too, particularly regarding its "ludicrous" prices. / www.gauchorestaurants.co.uk; 11 pm; EC3 & EC1 closed Sat & Sun, WC2 & EC2 closed Sat L & Sun.

GAUTHIER SOHO W1 £65 5 5 4
21 Romilly St 7494 3111 4–3A
"Ringing the doorbell adds to the special feel" of a trip to Alexis Gauthier's "beautiful, plush and quiet" Georgian townhouse, in the heart of Soho. But while it "oozes romance and decadence", it's first-and-foremost a gastronomic experience, with "unbelievably slick" service and some of London's best French cooking – "seasonal, classically based, and superb in taste and presentation". Top Menu Tip – leave space for the "always wonderful" signature Louis IV chocolate praline dessert. / W1D 5AF; www.gauthiersoho.co.uk; @GauthierSoho; 10.30 pm; closed Mon L & Sun.

LE GAVROCHE W1 £132 5 5 4
43 Upper Brook St 7408 0881 3–2A
Michel Roux's "iconic" Mayfair bastion (est 1967, by his father Albert) provides a "flawless and indulgent" treat, wherein "psychic" staff deliver "elegant" French cuisine and a "wine-lover's" list "full of gems". That the basement setting looks "a little dated" is all part of the traditional charm, and the main man's regular presence helps underpin "a truly magnificent experience". Top Tip – "the best value set lunch ever". / W1K 7QR; www.le-gavroche.co.uk; @legavroche_; 10 pm; closed Sat L & Sun; jacket required; set weekday L £87 (FP).

Gay Hussar W1 £50 2 2 5
2 Greek St 7437 0973 4–2A
"Go for the history, not the food", and you'll have a good time at this ancient Soho "institution" (famously "a venue for Socialist political intrigue"); the Hungarian scoff (goulash and so on) "ain't exactly fine dining", but the ambience is "terrific". / W1D 4NB; www.gayhussar.co.uk; @GayhussarsSoho; 10.45 pm; closed Sun; set pre theatre £37 (FP).

Gaylord W1 £58 3 3 3
79-81 Mortimer St 7580 3615 2–1B
"Approaching its 50th anniversary", this "'60s throwback" is a "civilised", "old-fashioned" venue, with "quality", "traditional" cuisine (recently jazzed up with a new menu) that fans find "a cut above"; it's "expensive" though, and sceptics feel it's still "in the dark ages". / W1W 7SJ; www.gaylordlondon.com; 10.45 pm, Sun 10.30 pm.

Gazette £39 244
79 Sherwood Ct, Chatfield Rd, SW11 7223 0999 10–1C
100 Balham High St, SW12 8772 1232 10–2C
147 Upper Richmond Rd, SW15 8789 6996 10–2B
These "little bits of La Belle France" in Balham, Clapham and Putney win praise for their "chilled" style, "heavily accented" but "friendly" Gallic staff, and "very French" cuisine; the food rating was hit though by one or two "disappointing" reports. / www.gazettebrasserie.co.uk; 11 pm.

Geales £50 233
1 Cale St, SW3 7965 0555 5–2C
2 Farmer St, W8 7727 7528 6–2B
"Delicious" fish 'n' chips wins consistent praise for these posh chippies in Notting Hill and Chelsea, but they come "at a price". / www.geales.com; @geales1; 10.30 pm, Sun 9.30 pm; Mon L.

Gelupo W1 £9 433
7 Archer St 7287 5555 3–2D
"Blood orange sorbet... be still my beating heart!" – opposite Bocca di Lupo (same owners) this tiny café has become a key West End pit stop, due to its "fabulous" and "so unusual" ices and granitas ("as good as in Rome!"); now also at Cambridge Circus, within the newly opened Vico. / W1D 7AU; www.gelupo.com; 11 pm, Fri & Sat midnight; no Amex; no booking.

Gem N1 £30 444
265 Upper St 7359 0405 8–2D
"Nothing flashy, but always reliable" – that's the approach at this "satisfying" Turkish/Kurdish spot near Angel, serving "very good mezze and kebabs"; "though it can be hard to hold an audible conversation, it's terrific value". / N1 2UQ; www.gemrestaurant.org.uk; @Gum_restaurant; 11 pm, Fri & Sat midnight, Sun 10.30 pm; no Amex; set weekday L £21 (FP).

La Genova W1 £60 333
32 North Audley St 7629 5916 3–2A
A "lovely old fashioned" Italian, beloved of an older fan club, whose quiet, central location makes it "a perfect retreat after shopping in the West End"; "the food varies from good to very good". / W1K 6ZG; www.lagenovarestaurant.com; 11 pm; closed Sun.

George & Vulture EC3 £44 225
3 Castle Ct 7626 9710 9–3C
This truly "Dickensian" chop house (Charles was a regular), is a treasured "timeless" period piece, serving "traditional City fare"; lad's business lunches aside though, "it's a disgrace that this wonderful venue has such poor food", and the wine choice isn't so hot either – "'Would you like red or white?' just doesn't cut it anymore!" / EC3V 9DL; 2.15 pm; L only, closed Sat & Sun.

German Gymnasium N1 NEW
26 Pancras Rd 7287 8000 8–3C
In November 2015, D&D London have promised to open the doors to this long-anticipated renovation of a Grade II Victorian landmark by King's Cross, incorporating restaurant, grand café, bars and terrace, with cooking of the Mittel-European school – all sounds a bit Corbin & King? / N1C 4TB; www.germangymnasium.com.

Giacomo's NW2 £37 453
428 Finchley Rd 7794 3603 1–1B
"Everyone is greeted like family" at this "small", "noisy" and "kid-friendly" Child's Hill Italian – a "cosy local" with "fresh if unsophisticated" cooking. / NW2 2HY; www.giacomos.co.uk; 11 pm.

Gifto's Lahore Karahi UB1 £22 432
162-164 The Broadway 8813 8669 1–3A
"Still buzzy and still producing delicious food!" – a large, Pakistani, Formica-topped canteen that's something of a Southall landmark. / UB1 1NN; www.gifto.com; 11.30 pm, Sat & Sun midnight.

Gilbert Scott, St Pancras Renaissance NW1 £68 223
Euston Rd 7278 3888 8–3C
Undeniably handy for the Eurostar, with a "gorgeous" historic interior, but otherwise Marcus Wareing's St Pancras dining room receives a mixed rep – what, to fans, is "classic British cooking" can also seem "very average for its elevated price", and service often "leaves a lot to be desired". / NW1 2AR; www.thegilbertscott.co.uk; @Thegilbertscott; 10.45 pm; set weekday L & pre-theatre £50 (FP).

Gilgamesh NW1 £69 223
The Stables, Camden Mkt, Chalk Farm Rd 7428 4922 8–3B
"Dauntingly large" Camden Lock venue, with crazy-lavish wood-carved décor; its "pricey", surprisingly ambitious Pan-Asian cuisine has never really lived up, but it's not terrible, and fans say the overall experience is "good fun!!" / NW1 8AH; www.gilgameshbar.com; Sun-Thu 10 pm, Fri & Sat 11 pm.

Gin Joint EC2 £52 233
Barbican Centre, Silk St 7588 3008 12–2A
"Lovely views over the lake" are a highlight at Searcy's "spacious" Barbican Centre brasserie, which despite its trendy name (and gin-based cocktails) is like most of its forebears on this site – the food's "pedestrian", but it's a "top bet if you're going to an event", and "always quiet enough for conversation". / EC2Y 8DS; www.searcys.co.uk/venues/gin-joint; @ginjoint_london; 10 pm.

Ginger & White **£17** 3 3 3
2 England's Ln, NW3 7722 9944 8–2A
4a-5a, Perrins Ct, NW3 7431 9098 8–2A
"Hang out all day" if you're part of the "NW3 in-crowd", at these stylish cafés in Belsize Park and Hampstead – 'go-to' locals for coffee or brunch. / www.gingerandwhite.com; 5.30 pm, W1 6 pm; W1 closed Sun.

Giraffe **£40** 1 1 1
Branches throughout London
"Average in all respects save for the fact that they are great with kids" – these World Food diners (nowadays owned by Tesco!) are "crowded", with "stodgy" fare, but are second only in the survey to PizzaExpress for being impeccably "tolerant of exuberant little ones". / www.giraffe.net; 10.45 pm, Sun 10.30 pm; no booking, Sat & Sun 9 am-5 pm.

The Glasshouse TW9 **£71** 4 4 3
14 Station Pde 8940 6777 1–3A
"From the Chez Bruce stable", this "consistently excellent" neighbourhood spot by Kew Gardens tube continues to win acclaim for its "subtle" and "beautifully judged" cuisine; the interior doesn't suit everyone however, and "though it shares the ambition of CB, it doesn't achieve quite the same level". / TW9 3PZ; www.glasshouserestaurant.co.uk; @The_Glasshouse; 10.15 pm, Sun 9.45 pm; set weekday L £50 (FP), set Sun L £53 (FP).

Gökyüzü N4 **£33** 4 3 3
26-27 Grand Pde, Green Lanes 8211 8406 1–1C
"Deservedly the most popular of all the Turks on Harringay's Grand Parade" – "you cram in" but it's worth it for the "meat feasts" and "exceptionally fresh and zingy salads", all at cheapo prices. / N4 1LG; www.gokyuzurestaurant.co.uk; @Gokyuzulondon; midnight, Fri & Sat 1 am.

Gold Mine W2 **£34** 5 2 1
102 Queensway 7792 8331 6–2C
"I'd travel from Sheffield to London, just for its succulence!" – this Bayswater Chinese competes with its better known local rival, The Four Seasons, as the home of "the Capital's best crispy duck"; likewise it too is "noisy and cramped". / W2 3RR; 11 pm.

Golden Dragon W1 **£34** 3 2 2
28-29 Gerrard St 7734 1073 4–3A
"A better-than-average dim sum option in the heart of Chinatown"; "arrive early to avoid the queue!" / W1 6JW; goldendragonlondon.com; Mon-Thu 11.15 pm, Fri & Sat 11.30 pm, Sun 11 pm.

Golden Hind W1 **£26** 4 4 3
73 Marylebone Ln 7486 3644 2–1A
"A joy for lovers of fish 'n' chips" – this "very basic" Marylebone institution's "unbeatable" scoff and "welcoming" style have only improved since its renovation after a fire in June; "it's also great value as you can BYO". / W1U 2PN; 10 pm; closed Sat L & Sun.

Good Earth **£56** 3 3 2
233 Brompton Rd, SW3 7584 3658 5–2C
143-145 The Broadway, NW7 8959 7011 1–1B
11 Bellevue Rd, SW17 8682 9230 10–2C
"A cut above the usual Chinese" – this quality chain is "always reliable" and its two-year-old Balham branch is proving "a marvellous addition to the area"; never a cheap option, some fans now fear they are "in danger of pricing themselves out of the market". / www.goodearthgroup.co.uk; Mon - Sat 10.30pm, Sun 10 pm.

Goodman **£69** 4 4 3
24-26 Maddox St, W1 7499 3776 3–2C
3 South Quay, E14 7531 0300 11–1C
11 Old Jewry, EC2 7600 8220 9–2C
"Carnivore heaven" – these "macho" haunts are "the best of the upmarket steak chains" (significantly out-gunning Hawksmoor this year), and "superb for old-school business lunches". The steaks of course are "not cheap", but "huge", "cooked to perfection", and served with "great truffle chips". Other attractions include the "interesting specials board with rare cuts", plus "excellent wines at fair mark-ups". / www.goodmanrestaurants.com; 10.30 pm; E14 & EC2 closed Sat & Sun.

GORDON RAMSAY SW3 **£128** 3 4 3
68-69 Royal Hospital Rd 7352 4441 5–3D
Slowly but surely, GR's Chelsea flagship is clawing its way back into London's very top tier. As yet, it still inspires too many gripes about a "boring" experience at "stratospheric" prices, but year-on-year the 'swingometer' is steadily heading in the direction of its admirers who – lauding Clare Smyth's "absolutely impeccable" cuisine – say "the bill is eye-watering, but after such a superb meal, you won't care!" Stop Press – in early October 2015, Clare Smyth announced that she was stepping back, to open her own place in Autumn 2016. Her No 2. Matt Abe will succeed her here. / SW3 4HP; www.gordonramsay.com; @GordonRamsey; 10.15 pm; closed Sat & Sun; no jeans or trainers; booking: max 8; set weekday L £82 (FP).

Gordon's Wine Bar WC2 £33 235
47 Villiers St 7930 1408 4–4D
Just about everyone in London has supped a glass of vino at one time or another at this "one-of-a-kind" ancient wine bar, by Embankment tube; the food – cheese, cold cuts, hot dishes, salads – is "nothing special", but the cave-like interior is "amazing", and it has one of the West End's nicest (and biggest) outdoor terraces. / WC2N 6NE; www.gordonswinebar.com; @gordonswinebar; 11 pm; no booking.

The Goring Hotel SW1 £80 355
15 Beeston Pl 7396 9000 2–4B
"Marvellously discreet" bastion near Victoria (complete with royal warrant) – "a fine example of everything old-fashioned and English", not least its "magnificent" staff. "Superb" traditional fare is served in the "beautiful" and "civilised" dining room, with top billing going to the "breakfast fit for a queen" and "quintessential afternoon tea". / SW1W 0JW; www.thegoring.com; @thegoring; 10 pm; closed Sat L; no jeans or trainers; booking: max 8; set Sun L £0 (FP), set pre-theatre £55 (FP).

Gourmet Burger Kitchen £30 222
Branches throughout London
"GBK always delivers what it says on the tin!", say loyalists of this still-popular burger franchise; "it nowadays lags a market it once led" however, and even if it's still "always solid and enjoyable" it's also arguably "nothing to write home about". / www.gbkinfo.com; most branches close 10.30 pm; no booking.

Gourmet Pizza Company Gabriels Wharf SE1 £38 333
56 Upper Ground 7928 3188 9–3A
"Superb views over the River Thames" and a lovely terrace add to the "fun" of this South Bank spot (run by PizzaExpress); "great toppings as well as the usual ones". / SE1 9PP; www.gourmetpizzacompany.co.uk; 11.30 pm.

Gourmet San E2 £25 421
261 Bethnal Green Rd 7729 8388 12–1D
"Horrible setting, but top notch food" – that's the deal at this well-priced Sichuanese, in Bethnal Green. / E2 6AH; www.oldplace.co.uk; 11 pm; D only.

Les Gourmets des Ternes £60 223
9 Knightsbridge Grn, SW1 3092 1493 5–1D
NEW
18 Formosa St, W9 7286 3742 8–4A
This tiny, "very French" Maida Vale spin-off from a Parisan bistro of the same name (now also with a Knightsbridge sibling on the site that was Chabrot d'Amis, RIP) inspires middling feedback – the "standard, simple Gallic fare" can be "delicious", but can also seem "average". / SW1 closed Sun – W9 closed Sun & Mon.

The Gowlett SE15 £32 434
62 Gowlett Rd 7635 7048 1–4D
"Super-thin crust pizzas with delicious toppings" and "the occasional beer festival" help win a thumbs up for this Peckham pub, now with a trendy small curing and smoke house in the cellar. / SE15 4HY; www.thegowlett.com; @theGowlettArms; 10.30 pm, Sun 9 pm; no credit cards.

Goya SW1 £45 333
34 Lupus St 7976 5309 2–4C
For "easygoing tapas on a sunny corner in Pimlico" this is a useful neighbourhood "staple" – there's a popular bar on the ground floor, so for a quiet dinner "seek a table upstairs". / SW1V 3EB; www.goyarestaurant.co.uk; 11.30 pm, Sun 11 pm.

Grain Store N1 £55 223
1-3 Stable St, Granary Sq 7324 4466 8–3C
Bruno Loubet's "NYC warehousy" King's Cross two-year-old divided opinions this year; to its fans this "wonderfully bustling space" remains "an absolute revelation" thanks to "endlessly inventive", "veg-a-centric" cooking, but a few doubters had meals that were "absolutely awful". (Flying from Gatwick? – there's now a branch there too.) / N1C 4AB; www.grainstore.com; @GrainStoreKX; Mon-Wed 11.30 pm, Thu-Sat midnight; closed Sun D; booking: max 14.

The Grand Imperial Guoman Grosvenor Hotel SW1 £65 332
101 Buckingham Palace Rd 7821 8898 2–4B
"Surprisingly good for this location!"; a "strangely grand, station-hotel dining room" adjacent to Victoria, where – despite "steep" prices – "delicious dim sum" and other "tasty" Cantonese fare make it "worth a visit". / SW1W 0SJ; www.grandimperiallondon.com; @grand_imperial; Thu-Sat 11, Sun-Wed 10.30 pm.

Granger & Co £49 324
175 Westbourne Grove, W11 7229 9111 6–1B
Stanley Building, St Pancras Sq, N1 3058 2567 8–3C NEW
The Buckley Building, 50 Sekforde St, EC1 7251 9032 9–1A
"There's a permanent queue around the corner", at these "laid back" Antipodean haunts, rammed with "yummy mummies" and "ladies who lunch"; brunch is the massive deal here – "lo-cal tasty combos" that "draw inspiration from all over the world". / Mon - Sat 10pm, Sun 5pm.

The Grapes E14 £47 2 3 5
76 Narrow St 7987 4396 11–1B
One of the oldest pubs in East London, this "tiny" Thames-side treasure in Limehouse offers a limited menu in the bar (a full roast on Sundays), and "great fish 'n' chips" in the upstairs dining room. Its interesting associations are many – not least that it's currently owned by Gandalf himself (Sir Ian McKellen)! / E14 8BP; www.thegrapes.co.uk; @TheGrapesLondon; 11 pm, Sun 10.30 pm; no Amex.

The Grazing Goat W1 £56 3 3 3
6 New Quebec St 7724 7243 2–2A
This "posh pub", quietly located near Marble Arch, is proving "a great addition to Marylebone" with "hearty, satisfying fare" and "a nice if noisy vibe". / W1H 7RQ; www.thegrazinggoat.co.uk; @TheGrazingGoat; 10 pm, Sun 9.30 pm;.

Great Nepalese NW1 £36 3 3 2
48 Eversholt St 7388 6737 8–3C
"They're such lovely people" at this ancient stalwart, in a grungy Euston side street, where a dedicated fanclub hail its "top curries" (incorporating some not-particularly-spicey Nepalese specials). / NW1 1DA; www.great-nepalese.co.uk; 11.30 pm, Sun 10 pm.

Great Queen Street WC2 £49 2 2 3
32 Great Queen St 7242 0622 4–1D
Fans still laud it for its "rare assurance" and its "hearty and bold" British fare, but this "buzzy" and "un-flashy" ("cramped and noisy") Covent Garden dining room is increasingly "resting on its laurels" nowadays, producing some meals that are "surprisingly average". / WC2B 5AA; www.greatqueenstreetrestaurant.co.uk; @greatqueenstreet; 10.30 pm; closed Sun D; no Amex.

The Greedy Buddha SW6 £32 3 2 2
144 Wandsworth Bridge Rd 7751 3311 10–1B
"Nothing too glamourous, but it does the job!" – a "cramped" curry house, near Parson's Green, where "very good food at low prices" makes it worth enduring service that's "erratic". / SW6 2UH; www.thegreedybuddha.com; @thegreedybudha; 10.30 pm, Fri & Sat 11.30 pm; no Amex.

The Greek Larder Arthouse N1 NEW £50 3 3 2
1 York Way 3780 2999 8–3C
A "welcome addition" to King's Cross – this modern Greek newcomer (from the original founder of The Real Greek) is "authentically chaotic", serving "strongly flavoured" small plates at "good prices". / N1C 4AS; www.thegreeklarder.co.uk; @thegreeklarder; 10.30 pm, Sun 5 pm.

Green Cottage NW3 £38 3 2 2
9 New College Pde 7722 5305 8–2A
"Long established, popular Chinese" in Swiss Cottage, where "tasty food" comes in "large portions"; ignore the ambience ("not great") and service ("can be abrupt"). / NW3 5EP; 10.30 pm; no Amex.

The Green Room, The National Theatre SE1 NEW £42 2 2 2
South Bank 7452 3630 2–3D
The NT's new 'neighbourhood diner' and "beautiful" garden is "a very nice addition to the South Bank"; the food is "not particularly inspiring", but it's "good value" and "you can forgive the slightly pretentious presentation, given its emphasis on sustainability and quality". / SE1 9PX; www.nationaltheatre.org.uk; @greenroomSE1; 11 pm, Sun 10.30 pm .

Green's SW1 £75 3 3 3
36 Duke St 7930 4566 3–3D
"A choice of booths or tables" adds to the "discreet", "quiet" and business-friendly, clubland-appeal of the Parker Bowles family's St James's "stalwart"; "very classic British food" (majoring in fish) is well-served – "the quality is the highest... and so are the prices". / SW1Y 6DF; www.greens.org.uk; 10.30 pm; closed Sun; no jeans or trainers; set pre theatre £49 (FP).

Greenberry Café NW1 £50 2 2 3
101 Regent's Park Rd 7483 3765 8–2B
"Much favoured by locals with laptops and buggies" – this "eating and meeting spot" in Primrose Hill is tipped as a particularly handy option for breakfast, but serves coffee, cakes and light meals throughout the day. / NW1 8UR; greenberrycafe.co.uk; @Greenberry_Cafe; 10 pm, Mon & Sun 4 pm; closed Sun D; no Amex; set always available £29 (FP).

The Greenhouse W1 £130 3 4 4
27a Hays Mews 7499 3331 3–3B
Arnaud Bignon's cuisine is "top notch", but it's the "hugely impressive wine list" ("What breadth! What depth!") that draws connoisseurs to Marlon Abela's "spacious", "lovely" and luxurious haunt, "tucked away" in a Mayfair mews; the food can seem "a bit frothy and fancy" though... and "fiendishly expensive". / W1J 5NY; www.greenhouserestaurant.co.uk; 10.15 pm; closed Sat L & Sun; booking: max 8.

Gremio de Brixton, St Matthew's Church SW2 NEW £42 3 2 4
Effra Rd 7924 0660 10–2D
The "very snug and atmospheric" crypt of St Matthew's Church in Brixton, hosts this new tapas joint, which is consistently well-rated. / SW2 1JF; www.gremiodebrixton.com; 11 pm, Sat 11.30 pm, Sun 9 pm.

Grind Coffee Bar SW15 £15 424
79 Lower Richmond Rd 8789 9073 10–2A
"Better than many of the more central indie coffee houses" – a Putney outfit that does very "tasty" breakfasts in particular; but waiting for the brews themselves can be "painstakingly slow" – "the price of true craftsmanship?" / SW15 1ET; grindcoffeebar.co.uk; 6 pm.

Grumbles SW1 £43 233
35 Churton St 7834 0149 2–4B
"Wonderfully, reassuringly old-fashioned" local bistro in Pimlico, complete with "rustic" interior; expect no fireworks, but "ever-dependable" scran at a "cheap" price. / SW1V 2LT; www.grumblesrestaurant.co.uk; 10.45 pm; set Sun L £32 (FP).

Guglee £33 333
7 New College Pde, NW3 7722 8478 8–2A
279 West End Ln, NW6 7317 8555 1–1B
"Not your average local cuzza" – a duo of "welcoming" West Hampstead and Swiss Cottage Indians serving "light and tasty" street food. / www.guglee.co.uk; 11 pm.

The Guinea Grill W1 £75 233
30 Bruton Pl 7499 1210 3–3B
"In a back mews in the heart of posh London" – an old-fashioned ("cramped") Mayfair stalwart attached to a cute pub, acclaimed for its pies; it's "not so cheap" and sceptics fear "well past its prime" nowadays, but fans still approve its quaint style and "great steaks". / W1J 6NL; www.theguinea.co.uk; @guineagrill; 10.30 pm; closed Sat L & Sun; booking: max 8.

The Gun E14 £58 324
27 Coldharbour 7515 5222 11–1C
This "quaint riverside tavern has so much charm and history" – not to mention a big terrace, and fab river views over to the O2 – and makes "a refreshing escape from Canary Wharf" (a short walk away); "the food's fancy for a pub, if not quite in the upper echelons for a gastropub". / E14 9NS; www.thegundocklands.com; @thegundocklands; 10.30 pm, Sun 9.30 pm.

Gung-Ho NW6 £40 232
328-332 West End Ln 7794 1444 1–1B
For supporters this West Hampstead stalwart is "still going strong" – "a consistently good and delightful neighbourhood Chinese"; the ambience is more "flat" than once it was however, and quite a few sceptical former fans feel it's "lost its former star quality". / NW6 1LN; www.stir-fry.co.uk; 11.30 pm; no Amex.

Gustoso Ristorante & Enoteca SW1 £43 353
33 Willow Pl 7834 5778 2–4B
"As the word spreads it's getting harder to get into this super local" in the backstreets of Westminster – "a welcome addition to an area lacking decent places"; service is very "warm", and "there's no need to rely on expenses" to enjoy the "simple and authentic" cooking. / SW1P 1JH; ristorantegustoso.co.uk; @GustosoRist; 10.30 pm, Fri & Sat 11 pm, Sun 9.30 pm; set always available £32 (FP).

GYMKHANA W1 £63 544
42 Albemarle St 3011 5900 3–3C
"Exceeding all my high expectations!" – this "delightfully cosseting" nouvelle Indian, near The Ritz, has quickly become one of London's top destinations; "immensely flavourful", "properly exquisite" dishes (plus "top quality cocktails" and "heroic wine matches") are served, in a "quaint and exotic", "faux-colonial" setting. / W1S 4JH; www.gymkhanalondon.com; @GymkhanaLondon; 10.30 pm; closed Sun.

Habanera W12 NEW £38 323
280 Uxbridge Rd 8001 4887 7–1C
With its yummy cocktails, "interesting Mexi-vibe" and "decent (if pricey)" tacos and burritos, this new Latino has broken the local W12 ordinance that forbids the opening of half-decent restaurants on the tacky strip running north of Shepherd's Bush Green. / W12 7JA; www.habanera.co.uk; 11 pm, Fri & Sat midnight, Sun 10.30 pm.

Haché £35 334
329-331 Fulham Rd, SW10 7823 3515 5–3B
24 Inverness St, NW1 7485 9100 8–3B
37 Bedford Hill, SW12 8772 9772 10–2C
153 Clapham High St, SW4 7738 8760 10–2D
147-149 Curtain Rd, EC2 7739 8396 12–1B
"Of the chain burger choices, this is consistently good" – this small group provides excellent "gourmet" options "with some unexpected combinations", and its SW10 branch in particular has an enjoyably "buzzy" atmosphere. / www.hacheburgers.com; 10.30 pm, Fri-Sat 11 pm, Sun 10 pm.

Hakkasan £89 434
17 Bruton St, W1 7907 1888 3–2C
8 Hanway Pl, W1 7927 7000 4–1A
"Dark", "seductive" and "very sexy" styling – "like a nightclub" (and with "loud" noise levels to match) – provide a "funky" backdrop to a meal at these "dramatic" venues (the cradle of what's a growing global franchise). Though "not cheap", the Chinese cuisine's "top notch" too, especially the "superbly original" dim sum. / www.hakkasan.com; midnight, Sun 11 pm.

Ham Yard Restaurant, Ham Yard Hotel W1 £50 [1][1][4]
1 Ham Yd 3642 2000 3–2D
"The design is super... the courtyard a wonderful addition to Soho", but in other respects the restaurant at this Firmdale hotel is "a shame" – the service can be "dire", and the food is a total "sideshow". / W1D 7DT; www.hamyardhotel.com; @ham_yard; 11.30 pm, Sun 10.30 pm.

The Hampshire Hog W6 £52 [2][2][3]
227 King St 8748 3391 7–2B
With its "fashionable looks", "eclectic mix of seating" and "delightful garden", this "friendly" large pub has brightened up the grungy environs of Hammersmith Town Hall; quibbles? – service is "charming but can be wayward". / W6 9JT; www.thehampshirehog.com; @TheHampshireHog; 11 pm, Sun 10 pm; closed Sun D.

Harbour City W1 £38 [2][1][1]
46 Gerrard St 7439 7859 4–3B
"Tasty, fresh, quick, filling" – the wide range of "amazingly cheap" lunchtime dim sum at this "Chinatown stalwart"; otherwise, don't bother. / W1D 5QH; www.harbourcity.com.hk; 11.30 pm, Fri & Sat midnight, Sun 10.30 pm.

Hard Rock Café W1 £59 [2][2][4]
150 Old Park Ln 7629 0382 3–4B
"You wouldn't go for a quiet or romantic meal", but "if you can bear the volume", the 40-year-old cradle of the Hard Rock brand works "for a noisy, fun, burger with teens". / W1K 1QZ; www.hardrock.com/london; @HardRock; midnight; need 20+ to book.

Hardy's Brasserie W1 £49 [2][3][3]
53 Dorset St 7935 5929 2–1A
"Largely unchanged since the '80s" – a Marylebone bistro "stalwart" liked for its "welcoming and comforting" style; the food's fairly "reliable" – "excellent weekend brunch" is a relatively recent innovation. / W1U 7NH; www.hardysbrasserie.com; @hardys_W1; 10 pm; closed Sat & Sun.

Hare & Tortoise £32 [3][2][3]
11-13 The Brunswick, WC1 7278 9799 2–1D
373 Kensington High St, W14 7603 8887 7–1D
156 Chiswick High Rd, W4 8747 5966 7–2A NEW
38 Haven Grn, W5 8810 7066 1–2A
296-298 Upper Richmond Rd, SW15 8394 7666 10–2B
90 New Bridge St, EC4 7651 0266 9–2A
"A definite step-up from Wagamama" – these "always packed" Pan-Asian diners offer "fresh and tasty" snacks (notably "great-value noodles and sushi"), all "at decent prices" and served "hot and quickly". / www.hareandtortoise-restaurants.co.uk; 10.45 pm, Fri & Sat 11.15 pm, EC4 10 pm; W14 no bookings.

Harry Morgan's NW8 £42 [2][2][1]
31 St John's Wood High St 7722 1869 8–3A
Classic Jewish Deli that's long been a feature of St John's Wood's main drag; it's still regularly acclaimed by its devotees for kosher treats "like mum used to make" and "the best salt beef sarnies", but dissenters feel it's "gone way downhill" and is "really awful" nowadays. / NW8 7NH; www.harryms.co.uk; 10.30 pm.

Harwood Arms SW6 £62 [5][3][3]
Walham Grove 7386 1847 5–3A
The "unassuming frontage" gives no hint of the "gorgeous" British cooking – some of London's best in either a pub or restaurant – at this "marvellous" gastropub "par excellence" in an obscure Fulham backstreet; and at the bar, "you wont find a better Scotch Egg anywhere". / SW6 1QP; www.harwoodarms.com; 9.15 pm, Sun 9 pm; closed Mon L; set weekday L £45 (FP).

Hashi SW20 £36 [4][4][3]
54 Durham Rd 8944 1888 10–2A
"Already popular with the locals, but should be better-known" – a "cosy little Raynes Park Japanese in an otherwise ordinary suburban road", with "delightful" staff that's "as good as any West End Japanese". / SW20 0TW; www.hashicooking.co.uk; 10.30 pm; closed Mon; no Amex.

The Havelock Tavern W14 £45 [3][2][4]
57 Masbro Rd 7603 5374 7–1C
"Classic, always buzzing gastropub" in the backstreets of Olypmia; its culinary ratings don't scale the heights they once did, but it still has a large fanclub drawn by its "delicious cooking, from outstanding Sunday roast beef to inventive and daily changing mains". / W14 0LS; www.havelocktavern.com; @HavelockTavern; 10 pm, Sun 9.30 pm; no booking.

The Haven N20 £50 [2][2][2]
1363 High Rd 8445 7419 1–1B
"A good local choice" in Whetstone, if a "rather noisy" one; "the food is never bad or great", but "reliable". / N20 9LN; www.haven-bistro.co.uk; 11 pm; set always available £31 (FP).

Hawksmoor £64 [3][3][3]
5a, Air St, W1 7406 3980 3–3D
11 Langley St, WC2 7420 9390 4–2C
3 Yeoman's Row, SW3 7590 9290 5–2C
157 Commercial St, E1 7426 4850 12–2B
10-12 Basinghall St, EC2 7397 8120 9–2C
"Utterly brilliant steaks" and "professional" cocktails have won cult status for Huw Gott and Will Beckett's "lively and clubby" steak houses (a fave rave for "boozy business lunches"); they risk starting to seem "up themselves", however, not helped by increasingly "stupid prices". / www.thehawksmoor.com; all branches between 10 pm & 11 pm; EC2 closed Sat & Sun; SRA-3.*

Haz £37 2 3 2
9 Cutler St, E1 7929 7923 9–2D
34 Foster Ln, EC2 7600 4172 9–2B
112 Houndsditch, EC3 7623 8180 9–2D
6 Mincing Ln, EC3 7929 3173 9–3D
"Always a safe bet" for "an informal business lunch" or "a dinner after work" – these large, "crowded" Turkish operations are "well-priced" and "efficient", and even if the "tasty" sustenance is arguably "without flair", it's also "without offence". / www.hazrestaurant.co.uk; 11.30 pm; EC3 closed Sun.

Heddon Street Kitchen W1 £59 2 3 3
3-9 Heddon St 7592 1212 3–2C
It's hard to get excited for or against Gordon Ramsay's "informal" bar and grill concept, just off Regent Street; its best point is its "fun, laid back style", but the whole set-up is rather "mid-range", with food that's "OK" but "unmemorable", and service that's "fine but not stand-out". / W1B 4BW; www.gordonramsay.com/heddon-street; @heddonstkitchen; 11 pm, Sun 10 pm.

HEDONE W4 £104 4 3 3
301-303 Chiswick High Rd 8747 0377 7–2A
"The best ingredients in London" and "unique, technical mastery" underpin "staggering", "cutting-edge cuisine at its finest" for most who trek to Mikael Jonsson's open-kitchen HQ, in outer Chiswick. It's an "idiosyncratic" experience however, and sceptics feel there's just "too much fuss and self regard", especially given the "eye-watering expense". Stop Press – In October 2015 the restaurant will close and re-open with half the number of covers, more complicated cooking, and a focus on rare ingredients and wines. Pricing may change too. / W4 4HH; www.hedonerestaurant.com; @HedoneLondon; 9.30 pm; closed Mon, Tue L, Wed L & Sun; set weekday L £70 (FP).

Heirloom N8 £46 3 4 3
35 Park Rd 8348 3565 1–1C
"Field-to-table" is the concept at this Crouch End yearling, where "lots of the produce comes from a farm in rural Bucks"; its "regularly changing" menu and "attentive" service help make it "a good addition to the N8 restaurant-stable". / N8 8TE; heirloomn8.com; @HeirloomN8; 11.30 pm.

Hélène Darroze, The Connaught Hotel W1 £128 2 3 3
Carlos Pl 3147 7200 3–3B
This "elegant", panelled Mayfair dining room (where a "posh brunch" is a recent innovation) continues to inspire mixed feelings; even many hailing "outstanding" cuisine fret at the bills, while those who find the cooking "over-contrived" or "lacking wow" think prices are utterly "gob-smacking". / W1K 2AL; www.the-connaught.co.uk; @TheConnaught; 9.30 pm; closed Mon & Sun; jacket & tie required; SRA-2.*

Hereford Road W2 £49 4 2 3
3 Hereford Rd 7727 1144 6–1B
"Interesting, full-on flavours" from a "simple, high-quality British menu" inspire some foodies to suggest that Tom Pemberton's "stylish" Bayswater fixture is "under-rated". Top Tip – fans say the set lunch deal is "beyond incredible". / W2 4AB; www.herefordroad.org; @3HerefordRoad; 10.30 pm, Sun 10 pm; set weekday L £32 (FP).

The Heron W2 £32 5 2 1
1 Norfolk Cr 7706 9567 8–4A
"Like a trip to Bangkok without the airfare" – a "brilliant, authentic Thai" in a "tiny, no-frills" Bayswater basement, serving a "varied menu" ("heavy spice available for the brave") at "incredible, low prices". / W2 2DN; no website; 11 pm.

Hibiscus W1 £126 4 4 3
29 Maddox St 7629 2999 3–2C
Stronger showing this year for Claude Bosi's low-key foodie temple in Mayfair; a few critics still "expected more" at the "astronomical" prices, but overall there was much more consistent praise for his famously "adventurous" approach, "exciting" tastes, and "beautiful" presentation. Top Tip – "give the fantastic chef's table a try". / W1S 2PA; www.hibiscusrestaurant.co.uk; @HibiscusLondon; 11 pm; closed Mon & Sun; set weekday L £56 (FP).

High Road Brasserie W4 £50 1 1 3
162-166 Chiswick High Rd 8742 7474 7–2A
All the worst DNA of the Soho House group is expressed by its "pretentious" W4 offshoot; the Chiswick set still like posing on the terrace at brunch, but prices are "sky high", and even those who "love the genuine local buzz" say its standards are "very disappointing". / W4 1PR; www.brasserie.highroadhouse.co.uk; @sohohouse; 10.45 pm, Fri & Sat 11.45 pm, Sun 10 pm.

High Timber EC4 £62 2 2 3
8 High Timber 7248 1777 9–3B
"Excellent South African wines can be chosen after a wander through the wine cellars" at this Thames-side spot (owned by a Stellenbosch vineyard), near the Wobbly Bridge (fab views, but only from the outside tables); as for the "rustic" sustenance, it's pricey and "nothing exceptional". / EC4V 3PA; www.hightimber.com; @HTimber; 10 pm; closed Sat & Sun.

Hill & Szrok E8 £42 5 4 4
60 Broadway Mkt 7833 1933 1–2D
"Sitting around a big butcher's block doesn't sound very romantic, but it gives you lots to talk about!" – this "butcher-by-day, meat-feast-at-night" in Broadway Market provides "an unusual and well-lit setting" for "a fantastic meat experience". / E8 4QJ; www.hillandszrok.co.uk; @hillandszrok; 11 pm, Sun 9 pm.

Hilliard EC4 £28 443
26a Tudor St 7353 8150 9–3A
"Full of lawyers getting a health fix" – a "busy", all-day Temple haunt where "they care about the details, reflecting their demanding customers!"; "wonderful fresh ingredients" from a "menu that changes daily", plus superior coffee and "excellent cakes". / EC4Y 0AY; www.hilliardfood.co.uk; 6 pm; L only, closed Sat & Sun; no booking.

Hix W1 £65 222
66-70 Brewer St 7292 3518 3–2D
As the HQ of a 'name' chef, Mark Hix's potentially "stylish" and "buzzy" Soho venture (with basement bar) is a total yawn nowadays, and monumentally overpriced for what you get – i.e. so so service, and food that's "nothing special". / W1F 9UP; www.hixsoho.co.uk; @HixRestaurants; 11.30 pm, Sun 10.30 pm.

Hix Oyster & Chop House EC1 £58 333
36-37 Greenhill Rents, Cowcross St 7017 1930 9–1A
"Great British dishes using the highest quality of raw materials" (eg "Barnsley chop to die for", and a wide selection of oysters) do win fans for Mark Hix's Smithfield operation; there are quibbles though – primarily that it's "not cheap". / EC1M 6BN; www.restaurantsetcltd.com; @HixRestaurants; 11 pm, Sun 10 pm; closed Sat L.

HKK EC2 £70 543
Broadgate Quarter, 88 Worship St 3535 1888 12–2B
"Challenging, interesting and fun" – the Chinese cuisine (much of it served from extensive multi-course tasting menus) at this Hakkasan-cousin, near Liverpool Street, is London's highest rated; the interior "looks lovely" but is "a little quiet". Top Menu Tip – "the best duck ever". / EC2A 2BE; www.hkklondon.com; @HKKlondon; 10 pm; closed Sun.

Hoi Polloi Ace Hotel E1 £56 234
100 Shoreditch High St 8880 6100 12–1B
"Achingly trendy" Shoreditch hotel, where the grub's overseen by the team that created Bistrotheque; like its forebear, it's more the scene you go for – the "innovative" food's arguably too "expensive". / E1 6JQ; hoi-polloi.co.uk; @wearehoipolloi; Sun-Wed midnight, Thu-Sat 1 am; cancellation charge for larger bookings.

Holborn Dining Room, Rosewood London WC1 £62 234
252 High Holborn 3747 8633 2–1D
With its "old school glamour", this "impressive"-looking operation (on the site that was once Pearl, RIP) is quite "a wow", and its "spacious" and "buzzy" quarters are ideal for business; food-wise, however, it's "nothing out of this world". Top Tip – Check out the "wonderful" adjoining Scarfes Bar. / WC1V 7EN; www.holborndiningroom.com; @HolbornDining; 11.15 pm, Sun 10.30 pm.

Homeslice £24 544
52 Wells St, W1 3151 7488 2–1B NEW
13 Neal's Yd, WC2 7836 4604 4–2C
"Awesome pizza" – "huge", and with "obscure combinations that work" – are well "worth the wait" (you can't book) at these "fun", but "crammed" and "loud" pit stops, whose Fitzrovia outpost opened in August 2015. /

Honest Burgers £28 443
Branches throughout London
"Not fancy, just bloody good!" – "of all the burger chains that have proliferated in recent years, this is the tops" (the original Brixton branch rating particular mention). Why? – they're "brilliantly sourced", "the specials are more special", and the "unique" rosemary flavoured fries are "seriously addictive". Queues, though, are "daunting". / www.honestburgers.co.uk; @honestburgers; 10 pm - 11 pm; SW9 closed Mon D.

Honey & Co W1 £48 542
25a Warren St 7388 6175 2–1B
"Exhilarating" modern Middle Eastern dishes (not least the "extraordinary cakes") inspire adulatory reviews for this "Lilliputian-sized" café, near Warren Street tube; size constraints mean "it's hard to get a table" though, and once you have conditions are "squashed". / W1T 5JZ; www.honeyandco.co.uk; @Honeyandco; Mon-Sat 10.30 pm; closed Sun.

Hood SW2 NEW £42 442
67 Streatham Hill 3601 3320 10–2D
"Already a regular haunt in Streatham Hill (book!)" – a welcoming "if slightly spartan" new, little neighbourhood café with a "small but well cooked" menu, plus an "interesting" list of English wines and craft beers; brunch with kids "is a real winner" too. / SW2 4TX; www.hoodrestaurants.com; @hoodStreatham; 11 pm.

Hoppers W1 NEW
49 Frith St no tel 4–2A
The sharp-eyed Sethi siblings – the team behind Gymkhana and Trishna (as well as backers of Bao, Lyle's and Bubbledogs) – aim to turn their Midas touch to street food, with this Soho café inspired by the road shacks of Tamil Nadu and Sri Lanka, due to open October 2015. / W1D 4SG; www.hopperslondon.com; 10.30 pm.

The Horseshoe NW3 £48 322
28 Heath St 7431 7206 8–2A
The "unbeatable combination" of Camden Brewery beers (which used to be brewed on this very site), and some of Hampstead's better pub grub win praise for this popular hostelry. / NW3 6TE; www.thehorseshoehampstead.com; @getluckyatthehorseshoe; 10 pm, Fri & Sat 11 pm.

Hot Stuff SW8 £22 442
23 Wilcox Rd 7720 1480 10–1D
"Top curries at super-cheap prices" continue to win enthusiastic recommendations for this BYO Indian, in deepest Vauxhall (on the stretch of road immortalised in 'My Beautiful Laundrette'). / SW8 2XA; www.eathotstuff.com; 9.30 pm; closed Mon; no Amex.

House of Ho £57 322
1 Percy St, W1 awaiting tel 2–1C NEW
57-59 Old Compton St, W1 7287 0770 4–3A
Fans praise "an interesting take on Vietnamese food" and "funky" styling at this well-publicised yearling; but critics say the nosh is "nothing special", that service is "not up to much", and think "the feel of the place is frankly depressing". A new HQ (on the site of Bam-Bou, RIP) is expected late-2015. /

House Restaurant, National Theatre SE1 NEW £52 232
Royal National Theatre, Belvedere Rd 7452 3600 2–3D
Views divide on this re-staging of the National's main restaurant space (fka 'Mezzanine'); undoubtedly it's "useful for a show", but while fans say it's "a lot better than its predecessor", those who found it "inconsistent" say "work is needed if we are to return for an encore". / SE1 9PX; @NT_House; 10 pm.

The Hoxton Grill EC2 £52 234
81 Great Eastern St 7739 9111 12–1B
"Everything is slick" at this large and "very cool" Shoreditch venue, serving "enjoyable" diner-style grub; not everyone 'gets it' though – "with its DJ and noise from drinkers, it doesn't know if it's a disco, bar or restaurant!" / EC2A 3HU; www.hoxtongrill.co.uk; @hoxtongrill; 11.45 pm.

Hubbard & Bell, Hoxton Hotel WC1 £56 334
199-206 High Holborn 7661 3030 2–1D
Soho House's "fun cross between a diner and a grill" is great for "people watching" and gets "very lively" ("noisy") in the evenings with a DJ and large groups; the food "can become incidental", so "better to go at lunchtime" (or for the excellent breakfasts). / WC1V 7BD; www.hubbardandbell.com; @hubbardandbell; 2 am, Sunday midnight.

Hunan SW1 £79 521
51 Pimlico Rd 7730 5712 5–2D
"Let the owner order for you", then sit back for "a roller coaster ride of endless one-mouthful plates" when you visit this "cramped" Pimlico veteran. The "truly original and exciting" cooking is arguably "London's best Chinese food" and the Peng family's "haphazard, grace-under-pressure" service helps create "an experience like no other". / SW1W 8NE; www.hunanlondon.com; 11 pm; closed Sun; set weekday L £56 (FP).

Hungry Donkey E1 NEW £42
56 Wentworth St 7392 9649 9–2D
Attractive-looking, airy, all-day operation in Aldgate inspired by Hellenic street food (eat in or take out), majoring in souvlaki cooked on the Josper grill and a wide range of Greek tipples; it opened too late for the survey, hence it's un-rated. / E1 7AL; www.hungrydonkey.co.uk; @thehungrydonkey; Mon-Wed 10 pm, Thu-Sat 10.30 pm, Sun 6 pm.

Hush £61 233
8 Lancashire Ct, W1 7659 1500 3–2B
95-97 High Holborn, WC1 7242 4580 2–1D
A "posh" location (tucked-away off Bond Street, with a large terrace), "buzzy" bar and "spacious" dining room have won a fashionable following for the Mayfair original of this small group, even if it's "not as good as it thinks it is"; its straightforward Holborn spin-off is akin to an upmarket Côte. / www.hush.co.uk; @Hush_Restaurant; W1 10.45 pm; WC1 10.30 pm, Sun 9.30 pm; WC1 closed Sun.

Hutong The Shard SE1 £87 224
31 St Thomas St 3011 1257 9–4C
"Up high, overlooking London is breathtaking", at this "slick and graceful" 33rd-floor perch; but while fans find the Chinese cuisine "astonishingly good" for a room with a such an "exceptional" view, others find it "unspectacular" especially given the "crazy prices". / SE1 9RY; www.hutong.co.uk; @HutongShard; 11 pm.

Ibérica £46 334

Zig Zag Building, 70 Victoria St, SW1 7636 8650 2–4B NEW
195 Great Portland St, W1 7636 8650 2–1B
12 Cabot Sq, E14 7636 8650 11–1C
89 Turnmill St, EC1 7636 8650 9–1A

These "cool-ish" modern Spaniards offer an "inexpensive and delicious" selection of tapas; "for a fairly quick business lunch" the E14 branch is one of the Wharf's better options, and the "large" and "lively" Clerkenwell outlet is perhaps their best opening yet. A further outpost opened in Victoria as this guide went to press. / 11 pm; W1 closed Sun D.

Iddu SW7 NEW £49 212

44 Harrington Rd 7581 8088 5–2B

Not far from Gloucester Road tube, a new café and wine bar; its "interesting" Sicilian dishes and wines show some promise, but it can seem "pricey", and service can be "hopeless". / SW7 3ND; www.iddulondon.com; 10 pm.

Imli Street W1 £40 322

167-169 Wardour St 7287 4243 3–1D

With its "interesting", affordable Indian street food 'tapas', plus the odd cocktail if you so fancy, this sizeable Soho operation is "a handy drop-in", and one that can be "fun" too. / W1F 8WR; www.imlistreet.com; @imlistreet; 11 pm, Sun 10 pm.

Inaho W2 £44 515

4 Hereford Rd 7221 8495 6–1B

"Better than Nobu!" might seem a surprising claim for this "eccentric", "little" Japanese shed in Bayswater, but it's regularly praised for "the best sushi and sashimi ever"; the service though could not be described as 'rapid'. / W2 4AA; 10.30 pm; closed Sat L & Sun; no Amex or Maestro.

Inamo £46 222

4-12 Regent St, SW1 7484 0500 3–3D
134-136 Wardour St, W1 7851 7051 3–1D

The "quirky" touchscreen table ordering system is by far the best feature of this Asian chain – the food is secondary (but "tasty nonetheless"); the odd critic says it's "a rubbish concept", but for most reporters it's "fun for a night out with friends, or with kids, or maybe even a date". / www.inamo-restaurant.com; @InamoRestaurant; W1: Mon - Thu 11.30pm, Fri & Sat midnight, Sun 10.30 pm – SW1: Mon - Thu 11pm, Fri & Sat 12.30pm, Sun 10.30pm.

India Club, Strand Continental Hotel WC2 £29 321

143 Strand 7836 4880 2–2D

A scruffy old relic, near the Indian High Commission (where you BYO, or pick up a pint in the hotel bar); "it's the authenticity of the cooking, the eternal pre-war atmosphere, and very fair prices that keep us going back". / WC2R 1JA; www.strand-continental.co.uk; 10.50 pm; no credit cards; booking: max 6.

Indian Moment SW11 £35 343

44 Northcote Rd 7223 6575 10–2C

"A pre-drink curry, rather than a post-session, end-of-the-night filler!", say fans of this much-appreciated Battersea local, with its "interesting" cooking and "classy and modern" interior. / SW11 1NZ; www.indianmoment.co.uk; @indianmoment; 11.30 pm, Fri & Sat midnight; no Amex.

Indian Ocean SW17 £33 453

214 Trinity Rd 8672 7740 10–2C

"It never ever fails!" – a "stalwart" Wandsworth Indian, acclaimed for its "very tasty" cooking, and "some of the best service ever". / SW17 7HP; www.indianoceanrestaurant.com; 11.30 pm.

Indian Rasoi N2 £36 433

7 Denmark Ter 8883 9093 1–1B

"If you don't know it, you're missing out!"; this "tiny" Muswell Hill Indian draws fans from across north London for its "unusual" cooking with "lovely, individual flavours". / N2 9HG; www.indian-rasoi.co.uk; 10.30 pm; no Amex.

Indian Veg N1 £11 433

92-93 Chapel Mkt 7833 1167 8–3D

"Colourful, veggie propaganda posters all over the walls make for a diverting read" at this age-old, self-service, "buffet-style" vegan in Islington, where it's "hard not to overeat", given the "tasty curries at crazy prices". / N1 9EX; 11.30 pm.

Indian Zilla SW13 £46 332

2-3 Rocks Ln 8878 3989 10–1A

"Ace" and "original" cooking continues to win many fans for this Barnes sibling to Indian Zing; its ratings slipped this year though – a couple of reporters had "iffy" meals, and the ambience has suffered when it's empty. / SW13 0DB; www.indianzilla.co.uk; 11 pm; closed weekday L.

Indian Zing W6 £49 532

236 King St 8748 5959 7–2B

"Even my Punjabi mother-in-law swooned!" – Manoj Vasaikar's "very distinctive" modern Indian cuisine remains "worth the trip" to this very well-known, but somewhat "oddly located" little "gem", near Ravenscourt Park. / W6 0RS; www.indianzing.co.uk; @IndianZing; 11 pm, Sun 10 pm.

Indigo One, Aldwych WC2 £65 [2][4][3]
1 Aldwych 7300 0400 2–2D
A "dependable spot for a quick bite to eat pre-theatre" – this Theatreland mezzanine dining room benefits from the buzz of the foyer below and is "all-round a very good experience", enhanced by a successful revamp in spring 2015. / WC2B 4BZ; www.onealdwych.com; @OneAldwych; 10.15 pm.

Inside SE10 £45 [4][4][1]
19 Greenwich South St 8265 5060 1–3D
Guy Awford's "sparkling gem" is "still the best in Greenwich", serving "excellent value" cuisine (both "classic and with a twist"); its premises aren't a huge plus however – they're "cramped, noisy and dowdy". / SE10 8NW; www.insiderestaurant.co.uk; @insideandgreenwich; Tue-Sat 10 pm, Sun 3 pm; closed Mon & Sun D; SRA-1.*

Ippudo London £38 [2][3][2]
Central St Giles Piazza, WC2 7240 4469 4–1B NEW
1 Crossrail Pl, E14 3326 9485 11–1C NEW
"It shouldn't be hard to take a reliable international formula and clone it", but these new outposts of the global Japanese tonkotsu chain get a mixed rep – even those who rate its first branch as "very good" say "it's inferior to Kanada-Ya across the road", and the worst reports are of food that's "watery and greasy". / www.ippudo.co.uk; @IppudoLondon.

Isarn N1 £46 [4][3][2]
119 Upper St 7424 5153 8–3D
"They put love into their authentic cooking" at this "tranquil" and affordable Thai – a very "dependable" feature of the Islington restaurant strip. / N1 1QP; www.isarn.co.uk; 11 pm, Sat & Sun 10 pm.

Ishtar W1 £46 [3][3][2]
10-12 Crawford St 7224 2446 2–1A
"Steady cooking, kind staff, fair prices... and that's over a dozen visits – what more can you ask?", say fans of this "accommodating" Turkish "gem", in Marylebone. / W1U 6AZ; www.ishtarrestaurant.com; 11.30 pm, Sun 10.30 pm; set weekday L £28 (FP).

The Italian Job W4 NEW £30 [2][2][4]
13 Devonshire Rd 8994 2852 7–2A
"The food's not really the point here (even if it's very serviceable none the less)" – it's the rotating list of Italian craft beer that makes this new Chiswick bar, just beside La Trompette, worth seeking out. / W4 2EU; www.theitalianjobpub.co.uk; @TheItalianJobW4.

Itsu £33 [2][3][3]
Branches throughout London
"A gym day feels more healthy" if you snack at these "refreshingly lo-cal" Pan-Asian pit-stops, whose sushi, "slurpy soups" and other "innovative bites" are "not the tastiest, but generally good quality". / www.itsu.co.uk; 11 pm, E14 10 pm; some are closed Sat & Sun; no booking.

The Ivy WC2 £69
1-5 West St 7836 4751 4–3B
Richard Caring's famous Theatreland idol – now the original of a fast expanding brand – emerged from a massive overhaul too late to be rated (just before the survey closed). Too often a let down in recent years, a handful of first-days reports say its "beautiful refurb" is "superb in every detail" – "wow, wow, wow!" / WC2H 9NQ; www.the-ivy.co.uk; @CapriceHoldings; 11 pm, Sun 10 pm; no shorts; booking: max 6; set weekday L & pre-theatre £45 (FP).

The Ivy Café W1 NEW
96 Marylebone Ln 3301 0400 2–1A
Richard Caring continues to expand his most bankable brand, The Ivy, with a casual café offering due to open November-2015 on the former site of Union Café (RIP) in Marylebone; let's hope it has better food than the other recent spin-offs. / W1U 2QA; www.theivycafemarylebone.com; 11 pm, Fri & Sat 11.30 pm, Sun 10.30 pm.

The Ivy Chelsea Garden SW3 NEW £57 [2][2][5]
197 King's Rd 3301 0300 5–3C
You need to be "Prince William or Lady Gaga to get a table before 2050", at the Ivy's new, all-day west London cousin (on the site that in the late '80s was famous as Henry J Beans). "Like the original Ivy, the food's not the point" – in fact, it's really "dreary" here – "it's the beautiful design and glorious, not-so-secret garden that make it a sublime addition to the King's Road". / SW3 5ED; www.theivychelseagarden.com; @ivychelsgarden; 11.30 pm.

The Ivy Kensington Brasserie W8 NEW
96 Kensington High St awaiting tel 5–1A
On the site of Jon (Foxtons) Hunt's short-lived Pavilion (RIP), yet another Ivy spin-off from the Caprice Group, due to open late-2015; whatever the outcome food-wise, it's good to know that more will be made of this barmily luxurious, but previously under-utilised, space. / W8 4SG.

The Ivy Market Grill WC2 NEW £57 223
1a Henrietta St 3301 0200 4–3D
If you're going to roll out a brand like 'The Ivy', for Pete's sake, do better than this new lukewarm knock-off, right by Covent Garden market; apologists say it's handy with a "nice al fresco" area, but given its "bland" food, "perfunctory" service and "lack of ambience" you "expect better of the Caprice stable". / WC2E 8PS; www.theivymarketgrill.com; @ivymarketgrill; midnight, Sun 11.30 pm; set weekday L £36 (FP).

Izgara N3 £34 322
11 Hendon Lane 8371 8282 1–1B
A recently refurbished Turkish grill in Finchley with a "wonderful array of meat skewers", and a "buzzy" (if rather "noisy") setting. / N3 1RT; www.izgararestaurant.net; midnight; no Amex.

Jackson & Rye £46 123
56 Wardour St, W1 7437 8338 3–2D
219-221 Chiswick High Rd, W4 8747 1156 7–2A NEW
Hotham House, 1 Heron Sq, TW9 8948 6951 1–4A
"A trick missed" – these "smart", US-style diners are a case of "style over substance"; they're "buzzing" (and Richmond has "a lovely riverside location"), but the food is "poor" (stick to breakfast) and service is "friendly" but "lackadaisical" – "employ some Americans!" / www.jacksonrye.com.

Jaffna House SW17 £16 542
90 Tooting High St 8672 7786 10–2C
"Despite its humble interior, well worth a visit" – a family-run Tooting Sri Lankan (the dining space is a converted living room) where the "tasty" grub is "ridiculously good value". / SW17 0RN; www.jaffnahouse.co.uk; midnight.

Jago Second Home E1 NEW £49 323
60-80 Hanbury St 3818 3241 12–2C
If you're a lover of '70s SciFi movies, you'll love this "slightly weird" (and very orange) new conservatory annex to a so-now East End tech office space. Arguably "it's trying too hard to be hip", and the modern Middle Eastern-inspired food is "a bit mixed", but some dishes are "brilliantly executed". (The name? apparently slang for the slums that once inhabited this part of Shoreditch). / E1 5JL; www.jagorestaurant.com; @jagorestaurant; 10.30 pm .

Jamaica Patty Co. WC2 £10 332
26 New Row 7836 3334 4–3C
A handy Covent Garden pit stop, serving "above average patties" – "good grub, good prices, great tastes!" / WC2N 4LA; www.jamaicapatty.co.uk; @JamaicaPattyCo; 11 pm, Sun 7 pm.

Jamie's Diner W1 £48 222
23a Shaftesbury Ave 3697 4117 3–3D
Jamie Oliver's year-old, family-friendly Soho diner disappoints half those who comment on it – it's "ordinary at best". / W1D 7EF; www.jamieoliversdiner.com; @jamiesdiner; Mon-Fri 11 pm, Sat & Sun 10.30 pm.

Jamie's Italian £44 112
Branches throughout London
"Avoid!"; Jamie Oliver risks becoming "synonymous with poor food" with his chain of Italian diners, which inspire far too many "embarrassingly bad" reports of "really weak" results, and "shrugging" service. / www.jamiesitalian.com; @JamiesItalianUK; 11.30 pm, Sun 10.30 pm; booking: min 6.

Jar Kitchen WC2 NEW £48 333
Drury Ln 7405 4255 4–1C
The owners are first-time restaurateurs, so there are still "some things to iron out" at this tiny rookie, on the fringes of Covent Garden; that said it has "tasty home cooking" and "lovely staff" to recommend it. / WC2B 5QF; www.jarkitchen.com; @JarKitchen; 11.30 pm .

Jashan N8 £32 542
19 Turnpike Ln 8340 9880 1–1C
"Incredibly popular with anyone within easy reach of Turnpike Lane" – a "fantastic" (if slightly "tired" looking) Indian, whose "extensive, wide-ranging menu is a departure from what you'd expect of a local", and "amazing for the price". / N8 0EP; www.jashanturnpikelane.co.uk; 11.30 pm; D only; no Amex; need 6+ to book, Sat & Sun.

Jin Kichi NW3 £44 543
73 Heath St 7794 6158 8–1A
"Just like Tokyo!"; this "real Japanese" in the heart of Hampstead may be "tiny" and "cramped", but "it never fails to deliver wonderful food" and "without ridiculous prices" too. / NW3 6UG; www.jinkichi.com; 11 pm, Sun 10 pm; closed Mon L.

Jinjuu W1 NEW £47 333
16 Kingly St 8181 8887 3–2C
Korean-inspired bar snacks and larger dishes "are not quite elevated to an art form, but to a good level" at the first solo venture from TV Iron Chef star Judy Joo, where you can eat in the ground floor bar (DJs on some nights), or basement dining room. / W1B 5PS; www.jinjuu.com; @JinjuuLDN; midnight.

Joanna's SE19 £44 334
56 Westow Hill 8670 4052 1–4D
An "institution" in Crystal Palace – this atmospheric neighbourhood stalwart of three decades standing remains "a firm favourite" thanks to its "consistently good" all-round standards; just one gripe – "bring back the table cloths!" / SE19 1RX; www.joannas.uk.com; @JoannasRest; 10.45 pm, Sun 10.15 pm.

Joe Allen WC2 £53 124
13 Exeter St 7836 0651 4–3D
A "Theatreland favourite since it opened in the mid-'70s" – this "fun and buzzy", occasionally star-studded, old, Covent Garden basement hangs on to its fan club despite perennially "tired" cooking. Top Menu Tip – the "delicious under-the-counter burgers" which "strangely have never made the menu". / WC2E 7DT; www.joeallen.co.uk; @JoeAllenWC2; Sun-Thu 11.45 pm, Fri & Sat 12.45 am; set weekday L £34 (FP).

Joe's Brasserie SW6 £43 233
130 Wandsworth Bridge Rd 7731 7835 10–1B
The "comfort food" is "good standard stuff" and there's "very well-priced wine" at John Brinkley's stalwart brasserie in deepest Fulham; "enjoyable outside terrace" too. / SW6 2UL; www.brinkleys.com; @BrinkleysR; 11.30 pm, Sun 10.30 pm.

John Doe W10 NEW £49 433
46 Golborne Rd 8969 3280 6–1A
On-trend for slow-cooking and smoking, but doing it rather better than most – a "wonderful" north Kensington newcomer serving "fabulous game, fish, bone marrow and veg" straight from the charcoal grill; "sit at the bar and watch your meal being prepared". / W10 5PR; www.johndoerestaurants.com; @johndoegolborne; midnight, Sun 4 pm.

The Joint £26 532
19 New Cavendish St, W1 7486 3059 2–1A
NEW
87 Brixton Village, Coldharbour Ln, SW9 0 7717 6428 12 10–1D
"The best pulled pork this side of anywhere", and "ribs and wings like you get in the deep South" are plain "brilliant" at this "lip-smackin'" BBQ duo; "you have to queue around the block at the hustling and bustling Brixton Market original, but boy is it worth it!" / www.the-joint.co; closed Mon.

Jolly Gardners SW15 £49 433
61-63 Lacey Rd 8870 8417 10–2A
"Masterchef winner Dhruv Baker uses seasonal produce to create interesting alternatives to traditional pub fare" at this "stark" Earlsfield gastropub, which wins ringing endorsements from most (if not quite all) who report on it. / SW15 1NT; www.thejollygardeners.co.uk; @JollyGardeners; 11 pm, Sun 6 pm.

Jones & Sons E8 NEW £54 444
22-27 Arcola St 7241 1211 1–1C
"Many places in smarter postcodes would charge a heck of a lot more" than this open-kitchen operation, in a converted Dalston factory (nowadays trendy studios), which fans say "deserves proper recognition" for its cooking, in particular "outstanding" char-grilled steaks. / E8 2DJ; www.jonesandsonsdalston.com; 10 pm, Fri & Sat 11 pm.

The Jones Family Project EC2 £50 243
78 Great Eastern St 7739 1740 12–1B
"Staff couldn't be friendlier" at this sizeable Shoreditch bar (street level) / restaurant (basement); steak is the menu highlight, but top billing goes to the "fab cocktails". / EC2A 3JL; www.jonesfamilyproject.co.uk; @jonesshoreditch; 10.30 pm, Sun 6 pm.

José SE1 £47 555
104 Bermondsey St 7403 4902 9–4D
"It's worth fighting to get in" to José Pizarro's "tiny" and "cramped" little "piece of Spain" in Bermondsey – you enjoy "masterful" tapas, served by "staff who take tremendous pride in their work", in a marvellously "vibrant" setting. / SE1 3UB; www.josepizarro.com; @Jose_Pizarro; Mon-Sat 10.15 pm, Sun 5.15 pm; closed Sun D.

José Pizarro EC2 NEW £58 443
Broadgate Circle 3437 0905 12–2B
From hip Bermondsey (José, Pizarro) to the heart of the Square Mile – cynics might say JP has sold out with this Broadgate Circle newcomer; early reports though say "it's a great addition to the City", with an "extensive" array of "superb" tapas, and "a super terrace for a sunny day". / EC2M 2QS; www.josepizarro.com; @JP_Broadgate; 10.45 pm, Sun 9.45 pm .

Joy King Lau WC2 £38 322
3 Leicester St 7437 1132 4–3A
"Four crowded floors of bustle" that are "very much better-than-average for Chinatown", if "looking a bit dated now"; the Cantonese chow's "not the most sophisticated", but "dim sum and char sui are all excellent". / WC2H 7BL; www.joykinglau.com; 11.30 pm, Sun 10.30 pm.

The Jugged Hare EC1 £66 323
49 Chiswell St 7614 0134 12–2A
"Really good game in season" is a highlight at this "countryman's oasis" near The Barbican – a "stylish" and "buzzy" ("packed") gastropub serving "lovely" British food. / EC1Y 4SA; www.thejuggedhare.com; @juggedhare; Mon-Wed 11 pm, Thu-Sat midnight, Sun 10.30 pm.

Julie's W11 **£65**
135 Portland Rd 7229 8331 6–2A
"Those cubbyhole niches have seen a lot of action" over the years, at this famously sexy, '70s basement warren in Holland Park; just as the food (never great) showed some signs of improving, they closed it till Spring 2016 for a huge refurb – let's hope it emerges as the knock-out place it has the potential to be. / W11 4LW; www.juliesrestaurant.com; @JuliesW11; 11 pm.

Jun Ming Xuan NW9 **£42** 442
28 Heritage Ave 8205 6987 1–1A
In the new Beaufort Park area of Colindale, a modern Chinese at the foot of a recent development; even if The Times review hailing it as the UK's best is a tad wide of the mark, it wins enthusiastic praise for its "terrific dim sum and other classic dishes". / NW9 5GE; 11 pm.

The Junction Tavern NW5 **£48** 333
101 Fortess Rd 7485 9400 8–2B
A "high-quality gastropub" on the Tufnell Park/ Kentish Town borders, that generates consistently upbeat feedback; cute courtyard. / NW5 1AG; www.junctiontavern.co.uk; @Junction Tavern; 11 pm, Mon 10.30 pm; Mon-Thu D only, Fri-Sun open L & D; no Amex.

K10 **£38** 332
20 Copthall Ave, EC2 7562 8510 9–2C
3 Appold St, EC2 7539 9209 12–2B
Minster Ct, Mincing Ln, EC3 3019 2510 9–3D NEW
"Better than the big-name conveyor chains" – these well-run, slightly "spartan" City operations have very "decent" standards, and serve "a great selection of sushi and other delicacies"; "arrive early to avoid the queues". / www.k10.com; Appold 9 pm, Wed-Fri 9.30 pm.

Kadiri's NW10 **£24** 432
26 High Rd 8459 0936 1–1A
"Every dish – mild or very hot – is delicious", say fans of this cramped, '70s subcontinental in Willesden; there's the odd gripe though that "they've pared back on what was a very varied menu to something more bog standard". / NW10 2QD; www.kadiris.com; @kadirislondon; 11 pm.

Kaffeine **£12** 455
15 Eastcastle St, W1 7580 6755 3–1D NEW
66 Great Titchfield St, W1 7580 6755 3–1C
"The coffee never disappoints" – "it's the best, no doubts" – at these "always packed" Fitzrovia haunts; "inventive" nibbles too, and "an amazing emphasis on top-quality service". / www.kaffeine.co.uk.

Kai Mayfair W1 **£97** 322
65 South Audley St 7493 8988 3–3A
This luxurious Chinese is "all a bit Mayfair", especially its Claret-heavy wine list, non-oriental waiters, and prices off the Richter scale; perhaps surprisingly though, it's generally "worth it". / W1K 2QU; www.kaimayfair.co.uk; @kaimayfair; 10.45 pm, Sun 10.15 pm.

Kaifeng NW4 **£62** 323
51 Church Rd 8203 7888 1–1B
Hendon's stalwart kosher Chinese restaurant is, say fans, "as good as ever", and unusually flexible (they "cater for coeliacs" and "even a guest who didn't fancy Chinese was given a suitable dinner!"); not everyone's wowed though, especially by prices some consider a "rip off". / NW4 4DU; www.kaifeng.co.uk; 10 pm; closed Fri & Sat.

Kanada-Ya **£19** 532
3 Panton St, SW1 awaiting tel 4–4A NEW
64 St Giles High St, WC2 7240 0232 4–1B NEW
"The hoards queuing outside know they're in for a treat" at these cheap, "truly genuine", "cheek-by-jowl" ramen newcomers in the West End (outposts of a chain originating in Fukuoka, in southern Japan); "the broth is so rich, the meat so unctuous, you'll finish the bowl, even if you feel you're about to burst!" / www.kanada-ya.com/home/.

Kaosarn **£26** 343
110 St Johns Hill, SW11 7223 7888 10–2C
Brixton Village, Coldharbour Ln, SW9 7095 8922 10–2D
"Always hopping" – these "vibrant" ("if not exactly plush") cafés in Brixton Village and Battersea, are "spot on", with "fresh, home-cooked Thai flavours" ("no hint of generic gloop") and "a BYO policy that keeps prices down". / SW9 10 pm, Sun 9 pm; SW11 closed Mon L.

Kappacasein SE16 **£6** 532
1 Voyager Industrial Estate 0 7837 7568 52 11–2A
"The best toasted cheese sandwich in the history of the world" (and also "very good raclettes") inspire love (and long queues) for the Borough Market stall of this Bermondsey dairy (which itself opens on Saturdays). / SE16 4RP; www.kappacasein.com; Thu 5 pm, Fri 6 pm, Sat 5 pm .

Karma W14 **£40** 432
44 Blythe Rd 7602 9333 7–1D
"In a hidden corner of Olympia", this "quiet" Indian is well worth discovering – "decidedly not your average cuzza", it serves "superb, authentic curries". / W14 0HA; www.k-a-r-m-a.co.uk; @KarmaKensington; 11 pm; no Amex.

Kaspar's Seafood and Grill The Savoy Hotel WC2 £79 333

100 The Strand 7836 4343 4–3D

Critics decry a "characterless" space and "unspectacular" cooking at the Savoy's former River Restaurant; on balance, though, most reporters approve of its "OTT" Deco décor and say the food is "excellent, if pricey". Top Tip – "good value pre-theatre menu". / WC2R 0EU; www.kaspars.co.uk; @KasparsLondon; 11 pm.

Kateh £43 542

9 Knightsbridge Grn, SW1 7289 3393 5–1D

NEW

5 Warwick Pl, W9 7289 3393 8–4A

A tiny outfit in Little Venice, which comes "absolutely recommended" thanks to the "beautiful blend of magical Persian dishes, served by its attentive and friendly staff"; it's "very (perhaps too) cosy" too – "it's hard to fit all the plates on the table!"; still no feedback on its year-old Knightsbridge branch. / www.katehrestaurant.co.uk; @KatehRestaurant.

Kazan £48 342

77 Wilton Rd, SW1 7233 8298 2–4B

93-94 Wilton Rd, SW1 7233 7100 2–4B

"Deservedly successful", "very busy" Pimlico duo, with restaurant and café spin-off on the same street; their looks are "quite ordinary", but service is "accommodating", and there's high praise for the "sparkling fresh" salads and mezze and other well-prepared Turkish fare. / www.kazan-restaurant.com; 10 pm.

The Keeper's House Royal Academy W1 £65 222

Royal Academy Of Arts, Piccadilly 7300 5881 3–3D

"It's handy when visiting an exhibition", but many reporters "expected more" of this "prestigious" basement two-year-old ("tucked away" below the RA) – the food "goes from excellent to meh", service can be "novice", and overall it can all seem "fairly ordinary". / W1J 0BD; www.keepershouse.org.uk; @KHRestaurant; 11.30 pm; closed Sun; set pre theatre £41 (FP).

Ken Lo's Memories SW1 £60 342

65-69 Ebury St 7730 7734 2–4B

"I love the place, and so do many regulars!" – this once-famous Belgravia Chinese remains a "calm and civilised" venue, and though oft-accused of "living on its past reputation", its ratings are remarkably steady; the food is "unadventurous by the standards of some newer Chinese places, but high quality". / SW1W 0NZ; www.memoriesofchina.co.uk; 10.45 pm, Sun 10 pm.

Kennington Tandoori SE11 £45 333

313 Kennington Rd 7735 9247 1–3C

"Preppy young locals rub shoulders with older politicos" at this "neighbourhood gossip shop" – a "consistently good local curry house", within easy striking distance of the Palace of Westminster. / SE11 4QE; www.kenningtontandoori.com; @TheKTL; 11 pm; no Amex.

Kensington Place W8 £60 333

201-209 Kensington Church St 7727 3184 6–2B

This seminal '90s venue, off Notting Hill Gate – with its "bright windows and open interior" – was "reinvented after the post-Rowley Leigh wilderness years" and is now biased to "delicious" fish and seafood (with shop attached); sceptics still find the food a tad "ordinary" however, and the setting's "noisy" as ever. / W8 7LX; www.kensingtonplace-restaurant.co.uk; @kprestaurantW8; 10.30 pm; closed Mon L & Sun D; set weekday L £45 (FP).

Kensington Square Kitchen W8 £33 343

9 Kensington Sq 7938 2598 5–1A

For "a top brunch in Kensington" (or an affordable "straightforward" bite at any time), winkle out this cute, cramped little indie café, tucked away off a picturesque old square. / W8 5EP; www.kensingtonsquarekitchen.co.uk; @KSKRestaurant; 4.30 pm, Sun 4 pm; L only; no Amex.

The Kensington Wine Rooms W8 £55 223

127-129 Kensington Church St 7727 8142 6–2B

"I'm at the age when reading wine lists is my form of porno, and a long lunch here is very enjoyable...!"; this Kensington bar-dining room provides an "extensive and varied list" (including plenty of wines by the glass), washed down with tapas-style food that's "pleasant". / W8 7LP; www.greatwinesbytheglass.com; @wine_rooms; 10.45 pm.

(Brew House) Kenwood House NW3 £32 224

Hampstead Heath 8348 4073 8–1A

"Luxuriate in the sunshine at the outdoor tables" of Kenwood's beautifully located self-service café, at the top of Hampstead Heath; stick to breakfasts, coffee and cakes though – other options are "very variable and not great value, but the surroundings make every latte a joy!" / NW3 7JR; www.companyofcooks.com; @EHKenwood; 6 pm (summer), 4 pm (winter); L only.

Kerbisher & Malt £20 332

53 New Broadway, W5 8840 4418 1–2A
164 Shepherd's Bush Rd, W6 3556 0228 7–1C
170 Upper Richmond Road West, SW14 8876 3404 1–4A
50 Abbeville Rd, SW4 3417 4350 10–2D
59-61 Rosebery Ave, EC1 7833 4434 9–1A NEW

"Flaky, fresh fish, and proper fat chips" – plus funkier menu options (eg fennel salad!) – have fuelled growth at this chippy-chain, which fans say is "traditional where it counts, but stylish and modern too"; the design can seem "a bit dull" however, and sceptics say they're "only a bit better than an average chippy". / www.kerbisher.co.uk; 10 pm - 10.30pm, Sun 9 pm - 9.30 pm; W6 closed Mon; no booking.

Kettners W1 £58

29 Romilly St 7734 6112 4–2A

Will the Soho House group finally succeed where all else have failed in revivifying this magnificent Victorian landmark in Soho (founded in 1867), which – aside from its jolly champagne bar – has been perennially disappointing for as long as most folk can remember. When it re-opens in 2018, it will be as part of a new hotel complex. / W1D 5HP; www.kettners.com; @KettnersLondon; 11 pm, Fri & Sat 11.30 pm, Sun 9.30 pm.

Khan's W2 £23 332

13-15 Westbourne Grove 7727 5420 6–1C

For a "cheap 'n' cheerful" Indian meal, this large veteran canteen in Bayswater has its plus points; it's hectic though, and don't go if you want to booze (it's alcohol free). / W2 4UA; www.khansrestaurant.com; @khansrestaurant; 11.30 pm, Sat & Sun midnight.

Kiku W1 £55 432

17 Half Moon St 7499 4208 3–4B

"Marvellous sushi" is the draw to this "bustling" but "bland"-looking Mayfair fixture; a catch? – it's really "not cheap". / W1J 7BE; www.kikurestaurant.co.uk; 10.15 pm, Sun 9.45 pm; closed Sun L.

Kikuchi W1 £52 532

14 Hanway St 7637 7720 4–1A

"To-die-for sushi" – "better than much of what I tasted in Japan" – is the (only) reason to seek out this "simple" venture, tucked-away off Tottenham Court Road; it's "expensive" though, and with the service "there are some language barriers". / W1T 1UD; 10.30 pm; closed Sun.

Kimchee WC1 £42 322

71 High Holborn 7430 0956 2–1D

"The Korean Wagamama" in 'Midtown' is consistently well-rated, for both food that's "OK rather than exceptional", and also its "well designed space", but not for its sometimes "lousy" service. / WC1V 6EA; www.kimchee.uk.com; @kimcheerest; 10.30 pm.

Kintan WC1 £44 433

34-36 High Holborn 7242 8076 9–2A

London's first yakiniku-style outpost (a Japanese take on Korean BBQ) – this Holborn yearling wins praise for its "great-tasting" meaty fare; "kids love cooking their own dinner at the table too". / WC1V 6AE; www.kintan.uk/about; 10 pm.

Kipferl N1 £45 333

20 Camden Pas 77041 555 8–3D

"Without all the kitsch of lederhosen and dirndls" – an "obliging" Islington deli-restaurant offering "lovely Austrian food that's authentic but not too heavy" (eg schnitzels, Bergkäse omelette) plus "top coffee", and a "great selection of gateaux and Austrian wines"; just the job for brunch. / N1 8ED; www.kipferl.co.uk; @KipferlCafe; 9.30 pm; closed Mon.

Kiraku W5 £35 532

8 Station Pde 8992 2848 1–3A

"Exceptional Japanese food justifies the trek to this friendly, izakaya-style café", near Ealing Common Tube, "hence why it's always packed", typically with the local Japanese community. / W5 3LD; www.kiraku.co.uk; @kirakulondon; 10 pm; closed Mon; no Amex.

Kishmish SW6 £50 443

448-450 Fulham Rd 7385 6953 5–4A

Not far from Stamford Bridge – a "non-standard" Indian whose interesting menu offers a "different take" on the average curry ("delicious buffalo vindaloo" for example). / SW6 1DL; www.kishmish.biz; @KishmishFulham; 11 pm.

Kitchen, National Theatre SE1 NEW £26 222

South Bank 7452 3600 2–3D

"Not fine dining", and "not with a lot of choice", but "for a quick bite before a play" or when on the South Bank, the NT's "very reasonably priced" new "cheap 'n cheerful self-service option" is "worth considering". / SE1 9PX; www.nationaltheatre.org; 8 pm, Sun 6 pm.

Kitchen W8 W8 £69 543

11-13 Abingdon Road 7937 0120 5–1A

"Phil Howard has worked his magic" in overseeing this "smart but unpretentious" neighbourhood spot, just off Ken' High Street; "nuanced" and "very fine" cuisine is "excellently served" in a setting that's "not hugely distinctive" but "calm and serene". / W8 6AH; www.kitchenw8.com; @KitchenW8; 10.30 pm, Sun 9.30 pm; set weekday L £42 (FP), set pre-theatre £44 (FP), set Sun L £52 (FP).

Kitty Fisher's W1 NEW £67 444

10 Shepherd's Mkt 3302 1661 3–4B

If you can nab a table (ay, there's the rub), you should find your efforts amply-rewarded by this "cramped" newcomer in Mayfair's Shepherd's Market – one of 2015's hottest tickets thanks to its "genial" service, "romantic" style, and Tomos Parry's "very different and impressive, yet un-fussy cooking". Top Menu Tip – "the burnt onion butter alone is worth a trip". / W1J 7QF; www.kittyfishers.com; @kittyfishers; 9.30 pm .

Koba W1 £42 333

11 Rathbone St 7580 8825 2–1C

"Fun for a change" – a Korean table-BBQ celebrating its 10th year, that makes a good introduction to the cuisine, and is consistently well-rated. / W1T 1NA; 11 pm; closed Sun L.

Koffmann's The Berkeley SW1 £86 553

The Berkeley, Wilton Pl 7107 8844 5–1D

"Masterful" veteran chef, Pierre Koffmann uses his "magic touch" to render "fabulous flavours from relatively humble ingredients" via an "old school", "gutsy" French menu at this Knightsbridge basement, where "wonderful" service helps enliven the potentially "sterile" interior. Top Menu Tip – "pistachio soufflé is an attraction in itself". / SW1X 7RL; www.the-berkeley.co.uk; @TheBerkeley; 10.30 pm; set weekday L £50 (FP), set pre-theatre £52 (FP).

Kolossi Grill EC1 £33 343

56-60 Rosebery Ave 7278 5758 9–1A

"Almost as good as a Greek holiday", say fans of this "cheap 'n' cheerful" taverna near Sadler's Wells – "ancient waiters" provide "a warm welcome" and the nosh has been "consistent over decades". / EC1R 4RR; www.kolossigrill.com; 11 pm; closed Sat L & Sun; set weekday L £17 (FP).

Konditor & Cook £22 332

Curzon Soho, 99 Shaftesbury Ave, W1 0844 854 9367 4–3A

46 Gray's Inn Rd, WC1 0844 854 9365 9–1A

10 Stoney St, SE1 0844 854 9363 9–4C

22 Cornwall Road, SE1 0844 854 9361 9–4A

30 St Mary Axe, EC3 0844 854 9369 9–2D

"Exquisite cakes", "top sarnies" and "fabulous" coffee are a particular danger at these "cramped" cafés – "I'd be fat as a barrel if I lived nearby!". / www.konditorandcook.com; 6 pm, W1 11 pm; WC1 & EC3 closed Sat & Sun; SE1 closed Sun; no booking.

Kopapa WC2 £65 222

32-34 Monmouth St 7240 6076 4–2B

For brunch especially, Peter Gordon's "busy" Pacific-fusion café in Theatreland is often recommended; one or two reporters really don't dig it though, describing "supposedly Maori-influenced" food that "sounds much better than it tastes". / WC2H 9HA; www.kopapa.co.uk; @Kopapacafe; 11 pm, Sun 9.45 pm; set pre theatre £42 (FP).

Koya-Bar W1 £34 444

50 Frith St 7434 4463 4–2A

Koya's gone, but its neighbouring atmospheric, if utilitarian bar sails on, serving "always interesting" udon noodle and donburi (rice-based) dishes; expansion beyond Soho is on the cards, with a spin-off planned for 2016. / W1D 4SQ; www.koyabar.co.uk; @KoyaBar; Mon-Wed 10.30 pm, Thu-Sat 11 pm, Sun 10 pm; no Amex.

Kricket Pop Brixton SW9 NEW £44

53 Brixton Station Rd no tel 10–1D

Part of a Brixton community project built around old freight containers and championing budding food and drink entrepreneurs – a new Indian-inspired concept mixing small plates and cocktails, that wins positive early reports. / SW9 8PQ; www.kricket.co.uk; @KricketBrixton; 10 pm.

Kulu Kulu £32 312

76 Brewer St, W1 7734 7316 3–2D

51-53 Shelton St, WC2 7240 5687 4–2C

39 Thurloe Pl, SW7 7589 2225 5–2C

"Don't go if you're a sushi aficionado", but "for a quick fix" these "old-timer" conveyor-cafés "tick every box for easy grub". / 10 pm, SW7 10.30 pm; closed Sun; no Amex; no booking.

Kurobuta £55 4 2 3

Harvey Nichols, Knightsbridge, SW1 7920 6440 5–1D NEW
312 King's Rd, SW3 3475 4158 5–3C
17-20 Kendal St, W2 3475 4158 6–1D
"Super oishi!" (as they say in Japan) – ex-Nobu supremo Scott Hallsworth's "funky, young and vibey" Izakayas have won fame with "amazing dishes, bursting with big bold flavours". Staff can be "overwhelmed" though, and his W2 branch dished up some "disastrous" meals this year, in contrast to his well-rated newcomer in SW3 (near his original pop-up). / www.kurobuta-london.com.

The Ladbroke Arms W11 £53 4 3 4

54 Ladbroke Rd 7727 6648 6–2B
"One of the prettiest pubs in London" – this fine Notting Hill tavern "never fails to come up trumps" with its "always delicious" food and "friendly" (if occasionally "disorganised") service; "try to get a table outside". / W11 3NW; www.capitalpubcompany.com; @ladbrokearms; 11 pm, Sun 10.30 pm; no booking at D.

The Lady Ottoline WC1 £50 3 3 3

11a Northington St 7831 0008 2–1D
Centrally located (Bloomsbury) yet somehow still feeling "tucked away", this handsomely restored Victorian pub is "more restaurant than boozer" with a "comforting", "seasonal" menu that's "not overly elaborate". / WC1N 2JF; www.theladyottoline.com; @theladyottoline; 10 pm, Sun 8 pm.

Lahore Karahi SW17 £23 4 1 2

1 Tooting High Street, London 8767 2477 10–2C
"Cheap thrills in Tooting" – even if service is "patchy", the food at this "buzzing", "no-frills" Pakistani canteen-landmark is worth queueing for; BYO. / SW17 0SN; www.lahorekarahi.co.uk; midnight; no Amex.

Lahore Kebab House £24 4 1 2

668 Streatham High Rd, SW16 8765 0771 10–2D
2-10 Umberston St, E1 7481 9737 11–1A
"A place of pilgrimage" for decades, this "noisy and frantic" Pakistani "bedlam" in Whitechapel is renowned for its "incredible food at incredible prices" (in particular its "stupendous lamb chops"); it provoked a couple of 'off' reports this year though – hopefully just a blip. It also has a well-rated, but much less well-known Streatham sibling. BYO. / midnight.

Lamberts SW12 £50 5 5 4

2 Station Pde 8675 2233 10–2C
"Approaching Chez Bruce standards but less expensive!" – this Balham neighbourhood favourite "hits all the right notes", with its "subtle" décor, "helpful" service and "unfailingly impressive" cooking that's "really exceptional value". / SW12 9AZ; www.lambertsrestaurant.com; @lamberts_balham; 10 pm, Sun 5 pm; closed Mon & Sun D; no Amex; set always available £36 (FP); SRA-3.*

(Winter Garden) The Landmark NW1 £78 2 3 4

222 Marylebone Rd 7631 8000 8–4A
The "formidable" Sunday brunch – with "unlimited champagne, live music and excellent food" – satisfies visitors to this "beautiful" Marylebone destination time and again, as does the ambience of the "wonderful, light atrium" with "lights twinkling in the trees". / NW1 6JQ; www.landmarklondon.co.uk; @landmarklondon; 10.15 pm; no trainers; booking: max 12; set always available £55 (FP).

Langan's Brasserie W1 £68 2 2 4

Stratton St 7491 8822 3–3C
With its "chatterbox-y" buzz, this famous and "delightfully furnished" old-timer, near The Ritz, is "a long time favourite" for its older fan club, in particular as an "impressive but laid back venue for business"; its culinary standards, however, have long been well "past it". / W1J 8LB; www.langansrestaurants.co.uk; @langanslondon; 11 pm, Fri & Sat 11.30 pm; closed Sun.

Lantana Cafe £35 3 3 3

13-14 Charlotte Pl, W1 7323 6601 2–1C
45 Middle Yd, Camden Lock Pl, NW1 7428 0421 8–2B NEW
Unit 2, 1 Oliver's Yd, 55 City Rd, EC1 7253 5273 12–1A
"Sweet mate!"; one of the first Aussie-style coffee bars to bring Antipodean-style brunching to the capital – the Fitzrovia side street original is still "the best" ("be prepared to queue at weekends"), but the "EC1 canteen for Shoreditch hipsters" is gaining fans too. / www.lantanacafe.co.uk.

Lardo £40 3 3 4

158 Sandringham Rd, E8 3021 0747 1–1D NEW
197-201 Richmond Rd, E8 8965 2683 1–2D
"Tattooed diners and china crockery" abound at this "classic Hackney hipster venue" near London Fields (now with nearby offshoot, Lardo Bebé) – but if you can withstand the beards and beanies then you'll enjoy "pizza with gravitas". / www.lardo.co.uk; @lardolondon.

Latium W1 £53 453
21 Berners St 7323 9123 3–1D
"There's nothing in your face" about Maurizio Morelli's "grown up" and "unpretentious" Fitzrovia favourite; "subtle" cooking ("awesome ravioli") is very professionally served in a "spacious" room that's "smart, if slightly austere". / W1T 3LP; www.latiumrestaurant.com; @LatiumLondon; 10.30 pm, Sat 11 pm; closed Sat L & Sun L.

Launceston Place W8 £79 454
1a Launceston Pl 7937 6912 5–1B
In a Kensington backstreet, this "very quiet and romantic" townhouse is a classic choice for an "intimate" date; it's currently on a high – "nothing seems too much trouble" for the "attentive" staff, and the cuisine has been consistently "excellent" in recent times – let's hope it survives the August 2015 departure of chef Tim Allen. / W8 5RL; www.launcestonplace-restaurant.co.uk; @LauncestonPlace; 10 pm, Sun 9.30 pm; closed Mon & Tue L; set weekday L £55 (FP), set Sun L £62 (FP).

THE LEDBURY W11 £133 555
127 Ledbury Rd 7792 9090 6–1B
"Brett Graham simply doesn't falter" at this "utterly brilliant" Notting Hill champion – yet again London's No. 1 foodie address thanks to his "adventurous" culinary creations "perfectly executed with panache". The "muted luxury" of the room is all part of an experience combining "subtle understated elegance, and care given to every detail". / W11 2AQ; www.theledbury.com; @theledbury; 9.45 pm; closed Mon L & Tue L; set weekday L £82 (FP).

Lemonia NW1 £45 245
89 Regent's Park Rd 7586 7454 8–3B
"What do they put in the water?" to drive the "terrific" buzz at this "always packed" Primrose Hill mega-taverna; "obliging" long-serving staff ("you feel like they know you") are key to its magic, but less so the Greek fodder – "I've complained about the boring, unchanging food since about 1975, but keep on going back!" / NW1 8UY; www.lemonia.co.uk; @Lemonia_Greek; 11 pm; closed Sun D; no Amex; set weekday L £29 (FP).

Leon £26 232
Branches throughout London
"Fast food as in quick, not cheap and nasty" – so say devotees of the "wholesome", "healthy" snacks at this much-lauded chain; no escaping, however, that a fair few old fans feel it's "losing its edge", offering "nothing overly exciting" these days. / www.leonrestaurants.co.uk; 10 pm, W1 8.45 pm, E14 8 pm; EC4 closed Sun, W1 closed Sat & Sun; no booking L.

Leong's Legends W1 £37 422
3 Macclesfield St 7287 0288 4–3A
"Wow those soup dumplings are good!" – Chinatown Taiwanese with "consistently interesting food, especially the signature Xiao Long Bao"; "you knock on the door to get in" – it's "not very comfortable, but who cares with tastes and flavours like this". / W1D 6AX; www.leongslegend.com; 11 pm, Sat 11.30 pm; no booking.

The Lido Café, Brockwell Lido SE24 £43 334
Dulwich Rd 7737 8183 10–2D
"It's fun watching the early swimmers" if you try the "wonderful breakfast" at this "relaxing" café, which enjoys "a lovely setting next to the Lido"; at other times the Mediterranean fare is "of a good standard and fairly priced" too. / SE24 0PA; www.thelidocafe.co.uk; @thelidocafe; 9.30 pm; closed Sun D; no Amex.

The Light House SW19 £56 222
75-77 Ridgway 8944 6338 10–2B
"Innovative dishes, from an ever-changing menu" still lead some fans to tip this airy ("noisy") fixture as "Wimbledon's premier dining experience"; "it's time for a shake-up" though – too many other reports suggest "it's lazy, and resting on its laurels". / SW19 4ST; www.lighthousewimbledon.com; 10.30 pm; closed Sun D.

Lima £65 332
31 Rathbone Pl, W1 3002 2640 2–1C
14 Garrick St, WC2 7240 5778 4–3C
"Sensational" ceviches and other "mind-blowing" Peruvian fare – with "unfamiliar ingredients" and "a bit of a kick" – quickly won renown for the Fitzrovia original, but both it, and its new Covent Garden ('Lima Floral') spin-off can suffer from seeming "over-hyped", not helped by slightly "soulless" decor. /

Linnea TW9 £50 443
Kew Green 8940 5696 1–3A
"Wonderful simple food, well presented" again wins lofty ratings for Jonas Karlsson's Kew Green yearling; but while fans "are amazed it's not more popular" there are quibbles – "the room is a little bleak", and the odd reporter finds prices "toppy". / TW9 3BH; www.linneakew.co.uk; 10 pm; closed Mon & Sun; set weekday L £30 (FP).

Lisboa Pâtisserie W10 £10 335
57 Golborne Rd 8968 5242 6–1A
"A trip to Portobello market is incomplete without a visit to this mythical café"; "it's like walking into somewhere in Lisbon itself", with "strong coffee, lots of chatter, and piles of heavenly, sticky sweet cakes". / W10 5NR; 7 pm; L & early evening only; no booking.

Little Bay £28 [2][3][5]

228 Belsize Rd, NW6 7372 4699 1–2B
171 Farringdon Rd, EC1 7278 1234 9–1A

"Its all about the ambience in these eccentric and outlandish theatre-themed bistros (just the right side of tacky)"; the food's not award-winning, but "it's so cheap and excellent for the price, there are never any complaints!" / www.little-bay.co.uk; @TheLittleBay; 11.30 pm, Sun 11 pm; no Amex, NW6 no credit cards.

Little Georgia Café £35 [3][3][4]

14 Barnsbury Rd, N1 7278 6100 8–3D
87 Goldsmiths Row, E2 7739 8154 1–2D

"The unusual combinations of flavours all seem to work", when it comes to the "solid Georgian cooking" at these "very cute" cafés, in Hackney and Islington. / www.littlegeorgia.co.uk; 10 pm.

Little Social W1 £76 [3][3][3]

5 Pollen St 7870 3730 3–2C

The "petite and cosy" style of this Mayfair mews haunt can make it seem a more "easygoing" choice than its showier sibling, Pollen Street Social, opposite; it too serves some "classy" and "clever" cooking, but like other Atherton places is drawing increasing flak for being "overpriced" and "underwhelming". / W1S 1NE; www.littlesocial.co.uk; @_littlesocial; 10.30 pm; closed Sun; set weekday L £48 (FP).

Lobster Pot SE11 £62 [4][3][3]

3 Kennington Ln 7582 5556 1–3C

An "idiosyncratic but charming", family-run stalwart in a "terrible" Kennington location, where you eat surrounded by engagingly "weird" nautical décor ("complete with seagull noises"); the overall effect is "very French", helped by the "splendid", "real" Breton fish and seafood. / SE11 4RG; www.lobsterpotrestaurant.co.uk; 10.30 pm; closed Mon & Sun; booking: max 8.

Locanda Locatelli Hyatt Regency W1 £78 [3][3][3]

8 Seymour St 7935 9088 2–2A

"Creative and expertly presented cuisine" has long made Giorgio Locatelli's "civilised" Marylebone dining room one of London's better-known Italian destinations; it is "hugely expensive" though, and while it feels "romantic" to some, it's "too corporate" for other tastes. / W1H 7JZ; www.locandalocatelli.com; @LocLocatelli; 11 pm, Thu-Sat 11.30 pm, Sun 10.15 pm; booking: max 8.

Locanda Ottomezzo W8 £67 [3][4][3]

2-4 Thackeray St 7937 2200 5–1B

"An excellent range of food and enthusiastic staff" help win praise for this Kensington Italian, whose "niche-y" interior is "somewhat cramped" but pleasantly "rustic". / W8 5ET; www.locandaottoemezzo.co.uk; 10.30 pm; closed Mon L, Sat L & Sun.

Loch Fyne £45 [2][2][3]

Branches throughout London

"You go knowing what to expect" to this fish and seafood franchise – even if the performance is rather "formulaic", there's "a very good range of options" and for "a decent meal in nice surroundings" it is "unexceptional but reliable". / www.lochfyne-restaurants.com; 10 pm, WC2 10.30 pm.

The Lockhart W1 £56 [2][2][2]

22-24 Seymour Pl 3011 5400 2–2A

"A different style of food for London" – "real American cooking" from the Deep South, served in an increasingly hip corner of Marylebone; fans love the "refined big flavours", but sceptics say dishes can "lack delicious-ness". Top Menu Tip – all agree on one thing: "the corn bread is phenomenal". / W1H 7NL; www.lockhartlondon.com; @LockhartLondon; 10 pm, Sun 3.30 pm; closed Mon & Sun D.

Lola Rojo SW11 £43 [4][3][4]

78 Northcote Rd 7350 2262 10–2C

"A fantastic Spanish spot" in Battersea, with a crisp modern interior, where "excellent tapas are creative yet authentic" and "superb value". / SW11 6QL; www.lolarojo.net; @LolaRojoSW11; 10.30 pm, Sat & Sun 11 pm; no Amex.

London House SW11 £62 [3][3][2]

7-9 Battersea Sq 7592 8545 10–1C

Gordon Ramsay's Battersea yearling splits opinion; fans say it's "an unexpected pleasure" with "stylish" looks and "complex and rich" cuisine – to sceptics though it's "missing that certain je ne sais quoi". / SW11 3RA; www.gordonramsay.com/london-house; @londonhouse; Tue-Fri 10 pm; closed Mon, Tue L & Wed L.

The Lord Northbrook SE12 £39 [4][4][4]

116 Burnt Ash Rd 8318 1127 1–4D

There's "a great community feel" to this large Lea Green hostelry which "underwent a 1000% makeover a few years ago"; "in an area lacking good eating options", it "always comes up trumps". / SE12 8PU; www.thelordnorthbrook.co.uk; @LordNorthbrook; 9 pm, Fri & Sat 10 pm.

Lorenzo SE19 £46 [2][2][3]

73 Westow Hill 7637 0871 1–4D

This "bustling", Italian local is an Upper Norwood "staple", liked for its "lively" style and "reasonable prices"; food-wise, it "can be disappointing nowadays", but most reports say it's still "reliable". Top Tip – avoid the "crowded and slightly claustrophobic basement". / SE19 1TX; www.lorenzo.uk.com; 10.30 pm.

Luce e Limoni WC1 £52 444
91-93 Gray's Inn Rd 7242 3382 9–1A
"Sister restaurant of nearby Fabrizio" in Bloomsbury, but "quieter" and more "high end"; it's a very solid all-rounder combining "a hugely congenial" interior with "welcoming" service and accomplished Sicilian food at "honest prices". / WC1X 8TX; www.luceelimoni.com; 10 pm, Fri-Sat 11 pm.

Lucio SW3 £68 333
257 Fulham Rd 7823 3007 5–3B
"Lucio is there to greet and meet" at his "friendly" Chelsea Italian, where the food and "excellent" wines are rather toppishly priced but "never fail to deliver". Top Tips – "amazing" pasta, and "incredible value" set lunch. / SW3 6HY; www.luciorestaurant.com; 10.45 pm; set weekday L £38 (FP).

The Lucky Pig Fulham SW6 NEW £50
374 North End Rd 7385 1300 5–4A
Regular music is a feature at this slightly glam new bar-cum-restaurant (a spin-off from a Fitzrovia cocktail den), occupying the large site that was once Sugar Hut (long RIP); no feedback yet for a rating. / SW6 1LY; www.theluckypig.co.uk; @LuckyPigFulham; midnight; set weekday L £29 (FP).

Lucky Seven W2 £35 333
127 Westbourne Park Rd 7727 6771 6–1B
Teleport yourself to '50s America at Tom Conran's vintage US diner, on the fringe of Notting Hill; expect to queue and share a booth, but its yummy burgers and shakes "justify the wait". / W2 5QL; www.lucky7london.co.uk; @Lucky7London; 10.15 pm, Sun 10 pm; no Amex; no booking.

Lupita WC2 £44 332
13-15 Villiers St 7930 5355 4–4D
For a "snappy" bite right in the heart of town – an "unpretentious and good value" Mexican, with "unusual" and "authentic" dishes – a "surprise find" in the grungy, touristy environs of Charing Cross station. / WC2N 6ND; www.lupita.co.uk; @LupitaUK; 11 pm, Fri & Sat 11.30 pm, Sun 10 pm.

Luppolo E11 NEW £32
34-38 High St 8530 8528 1–1D
Deriving its name from the Italian word for hops – a new Wanstead pizzeria specialising in craft beers, including their own-brand pale ale. / E11 2RJ; www.luppolopizza.com; @LuppoloWanstead; 11 pm, Sun 10.30 pm.

Lure NW5 £40 433
56 Chetwynd Rd 7267 0163 8–1B
"A beautiful range of fish, and some interesting sides" have won instant raves for this Aussie-run, "upmarket chippy with a twist" – "a welcome arrival" to Dartmouth Park. / NW5 1DJ; www.lurefishkitchen.co.uk; 10 pm.

Lurra W1 NEW £52
9 Seymour Pl 7724 4545 2–2A
Just as this guide went to the printers, a sister to the highly-esteemed Donostia in Marble Arch opened up nearby, offering food from the 'erretegia' (charcoal and wood grills, traditional to the Basque Country). / W1H 5BA; www.lurra.co.uk; @LurraW1.

Lutyens EC4 £74 222
85 Fleet St 7583 8385 9–2A
As "a very solid business lunch venue", Sir Terence Conran's "smart" City-fringe brasserie is a reasonably "classy" choice; given its "antiseptic" ambience and cuisine that's "OK, but no more", there's no other reason to seek it out. / EC4Y 1AE; www.lutyens-restaurant.com; @LutyensEC4; 9.45 pm; closed Sat & Sun.

Lyle's E1 £66 553
The Tea Building, 56 Shoreditch High St 3011 5911 12–1B
"The food speaks for itself" – "memorable" combinations, sourced "with real care", prepared with "passion" and presented "with a lack of hype" – when you visit this agreeably "austere" and "honest" Shoreditch yearling (founded by alumni of St John). / E1 6JJ; www.lyleslondon.com; @lyleslondon; 10 pm; closed Sat L & Sun.

M Restaurants £74 433
Zig Zag Building, Victoria St, SW1 3327 7770 2–4B NEW
2-3 Threadneedle Walk, EC2 3327 7770 9–2C
Ex-Gaucho supremo, Martin Williams, is the man behind this large, extremely ambitious City entertaining complex, incorporating a sushi-to-ceviche 'Raw' restaurant, alongside a more familiar 'Grill', the latter acclaimed for its formidable selection of steaks; to critics it can all seem "too like Las Vegas", but fans – particularly for a "discreet" business occasion – say it's "wonderful". A Victoria outpost is due to open in November 2015. / www.mrestaurants.co.uk.

Ma Cuisine TW9 £43 222
9 Station Approach 8332 1923 1–3A
"No effort to be modern or fashionable" is a plus-point for fans of this "'70s-style bistro throwback", near Kew Gardens station; sceptics say "it owes its popularity to a lack of local oppo'", but most reporters applaud its "timeless" appeal and "reasonable prices". / TW9 3QB; www.macuisinekew.co.uk; @MaCuisineKew; 10 pm, Fri & Sat 10.30 pm; no Amex.

Ma Goa SW15 **£40** 4 4 2
242-244 Upper Richmond Rd 8780 1767 10–2B
"There's a good reason it's been around for years!" – this family-run, "hidden gem" in Putney has "charming" service and "offbeat Indian home cooking" featuring "distinctly Goan flavours" at "great prices"; it's not quite as highly rated as it once was though. / SW15 6TG; www.ma-goa.com; @magoarestaurant; 10.30 pm, Fri-Sat 11 pm, Sun 10pm.

MacellaioRC SW7 **£52** 5 3 4
84 Old Brompton Rd 7589 5834 5–2B
"Knocking more macho steak houses into a cock hat" – this offbeat grill occupies an Italian butcher's shop in South Kensington, where "an enthusiastic owner" serves "the best steaks ever", and where the ingenious wine list is arranged according to how rare or well done you like your meat. Staff can be a tad "patronising" though – "Italians who assume we all live on Spam and Sunblest!" / SW7 3LQ; www.macellaiorc.com; @MaxelaUk; 11 pm.

Made In Camden, Roundhouse NW1 **£44** 2 2 2
Chalk Farm Rd 7424 8495 8–2B
"For a casual meal after the Roundhouse (in whose entrance it's located)", this well-designed bar/dining room is ideal; but while its cooking can come as "a pleasant surprise", it's not as highly-rated as once it was. / NW1 8EH; www.madeincamden.com; 10.15 pm.

Made in Italy **£40** 3 3 3
50 James St, W1 7224 0182 3–1A
249 King's Rd, SW3 7352 1880 5–3C
"Excellent pizzas" (served by the metre), "switched on" service and "good VFM" continue to impress at this small Italian chain; as always the "buzzy King's Road classic" is tops (but SW19 also got a thumbs up this year). / www.madeinitalygroup.co.uk; 11 pm, Sun 10 pm; SW3 closed Mon L.

Madhu's UB1 **£36** 4 3 3
39 South Rd 8574 1897 1–3A
A legendary Southall curry house, whose "minimalist interior makes a refreshing change from typical chintz", and which provides "friendly" service and high-quality cooking; (it's part of an eponymous empire incorporating outside catering, and a branch at the Sheraton Skyline Heathrow). / UB1 1SW; www.madhus.co.uk; 11.30 pm; closed Tue, Sat L & Sun L.

The Magazine Restaurant Serpentine Gallery W2 **£57** 3 4 5
Kensington Gdns 7298 7552 6–2D
"If you want something a bit different for a romantic meal", Zaha Hadid's "sleek" structure, leafily located in Hyde Park, is "a very pleasant place to eat, drink and while away time", and the food's not bad either. / W2 2AR; www.magazine-restaurant.co.uk; @TheMagazineLDN; Tue & Sun 6 pm, Wed-Sat 10.45 pm; closed Mon, Tue D & Sun D.

Magdalen SE1 **£55** 4 4 3
152 Tooley St 7403 1342 9–4D
"An oasis in a desert of mediocrity around London Bridge" – this "grown up" gem has won a strong following over the years with its "unobtrusive" service, "understated" style, and – last but not least – its "rich and complex" cuisine (emphasising meat and offal), matched with "lovely" wine. / SE1 2TU; www.magdalenrestaurant.co.uk; @Magdalense1; 10 pm; closed Sat L & Sun; set weekday L £37 (FP).

Maggie Jones's W8 **£55** 2 3 5
6 Old Court Pl 7937 6462 5–1A
With its "intimate wooden booths and rustic fare" (in "hearty portions"), this "quirky" hideaway, near Kensington Palace (named for the pseudonym Princess Margaret used to book under) is "one of the cosiest restaurants in London". It's fair to say, however, that the cooking is a little "'70s-bistro... and that's not a compliment". / W8 4PL; www.maggie-jones.co.uk; 11 pm, Sun 10.30 pm.

Maguro W9 **£38** 3 4 3
5 Lanark Pl 7289 4353 8–4A
A "tiny" Maida Vale Japanese, serving "delicious" sushi and other fare; "it's clearly doing something right as it's always busy and buzzy". / W9 1BT; www.maguro-restaurant.com; 11 pm, Sun 10.30 pm; no Amex.

Maison Bertaux W1 **£16** 4 2 3
28 Greek St 7437 6007 4–2A
"So oblivious of trends and fashions"; "there's nowhere else like" this "eccentric" Soho treasure (est 1871) – "just a great place to sit for a really good, big cup of black coffee and a croissant or cake". / W1D 5DQ; www.maisonbertaux.com; @Maison_Bertaux; 10.15 pm, Sun 8 pm.

Malabar W8 **£42** 4 4 2
27 Uxbridge St 7727 8800 6–2B
"Going great guns after over 25 years" – this curry house just off Notting Hill Gate is "a neighbourhood classic", and, though its "graceful", "modern" décor is a tad "soulless", service is "charming" and the cooking is "very strong". / W8 7TQ; www.malabar-restaurant.co.uk; 11.30 pm.

Malabar Junction WC1 £41 343
107 Gt Russell St 7580 5230 2–1C
"Don't be fooled by the modest entrance" if you seek out this calming Keralan, near the British Museum – even those who find the interior "hotel-y" approve of its "very attentive" service and high-quality South Indian fare. / WC1B 3NA; www.malabarjunction.com; 11 pm.

Mamma Dough £28 333
76-78 Honor Oak Pk, SE23 8699 5196 1–4D NEW
354 Coldharbour Ln, SW9 7095 1491 10–1D NEW
The Honor Oak Park original may be "overrun by children with beardy fathers – but the pizzas make it worth it!", as do the "brilliant staff"; a Brixton branch opened in September 2015. /

Mandalay W2 £30 221
444 Edgware Rd 7258 3696 8–4A
"Scuzzy in looks, but packed for a reason!" – the Ally family's "small and friendly" shop-conversion, near Edgware Road tube still draws a crowd thanks to its "fresh and inexpensive" Burmese chow (think Indian meets Chinese). / W2 1EG; www.mandalayway.com; 10.30 pm; closed Sun.

Mandarin Kitchen W2 £41 422
14-16 Queensway 7727 9012 6–2C
"Very busy" and "very crowded" Bayswater Chinese, famous for its seafood, and in particular its "succulent" lobster noodles; what a loss though – the hilariously bad décor "had a bit of a spruce up" this year. / W2 3RX; 11.15 pm.

Mangal 1 E8 £31 544
10 Arcola St 7275 8981 1–1C
"The smell alone gets my vote!" – "the huge, roaring furnace of a charcoal grill" produces some of London's best kebabs at this "consistently brilliant" Turk, which was a cheap 'n' cheerful, cross-town destination long before Dalston was trendy; "BYO is a bonus". / E8 2DJ; www.mangal1.com; @Mangalone; midnight, Sat & Sun 1 am; no credit cards.

Mangal II N16 £35 432
4 Stoke Newington Rd 7254 7888 1–1C
Although less acclaimed than the nearby original, this Dalston spin-off "continues to excel in Turkish grills and salads in an area with many competitors" – "it is what it is, but it's always fun, always consistent". / N16 8BH; www.mangal2.com; 1 am, Sun midnight.

Manicomio £60 223
85 Duke of York Sq, SW3 7730 3366 5–2D
6 Gutter Ln, EC2 7726 5010 9–2B
"The best al-fresco dining" – particularly at SW3 – is a major boost to the popularity of these "safe, if pretty unremarkable" Italians, ideal for a light lunch over business (in the City) or "as a hideaway for a break from shopping" (in Chelsea). / www.manicomio.co.uk; SW3 10.30 pm, Sun 10 pm; EC2 10 pm; EC2 closed Sat & Sun.

Manna NW3 £57 332
4 Erskine Rd 7722 8028 8–3B
The UK's oldest veggie is an obscure little café in Primrose Hill; reports from its tiny fan club are all upbeat though – they say it's "enjoying a new lease of life", with "great vegan dishes". / NW3 3AJ; www.mannav.com; @mannacuisine; 10 pm; closed Mon.

The Manor SW4 £57 543
148 Clapham Manor St 7720 4662 10–2D
With the opening of this "stellar" new sibling to the nearby Dairy, this "underwhelming corner of Clapham" now has two stand-out venues; "genuinely passionate" staff provide "terrific" small plates that are "ingenious without being daft" in a "designer-grungy" setting. Top Menu Tip – "incredible tasting menu here" too. / SW4 6BS; www.themanorclapham.co.uk; @TheManorClapham; 10 pm, Sun 4pm.

Manuka Kitchen SW6 £45 444
510 Fulham Rd 7736 7588 5–4A
With its "concise but perfect" wine list, "exceptional quality" menu and overall "incredible value", this "tiny" New Zealand-inspired two-year-old in Fulham is already a firm favourite, with brunch a particular highlight; don't forget to check out the downstairs gin bar. / SW6 5NJ; www.manukakitchen.co.uk; @ManukaKitchen; 11 pm, Sun 5 pm.

Mar I Terra SE1 £31 232
14 Gambia St 7928 7628 9–4A
"A very unpretentious, friendly and reliable, hidden-away Spanish place", near Southwark tube, praised for its "authentic", if "basic", tapas and other fare. / SE1 0XH; www.mariterra.co.uk; 11 pm; closed Sat L & Sun.

Marcus The Berkeley SW1 £118 2 3 2

Wilton Pl 7235 1200 5–1D

Since its March 2014 refit, Marcus Wareing's celebrated Knightsbridge chamber has lost its momentum. Fans do still extol a "completely fabulous" experience with "cracking" cuisine, but even they often note how "expensive" it is. And there are now far too many critics – citing a "pompous" approach and cooking "lacking wow factor" – who say its prices are plain "outrageous". / SW1X 7RL; www.marcus-wareing.com; @Marcussw1; 10.45 pm; closed Sun; no jeans or trainers; booking: max 8; set weekday L £82 (FP).

Margaux SW5 £64 3 2 3

152 Old Brompton Rd 7373 5753 5–2B

"A good addition to Earl's Court" – a "bare-brick" local yearling, with "delicious" cooking and an enjoyable wine selection. See also Bandol. / SW5 0BE; www.barmargaux.co.uk; @BarMargaux; 11 pm, Sun 10 pm.

Mari Vanna SW1 £70 2 3 4

116 Knightsbridge 7225 3122 5–1D

"The splendid recreation of a Russian interior" ("like your rich grandma's beautiful dacha") is a highpoint of this luxurious Knightsbridge haunt; the "very expensive" Russian scoff is middling, but "add vodka in all its varieties" and the experience can be "fun". / SW1X 7PJ; www.marivanna.co.uk; @marivannalondon; 11.30 pm.

Marianne W2 £122 4 5 4

104 Chepstow Rd 3675 7750 6–1B

Marianne Lumb's "tiny treasure" (just 14 covers) in Bayswater is "an absolute joy that's worth every penny!", with "passionate" personal service, and "confident", "exquisite" cooking, which create a "wonderfully intimate" experience; "it's easier to get into Downing Street than to reserve" though. / W2 5QS; www.mariannerestaurant.com; @Marianne_W2; 11 pm; closed Mon.

Market NW1 £50 3 3 2

43 Parkway 7267 9700 8–3B

"We envy the locals!", say further-afield fans of this well-established brasserie in the centre of Camden Town; "the tables are almost on top of one another", but it's "buzzy and fun", and the cooking's "really good, honest fare". / NW1 7PN; www.marketrestaurant.co.uk; @MarketCamden; 10.30 pm, Sun 3 pm; closed Sun D; set weekday L £30 (FP).

The Marksman E2 NEW £50

254 Hackney Rd 7739 7393 1–2D

There's some pedigree behind this freshly refitted and relaunched Hackney pub with Tom Harris and Jon Rotheram – alumni of the St John Hotel, Nobu and Fifteen – at the helm; we await the survey, for a full report next year. / E2 7SJ; www.marksmanpub.com; @marksman_pub; midnight, Sun 11 pm.

Maroush £53 3 2 2

I) 21 Edgware Rd, W2 7723 0773 6–1D
II) 38 Beauchamp Pl, SW3 7581 5434 5–1C
V) 3-4 Vere St, W1 7493 5050 3–1B
VI) 68 Edgware Rd, W2 7224 9339 6–1D
'Garden') 1 Connaught St, W2 7262 0222 6–1D

"Consistent quality over numerous years" has won a big following for this well-known Lebanese chain, some of whose branches (I & II) have bustling café/take-aways alongside more serious restaurants; especially at the latter however, "the décor could be fresher". Top Menu Tip – in the cafés, if you're on a budget, ask for the menu of wraps. / www.maroush.com; most branches close between 12.30 am-5 am.

Masala Grill SW10 NEW £54 4 4 4

535 King's Rd 7351 7788 5–4B

Though in a simpler vein, "standards are being maintained at the former Chutney Mary"; this new Indian (same owners) offers "a different slant to the original on the site" but is "very professional" with some "excellent and unusual" dishes. / SW10 0SZ; www.masalagrill.co.

Masala Zone £32 2 3 3

Branches throughout London

"For a quick, cheap 'n' cheerful meal", this "bustling", "interestingly decorated", Indian-street-food chain is just the job, with its "good-value thalis" and other "simple" fare; WC2 in particular is "ideal pre-theatre". / www.realindianfood.com; 11 pm, Sun 10.30 pm; no Amex; booking: min 10.

MASH Steakhouse W1 £83 2 2 1

77 Brewer St 7734 2608 3–2D

No-one doubts the quality of the meat at this "swanky" steakhouse, "deep underground" near Piccadilly Circus; it's so "overpriced" it can seem "average" however, and the "cavernous" interior is "too large" and "brash". / W1F 9ZN; www.mashsteak.co.uk; @mashsteaklondon; 11.30 pm, Sun 11 pm; closed Sun L.

Massimo, Corinthia Hotel WC2 £76 243
10 Northumberland Ave 7998 0555 2–3D
Few chambers boast such dazzlingly OTT décor as this luxurious five-star dining room, near Embankment tube; its "high-end Italian fare" has always struggled to find a constituency, but fans say "the pre-theatre meal is a great experience". / WC2N 5AE; www.corinthia.com; @massimorest; 10.45 pm; closed Sun; set weekday L £55 (FP).

Masters Super Fish SE1 £25 422
191 Waterloo Rd 7928 6924 9–4A
"Queues of parked cabs while drivers grab a refuel say all you need to know" about the "terrific" fish 'n' chips at this "basic" SE1 pit-stop – "the wonderfully light batter and perfectly crispy chips are a thing of joy, while the mustard-crust option is ideal for carb-avoiders". / SE1 8UX; @MSuperfish; 10.30 pm; closed Sun; no Amex; no booking, Fri D.

Matsuba TW9 £46 443
10 Red Lion St 8605 3513 1–4A
"A small room" hosts this "independent Japanese" on the fringes of Richmond town centre; its sushi and other Japanese/Korean fare is "decent rather than great", but there's no doubting that it's "a real treat for the 'burbs". / TW9 1RW; www.matsuba-restaurant.com; @matsuba; 10.30 pm; closed Sun.

Matsuri SW1 £85 331
15 Bury St 7839 1101 3–3D
"Great teppanyaki in the traditional style" is an "entertaining experience" (especially for a business occasion) at this pricey St James's Japanese; not so the "drab" interior however. / SW1Y 6AL; www.matsuri-restaurant.com; @MatsuriJ; 10.30 pm, Sun 10 pm.

Max's Sandwich Shop N4 NEW £20 422
19 Crouch Hill awaiting tel 1–1C
Not your traditional sandwich shop; this Crouch Hill creation serves hot sarnies and boozy cocktails till midnight – "not flashy, but highly underrated!". / N4 4AP; @lunchluncheon; 11 pm, Sun 6 pm.

Mayfair Pizza Company W1 NEW £47 334
4 Lancashire Ct 7629 2889 3–2B
"Tucked away" in a cute enclave off Bond Street, a "lovely pizza spot" (formerly a branch of Rocket) that's "consistently good value for Mayfair". / W1S 1EY; www.mayfairpizzaco.com; 11 pm .

maze W1 £84 222
10-13 Grosvenor Sq 7107 0000 3–2A
It seems a long time since this Gordon Ramsay operation in Mayfair was the talk of the town; fans do still proclaim its "well-executed fusion combinations", but oftentimes reporters think it's borderline "awful", and "hugely overpriced". / W1K 6JP; www.gordonramsay.com/maze; @mazerestaurant; 11 pm; set always available £56 (FP).

maze Grill W1 £76 222
10-13 Grosvenor Sq 7495 2211 3–2A
Gordon Ramsay's Mayfair grill room is a shadow of its former self nowadays, attracting few and mixed reports; but while too many critics still gripe about the cooking ("rubbish") or the prices ("really??!!"), more positive types say its steaks and sides are "reliably good" and that it makes "a discreet venue for business". / W1K 6JP; www.gordonramsay.com; @mazegrill; 11 pm; no shorts; set always available £50 (FP).

maze Grill SW10 £74 222
11 Park Wk 7255 9299 5–3B
Gordon Ramsay's return to the Chelsea site where he earnt his stripes (when it was Aubergine) – a new offshoot of his maze brand – is a bit of a damp squib; fans do say it's "lovely", with "excellent steak", but feedback is muted, and even supporters say "it's highly priced for what's only good execution". / SW10 0AJ; www.gordonramsay.com/mazegrill/park-walk; @mazegrill; 11 pm; set always available £47 (FP).

Mazi W8 £62 334
12-14 Hillgate St 7229 3794 6–2B
"Sophisticated Greek-inspired cooking with a twist" has won quite a fan club for this "cheap 'n' cheerful" (quite cramped) two-year-old, off Notting Hill Gate. / W8 7SR; www.mazi.co.uk; @mazinottinghill; 10.30 pm; closed Mon L & Tue L; set weekday L £34 (FP).

Meat Mission N1 £33 334
14-15 Hoxton Mkt 7739 8212 12–1B
"When a dirty burger is required", you're "up to your elbows in deliciousness" at this "cracking" Hoxton Square operation (part of the 'Meat' franchise); it's "fun" (if "noisy") too. / N1 6HG; www.meatmission.com; @MEATmission; midnight, Sun 10 pm.

MEATLiquor £38 324
74 Welbeck St, W1 7224 4239 3–1B
133b Upper St, N1 awaiting tel 8–3D NEW
The self-consciously "dingy", "so-loud" vibe – "like a cross between a biker bar and a branch of Hollisters" – underpins the "hip" appeal of these notorious dives; "the long queues are justified" though for a fix of the "brill cocktails", "lovely dirty burgers" and other cholesterol-laden treats.

MEATmarket WC2 **£30** 4 2 2
Jubilee Market Hall, 1 Tavistock Ct 7836 2139 4–3D
"Forget the fakery of crinkly sided food trucks with old Etonian owners" – for "a rough and ready, but brilliant burger", this "honest" Covent Garden joint makes a superb "guilty treat"; "great rum cocktails too". / WC2E 8BD; www.themeatmarket.co.uk; @MEATLiquor; midnight, Sun 10 pm; no Amex.

Mediterraneo W11 **£60** 3 3 4
37 Kensington Park Rd 7792 3131 6–1A
Even devotees concede this "long-time favourite" in Notting Hill is "a bit dear for a local", but they say it's "worth it" thanks to its "warm, lively and intimate" atmosphere, and "traditional Italian fare that's very well done". / W11 2EU; www.mediterraneo-restaurant.co.uk; 11.30 pm, Sun 10.30 pm; booking: max 10.

Medlar SW10 **£71** 4 4 3
438 King's Rd 7349 1900 5–3B
"Well-hidden in the red-trouser-wearing Chelsea hinterlands", this unexpectedly accomplished neighbourhood spot (run by some alumni of Chez Bruce) has won an impressive fan club. Perhaps the interior is a tad "subdued", but staff are "incredibly friendly and efficient", the "sensitive" cooking is "stunning", and there's a "remarkably varied" wine list. Top Tip – "amazing value lunch". / SW10 0LJ; www.medlarrestaurant.co.uk; @medlarchelsea; 10.30 pm; set Sun L £0 (FP), set weekday L £51 (FP).

Megan's **£45** 2 2 4
571 Kings Rd, SW6 7371 7837 5–4A
120 St John's Wood High St, NW8 7183 3138 8–3A
"The enchanting, tucked-away covered garden keeps us going back for more", but the provisions at this Chelsea neighbourhood haunt – which now also has a very cute St John's Wood spin off – has "lost a little sparkle since its change of management". / www.megans.co.uk.

Mele e Pere W1 **£50** 3 3 3
46 Brewer St 7096 2096 3–2D
"Why is it not more popular?"; this (slightly "dull-looking") Soho basement is "worth knowing about in this bit of town" – the food's "reliable" and "reasonably priced" and it's "noisy" but "great fun". Top Menu Tips – "to-die-for gelatos", "Prosecco on tap", and an interesting list of vermouths. / W1F 9TF; www.meleepere.co.uk; @meleEpere; 11 pm; set weekday L £31 (FP).

The Melt Room W1 NEW **£18**
26 Noel St 7096 2002 3–1D
Single concept restaurants are all the rage, but perhaps we have reached the fashion's ne plus ultra with this May 2015 Soho arrival? – a restaurant dedicated to the art of the cheese toastie! / W1F 8GY; www.meltroom.com; @melt_room; 9 pm, Sun 6.30 pm.

Menier Chocolate Factory SE1 **£52** 1 2 3
51-53 Southwark St 7234 9610 9–4B
"Excellent-value, meal-and-show ticket deals" are the way to go at this intriguing South Bank venue, which combines a restaurant and small theatre; otherwise "you wouldn't make the trip" for its "no-frills" fodder from a "limited" menu. / SE1 1RU; www.menierchocolatefactory.com; @MenChocFactory; 11 pm; closed Mon & Sun D.

The Mercer EC2 **£62** 2 2 2
34 Threadneedle St 7628 0001 9–2C
"There's elbow room to talk shop" at this "airy", City "staple" – a converted banking hall, in the heart of the Square Mile, with a "very strong business clientele"; its ratings have drifted though – the "broadly British" food is "OK, but nothing special", and service "patchy at times". / EC2R 8AY; www.themercer.co.uk; 9.30 pm; closed Sat & Sun.

Merchants Tavern EC2 **£58** 3 3 4
36 Charlotte Rd 7060 5335 12–1B
Angela Hartnett's "superbly buzzy and attractive" Shoreditch two-year-old – complete with large open kitchen – continues to draw enthusiastic praise for its "relaxed" vibe and "unpretentious and delicious" (if sometimes "variable") cooking. Top Tip – superior quick bites in the front bar. / EC2A 3PG; www.merchantstavern.co.uk; @merchantstavern; 11 pm, Sun 9 pm; set weekday L £38 (FP), set Sun L £43 (FP).

Le Mercury N1 **£32** 2 3 4
154-155 Upper St 7704 8516 8–2D
"No frills", but "cosy" bistro that's been a "cheap 'n' cheerful" Islington institution for as long as most people can remember; the scoff is only "standard French fare", but "for the price you can't beat it". / N1 1QY; www.lemercury.co.uk; @Le_Mercury; midnight, Sun 11 pm; Mon-Thu D only, Fri-Sun open L & D.

Meson don Felipe SE1 **£40** 2 2 3
53 The Cut 7928 3237 9–4A
A "very old-school, and over-crowded tapas bar, with haphazard service"; "excellent, keenly-priced wines" add to an overall effect that's surprisingly pleasing (especially when the Flamenco guitarist is playing) and it's "a really fun place to eat around a show at the Old Vic". / SE1 8LF; www.mesondonfelipe.com; @MesonDonFelipe1; 11 pm; closed Sun; no Amex; no booking at D.

Mews of Mayfair W1 £68 234
10 Lancashire Ct, New Bond St 7518 9388 3–2B
Luscious cocktails fuel the "great buzz" at this well-located Mayfair haunt, tucked-away just off Bond Street, and with "lovely outside tables in summer"; the food though is "pretty average" and (unless you go on an offer) "pricey" too. / W1S 1EY; www.mewsofmayfair.com; @mewsofmayfair; 10.45 pm; closed Sun D; SRA-3.*

Meza £30 532
34 Trinity Rd, SW17 0772 211 1299 10–2C
70 Mitcham Rd, SW17 8672 2131 10–2C
"The cat is well and truly out of the bag on this one!" – this "teeny-tiny" Tooting Lebanese is permanently "full to bursting" thanks to its "hospitable" style, and "simple", but "unfailingly good", mezze and other "delicious" fare at "startlingly cheap" prices. There's now a second site nearby. /

Michael Nadra £57 432
6-8 Elliott Rd, W4 8742 0766 7–2A
42 Gloucester Ave, NW1 7722 2800 8–2B
Michael Nadra's "first class" modern French cuisine wins high acclaim for both his very "cramped" Chiswick original, and also for his cavernous two-year-old spin-off in Camden Town; NW1 isn't quite as well-rated or well-known as W4, but more worth knowing about in the locale. / www.restaurant-michaelnadra.co.uk; @michaelnadra; W4 10 pm, Fri-Sat 10.30 pm, NW1 10.30 pm, Sun 9 pm; NW1 closed Mon, W4 closed Sun.

Mien Tay £31 311
180 Lavender Hill, SW11 7350 0721 10–1C
122 Kingsland Rd, E2 7729 3074 12–1B
"Massive bowls of pho and two can eat until stuffed for about £20" – that's the attraction of these "busy and buzzy" pitstops in Battersea and Shoreditch; the trade-offs are "shabby" décor and "perfunctory" service. / 11 pm, Fri & Sat 11.30 pm, Sun 10.30 pm; cash only.

Mildreds W1 £42 332
45 Lexington St 7494 1634 3–2D
"Reliable", "buzzy" veggie canteen that's something of a Soho institution; it serves "hearty food that really fills you up", "if you don't mind a queue..." / W1F 9AN; www.mildreds.co.uk; @mildredssoho; 10.45 pm; closed Sun; no Amex; no booking.

Milk SW12 £14 444
20 Bedford Hill 8772 9085 10–2C
"So lucky to have this great independent in Balham" – a "little (and I do mean little)" caff serving "amazing coffee and inspirational all-day brunch"; "you inevitably queue, but it's worth the wait". / SW12 9RG; www.milk.london.

Mill Lane Bistro NW6 £53 232
77 Mill Ln 7794 5577 1–1B
Mixed reports of late on this "little bit of France in West Hampstead", whose repertoire includes "Full French Breakfast"; to many it's still "an all-round great local", but a worrying number this year were "totally underwhelmed". / NW6 1NB; www.milllanebistro.com; @millanebistro; 10 pm; closed Mon & Sun D; no Amex.

Min Jiang, The Royal Garden Hotel W8 £77 435
2-24 Kensington High St 7361 1988 5–1A
"Peking duck to die for", "fantastic dim sum", and "a superb panorama as a bonus" – that's the "rare combination" at this 8th-floor dining room overlooking Kensington Gardens, which – as one of London's top Chinese destinations – breaks all the rules for rooms with a view. / W8 4PT; www.minjiang.co.uk; @royalgdnhotel; 10 pm.

Mint Leaf £51 332
Suffolk Pl, Haymarket, SW1 7930 9020 2–2C
Angel Ct, Lothbury, EC2 7600 0992 9–2C
The low profile of these designer Indians – in a "dim-lit" basement near Trafalgar Square, and near Bank – is at odds with the big sums lavished on their slick décor; feedback is thin but upbeat – the food's "not cheap" but "very well prepared", and they serve "great bar snacks along with full meals". / www.mintleafrestaurant.com; SW1 11 pm, Sun 10.30 pm – EC2 10.30 pm; SW1 closed Sat & Sun L, EC2 closed Sat & Sun.

Mirch Masala SW17 £25 521
213 Upper Tooting Rd 8767 8638 10–2D
"You get no pretentions, just great flavours" at this "high turnover", "café-style Pakistani" in Tooting, serving "really tasty food at incredible prices". / SW17 7TG; www.mirchmasalarestaurant.co.uk; midnight; no credit cards.

Mishkin's WC2 £43 123
25 Catherine St 7240 2078 4–3D
"They wouldn't know their challah from their cholent" at Russell Norman's "trendy" Covent Garden diner; admittedly "it's no small trick making Jewish food cool", but its "deli treats" are "lacklustre" and "couldn't be much less authentic". / WC2B 5JS; www.mishkins.co.uk; @MishkinsWC2; 11.15 pm, Sun 10.15 pm.

Mission E2 NEW £55 234
250 Paradise Row 7613 0478 12–1D
"What a list! What a venue!" – the team behind Sager + Wilde have created a "fantastic" new space, in this Bethnal Green railway arch, where the focus is on a "brilliant and interesting wine selection" dominated by Californian vintages; the sharing plates? – a mite "unremarkable". / E2 9LE; missione2.com; @mission-e2; midnight.

The Modern Pantry £58 334
47-48 St Johns Sq, EC1 7553 9210 9–1A
14 Finsbury Sq, EC2 7553 9210 12–2A NEW
"You could be in Sydney", say fans of the "exciting combinations" at Anna Hansen's foodie hotspot in Clerkenwell, known particularly as a top brunch destination; critics complain of "bland" results though, and say the interior's "not the most luxurious". New City-fringe branch opened in September 2015. / www.themodernpantry.co.uk; @TheModernPantry; SRA-3.*

MOMMI SW4 NEW £39
44 Clapham High St 3814 1818 10–2D
Another Japanese–South American fusion hang-out, this time in Clapham; it opened too late for our survey, but apparently marries the 'vibrancy of Miami and the eclecticism of Venice Beach'. / SW4 7UR; www.wearemommi.com; @wearemommi; 11 pm, Thu-Sun midnight.

Momo W1 £69 223
25 Heddon St 7434 4040 3–2C
"Lovely" (if "loud and squashed") souk-style, glam-crowd, party-Moroccan, off Regent Street, with a vibey basement bar, and "great summer terrace"; service is very "variable" however, and the food is "totally overpriced" and "just not worth it..." / W1B 4BH; www.momoresto.com; @momoresto; 11.30 pm, Sun 11 pm.

Mon Plaisir WC2 £59 224
19-21 Monmouth St 7836 7243 4–2B
This "delightful" 70-year-old, Gallic veteran in Covent Garden, is "a staunch friend" to its big, devoted following; especially compared with yesteryear however, the "classic" brasserie fare is "never going to set the world alight", but it's certainly still "good value pre-theatre". / WC2H 9DD; www.monplaisir.co.uk; @MonPlaisir4; 11 pm; closed Sun; set pre-theatre £32 (FP), set weekday L £33 (FP).

Mona Lisa SW10 £28 332
417 King's Rd 7376 5447 5–3B
"It's cheap as chips, so long as you don't stray from the set offer", at this veteran World's End greasy spoon, whose ace three-courses-for-a-tenner evening deal draws in a 'dukes-to-dustmen' clientele. / SW10 0LR; 11 pm, Sun 5.30 pm; closed Sun D; no Amex.

Monmouth Coffee Company £12 554
27 Monmouth St, WC2 7232 3010 4–2B
Arches Northside, Dockley Rd, SE16 7232 3010 9–4D
2 Park St, SE1 7232 3010 9–4C
The coffee is "a miracle" – and "there's a wonderful range" too (plus "super" pastries, and at SE1 "fabulous bread 'n' jam") – at these "totally friendly", if "crowded" communal café-classics. / www.monmouthcoffee.co.uk; 6 pm-6.30 pm, SE16 12 pm; closed Sun; SE16 open Sat only; no Amex; no booking.

Morada Brindisa Asador W1 NEW £43 224
18-20 Rupert St 7478 8758 4–3A
Opinions split on this "ambitious" (and pricey) new Hispanic venture, just off Shaftesbury Avenue, with its "huge central bar". To fans it's "a triumphant opening" with "wonderful BBQ meats and fish" ("the roasted whole leg of suckling pig is quite a centrepiece"), plus "super sherries and wines". "Ragged" service is a repeat complaint however, as is "unexciting" results. / W1D 6DE; www.brindisatapaskitchens.com/morada; @Brindisa.

Morden & Lea W1 NEW £43
17 Wardour St 3764 2277 4–3A
Ex-Ramsay henchman, Mark Sargeant, is the driving force behind this two-floor Soho newcomer (ground floor, sharing plates – upstairs, proper dining room), whose staid, trad' looks (lots of leather and Farrow & Ball) might seem more at home in Bath than just by Chinatown; no feedback yet for a rating. / W1D 6PJ; www.mordenandlea.com; @MordenAndLea; 11 pm, Sun 10 pm.

Morelli's Gelato WC2 NEW £22
20a The Piazza, The Mkt 0 7479 8568 89 4–3D
Surprisingly few mentions for this recent addition to Covent Garden Market – an outpost of a much-loved Broadstairs ice cream institution (est 1932); as well as gelato you'll find prosecco and coffee. / WC2 8RB; @morellisgelato; 8 pm.

The Morgan Arms E3 £50 433
43 Morgan St 8980 6389 1–2D
After a recent update, locals feel this "brilliant" Mile End gastropub is "coming back" into its own – the grub is "about as good as it gets", and at "reasonable" prices too. / E3 5AA; www.morganarmsbo.com; @TheMorganArms; 10 pm.

Morito EC1 £36 432

32 Exmouth Mkt 7278 7007 9–1A

"If you're looking for a not-too-pricey quality bite", try to grab one of the "small stools" at Moro's "buzzy" little sister – it's a bit "cramped and uncomfortable", but the tapas are "truly scrumptious". / EC1R 4QE; www.morito.co.uk; @moritotapas; 11 pm, Sun 4 pm; closed Sun D; no Amex; no booking at D.

MORO EC1 £60 543

34-36 Exmouth Mkt 7833 8336 9–1A

"Amazingly consistent over the years, and still in a league of its own" – this "mad busy", but "laid back and friendly" Exmouth Market favourite "still retains its zing", serving "inventive riffs on Spanish/North African dishes" showcasing "clear, clean flavours", and "an exciting wine list" that's "particularly strong on sherries"; "it's still too noisy", though. / EC1R 4QE; www.moro.co.uk; @RestaurantMoro ; 10.30 pm; closed Sun D.

Motcombs SW1 £62 233

26 Motcomb St 7235 6382 5–1D

"You will meet interesting rogues and nobs mixing happily together in the upstairs winebar, before winding your way downstairs to the 'serious' restaurant below", at this long-established Belgravia den; food-wise it's "very reliable, but never exceptional". / SW1X 8JU; www.motcombs.co.uk; @Motcombs; 11 pm; closed Sun D.

Moti Mahal WC2 £65 332

45 Gt Queen St 7240 9329 4–2D

A "classic West End Indian" on the fringe of Covent Garden that's part of a Delhi-based chain; its cooking "doesn't quite blow the lights out, but is reliably interesting". / WC2B 5AA; www.motimahal-uk.com; @motimahal59; 10.45 pm; closed Sat L & Sun.

Mr Chow SW1 £86 333

151 Knightsbridge 7589 7347 5–1D

Still inspiring loyalty after nearly 50 years, this once-glamourous Knightsbridge haunt pleases its dedicated fan club; whether it's still truly, as some suggest, "a place to be seen" is very debatable, but its "very expensive" Chinese fare remains solidly rated. / SW1X 7PA; www.mrchow.com; @MRCHOW; midnight; closed Mon L.

Murakami WC2 NEW £45

63-66 St Martin's Ln 3417 6966 4–3B

A big, Japanese newcomer in Covent Garden, offering a wide menu incorporating sushi, sashimi and robata-grilled meats; limited feedback so far (but all upbeat). / WC2N 4JS; www.murakami-london.co.uk; @hello_murakami; 10.30 pm.

Murano W1 £95 333

20-22 Queen St 7495 1127 3–3B

Angela Hartnett's "quietly sophisticated" Mayfair flagship is a "classy" mix of "sleek" (slightly anonymous) décor and "superb" cuisine (that's "not really that Italian"); its ratings were hit this year however, by incidents of "inattentive" cooking and "disinterested" service. / W1J 5PP; www.muranolondon.com; @muranolondon; 11 pm; closed Sun; set weekday L £57 (FP).

Namaaste Kitchen NW1 £44 442

64 Parkway 7485 5977 8–3B

A comfortable, Camden Town curry house that's consistently well-rated for its "excellent and different modern Indian cooking". / NW1 7AH; www.namaastekitchen.co.uk; @NamaasteKitchen; 11 pm.

The Narrow E14 £50 113

44 Narrow St 7592 7950 11–1B

Gordon Ramsay, please either ditch or sort out this under-performing Limehouse pub – with its "laid-back" style and smashing views from the conservatory, it could be a Docklands destination, but too often its standards are "truly dreadful". / E14 8DP; www.gordonramsay.com/thenarrow/; @thenarrow; 10.30 pm, Sun 8 pm.

The National Dining Rooms National Gallery WC2 £51 113

Sainsbury Wing, Trafalgar Sq 7747 2525 2–2C

"Lovely space, shame about the food!"; as "a convenient option for a light bite", this attractive dining room "overlooking bustling Trafalgar Square" would be ideal... were it not for Peyton & Byrne's "atrocious" service and inept catering. / WC2N 5DN; www.thenationaldiningrooms.co.uk; @PeytonandByrne; 5 pm, Fri 8.30 pm; Sat-Thu closed D, Fri open L & D; no Amex.

Naughty Piglets SW2 NEW £46 452

28 Brixton Water Ln 7274 7796 10–2D

A "lovely new local" in the "unpromising area between Brixton and Herne Hill" featuring "amazing wine options" (many of them "natural and unusual"); "it's the sort of place you want to do well", with "ultra-charming" service and "simple" tapas. / SW2 1PE; www.naughtypiglets.co.uk; 11 pm, Sun 4 pm .

Nautilus NW6 £41 441

27-29 Fortune Green Rd 7435 2532 1–1B

"The matzo meal batter is so light and the fish always so über fresh" that it's inevitably a delight to visit this "truly excellent" – if "basic and functional" – West Hampstead chippy. / NW6 1DU; 10 pm; closed Sun; no Amex.

Nayaab SW6 £36 432
309 New King's Rd 7731 6993 10–1B
"Proper Indian cooking from a wide-ranging menu" wins high praise for this well-established Punjabi, near Parsons Green. / SW6 4RF; 11 pm.

Needoo E1 £28 422
87 New Rd 7247 0648 12–2D
"You could walk past it and not look twice", but this East End Pakistani (somewhat eclipsed by its near neighbour Tayyabs) offers "cheap 'n' cheerful meals in abundance" – "great, simple curries" and magnificent lamb chops. / E1 1HH; www.needoogrill.co.uk; @NeedooGrill; 11.30 pm.

New Mayflower W1 £42 322
68-70 Shaftesbury Ave 7734 9207 4–3A
"You don't go for the average service or ambience", but for the "reliably good Cantonese/Peking cuisine" offered by this "reliable" Chinatown stalwart, which serves well into the wee hours of early morning. / W1D 6LY; www.newmayflowerlondon.com; 4 am; D only; no Amex.

New Street Grill EC2 £59 233
16a New St 3503 0785 9–2D
D&D London's spacious, characterful and well-appointed warehouse conversion near Liverpool Street is primarily tipped for business occasions; but while fans applaud its "excellent" steaks, its ratings are held back by a minority who find the whole package "expensive" and "unimpressive". / EC2M 4TR; www.newstreetgrill.co.uk; @newstreetgrill; 10.30 pm; closed Sun D.

New World W1 £38 323
1 Gerrard Pl 7434 2508 4–3A
"Old-school Hong Kong dim sum on a trolley – the only way to have it!"; "be prepared to queue" for this massive Chinatown landmark – "there are classier restaurants by far", but "the fun factor of the circulating food makes the experience". / W1D 5PA; www.newworldlondon.com; 11.30 pm, Sun 11 pm.

The Newman Arms W1 £46
Rathbone St 3643 6285 4–1A
Apparently Orwell's 'proles pub' in 1984, this old Fitzrovian boozer was taken over by the owner of The Cornwall Project, Matt Chatfield, too late for significant survey feedback; enthusiastic early press reports on its farm-to-fork approach (with the aim of 'providing the freshest Cornish fish and veg'). / W1T 1NG; www.newmanarms.co.uk; @NewmanArmsPub; 11 pm.

Newman Street Tavern W1 £45 334
48 Newman St 3667 1445 3–1D
It's "under-appreciated", say fans of this "classic gastropub" in Marylebone, applauded for its "grown-up" cooking – with a strong emphasis on "always being fresh and seasonal" – and "genial" style. / W1T 1QQ; www.newmanstreettavern.co.uk; @NewmanStTavern; 10.30 pm; closed Sun D; SRA-2.*

Nobu Metropolitan Hotel W1 £90 332
19 Old Park Ln 7447 4747 3–4A
"Still doing amazing sushi... still incredibly expensive" – London's original Japanese-fusion haunt is increasingly overlooked nowadays, but it remains a "classic" for some reporters; the odd celeb still pops up now and again, but even so the dining room "lacks atmosphere". / W1K 1LB; www.noburestaurants.com; @NobuOldParkLane; 10.15 pm, Fri & Sat 11 pm, Sun 10 pm; set weekday L £58 (FP).

Nobu, Berkeley W1 £90 322
15 Berkeley St 7290 9222 3–3C
"Expensive but amazing" sushi and other "fabulous" fusion fare underpins support for this large, showy Mayfair Japanese; it can seem "impersonal" and "charmless" however, and sceptics say it's overrun by a "selfie-stick clientele" nowadays. / W1J 8DY; www.noburestaurants.com; @NobuBerkeleyST; 11 pm, Sun 9.45 pm; closed Sun L; set weekday L £58 (FP).

Noor Jahan £40 433
2a Bina Gdns, SW5 7373 6522 5–2B
26 Sussex Pl, W2 7402 2332 6–1D
These gloomily "upmarket", "always busy" neighbourhood curry houses are the "perfect" local for the well-heeled denizens of Earl's Court and Bayswater looking for a "reliable" fix of "classic Indian tandoori fare". / 11.30 pm, Sun 10 pm.

Nopi W1 £70 322
21-22 Warwick St 7494 9584 3–2D
"Sublime flavour combos that both excite and comfort" have carved a huge name for Yotam Ottolenghi's modern Middle Eastern spot, just off Regent Street; ratings slid across the board this year though, and it took flak for some "ordinary" meals, its "eye-watering" expense, "offhand" service and "sterile" ambience. / W1B 5NE; www.nopi-restaurant.com; @ottolenghi; 10.15 pm, Sun 4 pm; closed Sun D.

Nordic Bakery **£15** 333
14a Golden Sq, W1 3230 1077 3–2D
37b New Cavendish St, W1 7935 3590 2–1A
48 Dorset St, W1 7487 5877 2–1A
You suffer "Soho media types networking over a coffee and a delicious cinnamon bun" but it's worth "squeezing yourself into" one of these "authentic" Scandi coffee shops. / Golden Square 8 pm, Sat 7 pm, Sun 7 pm, Cavendish Street & Dorset Street 6 pm.

The Norfolk Arms WC1 **£44** 433
28 Leigh St 7388 3937 8–4C
"A real find near King's Cross" – a "pleasantly chaotic" hybrid of gastropub and tapas bar, serving "unpretentious but delicious" Spanish-inspired food. / WC1H 9EP; www.norfolkarms.co.uk; 10.15 pm.

North China W3 **£42** 432
305 Uxbridge Rd 8992 9183 7–1A
One of Acton's few claims to gastronomic heights, this long-established, family-run Chinese is "so busy" because it's unusually good for somewhere out in the boonies, and "prices are more than reasonable". / W3 9QU; www.northchina.co.uk; 11 pm, Fri & Sat 11.30 pm.

The North London Tavern NW6 **£46** 333
375 Kilburn High Rd 7625 6634 1–2B
Handy for Kilburn's Tricycle Theatre – a "surprisingly good gastropub", with "genuine service" and "very decent food"; it's part of the Metropolitan Pub Company. / NW6 7QB; www.northlondontavern.co.uk; @NorthLondonTav; 10.30 pm, Sun 9.30 pm.

North Sea Fish WC1 **£38** 332
7-8 Leigh St 7387 5892 8–4C
"Some of the customers may look on their last legs, but for fine fish 'n' chips at fair prices" seek out this old-fashioned Bloomsbury chippy, whose "faded '70s décor has its own character". / WC1H 9EW; www.northseafishrestaurant.co.uk; 10 pm, Sun 5.30 pm; closed Sun D; no Amex.

The Northall, Corinthia Hotel SW1 **£85** 344
10a Northumberland Ave 7321 3100 2–3C
"No need to worry about the office bean counters getting stressed over pricey client lunches" if you entertain at this "very classy"-looking brasserie, near Embankment; "for part of such an extravagant 5-star hotel" it's "not too expensive" (set lunch in particular) and the grub's very "decent". / SW1A 2BD; www.thenorthall.co.uk; @CorinthiaLondon; 10.45 pm; set pre theatre £56 (FP).

Northbank EC4 **£56** 344
1 Paul's Walk 7329 9299 9–3B
"Great views of the Shard and Tate Modern" are the star turn at this business-friendly bar-restaurant, by the Wobbly Bridge; the food can still be "lovely", but it's looking "a little tired" these days with "haphazard" service – time for a revamp? / EC4V 3QH; www.northbankrestaurant.co.uk; @NorthbankLondon; 10 pm; closed Sun.

Novikov (Asian restaurant) W1 **£102** 112
50a Berkeley St 7399 4330 3–3C
"Glamorous... if you're into big tables of overdressed Euros, yelling at the top of their voices!" – this Russian-owned Pan-Asian is praised by fans for its "stunning" food and "electric" ambience, but dismissed by critics for its "inferior" fare, and prices on a par with an EU bailout. / W1J 8HA; www.novikovrestaurant.co.uk; @NovikovLondon; 11.15 pm; set weekday L £57 (FP).

Novikov (Italian restaurant) W1 **£110** 222
50a Berkeley St 7399 4330 3–3C
That it's "ludicrously expensive", is the main drawback of the "OTT" Italian section of this ostentatious, Russian-run Mayfair bling-fest – the food's actually "better than you'd imagine"; and if you like this sort of thing, it's "great for people watching". / W1J 8HA; www.novikovrestaurant.co.uk; @NovikovLondon; 11.15 pm.

Numero Uno SW11 **£53** 444
139 Northcote Rd 7978 5837 10–2C
A quintessential "neighbourhood Italian" bordering the Nappy Valley – "friendly and authentic", with "slick service, matched by a range of traditional dishes". / SW11 6PX; 11.30 pm; no Amex.

Nuovi Sapori SW6 **£45** 343
295 New King's Rd 7736 3363 10–1B
"Friendly and welcoming" owners contribute much to the appeal of this well-established local near Parsons Green, serving a "reliable" menu of "traditional Italian cuisine". / SW6 4RE; 11 pm; closed Sun.

Nusa Kitchen **£12** 443
9 Old St, EC1 7253 3135 9–1B
2 Adam's Ct, EC2 7628 1149 9–2C
88 Cannon St, EC4 7621 9496 9–3C
"Transforming the lunch time soup experience" – City and Farringdon pit stops which serve "utterly amazing" Asian broths. / www.nusakitchen.co.uk; 4 pm; closed Sat & Sun; no booking.

Oak £50 [4][2][4]
243 Goldhawk Rd, W12 8741 7700 7–1B
137 Westbourne Park Rd, W2 7221 3355 6–1B
There's something so "cool" about the "really buzzing" style of these "transformed old boozers" in Bayswater and Shepherd's Bush, which serve "scrumptious", "thin and crispy" pizza – "some of the finest in town!" Top Tip – the upstairs bar in W2 is "a real gem". / W12 Mon - Sat 10:30pm / SUn 9:30pmW2 Mon-Thurs 10:30pm / Fri - Sat 11pm / Sun 10pm.

Obicà £46 [3][3][2]
11 Charlotte St, W1 7637 7153 2–1C
19-20 Poland St, W1 3327 7070 3–1D
96 Draycott Ave, SW3 7581 5208 5–2C
35 Bank St, E14 7719 1532 11–1C
"For some reason they've changed their name (from Obika)", but these 'Mozzarella bars' "make a solid choice for some excellent produce and a drink or two", and win tips for their superior pizza too. / www.obika.co.uk; 10 pm - 11 pm; E14 Closed Sun.

Oblix The Shard SE1 £88 [2][2][4]
31 St Thomas St 7268 6700 9–4C
"To woo a date" the view is "stunning" at this 32nd-floor South Bank roost (run by the owners of Zuma, et al); so are the "extortionate" prices though, and sceptics suggest you "go to the bar, and eat elsewhere". (Stop Press – will new Pied à Terre chef, Marcus Eaves – who joined in September 2015 – finally make it a foodie hotspot?) / SE1 9RY; www.oblixrestaurant.com; @OblixRestaurant; 11 pm.

Odette's NW1 £62 [3][3][3]
130 Regent's Park Rd 7586 8569 8–3B
"For an unhurried journey of sensory delight", Bryn William's "cosy", "slightly old-fashioned" romantic classic in Primrose Hill remains well-rated as "a lovely all-round experience" with "first-rate" cuisine; for a few doubters though, it "just doesn't quite hit the spot". / NW1 8XL; www.odettesprimrosehill.com; @Odettes_rest; 10 pm, Fri & Sat 10.30 pm; closed Mon; no Amex.

Ognisko Restaurant SW7 £51 [3][3][4]
55 Prince's Gate, Exhibition Rd 7589 0101 5–1C
"The old-fashioned dining room is a delight", at this émigrés club near the Science Museum, which also boasts "a wonderful rear terrace, on a garden square"; Jan Woroniecki's year-old regime doesn't please all its old regulars, but the "hearty" Polish fare and "exotic house cocktails" were well-rated this year. / SW7 2PN; www.ogniskorestaurant.co.uk; 11.15 pm ; closed Mon L; no trainers.

Oka Kingly Court W1 NEW £47 [4][3][3]
Kingly St 7734 3556 3–2D
In Soho and Primrose Hill, a duo of Pan-Asian restaurants offering "excellent quality" sushi and a smattering of "unusual" but "clever" dishes – Marmite chicken anyone? / W1B 5PW; www.okarestaurant.co.uk; @RestaurantOka; 10.30 pm.

Old Tom & English W1 NEW £49
187b Wardour St 7287 7347 3–1D
A Soho hang out that only takes reservations? – a nowadays radical premise for this low-lit basement hideaway, entered speakeasy-style via a "discreet" entrance, and with "quirky" '60s styling; cocktails are a big deal here, but early reports say the food is better than incidental. / W1F 8ZB; oldtomandenglish.com/; @oldtomsoho; 11.30 pm, Sat midnight.

Oldroyd N1 NEW £42
344 Upper St 8617 9010 8–3D
Tom Oldroyd (formerly chef-director of Polpo group) goes it alone at this pocket-sized, new modern bistro in Islington, serving a variety of funky sharing plates; it opened too late for our survey, but early press feedback hails it as a bargain. / N1 0PD; www.oldroydlondon.com; @oldroydlondon.

Oliveto SW1 £63 [4][2][2]
49 Elizabeth St 7730 0074 2–4A
"Wonderful pizza and pasta, at prices that don't frighten Belgravians one little bit" make this "family-friendly" Sardinian a choice that's relatively "cheap 'n' cheerful", if only by the standards of this swanky 'hood. / SW1W 9PP; www.olivorestaurants.com/oliveto; @OlivoGroup; 10.30 pm; booking: max 7 at D.

Olivo SW1 £58 [3][4][2]
21 Eccleston St 7730 2505 2–4B
"Dated" '90s Belgravian, with "tables too close together and dreadful acoustics"; "it's very popular for good reason" though – its Sardinian cuisine is "consistently excellent" and matched with "interesting Sardinian wines". / SW1 9LX; www.olivorestaurants.com/olivo; @OlivoGroup; 10.30 pm; closed Sat L & Sun L.

Olivocarne SW1 £61 [4][4][2]
61 Elizabeth St 7730 7997 2–4A
"Upscale sister to Olivo, Oliveto etc. with more of a focus on meat" – this Belgravia's Sardinian has "excellent" cooking to offset its rather "reserved" ambience. / SW1W 9PP; www.olivorestaurants.com/olivocarne; @OlivoGroup; 11 pm, Sun 10.30 pm.

Olivomare SW1 £61 [4][3][2]
10 Lower Belgrave St 7730 9022 2–4B
Stark, "Barbarella-esque" decor creates a "bare-bones" ambience at this very "contemporary" Belgravian; this "does nothing to detract", however, from the "brilliant and resolutely Sardinian menu", majoring in "super-fresh" fish and seafood; the wine list's "a joy" too. / SW1W 0LJ; www.olivorestaurants.com/olivomare; @OlivoGroup; 11 pm, Sun 10.30 pm; booking: max 10.

Olympic Olympic Studios SW13 £50 [2][2][4]
117-123 Church Rd 8912 5170 10–1A
"A roaring success among trendier Barnes types" – this converted Edwardian cinema (for much of its life, famous recording studios, but nowadays again also showing movies) makes "a great local meeting place", especially for brunch; "both food and service are hit-and-miss though... when they get it right it's really good, but it's very inconsistent". / SW13 9HL; www.olympiccinema.co.uk; @Olympic_Cinema; 11 pm, Sat & Sun midnight.

Olympus Fish N3 £34 [4][5][2]
140-144 Ballards Ln 8371 8666 1–1B
"Wonderful, fresh, char-grilled fish" is an alternative to the "succulent non-greasy fish 'n' chips" at this "unpretentious" Finchley chippy, whose longstanding owners give a notably "warm welcome". Top Menu Tip – "divine sea bass cooked in sea salt". / N3 2PA; www.olympusrestaurant.co.uk; @Olympus_London; 11 pm; set weekday L £17 (FP).

On The Bab £36 [4][3][2]
39 Marylebone Ln, W1 7935 2000 2–1A NEW
36 Wellington St, WC2 7240 8825 4–3D NEW
305 Old St, EC1 7683 0361 12–1B
"Korean food is so hot right now", and these energetic, "cheap 'n' cheerful" pit-stops and their "delicious" anju (street-food dishes) are a "must try"; very handy new Covent Garden branch that "makes a good fist of fast turnarounds". / www.onthebab.co.uk; @onthebab.

One Canada Square E14 £58 [2][2][2]
1 Canada Sq 7559 5199 11–1C
For a business lunch this two-year-old bar/brasserie, in the lobby of Canary Wharf's main skyscraper, couldn't have a better location; it's "a bit of a goldfish bowl" however (which at night is "rammed with loud City types"), and the "pricey" food is "not as good as they think it is". / E14 5AB; www.onecanadasquarerestaurant.com; @OneCanadaSquare; 10.45 pm; closed Sun; set pre theatre £36 (FP).

101 Thai Kitchen W6 £33 [4][2][1]
352 King St 8746 6888 7–2B
"Mind-blowing spicing" ("not for the faint hearted!") vouches for the authenticity of this Thai caff near Stamford Brook; it's a "no-nonsense, straightforward place" but "look past the décor – you'll be in south east Asia!". / W6 0RX; www.101thaikitchen.com; 10.30 pm, Fri & Sat 11 pm; no Amex.

1 Lombard Street EC3 £69 [2][3][3]
1 Lombard St 7929 6611 9–3C
"The buzz is returning to pre-crash heights" at this Square Mile linchpin; OK, the food is only "satisfactory" and the ex-banking-hall interior is a "bit cavernous and plain", but tables are "well-spaced", and its "capable" style and central location make it "a perfect setting for the City". / EC3V 9AA; www.1lombardstreet.com; @1lombardstreet; 10 pm; closed Sat & Sun; booking: max 6.

One Sixty Smokehouse £52 [4][4][3]
291 West End Ln, NW6 7794 9786 1–1B
9 Stoney Ln, E1 7283 8367 9–2D NEW
"Comfort food at its American best" – "sensational" ribs, wings, soft-shell crab burgers, etc – wins raves for David Moore and Sean Martin's year-old "edgy West Hampstead smokehouse", now also with a branch in the City. / www.one-sixty.co.uk; @onesixtylondon.

One-O-One, Sheraton Park Tower SW1 £100 [5][2][1]
101 Knightsbridge 7290 7101 5–1D
"Off-the-charts-good" Breton fish cuisine makes Pascal Proyart's Knightsbridge HQ "London's best-kept secret for seafood"; there is, however, a catch – the hotel dining room it occupies is "absolutely ghastly", with a "dead", "business-lounge" ambience. / SW1X 7RN; www.oneoonerestaurant.com; @oneoone; 10 pm; closed Mon & Sun; booking: max 6; set weekday L £55 (FP).

The Only Running Footman W1 £61 [3][3][3]
5 Charles St 7499 2988 3–3B
"There's plenty of elbow room in the spacious dining room" of this boozer, near Berkeley Square – "very handy for a Mayfair working lunch", or indeed any other kind of occasion. / W1J 5DF; www.therunningfootmanmayfair.com; @theorfootman; 10 pm.

Les 110 de Taillevent W1 NEW

16 Cavendish Sq awaiting tel 3–1B

In Autumn 2015 (as we were going to press) the first London outpost of the fabled Parisian brasserie's spin-off brand was due to open on the former site of a branch of Her Majesty's banker Coutts & Co, just north of Oxford Street; wine and pairing menus are set to be a major feature of what should be an interesting opening (the 'cent dix' of the title refers to the number of wine bins). / W1G 9DD; www.taillevent.com; @LeTaillevent.

Opera Tavern WC2 £46 444

23 Catherine St 7836 3680 4–3D

"The best ever small tasty treats" are provided by "willing" staff at this "very cute" (but at times very "noisy") pub-conversion sibling to Salt Yard, well-located near Covent Garden. Top Menu Tips – "Morcilla Scotch eggs to die for"; and "outstanding mini Ibérico pork and foie gras burgers". / WC2B 5JS; www.operatavern.co.uk; @saltyardgroup; 11.15 pm, Sun 9.45 pm; SRA-2.*

Opso W1 £44 224

10 Paddington St 7487 5088 2–1A

All acknowledge the "beautiful" interior of this Marylebone yearling, but its modern Greek cooking splits opinion – to fans it's a solid "cheap 'n' cheerful" choice, but to critics it's "disappointing" and "highly priced". / W1U 5QL; opso.co.uk; @OPSO_london; 10 pm, Fri & Sat 10.30 pm; closed Sun D.

The Orange SW1 £59 334

37 Pimlico Rd 7881 9844 5–2D

"Fun and atmospheric" Pimlico gastropub which "draws an attractive younger crowd" with its "fab" pizza, and other fare. / SW1W 8NE; www.theorange.co.uk; @TheOrangeSW1; 10 pm, Sun 9.30 pm.

Orange Pekoe SW13 £26 344

3 White Hart Ln 8876 6070 10–1A

"A unique and lovely tea room and café" in Barnes – a "superb selection of teas" is served "with flair", plus "well-chosen" bites including "salads to die for", "filling sarnies" and "very good cakes". / SW13 0PX; www.orangepekoeteas.com; @OrangePekoeTeas; 5 pm; L only.

The Orange Tree N20 £46 223

7 Totteridge Ln 8343 7031 1–1B

A popular Totteridge linchpin that again divides the locals – to critics it's "a waste of a prime location", but fans say it's "always good". / N20 8NX; www.theorangetreetotteridge.co.uk; @orangetreepub; 9.45 pm, Fri & Sat 10.30 pm, Sun 9 pm; set weekday L £28 (FP).

Orpheus EC3 £48 431

26 Savage Gdns 7481 1931 9–3D

"It looks awful, but that's a good thing – I don't want anyone else to know about it!"; this "throwback" in a railway arch near Tower Hill is little known, but its fish dishes are "unusually good", featuring "simple yet elegant saucing". / EC3N 2AR; www.orpheusrestaurant.co.uk; 3 pm; L only, closed Sat & Sun.

Orrery W1 £80 343

55 Marylebone High St 7616 8000 2–1A

A "bright and airy" first-floor room – above Marylebone's Conran Shop, and overlooking a churchyard – provides the "spacious" and "calm" setting for this well-known D&D London venture, whose "efficient" service further boosts its appeal for business; the food is "expensive" but usually "lovely" too. / W1U 5RB; www.orreryrestaurant.co.uk; @orrery; 10.30 pm, Fri & Sat 11 pm; set weekday L £52 (FP), set Sun L £55 (FP).

Orso WC2 £55 222

27 Wellington St 7240 5269 4–3D

"Very convenient for the ROH" – this once-exciting, Covent Garden basement remains a treasured "stalwart" for a devoted fanclub, who say it's "charming" and "solid"; ratings-wise, it "continues to go downhill", however – its performance can just seem too "stale". / WC2E 7DB; www.orsorestaurant.co.uk; @Orso_Restaurant; 11.30 pm; set always available £36 (FP).

Oslo Court NW8 £62 354

Charlbert St, off Prince Albert Rd 7722 8795 8–3A

"It is as though the last 30 years never happened", at this "unique" time-warp at the foot of a Regent's Park apartment block – a fave rave for silver-haired north Londoners with birthdays to celebrate. For most reporters, it remains an utter "treasure" thanks to its "wonderful", "retro" '70s menu, "fun" style and "long serving staff" who help "put a smile on your face", but for a few (including former fans) it's starting to feel like it's "gone over". Top Menu Tip – "the famed dessert trolley". / NW8 7EN; www.oslocourtrestaurant.co.uk; 11 pm; closed Sun; no jeans or trainers.

Osteria Antica Bologna SW11 £43 433

23 Northcote Rd 7978 4771 10–2C

"A light and accessible makeover" has revivified this "busy and cheerful" age-old osteria, near Clapham Junction – the food's "nothing fancy, but genuine northern Italian cuisine, mixing staples and specials of the day". / SW11 1NG; www.osteria.co.uk; @OsteriaAntica; 10.30 pm, Sun 10 pm.

Osteria Basilico W11 **£58** 3 2 4
29 Kensington Park Rd 7727 9957 6–1A
An enduring pillar of Notting Hill dining that's still "consistently good", particularly its "fun atmosphere";"don't forget to book if you want a table on the ground floor". / W11 2EU; www.osteriabasilico.co.uk; 11.30 pm, Sun 10.15 pm; no booking, S.

Osteria Tufo N4 **£47** 4 5 3
67 Fonthill Rd 7272 2911 8–1D
"There's no need to go to the West End any more", when you can visit this "fabulous" two-year-old in Finsbury Park – "the best kind of neighbourhood place","run with love" and with "top-notch", "reasonably priced" Italian cooking. / N4 3HZ; www.osteriatufo.co.uk; @osteriatufo; 10.30 pm; closed Mon & Sun L; no Amex.

Ostuni NW6 **£49** 3 3 4
43-45 Lonsdale Rd 7624 8035 1–2B
A converted Victorian workshop, in Queen's Park, provides a "very attractive and very spacious" venue for this "lively" two-year-old Puglian, whose "authentically Italian" décor is carried off with "pizzazz", and which serves "great food at reasonable prices". / NW6 6RA; www.ostunirestaurant.co.ukwww.ostunirestaurant.co.uk; @OstuniLondon; 10 pm, Sun 9 pm.

Otto's WC1 **£65** 4 5 4
182 Grays Inn Rd 7713 0107 2–1D
"The old-school French cuisine you thought had died a death" makes an unlikely find behind an unassuming façade in an "out-of-the-way" corner of Bloomsbury; the "eccentric" interior is "charming in a quiet, old-fashioned way", but the stand-out attractions are "Otto himself, who's a star","superb" food and "excellent" wine. Top Menu Tips – "sublime" steak tartare, and the "to die for" Canard à la Presse (for which you must pre-order). / WC1X 8EW; www.ottos-restaurant.com; @OttosRestaurant; 9.45 pm; closed Sat L & Sun; set weekday L £47 (FP).

Ottolenghi **£52** 4 2 2
13 Motcomb St, SW1 7823 2707 5–1D
63 Ledbury Rd, W11 7727 1121 6–1B
1 Holland St, W8 7937 0003 5–1A
287 Upper St, N1 7288 1454 8–2D
50 Artillery Pas, E1 7247 1999 9–2D
"You discover tastebuds you never knew existed!", say fans of the "revelatory" salads and "insanely good" cakes at Yotam Ottolenghi's "chic" (but slightly "sterile") communal deli/cafés; "ridiculous queues" are a perennial hazard however, and a dip in ratings supports those who say "it's suffering from its own success". / www.ottolenghi.co.uk; N1 10.15 pm, W8 & W11 8 pm, Sat 7 pm, Sun 6 pm; N1 closed Sun D; Holland St takeaway only; W11 & SW1 no booking, N1 booking for D only.

Outlaw's Seafood and Grill The Capital Hotel SW3 **£84** 4 4 2
22-24 Basil St 7589 5171 5–1D
Nathan Outlaw's "rare and outstanding" treatment of fish and seafood underpins the "first class" experience at this "calm" chamber, just a stone's throw from Harrods, although the room is too small and "too formal" for some tastes. Top Tip – on Thursday you can BYO with no corkage. / SW3 1AT; www.capitalhotel.co.uk; @hotelcapital; 10 pm; closed Sun; set weekday L £52 (FP).

(Brasserie) Oxo Tower SE1 **£73** 1 1 2
Barge House St 7803 3888 9–3A
"Urgh!" – the brasserie section of this South Bank landmark also "consistently trades on its name and great Thames view" with "terrible service and very ordinary food"; what's more it's "very, very expensive". / SE1 9PH; www.harveynichols.com/restaurants/oxo-tower-london; @OXO_Tower; 11 pm, Sun 10 pm; set weekday L & pre-theatre £51 (FP).

(Restaurant) Oxo Tower SE1 **£89** 1 1 1
Barge House St 7803 3888 9–3A
"Stunning view, shame about the food" – year-in-year-out it's plus ça change at this famous South Bank fixture, whose "rubbish" cooking, "purposeless" service and hefty bills make it nigh on "the worst bang for your buck in town". / SE1 9PH; www.harveynichols.com/restaurants; @OXO_Tower; 11 pm, Sun 10 pm; set weekday L £59 (FP); SRA-3.*

Pachamama W1 **£56** 3 3 2
18 Thayer St 7935 9393 2–1A
"Intriguing sharing plates inspired by Peru", all "washed down with good Pisco cocktails" win a big thumbs-up for this Marylebone yearling; on the downside, its basement setting is "soulless", and "the acoustics are terrible". / W1U 3JY; www.pachamamalondon.com; @pachamama_ldn; 10.45 pm; closed Mon L.

Le Pain Quotidien **£31** 2 2 4
Branches throughout London
"Nothing to get too excited about", but this "rustic" chain makes a great standby for a bowlful of coffee, or "handy refuel" (especially breakfast) – "there's just something about the ambience... it feels very relaxed". / www.painquotidien.com; most branches close between 7 pm-10 pm; no booking at some branches, especially at weekends.

The Painted Heron SW10 £56 443
112 Cheyne Walk 7351 5232 5–3B
"Hidden away but worth finding" – this "understated but excellent" Indian fixture off the Chelsea Embankment provides "friendly and eager" service and "is an oasis of adventurous, impeccably spiced cuisine". / SW10 0DJ; www.thepaintedheron.com; @thepaintedheron; 10.30 pm, Sun 10 pm; no Amex.

The Palmerston SE22 £55 433
91 Lordship Ln 8693 1629 1–4D
Superior East Dulwich gastropub that's a haven of "good value", "great seasonal pub food" and "a big range of wines by the glass" – the kind of place "you'd happily eat almost everything on the menu". / SE22 8EP; www.thepalmerston.co.uk; @thepalmerston; 10 pm, Sun 9.30 pm; no Amex; set always available £31 (FP).

The Palomar W1 £48 444
34 Rupert St 7439 8777 4–3A
"Israeli cooking as in Jerusalem" ("brilliant, punchy, sparky" small dishes), plus "super-keen and knowledgeable" service have made a smash-hit of this "bare-walled" yearling, in the heart of the West End – "the joint is jumping!" and it's superb "fun" (if "squashed" and "extremely noisy"). There's a little, tough-to-book, dining room, or sit at the bar and watch the chefs in action. / W1D 6DN; www.thepalomar.co.uk; @palomarsoho; 11 pm, Fri-Sat 11.30 pm; closed Sun L; SRA-1.*

The Pantechnicon SW1 £58 334
10 Motcomb St 7730 6074 5–1D
This "professionally run" Belgravian combines a "buzzy ground floor bar", with a "quieter", grand and comfortable upstairs dining room, which "still feels like a pub... just". / SW1X 8LA; www.thepantechnicon.com; @ThePantechnicon; 10 pm, Sun 9.30 pm.

Pappa Ciccia £34 444
105 Munster Rd, SW6 7384 1884 10–1B
41 Fulham High St, SW6 7736 0900 10–1B
"Outstanding pizza (crispy and doughy without being burnt)" is a highlight of the "tasty, traditional Italian fare, in generous portions" at these BYO spots in Fulham – "for the price you pay, the food's extremely good". / www.pappaciccia.com; 11 pm, Sat & Sun 11.30 pm; Munster Rd no credit cards.

Paradise by Way of Kensal Green W10 £50 225
19 Kilburn Ln 8969 0098 1–2B
Rambling, "shabby-chic" Kensal Green landmark, still ticking all the right boxes for its glam' 20/30-something following; in its large, "laid-back" dining room, the food's "nothing too exciting" but "enjoyable". / W10 4AE; www.theparadise.co.uk; @weloveparadise; 10.30 pm, Fri & Sat 11 pm, Sun 9 pm; closed weekday L; no Amex.

Paradise Garage E2 NEW £45
254 Paradise Row 7613 1502 12–1D
New debut from foodie darling Robin Gill (he of Clapham's The Manor, and The Dairy) in an oh-so-hip railway arch, in the beating heart of trendy Bethnal Green; it opened too late for survey feedback on its funky small plates, but the word on the street is encouraging. / E2 9LE; paradise254.com; @ParadiseRow254; 9.30 pm; closed Mon, Tue L & Sun D.

Paradise Hampstead NW3 £33 454
49 South End Rd 7794 6314 8–2A
"The friendly owner goes the extra mile" at this "classic, traditional, British Indian of decades' standing" – an "insufferably popular" neighbourhood "hotspot" by Hampstead Heath overground; everything about the place is "a cut above". / NW3 2QB; www.paradisehampstead.co.uk; 10.45 pm.

El Parador NW1 £38 454
245 Eversholt St 7387 2789 8–3C
"It looks nothing from the outside", but this "terrific" spot, near Mornington Crescent, is a great all-rounder, not least its "dreamy" tapas ("there's always something new and different") that's "well-priced" to boot; "cosy little courtyard in summer". / NW1 1BA; www.elparadorlondon.com; 11 pm, Fri & Sat 11.30 pm, Sun 9.30 pm; closed Sat L & Sun L; no Amex.

Parlour NW10 £49 444
5 Regent St 8969 2184 1–2B
Jesse Dunford Wood's "unique and quirky venue" occupies "a converted Kensal Rise boozer", but "it's no normal gastropub" – the food's "really interesting and delicious". Top Tips – the "amazing cow pie in huge portions" (and a meal at the chef's personal table). / NW10 5LG; www.parlourkensal.com; @ParlourUK; 10 pm; closed Mon.

Patara £56 3 3 3

15 Greek St, W1 7437 1071 4–2A
5 Berners St, W1 8874 6503 3–1D NEW
7 Maddox St, W1 7499 6008 3–2C
181 Fulham Rd, SW3 7351 5692 5–2C
9 Beauchamp Pl, SW3 7581 8820 5–1C

"Delicate" cooking, "unobtrusive" service and "subtle" décor combine to make this popular and rather superior Thai chain "an all-round good effort". / www.pataralondon.com; 10.30 pm; Greek St closed Sun L.

Paternoster Chop House EC4 £55 3 3 2

Warwick Ct, Paternoster Sq 7029 9400 9–2B

Poor feedback this year, on this "expensive" D&D London's steakhouse, which critics feel seems to "trade on its location" (it's right by St Paul's, with many al fresco tables); "at lunch, it's 95% business", and hard to give it any wider recommendation. / EC4M 7DX; www.paternosterchophouse.co.uk; @paternoster1; 10.30 pm; closed Sat & Sun D.

Patio W12 £36 3 5 5

5 Goldhawk Rd 8743 5194 7–1C

"Old-fashioned, in the nicest possible way" – a "warm and cosy" spot, right by Shepherd's Bush Green, that's a top budget choice thanks to its super-friendly service, affordable Polish fodder, and wide range of flavoured vodkas. / W12 8QQ; www.patiolondon.com; 11 pm, Sat & Sun 11.30 pm; closed Sat L & Sun L.

Pâtisserie Valerie £28 2 2 2

Branches throughout London

Luke Johnson is laughing all the way to the bank with his partial June 2015 sale of this once-tiny pâtisserie chain; some reporters think it can be "dire" nowadays (the new branches in particular), but others do praise the "wonderful" cakes and "yummy brunches", especially at the "tatty but charming Old Compton Street original". / www.patisserie-valerie.co.uk; most branches close between 5 pm-8 pm; no booking except Old Compton St Sun-Thu.

Patogh W1 £22 4 4 4

8 Crawford Pl 7262 4015 6–1D

A "lovely, little Middle Eastern spot", just off the Edgware Road – "simple but very atmospheric", serving "authentic, basic dishes" featuring "large portions of freshly grilled meat"; BYO. / W1H 5NE; 11 pm; no credit cards.

Patron NW5 NEW £47 3 3 4

26 Fortress Rd 7813 2540 8–2C

A cute, little, new 'Cave à Manger' in Kentish Town, "already very busy" thanks to its "simple but good, traditional French fare". / NW5 2HB; www.patronlondon.com.

Patty and Bun £23 4 3 3

54 James St, W1 7487 3188 3–1A
22-23 Liverpool St, EC2 7621 1331 9–2D

"Just wow!"; the "revelatory" burgers are "a sloppy sensation" – "so juicy, moist and cooked to perfection" – at these "loud", "indie-vibe" pitstops, whose branch near Selfridges is the highest-rated burger-joint in town. / www.pattyandbun.co.uk; Mon - Wed 10pm, Thu - Fri 11pm, Sat 9pm, Sun 6pm.

The Pear Tree W6 £43 3 3 4

14 Margravine Rd 7381 1787 7–2C

A "lovely and intimate" little Victorian gastropub (with cute garden), tucked way behind the Charing Cross Hospital, serving a "limited" menu of "surprisingly good" food. / W6 8HJ; www.thepeartreefulham.com; Mon-Thu D only, Fri-Sun open L & D.

Pearl Liang W2 £47 4 3 2

8 Sheldon Sq 7289 7000 6–1C

A hotspot for dim sum – this big, dim-lit basement Chinese has an out-on-a-limb, Paddington Basin location, but is worth truffling out for its "top notch" cooking. / W2 6EZ; www.pearlliang.co.uk; @PearlLiangUK; 11 pm.

Peckham Bazaar SE15 £46 4 4 4

119 Consort Rd 7732 2525 1–4D

"Different... in a good way" – a "really interesting menu of mainly Greek Albanian food" (much of it barbecued) earns many recommendations for this "buzzy little Balkan place in an unlikely part of Peckham"; its "mysterious wines" add to the appeal – "I just do a lucky dip and it's always fine". / SE15 3RU; www.peckhambazaar.com; @PeckhamBazaar; 10 pm, Sun 8 pm; closed Mon, Tue-Fri D only, Sat & Sun open L & D; no Amex.

Peckham Refreshment Rooms SE15 £40 3 2 3

12-16 Blenheim Grove 7639 1106 1–4D

On a Friday and Saturday night this Peckham two-year-old can be "a bit too manic with young drinkers", but most locals cherish it as a "chilled" spot (notwithstanding the "uncomfortable bar stools") for a "quality", "casual" bite. / SE15 4QL; www.peckhamrefreshment.com; @PeckhamRefresh; midnight; closed Sun D.

Pedler SE15 NEW £37 3 2 4

58 Peckham Rye 3030 5015 1–4D

"A welcome addition to the trendy Peckham scene" – a "busy" if "crammed-in" bistro dishing up "simple, tasty" meals at "reasonable prices"; "fantastic brunch" too, with an "extremely impressive variety" of "thoughtful" options. / SE15 4JR; www.pedlerpeckhamrye.com; @pedlerpeckham; 10.45 pm; closed Mon, Tue L, Wed L, Thu L & Sun D.

Pellicano **£59** 3 4 3
19-21 Elystan St, SW3 7584 1789 5–2C
MyHotel, 35 Ixworth Pl, SW3 7589 3718 5–2C
"The move to myHotel hasn't made me love it any less!" – a Chelsea old favourite that was rehoused on the same street a couple of years ago, but is "as good as ever", with "well-prepared, reasonably priced Sardinian cooking". It leaves behind Pellicanino – a more informal spot for pizza and pasta on the original site. /

E Pellicci E2 **£19** 3 4 5
332 Bethnal Green Rd 7739 4873 12–1D
"Lashings of Cockney charm" are on the menu of this "consistently marvellous" East End caff, known for its listed Art Deco interior, and "delicious, old-fashioned breakfast fry-ups". / E2 0AG; 4.15 pm; L only, closed Sun; no credit cards.

Pennethorne's Cafe Bar Somerset House WC2 NEW **£38**
The New Wing, Somerset Hs, Strand 3751 0570 2–2D
A recent addition to the increasingly well-served New Wing of Somerset House; not enough reviews for a rating this year, but initial reports tip it as a "smart, grown-up place to meet friends" for a glass of vino and a snack. / WC2R 1LA; www.pennethornescafe.co.uk; @pennethornes; 9.45 pm; closed Sun; no Amex.

Pentolina W14 **£47** 4 5 4
71 Blythe Rd 3010 0091 7–1C
"What a jewel!" – this "massively popular" Olympia spot is "heaven-around-the-corner" for locals; it's "cramped and noisy", but very "attractive" looking, with "extremely welcoming" service from the chef's wife and "fresh and imaginative" Italian cooking. / W14 0HP; www.pentolinarestaurant.co.uk; 10 pm; closed Mon & Sun; no Amex.

The Pepper Tree SW4 **£30** 3 3 3
19 Clapham Common S'side 7622 1758 10–2D
"There's no time to hang around", at this "always crowded" Clapham canteen; "you do have to queue, but give it a go for its modestly priced nosh that's simple, unfussy, and filling". / SW4 7AB; www.thepeppertree.co.uk; @PepperTreeSW4; 10.45 pm, Sun & Mon 10.15 pm; no booking.

Percy & Founders W1 NEW **£54** 3 3 3
1 Pearson Sq, Fitzroy Pl 3761 0200 2–1B
There's "a real wow factor" to the "smart and American-feeling" decor of this big new watering hole – the "open and spacious ground floor of a Fitzrovia office building"; fans say the food is "surprisingly good" too, but others – judging it "over-designed and inauthentic" – find its appeal "hollow". / W1T 3BF; percyandfounders.co.uk; @PercyFounders; 10.30 pm; closed Sun D.

Pescatori **£56** 3 2 2
11 Dover St, W1 7493 2652 3–3C
57 Charlotte St, W1 7580 3289 2–1C
These West End Italians may "lack that friendly local feel" but even their worst critic says the fish and seafood here is consistently "well done". / www.pescatori.co.uk; 11 pm; closed Sat L & Sun.

Petersham Hotel TW10 **£65** 3 4 5
Nightingale Ln 8940 7471 1–4A
"Unbeatable views of the Thames" are the stand-out feature of this "elegant" (if "rather dated") traditional dining room in a "lovely, old, grand hotel", near Richmond Park – a particular hit with its silver-haired clientele; service is "gracious" and "un-rushed", and it's just the job for a special family meal. / TW10 6UZ; www.petershamhotel.co.uk; @ThePetersham; 9.45 pm, Sun 8.45 pm; set Sun L £57 (FP).

Petersham Nurseries TW10 **£72** 2 2 4
Church Ln, Off Petersham Rd 8940 5230 1–4A
"Down a narrow lane, near Richmond Park, an idyllic and unique greenhouse setting, with earthen floor, greenery and pleasantly distressed antiques creates a magical atmosphere"; food-wise, though, this now-famous garden centre café "is not what it used to be" – "uninspiring", yet "priced like the West End". / TW10 7AG; www.petershamnurseries.com; @PetershamN; L only, closed Mon.

The Petite Coree NW6 NEW **£39** 5 4 2
98 West End Ln 7624 9209 1–1B
"A former Nobu chef brings his magic touch to NW6", with the opening of this "really sweet little neighbourhood find"; while the "cramped" interior "leaves something to be desired", the "unlikely sounding Korean/Euro fusion fare" is "somehow made to work" – "it's truly wonderful and inexpensive". / NW6 2LU; www.thepetitecoree.com.

La Petite Maison W1 £83 434
54 Brook's Mews 7495 4774 3–2B
"You're whisked to the South of France", when you visit this "sophisticated", "noisy" and "crowded" Mayfair haunt; few seem to begrudge the dizzying prices, as the "gimmick-free" Mediterranean-style sharing plates are "simply stunning" – "appealingly light" and so, so fresh. / W1K 4EG; www.lpmlondon.co.uk; @lpmlondon; 10.45 pm, Sun 9.45 pm.

Pétrus SW1 £108 343
1 Kinnerton St 7592 1609 5–1D
The "stunning" wine selection is the centrepiece of Gordon Ramsay's swish and discreet Belgravian; on most accounts it's "stunningly good in every way", but it's also "extremely expensive" and a tad "too corporate" for some tastes. / SW1X 8EA; www.gordonramsay.com/petrus; @petrus; 10.15 pm; closed Sun; no trainers; set weekday L £66 (FP).

Peyote W1 £70 223
13 Cork St 7409 1300 3–3C
Mayfair Latino overseen by Mexico City legend, chef Eduardo Garcia, that's not made huge waves, but undoubtedly has a "trendy, buzzing atmosphere"; fans do hail its "delicious" Mexican tucker, but even they say it's "dear" – to foes it's "disappointing with the owner's pedigree" and, at the price, "exorbitant". / W1S 3NS; www.peyoteresaurant.com; @Peyotelondon; Mon-Thu 1 am, Fri & Sat 2 am; closed Sat L & Sun.

Pham Sushi EC1 £36 531
159 Whitecross St 7251 6336 12–2A
"You don't go for the ambience!"; you go to this "basic" Barbican fixture for "fabulous" sushi and sashimi that's "incredible value". / EC1Y 8JL; www.phamsushi.co.uk; @phamsushi; 9.45 pm; closed Sat L & Sun.

Pho £35 223
Branches throughout London
"For a wholesome steaming hot bowl of noodles", these popular Vietnamese pitstops remain a "reliable option", but "quality has dropped since its early days" and its overall performance is now "OK but unspectacular". / www.phocafe.co.uk; EC1 10 pm, Fri & Sat 10.30 pm, W1 10.30 pm, W12 9 pm, Sat 7 pm, Sun 6 pm; EC1 closed Sat L & Sun, W1 closed Sun; no Amex; no booking.

The Phoenix SW3 £49 233
23 Smith St 7730 9182 5–2D
"Wonderfully atmospheric" backstreet boozer (part of Geronimo Inns) that's "always good fun", and with food that's "decently priced for Chelsea". / SW3 4EE; www.geronimo-inns.co.uk; @ThePhoenixSW3; 10 pm; SRA-3.*

Phoenix Palace NW1 £56 322
5-9 Glentworth St 7486 3515 2–1A
"Giant green and gold fixture", near Baker Street, that's "well-favoured by the Chinese community", particularly for dim sum; it's not as highly rated as it once was however – dishes can be "matchless" but they can also be "so-so" nowadays. / NW1 5PG; www.phoenixpalace.co.uk; 11.15 pm, Sun 10.15 pm.

Picture W1 £49 343
110 Great Portland St 7637 7892 2–1B
An "epic tasting menu" is a highlight of the "interesting" and "good value" small-plate formula, at this "sparse"-looking two-year-old near Broadcasting House, "decorated with the usual exposed brick, concrete and naked bulbs". / W1W 6PQ; www.picturerestaurant.co.uk; @picturerest; 10 pm; closed Sun.

Piebury Corner N7 £19 433
209-211 Holloway Rd 7700 5441 8–2D
It helps to be a fan of the Gunners if you visit this "small" 'pie deli' near the Emirates, whose "great range of pies, roasties and gravies" is named for members of the Arsenal team – "good grub at good prices", plus an "ever-changing" list of beers and wines. / N7 8DL; www.pieburycorner.com.

PIED À TERRE W1 £110 553
34 Charlotte St 7636 1178 2–1C
David Moore's "perennially excellent!" foodie temple in Fitzrovia remains one of London's prime gastronomic 'heavy hitters' – service is "outstanding", the "very clever" cuisine is "a joy", and a friendly sommelier oversees a "treasure trove" of wine. Stop Press – chef Marcus Eaves left in early September 2015, but David Moore has a good track record of attracting the best talent here. / W1T 2NH; www.pied-a-terre.co.uk; @PiedaTerreUK; 10.45 pm; closed Sat L & Sun; booking: max 7; set weekday L £60 (FP), set pre-theatre £64 (FP).

Pig & Butcher N1 £52 444
80 Liverpool Rd 7226 8304 8–3D
"Beautiful meats cooked to perfection" are the highlight of the daily changing menu of this "very decent" Islington gastropub – "it's very busy, and rightly so". / N1 0QD; www.thepigandbutcher.co.uk; @pigandbutcher; 10 pm, Sun 9 pm; Mon-Thu D only, Fri-Sun open L & D.

Pilpel £9 442
38 Brushfield Street, London, E1 7247 0146 12–2B
Old Spitalfields Mkt, E1 7375 2282 12–2B
146 Fleet St, EC4 7583 2030 9–2A
Paternoster Sq, EC4 7248 9281 9–2B
"Just really really good falafel" from this small chain – "crisp but never dry", "deeply flavoured", "always fresh", and pleasantly "fluffy". / www.pilpel.co.uk; (1) MON - FRI 4pm (2) Mon-Fri 4pm / Sun 5pm(3) Mon -Thirs 8pm / Fri 4pm(4) Mon -Thurs 9pm / Fri 4pm / Sun 6pm; some branches closed Sat & Sun.

Piquet W1 NEW £55
92-94 Newman St 3826 4500 3–1D
The first solo effort from chef Allan Pickett (last seen at D&D London's Plateau) is set to open in Autumn 2015, backed by Bodean's founder André Blais – expect classic French-style cuisine using British ingredients. / W1T 3EZ; www.piquet-restaurant.co.uk.

El Pirata W1 £39 344
5-6 Down St 7491 3810 3–4B
"Mad, slightly Bohemian bar" (well, by Mayfair's stodgy standards anyway) whose "lively" style and "good-value tapas" makes for "a lot of fun at very reasonable prices" for such an expensive area. / W1J 7AQ; www.elpirata.co.uk; @ElPirataMayfair; 11.30 pm; closed Sat L & Sun.

Pitt Cue Co W1 £25 533
1 Newburgh St 7287 5578 3–2D
"Pulled pork the best this side of Austin, TX" and other meaty-licious treats induce severe "cravings" in fans of this "brilliant BBQ", just off Carnaby Street; "you find queues and end up sharing tables, but this is part of the experience!" / W1F 7RB; www.pittcue.co.uk; @PittCueCo.

Pizarro SE1 £50 344
194 Bermondsey St 7407 7339 9–4D
José P is "a genuine star" and his "ebullient" Bermondsey favourite inspires rave reviews for its "helpful" service and "absolutely delicious" cooking; it's somewhat overshadowed by its nearby tapas bar sibling however. See also José Pizarro, EC2. / SE1 3TQ; www.josepizarro.com/restaurants/pizarro; @Jose_Pizarro; 11 pm, Sun 10 pm.

Pizza East £48 434
310 Portobello Rd, W10 8969 4500 6–1A
79 Highgate Rd, NW5 3310 2000 8–1B
56 Shoreditch High St, E1 7729 1888 12–1B
"Get your skinnys on, brush up the face fur and maybe have a tattoo also" if you visit these "too-cool-for-school, hipster heavens". But it seems "you can have both style and substance" – staff are "friendly" and the pizza is "totally inauthentic yet utterly delicious". / www.pizzaeast.com; @PizzaEast; E1 Sun-Wed 11 pm, Thu 12 am, Fri-Sat 1am; W10 Mon-Thu 11.30 pm, Fri-Sat 12 am, Sun 10.30 pm.

Pizza Metro £43 432
147-149 Notting Hill Gate, W11 7727 8877 6–2B
64 Battersea Rise, SW11 7228 3812 10–2C
"Proper, Neapolitan wood-fired pizza" (served al metro) drags fans from all over town to this "busy" old-favourite in Battersea, which always delivers a "fun" (if "noisy") night out; it has a similar, but less well-known, sibling in Notting Hill. /

Pizza Pilgrims £33 334
102 Berwick St, W1 0778 066 7258 3–2D
11-12 Dean St, W1 7287 8964 3–1D
Kingly Ct, Carnaby St, W1 7287 2200 3–2C
"I don't like pizza, but I LOVE this pizza!" – the Elliot brothers' "funky and fun" Soho pitstops are "worth the pilgrimage" thanks to "authentic" fare that's "a slice above the chains". / Mon - Sat 10.30pm, Sun 9.30 pm.

PizzaExpress £41 222
Branches throughout London
"Still the Daddy!" – this "amazingly consistent", 50-year-old chain remains formidably successful, not least as an "ultra-reliable, go-to-destination with the kids"; its ambience rating took a swallow dive this year however – something about the management style of new owners Hony Capital? / www.pizzaexpress.co.uk; 11.30 pm - midnight; most City branches closed all or part of weekend; no booking at most branches; SRA-1.*

Pizzeria Oregano N1 £41 443
18-19 St Albans Pl 7288 1123 8–3D
"Shhh don't tell anyone!" – fans of this "tucked-away Italian, hidden off Upper Street", say "its pizzas can't be beat"; "one of the best places hereabouts for a family meal". / N1 0NX; www.pizzaoregano.co.uk; @PizzeriaOregano; 11 pm, Fri 11.30 pm, Sun 10.30 pm; closed weekday L.

Pizzeria Pappagone N4 £36 344
131 Stroud Green Rd 7263 2114 8–1D
"Make sure you book at the weekends", for this "bustling" Stroud Green Italian ("the perfect spot for any family that doesn't want to be the noisiest one there"); "speedy" service is "the friendliest ever", and "outstanding" pizza is the highlight of a wide menu. / N4 3PX; www.pizzeriapappagone.co.uk; @Pizza_Pappagone; midnight.

Pizzeria Rustica TW9 £41 443
32 The Quadrant 8332 6262 1–4A
"Genuinely 'home-made' pizza" wins fans for this "hectic, not exactly spacious, but efficient and jolly" outfit, handy for Richmond station. / TW9 1DN; www.pizzeriarustica.co.uk; @RusticaPizzeria; Mon-Sat 11 pm, Sun 10 pm; no Amex.

PJ's Bar and Grill SW3 £58 3 4 4
52 Fulham Rd 7581 0025 5–2C
"Great brunch on weekends" is a well-established Chelsea ritual at this large, polo-themed venue, where "fun at the bar" is a greater draw than the "wide choice of sometimes unimaginative fare". / SW3 6HH; www.pjsbarandgrill.co.uk; @PJsBARANDGRILL; 10.30 pm, Sun 10 pm.

Plateau E14 £70 2 3 3
Canada Pl 7715 7100 11–1C
"My go-to place for a business meal in Canary Wharf" is how many E14 worker bees think of D&D London's elevated vantage-point ("lovely views" of Docklands), despite its "hard furnishings" and food that's "good not great". Top Menu Tip – "super dinner-time special offers". / E14 5ER; www.plateau-restaurant.co.uk; @plateaulondon; 10.15 pm; closed Sat L & Sun; set weekday L £47 (FP).

The Plough SW14 £45 3 4 4
42 Christ Church Rd 8876 7833 10–2A
"After a walk in Richmond Park, this traditional East Sheen pub is a wonderful destination"; the food – "a combination of pub grub and 'smarter' dishes" – is "reliably good", service makes an effort, and as well as an atmospheric interior, there's a big outside area with heaters. / SW14 7AF; theplough.com; Mon-Thu 9.30 pm, Fri & Sat 10 pm, Sun 9 pm; no Amex.

Plum + Spilt Milk Great Northern Hotel N1 £64 2 3 3
King's Cross 3388 0800 8–3C
"Very convenient for the Eurostar", this "comfortable" and "beautifully-lit" operation is "ideal for business meetings", or "to make the start of a journey special"; its cooking – if sometimes "uninspiring" – is "pretty solid" too. / N1C 4TB; www.plumandspiltmilk.com; @PlumSpiltMilk; 11 pm, Sun 10 pm; set weekday L £44 (FP).

Plum Valley W1 £51 3 2 3
20 Gerrard St 7494 4366 4–3A
"Rising above the mundane standards of Chinatown" – this somewhat superior venture particularly wins praise for its "great dim sum with a twist". / W1D 6JQ; www.plumvalleylondon.com; 11.30 pm.

Poissonnerie de l'Avenue SW3 £70 3 3 3
82 Sloane Ave 7589 2457 5–2C
"Just where to take an aged relative" – this "elegant" Brompton Cross stalwart is "reminiscent of a bygone age"; "the bill mounts up", but its loyal, silver-haired following just say "thank goodness for a place like this", with "courteous" service and "unfailingly good fish". / SW3 3DZ; www.poissonnerie.co.uk; 11.30 pm, Sun 10,30 pm.

POLLEN STREET SOCIAL W1 £95 2 2 2
8-10 Pollen St 7290 7600 3–2C
Eeeessh! – turns out Jason Atherton isn't superhuman after all, as falling ratings at his original solo venture give the first hints of growing pains amidst his burgeoning (but hitherto seemingly bulletproof) empire. This, the original Social, still has legions of fans who laud its "utterly inventive" cuisine and "buzzy" (if "downright noisy") vibe, but its performance has seemed more "generic" and "passionless" of late, with gripes over "unmemorable" meals at high prices, and "conveyor-belt" service. / W1S 1NQ; www.pollenstreetsocial.com; @PollenStSocial; 10.45 pm; closed Sun; set weekday L £63 (FP).

Polpetto W1 £48 3 3 3
11 Berwick St 7439 8627 3–2D
Fans of this Soho branch of Russell Norman's Venetian tapas empire say it's "easily his best" – "a great little 'bacaro', oozing atmosphere, matched by delicious small plates"; even so, there are one or two reporters for whom "it's not as good as expected". / W1F 0PL; www.polpo.co.uk; @PolpettoW1; 11 pm.

Polpo £40 2 2 3
41 Beak St, W1 7734 4479 3–2D
142 Shaftesbury Ave, WC2 7836 3119 4–2B
6 Maiden Ln, WC2 7836 8448 4–3D
Duke Of York Sq, SW3 7730 8900 5–2D NEW
126-128 Notting Hill Gate, W11 7229 3283 6–2B
2-3 Cowcross St, EC1 7250 0034 9–1A
"Are they starting to believe their own PR" at Russell Norman's NYC-style hang-outs? Legions of fans still say they're "such fun" with "tasty", "simple" Venetian tapas, but a growing number – citing "erratic" service and "mediocre" food – believe "it's all beginning to feel a little dispiriting and chain-y". / www.polpo.co.uk; W1 & EC1 11 pm; WC2 11 pm, Sun 10.30 pm; W1 & EC1 closed D Sun.

Le Pont de la Tour SE1 £80 2 2 4
36d Shad Thames 7403 8403 9–4D
It has "stunning views" of Tower Bridge, but D&D London's "elegant" landmark has seemed "stuck in the '90s" in recent years, and – aided by its "serious" wine list – appeals most as a business venue nowadays. In October 2015 it re-opens after a major two-month face-lift – let's hope they will pep up the "decent" but pricey cooking too. / SE1 2YE; www.lepontdelatour.co.uk; @lepontdelatour; 10.30 pm, Sun 9.30 pm; no trainers; set Sun L £54 (FP).

Scott's
Inamo
Trinity

Popeseye £47 342
108 Blythe Rd, W14 7610 4578 7–1C
36 Highgate Hill, N19 3601 3830 8–1B
277 Upper Richmond Rd, SW15 8788 7733 10–2A
"Unerringly succulent steaks" plus "quality, affordable red wines" is a "straightforward" formula that's sustained these "cosy", if basic local bistros since way before the current steakhouse craze; the Olympia original has always eclipsed its Putney spin-off, but feedback is good on the new Highgate branch. / www.popeseye.com; 10.30 pm; D only, closed Sun; no credit cards.

Poppies £29 434
30 Hawley Cr, NW1 7267 0440 8–2B
6-8 Hanbury St, E1 7247 0892 12–2C
"No-frills", fish 'n' chip restaurants in Spitalfields and Camden Town where "you eat surrounded by Post-War memorabilia, and served by staff in period dress"; it's all done "with style and zing", and "serves better food than you might expect"; live music in NW1 too. /

La Porchetta Pizzeria £34 233
33 Boswell St, WC1 7242 2434 2–1D
141-142 Upper St, N1 7288 2488 8–2D
147 Stroud Green Rd, N4 7281 2892 8–1D
74-77 Chalk Farm Rd, NW1 7267 6822 8–2B
84-86 Rosebery Ave, EC1 7837 6060 9–1A
Of all the wide variety of dishes, it's particularly the "genuine pizzas" in "good portions" (and at "fair value" prices) that keep packing in punters at these upbeat north London stand-bys; "lovely", "no fuss" service too. / www.laporchetta.net; Mon - Sat 11pm, Sun 10 pm; WC1 closed Sat L & Sun; N1, EC1 & NW1 closed Mon-Fri L; N4 closed weekday L; no Amex.

La Porte des Indes W1 £65 334
32 Bryanston St 7224 0055 2–2A
"From the outside it appears ordinary", but inside this "Tardis-like" space near Marble Arch is "vast, exotic and beautiful", complete with "a waterfall and costumed waiters"; it's all good "fun", and "complemented by great food" from an "upmarket" French-colonial Indian menu. / W1H 7EG; www.laportedesindes.com; @LaPorteDesIndes; 11.30 pm, Sun 10.30 pm.

Il Portico W8 £54 354
277 Kensington High St 7602 6262 7–1D
"You get treated like the prodigal son returning home", if you're one of the many regulars at this easily-missed, "convivial" stalwart, near Kensington Odeon, "run by the same family since its inception back in the 1970's"; "all the old favourites are on the menu" and realised to a very dependable standard. / W8 6NA; www.ilportico.co.uk; 10.45 pm; closed Sun.

Portland W1 NEW £58 553
113 Great Portland St 7436 3261 2–1B
Outstanding "new kid-on-the-foodie-block", which crept into Fitzrovia without fanfare, but is proving one of the year's gastronomic highlights; its "functional" and "echo-y" design covers the "bare essentials", the notably "genuine" service (led by co-owner Will Lander) is "spot on", and the "eclectic" cuisine is "novel" and "exciting". / W1W 6QQ; www.portlandrestaurant.co.uk; @portland113; 9.45 pm; closed Sun.

Portobello Ristorante W11 £50 333
7 Ladbroke Rd 7221 1373 6–2B
It's well worth knowing about this "very friendly and VERY Italian" spot, just off Notting Hill Gate; the welcome is "warm", they serve "wonderful" pizza, there's a superb outside terrace in summer, and it's a winner if you have kids too. / W11 3PA; www.portobellolondon.co.uk; 10 pm, Fri-Sat 11 pm.

The Portrait National Portrait Gallery WC2 £58 234
St Martin's Pl 7312 2490 4–4B
"Stunning views towards Nelson and Parliament" are the exceptional talking points of this top-floor dining room, by Trafalgar Square; fans say the cooking is "amazingly good for a gallery" too, but to harsher critics that translates as "reliable but unexciting" (maybe go for an "impressive brunch"). / WC2H 0HE; www.npg.org.uk/visit/shop-eat-drink.php; @NPGLondon; Thu-Fri 8.30 pm; Sun-Wed closed D.

Potli W6 £42 433
319-321 King St 8741 4328 7–2B
"No idea why it's still second to Indian Zing!" – this nearby, sparky-looking Hammersmith hang-out serves "inventive and big-flavoured" cuisine that's only a smidgeon less highly rated than at its better known local rival. Top Menu Tip – "fantastic fish curries". / W6 9NH; www.potli.co.uk; @Potlirestaurant; 10.30 pm, Fri & Sat 11.30 pm.

La Poule au Pot SW1 £63 335
231 Ebury St 7730 7763 5–2D
"For romantic gazing across a candle into the eyes of your beloved", there is no better choice than this famously "seductive" haven of "dark corners and intimacy" in Pimlico. The hearty, "classic" Gallic sustenance carries "no surprises", but it and the "colourful", "resolutely French" service all "add to the rustic charm". / SW1W 8UT; www.pouleaupot.co.uk; 11 pm, Sun 10 pm; set weekday L £45 (FP).

Prawn On The Lawn N1 £47 4 4 3
220 St Paul's Rd 3302 8668 8–2D
A short hop from Highbury & Islington tube, this fishmonger-cum-restaurant is well worth tracking down for its "amazingly fresh fish, simply prepared", and "knowledgeable owner and staff" – but you may have to squeeze in like the proverbial sardine! / N1 2LY; prawnonthelawn.com; @PrawnOnTheLawn; 11 pm; closed Mon & Sun; no Amex.

Primeur N5 £48 4 3 3
116 Petherton Rd 7226 5271 1–1C
"Just what N5 needed!" – an "amazing neighbourhood winner" that's "hard to find and hard to book" but serves "beautiful, simple dishes" and "very good", somewhat "esoteric" wine; negatives? – get on their wrong side, and staff can display a "bad attitude". / N5 2RT; www.primeurn5.co.uk; @Primeurs1; 10 pm; closed Mon, Tue L, Wed L, Thu L & Sun D; no booking.

The Prince Of Wales SW15 £48 4 3 4
138 Upper Richmond Rd 8788 1552 10–2B
Ratings are consistently positive for this local, near East Putney station – part of the dependable Food & Fuel chain – praised for its "excellent gastropub fare". / SW15 2SP; www.princeofwalesputney.co.uk; @princeofwalessw; 10 pm, Sun 9.30 pm.

Princess Garden W1 £50 3 3 3
8-10 North Audley St 7493 3223 3–2A
You're not in Chinatown now! – this "plush" Mayfair Chinese is an "elegant" ("slightly clinical") spot with "smartly dressed" staff and a "comfortable" interior; the Cantonese cooking is "consistent" and "surprisingly good value" too. / W1K 6ZD; www.princessgardenofmayfair.com; 11 pm.

Princess of Shoreditch EC2 £50 3 4 4
76 Paul St 7729 9270 12–1B
"Downstairs, they still know how to do proper pub food" – up the spiral stairs there's a "relaxed" restaurant serving "surprisingly good" grub – at this "unpretentious" but happening Shoreditch boozer. / EC2A 4NE; www.theprincessofshoreditch.com; @princessofs; 10 pm, Sun 8 pm; no Amex.

Princess Victoria W12 £46 3 3 3
217 Uxbridge Rd 8749 5886 7–1B
This "beautifully restored, Victorian gin palace" makes a "lovely" and "bustling" retreat from a busy highway, deep in Shepherd's Bush; it's become a major local destination thanks to its "enticing" food and "very strong wine list for a pub". / W12 9DH; www.princessvictoria.co.uk; @pvwestlondon; 10.30 pm, Sun 9.30 pm; no Amex.

Princi W1 £35 3 2 4
135 Wardour St 7478 8888 3–2D
"Late-night munchies?"... "pre-theatre snack?"... "need a quick light lunch?" – this "vibrant and fun" (if "jammed") Milanese-inspired deli-patisserie in Soho is just the job, with a "tempting" array of dishes ranging from "top" pizza to "sinful" cakes. / W1F 0UT; www.princi.com; midnight, Sun 10 pm; no booking.

Prix Fixe W1 £39 3 2 3
39 Dean St 7734 5976 4–2A
"For an enjoyable evening of classic French food that doesn't break the bank, this little bit of France in Soho delivers with remarkable reliability", and offers "good value for money". / W1D 4PU; www.prixfixe.net; @prixfixelondon; 11.30 pm.

Provender E11 £39 4 4 3
17 High St 8530 3050 1–1D
"Proof the east is on the up!" – well-known restaurateur, Max Renzland's "bourgeois" café/ bistro in Wanstead is a "classic" Gallic venture, "with a proper French attitude" and very "well-executed" cooking. Top Menu Tip – the set lunch menu is "amazing value for money". / E11 2AA; www.provenderlondon.co.uk; @ProvenderBistro; Sun 9 pm, Mon-Fri 10 pm.

The Providores W1 £70 3 3 2
109 Marylebone High St 7935 6175 2–1A
Increasingly it is the "consistently interesting" list of NZ wines, visiting makers and "phenomenal" wine dinners that reporters note at this first-floor Marylebone dining room; leaving aside its "terrific" and "innovative" brunch, the Pan-Pacific cuisine is less in the spotlight. / W1U 4RX; www.theprovidores.co.uk; 10.30 pm; SRA-2.*

(Tapa Room) The Providores W1 £58 3 3 3
109 Marylebone High St 7935 6175 2–1A
"Still exciting!" – even after 15 years, support for Peter Gordon's "imaginative" Pan-Pacific Marylebone tapas bar is very solid – if you're prepared to be "squashed" into the "crowded" dining room, results can still "surprise". / W1U 4RX; www.theprovidores.co.uk; @theprovidores; 10.30 pm, Sun 10 pm.

Prufrock Coffee EC1 £13 3 4 4
23-25 Leather Ln 0785 224 3470 9–2A
"Much beard stroking" is a hazard at this "coffee geek heaven" near Chancery Lane, where "brews are pulled with excruciating care on a Marzocco machine" – a "buzzy" spot with "very decent" snacks too. / EC1N 7TE; www.prufrockcoffee.com; @PrufrockCoffee; L only; no Amex.

Pulia SE1 NEW **£38**
36 Stoney St 7407 8766 9–4C
Already an established chain of café/delis in its homeland, this Italian newcomer – right in the scrum of London's criminally busy Borough Market – has yet to inspire sufficient reports for a rating. / SE1 9AD; www.pulia.it/en; @Pulia; 8.30 pm.

The Punchbowl W1 **£48** 3 3 4
41 Farm St 7493 6841 3–3A
Serving the well-heeled residents of Mayfair since 1750, this characterful, tastefully revamped Georgian boozer (owned till recently by Madonna-ex, Guy Ritchie) wins decent ratings across the board, albeit from a smattering of reporters. / W1J 5RP; www.punchbowllondon.com; @ThePunchBowlLDN; closed Sun D.

Punjab WC2 **£32** 3 3 3
80 Neal St 7836 9787 4–2C
This "faded" Covent Garden veteran is "one of London's oldest" and "much better than you might expect from its touristy location"; service is good too, although "you do sometimes get the feeling that the quicker they can get it to you, the quicker you'll go". / WC2H 9PA; www.punjab.co.uk; 11 pm, Sun 10.30 pm.

Quaglino's SW1 **£65** 2 2 3
16 Bury St 7930 6767 3–3D
Fans hail the "third coming" of this "glitzy" D&D London veteran – relaunched in 2014 with more regular entertainment – applauding its "much busier and buzzier" vibe in particular; its ratings are still dragged down though by too many "very, very average" reports. / SW1Y 6AJ; www.quaglinos-restaurant.co.uk; @quaglinos; 10.30 pm, Fri & Sat 11 pm; closed Sun; no trainers; set dinner £43 (FP), set weekday L £47 (FP).

The Quality Chop House EC1 **£47** 3 5 3
94 Farringdon Rd 7278 1452 9–1A
"Retaining the era of a bygone age" – this restored 'Working Class Caterer' is a foodie linchpin of Farringdon, despite its "bum-numbingly, cripplingly-uncomfy, bench-seating booths"; "honest" British grub is "prepared with care", but it's somewhat secondary to the "brief but intriguing and fairly priced" wine list. / EC1R 3EA; www.thequalitychophouse.com; @QualityChop; 10.30 pm; closed Sun.

Quantus W4 **£41** 4 5 4
38 Devonshire Rd 8994 0488 7–2A
"Leo, the owner, is very entertaining" and the "amiable" staff set up a "welcoming" vibe at this "snug" Chiswick favourite; food-wise it's rather "in the shadow of La Trompette opposite", but the Latin-influenced cuisine is "always interesting". / W4 2HD; www.quantus-london.com; 10 pm; closed Mon L, Tue L & Sun.

Quattro Passi W1 **£95** 2 3 2
34 Dover St 3096 1444 3–3C
"The sister restaurant of one with the same name on the Amalfi coast" – this Mayfair yearling does win praise (especially from expense accounters) for its "proper Italian cooking" and "spacious" interior, but the "3-digit wine list" is a total shocker ("I actually gasped out loud"), and "at these prices, they must be having a laugh". / W1S 4NG; www.quattropassi.co.uk; @quattropassiuk; 10.30 pm; closed Sun D; set weekday L £38 (FP).

The Queens Arms SW1 **£43** 3 4 4
11 Warwick Way 7834 3313 2–4B
"Cheerful and helpful" staff contribute to the appeal of this popular Pimlico gastropub, where menu staples ("excellent burgers and fish 'n' chips") come particularly recommended; eat in the "crowded" bar or "quieter upstairs". / SW1V 1QT; www.thequeensarmspimlico.co.uk; @thequeensarms; 10 pm.

Queenswood SW11 NEW **£46** 2 2 3
15 Battersea Sq 7228 8877 5–4C
In deepest Battersea, a new bistro featuring extensive drinks options, and with a wider-than-usual array of veggie dishes; fans say it's a "lively addition to the area", but others give it a more lukewarm reception. / SW11 3RA; queenswoodldn.com; @QueenswoodLDN; 10.30 pm; no Amex.

Le Querce SE23 **£38** 4 4 3
66-68 Brockley Rise 8690 3761 1–4D
"The specials board is particularly interesting" at this "fantastic", "family-run" Sardinian – Brockley Park's greatest contribution to London gastronomy, with "very industrious" service. Top Menu Tips – "wonderful homemade pasta" and funky ice creams (e.g. beetroot and basil). / SE23 1LN; www.lequerce.co.uk; 10 pm, Sun 8.30 pm; closed Mon & Tue L.

Quilon SW1 £71 442

41 Buckingham Gate 7821 1899 2–4B

"It looks a little bit like an airport departure lounge", but the Taj Group's "understated", "well-spaced" and luxurious dining room, near Buck House, is a seriously good gastronomic destination with "fragrant", "delightfully subtle" Keralan cuisine that, at its best, is "unbeatable". / SW1E 6AF; www.quilon.co.uk; @TheQuilon; 11 pm, Sun 10.30 pm; set weekday L £50 (FP); SRA-1.*

Quirinale SW1 £60 332

North Ct, 1 Gt Peter St 7222 7080 2–4C

"You may spot the odd politico or two" at this Westminster basement, whose "bright, spacious, high-ceilinged interior" lifts its slightly "sterile" ambience; "in a neighbourhood without too many choices", its "fine" Italian cuisine is all the more notable. / SW1P 3LL; www.quirinale.co.uk; @quirinaleresto; 10.30 pm; closed Sat & Sun; set weekday L £42 (FP).

Quo Vadis W1 £56 354

26-29 Dean St 7437 9585 4–2A

Under the Hart Bros, this well-known Soho veteran is really on song, and the "particularly charming" staff contribute to the "bag-loads of character" in its "bright, spacious and gloriously flower-filled" dining room; Jeremy Lee's food is "not centre stage" but "unfussy, un-showy and very capable". / W1D 3LL; www.quovadissoho.co.uk; 10.45 pm; closed Sun; set pre-theatre £38 (FP), set weekday L £42 (FP).

Rabbit SW3 £47 444

172 King's Rd 3750 0172 5–3C

What is this "fun and original" sibling to Notting Hill's Shed doing in the heart of the King's Road? Its "innovative" British sharing plates can be a bit "microscopic", but are "superbly executed" with "farm-fresh" flavours, and the "creative", "barn-like" decor "works well in the crazy L-shaped space". / SW3 4UP; www.rabbit-restaurant.com; @RabbitResto; closed Mon L & Sun D.

Rabot 1745 SE1 £58 223

2-4 Bedale St 7378 8226 9–4C

"Not as gimmicky as it sounds, but not amazing either" – a fair summary of views on this Hotel Chocolat-backed yearling (with an atmospheric covered terrace overlooking Borough Market), that features "a very original menu with cocoa in every dish". / SE1 9AL; www.hotelcholcolat.com/uk/restaurant/rabot-1745; @rabot1745; 9.30 pm; closed Mon & Sun.

Radha Krishna Bhaven SW17 £29 332

86 Tooting High St 8682 0969 10–2C

Limited feedback on this well-established Tooting curry house – its South Indian cuisine is highly rated by those who do comment however. / SW17 0RN.

Ragam W1 £28 542

57 Cleveland St 7636 9098 2–1B

"Standing the test of time over many years" – this "bright-lit" gem "in the shadow of the Telecom Tower" is arguably "the best cheap curry in central London", serving "terrific South Indian food at great prices"; looks-wise it's always been totally "nondescript", but they refurbished in summer 2015. Top Menu Tip – "dosas are a revelation". / W1T 4JN; www.ragam.co.uk; 11 pm.

Rainforest Café W1 £58 123

20-24 Shaftesbury Ave 7434 3111 3–3D

"I hate it... but kids love it!"; animatronic jungle creatures and real rain are a hazard at this theme diner near Piccadilly Circus, but even those who say it's "severely overpriced" sometimes admit (if through gritted teeth) that it can be great fun! / W1V 7EU; www.therainforestcafe.co.uk; @RainforestCafe; 10 pm, Fri & Sat 8 pm.

Randall & Aubin W1 £58 444

16 Brewer St 7287 4447 3–2D

"It just rocks!"; this "cool little Soho haven" is "a bit cramped and insanely busy" thanks to its "fabulous" seafood ("proper fruits de mer") and "top rotisserie chicken"; in September 2015, its once notoriously uncomfortable tall stools received a plush makeover, making them an even better perch for people-watching! / W1F 0SG; www.randallandaubin.com; @randallandaubin; 11 pm, Sat midnight, Sun 10 pm; no booking at D.

Rani N3 £29 322

7 Long Ln 8349 4386 1–1B

Finchley's Gujarati veggie-veteran is (on most accounts), "an old favourite back on form", serving a "delicious and varied selection" of "great-value dishes", with "fab homemade condiments". / N3 2PR; www.raniuk.com; @RaniVegetarian; 10.30 pm.

Raoul's Café £46 223

105-107 Talbot Rd, W11 7229 2400 6–1B

13 Clifton Rd, W9 7289 7313 8–4A

"Perfect eggs" – and "when it's warm, being able to sit out" – are the key selling points of this laid-back brunch favourite in Maida Vale, where "you often queue even though it's not cheap"; the Hammersmith branch has closed, but there's also a (little-commented-on) Notting Hill spin-off. / www.raoulsgourmet.com; 10.15 pm, W11 6.15 pm; booking after 5 pm only.

Rasa £38 433
6 Dering St, W1 7629 1346 3–2B
Holiday Inn Hotel, 1 Kings Cross, WC1 7833 9787 8–3D
55 Stoke Newington Church St, N16 7249 0344 1–1C
56 Stoke Newington Church St, N16 7249 1340 1–1C
"Ridiculously affordable", "delicately flavoured" (and "relatively healthy") Keralan cooking still wins rave reviews for this small South Indian chain, whose Stokey original remains "a go-to local gem". / www.rasarestaurants.com; 10.45 pm; WC1 & W1 closed Sun.

Rasoi SW3 £99 423
10 Lincoln St 7225 1881 5–2D
"Set in a beautiful townhouse in a side street near Sloane Square" – Vineet Bhatia's "calm" and "elegant" Chelsea HQ is, for fans, "the definition of innovative Indian cuisine", with each dish "a symphonic composition"; not everyone's impressed though, and even supporters can find it "horrifically expensive". / SW3 2TS; www.rasoirestaurant.co.uk; @GujaratiRasoi; 10.30 pm, Sun 9.45 pm; closed Sat L; set weekday L £58 (FP).

Ravi Shankar NW1 £32 322
132-135 Drummond St 7388 6458 8–4C
"Mercifully, little changes at this Little India veggie stalwart" – "a complete bargain" that's "the best of the buffet choices hereabouts"; "amazingly cheap at lunch". / NW1 2HL; 10.30 pm.

Red Dog £41 323
37 Hoxton Sq, N1 3551 8014 12–1B
27-31 Bedford Rd, SW4 3714 2747 10–2D
The "Devastator Burger" is a hallmark of this "crowded and noisy" Kansas City BBQ concept, in Hoxton and now also in Clapham too, but like most of the fare here, while "substantial", it's "fairly expensive". / www.reddogsaloon.co.uk; @reddogsaloonn1.

Red Fort W1 £65 222
77 Dean St 7437 2525 4–2A
This landmark curry-stalwart in Soho has revamped over the years, but its ratings waned sharply this year; for fans it's still a big favourite, but for others it's now a big let-down – "it made me think of an averagely 'premium' restaurant, in an averagely 'premium' hotel". / W1D 3SH; www.redfort.co.uk; @redfortlondon; 11.15 pm, Sun 10.15 pm; closed Sat L & Sun L; set weekday L & pre-theatre £38 (FP).

The Red Pepper W9 £48 322
8 Formosa St 7266 2708 8–4A
"Shame it's so cramped and uncomfortable", and "very noisy" too – the wood-fired pizza at this long-running Maida Vale fixture can be "excellent". / W9 1EE; www.theredpepperrestaurant.co.uk; Sat 11 pm, Sun 10 pm; closed weekday L; no Amex.

The Refinery NW1 NEW £49 233
5 Brock St, Regent's Pl 3002 5524 8–4C
Part of the Drake & Morgan empire (and sharing its name with the group's Bankside branch), this "light and spacious" arrival is a handy option near Euston station, serving "British staples at reasonable prices". / NW1 3FG; www.therefinerybar.co.uk; @therefinerybar; 10 pm; closed Sun; SRA-3.*

Le Relais de Venise L'Entrecôte £46 322
120 Marylebone Ln, W1 7486 0878 2–1A
18-20 Mackenzie Walk, E14 3475 3331 11–1C
5 Throgmorton St, EC2 7638 6325 9–2C
"A very simple concept that works every time" – this Gallic steakhouse chain offers little choice – you get "a rather tasty green salad", steak with secret sauce, "addictive fries", and second helpings if needed; the setting is "bustling", but "brusque-verging-on-rude" service can leave branches feeling "soulless". / www.relaisdevenise.com; W1 11 pm, Sun 10.30 pm; EC2 10 pm; EC2 closed Sat & Sun; no booking.

Resident Of Paradise Row E2 NEW £46
Arch 252 Paradise Row 7729 9609 12–1D
Locals tip it as a "great Sunday roast and brunch" spot, but otherwise there's limited feedback for this year-old bar/restaurant in Bethnal Green, sheltered by increasingly fashionable railway arches (and with a sizeable outside terrace). / E2 9LE; www.residentlondon.com; @ResidentPR; Tue-Sat 10.15 pm, Sun 8 pm; Kitchen is closed on Mondays but they still serve snacks.

Le Restaurant de Paul £38 443
29-30 Bedford St, WC2 7836 3304 4–3C
Tower 42, Old Broad St, EC2 7562 5599 9–2C NEW
Covent Garden HQ of the famous pâtisserie chain, where fans "are delighted they have a full-blown restaurant" – a civilised chamber, off the main shop. "Ideal for an afternoon-tea break" or light bite anytime (salads, charcuterie, omelettes, etc), a second full-service outpost opened in the City's Tower 42 as we went to press.

Reubens W1 £55 332
79 Baker St 7486 0035 2–1A
The "best salt beef in London" is hailed by fans of this long-established Marylebone deli-restaurant (the latter in the basement), serving "delicious kosher food in massive portions". / W1U 6RG; www.reubensrestaurant.co.uk; 9.45 pm; closed Fri D & Sat; no Amex.

Rex & Mariano W1 NEW £47 543
St Anne's Ct 7437 0566 4–2A
"A great attempt to redefine seafood dining!"; the Goodman Group have hit another home run with this "bright and airy" newcomer, tucked away down a Soho alleyway, where "sensational" dishes are "extraordinary value". The "waiter-free", iPad ordering can be "confusing", but fans say "it puts the diner at the heart of the meal". Top Menu Tip – raw items, grills, plus "outstanding" salads, ceviches, and courgette fries. Stop Pess – In September 2015, it was announced that Rex & Mariano would move elsewhere – these premises will become another new concept: Zelman Meats. / W1F 0BD; rexandmariano.com; @RexandMariano; Sun-Thu 10.30 pm, Fri & Sat 11 pm.

Rextail W1 £83 333
13 Albermarle St 3301 1122 3–3C
Arkady Novikov's year-old basement (a stylish, but "cramped" space of railway-carriage proportions) put in a better performance this year – "the price reflects its Mayfair setting", but it's overall "very enjoyable". / W1S 4HJ; www.rextail.co.uk; @Rextail_London; midnight; closed Sun.

The Rib Man E1 £12 53
Brick Lane, Brick Lane Market no tel 12–2C
Mark Gevaux's "meltingly tender ribs and rolls of porky greatness" can no longer be found at KERB – now you need to go to Brick Lane on Sundays instead; his "fiery" sauces are the stuff of urban legend – "Look out! They'll blow your head off!" / E1 6HR; www.theribman.co.uk; @theribman.

Rib Room, Jumeirah Carlton Tower Hotel SW1 £103 342
Cadogan Pl 7858 7250 5–1D
"A real treat in every respect" – this luxurious, well-spaced Belgravia dining room is firing on all cylinders after its revamp last year; as well as the top-quality roast beef and grills for which it's long been famous, the "seasonal menus show true skill and inventiveness". / SW1X 9PY; www.theribroom.co.uk; @RibRoomSW1; 11 pm, weekends 10.30 pm; set weekday L £69 (FP).

Riccardo's SW3 £43 233
126 Fulham Rd 7370 6656 5–3B
"If you have a table on the terrace, the ambience is great" at this "crowded" (and kid-friendly) "local favourite" in Chelsea, where "amiable Riccardo is usually in attendance"; its "simple" staples are regularly "well-prepared", but can also disappoint nowadays. / SW3 6HU; www.riccardos-italian-restaurant.co.uk; @riccardoslondon; 11.30 pm.

The Richmond E8 NEW £52 433
316 Queensbridge Rd 7241 1638 1–2D
Bargain bivalves (£1 an oyster at happy hour) are a mainstay of east London's only raw seafood bar – a feature of Brett Redman's new Hackney hang out (on the site of LMNT, RIP), which also boasts a "superb fish menu" and "good list of wines by the glass". / E8 3NH; therichmondhackney.com; @The Richmond; Mon-Thu 10 pm, Fri & Sat 10.30 pm; closed Sun D.

Riding House Café W1 £56 224
43-51 Great Titchfield St 7927 0840 3–1C
"Capturing the perfect brunch vibe" – this "buzzy", "NYC-style" haunt in Fitzrovia has a "very media" following that adores it, especially at breakfast (or for a business lunch), and it's "always busy"; even fans concede however, that the cooking here generally is "nothing to shout about". / W1W 7PQ; www.ridinghousecafe.co.uk; @ridinghousecafe; 10.30 pm, Sun 9.30 pm.

Rising Sun NW7 £48 343
137 Marsh Ln, Highwood Hill 8959 1357 1–1B
"An interesting Italian menu" helps differentiate this "picturesque", "small", "very friendly" family-run pub in Mill Hill; "prices seem to have edged up" in recent times, but even so "it's the best for miles around". / NW7 4EY; www.therisingsunmillhill.co.uk; @therisingsunpub; 9.30 pm, Sun 8.30 pm; closed Mon L.

Ristorante Frescobaldi W1 NEW £75 344
15 New Burlington Pl 3693 3435 3–2C
"The name is very '70s" – not so the "amazing and modern but comfy" design of this Mayfair newcomer, the first UK venture of a 700-year-old Italian wine dynasty; chef Roberto Reatini's food is well-praised, but, as one would expect, it's the "incredible" cellar that's the real draw here. / W1S 5HX; frescobaldirestaurants.com; @frescobaldi_london; 10.45 pm.

(Palm Court) The Ritz W1 £69 245
150 Piccadilly 7493 8181 3–4C
Loved by some ("the afternoon tea is unparalleled!"), but this famous and elegant chamber is to many disappointing ("dry, mechanically-cut sandwiches with fillings I had not seen since a wartime Sunday School party, aimed at naive tourists!"); whichever camp you're in, it's not cheap. / W1C 9BR; www.theritzlondon.com; 7.30 pm; jacket & tie required.

The Ritz Restaurant, The Ritz W1 £125 245
150 Piccadilly 7493 8181 3–4C
"The loveliest dining room in London" – this "wonderfully romantic" Louis XVI-style chamber is "a proper, old-school, fine-dining experience"; it's not a reliable one, however, given food that can be "poor", and even ardent fans can find the bill "shocking". / W1J 9BR; www.theritzlondon.com; @theritzlondon; 10 pm; jacket & tie required.

Riva SW13 £65 442
169 Church Rd 8748 0434 10–1A
With its "exceptional" north Italian cooking and "brilliantly knowledgeable" service – much of it from owner Andreas Riva – this "pricey but first-rate" Barnes fixture remains a place of foodie pilgrimage, and it inspired few gripes this year, despite its rather "drab" interior. Top Menu Tip – "the cinnamon ice cream with balsamic sounds weird but is the best dessert in town". / SW13 9HR; 10.30 pm, Sun 9 pm; closed Sat L.

Rivea Bulgari Hotel SW7 £70 242
171 Knightsbridge 7151 1025 5–1C
"Alain Ducasse is a genius", say fans of his Knightsbridge basement yearling, hailing its "sublime" small plates (prepared by protégé Damien Leroux), and "effortlessly smooth" service; however at its hefty prices, it can be "short on memorable dishes", and what is a "hip" and "magnificent" setting to some is to others plain "vulgar". / SW7 1DW; www.bulgarihotels.com; 10.15 pm; set weekday L £44 (FP).

THE RIVER CAFÉ W6 £100 323
Thames Wharf, Rainville Rd 7386 4200 7–2C
"Eye-wateringly expensive, but brilliant", say disciples of this world-famous Italian café (part of a Thames-side wharf in a Hammersmith backwater), for whom the "sophistication" of the "freshest ingredients prepared for maximum flavour" have long put it "in a league of its own" (especially outside on a sunny day). "Cramped" conditions and "brusque" service can "leave a lot to be desired" however, and there are many, many sceptics who – though not disputing that the grub's good – say prices are just "insane for a bit of al dente pasta". / W6 9HA; www.rivercafe.co.uk; @RiverCafeLondon; 9 pm, Sat 9.15 pm; closed Sun D.

Rivington Grill £52 333
178 Greenwich High Rd, SE10 8293 9270 1–3D
28-30 Rivington St, EC2 7729 7053 12–1B
"Efficient", somewhat "grown-up" Shoreditch and Greenwich brasseries, whose "straightforward" grills and burgers mean they are "always a safe bet", if an "unexciting" one. / www.rivingtongrill.co.uk; 11 pm, Sun 10 pm; SE10 closed Mon, Tue L & Wed L.

Roast SE1 £70 222
Stoney St 3006 6111 9–4C
A "top notch breakfast" with "sun streaming through those huge windows" is the most reliable attraction in this "light and airy" (but "soulless") dining room, over Borough Market; however at other times its British fare can seem "severely overpriced" given the "un-memorable" results – "I've had better £10 roasts in a pub!". / SE1 1TL; www.roast-restaurant.com; @roastrestuarant; 10.45 pm; closed Sun D; set Sun L £60 (FP); SRA-2.*

Rocca Di Papa £37 234
73 Old Brompton Rd, SW7 7225 3413 5–2B
75-79 Dulwich Village, SE21 8299 6333 1–4D
Even if the fare is "fairly standard stuff", these "always very busy" and "noisy" Italians in South Kensington and Dulwich Village win little but praise; a visit is "always fun". / SW7 11.30 pm; SE21 11 pm.

Rochelle Canteen E2 £50 433
Arnold Circus 7729 5677 12–1C
If you're not a "trendy youngster from a Shoreditch start-up" then prepare to "rough it" at Melanie Arnold & Margot Henderson's "almost secret" venture near Spitalfields Market ("you feel like you're eating in a school playground") – those who do are in for "a hidden world of delight", lovely garden and "imaginative" meals; you can even BYO. / E2 7ES; www.arnoldandhenderson.com; L only, closed Sat & Sun; no Amex.

Rocket £46 333
36-38 Kingsway, WC2 7242 8070 2–1D
2 Churchill Pl, E14 3200 2022 11–1C
201 Bishopsgate, EC2 7377 8863 12–2B
6 Adams Ct, EC2 7628 0808 9–2C
For a "cheap and cheerful" meal in areas like Canary Wharf and Bank this chain of "buzzing" diners generally proves an effective standby (even if it doesn't quite convince all reporters) – pizzas are "authentic" and portions "generous". / 10.30 pm, Sun 9.30 pm; W1 closed Sun; EC2 closed Sat & Sun; SW15 Mon-Wed D only, Bishopsgate closed Sun D, E14.

Roka £83 [4][3][3]
30 North Audley St, W1 7305 5644 3–2A
37 Charlotte St, W1 7580 6464 2–1C
Aldwych House, 71-91 Aldwych, WC2 7294 7636 2–2D
Unit 4, Park Pavilion, 40 Canada Sq, E14 7636 5228 11–1C
"Stunning" sushi and "exquisite robatayaki" again win acclaim for this venerated and recently-expanded Japanese-fusion group (whose Charlotte Street original is the best of the bunch). Enthusiasm dipped a little this year, however, with gripes that the newer siblings in particular seem more "noisy" and "corporate". / www.rokarestaurant.com; 11.15 pm, Sun 10.30 pm; booking: max 8.

The Rooftop Café, The Exchange SE1 £47 [3][3][5]
28 London Bridge St 3102 3770 9–4C
Don't be put off by the "very unwelcoming office-building entrance and a climb up some very shabby stairs" – once you emerge onto the terrace you're greeted by "incredible views" of the Shard and "very dependable" cooking at this "light and airy" hidden gem. / SE1 9SG; therooftopcafe.co.uk; @rooftopcafeldn; closed Mon D, Tue D & Sun.

Roots at N1 N1 £48 [5][5][3]
115 Hemingford Rd 7697 4488 8–3D
"Breathtakingly good" cuisine at very "sensible prices" wins rave reviews for this "very interesting" Indian, "tucked away in Islington"; this "candle-lit, high-ceilinged ex-pub" is "a lovely space" too, and the "gracious" staff "always have a smile for guests". / N1 1BZ; www.rootsatn1.com; @rootsatn1; 10 pm, Sun 9 pm; closed Mon, Tue–Sat D only, Sun open L & D.

Rosa's £35 [4][3][2]
23a Ganton St, W1 7287 9617 3–2C
48 Dean St, W1 7494 1638 4–3A
246 Fulham Rd, SW10 7583 9021 5–3B
Westfield Stratford City, E15 8519 1302 1–1D
12 Hanbury St, E1 7247 1093 12–2C
"Zingy", "simple" dishes "with a decent kick" at "reasonable prices" win praise for this high quality chain of straightforward, "busy" Thai cafés; the original near Brick Lane is still the highest rated, and there's a new Islington branch that's "airier than most". / www.rosaslondon.com; 10.30 pm, Fri & Sat 11 pm, Ganton St Sun 10 pm; some booking restrictions apply.

Rossopomodoro £38 [2][2][2]
50-52 Monmouth St, WC2 7240 9095 4–3B
214 Fulham Rd, SW10 7352 7677 5–3B
1 Rufus St, N1 7739 1899 12–1B
10 Jamestown Rd, NW1 7424 9900 8–3B
46 Garrett Ln, SW18 8877 9903 10–2B
"It's a chain, but it's a good chain" – the consensus on these "buzzing" Italians, particularly praised for their "fantastic pizza"; that said, for a business actually based in Naples, results overall are surprisingly MOR. / www.rossopomodoro.co.uk; 11.30 pm, WC2 Sun 11.30 pm.

Roti Chai W1 £46 [4][4][3]
3 Portman Mews South 7408 0101 3–1A
"Really authentic" but "not overpowering" flavours characterise the "exciting Indian street food" at this contemporary-style venue near Selfridges, where there's both a no-booking ground floor, and more formal basement. / W1H 6HS; www.rotichai.com; @rotichai; 10.30 pm.

Roti King, Ian Hamilton House NW1 £22 [5][1][1]
40 Doric Way 0 7966 0934 67 8–3C
"Nothing prepares you for the simply wonderful Malaysian rotis" freshly made "in front of your eyes" at the counter of this "tiny", "brusque" and "in-no-way-pretty" basement "dive" in "a grotty bit of Euston". / NW1 1LH; www.facebook.com/rotikinglondon.

Rotorino E8 £48 [3][3][3]
434 Kingsland Rd 7249 9081 1–1D
"Book a booth, and stay till late", say fans of Stevie Parle's Dalston spin-off, whose "fabulous, stylish interior and seductive low lighting" lends it a "buzzy" and "romantic" aura; it's "slightly pricey" however, and "the food ranges from very good to ordinary". / E8 4AA; www.rotorino.com; @Rotorino; 11 pm.

Rotunda Bar & Restaurant, Kings Place N1 £54 [2][2][3]
90 York Way 7014 2840 8–3C
With its beautiful canal-side terrace, this "buzzy" arts centre brasserie is ideal in summer, especially on business; realisation of the dishes – meat in particular – can be "wonderful", but can also be "way off-the-mark". / N1 9AG; www.rotundabarandrestaurant.co.uk; @rotundalondon; 11 pm; closed Sun.

Roux at Parliament Square RICS SW1 £88 553
12 Great George St 7334 3737 2–3C
The Roux family don't seem to have told Masterchef winner Steve Groves that MPs aren't the most discerning bunch! – his cooking at this elegant dining room near Parliament is "truly noteworthy", with many reports of "absolutely brilliant" meals and "exemplary service". / SW1P 3AD; www.rouxatparliamentsquare.co.uk; @RouxAPS; 10 pm; closed Sat & Sun.

Roux at the Landau, The Langham W1 £100 234
1c Portland Pl 7965 0165 2–1B
"There's a peaceful serenity" to this "beautiful" chamber, over the road from Broadcasting House, suiting it to either a "comfortable" business lunch or "romantic treat"; most reporters praise the "fabulous" cuisine too, although one or two "expected more" of the illustrious Roux brand. / W1B 1JA; www.thelandau.com; @Langham_Hotel; 10.30 pm ; closed Sat L & Sun; no trainers; set weekday L £68 (FP).

Rowley's SW1 £69 222
113 Jermyn St 7930 2707 3–3D
Fans of this St James's veteran (occupying the original Wall's Butchers Shop) hail its Chateaubriand as "among the best in London", and say its "unlimited frites are a joy!"; it's "not cheap" though, and its wine list can seem particularly "ordinary and overpriced". / SW1Y 6HJ; www.rowleys.co.uk; @rowleys_steak; 10.30 pm.

Rox Burger SE13 NEW £26 433
82 Lee High Rd 3372 4631 1–4D
In Lewisham, a tiny burger bar serving "fantastic homemade burgers" and "unusual sides" too; if there's a complaint it's that the "simple" premises are just "too small". / SE13 5PT; www.roxburger.com.

Royal Academy W1 £48 222
Burlington Hs, Piccadilly 7300 5608 3–3D
"They always seem to be trying to improve this barn of a restaurant" – a potentially charming chamber at the heart of the famous galleries; but while fans rate it as a handy West End standby, too often its performance is "lacking". / W1J 0BD; www.royalacademy.org.uk; @khrestaurant; 10.30 pm; L only, ex Fri open L & D; no booking at L.

Royal China £48 412
24-26 Baker St, W1 7487 4688 2–1A
805 Fulham Rd, SW6 7731 0081 10–1B
13 Queensway, W2 7221 2535 6–2C
30 Westferry Circus, E14 7719 0888 11–1B
"If you love Hong Kong, you'll feel right at home" at these "wonderfully garish" Cantonese stalwarts, which attract "overwhelming queues" to enjoy what many fans consider "the best dim sum in London"; service, though, is of the "couldn't-give-a-fig" variety. / www.royalchinagroup.co.uk; 10.45 pm, Fri & Sat 11.15 pm, Sun 9.45 pm; no booking Sat & Sun L.

Royal China Club W1 £74 432
40-42 Baker St 7486 3898 2–1A
"Extremely good Chinese fare is cooked with real class" at the Royal China group's "pricey but superior" Marylebone flagship; no great prizes for decor however, which "lacks warmth". / W1U 7AJ; www.rcguk.co.uk; 11 pm, Sun 10.30 pm.

The Royal Exchange Grand Café The Royal Exchange EC3 £55 224
The Royal Exchange Bank 7618 2480 9–2C
The "beautiful", ultra-impressive location (a majestic covered courtyard) eclipses all other aspects of this heart-of-the-City seafood operation – "a great venue for business" from breakfast on. / EC3V 3LR; www.royalexchange-grandcafe.co.uk; @rexlondon; 10 pm; closed Sat & Sun; set weekday L £39 (FP).

RSJ SE1 £50 332
33 Coin St 7928 4554 9–4A
"A remarkable and superb Loire wine list" is the crown jewel feature of this "unfailing" old timer near the National Theatre; OK, "the décor is 20 years out of date" (and wasn't great then), but staff are "welcoming", and you get "really good French food at reasonable prices". / SE1 9NR; www.rsj.uk.com; @RSJWaterloo; 11 pm; closed Sat L & Sun; set always available £36 (FP).

Rucoletta EC2 £47 432
6 Foster Lane 7600 7776 9–2C
"A very serviceable Italian, near St Paul's" that's "efficient for hungry bankers and industrialists", and whose "enjoyable and steady" cooking is "a big step-up from the surrounding chains". / EC2V 6HH; www.rucoletta.co.uk; @RucolettaLondon; 9.30 pm, Thu-Sat 10 pm; closed Sat D & Sun; no Amex.

Rugoletta £38 333
308 Ballards Ln, N12 8445 6742 1–1B
59 Church Ln, N2 8815 1743 1–1B
"A traditional, warm Italian welcome" (including to kids) adds to the appeal of these Barnet and East Finchley locals, where the "pizza, pasta and well-presented main dishes" are "for the price, fantastico!" (and you can BYO).

Rules WC2 £78 [3][2][5]
35 Maiden Ln 7836 5314 4–3D
"Even if you would normally avoid tourist spots like the plague", London's oldest restaurant (Covent Garden, 1798) satisfies even sceptical visitors with its "truly historic" interior and "proud-to-be-old-fashioned" menu, majoring in meat, game and "old-school puds"; one caution though – it's getting "oh oh so expensive". / WC2E 7LB; www.rules.co.uk; @RulesRestaurant; 11.30 pm, Sun 10.30 pm; no shorts.

Sackville's W1 NEW £68
8a Sackville St 7734 3623 3–3D
Chef/patron Wayne Dixon trained at Ramsay's 'maze Grill' and it certainly shows when it comes to the pricing at this new Mayfair venture; the focus is on posh patties (including the Wagyu Sackville burger at £38), plus expensive cuts of steak with lashings of shaved truffles. / W1S 3DF.

Le Sacré-Coeur N1 £36 [3][3][4]
18 Theberton St 7354 2618 8–3D
"A cheerful piece of Paris, just north of Angel," this well-loved veteran serves "delightful" French fare with "charm and verve"; it is perhaps "a bit tatty" nowadays, but no denying the "brilliant value for money". / N1 0QX; www.lesacrecoeur.co.uk; 11 pm, Sat 11.30 pm, Sun 10.30 pm; set weekday L £24 (FP).

Sacro Cuore NW10 £36 [4][3][3]
45 Chamberlayne Rd 8960 8558 1–2B
"The best pizza in North West London by far" – this "cool" Kensal Rise three-year-old makes "handmade pizza" that's "just like in Naples". / NW10 3NB; www.sacrocuore.co.uk/menu.html; @SacroCuorePizza; 10.15 pm; no Amex; no booking at certain times.

Sagar £35 [4][4][3]
17a Percy St, W1 7631 3319 3–2B
31 Catherine St, WC2 7836 6377 4–3D
157 King St, W6 8741 8563 7–2C
"Delicious" dosas and "excellent breads" are highlights of the "fabulous and very reasonably priced" veggie South Indian dishes at these low-key, but "pleasant and efficient" (and vegan-friendly) cafés. / www.sagarveg.co.uk; Sun-Thu 10.45 pm, Fri & Sat 11.30 pm.

Sager & Wilde E2 £38 [3][4][4]
193 Hackney Rd 8127 7330 12–1C
"The nibbles are fine", but it's the "fabulous and intriguing wine selection", "enthusiastic" staff and "relaxed vibe" which drive the appeal of this Haggerston "jewel". / E2 8JP; www.sagerandwilde.com; 10 pm; closed weekday L.

Saigon Saigon W6 £39 [3][4][4]
313-317 King St 8748 6887 7–2B
"Staff are lovely" and add to the engagingly rickety and "authentic" vibe of this well-established Hammersmith Vietnamese, praised for its "powerful flavours" and "great value". / W6 9NH; www.saigon-saigon.co.uk; @saigonsaigonuk; 11 pm, Sat & Mon 10 pm.

St John EC1 £62 [5][4][3]
26 St John St 7251 0848 9–1B
"Still brilliant after all this time" – Fergus Henderson's white-walled, Smithfield legend continues to produce supremely "honest" offal-heavy dishes based on "awesome ingredients" (most famously the "hugely addictive bone marrow"). Top Tip – the "rowdy" adjacent bar is as good in its way as the main dining room. / EC1M 4AY; www.stjohngroup.uk.com; @SJRestaurant; 11 pm; closed Sat L & Sun D.

St John Bread & Wine E1 £56 [5][3][3]
94-96 Commercial St 7251 0848 12–2C
"The finest bacon butties in the universe" are but one highlight of the "otherworldly" small plates (majoring in "offal-y wonders") served at this marvellously "vibrant" (if "noisy") Shoreditch canteen; "service can be prickly, but hey ho". / E1 6LZ; www.stjohngroup.uk.com/spitalfields; @StJBW; 10.30 pm, Sun 9.30 pm.

St Johns N19 £46 [4][3][5]
91 Junction Rd 7272 1587 8–1C
"A longstanding neighbourhood favourite" in Archway (George Michael's no. 1 pub, apparently), whose huge, "always buzzing" dining room occupies a lovely converted old ballroom; it serves an "intriguing" mix of "traditional-with-a-twist" dishes. / N19 5QU; www.stjohnstavern.com; @stjohnstavern; 11 pm, Sun 9.30 pm; Mon-Thu D only, Fri-Sun open L & D; no Amex; booking: max 12.

St Pancras Grand, St Pancras Int'l Station NW1 £53 [1][2][3]
The Concourse 7870 9900 8–3C
It occupies a "beautiful space", and – if you're waiting for a train – this grand railway brasserie is "a haven from the busy concourse"; the food doesn't live up to the interior however, and "they know how to charge for the experience". / NW1 2QP; www.saintpancrasgrand.co.uk; @SearcyStPancras; 10.30 pm, Sun 8 pm.

Sakana-tei W1 £45 [5][2][1]
11 Maddox St 7629 3000 3–2C
For "the most authentic Japanese in London", some Asian ex-pats tip this "decrepit" Mayfair basement – "it's the best in the west (and that's not me, but a Japanese CEO with a jaw-dropping expense account!)" / W1S 2QF; 10 pm; closed Sun.

Sake No Hana SW1 £75 3 1 2
23 St James's St 7925 8988 3–4C
You take "a weirdly shopping-centre-esque escalator" to this slickly designed Japanese, in a '60s St James's development next to The Economist; its "Asian-fusion" cuisine can be "very enjoyable", but it's "expensive", service can be "un-welcoming" and too often there's "no atmosphere". / SW1A 1HA; www.sakenohana.com; @sakenonhana; 11 pm, Fri & Sat 11.30 pm; closed Sun.

Salaam Namaste WC1 £36 3 2 2
68 Millman St 7405 3697 2–1D
"Excellent Indian food with a twist" rewards a visit to this "busy", brightly lit Bloomsbury venture. / WC1N 3EF; www.salaam-namaste.co.uk; @SalaamNamasteUK; 11.30 pm, Sun 11 pm.

Sale e Pepe SW1 £66 3 4 3
9-15 Pavilion Rd 7235 0098 5–1D
"It feels like the heydey of the 1980s", at this "always lively" old faithful trattoria, near Harrods; "prices are a bit high", and "it can be so noisy", but the grub's "tasty", service is "with a smile", and it's good "fun". / SW1X 0HD; www.saleepepe.co.uk; 11.30 pm; no shorts.

Salloos SW1 £58 4 4 3
62-64 Kinnerton St 7235 4444 5–1D
"Wonderful, old-style Pakistani", in a posh Belgravia mews – "the marinated lamb chops are to die for", but "it's a shame it's so expensive". / SW1X 8ER; www.salloos.co.uk; 11 pm; closed Sun; need 5+ to book.

Salmontini SW1 NEW £71
1 Pont St 7118 1999 5–1D
On a Belgravia site some still recall as Drones (long RIP), a plush new cocktail bar and restaurant, backed by a Beirut-based brand; early reports are very enthusiastic about its "knowledgeable" staff and "Japanese/European menu" majoring in smoked fish and sushi. / SW1X 9EJ; salmontini.co.uk; @Salmontini_Uk; 10.45pm, Fri & Sat 11.15 pm, Sun 10.30 pm.

The Salon, Somerset House WC2 NEW £74
Lancaster Pl 3693 3247 2–2D
A recently added annex to Skye Gyngell's Somerset House dining room (Spring), serving a very pared down menu and drinks to drop-ins only (no reservations); it opened too late for a rating, but it's certainly a relatively affordable option at this beautiful landmark. / WC2R 1LA; www.springrestaurant.co.uk/salon; @Spring_Rest; 10.30 pm; closed Sun D; no booking.

Le Salon Privé TW1 NEW £46 3 4 5
43 Crown Rd 8892 0602 1–4A
Hopeful early-days reports on this "newly revitalised" St Margarets bistro (previously Brula, RIP) – under new owners, the small space "is much improved", and the "genuine French cuisine" is at least as good, if not better than before. / TW1 3EJ; 10.30 pm.

Salt & Honey W2 NEW £45
28 Sussex Pl 7706 7900 6–1D
From the duo behind Manuka Kitchen in Fulham, a new, little neighbourhood bistro in Bayswater serving British-Antipodean food – it opened after our survey closed so we look forward to a full review next year. / W2 2TH; www.saltandhoneybistro.com; @Salthoneybistro; 10 pm, Sun 9 pm; closed Mon.

The Salt House NW8 £49 3 3 3
63 Abbey Rd 7328 6626 8–3A
Near that famous zebra crossing, an attractive and consistent St John's Wood gastropub with good outdoor seating, that's a "useful" option hereabouts. / NW8 0AE; www.salthouseabbeyroad.com; @thesalthousenw8; 11 pm, Fri & Sat midnight.

Salt Yard W1 £49 3 2 3
54 Goodge St 7637 0657 2–1B
Devotees still hail the "sheer deliciousness" of the Italian/Spanish tapas at this convivial Fitzrovia haunt, whose "relaxing" style is fine for a more informal business lunch; compared with its glory days though, it's "lost its edge", and former fans can find it "average" nowadays. / W1T 4NA; www.saltyard.co.uk; @SaltYardLdn; 10.45 pm, Sun 9.45 pm; .

Salvation In Noodles £34 3 2 2
122 Balls Pond Rd, N1 7254 4534 1–1C
2 Blackstock Rd, N4 7254 4534 8–1D NEW
"The outside bike-parking is a nice touch" at this trendy Dalston yearling, but while fans love its "huge and delicious" pho and other fare, critics say "there are better Vietnamese a short distance away"; they must be doing something right though, as a new branch opened in Finsbury Park in July. /

San Carlo Cicchetti £50 3 3 3
215 Piccadilly, W1 7494 9435 3–3D
30 Wellington St, WC2 7240 6339 4–3D
Yes, they're a bit "OTT, camp, bright and flashy", but these "efficient" tourist-land outposts of a national Italian chain generally come recommended, thanks to their "fun and bustling style" and "tasty", "relatively well-priced" sharing dishes.

San Daniele del Friuli N5 £44 3 4 3
72 Highbury Park 7226 1609 8–1D
The daily specials on the blackboard are a good bet if you visit this engaging, family-run "local favourite", in Highbury Park, with enjoyable, seasonal Italian cooking. / N5 2XE; www.sandanielehighbury.co.uk; 10.30 pm; closed Mon L, Tue L, Wed L & Sun; no Amex.

The Sands End SW6 **£51** 3 4 4
135 Stephendale Rd 7731 7823 10–1B
It's "a bit stereotypically Sloaney" (and pricey), but this popular gastropub in deepest Fulham is "super" – the scoff's "consistently good", and its "lovely interior" helps it feel very "chilled out". / SW6 2PR; www.thesandsend.co.uk; @thesandsend; 10 pm.

Santa Maria W5 **£32** 5 3 3
15 St Mary's Rd 8579 1462 1–3A
"I've seen Italians travel from East London just to get their fix!" – this "superb" Ealing outfit arguably serves "the best pizza in London"; "it's hard to secure a table though, and sometimes they want you out pretty rapido". / W5 5RA; www.santamariapizzeria.com; @SantaMariaPizza; 10.30 pm.

Santini SW1 **£75** 2 2 2
29 Ebury St 7730 4094 2–4B
"Professional" Belgravia stalwart, with a swish "light and airy" interior, and lovely sunny terrace – the "authentic" Italian cooking is "competent" too; the problem is that it is decidedly "not cheap". / SW1W 0NZ; www.santini-restaurant.com; 10 pm, Sat 11 pm.

Santore EC1 **£44** 4 3 3
59 Exmouth Mkt 7812 1488 9–1A
"Genuine Neapolitan" in Exmouth Market majoring in "winning pizza"; inside is "crowded and noisy", but "outside it's wonderful on a warm evening" – "greet the waiter with a 'Buona Sera' and you might get a better table". / EC1R 4QL; www.santorerestaurant.co.uk; 11 pm.

Sapori Sardi SW6 **£48** 4 4 2
786 Fulham Rd 7731 0755 10–1B
"Simple fresh ingredients, beautifully cooked" inspire rave reviews for this Fulham Sardinian – "a top local", with "friendly" service and a "relaxed" style. / SW6 5SL; www.saporisardi.co.uk; @saporisardi; 11 pm; no Amex.

Sardo W1 **£57** 3 2 2
45 Grafton Way 7387 2521 2–1B
"Really solid, interesting and unfussy" – such are the virtues of this "traditional" Fitzrovia Sardinian, indeed fans of its "authentic" and "copious" cooking, enjoyable wines, and "buzzy" style say it's "under-rated"; "slightly cramped in the back room". / W1T 5DQ; www.sardo-restaurant.com; 11 pm; closed Sat L & Sun.

Sarracino NW6 **£45** 4 2 2
186 Broadhurst Gdns 7372 5889 1–1B
"Totally authentic Neapolitan pizza" (served by the metre) is the top draw to this West Hampstead trattoria, although "the Italian chef's pastas and mains are worth a visit in their own right". / NW6 3AY; www.sarracinorestaurant.com; 11 pm; closed weekday L.

Sartoria W1 **£69**
20 Savile Row 7534 7000 3–2C
Ex L'Anima chef, Francesco Mazzei is – in something of a coup for D&D London – to relaunch this grand, spacious and perennially promising-but-under-performing Mayfair Italian in early November 2015; it's closed till then for a major refit – this should be one to watch. / W1S 3PR; www.sartoria-restaurant.co.uk; @SartoriaRest; 10.45 pm; closed Sat L & Sun; set weekday L £38 (FP).

Satay House W2 **£35** 3 2 2
13 Sale Pl 7723 6763 6–1D
A "cheerful" Malaysian veteran, in a "pleasantly quiet street off Edgware Road", providing a "wide variety of dishes", at a "decent" price. / W2 1PX; www.satay-house.co.uk; 11 pm.

Sauterelle Royal Exchange EC3 **£72** 3 3 3
Bank 7618 2483 9–2C
"A great view of the Royal Exchange courtyard" (from the right tables) adds to the "surprisingly good" ambience of this mezzanine-level D&D London venture, and "although it's not cheap, prices compare well with places of a similar standard in the City". / EC3V 3LR; www.royalexchange-grandcafe.co.uk/at/sauterelle-bank; @REXLondon; 9.30 pm; closed Sat & Sun; no trainers.

Savoir Faire WC1 **£39** 3 3 2
42 New Oxford St 7436 0707 4–1C
Handy for the British Museum, a budget Gallic spot, where "charming staff serve well-cooked bistro fare to a regular clientele". / WC1A 1EP; www.savoir.co.uk; 10.30 pm, Sun 10 pm.

(Savoy Grill) The Savoy Hotel WC2 **£89** 2 3 3
Strand 7592 1600 4–3D
This "impressive" panelled chamber – once London's pre-eminent power-dining scene – still looks the part, and can still deliver some "accomplished" traditional British cuisine; prices are "ridiculous" however, especially given the fairly "unimaginative" repertoire. / WC2R 0EU; www.gordonramsay.com/thesavoygrill; @savoygrill; 11 pm, Sun 10.30 pm; set pre-theatre £55 (FP), set weekday L £57 (FP).

Scalini SW3 **£75** 3 3 3
1-3 Walton St 7225 2301 5–2C
"Excellent old-school Italian" buoyed along by its supremely "buzzy", "noisy yet intimate" style; given its ultra-chichi location on the fringes of Knightsbridge it's unsurprisingly no bargain, but on all accounts "worth every penny". / SW3 2JD; www.scalinionline.com; 11.30 pm; no shorts.

Scandinavian Kitchen W1 £14 353
61 Great Titchfield St 7580 7161 2–1B
"Overwhelming friendliness and lack of snootiness" win lots of brownie points for this "charming" (if "cramped") Scandi-"fuel-stop"/grocer, near the Beeb; grab an open sarnie, meatballs, herrings or salad, and check out the Scandi-themed pun of the day on the A board; spiffing Monmouth coffee too. / W1W 7PP; www.scandikitchen.co.uk; @scanditwitchen; 7 pm, Sat 6 pm, Sun 4 pm; L only; no Maestro; no booking.

The Scarsdale W8 £42 234
23a Edwardes Sq 7937 1811 7–1D
Nestled in the corner of a gorgeous, old Kensington Square, this picturesque tavern (with small garden) is a classic of its genre, with pub grub that's not achingly 'gastro', but perfectly palatable. / W8 6HE; www.scarsdaletavern.co.uk; @onlyatfullers; 10 pm, Sun 9.30 pm.

SCOTT'S W1 £80 444
20 Mount St 7495 7309 3–3A
"For glam, glam, and more glam", it's hard to out-do Richard Caring's "über-slick" Mayfair veteran – a "very grown-up" affair combining "expensive but lovely" fish and seafood and "always professional" service. It does attract the odd cynical report too though – in fact a few more this year than previously. / W1K 2HE; www.scotts-restaurant.com; 10.30 pm, Sun 10 pm; booking: max 6.

Sea Containers Mondrian London SE1 £67 233
20 Upper Ground 3747 1020 9–3A
It looks knockout, and has "wonderful views of the river", but this much-hyped, nautically-themed NYC import, on the South Bank, "is going the same way as the Oxo Tower" – "you pay a lot for average food and nice décor, and overall it's not worth it". / SE1 9PD; www.mondrianlondon.com; @MondrianLDN; 11 pm.

The Sea Cow SE22 £36 332
37 Lordship Ln 8693 3111 1–4D
"The kind of chippy serving grilled tuna, salad, with fries optional... perfect!" – you eat on communal benches at this "upmarket" East Dulwich spot, which provides "a good choice of fish that's very fresh, grilled or fried, with chips or greenery". / SE22 8EW; www.theseacow.co.uk; @seacowcrew; 11 pm, Sun 10 pm; closed Mon; no Amex.

Seafresh SW1 £37 432
80-81 Wilton Rd 7828 0747 2–4B
"Excellent traditional fish 'n' chips" is "efficiently served in an authentic and basic setting", in this veteran Pimlico chippy, whose menu also includes various "upmarket" options ("wonderful fresh lobster at bargain prices and superb Essex oysters"). / SW1V 1DL; www.seafresh-dining.com; 10.30 pm; closed Sun.

The Sea Shell NW1 £44 322
49 Lisson Grove 7224 9000 8–4A
Despite its "dreary" appearance, this sizeable Marylebone café/take-away has some renown as one of London's top chippies; some would say that's over-egging it, but numerous fans do still acclaim it as "one of the best around". / NW1 6UH; www.seashellrestaurant.co.uk; @SeashellRestaur; 10.30 pm; closed Sun.

Season Kitchen N4 £42 333
53 Stroud Green Rd 7263 5500 8–1D
"A stand-out for Finsbury Park" – a "friendly local", where "ever-changing", "always original" dishes from "a well thought-out seasonal menu" are served in "a little, characterful room". / N4 3EF; www.seasonkitchen.co.uk; 10.30 pm, Sun 9 pm; D only.

Señor Ceviche W1 NEW £42 334
Kingly Ct 7842 8540 3–2C
"Funky", new Peruvian pop-up-turned-permanent in Soho's growing Kingly Court; fans extol its "exquisite ceviche", but "creeping" prices spoil the fun for sceptics for whom it's now too "mainstream" and "unremarkable"; still "great frozen Pisco sours". / W1B 5PW; www.senor-ceviche.com; @SenorCevicheLDN; 10.30 pm, Thu-Sat 11 pm.

Sesame WC2 NEW £21 222
23 Garrick St 7240 4879 4–3C
From the Ottolenghi stable, a new "bench and stool" Covent Garden pitstop offering Middle Eastern street-food; initial reports suggest the overall experience is only "so-so", but it certainly provides "quick, healthy" fare, and is pretty "cheap" too. / WC2E 9BN; www.sesamefood.co.uk; @SesameFood; 11 pm; no booking.

Seven Park Place SW1 £95 334
7-8 Park Pl 7316 1615 3–4C
"To hell with the cost!" – this "charming restaurant attached to a St James's hotel" is often nominated for business entertaining but deserves more attention generally, as William Drabble's "highly accomplished" cuisine is "remarkably good". Top Tip – "excellent value set lunch". / SW1A 1LS; www.stjameshotelandclub.com; @SevenParkPlace; 10 pm; closed Mon & Sun; set weekday L £56 (FP).

Seven Stars WC2 £34 3 2 3
53 Carey St 7242 8521 2–2D
Larger-than-life landlady, 'Roxy Beaujolais' and her crew "continue to rustle up above-average pub food" at her quaint, tightly packed tavern, behind the Royal Courts of Justice. / WC2A 2JB; 9 pm; no booking.

Sexy Fish, Berkeley Square House W1 NEW £68
1-4 Berkeley Sq 3764 2000 3–3B
Sitting pretty alongside Bentley and Bugatti showrooms, members' clubs and purveyors of haute couture, Richard Caring's latest venture (on the site of a former Mayfair NatWest bank) adds another seafood specialist to the Caprice empire; it's set to open in October 2015. / W1J 6BR; www.sexyfish.com.

Shackfuyu W1 NEW £34 5 4 4
14a, Old Compton St 7734 7492 4–2B
"Small", "US/Asian-fusion" dishes, with "enormous flavours" win rave reviews for this new Bone Daddies pop-up-turned-permanent, on the Soho site that was Made In Italy (RIP); it's "brilliant value" too. Top Menu Tip – "super yummy prawn toast, and also the matcha ice cream – a total revelation of amazing tastes". / W1D 4TH; www.bonedaddies.com; @BoneDaddiesLDN.

Shake Shack £24 3 2 2
80 New Oxford St, WC1 awaiting tel 4–1B NEW
24 The Market, WC2 3598 1360 4–3D
The Street, Westfield Stratford, E20 awaiting tel 1–1D NEW
"Yummmmmmmmm" – "lovely burgers", and "the best crinkle chips" win the thumbs-up for Danny Meyer's US-import, which is now in Westfield Stratford as well as Covent Garden; even fans though note it's "quite expensive". /

Shampers W1 £49 2 4 5
4 Kingly St 7437 1692 3–2D
"Often full of bibulous professional-types", this "noisy and crowded", "'70s time warp" in Soho "always comes up trumps"; longstanding owner Simon is "hands on" and "utterly charming", and presides over the "reliable" fare, "fantastic" atmosphere and "wine list to die for". / W1B 5PE; www.shampers.net; @Shampers_Soho; 10.45 pm; closed Sun.

Shanghai E8 £38 3 2 3
41 Kingsland High St 7254 2878 1–1C
The splendid (listed) tiled front section of this former pie 'n' eel shop is one draw to this Dalston Chinese – the other is its "super dim sum". / E8 2JS; www.shanghaidalston.co.uk; 11 pm; no Amex.

Shanghai Blues WC1 £62 3 3 3
193-197 High Holborn 7404 1668 4–1D
"Pretty, old Shanghainese décor" helps create this Holborn Chinese's "relaxing", rather "sophisticated" ambience (as do the listed surroundings of what was once St Giles Library); lunchtime dim sum is the main event here – "the very high quality and range is the real deal". / WC1V 7BD; www.shanghaiblues.co.uk; 11 pm, Sun 10.30 pm.

The Shed W8 £48 3 3 3
122 Palace Gardens Ter 7229 4024 6–2B
If you like the idea of "slumming it" in what feels like "an actual country shed", this "cute" faux-rustic spot, off Notting Hill Gate, can be "fun", and fans praise its "super-tasty", "farm-to-table British tapas" too; to cynics though, it appears "odd", "over-rated" and "overpriced". / W8 4RT; www.theshed-restaurant.com; @theshed_resto; 11 pm; closed Mon L & Sun.

J SHEEKEY WC2 £75 4 4 4
28-34 St Martin's Ct 7240 2565 4–3B
"Set in the hustle and bustle of Theatreland" – down a cute alleyway – this "star-studded", "old-school" legend (est 1896, but dating its current celebrity to a late '90s relaunch) is yet again London's most talked-about destination. Nowadays owned by Richard Caring, it beat its sibling Scott's to another crown: "the capital's top seafood" (in particular "the world's best fish pie"), which is "immaculately" served in a series of "old-fashioned panelled rooms" – "noisy and crowded", but superbly "clubby" and "charismatic". / WC2N 4AL; www.j-sheekey.co.uk; @CapriceHoldings; 11.30 pm, Sun 10.30 pm; booking: max 6; set weekday L £51 (FP).

J Sheekey Oyster Bar WC2 £76 4 4 5
28-34 St Martin's Ct 7240 2565 4–3B
"Slurping down quality oysters perched on a stool – is there a better way of spending an evening?" Not according to many devotees of the "brilliant", "friendly" and "glamorous" bar attached to the adjacent "doyenne of seafood restaurants". / WC2N 4AL; www.j-sheekey.co.uk; @CapriceHoldings; 11.30 pm, Sun 10.30 pm; booking: max 3; set weekday L £53 (FP).

Shepherd's SW1 £52 3 4 3
Marsham Ct, Marsham St 7834 9552 2–4C
"It looks as though this Tory watering hole has returned to action just at the right time!" – this archetypal politico bastion near Westminster re-opened after a period of closure this year, and though some "wobbly" meals from its menu of advanced comfort food were reported, most reports say "it's a bonus to have it back". / SW1P 4LA; www.shepherdsrestaurant.co.uk; 10.45 pm; closed Sat & Sun.

Shikumen, Dorsett Hotel W12 NEW £39 5 2 2

58 Shepherd's Bush Grn 8749 9978 7–1C

"A new kid on the block with out-of-this-world dim sum" – this new Chinese in a recently opened W12 boutique hotel "can amaze" with its "exceptional offerings". On the downside, "the atmosphere's a bit stiff and unmistakably hotel-y", but "the so-so ambience isn't all their fault – you are right on Shepherd's Bush Green after all!" (This place has eclipsed its eponymous year-old sibling in Ealing – worth remembering though in case you find yourself in W5). / W12 5AA; shikumen.co.uk; @ShikumenUK; 10.45 pm.

Shilpa W6 £31 5 4 2

206 King St 8741 3127 7–2B

An "ordinary façade belies the quality" of this "honest" Hammersmith Indian, which continues to churn out "glorious Keralan food" at "unbelievably low prices". / W6 0RA; www.shilparestaurant.co.uk; 11 pm, Thu-Sat midnight.

The Ship SW18 £52 3 3 4

41 Jews Row 8870 9667 10–2B

Steadfast support for this "must-see" boozer, which benefits from a "great riverside" location (with vast terrace) by Wandsworth Bridge and "good pub food", including a summer BBQ. / SW18 1TB; www.theship.co.uk; @shipwandsworth; 10 pm; no booking, Sun L.

Shoe Shop NW5 NEW £45 5 4 2

122 Fortess Rd 7267 8444 8–2C

"Giaconda is reborn – Hallelujah!" – Paul Merrony and Tracey Petersen are back with a bang at this "tiny", year-old Tuffnell Park shop-conversion; the decor is "basic", but there's "a happy vibe", and the "robust", "intelligent and original cooking" is "a masterclass of what's possible at a reasonable price". / NW5 2HL; www.shoeshoplondon.com; 9 pm; closed Mon & Sun.

Shoryu Ramen £42 4 2 2

9 Regent St, SW1 no tel 3–3D
3 Denman St, W1 no tel 3–2D
5 Kingly Ct, W1 no tel 3–2C
Broadgate Circle, EC2 no tel 12–2B NEW

"Mad popularity creates a rather hectic ambience", at these "crowded and packed-in" Japanese pit-stops; still "you can expect quality food" – "amazing fresh noodles, broth and steamed buns". / Regent St 11.30 pm, Sun 10.30 pm – Soho midnight, Sun 10.30 pm; no booking (except Kingly Ct).

Shotgun W1 NEW

26 Kingly St awaiting tel 3–3C

American chef Brad McDonald (The Lockhart, Marylebone) whose talents divide opinion among our reporters (apart from when it comes to his cornbread) brings more cooking from the Deep South to Soho with a new BBQ, due to open in Autumn 2015. / W1B 5QD; www.shotgunbbq.com.

Sichuan Folk E1 £44 4 4 2

32 Hanbury St 7247 4735 12–2C

"An excellent Chinese within a stone's throw of the touristy Brick Lane Indians" – a small, closely packed spot bringing "sensationally good-value", supremely "spicy" Sichuan scoff to this stretch of the East End; staff are "lovely and welcoming" too. / E1 6QR; www.sichuan-folk.co.uk; 10.30 pm; no Amex; set weekday L £18 (FP).

The Sign of The Don Bar & Bistro EC4 £53 2 4 4

21 St Swithin's Ln 7626 2606 9–3C

"A more casual version of its elder sibling" next door, the Don's year-old spin-off is "a good alternative", particularly for "more relaxed business lunches", even if the brasserie fare is "not especially notable". / EC4N 8AD; www.thesignofthedon.com; @signofthedon; 10 pm; closed Sat & Sun; set always available £41 (FP).

Signor Sassi SW1 £65 3 3 4

14 Knightsbridge Grn 7584 2277 5–1D

"There's never a dull moment", say fans of this "fun", old-school Knightsbridge trattoria – "if you're lost for words on a first date, the waiters are sure to help you out!" / SW1X 7QL; www.signorsassi.co.uk; 11.30 pm, Sun 10.30 pm.

Silk Road SE5 £24 5 2 2

49 Camberwell Church St 7703 4832 1–3C

"A whole new take on Chinese food" – the "bold" and "amazingly unusual" Xinjiang dishes shine at this Camberwell café; "it's all a bit spit and sawdust" though, and "the line of hipsters outside the door can be tedious". / SE5 8TR; 10.30 pm; closed Sat L & Sun L; no credit cards.

Simpson's Tavern EC3 £38 2 4 5

38 1/2 Ball Ct, Cornhill 7626 9985 9–2C

"The food is almost a side show to the surroundings" at this Dickensian chophouse (fka Simpson's of Cornhill) in a City alleyway, which offers "a real taste of history" in an "unpretentious and thoroughly enjoyable" manner; good breakfasts too. / EC3V 9DR; www.simpsonstavern.co.uk; @SimpsonsTavern; 3 pm; L only, closed Sat & Sun.

Simpsons-in-the-Strand WC2 £76 [1][1][1]
100 Strand 7836 9112 4–3D
"Pity the tourists who go believing it's the home of real English cooking!" – this famous temple to Roast Beef is "a shadow of its former self", with "sloppy" staff serving "school dinners" in a "gloomy" chamber; for a business breakfast, it's just about tolerable. / WC2R 0EW; www.simpsonsinthestrand.co.uk; 10.45 pm, Sun 9 pm; no trainers.

Singapore Garden NW6 £43 [4][3][3]
83a Fairfax Rd 7624 8233 8–2A
"They've maintained quality over three decades" at this "always-packed" north London favourite, which can come as a "surprise" given its off-the-beaten-track location in a Swiss Cottage parade; service is "smiling", and the Chinese/Malaysian/Singaporean fare is "expensive-but-worth-it". / NW6 4DY; www.singaporegarden.co.uk; @SingaporeGarden; 11 pm, Fri & Sat 11.30 pm.

(Gallery) Sketch W1 £80 [2][2][4]
9 Conduit St 7659 4500 3–2C
Fans of this funky Mayfair fashionista-favourite admit it's "very expensive", but say it's a "cool" joint, with an "always inventive menu, full of surprises"; the less rose-tinted view is that it's "too gimmicky and over-crowded – like a factory processing posh meals for the young and loaded". / W1S 2XG; www.sketch.uk.com; @sketchlondon; 11 pm; booking: max 10.

(Lecture Room) Sketch W1 £134 [3][3][5]
9 Conduit St 7659 4500 3–2C
"The magnificence of the space" certainly makes for "an experience" at this barmily opulent Mayfair dining room, overseen by Parisian supremo Pierre Gagnaire; fans – particularly of the "steal" of a set lunch – hail its "amazing" and "innovative" cuisine too, but sceptics say it's "so over-priced". / W1S 2XG; www.sketch.uk.com; @sketchlondon; 10.30 pm; closed Mon, Sat L & Sun; no trainers; booking: max 8; set weekday L £65 (FP).

Skipjacks HA3 £30 [4][4][3]
268-270 Streatfield Rd 8204 7554 1–1A
"Fish lovers travel for miles to eat here", at this Harrow chippy, which is "never without a takeaway queue and full restaurant"; "you don't come for the ambience" but "everyone is happy knowing that results will be first rate". / HA3 9BY; 10.30 pm; closed Sun; no Amex.

Skylon South Bank Centre SE1 £75 [1][2][2]
Belvedere Rd 7654 7800 2–3D
"If you have a window table, it ameliorates some of the drawbacks" of this huge, Thames-side chamber; for somewhere so "expensive" however, service can be "chaotic", and the cooking is too often "nothing special". / SE1 8XX; www.skylon-restaurant.co.uk; @skylonsouthbank; 10.30 pm; closed Sun D; no trainers; booking: max 12; set weekday L £53 (FP), set pre-theatre & Sun L £56 (FP).

Skylon Grill SE1 £61 [1][1][3]
Belvedere Rd 7654 7800 2–3D
"Location, location and location" – including the "wonderful" Thames view – are all that "redeems" the cheaper option at the D&D London's massive South Bank complex, where service is "indifferent" and the "flair-free food offers much but delivers little". / SE1 8XX; www.skylon-restaurant.co.uk; @skylonsouthbank; 11 pm; closed Sun D.

Smith & Wollensky WC2 £102
1 John Adam St 2–2D
With a reputed £10m spent on converting the ground floor of The Adelphi, just off The Strand, this hallowed US steakhouse brand's first incursion into the UK market makes a bold statement, with 300 seats, endless leather and brass, and a menu packed with USDA cuts. It opened too late for survey feedback – early press reports suggest it may be heading down the same beserk over-pricing route pursued by other US imports like Palm (RIP) and Cut, but the business-friendly location here could prove a saving grace. / WC2N 6HT; www.smithandwollensky.co.uk; @sandwollenskyuk.

Smith's Of Ongar E1 £57 [3][3][4]
22 Wapping High St 7488 3456 11–1A
"Well worth a visit even though it's a bit off the beaten track" – this Wapping offshoot of a long-established Essex business "has got it all" – "a wide selection of beautiful fish" ("well cooked, but with nothing too clever"), "attentive staff", and "impressive views" of Tower Bridge and the Thames. / E1W 1NJ; smithsrestaurant.com; @Smithsofwapping; 10 pm; closed Sun D.

(Top Floor) Smiths of Smithfield EC1 £75 [3][3][4]
67-77 Charterhouse St 7251 7950 9–1A
"Fantastic views of the City" are a highpoint at this business-friendly rooftop destination, whose steak-focussed offerings have seemed "much more up-to-par" of late, and are generally judged "very good, if at a price". / EC1M 6HJ; www.smithsofsmithfield.co.uk; @thisismiths; 10.45 pm; closed Sat L & Sun; booking: max 10.

(Dining Room) Smiths of Smithfield EC1 £56 222
67-77 Charterhouse St 7251 7950 9–1A
"Reliable... OK... so very average" – this first-floor Smithfield brasserie is "nothing to write home about" nowadays; its steak-heavy formula is just about serviceable for an informal business lunch, but service is "haphazard" and "the acoustics suck"! / EC1M 6HJ; www.smithsofsmithfield.co.uk; @thisismiths; 10.45 pm; closed Sat L & Sun; booking: max 12.

(Ground Floor) Smiths of Smithfield EC1 £32 223
67-77 Charterhouse St 7251 7950 9–1A
Hung over and in need of brunch? – this big and "buzzy" Smithfield venue is a seminal choice for weekend mornings, with "Bloody Mary on hand to remove the cobwebs", and an "SOS English breakfast". / EC1M 6HJ; www.smithsofsmithfield.co.uk; @thisismiths; 5 pm; L only; no booking.

Smokehouse Chiswick W4 NEW £47 333
12 Sutton Lane North 7354 1144 7–2B
"A bizarre smorgasbord of smoked meat, Korean spices and whisky – somehow it works!"; this new outer-Chiswick outpost of Ian Rankin's Smokehouse Islington (on the pub site that was the Hole in the Wall, RIP) wins fans both for its "interesting" food and "wonderful garden". By the indifferent standards of W4, "it's a step up for an area desperate for quality". / W4 4LD; www.smokehousechiswick.co.uk; @smokehousen1; 10 pm, Sun Sun 9 pm; Mon-Thu D only, Fri-Sun open L & D.

The Smokehouse Islington N1 £53 333
63-69 Canonbury Rd 7354 1144 8–2D
"For an indulgent meat-oriented treat", this "bustling" Canonbury gastropub serves "super-rich", smoked dishes, although the menu is too "limited" for some tastes; see also Smokehouse Chiswick. / N1 2RG; www.smokehouseislington.co.uk; @smokehouseN1; 10 pm, Sun 9 pm; closed weekday L.

Smoking Goat WC2 NEW £35 523
7 Denmark St no tel 4–1B
"The lights are low, the air is smoky", at Ben Chapman's "tiny", no-bookings, Thai BBQ-newcomer in Soho, whose "short menu" focuses on "hefty chunks of meat, marinated and grilled to perfection"; service though can be a bit "too cool to smile". Top Menu Tip – "the fish sauce wings alone are worth the visit!" / WC2H 8LZ; www.smokinggoatsoho.com; @smokinggoatsoho; no booking.

Snaps & Rye W10 NEW £40 434
93 Golborne Rd 8964 3004 6–1A
"Slightly out of the way, but well worth the trip" – this contemporary, Danish dining room in North Kensington is extolled for its "delicious Scandi food with a modern twist", "light and airy" atmosphere and house-infused Akvavit snaps. / W10 5NL; www.snapsandrye.com; @snapsandrye; 9 pm; closed Mon, Tue D, Wed D, Thu D, Sat D & Sun D.

Social Eating House W1 £74 443
58-59 Poland St 7993 3251 3–2D
"A favourite of the Atherton empire" for many reporters – this "trendy yet superb" Soho two-year-old offers "memorable" cuisine, plus "delightful" cocktails and wines; it has a "lovely loungey vibe" too (but can get "overwhelmingly loud"). Top Tip – "excellent value set lunch". / W1F 7NR; www.socialeatinghouse.com; @blindasapig; 10 pm; closed Sun; set weekday L £50 (FP).

Social Wine & Tapas W1 NEW £44
39 James St 7993 3257 3–1A
From the prolific stable of Jason Atherton – a svelte Marylebone newcomer with a heavy focus on wines, sherries and madeiras, plus funky tapas, served from open kitchens in both the tapas bar (ground floor) and cellar bar; it opened too late for the survey, but early press reviews are nothing short of adulatory. / W1U 1EB; www.socialwineandtapas.com; @socialwinetapas; 10.45 pm; closed Sun.

Soif SW11 £55 333
27 Battersea Rise 7223 1112 10–2C
"The very Gallic staff really know their off-the-beaten-track wines" (the list is "complex", "a bit of a lottery", and can be "excellent value") at this "lively bar-cum-restaurant" in Battersea (a sibling to Terroirs), which serves a "French-accented" menu of "simple and solid" bistro fare. / SW11 1HG; www.soif.co; @soifSW11; 10 pm; closed Mon L & Sun D.

Som Saa Climpson's Arch E8 NEW £38 533
Arch 374 Helmsley Place 7254 7199 1–2D
"Long may it continue to pop up!" – an "extended residency", in a no frills, no booking, railway arch behind London Fields, where "the cooking is done in a shipping container on the forecourt"; the result? – "some of the best Thai food in the UK" – "if it wasn't so archly hipster it would be perfect!" / E8 3SB; www.climpsonsarch.com; @somsaa_london; 10.30 pm; closed Mon, Tue, Wed, Thu L & Fri L.

Sông Quê E2 **£30** 2 1 2
134 Kingsland Rd 7613 3222 12–1B
"It looks a bit like a Hanoi works canteen", but "if you don't mind full-on and sharing tables", fans say you get "wonderful, no frills" chow at this Shoreditch Vietnamese; critics, though, "expect more" – they say the food's "not as fresh and delicate as it used to be". / E2 8DY; www.sonque.co.uk; 11 pm, Sun 10.30 pm; no Amex.

Sonny's Kitchen SW13 **£56** 2 2 2
94 Church Rd 8748 0393 10–1A
"Everything a local ought to be", claim loyal fans (and "a top spot for weekend brunch"), but compared to its excellence of yesteryear this "airy" Barnes favourite has "lost the plot"; food-wise? – it's "reasonable, but doesn't reflect its links to Phil Howard". / SW13 0DQ; www.sonnyskitchen.co.uk; @SonnysKitchen; Fri-Sat 11 pm, Sun 9.30 pm; set always available £36 (FP), set Sun L £42 (FP).

Sophie's Steakhouse **£59** 2 2 2
29-31 Wellington St, WC2 7836 8836 4–3D
311-313 Fulham Rd, SW10 7352 0088 5–3B
"Good steaks properly cooked – what more do you want of a steakhouse?!"; these Covent Garden and Fulham fixtures also win praise for "amazing" breakfasts and their "family-friendly" approach. / www.sophiessteakhouse.com; SW10 11.45 pm, Sun 11.15 pm; WC2 12.45 am, Sun 11 pm; no booking.

Sosharu Turnmill Building EC1 NEW
63 Clerkenwell Rd awaiting tel 9–1A
Jason Atherton's planned foray into izakaya-style dining (incorporating also teppanyaki, and a robata grill) will need to work well to fill this big Clerkenwell site (formerly Turnmills nightclub, RIP); as this guide goes to press, its debut has been postponed until December 2015. / EC1M 5NP; www.jasonatherton.co.uk/restaurants/sosharu.

Sotheby's Café W1 **£64** 3 3 2
34-35 New Bond St 7293 5077 3–2C
"For a people-watching lunch", try this small café off the foyer of the famous Mayfair auction house; "the choice is limited, but the food's always good", and there's "a wide selection of reasonable wines". / W1A 2AA; www.sothebys.com; @Sothebys; L only; L only, closed Sat & Sun; booking: max 8; set weekday L £52 (FP).

Source SW11 **£51** 2 2 4
Ransome's Dock, 35-37 Parkgate Rd 7350 0555 5–4C
Opinions divide on this year-old successor to Ransome's Dock (RIP), near the Thames in Battersea; to fans it's a "delightful" local, and "a big improvement on its tired predecessor" – to critics, however, it's "very disappointing", with an "aloof" attitude. / SW11 4NP; www.sourcebattersea.com; @SOURCEBattersea; 10 pm, Fri & Sat 10.30 pm; closed Sun D.

Spring, Somerset House WC2 **£88** 3 3 2
Lancaster Pl 3011 0115 2–2D
"A joyful addition to the London dining scene" is how most reporters greet Skye Gyngell's Somerset House yearling – a "magical", "light, bright and airy" new space (with courtyard) where staff "in Boho costumes" deliver her "deliciously balanced" and "wonderfully fragrant" cuisine. "Silly prices" are a big turn-off though, and lead a strident minority to gripe about "not enough ooomph" and "too much hype". / WC2R 1LA; springrestaurant.co.uk; @Spring_Rest; 10.30 pm; closed Sun D; set weekday L & pre-theatre £53 (FP).

Spuntino W1 **£44** 3 3 4
61 Rupert St no tel 3–2D
"The atmosphere's terrific and the cocktails knockout" at Russell Norman's "hipster" Soho bar (where you eat at the counter) – "a perfect spot for a glass of vino and a sharing plate". / W1D 7PW; www.spuntino.co.uk; 11.30 pm, Sun 10.30 pm.

THE SQUARE W1 **£126** 4 2 2
6-10 Bruton St 7495 7100 3–2C
With its "polished" style, "well-spaced tables" and "one of the Capital's finest wine lists", this Mayfair luminary would be a natural for besuited expense-accounters even without Phil Howard's "complex and highly innovative" cuisine; however, critics of its slightly "sterile" setting and "exorbitant" prices were again more vocal this year. / W1J 6PU; www.squarerestaurant.com; @square_rest; 9.45 pm, Sat 10.15 pm, Sun 9.30 pm; closed Sun L; booking: max 8; set weekday L £66 (FP).

Sree Krishna SW17 **£25** 4 3 2
192-194 Tooting High St 8672 4250 10–2C
"No, it still hasn't changed!" – a Tooting relic, particularly "renowned for its masala dosas" and South Indian specials (although its more "mainstream" fare also "satisfies completely"). / SW17 0SF; www.sreekrishna.co.uk; @SreeKrishnaUk; 10.45 pm, Fri & Sat 11.30 pm.

Star of India SW5 £54 3 2 3
154 Old Brompton Rd 7373 2901 5–2B
"No longer trendy", nor as engagingly camp as in its glory days – this Earl's Court veteran is sometimes accused of "trading on its reputation"; that said, for most reporters it remains an "old favourite", with "original and well-prepared dishes". / SW5 0BE; www.starofindia.eu; 11.45 pm, Sun 11.15 pm.

Sticks'n'Sushi £48 3 3 3
11 Henrietta St, WC2 3141 8810 4–3D
Nelson Rd, SE10 3141 8220 1–3D NEW
58 Wimbledon Hill Rd, SW19 3141 8800 10–2B
Crossrail Pl, E14 3141 8230 11–1C NEW
"Does what it says on the tin pretty well" – this "odd Asian/Scandi concept" (sushi with a Danish twist) wins consistent praise for its "inventive interpretation of dishes" and "gorgeous cocktails"; by the standards of Wimbledon, Greenwich or E14, it's quite "scene-y" too. / www.sticksnsushi.com; Sun-Tue 10 pm, Wed-Sat 11 pm; SRA-1.*

STK Steakhouse ME by Meliá London WC2 £72 1 1 2
336-337 Strand 7395 3450 2–2D
"Like a pulling joint, sponsored by Lycra!" – a "very busy and too noisy" Covent Garden steakhouse, which fans say is "fun for a night out with the girls", but which draws far too much flak for being "overpriced" and with "terrible" food and service too. / WC2R 1HA; www.stkhouse.com; @STKLondon; Mon-Wed 11 pm, Thu-Sat midnight, Sun 10 pm; D only.

Stock Pot £30 2 2 2
38 Panton St, SW1 7839 5142 4–4A
54 James St, W1 7935 6034 3–1A
273 King's Rd, SW3 7823 3175 5–3C
"You certainly don't visit these squished and basic '60s canteens for the ambience"; who cares? – they're "humming from sun-up to sundown with folks who've come for a big plate of tasty fodder" at rock-bottom prices. / SW1 11.30 pm, Wed-Sat midnight, Sun 11 pm SW3 10.15 pm, Sun 9.45 pm; no Amex.

STORY SE1 £103 5 4 3
199 Tooley St 7183 2117 9–4D
"Genius!" – "an incredible journey of flavour and excitement" is to be found at Tom Sellers's "Scandi-style" dining room, near Tower Bridge, whose "spectacular and truly exciting" multi-course menus are "akin to a trip to the Fat Duck, but at under half the price". / SE1 2UE; www.restaurantstory.co.uk; @Rest_Story; 9.30 pm; closed Mon & Sun; set weekday L £62 (FP).

Strand Dining Rooms WC2 £57
1-3 Grand Buildings, Strand 7930 8855 2–3C
"It has a great location", just off Trafalgar Square, but (aside from its "first-rate breakfast") this big, all-day British brasserie "could be so much better" – let's hope Mark Sargeant's April 2015 appointment (too late for survey feedback) will prove the catalyst for a shake-up. / WC2N 4JF; www.thestranddiningrooms.com; @StrandDining; 11 pm; closed Sun D.

Street Kitchen (van) EC2 £17 3 3
Finsbury Avenue Sq no tel 12–2B
"Queues are testament" to the "delicious" food ("top burgers" a highlight) from these superior pop-ups, operating from converted Airstream campers, near Broadgate Circle and also from the Battersea 'Hatch'. / EC2 2PG; www.streetkitchen.co.uk; @Streetkitchen; L only.

Suk Saran SW19 £56 3 3 2
29 Wimbledon Hill Rd 8947 9199 10–2B
"One of Wimbledon's better restaurants for food" – this Thai "winner" (part of a three-strong southwest London chain) perhaps "isn't cheap", but the style is "un-rushed and relaxed", staff are "an absolute pleasure", and dishes come "packed with flavour". / SW19 7NE; www.sukhogroups.com; 10.30 pm; booking: max 25.

Sukho Fine Thai Cuisine SW6 £55 5 4 3
855 Fulham Rd 7371 7600 10–1B
Some of "the best Thai food in London" – "beautifully presented, and served with great charm" – compensates for the "packed" conditions at this "fabulous" shop conversion in deepest Fulham. / SW6 5HJ; www.sukhogroups.com; 11 pm; set weekday L £38 (FP).

Suksan SW10 £49 4 4 3
7 Park Walk 7351 9881 5–3B
The sister restaurant to Fulham's outstanding 'Sukho Fine Thai Cuisine' – feedback on this more casual and family-friendly Chelsea corner café is more limited, but it's consistently highly rated. / SW10 0AJ; www.sukhogroups.com; 10.45 pm; set weekday L £30 (FP).

The Summerhouse W9 £57 2 2 5
60 Blomfield Rd 7286 6752 8–4A
"Grab a canal-side table" and choose a sunny day, if you visit this "romantic" small spot, in Little Venice; don't go with huge culinary expectations though – while fish is the menu highlight, too often results "could be so much better". / W9 2PA; www.thesummerhouse.co; 10.30 pm, Sun 10 pm; no Amex; set always available £42 (FP).

Sumosan W1 £78 432

26b Albemarle St 7495 5999 3–3C

"It's never been a popular, crowd-pulling destination" like nearby Nobu, but that's what fans love about this "relaxed yet classy" Japanese-fusion spot in Mayfair, where you can "still get a table on a Saturday night". / W1S 4HY; www.sumosan.com; @sumosan_; 11.30 pm, Sun 10.30 pm; closed Sat L & Sun L; set weekday L £48 (FP).

Sunday N1 £44 433

169 Hemingford Rd 7607 3868 8–2D

"The best brunch for miles around" is "recommended at any time of day" (but you queue at weekends), at this "gorgeous" local eatery, on the fringes of Islington; at night, they serve "a small, ever-changing seasonal menu" from the "tiny kitchen". / N1 1DA; @SundayBarnsbury; 10.30 pm; closed Mon, Tue D, Wed D & Sun D; no Amex.

Sushisamba EC2 £79 335

Heron Tower, 110 Bishopsgate 3640 7330 9–2D

"You can't argue with the view from the 39th floor!"; this dazzling City eyrie combines "amazing vistas and outside spaces" with "heavenly" Japanese/South American fusion fare – "incredibly fresh, zingy flavours, blended with panache". And yet... for some reporters "everything is slick, it looks brilliant, but it lacks heart and soul", not helped by the merciless prices. / EC2N 4AY; www.sushisamba.com; @Sushisamba; Sun-Mon 11.30 pm, Tue-Sat 12.30 am.

Sushi Tetsu EC1 £58 553

12 Jerusalem Pas 3217 0090 9–1A

"As close to the Japanese sushi-ya experience as it's possible to get outside Asia"; you sit at the bar, one of only 7 people face-to-face with the chef at this "amazing" Clerkenwell "hole in the wall", run by a "lovely husband and wife team" and serving sushi "like an incredible dream". ("It's akin to the Vienna Philharmonic performing just for you and six others, while explaining every note!") / EC1V 4JP; www.sushitetsu.co.uk; @SushiTetsuUK; 7.30 pm; closed Mon & Sun; set weekday L £37 (FP).

Sushi-Say NW2 £44 542

33b Walm Ln 8459 7512 1–1A

"The best thing in Willesden Green" – well, perhaps even better than that! – this obscure, "no frills", Japanese stalwart is a mecca for sushi lovers thanks to its "always faultless" dishes, and its "congenial and friendly" service; let's hope the owners never retire... / NW2 5SH; 10 pm, Sat 10.30 pm, Sun 9.30 pm; closed Mon, Tue, Wed L, Thu L & Fri L; no Amex.

The Swan W4 £48 455

119 Acton Ln 8994 8262 7–1A

"Strangely rustic in feel for somewhere in deepest Chiswick" – this tucked-away hostelry is "one of the best in West London"; the cooking is "surprisingly interesting and sophisticated", the service is a veritable "charm offensive", and the set-up works well both in winter (wood panels, fire, sofas) and summer ("luscious beer garden"). / W4 5HH; www.theswanchiswick.co.uk; @SwanPubChiswick; 10 pm, Fri & Sat 10.30 pm, Sun 10 pm; closed weekday L.

The Swan at the Globe SE1 £62 212

21 New Globe Walk 7928 9444 9–3B

"Thankfully the wonderful performance made us forget the grief of trying to get fed!" – service has cratered in recent times at this first-floor South Bank venture; the food is "OK" (from a "limited menu") and it has "top views of the North Bank of the Thames", but feels ever-more like a "tourist trap". / SE1 9DT; www.loveswan.co.uk; @swanabout; 10.30 pm, Sun 9 pm; set pre theatre £41 (FP).

Sweet Thursday N1 £40 333

95 Southgate Rd 7226 1727 1–2C

"Cool without trying too hard" – this "chilled" De Beauvoir outfit continues to thrive, "and deservedly so" on its "interesting, proper, thin crust" pizzas, and "a great choice of wines" from the little shop attached. / N1 3JS; www.sweetthursday.co.uk; @Pizza_and_Wine; 10 pm, Mon 9 pm, Sat 10.30 pm, Sun 9 pm.

Sweetings EC4 £75 223

39 Queen Victoria St 7248 3062 9–3B

"If you like an old-style City atmosphere", this "quirky" and "eccentric" Victorian time-warp is a treasured "institution", serving "classic", "plain" fish that's "dependably good, if rather highly priced"; arrive early for a table. / EC4N 4SA; www.sweetingsrestaurant.com; 3 pm; L only, closed Sat & Sun; no booking.

Taberna Do Mercado E1 NEW £44 433

Spitalfields Mkt 7375 0649 12–2B

A surprisingly low-key opening in a unit in Spitalfields Market from celeb chef du jour Nuno Mendes (Chiltern Firehouse, Viajante); clearly a passion-project, the focus is offbeat tapas from the chef's Portuguese homeland, which most (if not quite all) reports say is "superb". Top Menu Tip – "you must try the fish in a tin". / E1 6EW; www.tabernamercado.co.uk; @tabernamercado; 9.30 pm, Sun 7.30 pm; no booking at D.

Taberna Etrusca EC4 £54 2 4 4
9 - 11 Bow Churchyard 7248 5552 9–2C
"Very slick service" has long been a hallmark of this well-located City Italian, whose tucked-away al-fresco tables are lovely in the sunshine; all this plus "rustic cooking, and good value wine (for the ECs)". / EC4M 9DQ; www.etruscarestaurants.com; 10 pm; closed Sat & Sun.

The Table SE1 £38 3 3 3
83 Southwark St 7401 2760 9–4B
"Wonderful brunches" are the top draw to this "entertaining" and stylish café, over the road from Tate Modern; "it's packed out, and you queue round the block, but it's worth it". / SE1 0HX; www.thetablecafe.com; @thetablecafe; 10.30 pm; closed Mon D, Sat D & Sun D.

Taiwan Village SW6 £34 4 5 3
85 Lillie Rd 7381 2900 5–3A
"Amazing value, hidden gem off the gritty North End Road", with supremely "helpful" service, and where the "consistently delicious" Chinese cooking comes with "interesting" – and spicy – Taiwanese variations; "go with the superb let-us-feed-you chef's menu". / SW6 1UD; www.taiwanvillage.com; @taiwanvillage85; 11.30 pm, Sun 10.30 pm; closed weekday L; booking: max 20.

Tajima Tei EC1 £36 4 3 3
9-11 Leather Ln 7404 9665 9–2A
"Shame that the decor looks a bit cheap" – this busy Japanese hidden near Hatton Gardens has a choice of 19 set lunch menus, and is "very authentic and excellent". / EC1N 7ST; www.tajima-tei.co.uk; 10 pm; closed Sat & Sun; no booking at L.

Talad Thai SW15 £33 4 3 1
320 Upper Richmond Rd 8246 5791 10–2A
"A great stalwart for a cheap night out" – a Thai canteen, adjacent to an Asian supermarket in Putney, with "consistently tasty and enjoyable food" at un-scary prices. / SW15 6TL; www.taladthairestaurant.com; 10.30 pm, Sun 9.30 pm; no Amex.

Tamarind W1 £75 3 3 2
20 Queen St 7629 3561 3–3B
"Superior cooking with out-of-this-world fragrances and flavours" continues to rank this Mayfair fixture amongst London's top nouvelle Indians; "its basement location is a minus" however, and is it becoming more "corporate"? / W1J 5PR; www.tamarindrestaurant.com; @TamarindMayfair; 10.45 pm, Sun 10.30 pm; closed Sat L; booking: max 20; set weekday L £48 (FP).

Tandoori Nights SE22 £39 4 3 3
73 Lordship Ln 8299 4077 1–4D
"Reliably high quality, punchy cooking" keeps south Londoners going back time and again to this stalwart East Dulwich curry house – a "favourite local Indian". / SE22 8EP; www.tandoorinightsdulwich.co.uk; 11.30 pm, Fri & Sat midnight; closed weekday L & Sat L; no Amex.

Tapas Brindisa £45 3 3 3
46 Broadwick St, W1 7534 1690 3–2D
18-20 Southwark St, SE1 7357 8880 9–4C
41-43 Atlantic Rd, SW9 7733 0634 10–2D
The "ever-busy", "fun" (but "rushed") Borough Market original is the dominant member of this Spanish group, with wine and tapas that's "superb... but beware it's not cheap"; the Soho and Brixton spin-offs are less known, but in a similar vein. See also Morada Brindisa Asador. / 10.45 pm, Sun 10 pm; W1 booking: max 10.

Taqueria W11 £35 4 3 3
141-145 Westbourne Grove 7229 4734 6–1B
"Spot-on", "no frills" Mexican cantina, on the fringe of Notting Hill, with an "interesting" and "authentic" taco-focused menu, not to mention "delicious margaritas", and other Latino tipples; it's "cheap as chips" too. / W11 2RS; www.taqueria.co.uk; @TaqueriaUK; 11 pm, Fri & Sat 11.30 pm, Sun 10.30 pm; no Amex; no booking at weekends.

Taro £36 4 3 3
10 Old Compton St, W1 7439 2275 4–2B
61 Brewer St, W1 7734 5826 3–2D
"Delicious, cheap and quick" budget Japanese canteens in Soho, overseen by omnipresent Mr Taro – bento boxes are particularly good value. / www.tarorestaurants.co.uk; 10.30 pm, Sun 9.30 pm; no Amex; Brewer St only small bookings.

Tartufo SW3 £57 4 4 2
11 Cadogan Gdns 7730 6383 5–2D
"Tucked away at the base of a fusty old Chelsea block near Peter Jones", Alexis Gauthier's "surprising" two-year-old makes a "superb" find with its "professional" service and "refined" Italian-ish cooking (with truffles much in evidence); the "dungeon-like" setting is a bit of a downer though. / SW3 2RJ; www.tartufolondon.co.uk; @TartufoLondon; 10 pm; closed Mon & Sun D.

Tas £37 1 3 3
Branches throughout London
Is this popular and "well-located" Turkish chain just too "uninspired" nowadays? "For a quick cheap bite" many are still "happy to recommend" the mezze formula, but experiences seemed ever-more "busy and disappointing" this year. / www.tasrestaurant.com; 11.30 pm, Sun 10.30 pm; EC4 Closed Sun.

Tas Pide SE1 £40 233
20-22 New Globe Walk 7928 3300 9–3B
Cosy Anatolian, right by the Globe Theatre, which is "probably the most attractive Tas", and its "fairly traditional mezze and Turkish take on pizza" are similarly "reasonably priced". / SE1 9DR; www.tasrestaurants.co.uk/pide; 11.30 pm, Sun 10.30 pm.

(Whistler Restaurant) Tate Britain SW1 £54 235
Millbank 7887 8825 2–4C
Whistler's famous murals imbue this serene dining room with a "delightful" ambience, and its other claim to fame is Hamish Anderson's "exceptional" wine list ("from all corners of the globe, with many half-bottles, all at reasonable prices"); food-wise, though, it's "just OK". / SW1 4RG; www.tate.org.uk; @Tate; 3 pm, afternoon tea Sat-Sun 5 pm; L & afternoon tea only; set Sun L £50 (FP).

(Restaurant, Level 6) Tate Modern SE1 £59 214
Bankside 7887 8888 9–3B
You enjoy "stunning views" (some tables only) in the "airy" top-floor dining room of this south bank landmark; there's "an exceptional wine list" too, but the "mainly British food is mixed" ("some dishes good, some below par)", and service – though "pleasant" – is "shambolic". / SE1 9TG; www.tate.org.uk; @TateFood; 9 pm; Sun-Thu closed D, Fri & Sat open L & D.

Taylor St Baristas £16 344
Branches throughout London
"Unbelievable coffee" – "their roasts are unsurpassed" – win a big thumbs up for this Aussie chain, and it does "excellent healthy lunch salads and sandwiches" too; "its artisan-style service means your wait will be long", however. / EC2M 4TP; www.taylor-st.com; all branches 5 pm; Old Broad ST, Clifton St, W1, E14 closed Sat & Sun; New St closed Sat; TW9 closed Sun.

Tayyabs E1 £31 423
83 Fieldgate St 7247 9543 9–2D
"How do they keep it so good, while serving a gazillion people?!" – this "frantic" but "phenomenal" East End Pakistani enjoys "classic" status thanks to its "always fabulous and exceptional value" nosh (not least lamb chops that are "beyond superb"); "massive queues, even if you've booked!" / E1 1JU; www.tayyabs.co.uk; @1tayyabs; 11.30 pm.

Tem Tép W8 NEW £48 333
135 Kensington Church St 7792 7816 6–2B
"A great addition near Notting Hill Gate" – a new Vietnamese 'kitchen', with "wonderful" affordable food. / W8 7LP; temtep.co.uk; Sun-Thu 10 pm, Fri & Sat 10.30 pm; no Amex.

The 10 Cases WC2 £55 243
16 Endell St 7836 6801 4–2C
"Knowledgeable and passionate staff" advise on the "excellent wines by the glass" at this "fabulous and friendly" independent bistro/wine bar in Covent Garden; it serves a "short, simple menu" – "it's proper food, but the place is all about the vino". / WC2H 9BD; www.the10cases.co.uk; @10cases; 11 pm; closed Sun.

10 Greek Street W1 £46 543
10 Greek St 7734 4677 4–2A
"No flim-flam – just pure class!" – this Soho three-year-old may be "simple and basic" (and "a bit cramped" too), but it dishes up "brilliant", "sensitive" seasonal cuisine, and Luke's hand-written list provides "smashing wines at decent prices"; "book at lunch, to avoid the inevitable evening queue". / W1D 4DH; www.10greekstreet.com; @10GreekStreet; 11.30 pm; closed Sun.

Tendido Cero SW5 £52 333
174 Old Brompton Rd 7370 3685 5–2B
"Designer tapas" and "fabulous wine" buoy the "buzz" at this "crowded and noisy" South Kensington bar; it's "not cheap", but fans say "it's worth every penny!" / SW5 0BA; www.cambiodetercio.co.uk; @CambiodTercio; 11 pm.

Tendido Cuatro SW6 £48 232
108-110 New King's Rd 7371 5147 10–1B
Cambio de Tercio's Fulham venture dropped in ratings across the board this year; apologists insist the "cramped, crowded and noisy" tapas bar serves "excellent" food, but detractors feel prices are "totally inauthentic". / SW6 4LY; www.cambiodetercio.co.uk; @CambiodTercio; 11 pm, Sun 10.30 pm.

Tentazioni SE1 £63 223
2 Mill St 7394 5248 11–2A
"Off the beaten track" little Italian, near Shad Thames, which has long been a haven of "surprisingly accomplished" cooking; it has seemed more "impersonal" of late however, and the food "has gone from good to average". / SE1 2BD; www.tentazioni.co.uk; @TentazioniWorld; 10.45 pm, Sun 9 pm; closed Sat L.

Terra Vergine SW10 £53 433
442 King's Rd 7352 0491 5–3B
"Featuring food and wine from the Abruzzo" – a "very authentic" Chelsea operation, where "extremely fresh and unusual ingredients are prepared with great attention to detail"; "you could be in Italy, from the number of Italians who dine there". / SW10 0LQ; www.terravergine.co.uk; closed Mon L, Tue L & Wed L.

The Terrace on Holland Street W8 £67 344
33c Holland St 7937 9252 5–1A
The "cosy interior is complemented by the outside terrace", at this "lovely, tiny and intimate local", in a cute Kensington backwater, well-liked for its "unfussy, modern British cooking". / W8 4LX; www.theterraceonhollandstreet.co.uk; @HollandSt; 10.30 pm; closed Sun; set weekday L £40 (FP).

Terroirs WC2 £49 334
5 William IV St 7036 0660 4–4C
"Bold" and "so, so tasty" Gallic tapas dishes help soak up the many "esoteric" and "fascinating" organic wines at this wildly popular, "casual" bistro, just off Trafalgar Square; both the main room and hidden-away sub-basement are "buzzing" and "great fun". / WC2N 4DW; www.terroirswinebar.com; @terroirswinebar; 11 pm; closed Sun.

Texture W1 £97 442
34 Portman St 7224 0028 2–2A
"Absolutely divine" results from Agnar Sverrisson's "very creative" Icelandic menu, complemented by "stunning" wine matches (with an emphasis on champagnes), inspire raves for this foodie temple near Selfridges, where "charming and solicitous" service helps enliven the slightly "soulless" space. / W1H 7BY; www.texture-restaurant.co.uk; @TextureLondon; 10.30 pm; closed Mon & Sun; set weekday L £54 (FP).

Thali SW5 £48 444
166 Old Brompton Rd 7373 2626 5–2B
"Family recipes make this Indian restaurant special" – a stylish modern subcontinental in South Kensington (decorated with posters from Bollywood classics) serving slightly offbeat food with "fresh spicing and interesting flavours". / SW5 0BA; www.thali.uk.com; @Thali London; 11.30 pm, Sun 10.30 pm.

Theo Randall, InterContinental Hotel W1 £95 321
1 Hamilton Pl 7318 8747 3–4A
"Ambience has never been a strongpoint" of this "oddly corporate", windowless chamber, in the bowels of this Hyde Park Corner hotel; for fans, its "inspired" Italian cuisine is clear compensation, but a growing band of sceptics fear it's "not all it's cracked up to be" nowadays. / W1J 7QY; www.theorandall.com; @theorandall; 11 pm; closed Sat L & Sun; set weekday L £57 (FP).

34 W1 £75 333
34 Grosvenor Sq 3350 3434 3–3A
Richard Caring's "classy and elegant" operation "feels like it's been around for decades" and its "lively but discreet" quarters, "capable" service and "wide variety" of "excellent" grills make it a natural for business; prices, predictably, are "very Mayfair". / W1K 2HD; www.34-restaurant.co.uk; 10.30 pm.

The Thomas Cubitt SW1 £60 344
44 Elizabeth St 7730 6060 2–4A
"Catering to the well-heeled", this "posh pub" in Belgravia has a "wonderful atmosphere", even if it can be "very crowded" and "terribly noisy"; you can eat "classic pub grub" downstairs, but some prefer to "escape upstairs" to the "classy restaurant". / SW1W 9PA; www.thethomascubitt.co.uk; @TheThomasCubitt; 10 pm, Sun 9.30 pm.

3 South Place, South Place Hotel EC2 £62 323
3 South Pl 3503 0000 12–2A
"Smart, modern bar/restaurant" in D&D London's "funky hotel", by Liverpool Street, which is particularly tipped as "a superb spot for a business breakfast", although it's said to be "a solid choice for lunch" too. / EC2M 2AF; www.southplacehotel.com; @southplacehotel; 10.30 pm; booking: max 22.

tibits W1 £35 323
12-14 Heddon St 7758 4112 3–2C
"It's self-service, and you pay by weight from the great, wide-ranging, all-veggie buffet" – that's the concept at this very handy (and "family-friendly") Swiss-run operation, which is ideal for a healthy "quick bite" near Piccadilly Circus. / W1B 4DA; www.tibits.co.uk; @tibits_uk; 11.30 pm, Sun 10 pm; no Amex; need 8+ to book.

Tinello SW1 £55 444
87 Pimlico Rd 7730 3663 5–2D
With its "dark woods and low lighting", this "romantic" Pimlico Tuscan – a stablemate of Mayfair's Locanda Locatelli – is an all-round hit with its "rich" north Italian small dishes matched with "a well-thought-out and unusual wine list". / SW1W 8PH; www.tinello.co.uk; @tinello_london; 10.30 pm; closed Sun.

Ting Shangri-La Hotel at the Shard SE1 £88 224
Level 35, 31 St Thomas St 7234 8108 9–4C
"Astonishing views" of course accompany a trip to this "spacious and luxurious" 35th-floor chamber; as with all this landmark's other elevated eateries however, you pay through the nose for them, especially given the "disjointed" service and food that "verges on boring". / SE1 9RY; www.ting-shangri-la.com; 11.30 pm.

Toasted SE22 £49 233
38 Lordship Ln 8693 9021 1–4D
"An interesting wine list even if you don't like natural wines" helps win fans for this Caves de Pyrène outpost in East Dulwich; the food is no more than "perfectly pleasant" however, and some sceptics would say the same of the whole set-up. / SE22 8HJ; www.toastdulwich.co.uk; @toastdulwich; 9.45 pm; closed Sun D.

Toff's N10 £40 432
38 Muswell Hill Broadway 8883 8656 1–1B
"Utterly dependable fish 'n' chips" maintains this "always busy and welcoming" Muswell Hill institution as one of north London's most popular chippies. / N10 3RT; www.toffsfish.co.uk; @toffsfish; 10 pm; closed Sun.

Tokyo Diner WC2 £24 343
2 Newport Pl 7287 8777 4–3B
Battered stalwart Japanese caff that "feels just like Tokyo" (but is actually 'mislocated' in Chinatown); food-wise it's not earth-shattering, but "always reliable" for "freshly prepared" sushi and a good range of other dishes at "rock-bottom" prices. / WC2H 7JJ; www.tokyodiner.com; 11.30 pm; no Amex; no booking, Fri & Sat.

Tokyo Sukiyaji-Tei & Bar SW3 £46
85 Sloane Ave 3583 3797 5–2C
Formerly Sushi des Artistes (but under the same ownership), a Chelsea hideaway serving an eclectic range of fusion dishes as well as Japanese faves like sukiyaki, shabu-shabu and sashimi; feedback is limited, but fans say it's a "must visit". / SW3 3DX; www.tokyosukiyakitei.com.

Tom's Kitchen £63 121
Somerset House, 150 Strand, WC2 7845 4646 2–2D
27 Cale St, SW3 7349 0202 5–2C
11 Westferry Circus, E14 3011 1555 11–1C
1 Commodity Quay, E1 3011 5433 9–3D
"They need to up their game" at Tom Aikens's supposedly upmarket, casual bistro chain – with its "disorganised" service, "hit-and-miss" cooking and "lack of ambience", it's just "all a bit ordinary". / 10 pm - 10.45 pm; WC2 closed Sun D.

Tommi's Burger Joint £20 444
30 Thayer St, W1 7224 3828 3–1A
342 Kings Rd, SW3 7349 0691 5–3C
There's "always a mad rush" for a seat at these "no-frills", order-at-the-counter burger joints in Marylebone and Chelsea, on account of their "impressive steak-burgers and generally chilled-out vibe". / 9 pm.

The Tommy Tucker SW6 NEW £53 334
22 Waterford Rd 7736 1023 5–4A
Fulham's darling Claude Compton (Claude's Kitchen, Amuse Bouche) serves up another hit with his "upbeat and energetic" take on the British gastropub; the slow-cooked fare is "excellent" – particularly Sunday lunch – complemented by an "unusual wine cellar". / SW6 2DR; www.thetommytucker.com; @tommytuckerpub; Mon-Sat 10 pm, Sun 9 pm; set weekday L £30 (FP).

Tonic & Remedy, The M By Montcalm EC1 NEW £55
151-157 City Rd 3837 3102 12–1A
North of Old Street roundabout, a trendy-looking new hotel hang out, run by Searcys; not enough feedback for a rating, but one early reporter – lauding its "interesting mix of dishes" – says "it's a great place for after work drinks and dinner". / EC1V 1BE; www.tonicandremedy.co.uk; @tonicandremedy; Mon-Thu 10.30 pm, Fri & Sat 11 pm, Sun 10 pm.

Tonkotsu £32 443
Selfridges, 400 Oxford St, W1 7437 0071 3–1A
63 Dean St, W1 7437 0071 4–2A
4 Canvey St, SE1 7928 2228 9–4B
382 Mare St, E8 8533 1840 1–1D NEW
Arch 334 1a Dunston St, E8 7254 2478 1–2D
"Delicious hot and warming bowls of noodles" are the mainstay of these cramped bars in Soho, and now in Bankside, Haggerston and Hackney Central too; there's some dispute however as to whether they're "taking ramen to a new level", or are merely "fine". /

Tortilla £17 322
Branches throughout London
For a "fresh and satisfying burrito", these "speedy" operations – neck and neck with rival Chipotle – are "cheap and reasonably authentic". / www.tortilla.co.uk; W1 & N1 11 pm, Sun 9 pm, SE1 & E14 9 pm, EC3 7 pm, E14 Sun 7 pm; SE1 & EC3 closed Sat & Sun, N1 closed sun; no Amex.

Tosa W6 £35 332
332 King St 8748 0002 7–2B
"Freshly cooked over charcoal", the "excellent" yakitori is the speciality of this nondescript but "cosy" Japanese, near Stamford Brook tube, although the sushi and other fare is "very tasty" too. / W6 0RR; www.tosauk.com; 10.30 pm.

Toto's SW3 £88 2|3|3
Walton Hs, Lennox Gardens Mews 7589 2062 5–2C
"A beautiful, tucked-away Knightsbridge Italian, whose lovely courtyard is perfect when it's sunny"; "it's good to see it back in operation under its new owners" – "the resurrected incarnation is excellent" (if very expensive). / SW3 2JH; www.totosrestaurant.com; @TotosRestaurant; 11 pm.

Tozi SW1 £47 3|3|3
8 Gillingham St 7769 9771 2–4B
"Very useful in the Victoria desert" – this "accommodating" venture may be "pricey" and somewhat hotel-y, but fans love its "scrummy Venetian-inspired tapas", and praise the "flexible and welcoming" staff. / SW1V 1HN; www.tozirestaurant.co.uk; @ToziRestaurant; 10 pm.

The Trading House EC2 £42
89-91 Gresham St 7600 5050 9–1A
Newly-opened gastropub in the heart of the City – early days reports say it's "nicely-decorated", serving a wide range of food that's "well-made and well-presented". / EC2V 7NQ; www.thetradinghouse.uk.com; @tradinghouse; 10 pm; closed Sat L & Sun; no Amex.

The Tramshed EC2 £55 2|2|3
32 Rivington St 7749 0478 12–1B
"Impressive art including a Damien Hirst number in a tank of formaldehyde" sets the scene at Mark Hix's big Shoreditch shed; but while its "meat-centred" formula (chicken or steak 'n' chips) can be OK on business, it too often seems "all style over substance", delivering "not much flavour for the £££s". / EC2A 3LX; www.chickenandsteak.co.uk; @HIXrestaurants; Mon & Tue 11 pm, Wed-Sat 12.30 am, Sun 9.30 pm.

Trangallan N16 £44 5|4|4
61 Newington Grn 7359 4988 1–1C
"None of the plates or cutlery match, but in the quaintest way", at this Stoke Newington Hispanic; all reporters "love everything about the place" – "staff really know their stuff", there's "loads of interesting Spanish wines", and the food's "a revelation". / N16 9PX; www.trangallan.com; @trangallan_N16; 10.30 pm; closed Mon; no Amex; set weekday L £28 (FP).

Tredwell's WC2 £53 1|2|1
4 Upper St Martin's Ln 3764 0840 4–3B
"A let-down after such high hopes" – Marcus Wareing's casual West End haunt is "nearly so good... but somehow just isn't"; "is it a gourmet place or a brasserie for theatre-goers?" – "it's not good enough for the former, too expensive for the latter" – too often the service is "amateurish", and the decor strikes too many reporters as "bizarre: not relaxing, not cool, not quirky". / WC2H 9NY; www.tredwells.com; @tredwells; 10 pm, Thu-Sat 11 pm, Sun 9 pm; set weekday L & pre-theatre £35 (FP).

The Tree House SW13 £45 3|3|3
73 White Hart Ln 8392 1617 10–1A
"The outside area is a great place to eat in summer", say fans of this cute "pub-style" venue, on the fringes of Barnes, who praise its "reliable" standards generally. / SW13 0PW; www.treehousepeople.com; @TreeHouseBarnes; 11 pm, Fri & Sat midnight, Sun 10.30 pm.

Trinity SW4 £68 5|5|4
4 The Polygon 7622 1199 10–2D
"You feel the money's been well-spent" at Adam Byatt's fine-dining "oasis" in Clapham – "a superb all-rounder", where staff are "friendly without being overbearing", the room is "lovely and airy", the cuisine "consistently brilliant" and where "the Chef's Cellar wines are particularly well chosen". In October 2015 it is relaunching after a 3-month closure, with an open kitchen, new outside dining area, and a new 'casual dining' option on the first floor called 'Upstairs', with small plates and communal tables. / SW4 0JG; www.trinityrestaurant.co.uk; @TrinityLondon; 9.45 pm; closed Mon L & Sun D; set Sun L £0 (FP), set weekday L £46 (FP).

Trishna W1 £64 5|4|3
15-17 Blandford St 7935 5624 2–1A
Mumbai comes to Marylebone at this London offshoot of its legendary Indian forebear; despite a "trying-to-be-chic" revamp, the interior gets a slightly mixed rep, but the "extraordinarily good" cooking (in particular "memorable seafood and stand-out lamb chops") rivals that of its upstart Mayfair sibling, Gymkhana. / W1U 3DG; www.trishnalondon.com; @TrishnaLondon; 10.45 pm, Sun 9.45 pm; set weekday L & pre-theatre £35 (FP).

LA TROMPETTE W4 £71 4|4|4
5-7 Devonshire Rd 8747 1836 7–2A
"A good reason to live in Chiswick!" – this "dream local" is a worthy sibling to Chez Bruce, that's "well worth the trek to W4" for its "exemplary" classic cooking and "quiet wow factor"; a tiny minority, however, quibble that it's "not quite as special as prior to the extension" (a couple of years ago). / W4 2EU; www.latrompette.co.uk; @LaTrompetteUK; 10.30 pm, Sun 9.30 pm; set weekday L £50 (FP), set Sun L £54 (FP).

Troubadour SW5 £46 2|3|4
263-267 Old Brompton Rd 7370 1434 5–3A
"Still the same old Troubadour!" – but for how much longer? – this Bohemian relic is up for sale as we go to press; let's hope a buyer can be found, both to preserve the unique "arty" vibe of this "fun" '60s Earl's Court café (and live music venue), and also to improve its basic fodder. / SW5 9JA; www.troubadour.co.uk; @TroubadourLDN; 11 pm.

Trullo N1 **£59** 4 4 3
300-302 St Paul's Rd 7226 2733 8–2D
"A taste of Italy off Highbury Corner" – this "lovely" looking Italian continues to inspire north Londoners with its "simple", "dreamily authentic" cooking and "an amazing wine list that's both clever and good value"; some reports tip the ground floor over the basement. / N1 2LH; www.trullorestaurant.com; @Trullo_LDN; 10.30 pm; closed Sun D; no Amex; booking: max 12.

The Truscott Arms W9 **£56** 4 3 4
55 Shirland Rd 7266 9198 1–2B
"It's transformed the area!"; this "surprise gem" is "just what Maida Vale has been waiting for" – "an exceptional local", whose first-floor dining room provides quite "complex" cuisine, alongside matching wines. Top Menu Tip – an extensive gluten-free menu. / W9 2JD; www.thetruscottarms.com; @TheTruscottArms; 10 pm; SRA-3.*

The Truscott Cellar NW3 NEW **£39**
240 Haverstock Hill 7266 9198 8–2A
On the prominent Belsize Park site that was long Weng Wah House (RIP) – a new wine bar promising a 'British sharing plates' formula from the owners of Maida Vale's popular Truscott Arms; it opened in Autumn 2015. / NW3 2AE; www.twitter.com/TruscottCellar; @truscottcellar.

Tsunami **£46** 5 3 3
93 Charlotte St, W1 7637 0050 2–1C
5-7 Voltaire Rd, SW4 7978 1610 10–1D
"Terrific Japanese/Asian cuisine" – not just "spot-on sushi and sashimi" but also many "wonderful grazing options" – continue to win high acclaim for this Clapham outfit (whose more "basic" Fitzrovia spin-off is less well-known); "original cocktails" too, help make for a good night out. / www.tsunamirestaurant.co.uk; @Tsunamirest; SW4 10.30 pm, Fri & Sat 11 pm, Sun 9.30 pm; W1 11 pm; SW4 closed Mon - Fri L, W1 closed Sat L and Sun; no Amex.

Tulse Hill Hotel SE24 NEW **£46** 3 3 3
150 Norwood Rd 8671 7499 1–4D
Between Brixton and Dulwich, this newly-renovated gastropub is proving "a good addition to a rather bereft area"; the food's "a cut above", but "all the hipster beards on show can be a little distracting". / SE24 9AY; www.tulsehillhotel.com; @TulseHillHotel; 10 pm, Sun 9 pm.

28-50 **£54** 3 3 4
15 Maddox St, W1 7495 1505 3–2C
15-17 Marylebone Ln, W1 7486 7922 3–1A
140 Fetter Ln, EC4 7242 8877 9–2A
"Impressively knowledgeable staff make non-wine-buffs feel very comfortable" at these hugely popular bar/bistros, whose "wonderful" list has "many interesting options by the glass and bottle"; the food's "perfect for a business lunch" – "unadventurous but well-prepared". / www.2850.co.uk; EC4 9.30 pm, W1 Mon-Wed 10 pm, Thu-Sat 10.30 pm, Sun 9.30 pm; EC4 closed Sat & Sun.

Twist At Crawford W1 NEW **£59** 4 4 4
42 Crawford St 7723 3377 2–1A
"An innovative take" on tapas (mixing Mediterranean and Asian inspirations) wins praise for this "modest"-looking newcomer, and helps make it "a great new addition" to Marylebone. / W1H 1JW; www.twistkitchen.co.uk; @TwistKitchen; 11 pm, Fri 11.30 pm, Sat midnight; closed Sun; set weekday L £37 (FP).

Two Brothers N3 **£45** 3 3 2
297-303 Regent's Park Rd 8346 0469 1–1B
A recent refurb', with "smart new decor" divides fans of this Finchley fixture – thankfully the "family-friendly charm" is unwavering, and even those who say it's "gone off a bit", still say it's their No. 1 favourite chippie. / N3 1DP; www.twobrothers.co.uk; 10 pm; closed Mon; set weekday L £19 (FP).

2 Veneti W1 **£47** 3 4 3
10 Wigmore St 7637 0789 3–1B
"Interesting Venetian specialities" and "assiduous" service maintain the appeal of this "reliable", "high quality" (if rather "expensive") Italian, which is "very convenient for the Wigmore Hall" (and handy for business too). / W1U 2RD; www.2veneti.com; @2Veneti; 10.30 pm, Sat 11 pm; closed Sat L & Sun.

Typing Room Town Hall Hotel E2 **£88** 5 4 3
Patriot Square 7871 0461 1–2D
"Sublime food without snobbery"; Lee Westcott's "meticulous" dishes are delivered by staff who are "friendly, and absolutely on-the-ball" at this ("slightly sterile") Bethnal Green yearling, where "you watch the chefs work in the open kitchen"; it's fully as good as its legendary predecessor (Viajante, RIP). / E2 9NF; www.typingroom.com; @TypingRoom; 10 pm; closed Mon & Tue L; set weekday L £50 (FP).

Umu W1 **£120** 2 2 2
14-16 Bruton Pl 7499 8881 3–2C
"The kaiseki is a revelation, and a confirmation of chef Yoshi's vast talents", say fans of Marlon Abela's Kyoto-style venture in a tucked-away Mayfair mews, for whom this is "the best Japanese food outside of Japan"; almost as many reporters though, just obsess over the bill – "dear, oh dear, oh dear, oh dear..." / W1J 6LX; www.umurestaurant.com; 10.30 pm; closed Sat L & Sun; no trainers; booking: max 14.

Union Street Café SE1 **£57** 2 2 2
47-51 Great Suffolk St 7592 7977 9–4B
Fans of Gordon Ramsay's industrial-chic Italian two-year-old in Borough praise its "interesting and varied menu" and "casual" style; there are a number of sceptics though, who say it's merely "expensive and average", or just plain bad. / SE1 0BS; www.gordonramsay.com/union-street-cafe; @unionstreetcafe; Mon-Sat 10.45 pm; closed Sun D.

Le Vacherin W4 **£63** 3 2 2
76-77 South Pde 8742 2121 7–1A
Malcolm John's "off-the-beaten-track" Gallic classic by Acton Green, is known for its "delicious" bistro fare and "intimate" ambience; its ratings suffered this year though, with quite a number of reports of the "perhaps-they-were-having-a-bad-day" variety. / W4 5LF; www.levacherin.co.uk; @Le_Vacherin; 9.45 pm, Fri & Sat 10.15 pm, Sun 8.30 pm; closed Mon L; set dinner £35 (FP), set weekday L & pre-theatre £41 (FP).

Vanilla Black EC4 **£61** 4 3 2
17-18 Tooks Ct 7242 2622 9–2A
"Wowza!" – even "died-in-the-wool meat eaters" are bowled over by this "little veggie, down a small alley near Chancery Lane", whose "strange combinations" "never cease to surprise with their unimaginable mixture of flavours"; the same could not be said though for its "sombre" interior. / EC4A 1LB; www.vanillablack.co.uk; @vanillablack1; 10 pm; closed Sun; no Amex.

Vapiano **£30** 3 2 2
19-21 Great Portland St, W1 7268 0080 3–1C
90b Southwark St, SE1 7593 2010 9–4B
"For a quick bite at a reasonable price" – pizza, pasta, salads, etc – try this offbeat German-owned food-court concept, in the West End and also Bankside – you serve yourself, but the system of ordering food that's "freshly prepared in front of you to order" gets the thumbs-up. / www.vapiano.co.uk; Mon -Thu 11pm, SE1 Fri & Sat 10.30pm, W1 Fri & Sat 11.30 pm.

Vasco & Piero's Pavilion W1 **£59** 3 4 3
15 Poland St 7437 8774 3–1D
"A real gem for those nostalgic for a more civilised, less trendy past!" – this "unassuming", heart-of-Soho Italian is "untainted by hip décor or noise"; there are sceptics for whom it's too "boring" (and too "closely packed"), but most reports focus on its "friendly and professional" staff, and quality, "traditional" fare. / W1F 8QE; www.vascosfood.com; @Vasco_and_Piero; 10.15 pm; closed Sat L & Sun; set weekday L £41 (FP).

Veeraswamy W1 **£77** 3 3 3
Victory Hs, 99-101 Regent St 7734 1401 3–3D
From its contemporary design, you'd never know this "quiet oasis" near Piccadilly Circus was London's oldest Indian (est 1926); to say, as fans do, that "it's still the best" would over-egg it, but its "inventive and flavourful" food rescues it from any hint of tourist-trap status. / W1B 4RS; www.veeraswamy.com; 10.30 pm, Sun 10 pm; booking: max 14; set Sun L £51 (FP).

Verden E5 **£48** 4 4 4
181 Clarence Rd 8986 4723 1–1D
Rave reviews for this modern wine-bar yearling in increasingly gentrified Clapton (once upon a time 'Murder Mile'). There's a good selection of "eclectic wines" ("they even have a 'breakfast wine'!"), served by "knowledgeable staff", alongside a "limited" menu (that's "fairly short on cooked dishes"). / E5 8EE; www.verdene5.com; @VerdenE5; midnight, Sun 10.30 pm; closed Mon, Tue L, Wed L & Thu L.

Verdi's E1 NEW **£46** 4 4 3
237 Mile End Rd 7423 9563 1–2D
"What a brilliant addition to the Whitechapel Road!" – "an excellent and rare trattoria" that would be "well worth a visit in any neighbourhood" thanks to its "delicious, regional Italian food", but is "particularly welcome in under-endowed Stepney!" / E1 4AA; www.gverdi.uk.

El Vergel SE1 **£33** 4 4 4
132 Webber St 7401 2308 9–4B
"Mouthwatering empanadas, and other top authentic South American sarnies and snacks" inspire love – especially at brunch – for this upbeat, budget Latino canteen, near Borough tube. / SE1 0QL; www.elvergel.co.uk; @ElVergel_London; 3 pm, Sat-Sun 4 pm; closed D, closed Sun; no Amex.

Vico WC2 NEW **£58**
140a Shaftesbury Ave awaiting tel 4–2B
The duo behind Soho's marvellous Bocca di Lupo, Jacob Kenedy and Victor Hugo, branch out into street food with this new 'piazza-eria' in Cambridge Circus (a casual, no-cutlery restaurant offering take-away and Gelupo ice cream counter); it opened in August 2015, too late for our survey. / WC2H 8PA; www.boccadilupo.com; @boccadilupo.

Il Vicolo SW1 £49 344
3-4 Crown Passage 7839 3960 3–4D
Down a cute alley in St James's, a "great little family-run Italian" that's "well worth seeking out" in this über-pricey part of town – "you are always looked after" and the Sicilian cooking is "thoroughly enjoyable". / SW1Y 6PP; 10 pm; closed Sat L & Sun.

The Victoria SW14 £50 344
10 West Temple 8876 4238 10–2A
"A boon if you've got a young family, but adults are well-catered-for too!" – Paul Merrett's "lovely", large gastropub is "hidden away in residential Sheen, near Richmond Park"; "kids get to run around in the enclosed garden" (with playground), while others enjoy the "high quality" cooking. / SW14 7RT; www.thevictoria.net; @thevictoria_pub; winter 10 pm, Sun 8 pm – summer 9 pm; no Amex.

Viet Grill E2 £44 433
58 Kingsland Rd 7739 6686 12–1B
"Spicey and great value for money" – the Vietnamese cooking at this modern Shoreditch café and pho-bar; "it's packed, and no wonder!". / E2 8DP; www.vietnamesekitchen.co.uk; @CayTreVietGrill; 11 pm, Fri & Sat 11.30 pm, Sun 10.30 pm.

Vijay NW6 £32 341
49 Willesden Ln 7328 1087 1–1B
It "could do with a facelift" (no change for decades there then), but the cooking at this longstanding South Indian in Kilburn is as "reliably delicious" and well priced now, as it has been for many a moon. / NW6 7RF; www.vijayrestaurant.co.uk; 10.45 pm, Fri & Sat 11.45 pm.

Villa Bianca NW3 £58 232
1 Perrins Ct 7435 3131 8–2A
"Well-located off Hampstead High Street in a quaint little alleyway" – "an old school 'silver service' trattoria", where "all the standard Italian dishes are served"; to its very dedicated fan cub it's "not a wow, but a safe bet", but to its detractors "it's shocking and tired". / NW3 1QS; www.villabiancagroup.co.uk; @VBgroupNW3; 11.30 pm, Sun 10.30 pm.

Villa Di Geggiano W4 NEW £63 222
66-68 Chiswick High Rd 3384 9442 7–2B
"Sumptuous Italian newcomer", occupying the Chiswick site that was once Frankie's (long RIP); wines from the Tuscan estate of the same name are a prime feature, as is its outside terrace, but the food can be "disappointing", especially at prices that some find "grabby". / W4 1SY; www.villadigeggiano.com; @VilladiGeggiano; 10 pm; closed Mon.

Village East SE1 £56 333
171-173 Bermondsey St 7357 6082 9–4D
"Too many hipsters" is a hazard at this happening Bermondsey hang-out, tipped for brunch, and also as being "great with a group of friends". / SE1 3UW; www.villageeast.co.uk; @VillageEastSE1; 10 pm, Sun 9.30 pm; set weekday L £35 (FP).

Villandry £55 112
11-12 Waterloo Pl, SW1 7930 3305 3–3D
170 Gt Portland St, W1 7631 3131 2–1B
Their "elegant" looks and high prices show "pretentions to greatness", but these smart-looking grand cafés – in St James's and Marylebone – "could be so much better", if only they had "more professional" staff and made an effort with their "very disappointing" cooking. /

The Vincent Rooms, Westminster Kingsway College SW1 £37 333
76 Vincent Sq 7802 8391 2–4C
Despite the elegant Westminster location, "low prices reflect that this is a training ground" for one of London's main catering colleges; by nature "it's a bit hit and miss", but typically "you get great food that's good value", and the servers are "charming, and eager for comments and criticism". / SW1P 2PD; www.thevincentrooms.com; @TheVincentRooms; 7 pm; closed Mon D, Tue D, Fri D, Sat & Sun; no Amex.

Vinoteca £46 234
15 Seymour Pl, W1 7724 7288 2–2A
55 Beak St, W1 3544 7411 3–2D
18 Devonshire Rd, W4 3701 8822 7–2A
One Pancras Sq, N1 3793 7210 8–3C NEW
7 St John St, EC1 7253 8786 9–1B
The "well-curated" list of "fantastic", "eclectic" wines by the glass underpins the major success of these "buzzing" modern wine bars (but its bistro fare is "very sound" too). The new King's Cross branch is "a bit hangar-like" but most reporters give it "three cheers". Top Tip – "Magic Monday, with wines sold at shop prices". / www.vinoteca.co.uk.

Vintage Salt £44 443
189 Upper St, N1 3227 0979 8–2D
69 Old Broad St, EC2 7920 9103 9–2C NEW
"Quality remains high" at this rebranded chain (from Fish & Chip Shop), where the national staple "can be had grilled or steamed if you prefer"; the "noisy and crowded" Islington branch is still the best-known, and is pepped up by its "charming" staff.

Vivat Bacchus £51 222
4 Hay's Ln, SE1 7234 0891 9–4C
47 Farringdon St, EC4 7353 2648 9–2A
"A blinding South African wine list", and the "lovely cheeses" ("ask in advance, and they may let you into the cheese room") are the stand out features of these "packed" ventures, in the City and South Bank; the other simple fare plays second fiddle but is "dependable". / www.vivatbacchus.co.uk; 10.30pm; EC4 closed Sat & Sun, SE1 closed Sat L & Sun.

VQ £46 243
St Giles Hotel, Great Russell St, WC1 7636 5888 4–1A
325 Fulham Rd, SW10 7376 7224 5–3B
"Just the place for breakfast after a 5am release from hospital... a nightclub... the cells" – these dependable diners (the age-old SW10 original, and newer WC1 spin-off) serve "classic", "simple" fodder, 24/7. / www.vingtquatre.co.uk; open 24 hours.

Vrisaki N22 £37 332
73 Middleton Rd 8889 8760 1–1C
"It's still hard to finish all the food", at this ancient taverna, behind a Bounds Green take-away, whose mezze feasts are, for its devotees, a top "cheap 'n' cheerful" treat. / N22 8LZ; www.vrisaki.uk.com; @vrisakiuk; 11.30 pm, Sun 9 pm; closed Mon; no Amex.

Wagamama £39 232
Branches throughout London
For a "swift", "no-frills", "fuel stop" – particularly "with kids well catered for" – many still recommend these "casual" communal noodle-refectories, even while acknowledging that the food is "nothing special" nowadays. / www.wagamama.com; 10 pm - 11 pm; EC4 & EC2 closed Sat & Sun; no booking.

Wahaca £33 233
Branches throughout London
"Fun, fresh Mexican street food" served by "obliging" staff underpins the "cheap 'n' cheerful" appeal (and "unstoppable expansion") of Thomasina Miers' "colourful and casual" chain; even some who feel "the buzz has gone" since its early days say it's "still decent". / www.wahaca.com; 10 pm - 11 pm; no booking.

The Wallace The Wallace Collection W1 £55 225
Hertford Hs, Manchester Sq 7563 9505 3–1A
"The magnificent covered atrium" provides a "stunning" and "spacious" setting for this restaurant adjoining the famous 18th-century palazzo and art gallery; the food's usually "decent" enough, but "erratic and lacklustre" service is a hazard. / W1U 3BN; www.peytonandbyrne.co.uk/the-wallace-restaurant/index.html; @PeytonandByrne; Fri & Sat 9.30 pm; Sun-Thu closed D; no Amex.

Waterloo Bar & Kitchen SE1 £50 222
131 Waterloo Rd 7928 5086 9–4A
"A great place to meet fellow Waterloo commuters" or "for the Old Vic" – this "incredibly noisy and packed" venue is a "handy", "reasonably priced" standby in "a hard area for eateries". / SE1 8UR; www.barandkitchen.co.uk; @BarKitchen; 10.30 pm.

The Waterway W9 £50 234
54 Formosa St 7266 3557 8–4A
The hint is in the name – this Little Venice hang out (same ownership as the nearby Summerhouse) has an unbeatable canal-side terrace that's just the job for a lazy summer day. / W9 2JU; www.thewaterway.co.uk; @thewaterway_; 11 pm, Sun 10.30 pm.

The Wells NW3 £49 224
30 Well Walk 7794 3785 8–1A
"Well-behaved, four-legged customers are welcome to sit under the bench or table", at this hugely popular pub, "superbly located", about 100m from the Heath, serving "solid" nosh (from a rather "unchanging" menu); staff are "smiley" but service "gets wonky at peak times". / NW3 1BX; www.thewellshampstead.london; @WellsHampstead; 10 pm, Sun 9.30 pm.

West Thirty Six W10 NEW £65
36 Golborne Rd 3752 0530 6–1A
Aiming to become a major north Kensington hang-out – a big, three-story newcomer (incorporating grill, lounge, bar, terrace and BBQ), from the owners of Beach Blanket Babylon; perhaps they share the same DNA food-wise? – early feedback is very mixed. / W10 5PR; www.w36.co.uk; @WestThirtySix; 10 pm.

The Wet Fish Café NW6 £47 333
242 West End Ln 7443 9222 1–1B
"Situated in a former fishmongers", this West Hampstead "oasis" is – for its enthusiastic local following – "second to none"; the fish cooking is "delicious", but the place is also "especially good for breakfast and brunch". / NW6 1LG; www.thewetfishcafe.co.uk; @thewetfishcafe; 10 pm, Sun 9.30 pm; no Amex; set always available £25 (FP), set weekday L £27 (FP).

The White Onion SW19 NEW £62 443
67 High St 8947 8278 10–2B
Residents of Wimbledon can't quite believe their luck as Eric and Sarah Guignard, husband and wife behind Surbiton's "charming" French Table, arrive in the heart of the village – with "high quality" Gallic cuisine, "efficient service" and a "good-value set lunch", it's a most "welcome addition". / SW19 5EE; www.thewhiteonion.co.uk; @thewhiteonionSW; 10.30 pm; closed Mon, Tue L, Wed L & Thu L; set weekday L £37 (FP).

White Rabbit N16 £48 [4][3][4]

15-16 Bradbury St 7682 0163 1–1C

"Why isn't this gem loved more?" – so say fans of this Dalston two-year old, who insist its "funky" small-plates cuisine is "some of the cleverest food in London at the moment"; feedback is limited though, and sceptics feel "it's imaginative but overhyped". / N16 8JN; www.whiterabbitdalston.com; @WhiteRabbitEAT; 11 pm ; closed weekday L.

The White Swan EC4 £63 [3][4][3]

108 Fetter Ln 7242 9696 9–2A

"Even when the ground floor is heaving and loud, it's thankfully quiet" in the civilised dining room over this pub, off Fleet Street; the ambitious fare is "perfect for a business lunch", but its value fluctuates as "pricing seems to rely on the frequent 50% off food deals". / EC4A 1ES; www.thewhiteswanlondon.com; @thewhiteswanEC4; 10 pm; closed Sat & Sun.

Wild Honey W1 £73 [2][2][2]

12 St George St 7758 9160 3–2C

This "club-like" Arbutus sibling in Mayfair still wins some praise for its "clever" cooking and "cosy" ambience, but ratings cratered this year amidst encounters with "amateur" service, "average" results and – most notably – silly prices: "they should re-name it Wild Money!" / W1S 2FB; www.wildhoneyrestaurant.co.uk; @whrestaurant; 10.30 pm; closed Sun; set Sun L £50 (FP).

Wiltons SW1 £97 [3][3][4]

55 Jermyn St 7629 9955 3–3C

"Where Lord Grantham would surely have dined when in London!" – this "stuffy" pillar of the St James's Establishment (est 1742, here since 1984) is "as traditional as traditional can be", and its "womb-like comfort" and "wonderful" seafood make for "impressive" entertaining; one snag – "prices verge on robbery!" / SW1Y 6LX; www.wiltons.co.uk; @wiltons1742; 10.15 pm; closed Sat L & Sun; jacket required.

Wimsey's SW6 NEW £46 [3][3][3]

177 New King's Rd 7731 8326 10–1B

An agreeably straightforward Parsons Green newcomer – the first solo venture from Leith's scholar Gwyn Rees-Sheppard, offering seasonal British dishes and English wines; the odd critic says it's "nothing amazing", but prices are generous, and the overall intent very genuine. / SW6 4SW; www.wimseys.co.uk; @Wimseys; 10.30 pm, Sun 10 pm; closed Mon.

The Windmill W1 £41 [3][2][3]

6-8 Mill St 7491 8050 3–2C

"The best pies ever!", and other "good old-fashioned British fare" make this Mayfair gastropub the perfect place to over-indulge in suet pastry and ale – be sure to ask about the Pie Club! / W1S 2AZ; www.windmillmayfair.co.uk; @tweetiepie_w1; 10 pm, Sat 5 pm; closed Sat D & Sun.

The Wine Library EC3 £34 [1][4][4]

43 Trinity Sq 7481 0415 9–3D

"The clue is in the name" when it comes to visiting these "unique", ancient City cellars, where a "superb selection of wines" can be enjoyed "at terrific shop prices, plus corkage"; to accompany, it's "not the finest of dining (a cheese and pâté buffet)" but "adequate". / EC3N 4DJ; www.winelibrary.co.uk; 7.30 pm; closed Mon D, Sat & Sun.

Wolfe's WC2 £48 [3][2][2]

30 Gt Queen St 7831 4442 4–1D

A rather '70s-style family diner in Covent Garden, which feels like "a step back in time"; "excellent burgers" have been the house speciality since time immemorial – the most memorable nowadays is the "brilliant Wagyu/Kobe option". / WC2B 5BB; www.wolfes-grill.net; @wolfesbargrill; 10 pm, Fri & Sat 10.30 pm, Sun 9 pm.

THE WOLSELEY W1 £60 [3][4][5]

160 Piccadilly 7499 6996 3–3C

"It should be a national monument!" – Corbin & King's "tremendously atmospheric" ("mildly cacophonous") European Grand Café by the Ritz has become a "perennial" linchpin of "glamorous" London life ("there's always at least one A-list celeb eating at a nearby table!"). It's the "fun and the buzz" that set it apart, however – the large Mittel-European menu is "very adaptable" but decidedly "not exciting" (even if "it does the best breakfast in town, bar none!") / W1J 9EB; www.thewolseley.com; @TheWolseley; midnight, Sun 11 pm.

Wong Kei W1 £30 [2][2][2]

41-43 Wardour St 7437 8408 4–3A

"You can even now buy a T-shirt saying 'upstairs'!" (the famous rude bark of the waiters to non-Oriental guests) at this Chinatown landmark; under new management of late, service is "more polite than in the old days", but the décor still looks like "it really needs an overhaul" and – though "unbeatably cheap" – "you still come here to eat and go". / W1D 6PY; www.wongkeilondon.com; Mon-Sat 11.15 pm, Sun 10.30 pm ; no credit cards; no booking.

Woodlands £38 322

37 Panton St, SW1 7839 7258 4–4A
77 Marylebone Ln, W1 7486 3862 2–1A
102 Heath St, NW3 7794 3080 8–1A
"Nutritious, delicious, and very well priced"; these long-established South Indian veggies serve "genuine" dishes, and are "comfy" and "pleasant", if somewhat "bleak" looking. / www.woodlandsrestaurant.co.uk; Mon - Sun 10.45 pm ; NW3 no L Mon.

The Woodstock W1 NEW £34

11 Woodstock St 7499 4342 3–2B
A relative newcomer to London's izakaya dining scene, with a plum position just off Oxford Street, and an offering of grilled meat skewers and cocktails, alongside Japanese beers; no survey feedback as yet, hence we've left it un-rated. / W1C 2AE; www.thewoodstocklondon.co.uk; @thewoodstockldn; midnight.

Workshop Coffee £45 344

80a Mortimer St, W1 7253 5754 9–1A NEW
St Christopher's Place, W1 7253 5754 3–1A NEW
27 Clerkenwell Rd, EC1 7253 5754 9–1A
60a Holborn Viaduct, EC1 no tel 9–2A NEW
It's the brilliant blend of coffees ("roasted before your very eyes") which wins nominations for these "friendly and entertaining" independents ("the Cheers of coffee shops!"); brunch is a highlight too though – "a wide variety of delicious sweets and savouries". /

Wormwood W11 NEW £65 443

16 All Saints Rd 7854 1808 6–1B
"Delightful", new husband-and-wife project, in the "Notting Hill backwater" site that was once Uli (RIP); fans laud the "cornucopia of tastes" of its "experimental Mediterranean and North African-tinged sharing plates" – a minority of sceptics though, find it "heavily priced" for a "crammed-in" and "loud" experience, whose "over-fussy cooking" has "muddy flavours". / W11 1HH; wormwoodrestaurant.com; 9.30 pm, Fri & Sat 10 pm; closed Mon, Tue, Wed L, Thu L & Sun D.

Wright Brothers £58 443

13 Kingly St, W1 7434 3611 3–2D
56 Old Brompton Rd, SW7 7581 0131 5–2B NEW
11 Stoney St, SE1 7403 9554 9–4C
8 Lamb St, E1 7377 8706 9–2D
"Tanks full of sparkling sea food" showcase the "breathtakingly fresh" oysters, shellfish and other "flavoursome" fare at these "happy and bustling" outfits. Top Menu Tips – "an historic beef and oyster pie", and "blissful oyster Happy Hour". / 10.30 pm, Sun 9 pm; booking: max 8.

XO NW3 £46 222

29 Belsize Ln 7433 0888 8–2A
Will Ricker's "very relaxed" Belsize Park haunt still has fans for its Pan-Asian fusion tapas and cocktails, but seems increasingly "uninspired" – "when it opened it was so fresh and exciting: now it just seems like another boring local". / NW3 5AS; www.rickerrestaurants.com; 10.30 pm, Sun 10pm .

Yalla Yalla £37 334

1 Green's Ct, W1 7287 7663 3–2D
12 Winsley St, W1 7637 4748 3–1C
Greenwich Peninsula Sq, SE10 0772 584 1372 8–3C
A "fresh and filling" feast is to be had at these "buzzy" Lebanese cafés; the "cramped but cosy" original, just off Oxford Street, makes a good respite from shopping, but all locations get the thumbs up. / www.yalla-yalla.co.uk; Green's Court 11 pm, Sun 10 pm – Winsley Street 11.30 pm, Sat 11 pm; W1 Sun.

Yama Momo SE22 NEW £55 433

72 Lordship Ln 8299 1007 1–4D
"An impressive addition to the East Dulwich food scene" – this "fun" Japanese newcomer (sibling to Clapham's Tsunami) is an instant local hit, thanks to its "fantastic cooking (particularly sushi and sashimi)", and "fab cocktails". / SE22 8HF; www.yamamomo.co.uk; @YamamomoRest; 10 pm, Fri & Sat 10.30 pm, Sun 9.30 pm; closed weekday L.

Yashin W8 £78 532

1a Argyll Rd 7938 1536 5–1A
"Do sit at the bar" – "watch the chefs carefully seasoning or searing the fish" – if you visit this "pricey" Kensington venture; the result is "outstanding modern sushi and sashimi", amongst London's best, with "wonderful and innovative mixes of flavours"; NB the basement can feel a bit "dead". / W8 7DB; www.yashinsushi.com; 10 pm.

Yashin Ocean House SW7 £80 222

117-119 Old Brompton Rd 7373 3990 5–2B
Is Yashin's South Kensington spin-off "just too odd to be a success"? It occupies a potentially characterful site, but feedback remains very limited – even fans concede "the atmosphere could be warmer", and though the Japanese-fusion cuisine can be "very refined", prices are "extortionate". / SW7 3RN; www.yashinocean.com; @YashinLondon; 10 pm, Sun 8 pm; set always available & pre-theatre £46 (FP).

Yasmeen NW8 NEW £46

1 Blenheim Ter 7624 2921 8–3A
On the former site of One Blenheim Terrace (RIP) in St John's Wood, a "sumptuous" new Lebanese where "maitre d' Bashir is a star" – promising initial reports, let's hope for more feedback next year. / NW8 0EH; www.yasmeenrestaurant.com; @yasmeencafe.

Yauatcha £76 5 2 3
Broadwick Hs, 15-17 Broadwick St, W1 7494 8888 3–2D
Broadgate Circle, EC2 awaiting tel 12–2B NEW
"Perfectly executed" and "creative" dim sum – probably "the best in London" – have made the "trendy" Soho basement original a "classic" destination, and its new more "airy" sibling in Broadgate fully lives up. W1 also boasts an "HK-style pâtisserie selection – both breathtakingly beautiful and very delicious". /

The Yellow House SE16 £45 3 3 2
126 Lower Rd 7231 8777 11–2A
If you find yourself near Surrey Quays, check out this "good value local, with plenty of choice" (pizza is the top tip) and "lovely" service. / SE16 2UE; www.theyellowhouse.eu; @Theyellowhouse_; 10 pm, Sun 8 pm; closed Mon, Tue–Sat closed L, Sun open L & D.

Yi-Ban E16 £45 4 3 2
London Regatta Centre, Dockside Rd, Royal Albert Dock 7473 6699 11–1D
An interesting waterside location near City Airport helps justify the trek to this obscure Chinese in deepest Docklands, as does its "solid, very reasonably priced" dim sum and other fare. / E16 2QT; www.yi-ban.co.uk; 11 pm, Sun 10.30 pm.

Yipin China N1 £42 2 2 1
70-72 Liverpool Rd 7354 3388 8–3D
Some detect "a fall from grace" at this "stark" Sichuan three-year-old in Islington; fans still hail its "stunning" cooking, but others are "not sure why it's had such raves" given its "slow" service and food they say is "awful and way overpriced". / N1 0QD; www.yipinchina.co.uk; 11 pm.

Yming W1 £41 3 5 4
35-36 Greek St 7734 2721 4–2A
"The staff always smile" at Christine Yau's "serene" Soho "haven", "run admirably by the amazing William"; the "interesting" Chinese cuisine is "consistently good" and at times "cracking". / W1D 5DL; www.yminglondon.com; 11.45 pm; set weekday L & pre-theatre £23 (FP).

York & Albany NW1 £59 2 2 3
127-129 Parkway 7592 1227 8–3B
Gordon Ramsay's large, glammed-up tavern on the corner of Regent's Park generates mixed and limited feedback; to fans it's a great all-rounder, but the ambience can also seem "bland", and too often the cooking is "not up to scratch". / NW1 7PS; www.gordonramsay.com; @yorkandalbany; 11 pm, Sun 9 pm.

Yoshi Sushi W6 £35 3 4 2
210 King St 8748 5058 7–2B
In a nondescript run of Hammersmith restaurants, this low key stalwart is worth remembering for its "reasonably priced, very decent Japanese and Korean grub, served with a smile". / W6 0RA; www.yoshisushi.co.uk; 11 pm, Sun 10.30 pm; closed Sun L; set weekday L £17 (FP).

Yoshino W1 £44 4 3 2
3 Piccadilly Pl 7287 6622 3–3D
"A must for sushi-lovers, expert or novice!" – an "interesting" little Japanese café, tucked down an alley "around a corner near the Royal Academy". / W1J 0DB; www.yoshino.net; @Yoshino_London; 10 pm; closed Sun.

Yum Bun EC1 £15 5 2
31 Featherstone St 0 7919 4082 21 12–1A
"Great buns!" – the steamed Chinese variety, "cooked with passion and served with a smile" – make Lisa Meyer's pop-up-goes-permanent in Shoreditch (next to the Rotary Bar) "a must-go experience". / EC1Y 2BJ; www.yumbun.co.uk; @yum_bun; 10 pm; closed Mon D, Tue D, Wed D, Sat L & Sun.

Yum Yum N16 £42 3 4 4
187 Stoke Newington High St 7254 6751 1–1D
"Lovely cocktails" and dependable tucker has proved a very enduring formula for this large Thai stalwart, in Stoke Newington. / N16 0LH; www.yumyum.co.uk; @yumyum; 11 pm, Fri & Sat midnight.

Zafferano SW1 £80 2 2 2
15 Lowndes St 7235 5800 5–1D
Once London's top Italian, this "chic" looking Belgravian has fans for whom it's still "somewhere special"; ratings dipped again this year though, and critics feel "its formulaic food is not up to par", and "doesn't justify the prices". / SW1X 9EY; www.zafferanorestaurants.com; 11.30 pm, Sun 11 pm; set weekday L £54 (FP).

Zaffrani N1 £45 3 2 2
47 Cross St 7226 5522 8–3D
"On a quiet corner away from the hubbub of Upper Street" – a "comfortable" Indian whose "sophisticated" cooking is "much better than you'd expect from a local". / N1 2BB; www.zaffrani-islington.co.uk; 10.30 pm.

Zaibatsu SE10 £32 4 4 2
96 Trafalgar Rd 8858 9317 1–3D
"Don't judge a book by its cover!" – "it's so hard to get a booking" at this "tiny", "basic", "café-style" Japanese BYO in Greenwich; why? – "the sushi's just amazing" and "very cheap". / SE10 9UW; www.zaibatsufusion.co.uk; @ong_teck; 11 pm; closed Mon.

Zaika W8 **£60** 333
1 Kensington High St 7795 6533 5–1A
"Welcome back Zaika!"; after the briefest flirtation with a British format (as One Kensington, RIP), the Tamarind Collection turned back 180 degrees, "beautifully re-converting" this erstwhile banking hall back to a nouvelle Indian dining room; its authentic cuisine "without all that fusion nonsense" is as popular as ever. / W8 5NP; www.zaikaofkensington.com; @ZaikaLondon; 10.45 pm, Sun 9.45 pm; closed Mon L.

Zayna W1 **£47** 432
25 New Quebec St 7723 2229 2–2A
"Top Punjabi/Pakistani" dishes again score high marks for this handy Marble Arch operation; sit upstairs, as the basement lacks atmosphere. / W1H 7SF; www.zaynarestaurant.co.uk; @zaynarestaurant; Mon-Thu 10.30 pm, Fri & Sat 11 pm, Sun 10.30 pm; closed weekday L.

Zest JW3 NW3 **£49** 323
341-351 Finchley Rd 7433 8955 1–1B
For a "fresh and modern" take on kosher cooking ("i.e. Middle East not Mittel-European") try this West Hampstead Israeli; you pay "high prices for tiny portions", but results are "healthy" and "tasty", and its contemporary, basement setting "has a real buzz". / NW3 6ET; www.zestatjw3.co.uk; @ZestAtJW3; Sat-Thu 9.45 pm ; closed Fri & Sat L.

Ziani's SW3 **£57** 333
45 Radnor Walk 7351 5297 5–3C
"Always jolly", "traditional" Chelsea Italian, with "such friendly staff"; "much used by the locals", you need to "squash in", but "it's a great place to take the family". / SW3 4BP; www.ziani.co.uk; 11 pm, Sun 10 pm; bank holidays closed on sunday.

Zoilo W1 **£54** 433
9 Duke St 7486 9699 3–1A
A "wonderful", little Argentinean tapas spot tucked away near Selfridges, majoring in "wonderfully tasty and moist" meats and burger dishes, and with a "fine selection" of Malbecs too; grab a seat at the downstairs bar, where "watching the chefs at work is an experience". / W1U 3EG; www.zoilo.co.uk; @Zoilo_London; 10.30 pm; closed Sun.

Zucca SE1 **£59** 443
184 Bermondsey St 7378 6809 9–4D
"Not as pretty as the River Café, but about as good at a fraction of the price" – Sam Harris's "out-of-the-way", "canteen-like" Bermondsey Italian continues to draw crowds from across town with its "impeccably simple use of first-class ingredients" and "huge range of wines". Top Menu Tip – "fantastic veal chops". / SE1 3TQ; www.zuccalondon.com; @ZuccaSam; 10 pm; closed Mon & Sun D.

Zuma SW7 **£80** 534
5 Raphael St 7584 1010 5–1C
"It may be the haunt of hedgies and wealthy Euros", but this "always humming" Japanese-fusion hang-out, near Harrods, is "so goddamn good"! A few critics do feel "it's way too pricey", but most reporters are blown away by its "spectacular" fare and "terrific" vibe. / SW7 1DL; www.zumarestaurant.com; 10.45 pm, Sun 10.15 pm; booking: max 8.

LONDON INDEXES

BREAKFAST
(with opening times)

Central

Al Duca *(9)*
Asia de Cuba *(7)*
Athenaeum *(7)*
Babaji Pide *(Sat & Sun 11)*
Bageriet *(9, Sat 10)*
Balans: *W1 (8)*
Balthazar *(7.30 Mon-Fri, Sat & Sun 9)*
Bar Italia *(6.30)*
Bar Termini *(Mon-Fri 7.30, Sat 9, Sun 10.30)*
The Berners Tavern *(7)*
Bonhams Restaurant *(8)*
The Botanist: *SW1 (8, Sat & Sun 9)*
Bouillabaisse *(8)*
Boulestin *(7)*
Browns (Albemarle) *(7, Sun 7.30)*
Café Bohème *(8, Sat & Sun 9)*
Café in the Crypt *(Mon-Sat 8)*
Caffé Vergnano: *WC1 (6.30, Sun 8.30); WC2 (8, Sun 11)*
Carousel *(9)*
The Cavendish *(Sat & Sun 10)*
Cecconi's *(7, Sat & Sun 8)*
The Chiltern Firehouse *(7, Sat & Sun 9)*
Christopher's *(Sat & Sun 11.30)*
The Cinnamon Club *(Mon-Fri 7.30)*
Colbert *(8)*
Cut *(7am, Sat & Sun 7.30)*
Daylesford Organic: *SW1 (8, Sun 10); Oxford StW1 (9)*
Dean Street Townhouse *(Mon-Fri 7, Sat & Sun 8)*
The Delaunay *(7, Sat & Sun 11)*
Dishoom: *WC2 (8, Sat & Sun 10)*
Dorchester Grill *(7, Sat & Sun 8)*
Fernandez &Wells: *Beak StW1 (7.30, Sat & sun 9); Lexington StW1 (7); St Anne's CtW1 (8, Sat 10); WC2 (8am, Sat & Sun 9am)*
Franco's *(7, Sat 8)*
La Fromagerie Café *(8, Sat 9, Sun 10)*
The Goring Hotel *(7, Sun 7.30)*
The Grazing Goat *(7.30)*
Hélène Darroze *(Sat 11)*
Holborn Dining Room *(Mon-Fri 7, Sat & Sun 8)*
Honey & Co *(Mon-Fri 8, Sat 9.30)*
Hush: *WC1 (8)*
Indigo *(6.30)*
Kaffeine: *Great Titchfield StW1 (7.30, Sat 8.30, Sun 9.30)*
Kaspar's Seafood and Grill *(7)*
Kazan (Café): *Wilton Rd SW1 (8, Sun 9)*
Konditor & Cook: *WC1 (9.30); W1 (9.30, Sun 10.30)*
Kopapa *(8.30, Sat 9, Sun 9.30)*
Koya-Bar *(Mon-Fri 8.30, Sat & Sun 9:30)*
Lantana Café: *W1 (8, Sat & Sun 9)*
Maison Bertaux *(8.30, Sun 9.15)*
maze Grill *(6.45)*
Monmouth Coffee Company: *WC2 (8)*
The National Dining Rooms *(10)*
Nopi *(8, Sat & Sun 10)*
Nordic Bakery: *Dorset StW1 (8, Sat & Sun 9); Golden SqW1 (Mon-Fri 8, Sat 9, Sun 11)*
The Northall *(6.30, Sat & Sun 7)*
One-O-One *(7)*
The Only Running Footman *(7.30, Sat & Sun 9.30)*
Opso *(Sat & Sun 10)*
The Orange *(8)*
Ottolenghi: *SW1 (8, Sun 9)*
The Pantechnicon *(Sat & Sun 9)*
Pennethorne's Cafe Bar *(8, Sat 10)*
Percy & Founders *(Sat & Sun 7.30)*
The Portrait *(10)*
Princi *(8, Sun 8.30)*
The Providores *(9am)*
Providores (Tapa Room) *(9, Sat & Sun 10)*
Le Restaurant de Paul: *WC2 (7, Sat & Sun 8)*
Rib Room *(7, Sun 8)*
Riding House Café *(7.30, Sat & Sun 9)*
The Ritz Restaurant *(7, Sun 8)*
Roux at the Landau *(7)*
Royal Academy *(8)*
San Carlo Cicchetti: *W1 (8, Sat & Sun 9)*
Scandinavian Kitchen *(8, Sat & Sun 10)*
Sesame *(7, Sat 9, Sun 11)*
Simpsons-in-the-Strand *(Mon-Fri 7.30)*
Sophie's Steakhouse: *all branches (Sat & Sun 11)*
Sotheby's Café *(9)*
Stock Pot: *SW1 (9.30)*
Strand Dining Rooms *(7, Sat 8, Sun 10)*
Tate Britain (Rex Whistler) *(Sat & Sun 10)*
tibits *(9, Sun 11.30)*
Tom's Kitchen: *WC2 (Sat & Sun 10)*
Tredwell's *(8, Sat 9, Sun 9.30)*
Villandry: *W1 (Sat 8, Sun 9)*
The Wallace *(10)*
Wolfe's *(9)*
The Wolseley *(7, Sat & Sun 8)*
The Woodstock *(11)*
Yalla Yalla: *Green's CtW1 (Sat & Sun 10)*

West

Adams Café *(7.30)*
Angelus *(10)*
Annie's: *W4 (Tue-Thu 10, Fri & Sat 10.30, Sun 10)*
Balans: *W4, W8 (8)*
Best Mangal: *SW6 (10-12)*
La Brasserie *(8)*
Brasserie Gustave *(Sat & Sun 11)*
Bumpkin: *SW7 (11)*
Bush Dining Hall *(Tue-Fri 8.30)*
The Butcher's Hook *(10)*
Clarke's *(8)*
Daylesford Organic: *W11 (8, Sun 11)*
Electric Diner *(8)*
Gallery Mess *(Sat & Sun 10)*
Geales Chelsea Green: *SW3 (9 Sat & Sun)*
Granger & Co: *W11 (7)*
The Hampshire Hog *(8, Sat & Sun 9)*
High Road Brasserie *(7, Sat & Sun 8)*
Joe's Brasserie *(Sat & Sun 11)*
Julie's *(10)*
Kensington Square Kitchen *(8, Sun 9.30)*
Kurobuta: *W2 (9)*
Lisboa Pâtisserie *(7)*
Lucky Seven *(Mon noon, Tue-Thu 10, Fri-Sun 9)*
The Magazine Restaurant *(8)*
Megan's Delicatessen: *SW6 (8)*
Mona Lisa *(7)*
Ottolenghi: *W11 (8, Sun 8.30)*
Pappa Ciccia: *Fulham High St SW6 (7)*
Pellicano: *Ixworth Pl SW3 (Mon-Fri 7-10 Sat & Sun 8-11)*
Pizza East Portobello: *W10 (8)*
PJ's Bar and Grill *(Sat & Sun 10)*
Raoul's Café & Deli: *W11 (8.30); W9 (8.30)*
Salt & Honey *(Sat & Sun 10)*
Shikumen *(7, Sun 7.30)*
Snaps & Rye *(8, Sun 10)*
Sophie's Steakhouse: *all branches (Sat & Sun 11)*
Stock Pot: *SW3 (8)*
Tom's Kitchen: *SW3 (8, Sat & Sun 10)*
Troubadour *(9)*
VQ: *SW10 (24 hrs)*
The Waterway *(Sat & Sun 10)*

North

Anima e Cuore *(9)*
Banners *(9, Sat & Sun 10)*
The Bull & Gate *(11)*
Dirty Burger: *NW5 (Mon-Thu 7, Sat & Sun 9)*
Gallipoli: *Upper St N1, Upper St N1 (10.30)*
Gilbert Scott *(Mon-Fri 10)*
Ginger & White: *all branches (7.30, Sat & Sun 8.30)*
Greenberry Café *(9)*
Harry Morgan's *(9)*
Kenwood (Brew House) *(9)*
Kipferl *(9, Sun 10)*
Landmark (Winter Gdn) *(7)*
Made In Camden *(Mon-Fri 9.30)*
Megan's: *NW8 (8)*
Ottolenghi: *N1 (8, Sun 9)*
Plum + Spilt Milk *(7, Sat & Sun 8)*
The Refinery *(7.30, Sat 9)*
Rugoletta: *N2 (10)*
St Pancras Grand *(7, Sun 8)*
Shoe Shop *(9)*
Sweet Thursday *(Sat & Sun 9.30)*
Trangallan *(Sat & Sun 11)*
The Wet Fish Café *(10, not Mon)*
York & Albany *(7)*

South

Abbeville Kitchen *(Sat & Sun 9)*
Annie's: *SW13 (Tue-Sun 10)*
Aqua Shard *(7, Sat & Sun 10)*
The Bingham *(7, Sat & Sun 8)*
Bistrò by Shot *(7.30)*
Bistro Union *(Sat & Sun 9.30)*
Brasserie Toulouse-Lautrec *(11, Sat & Sun 10)*
Brunswick House Café *(8am, Sat & Sun 10am)*
Buenos Aires Café: *SE10 (7.30)*
Butcher & Grill *(8.30)*
Caffé Vergnano: *SE1 (8, Sat & Sun 11)*
Hotel du Vin *(7, Sat & Sun 8)*
Canteen: *SE1 (8, Sat & Sun 9)*
Cau: *SW19 (10)*
Ceru *(11)*
Chapters *(8, Sun 9)*
Cornish Tiger *(9, excl Sun)*
The Depot *(Sat 9.30)*
Dirty Burger: *SW8 (Mon-Thu 7, Sat 9, Sun 10)*
Eco *(Sat & Sun 9)*
Edwins *(10)*
Elliot's Café *(8, Sat 9)*
fish! *(Thu-Sat 8, Sun 10)*
Franklins *(Sat 10)*
Garrison *(8, Sat & Sun 9)*
Gazette: *SW12 (7); SW11 (8)*
Joanna's *(10)*
Konditor & Cook: *all south branches (7.30)*
The Lido Café *(9)*
Monmouth Coffee Company: *SE1 (7.30)*
Orange Pekoe *(8.30)*
Petersham Hotel *(Mon-Fri 7, Sat & Sun 8)*
Pulia *(8)*
Queenswood *(8, Sat & Sun 9)*
Rabot 1745 *(Sat 9)*
Riva *(7)*
Rivington Grill: *SE10 (Thu-Sun 10)*
Roast *(7, Sat 8.30)*
Sonny's Kitchen *(Sat & Sun 9)*
The Table *(7.30, Sat & Sun 8.30)*
Tapas Brindisa: *SE1 (Fri & Sat 9, Sun 11)*
Ting *(6.30)*
Toasted *(8.30, Sun 10)*
Tulse Hill Hotel *(7, Sat & Sun 8)*
El Vergel *(8, Sat & Sun 10)*
The Victoria *(8.30)*
Village East *(Sat & Sun 11)*
Waterloo Bar & Kitchen *(Sat & Sun 11)*
Wimsey's *(Sat & Sun 9.30)*

East

Albion: *E2 (8)*
Andina *(8, Sat & Sun 10)*
The Anthologist *(7.30)*
Bad Egg *(Mon-Fri 8, Sat 10)*
Bird: *E2 (11, Sat & Sun 9)*
Bird of Smithfield *(7.30, Sat 10.30 brunch)*
Bleeding Heart Restaurant *(Mon- Fri 7)*
Blixen *(Mon-Fri 8, Sat & Sun 9)*
Bread Street Kitchen *(Mon-Fri 7)*
Brick Lane Beigel Bake *(24 hrs)*
Café Below *(7.30)*
Café Pistou *(8.30, Sat & Sun 10)*
Caffé Vergnano: *EC4 (7)*
Canteen: *E1 (8, Sat & Sun 9)*
Caravan: *EC1 (8, Sat & Sun 10)*
Chicken Shop & Dirty Burger: *E1 (8)*
Chinese Cricket Club *(6.30)*
City Social *(9)*
Coco Di Mama *(6.30)*
Comptoir Gascon *(9 takeaway onl)*
Coq d'Argent *(Mon-Fri 7.30)*
Department of Coffee *(7, Sat & Sun 10)*
Duck & Waffle *(6)*
The Empress *(Sat & Sun 10 pm)*
The Fox and Anchor *(7, Sat & Sun 8.30)*
Hawksmoor: *E1 (Sat & Sun 11)*
Hilliard *(8)*
Hoi Polloi *(7)*
The Hoxton Grill *(7)*
The Jugged Hare *(7)*
Little Georgia Café: *E2 (9, Sun 10)*
Lutyens *(7.30)*
Lyle's *(8)*
Manicomio: *EC2 (Mon-Fri 7)*
The Mercer *(7.30)*
The Modern Pantry: *EC1 (8, Sat 9, Sun 10)*
Nusa Kitchen: *EC2 (7); EC1 (8)*
Obicà: *E14 (9)*
One Canada Square *(7, 9 Sat)*
1 Lombard Street *(7.30)*
Paternoster Chop House *(Mon-Fri 8)*
E Pellicci *(7)*
Resident Of Paradise Row *(11, Sat & Sun 10)*
Rivington Grill: *EC2 (Mon-Fri 8)*
Rochelle Canteen *(9)*
Rocket The City: *Adams Ct EC2 (9); E14 (9.30)*
St John Bread & Wine *(9, Sat & Sun 10)*
The Sign of The Don *(7.30)*
Simpson's Tavern *(Tue-Fri 8)*
Smiths (Ground Floor) *(7, Sat 10, Sun 9.30)*
Street Kitchen (van) *(6.30)*
Taberna Do Mercado *(8)*
Verden *(Sat & Sun 11)*
Vivat Bacchus: *EC4 (Mon-Fri 7)*
Yum Bun *(11.30)*

BRUNCH MENUS

Central

Aurora
Balans: *all branches*
Balthazar
Barnyard
Boisdale
Le Caprice
Cecconi's
Christopher's
Daylesford Organic: *all branches*
Dean Street Townhouse
The Delaunay
Dishoom: *all branches*
La Fromagerie Café
Galvin at Windows
Hardy's Brasserie
Hélène Darroze
Hubbard & Bell
Hush: *W1*
Indigo
The Ivy
Jackson & Rye: *all branches*
Joe Allen
Kopapa
Lantana Café: *all branches*
Nordic Bakery: *Golden SqW1*
Ottolenghi: *all branches*
La Porte des Indes
The Portrait
The Providores
Providores (Tapa Room)
Quaglino's
Riding House Café
Ristorante Frescobaldi
Scandinavian Kitchen
Sophie's Steakhouse: *all branches*
Strand Dining Rooms
Tom's Kitchen: *all branches*
Villandry: *W1*
VQ: *all branches*
The Wolseley
Workshop Coffee Fitzrovia: *all branches*

West

The Abingdon
Annie's: *all branches*
Balans: *all branches*
Beach Blanket Babylon: *W11*
Bluebird
Bodean's: *SW6*
La Brasserie
The Builders Arms
Bumpkin: *SW7, W11*
Bush Dining Hall
Cheyne Walk Brasserie
The Cross Keys
Daylesford Organic: *all branches*
Eelbrook
Electric Diner
The Enterprise
Ffiona's
The Frontline Club
Granger & Co: *all branches*
High Road Brasserie
Jackson & Rye Chiswick: *all branches*
Joe's Brasserie
Kensington Square Kitchen
Lucky Seven
Megan's Delicatessen: *SW6*
The Oak: *W2*
Ottolenghi: *all branches*
PJ's Bar and Grill
Raoul's Café & Deli: *all branches*
The Sands End

The Shed
Sophie's Steakhouse: *all branches*
Taqueria
Tom's Kitchen: *all branches*
Troubadour
VQ: *all branches*
Zuma

North

Banners
Caravan King's Cross: *all branches*
Dishoom: *all branches*
Friends of Ours
Ginger & White: *all branches*
Granger & Co: *all branches*
Greenberry Café
Kenwood (Brew House)
Kipferl
Landmark (Winter Gdn)
Lantana Cafe: *all branches*
Made In Camden
Mill Lane Bistro
Ottolenghi: *all branches*
Sunday
The Wet Fish Café

South

Abbeville Kitchen
Albion: *all branches*
Annie's: *all branches*
Bellevue Rendez-Vous
Blue Elephant
Brew: *all branches*
Butcher & Grill
Butlers Wharf Chop House
Canteen: *SE1*
Chapters
Counter
Fields
Flotsam and Jetsam
Garrison
Grind Coffee Bar
Hood
Inside
Jackson & Rye Richmond: *all branches*
Joanna's
Lamberts
The Lido Café
Manuka Kitchen
Milk
Olympic Café
Pedler
Petersham Hotel
Rabot 1745
Rivington Grill: *all branches*
Roast
Sonny's Kitchen
The Table
El Vergel
Village East

East

Albion: *all branches*
Bad Egg
Balans: *all branches*
Canteen: *E1*
Caravan: *all branches*
Dishoom: *all branches*
Duck & Waffle
The Fox and Anchor
Granger & Co: *all branches*
Hawksmoor: *E1*
The Hoxton Grill
Lantana Café: *all branches*
The Modern Pantry: *all branches*
Ottolenghi: *all branches*
Resident Of Paradise Row
Rivington Grill: *all branches*
St John Bread & Wine
Smiths (Ground Floor)
Tom's Kitchen: *all branches*
Workshop Coffee: *all branches*

BUSINESS

Central

Al Duca
Alain Ducasse at The Dorchester
Alyn Williams
Amaya
The Araki
Athenaeum
The Avenue
The Balcon
Bank Westminster
Bar Boulud
Bellamy's
Benares
Bentley's
Bob Bob Ricard
Boisdale
Bonhams Restaurant
The Botanist: *SW1*
Boudin Blanc
Boulestin
Brasserie Chavot
Browns (Albemarle)
Le Caprice
The Cavendish
Cecconi's
China Tang
Christopher's
Chutney Mary
Cigalon
The Cinnamon Club
Clos Maggiore
Corrigan's Mayfair
Dean Street Townhouse
The Delaunay
Les Deux Salons
Dinner
Dorchester Grill
Elena's L'Etoile
Engawa
L'Escargot
Fera at Claridge's
Fischer's
Franco's
Galvin at Windows
Galvin Bistrot de Luxe
Le Gavroche
La Genova
Goodman: *all branches*
The Goring Hotel
Green's
The Greenhouse
The Guinea Grill
Hakkasan: *Hanway Pl W1*
Hawksmoor: *all branches*
Hélène Darroze
Hibiscus
Holborn Dining Room
Hush: *all branches*
Indigo
The Ivy
Kai Mayfair
Ken Lo's Memories
Koffmann's
Langan's Brasserie
Latium
Locanda Locatelli
M Restaurant Victoria Street: *all branches*
Marcus
MASH Steakhouse
Massimo
Matsuri
maze Grill
Mon Plaisir
Murano
Nobu
The Northall
One-O-One
Les 110 de Taillevent
Orrery
Otto's
The Pantechnicon
Percy & Founders
Pétrus
Pied à Terre
Quilon
Quirinale
Quo Vadis
Le Relais de Venise L'Entrecôte: *W1*
Rib Room
Riding House Café
Roka: *Charlotte St W1*
Roux at Parliament Square
Roux at the Landau
Rules
Sackville's
Salmontini
Santini
Sartoria
Savoy Grill
Scott's
Seven Park Place
J Sheekey
Shepherd's
Simpsons-in-the-Strand
Social Eating House

Social Wine & Tapas
The Square
Tamarind
Texture
Theo Randall
34
28-50: *all branches*
2 Veneti
Veeraswamy
Il Vicolo
The Wallace
Wild Honey
Wiltons
The Wolseley
Zafferano

West

Bibendum
Edera
The Frontline Club
Gallery Mess
Garnier
Gordon Ramsay
Hawksmoor Knightsbridge: *all branches*
The Ivy Chelsea Garden
The Ivy Kensington Brasserie
The Ledbury
Manicomio: *all branches*
Outlaw's Seafood and Grill
Poissonnerie de l'Avenue
La Trompette
Zuma

North

Bellanger
Frederick's
German Gymnasium
Landmark (Winter Gdn)
Plum + Spilt Milk
Rotunda Bar & Restaurant
St Pancras Grand
York & Albany

South

Aqua Shard
La Barca
Blueprint Café
Brigade
Butlers Wharf Chop House
Hotel du Vin
Canteen: *SE1*
The Glasshouse
Hutong
Magdalen
Oblix
Oxo Tower (Brass')
Oxo Tower (Rest')
Le Pont de la Tour
Roast
Skylon
Skylon Grill
Trinity
Vivat Bacchus: *all branches*
Zucca

East

Angler
L'Anima
Barbecoa: *EC4*
Bleeding Heart Restaurant
Blixen
Boisdale of Bishopsgate
Boisdale of Canary Wharf
Bread Street Kitchen
Café du Marché
Caravaggio
Chamberlain's
The Chancery
Chinese Cricket Club
Chiswell Street Dining Rms
Cinnamon Kitchen
City Miyama
City Social
Club Gascon
Coq d'Argent
Darwin Brasserie
The Don
Eyre Brothers
Fish Market
The Fox and Anchor
Galvin La Chapelle
Gatti's: *all branches*
George & Vulture
Goodman: *all branches*
Hawksmoor: *all branches*
Haz: *all branches*
High Timber
The Hoxton Grill
Ibérica: *E14*
José Pizarro
Lutyens
M Grill & M Raw
Manicomio: *all branches*
The Mercer
Merchants Tavern
Moro
New Street Grill
Northbank
One Canada Square
1 Lombard Street
Paternoster Chop House
Plateau
Roka: *E14*
The Royal Exchange Grand Café
St John
Sauterelle
The Sign of The Don
Smith's Of Ongar
Smiths (Top Floor)
Smiths (Dining Rm)
Sushisamba
Sweetings
Taberna Etrusca
3 South Place
The Trading House
The Tramshed
28-50: *all branches*
Vivat Bacchus: *all branches*
The White Swan

BYO

(Bring your own wine at no or low – less than £3 – corkage. Note for £5-£15 per bottle, you can normally negotiate to take your own wine to many, if not most, places.)

Central

Golden Hind
India Club
Patogh
Ragam

West

Adams Café
Alounak: *all branches*
Café 209
Faanoos: *W4*
Fez Mangal
Outlaw's Seafood and Grill
Pappa Ciccia: *all branches*

North

Ali Baba
Ariana II
Chutneys
Diwana Bhel-Poori House
Roti King
Rugoletta: *all branches*
Toff's
Vijay

South

Apollo Banana Leaf
Cah-Chi: *all branches*
Faanoos: *SW14*
Hot Stuff
Kaosarn: *all branches*
Lahore Karahi
Lahore Kebab House: *all branches*
Mien Tay: *all branches*
Mirch Masala
Sree Krishna
Zaibatsu

East

Lahore Kebab House: *all branches*
Little Georgia Café: *E2*
Mangal 1
Mien Tay: *all branches*
Needoo
Rochelle Canteen
Tayyabs
Viet Grill

ROMANTIC

Central

Andrew Edmunds
L'Artiste Musclé
L'Atelier de Joel Robuchon
Aurora
Babbo

The Berners Tavern
Blanchette
Bob Bob Ricard
Boudin Blanc
Café Bohème
Le Caprice
Cecconi's
The Chiltern Firehouse
Chor Bizarre
Clos Maggiore
Corrigan's Mayfair
Coya
Crazy Bear
Dean Street Townhouse
The Delaunay
Les Deux Salons
Elena's L'Etoile
L'Escargot
Fera at Claridges
Galvin at Windows
Gauthier Soho
Le Gavroche
Gay Hussar
Gordon's Wine Bar
Hakkasan: *Hanway PlW1*
Honey & Co
Hush: *W1*
The Ivy
Kettners
Kitty Fisher's
Koffmann's
Langan's Brasserie
Locanda Locatelli
Marcus
Momo
Mon Plaisir
Orrery
Otto's
La Petite Maison
Pied à Terre
Polpo: *W1*
La Porte des Indes
La Poule au Pot
Ritz (Palm Court)
The Ritz Restaurant
Roux at the Landau
Rules
Scott's
Seven Park Place
J Sheekey
J Sheekey Oyster Bar
Social Wine & Tapas
Spring
Tinello
The Wolseley
Zafferano

West

Albertine
Angelus
Annie's: *all branches*
Babylon
Beach Blanket Babylon: *all branches*
Belvedere
Bibendum
Brinkley's
Charlotte's Place
Cheyne Walk Brasserie
Clarke's
Le Colombier
Daphne's
The Dock Kitchen
E&O
Eight Over Eight
La Famiglia
Ffiona's
The Five Fields
The Ivy Chelsea Garden
Julie's
Launceston Place
The Ledbury
The Magazine Restaurant
Maggie Jones's
Marianne
Mediterraneo
Polish Club
Osteria Basilico
Paradise byWay of Kensal Green
Patio
The Pear Tree
Pentolina
Portobello Ristorante
Rasoi
The River Café
Star of India
The Summerhouse
The Terrace
Toto's
La Trompette
Troubadour
Le Vacherin
Zuma

North

L'Absinthe
L'Aventure
Bistro Aix
La Cage Imaginaire
Frederick's
The Little Bay: *all branches*
Le Mercury
Odette's
Oslo Court
Villa Bianca

South

A Cena
Annie's: *all branches*
Antico
Bellevue Rendez-Vous
The Bingham
Blue Elephant
Blueprint Café
Al Boccon di'vino
La Buvette
Hotel du Vin
Champor-Champor
Chez Bruce
The Depot
Edwins
Emile's
Enoteca Turi
The Glasshouse
Hutong
Joanna's
Lobster Pot
Oblix
Oxo Tower (Brass')
Petersham Hotel
Petersham Nurseries
Le Pont de la Tour
Le Salon Privé
Skylon
The Swan at the Globe
The Tree House
Trinity

East

Beach Blanket Babylon: *all branches*
Bleeding Heart Restaurant
Café du Marché
Club Gascon
Comptoir Gascon
Galvin La Chapelle
The Little Bay: *all branches*
Moro
Pizza East: *E1*
Rotorino
Sushisamba

ROOMS WITH A VIEW

Central

aqua kyoto
Dinner
Galvin at Windows
Kaspar's Seafood and Grill
The National Dining Rooms
Orrery
The Portrait

West

Babylon
Belvedere
Cheyne Walk Brasserie
Gallery Mess
Min Jiang
The Summerhouse
The Waterway

North

Rotunda Bar & Restaurant

South

Alquimia
Aqua Shard
The Bingham
Blueprint Café
Butlers Wharf Chop House
Craft London
The Depot
Gourmet *Pizza* Company
Hutong
Joanna's
Oblix
Oxo Tower (Brass')

Oxo Tower (Rest')
Petersham Hotel
Le Pont de la Tour
Roast
The Rooftop Café
The Ship
Skylon
Skylon Grill
The Swan at the Globe
Tate Modern (Level 7)
Ting

East

Angler
Barbecoa: *EC4*
Boisdale of Canary Wharf
City Social
Coq d'Argent
Darwin Brasserie
Duck & Waffle
Gin Joint
The Grapes
The Gun
High Timber
The Narrow
Northbank
Plateau
Rocket Canary Wharf: *E14*
Smiths (Top Floor)
Sushisamba
Yi-Ban

NOTABLE WINE LISTS

Central

Alyn Williams
Andrew Edmunds
Antidote
Arbutus
L'Autre Pied
Barrica
Boisdale
Bonhams Restaurant
Cigala
Clos Maggiore
Compagnie des Vins S.
Cork & Bottle
Dehesa
Ebury Rest' & Wine Bar
L'Escargot
Fera at Claridge's
The Fifth Floor Restaurant
1707
La Fromagerie Café
Galvin Bistrot de Luxe
Gauthier Soho
Le Gavroche
Goodman: *all branches*
Gordon's Wine Bar
The Greenho
Hardy's Brasserie
Hibiscus
The Ivy
Kai Mayfair
Latium
Locanda Locatelli
Marcus
Olivo
Olivomare
Les 110 de Taillevent
Opera Tavern
Orrery
Otto's
Pétrus
Pied à Terre
The Providores
Providores (Tapa Room)
Quattro Passi
Quo Vadis
Ristorante Frescobaldi
The Ritz Restaurant
Salt Yard
Sardo
Sartoria
Savoy Grill
Shampers
Social Eating House
Social Wine & Tapas
Sotheby's Café
The Square
Tapas Brindisa Soho: *W1*
Tate Britain (Rex Whistler)
The 10 Cases
10 *Greek* Street
Terroirs
Texture
Tinello
28-50: *all branches*
Vinoteca Seymour Place: *all branches*
Wild Honey
Zafferano

West

Albertine
L'Amorosa
Angelus
Bibendum
Brinkley's
Cambio de Tercio
Capote Y Toros
Clarke's
Le Colombier
L'Etranger
The Frontline Club
Garnier
Gordon Ramsay
Hedone
Joe's Brasserie
The Kensington Wine Rooms
The Ledbury
Locanda Ottomezzo
Margaux
Medlar
Popeseye: *W14*
Princess Victoria
The River Café
Tendido Cero
Tendido Cuatro
La Trompette
The Truscott Arms
Villa Di Geggiano
Vinoteca: *all branches*

North

La Collina
8 Hoxton Square
Prawn On The Lawn
Primeur
Sweet Thursday
Trangallan
Trullo
The Truscott Cellar
Vinoteca: *all branches*

South

A Cena
Chez Bruce
Emile's
Enoteca Turi
40 Maltby Street
Fulham Wine Rooms
The Glasshouse
José
Magdalen
Meson don Felipe
Naughty Piglets
Peckham Bazaar
Pizarro
Le Pont de la Tour
Popeseye: *SW15*
Riva
RSJ
Soif
Tentazioni
Toasted
The Tommy Tucker
Trinity
Vivat Bacchus: *all branches*
Zucca

East

Bleeding Heart Restaurant
Brawn
Cellar Gascon
Club Gascon
Comptoir Gascon
Coq d'Argent
The Don
Enoteca Rabezzana
Eyre Brothers
Goodman: *all branches*
High Timber
The Jugged Hare
Mission
Moro
The Quality Chop House
Sager & Wilde
St John Bread & Wine
The Sign of The Don
Smiths (Top Floor)
28-50: *all branches*
Typing Room
Verden
Vinoteca: *all branches*
Vivat Bacchus: *all branches*
The Wine Library

Beast

Kitchen Table Bubbledogs

The Anglesea Arms

Typing Room

LONDON CUISINES

AMERICAN

Central

The Avenue *(SW1)*
Big Easy *(WC2)*
Bodean's *(W1)*
Bubbledogs *(W1)*
The Chiltern Firehouse *(W1)*
Christopher's *(WC2)*
Delancey & Co. *(W1)**
Hard Rock Café *(W1)*
Hubbard & Bell *(WC1)*
Jackson & Rye *(W1)*
Jamie's Diner *(W1)*
Joe Allen *(WC2)*
The Joint Marylebone *(W1)**
The Lockhart *(W1)*
Mishkin's *(WC2)*
Pitt Cue Co *(W1)**
Rainforest Café *(W1)*
Shake Shack *(WC1,WC2)*
Shotgun *(W1)*
Spuntino *(W1)*
Wolfe's *(WC2)*

West

Big Easy *(SW3)*
Bodean's *(SW6)*
Electric Diner *(W11)*
Jackson & Rye Chiswick *(W4)*
Lucky Seven *(W2)*

North

One Sixty Smokehouse *(NW6)**
Red Dog Saloon *(N1)*

South

Bodean's *(SW4)*
Jackson & Rye Richmond *(TW9)*
The Joint *(SW9)**
Oblix *(SE1)*
Red Dog South *(SW4)*

East

Big Easy *(E14)*
Bodean's *(EC1, EC3)*
The Hoxton Grill *(EC2)*
One Sixty Smokehouse *(E1)**
Shake Shack *(E20)*

AUSTRALIAN

Central

Lantana Café *(W1)*

West

Granger & Co *(W11)*

North

Friends of Ours *(N1)**
Granger & Co *(N1)*
Lantana Cafe *(NW1)*
Sunday *(N1)**

South

Brew *(SW11, SW18, SW19)*
Flotsam and Jetsam *(SW17)**

East

Granger & Co *(EC1)*
Lantana Café *(EC1)*

BELGIAN

Central

Belgo *(WC2)*
Belgo Soho *(W1)*

North

Belgo Noord *(NW1)*

BRITISH, MODERN

Central

Adam Handling at Caxton *(SW1)*
Alyn Williams *(W1)**
Andrew Edmunds *(W1)**
Arbutus *(W1)*
Athenaeum *(W1)*
Aurora *(W1)*
Balthazar *(WC2)*
Bank Westminster *(SW1)*
Barnyard *(W1)*
Bellamy's *(W1)*
The Berners Tavern *(W1)*
Blacklock *(W1)**
Bob Bob Ricard *(W1)*
Bonhams Restaurant *(W1)**
The Botanist *(SW1)*
Le Caprice *(SW1)*
The Cavendish *(W1)*
Coopers Restaurant & Bar *(WC2)*
Daylesford Organic *(SW1,W1)*
Dean Street Townhouse *(W1)*
Dorchester Grill *(W1)*
Ducksoup *(W1)*
Ebury Rest' & Wine Bar *(SW1)*
Fera at Claridge's *(W1)*
The Fifth Floor Restaurant *(SW1)*
45 Jermyn St *(W1)*
Gordon's Wine Bar *(WC2)*
The Goring Hotel *(SW1)*
The Grazing Goat *(W1)*
Ham Yard Restaurant *(W1)*
Hardy's Brasserie *(W1)*
Heddon Street Kitchen *(W1)*
Hix *(W1)*
Hush *(W1,WC1)*
Indigo *(WC2)*
The Ivy *(WC2)*
The Ivy Café *(W1)*
The Ivy Market Grill *(WC2)*
Jar Kitchen *(WC2)*
Kettners *(W1)*
Kitty Fisher's *(W1)**
Langan's Brasserie *(W1)*
Little Social *(W1)*
Mews of Mayfair *(W1)*
Morden & Lea *(W1)*
The Newman Arms *(W1)*
Newman Street Tavern *(W1)*
The Norfolk Arms *(WC1)**
The Northall *(SW1)*
Old Tom & English *(W1)*
The Only Running Footman *(W1)*
The Orange *(SW1)*
The Pantechnicon *(SW1)*
Pennethorne's Cafe Bar *(WC2)*
Percy & Founders *(W1)*
Picture *(W1)*
Pollen Street Social *(W1)*
Polpo at Ape & Bird *(WC2)*
Portland *(W1)**
The Portrait *(WC2)*
The Punchbowl *(W1)*
Quaglino's *(SW1)*
The Queens Arms *(SW1)*
Quo Vadis *(W1)*
Roux at Parliament Square *(SW1)**
Roux at the Landau *(W1)*
Seven Park Place *(SW1)*
Seven Stars *(WC2)*
1707 *(W1)*
Shampers *(W1)*
Social Eating House *(W1)**
Sotheby's Café *(W1)*
Spring *(WC2)*
Tate Britain (Rex Whistler) *(SW1)*
10 Greek Street *(W1)**
The Thomas Cubitt *(SW1)*
Tom's Kitchen *(WC2)*
Tredwell's *(WC2)*
Villandry *(W1)*
The Vincent Rooms *(SW1)*
Vinoteca *(W1)*
VQ *(WC1)*
Wild Honey *(W1)*
The Wolseley *(W1)*

West

The Abingdon *(W8)*
The Anglesea Arms *(W6)*
Babylon *(W8)*
Beach Blanket Babylon *(W11)*
Belvedere *(W8)*
Bluebird *(SW3)*
The Brackenbury *(W6)*
Brinkley's *(SW10)*
The Builders Arms *(SW3)*
Bush Dining Hall *(W12)*
The Butcher's Hook *(SW6)*
The Carpenter's Arms *(W6)*
Charlotte's W5 *(W5)*
City Barge *(W4)*
Clarke's *(W8)**
The Dartmouth Castle *(W6)*
Daylesford Organic *(W11)*
The Dock Kitchen *(W10)*
The Dove *(W6)*
Duke of Sussex *(W4)*
Ealing Park Tavern *(W5)*
The Enterprise *(SW3)*
The Five Fields *(SW3)**
The Frontline Club *(W2)*
Harwood Arms *(SW6)**
The Havelock Tavern *(W14)*
Hedone *(W4)**

High Road Brasserie *(W4)*
The Ivy Chelsea Garden *(SW3)*
The Ivy Kensington Bras' *(W8)*
Joe's Brasserie *(SW6)*
Julie's *(W11)*
Kensington Place *(W8)*
Kensington Square Kitchen *(W8)*
Kitchen W8 *(W8)**
The Ladbroke Arms *(W11)**
Launceston Place *(W8)**
The Ledbury *(W11)**
The Magazine Restaurant *(W2)*
Marianne *(W2)**
maze Grill *(SW10)*
Medlar *(SW10)**
Megan's Delicatessen *(SW6)*
Paradise by Way of Kensal Gn *(W10)*
The Pear Tree *(W6)*
The Phoenix *(SW3)*
Princess Victoria *(W12)*
Rabbit *(SW3)**
Salt & Honey *(W2)*
The Sands End *(SW6)*
The Shed *(W8)*
The Terrace *(W8)*
Tom's Kitchen *(SW3)*
The Truscott Arms *(W9)**
Vinoteca *(W4)*
VQ *(SW10)*
The Waterway *(W9)*

North

The Albion *(N1)*
Bald Faced Stag *(N2)*
The Booking Office *(NW1)*
Bradley's *(NW3)*
The Bull *(N6)*
Caravan King's Cross *(N1)*
Chriskitch *(N10)**
Crocker's Folly *(NW8)*
The Drapers Arms *(N1)*
Frederick's *(N1)*
Grain Store *(N1)*
The Haven *(N20)*
Heirloom *(N8)*
The Horseshoe *(NW3)*
The Junction Tavern *(NW5)*
Landmark (Winter Gdn) *(NW1)*
Made In Camden *(NW1)*
Market *(NW1)*
Megan's *(NW8)*
The North London Tavern *(NW6)*
Odette's *(NW1)*
Oldroyd *(N1)*
Parlour *(NW10)**
Pig & Butcher *(N1)**
Plum + Spilt Milk *(N1)*
The Refinery *(NW1)*
Rising Sun *(NW7)*
Rotunda Bar & Restaurant *(N1)*
St Pancras Grand *(NW1)*
Season Kitchen *(N4)*
Shoe Shop *(NW5)**
The Wells *(NW3)*
The Wet Fish Café *(NW6)*
White Rabbit *(N16)**

South

Abbeville Kitchen *(SW4)*
Albion *(SE1)*
Aqua Shard *(SE1)*
The Bingham *(TW10)*
Bistro Union *(SW4)*
Blueprint Café *(SE1)*
The Brown Dog *(SW13)*
Brunswick House Café *(SW8)*
The Camberwell Arms *(SE5)**
Hotel du Vin *(SW19)*
Chapters *(SE3)*
Chez Bruce *(SW17)**
Claude's Kitchen *(SW6)**
Counter *(SW8)*
Craft London *(SE10)*
The Crooked Well *(SE5)*
The Dairy *(SW4)**
The Depot *(SW14)*
The Dysart Petersham *(TW10)**
Earl Spencer *(SW18)**
Edwins *(SE1)*
Elliot's Café *(SE1)*
Emile's *(SW15)*
Fields *(SW4)*
40 Maltby Street *(SE1)**
Franklins *(SE22)**
The Garrison *(SE1)*
The Glasshouse *(TW9)**
The Green Room *(SE1)*
Hood *(SW2)**
House Restaurant *(SE1)*
Inside *(SE10)**
Lamberts *(SW12)**
The Lido Café *(SE24)*
Linnea *(TW9)**
The Lucky Pig Fulham *(SW6)*
Magdalen *(SE1)**
The Manor *(SW4)**
Manuka Kitchen *(SW6)**
Menier Chocolate Factory *(SE1)*
Olympic Café *(SW13)*
Oxo Tower (Rest') *(SE1)*
The Palmerston *(SE22)**
Peckham Refreshment Rms *(SE15)*
Petersham Hotel *(TW10)*
Petersham Nurseries *(TW10)*
Le Pont de la Tour *(SE1)*
The Prince Of Wales *(SW15)**
Rivington Grill *(SE10)*
RSJ *(SE1)*
Sea Containers *(SE1)*
Skylon *(SE1)*
Skylon Grill *(SE1)*
Sonny's Kitchen *(SW13)*
Source *(SW11)*
Story *(SE1)**
The Swan at the Globe *(SE1)*
The Table *(SE1)*
Tate Modern (Level 7) *(SE1)*
The Tommy Tucker *(SW6)*
The Tree House *(SW13)*
Trinity *(SW4)**
Union Street Café *(SE1)*
The Victoria *(SW14)*
Waterloo Bar & Kitchen *(SE1)*
Wimsey's *(SW6)*

East

The Anthologist *(EC2)*
Bad Egg *(EC2)**
Balans *(E20)*
Beach Blanket Babylon *(E1)*
Beagle *(E2)**
Bird of Smithfield *(EC1)*
Blackfoot *(EC1)*
The Botanist *(EC2)*
The Boundary *(E2)*
Bread Street Kitchen *(EC4)*
Café Below *(EC2)*
Cafe Football *(E20)*
Caravan *(EC1)*
The Chancery *(EC4)**
Chiswell Street Dining Rms *(EC1)*
City Social *(EC2)*
The Clove Club *(EC1)**
The Culpepper *(E1)**
Darwin Brasserie *(EC3)*
The Don *(EC4)*
Duck & Waffle *(EC2)*
Eat 17 *(E17)*
Ellory *(E8)*
The Empress *(E9)**
Gin Joint *(EC2)*
The Gun *(E14)*
High Timber *(EC4)*
Hilliard *(EC4)**
Hoi Polloi *(E1)*
Jones & Sons *(E8)**
The Jugged Hare *(EC1)*
Lyle's *(E1)**
The Mercer *(EC2)*
Merchants Tavern *(EC2)*
The Modern Pantry *(EC1, EC2)*
The Morgan Arms *(E3)**
The Narrow *(E14)*
Northbank *(EC4)*
One Canada Square *(E14)*
1 Lombard Street *(EC3)*
Paradise Garage *(E2)*
Princess of Shoreditch *(EC2)*
Resident Of Paradise Row *(E2)*
The Richmond *(E8)**
Rivington Grill *(EC2)*
Rochelle Canteen *(E2)**
Sager & Wilde *(E2)*
The Sign of The Don *(EC4)*
Smith's Of Ongar *(E1)*
Smiths (Ground Floor) *(EC1)*
Street Kitchen (van) *(EC2)*
3 South Place *(EC2)*
Tom's Kitchen *(E1, E14)*
Tonic & Remedy *(EC1)*
The Trading House *(EC2)*
Vinoteca *(EC1)*
The White Swan *(EC4)*

BRITISH, TRADITIONAL

Central

Boisdale (SW1)
Browns (Albemarle) (W1)
Corrigan's Mayfair (W1)
Dinner (SW1)
Great Queen Street (WC2)
Green's (SW1)
The Guinea Grill (W1)
Hardy's Brasserie (W1)
Holborn Dining Room (WC1)
The Keeper's House (W1)
The Lady Ottoline (WC1)
National Dining Rooms (WC2)
Rib Room (SW1)
Rules (WC2)
Savoy Grill (WC2)
Scott's (W1)*
Shepherd's (SW1)
Simpsons-in-the-Strand (WC2)
Strand Dining Rooms (WC2)
Wiltons (SW1)
The Windmill (W1)

West

The Admiral Codrington (SW3)
The Brown Cow (SW6)
Bumpkin (SW3, SW7, W11)
Ffiona's (W8)
The Hampshire Hog (W6)
Hereford Road (W2)*
Maggie Jones's (W8)

North

Gilbert Scott (NW1)
Piebury Corner (N7)*
St Johns (N19)*

South

The Anchor & Hope (SE1)*
Butlers Wharf Chop House (SE1)
Canteen (SE1)
Canton Arms (SW8)
The Lord Northbrook (SE12)*
Roast (SE1)

East

Albion (E2)
Boisdale of Bishopsgate (EC2)
Bumpkin (E20)
Canteen (E1, E14)
The Fox and Anchor (EC1)
George & Vulture (EC3)
Hix Oyster & Chop House (EC1)
The Marksman (E2)
Paternoster Chop House (EC4)
E Pellicci (E2)
The Quality Chop House (EC1)
St John (EC1)*
St John Bread & Wine (E1)*
Simpson's Tavern (EC3)
Sweetings (EC4)

DANISH

Central

Sticks'n'Sushi (WC2)

West

Snaps & Rye (W10)*

South

Sticks'n'Sushi (SE10, SW19)

East

Sticks'n'Sushi (E14)

EAST & CENT. EUROPEAN

Central

Boopshis (W1)
The Delaunay (WC2)
Fischer's (W1)
Gay Hussar (W1)
The Wolseley (W1)

North

Bellanger (N1)
German Gymnasium (N1)
Kipferl (N1)

FRENCH

Central

Alain Ducasse (W1)
Antidote (W1)*
L'Artiste Musclé (W1)
L'Atelier de Joel Robuchon (WC2)
L'Autre Pied (W1)*
The Balcon (SW1)
Bar Boulud (SW1)
Bellamy's (W1)
Blanchette (W1)
Boudin Blanc (W1)
Boulestin (SW1)
Brasserie Chavot (W1)
Brasserie Zédel (W1)
Café Bohème (W1)
Chez Antoinette (WC2)
Cigalon (WC2)
Clos Maggiore (WC2)*
Colbert (SW1)
Compagnie des Vins S. (WC2)
Les Deux Salons (WC2)
Elena's L'Etoile (W1)
L'Escargot (W1)
Galvin at Windows (W1)
Galvin Bistrot de Luxe (W1)*
Le Garrick (WC2)
Gauthier Soho (W1)*
Le Gavroche (W1)*
Les Gourmets des Ternes (SW1)
The Greenhouse (W1)
Hélène Darroze (W1)
Hibiscus (W1)*
Koffmann's (SW1)*
Marcus (SW1)
maze (W1)
Mon Plaisir (WC2)
Les 110 de Taillevent (W1)
Orrery (W1)
Otto's (WC1)*
La Petite Maison (W1)*
Pétrus (SW1)
Pied à Terre (W1)*
Piquet (W1)
La Poule au Pot (SW1)
Prix Fixe (W1)
Le Relais de Venise (W1)
Le Restaurant de Paul (WC2)*
The Ritz Restaurant (W1)
Savoir Faire (WC1)
Savoy Grill (WC2)
Sketch (Lecture Rm) (W1)
Sketch (Gallery) (W1)
The Square (W1)*
Terroirs (WC2)
28-50 (W1)
Villandry (W1)
Villandry St James's (SW1)
The Wallace (W1)

West

Albertine (W12)
Angelus (W2)
Bandol (SW10)
Bel Canto (W2)
Belvedere (W8)
Bibendum (SW3)
La Brasserie (SW3)
Brasserie Gustave (SW3)*
Charlotte's Place (W5)
Charlotte's W4 (W4)
Cheyne Walk Brasserie (SW3)
Chez Patrick (W8)
Le Colombier (SW3)
L'Etranger (SW7)
Garnier (SW5)*
Gordon Ramsay (SW3)
Les Gourmets des Ternes (W9)
Michael Nadra (W4)*
Poissonnerie de l'Avenue (SW3)
Quantus (W4)*
La Trompette (W4)*
Le Vacherin (W4)

North

L'Absinthe (NW1)
The Almeida (N1)
L'Aventure (NW8)*
Bistro Aix (N8)*
Bradley's (NW3)
La Cage Imaginaire (NW3)
Le Mercury (N1)
Michael Nadra (NW1)*
Mill Lane Bistro (NW6)
Oslo Court (NW8)
Patron (NW5)
Le Sacré-Coeur (N1)
The Wells (NW3)

South

Augustine Kitchen (SW11)
Bellevue Rendez-Vous (SW17)
Boro Bistro (SE1)
Brasserie Toulouse-Lautrec (SE11)
La Buvette (TW9)
Casse-Croute (SE1)*
Gazette (SW11, SW12, SW15)
Lobster Pot (SE11)*
Ma Cuisine (TW9)
Le Salon Privé (TW1)

Soif *(SW11)*
Toasted *(SE22)*
The White Onion *(SW19)**

East
Bleeding Heart Restaurant *(EC1)*
Brawn *(E2)**
Café du Marché *(EC1)*
Café Pistou *(EC1)*
Cellar Gascon *(EC1)*
Club Gascon *(EC1)*
Comptoir Gascon *(EC1)*
Coq d'Argent *(EC2)*
The Don *(EC4)*
Galvin La Chapelle *(E1)**
Lutyens *(EC4)*
Plateau *(E14)*
Provender *(E11)**
Relais de Venise *(E14, EC2)*
Restaurant de Paul *(EC2)**
Royal Exchange *(EC3)*
Sauterelle *(EC3)*
The Trading House *(EC2)*
28-50 *(EC4)*

FUSION

Central
Asia de Cuba *(WC2)*
Bubbledogs (Kitchen Table) *(W1)**
Carousel *(W1)**
Dabbous *(W1)*
Kopapa *(WC2)*
Providores (Tapa Room) *(W1)*
The Providores *(W1)*
The Salon *(WC2)*
Twist At Crawford *(W1)**

West
E&O *(W11)*
Eight Over Eight *(SW3)*
L'Etranger *(SW7)*

North
XO *(NW3)*

South
Bistrò by Shot *(SW6)*
Champor-Champor *(SE1)*
MOMMI *(SW4)*
Pedler *(SE15)*
Queenswood *(SW11)*
Tsunami *(SW4)**
Village East *(SE1)*

East
Amaru *(E1)*
Caravan *(EC1)*
Jago *(E1)*

GREEK

Central
Opso *(W1)*

West
Mazi *(W8)*

North
Carob Tree *(NW5)**
The Greek Larder *(N1)*
Lemonia *(NW1)*
Vrisaki *(N22)*

East
Hungry Donkey *(E1)*
Kolossi Grill *(EC1)*

HUNGARIAN

Central
Gay Hussar *(W1)*

INTERNATIONAL

Central
Balans *(W1)*
Café in the Crypt *(WC2)*
Canvas *(SW1)*
Colony Grill Room *(W1)*
Cork & Bottle *(WC2)*
Ember Yard *(W1)*
Gordon's Wine Bar *(WC2)*
Grumbles *(SW1)*
Motcombs *(SW1)*
Rextail *(W1)*
Rocket Holborn *(WC2)*
Stock Pot *(SW1, W1)*
The 10 Cases *(WC2)*

West
The Andover Arms *(W6)*
Annie's *(W4)*
Balans *(W12, W4, W8)*
Eelbrook *(SW6)*
Gallery Mess *(SW3)*
The Kensington Wine Rooms *(W8)*
Margaux *(SW5)*
Mona Lisa *(SW10)*
Rivea *(SW7)*
The Scarsdale *(W8)*
Stock Pot *(SW3)*
Troubadour *(SW5)*

North
Banners *(N8)*
8 Hoxton Square *(N1)**
The Haven *(N20)*
The Orange Tree *(N20)*
Primeur *(N5)**

South
Annie's *(SW13)*
Brew *(SW15)*
Brigade *(SE1)*
Joanna's *(SE19)*
The Light House *(SW19)*
London House *(SW11)*
The Plough *(SW14)*
Rabot 1745 *(SE1)*
The Rooftop Café *(SE1)*
The Ship *(SW18)*
Ting *(SE1)*
Tulse Hill Hotel *(SE24)*
Vivat Bacchus *(SE1)*
The Yellow House *(SE16)*

East
Blixen *(E1)*
Eat 17 *(E9)*
Mission *(E2)*
Typing Room *(E2)**
Verden *(E5)**
Vivat Bacchus *(EC4)*
The Wine Library *(EC3)*

IRISH

West
The Cow *(W2)**

ITALIAN

Central
Al Duca *(SW1)*
Amico Bio *(WC1)*
Assunta Madre *(W1)*
Babbo *(W1)*
Bar Termini *(W1)**
Il Baretto *(W1)*
Bocca Di Lupo *(W1)**
Briciole *(W1)*
C London *(W1)*
Café Murano *(SW1, WC2)**
Caffè Caldesi *(W1)*
Caffé Vergnano *(WC2)*
Caraffini *(SW1)*
Cecconi's *(W1)*
Ciao Bella *(WC1)*
Como Lario *(SW1)*
Il Convivio *(SW1)*
Da Mario *(WC2)*
Dehesa *(W1)*
Delfino *(W1)*
Franco's *(SW1)*
La Genova *(W1)*
Gustoso *(SW1)*
Latium *(W1)**
Locanda Locatelli *(W1)*
Luce e Limoni *(WC1)**
Made in Italy *(W1)*
Mele e Pere *(W1)*
Morelli's Gelato *(WC2)*
Murano *(W1)*
Novikov (Italian restaurant) *(W1)*
Obicà *(W1)*
Oliveto *(SW1)**
Olivo *(SW1)*
Olivocarne *(SW1)**
Olivomare *(SW1)**
Opera Tavern *(WC2)**
Orso *(WC2)*
Ottolenghi *(SW1)**
Pescatori *(W1)*
Polpetto *(W1)*
Polpo *(W1, WC2)*
La Porchetta Pizzeria *(WC1)*
Princi *(W1)*
Quattro Passi *(W1)*
Quirinale *(SW1)*
Rex & Mariano *(W1)**
Ristorante Frescobaldi *(W1)*

Rossopomodoro *(WC2)*
Sale e Pepe *(SW1)*
Salt Yard *(W1)*
San Carlo Cicchetti *(W1, WC2)*
Santini *(SW1)*
Sardo *(W1)*
Sartoria *(W1)*
Signor Sassi *(SW1)*
Theo Randall *(W1)*
Tinello *(SW1)**
Tozi *(SW1)*
2 Veneti *(W1)*
Vapiano *(W1)*
Vasco & Piero's Pavilion *(W1)*
Vico *(WC2)*
Il Vicolo *(SW1)*
Zafferano *(SW1)*

West

Aglio e Olio *(SW10)*
L'Amorosa *(W6)**
Bird in Hand *(W14)*
Buona Sera *(SW3)*
Canta Napoli *(W4)*
Cibo *(W14)**
Da Mario *(SW7)*
Daphne's *(SW3)*
La Delizia Limbara *(SW3)*
Edera *(W11)*
Essenza *(W11)*
La Famiglia *(SW10)*
Frantoio *(SW10)*
Iddu *(SW7)*
The *Italian* Job *(W4)*
Locanda Ottomezzo *(W8)*
Lucio *(SW3)*
Made in Italy *(SW3)*
Manicomio *(SW3)*
Mediterraneo *(W11)*
Mona Lisa *(SW10)*
Nuovi Sapori *(SW6)*
The Oak W12 *(W12, W2)**
Obicà *(SW3)*
Osteria Basilico *(W11)*
Ottolenghi *(W11, W8)**
Pappa Ciccia *(SW6)**
Pellicanino *(SW3)*
Pentolina *(W14)**
Polpo *(SW3, W11)*
Il Portico *(W8)*
Portobello Ristorante *(W11)*
The Red Pepper *(W9)*
Riccardo's *(SW3)*
The River Café *(W6)*
Rossopomodoro *(SW10)*
Scalini *(SW3)*
Tartufo *(SW3)**
Terra Vergine *(SW10)**
Toto's *(SW3)*
Villa Di Geggiano *(W4)*
Ziani's *(SW3)*

North

Anima e Cuore *(NW1)**
Artigiano *(NW3)*
L'Artista *(NW11)*
Il Bacio *(N16, N5)*
La Collina *(NW1)*
Fabrizio *(N19)*
Fifteen *(N1)*
500 *(N19)*
Giacomo's *(NW2)**
Osteria Tufo *(N4)**
Ostuni *(NW6)*
Ottolenghi *(N1)**
Pizzeria Oregano *(N1)**
Pizzeria Pappagone *(N4)*
Porchetta Pizzeria *(N1, N4, NW1)*
Rugoletta *(N2)*
The Salt House *(NW8)*
San Daniele del Friuli *(N5)*
Sarracino *(NW6)**
Trullo *(N1)**
Villa Bianca *(NW3)*
York & Albany *(NW1)*

South

A Cena *(TW1)**
Al Forno *(SW15, SW19)*
Antico *(SE1)*
Artusi *(SE15)**
Bacco *(TW9)*
La Barca *(SE1)*
Bibo *(SW15)**
Al Boccon di'vino *(TW9)**
Buona Sera *(SW11)*
Canta Napoli *(TW11)*
Donna Margherita *(SW11)**
Enoteca Turi *(SW15)**
Lorenzo *(SE19)*
Numero Uno *(SW11)**
Osteria Antica Bologna *(SW11)**
Pizza Metro *(SW11)**
Pulia *(SE1)*
Le Querce *(SE23)**
Riva *(SW13)**
Sapori Sardi *(SW6)**
The Table *(SE1)*
Tentazioni *(SE1)*
Vapiano *(SE1)*
Zucca *(SE1)**

East

Amico Bio *(EC1)*
L'Anima *(EC2)*
L'Anima Café *(EC2)**
Apulia *(EC1)*
Il Bordello *(E1)*
Caravaggio *(EC3)*
Coco Di Mama *(EC4)*
Enoteca Rabezzana *(EC1)*
Fabrizio *(EC1)**
Gatti's City Point *(EC2)*
Lardo & Lardo Bebè *(E8)*
Luppolo *(E11)*
Manicomio *(EC2)*
Obicà *(E14)*
E Pellicci *(E2)*
Polpo *(EC1)*
La Porchetta Pizzeria *(EC1)*
Rotorino *(E8)*
Rucoletta *(EC2)**
Santore *(EC1)**
Taberna Etrusca *(EC4)*
Verdi's *(E1)**

MEDITERRANEAN

Central

About Thyme *(SW1)*
Bistro 1 *(W1, WC2)*
Massimo *(WC2)*
Nopi *(W1)*
The Norfolk Arms *(WC1)**
Riding House Café *(W1)*

West

The Atlas *(SW6)**
The Cross Keys *(SW3)*
Cumberland Arms *(W14)**
Locanda Ottomezzo *(W8)*
Made in Italy *(SW3)*
Mediterraneo *(W11)*
Raoul's Café *(W9)*
Raoul's Café & Deli *(W11)*
The Swan *(W4)**
Troubadour *(SW5)*
Wormwood *(W11)**

North

The Little Bay *(NW6)*
Vinoteca *(N1)*

South

The Bobbin *(SW4)*
Ceru *(SE1)*
Fish in a Tie *(SW11)*
The Fox & Hounds *(SW11)**
Oxo Tower (Brass') *(SE1)*
Peckham Bazaar *(SE15)**

East

The Eagle *(EC1)**
The Little Bay *(EC1)*
Morito *(EC1)**
Rocket Bishopgate *(EC2)*
Rocket Canary Wharf *(E14)*
Vinoteca *(EC1)*

POLISH

West

Daquise *(SW7)*
Polish Club *(SW7)*
Patio *(W12)*

South

Baltic *(SE1)*

PORTUGUESE

West

Lisboa Pâtisserie *(W10)*

East

Corner Room *(E2)*
Eyre Brothers *(EC2)**
The Gun *(E14)*
Taberna Do Mercado *(E1)**

RUSSIAN

Central

Bob Bob Ricard *(W1)*
Mari Vanna *(SW1)*

SCANDINAVIAN

Central

Bageriet *(WC2)**
Nordic Bakery *(W1)*
Scandinavian Kitchen *(W1)*
Texture *(W1)**

West

Flat Three *(W11)*

SCOTTISH

Central

Boisdale *(SW1)*

East

Boisdale of Bishopsgate *(EC2)*
Boisdale of Canary Wharf *(E14)*

SPANISH

Central

Ametsa *(SW1)**
aqua nueva *(W1)*
Barrafina *(W1)**
Barrafina Drury Lane *(WC2)**
Barrica *(W1)*
Bilbao Berria *(SW1)*
Cigala *(WC1)*
Dehesa *(W1)*
Donostia *(W1)**
Drakes Tabanco *(W1)*
Goya *(SW1)*
Ibérica *(SW1,W1)*
Lurra *(W1)*
Morada Brindisa Asador *(W1)*
Opera Tavern *(WC2)**
El Pirata *(W1)*
Salt Yard *(W1)*
Social Wine & Tapas *(W1)*
Tapas Brindisa Soho *(W1)*

West

Cambio de Tercio *(SW5)*
Capote Y Toros *(SW5)*
Casa Brindisa *(SW7)*
Duke of Sussex *(W4)*
Tendido Cero *(SW5)*
Tendido Cuatro *(SW6)*

North

Bar Esteban *(N8)**
La Bota *(N8)*
Café del Parc *(N19)**
Camino *(N1)*
El Parador *(NW1)**
Trangallan *(N16)**

South

Alquimia *(SW15)*
Angels & Gypsies *(SE5)*
Boqueria *(SW2)*
Brindisa Food Rooms *(SW9)*
Camino *(SE1)*
Gremio de Brixton *(SW2)*
José *(SE1)**
Lola Rojo *(SW11)**
Mar I Terra *(SE1)*
Meson don Felipe *(SE1)*
Pizarro *(SE1)*
Tapas Brindisa *(SE1)*

East

Bravas *(E1)*
Camino Blackfriars *(EC4)*
Camino Monument *(EC3)*
Copita Del Mercado *(E1)**
Eyre Brothers *(EC2)**
Ibérica *(E14, EC1)*
José Pizarro *(EC2)**
Morito *(EC1)**
Moro *(EC1)**

AFTERNOON TEA

Central

Athenaeum *(W1)*
The Delaunay *(WC2)*
Diamond Jub' Salon (Fortnum's) *(W1)*
La Fromagerie Café *(W1)*
The Goring Hotel *(SW1)*
Maison Bertaux *(W1)**
Ritz (Palm Court) *(W1)*
Royal Academy *(W1)*
Villandry *(W1)*
Villandry St James's *(SW1)*
The Wallace *(W1)*
The Wolseley *(W1)*
Yauatcha *(W1)**

North

Kenwood (Brew House) *(NW3)*
Landmark (Winter Gdn) *(NW1)*

South

Hotel du Vin *(SW19)*

BURGERS, ETC

Central

Balls & Company *(W1)*
Bar Boulud *(SW1)*
Bobo Social *(W1)**
Bodean's *(W1)*
Burger & Lobster *(W1)*
Dub Jam *(WC2)**
Five Guys *(WC2)*
Goodman *(W1)**
Hard Rock Café *(W1)*
Hawksmoor *(W1,WC2)*
Joe Allen *(WC2)*
Kettners *(W1)*
MEATLiquor *(W1)*
MEATmarket *(WC2)**
Opera Tavern *(WC2)**
Patty and Bun *(W1)**
The Queens Arms *(SW1)*
Rainforest Café *(W1)*
Sackville's *(W1)*
Shake Shack *(WC1,WC2)*
Tommi's Burger Joint *(W1)**
Wolfe's *(WC2)*
Zoilo *(W1)**

West

The Admiral Codrington *(SW3)*
Big Easy *(SW3)*
Bodean's *(SW6)*
Boom Burger *(W10)*
Electric Diner *(W11)*
Haché *(SW10)*
Lucky Seven *(W2)*
Tommi's Burger Joint *(SW3)**
Troubadour *(SW5)*

North

Dirty Burger *(NW5)*
Duke's Brew & Que *(N1)*
Five Guys Islington *(N1)*
Haché *(NW1)*
Harry Morgan's *(NW8)*
Meat Mission *(N1)*
MEATLiquor Islington *(N1)*
One Sixty Smokehouse *(NW6)**
Red Dog Saloon *(N1)*

South

Bodean's *(SW4)*
Boom Burger *(SW9)*
Dip & Flip *(SW11, SW19)**
Dirty Burger *(SW8)*
Haché *(SW12, SW4)*
Red Dog South *(SW4)*
Rivington Grill *(SE10)*
Rox Burger *(SE13)**
Village East *(SE1)*

East

Bleecker Street Burger *(E1)**
Bodean's *(EC1, EC3)*
Burger & Lobster *(EC1, EC4)*
Caboose *(E1)*
Chicken Shop & Dirty Burger *(E1)*
Comptoir Gascon *(EC1)*
Dirty Burger Shoreditch *(E1)*
Goodman *(E14)**
Goodman City *(EC2)**
Haché *(EC2)*
Hawksmoor *(E1, EC2)*
One Sixty Smokehouse *(E1)**
Patty and Bun *(EC2)**
The Rib Man *(E1)**
Rivington Grill *(EC2)*
Shake Shack *(E20)*
Smiths (Dining Rm) *(EC1)*
Street Kitchen (van) *(EC2)*

CHICKEN

Central

Bao *(W1)**
Chicken Shop *(WC1)*
Clockjack Oven *(W1)*
Randall & Aubin *(W1)**

North
Bird Islington *(N7)*
Chicken Shop *(NW5)*
Chicken Town *(N15)*
Le Coq *(N1)*

South
Chicken & Egg Shop *(SW12)*
Chicken Shop *(SW17)*

East
Bird *(E2)*
Chick 'n' Sours *(E8)**
Chicken Shop & Dirty Burger *(E1)*
The Tramshed *(EC2)*

FISH & CHIPS

Central
Golden Hind *(W1)**
North Sea Fish *(WC1)*
Seafresh *(SW1)**

West
Geales *(W8)*
Geales Chelsea Green *(SW3)*
Kerbisher & Malt *(W5,W6)*

North
Nautilus *(NW6)**
Olympus Fish *(N3)**
Poppies Camden *(NW1)**
The Sea Shell *(NW1)*
Skipjacks *(HA3)**
Toff's *(N10)**
Two Brothers *(N3)*
Vintage Salt *(N1)**

South
Brady's *(SW18)*
Fish Club *(SW11, SW4)**
fish! *(SE1)*
Kerbisher & Malt *(SW14, SW4)*
Masters Super Fish *(SE1)**
The Sea Cow *(SE22)*

East
Ark Fish *(E18)**
The Grapes *(E14)*
Kerbisher & Malt *(EC1)*
Poppies *(E1)**
Vintage Salt *(EC2)**

FISH & SEAFOOD

Central
Belgo Centraal *(WC2)*
Bellamy's *(W1)*
Bentley's *(W1)**
Bonnie Gull *(W1)**
Bouillabaisse *(W1)*
Burger & Lobster *(W1)*
Fishworks *(W1)*
Green's *(SW1)*
Kaspar's Seafood and Grill *(WC2)*
Olivomare *(SW1)**
One-O-One *(SW1)**
The Pantechnicon *(SW1)*
Pescatori *(W1)*
Quaglino's *(SW1)*
Randall & Aubin *(W1)**
Rib Room *(SW1)*
Royal China Club *(W1)**
Salmontini *(SW1)*
Scott's *(W1)**
Sexy Fish *(W1)*
J Sheekey *(WC2)**
J Sheekey Oyster Bar *(WC2)**
Wiltons *(SW1)*
Wright Brothers *(W1)**

West
Bibendum Oyster Bar *(SW3)*
Big Easy *(SW3)*
Chez Patrick *(W8)*
The Cow *(W2)**
Geales *(W8)*
Kensington Place *(W8)*
Mandarin Kitchen *(W2)**
Outlaw's Seafood *(SW3)**
Poissonnerie de l'Avenue *(SW3)*
The Summerhouse *(W9)*
Wright Brothers *(SW7)**

North
Belgo Noord *(NW1)*
Bradley's *(NW3)*
Carob Tree *(NW5)**
Lure *(NW5)**
Olympus Fish *(N3)**
Prawn On The Lawn *(N1)**
Toff's *(N10)**

South
Applebee's Café *(SE1)**
Cornish Tiger *(SW11)*
fish! *(SE1)*
Lobster Pot *(SE11)**
Le Querce *(SE23)**
Wright Brothers *(SE1)**

East
Angler *(EC2)**
Bonnie Gull Seafood Bar *(EC1)*
Burger & Lobster *(EC1, EC4)*
Chamberlain's *(EC3)*
Fish Central *(EC1)*
Fish Market *(EC2)*
The Grapes *(E14)*
Hix Oyster & Chop House *(EC1)*
M Raw *(EC2)**
Orpheus *(EC3)**
Royal Exchange *(EC3)*
Sweetings *(EC4)*
Wright Brothers *(E1)**

GAME

Central
Bocca Di Lupo *(W1)**
Boisdale *(SW1)*
Rules *(WC2)*
Wiltons *(SW1)*

West
Harwood Arms *(SW6)**
John Doe *(W10)**

North
San Daniele del Friuli *(N5)*

South
The Anchor & Hope *(SE1)**

East
Boisdale of Bishopsgate *(EC2)*
The Jugged Hare *(EC1)*

ICE CREAM

Central
Gelupo *(W1)**
Morelli's Gelato *(WC2)*

ORGANIC

Central
Daylesford Organic *(SW1,W1)*

West
Daylesford Organic *(W11)*

East
Smiths (Dining Rm) *(EC1)*

PIZZA

Central
Il Baretto *(W1)*
Bianco43 *(WC2)*
Delfino *(W1)*
Fire & Stone *(WC2)*
Homeslice *(W1,WC2)**
Kettners *(W1)*
Mayfair *Pizza* Company *(W1)*
Oliveto *(SW1)**
The Orange *(SW1)*
Pizza Pilgrims *(W1)*
La Porchetta Pizzeria *(WC1)*
Princi *(W1)*
Rossopomodoro *(WC2)*

West
Bird in Hand *(W14)*
Buona Sera *(SW3)*
Canta Napoli *(W4)*
Da Mario *(SW7)*
La Delizia Limbara *(SW3)*
Fire & Stone *(W12)*
Made in Italy *(SW3)*
The Oak W12 *(W12,W2)**
Osteria Basilico *(W11)*
Pappa Ciccia *(SW6)**
Pizza East Portobello *(W10)**
Portobello Ristorante *(W11)*
The Red Pepper *(W9)*
Rocca Di Papa *(SW7)*
Rossopomodoro *(SW10)*
Santa Maria *(W5)**

North
L' Antica Pizzeria *(NW3)**
Il Bacio *(N16, N5)*
Fabrizio *(N19)*
Pizza East *(NW5)**
Pizzeria Oregano *(N1)**

Pizzeria Pappagone *(N4)*
La Porchetta Pizzeria *(N1, N4, NW1)*
Rossopomodoro *(N1, NW1)*
Sacro Cuore *(NW10)**
Sweet Thursday *(N1)*

South

Al Forno *(SW15, SW19)*
Bianco43 *(SE10, SE3)*
Buona Sera *(SW11)*
Donna Margherita *(SW11)**
Eco *(SW4)*
Gourmet Pizza Company *(SE1)*
The Gowlett *(SE15)**
Lorenzo *(SE19)*
Mamma Dough *(SE23, SW9)*
Pizza Metro *(SW11)**
Pizzeria Rustica *(TW9)**
Rocca Di Papa *(SE21)*
Rossopomodoro *(SW18)*
The Yellow House *(SE16)*

East

Il Bordello *(E1)*
Pizza East *(E1)**
La Porchetta Pizzeria *(EC1)*
Rocket Bishopgate *(EC2)*
Rocket Canary Wharf *(E14)*

SANDWICHES, CAKES, ETC

Central

Bageriet *(WC2)**
Bar Italia *(W1)*
Bea's Of Bloomsbury *(WC1)**
Caffé Vergnano *(WC1)*
Crosstown Doughnuts *(W1)*
Daylesford Organic *(W1)*
Fernandez & Wells *(W1, WC2)*
La Fromagerie Café *(W1)*
Kaffeine *(W1)**
Konditor & Cook *(W1, WC1)*
Maison Bertaux *(W1)**
The Melt Room *(W1)*
Monmouth Coffee Company *(WC2)**
Nordic Bakery *(W1)*
Royal Academy *(W1)*
Scandinavian Kitchen *(W1)*
Workshop Coffee Fitzrovia *(W1)*

West

Lisboa Pâtisserie *(W10)*

North

Ginger & White *(NW3)*
Greenberry Café *(NW1)*
Kenwood (Brew House) *(NW3)*
Max's Sandwich Shop *(N4)**

South

Caffé Vergnano *(SE1)*
Fulham Wine Rooms *(SW6)*
Grind Coffee Bar *(SW15)**
Kappacasein *(SE16)**
Kitchen *(SE1)*
Konditor & Cook *(SE1)*
Milk *(SW12)**
Monmouth Coffee Company *(SE1, SE16)**
Orange Pekoe *(SW13)*

East

Brick Lane Beigel Bake *(E1)**
Caffé Vergnano *(EC4)*
Department of Coffee *(EC1)**
Konditor & Cook *(EC3)*
Nusa Kitchen *(EC1, EC2)**
Prufrock Coffee *(EC1)*
Workshop Coffee Holborn *(EC1)*

SALADS

Central

Kaffeine *(W1)**

STEAKS & GRILLS

Central

Barbecoa Piccadilly *(W1)*
Beast *(W1)*
Bodean's *(W1)*
Christopher's *(WC2)*
Cut *(W1)*
Flat Iron *(W1, WC2)**
Goodman *(W1)**
The Guinea Grill *(W1)*
Hawksmoor *(W1, WC2)*
M Restaurant Victoria Street *(SW1)**
MASH Steakhouse *(W1)*
maze Grill *(W1)*
Le Relais de Venise L'Entrecôte *(W1)*
Rib Room *(SW1)*
Rowley's *(SW1)*
Sackville's *(W1)*
Sophie's Steakhouse *(WC2)*
STK Steakhouse *(WC2)*
34 *(W1)*
Wolfe's *(WC2)*
Zoilo *(W1)**

West

Bodean's *(SW6)*
Casa Malevo *(W2)*
Haché *(SW10)*
Hawksmoor Knightsbridge *(SW3)*
John Doe *(W10)**
MacellaioRC *(SW7)**
PJ's Bar and Grill *(SW3)*
Popeseye *(W14)*
Smokehouse Chiswick *(W4)*
Sophie's Steakhouse *(SW10)*
West Thirty Six *(W10)*

North

Foxlow *(N16)*
Haché *(NW1)*
Popeseye *(N19)*
The Smokehouse Islington *(N1)*

South

Archduke Wine Bar *(SE1)*
Bodean's *(SW4)*
Buenos Aires Café *(SE10, SE3)*
Butcher & Grill *(SW11)*
Cau *(SE3, SW19)**
Cornish Tiger *(SW11)*
Naughty Piglets *(SW2)**
Popeseye *(SW15)*

East

Barbecoa *(EC4)*
Bodean's *(EC1, EC3)*
Buen Ayre *(E8)**
Cau *(E1)**
Foxlow *(EC1)*
Goodman *(E14)**
Goodman City *(EC2)**
Hawksmoor *(E1, EC2)*
Hill & Szrok *(E8)**
Hix Oyster & Chop House *(EC1)*
Jones & Sons *(E8)**
The Jones Family Project *(EC2)*
M Grill *(EC2)**
New Street Grill *(EC2)*
Paternoster Chop House *(EC4)*
Relais de Venise *(E14, EC2)*
Simpson's Tavern *(EC3)*
Smiths (Top Floor) *(EC1)*
Smiths (Dining Rm) *(EC1)*
Smiths (Ground Floor) *(EC1)*
The Tramshed *(EC2)*

VEGETARIAN

Central

Amico Bio *(WC1)*
Chettinad *(W1)**
Ethos *(W1)**
Malabar Junction *(WC1)*
Mildreds *(W1)*
Ragam *(W1)**
Rasa *(W1)**
Rasa Maricham *(WC1)**
Sagar *(W1)**
tibits *(W1)*
Woodlands *(SW1, W1)*

West

The Gate *(W6)**
Sagar *(W6)**

North

Chutneys *(NW1)*
Diwana Bhel-Poori House *(NW1)*
Jashan *(N8)**
Manna *(NW3)*
Rani *(N3)*
Rasa Travancore *(N16)**
Vijay *(NW6)*
Woodlands *(NW3)*

South

Blue Elephant *(SW6)*
Ganapati *(SE15)**
Le Pont de la Tour *(SE1)*
Sree Krishna *(SW17)**

East

Amico Bio *(EC1)*

The Gate *(EC1)**
Vanilla Black *(EC4)**

ARGENTINIAN

Central
Zoilo *(W1)**

West
Casa Malevo *(W2)*
Quantus *(W4)**

South
Buenos Aires Café *(SE10, SE3)*

East
Buen Ayre *(E8)**

BRAZILIAN

East
Sushisamba *(EC2)*

MEXICAN/TEXMEX

Central
La Bodega Negra *(W1)*
Cantina Laredo *(WC2)**
Chilango *(WC2)*
DF Mexico *(W1)**
Lupita *(WC2)*
Peyote *(W1)*

West
Habanera *(W12)*
Taqueria *(W11)**

North
Chilango *(N1)*

East
Chilango *(E1, EC2, EC4)*
Daddy Donkey *(EC1)**
DF Mexico *(E1)**

PERUVIAN

Central
Ceviche Soho *(W1)*
Coya *(W1)*
Lima *(W1)*
Lima Floral *(WC2)*
Pachamama *(W1)*
Señor Ceviche *(W1)*

East
Andina *(E2)*
Ceviche Old St *(EC1)*
Sushisamba *(EC2)*

SOUTH AMERICAN

West
Casa Cruz *(W11)*
Quantus *(W4)**

South
El Vergel *(SE1)**

AFRO-CARIBBEAN

Central
Jamaica Patty Co. *(WC2)*

MOROCCAN

West
Adams Café *(W12)*

NORTH AFRICAN

Central
Momo *(W1)*

West
Azou *(W6)*

SOUTH AFRICAN

Central
Bunnychow *(W1)*

TUNISIAN

West
Adams Café *(W12)*

EGYPTIAN

North
Ali Baba *(NW1)*

ISRAELI

Central
Gaby's *(WC2)*
The Palomar *(W1)**

East
Ottolenghi *(E1)**

KOSHER

Central
Reubens *(W1)*

North
Kaifeng *(NW4)*
Zest *(NW3)*

East
Brick Lane Beigel Bake *(E1)**

LEBANESE

Central
Fairuz *(W1)*
Maroush *(W1)*
Yalla Yalla *(W1)*

West
Chez Abir *(W14)**
Maroush *(SW3)*
Maroush Gardens *(W2)*

South
Arabica Bar and Kitchen *(SE1)*
Meza Trinity Road *(SW17)**
Yalla Yalla *(SE10)*

MIDDLE EASTERN

Central
Honey & Co *(W1)**
Patogh *(W1)**
Sesame *(WC2)*

North
Yasmeen *(NW8)*

East
Berber & Q *(E8)**
Morito *(EC1)**
Nusa Kitchen *(EC4)**
Pilpel *(E1, EC4)**

PERSIAN

Central
Kateh Knightsbridge *(SW1)**

West
Alounak *(W14, W2)*
Faanoos *(W4, W5)*
Kateh *(W9)**

South
Faanoos *(SW14)*

SYRIAN

West
Abu Zaad *(W12)*

TURKISH

Central
Babaji Pide *(W1)*
Ishtar *(W1)*
Kazan (Café) *(SW1)*

West
Best Mangal *(SW6, W14)**
Fez Mangal *(W11)**

North
Durum Ocakbasi *(N3)*
Gallipoli *(N1)*
Gem *(N1)**
GoÅNkyüzü *(N4)**
Izgara *(N3)*
Mangal II *(N16)**

South
FM Mangal *(SE5)*
Tas Pide *(SE1)*

East
Chifafa *(EC1)**
Haz *(E1, EC2, EC3)*
Mangal 1 *(E8)**

AFGHANI

North
Afghan Kitchen *(N1)**
Ariana II *(NW6)**

BURMESE

West
Mandalay *(W2)*

CHINESE

Central

A Wong *(SW1)**
Baozi Inn *(WC2)**
Barshu *(W1)**
The Bright Courtyard *(W1)**
Chilli Cool *(WC1)*
China Tang *(W1)*
The Duck & Rice *(W1)*
The Four Seasons *(W1)**
Golden Dragon *(W1)*
The Grand Imperial *(SW1)*
Hakkasan Mayfair *(W1)**
Harbour City *(W1)*
Hunan *(SW1)**
Joy King Lau *(WC2)*
Kai Mayfair *(W1)*
Ken Lo's Memories *(SW1)*
Leong's Legends *(W1)**
Mr Chow *(SW1)*
New Mayflower *(W1)*
NewWorld *(W1)*
Plum Valley *(W1)*
Princess Garden *(W1)*
Royal China *(W1)**
Royal China Club *(W1)**
Shanghai Blues *(WC1)*
Wong Kei *(W1)*
Yauatcha *(W1)**
Yming *(W1)*

West

The Four Seasons *(W2)**
Gold Mine *(W2)**
Good Earth *(SW3)*
Mandarin Kitchen *(W2)**
Min Jiang *(W8)**
North China *(W3)**
Pearl Liang *(W2)**
Royal China *(SW6,W2)**
Shikumen *(W12)**
Taiwan Village *(SW6)**

North

Good Earth *(NW7)*
Green Cottage *(NW3)*
Gung-Ho *(NW6)*
Kaifeng *(NW4)*
Phoenix Palace *(NW1)*
Singapore Garden *(NW6)**
Yipin China *(N1)*

South

Dalchini *(SW19)*
Dragon Castle *(SE17)*
Good Earth *(SW17)*
Hutong *(SE1)*
Silk Road *(SE5)**

East

Chinese Cricket Club *(EC4)**
Gourmet San *(E2)**
HKK *(EC2)**
Royal China *(E14)**
Shanghai *(E8)*
Sichuan Folk *(E1)**
Yauatcha City *(EC2)**
Yi-Ban *(E16)**

CHINESE, DIM SUM

Central

The Bright Courtyard *(W1)**
Dumplings' Legend *(W1)**
Golden Dragon *(W1)*
The Grand Imperial *(SW1)*
Hakkasan Mayfair *(W1)**
Harbour City *(W1)*
Joy King Lau *(WC2)*
New World *(W1)*
Princess Garden *(W1)*
Royal China *(W1)**
Royal China Club *(W1)**
Shanghai Blues *(WC1)*
Yauatcha *(W1)**

West

Min Jiang *(W8)**
Pearl Liang *(W2)**
Royal China *(SW6,W2)**
Shikumen *(W12)**

North

Jun Ming Xuan *(NW9)**
Phoenix Palace *(NW1)*

South

Dragon Castle *(SE17)*

East

Royal China *(E14)**
Shanghai *(E8)*
Yauatcha City *(EC2)**
Yi-Ban *(E16)**

GEORGIAN

North

Little Georgia Café *(N1)*

East

Little Georgia Café *(E2)*

INDIAN

Central

Amaya *(SW1)**
Benares *(W1)*
Carom at Meza *(W1)*
Chettinad *(W1)**
Chor Bizarre *(W1)*
Chutney Mary *(SW1)**
The Cinnamon Club *(SW1)*
Cinnamon Soho *(W1)**
Dishoom *(W1,WC2)**
Gaylord *(W1)*
Gymkhana *(W1)**
Imli Street *(W1)*
India Club *(WC2)*
Malabar Junction *(WC1)*
Mint Leaf *(SW1)*
Moti Mahal *(WC2)*
La Porte des Indes *(W1)*
Punjab *(WC2)*
Ragam *(W1)**
Red Fort *(W1)*
Roti Chai *(W1)**
Sagar *(W1,WC2)**
Salaam Namaste *(WC1)*
Salloos *(SW1)**
Tamarind *(W1)*
Trishna *(W1)**
Veeraswamy *(W1)*
Woodlands *(SW1,W1)*
Zayna *(W1)**

West

Anarkali *(W6)*
Bombay Brasserie *(SW7)*
Bombay Palace *(W2)**
Brilliant *(UB2)**
Chakra *(W11)*
Gifto's *(UB1)**
The Greedy Buddha *(SW6)*
Indian Zing *(W6)**
Karma *(W14)**
Khan's *(W2)*
Madhu's *(UB1)**
Malabar *(W8)**
Masala Grill *(SW10)**
Nayaab *(SW6)**
Noor Jahan *(SW5,W2)**
The Painted Heron *(SW10)**
Potli *(W6)**
Rasoi *(SW3)**
Sagar *(W6)**
Star of India *(SW5)*
Thali *(SW5)**
Zaika *(W8)*

North

Abi Ruchi *(N16)**
Chutneys *(NW1)*
Delhi Grill *(N1)**
Dishoom *(N1)**
Diwana Bhel-Poori House *(NW1)*
Great Nepalese *(NW1)*
Guglee *(NW3, NW6)*
Indian Rasoi *(N2)**
Indian Veg *(N1)**
Jashan *(N8)**
Kadiri's *(NW10)**
Namaaste Kitchen *(NW1)**
Paradise Hampstead *(NW3)**
Rani *(N3)*
Ravi Shankar *(NW1)*
Roots at N1 *(N1)**
Vijay *(NW6)*
Woodlands *(NW3)*
Zaffrani *(N1)*

South

Apollo Banana Leaf *(SW17)**
Babur *(SE23)**
Bengal Clipper *(SE1)*
Dalchini *(SW19)*
Everest Inn *(SE3)**
Ganapati *(SE15)**
Hot Stuff *(SW8)**
Indian Moment *(SW11)*

Indian Ocean *(SW17)**
Indian Zilla *(SW13)*
Jaffna House *(SW17)**
Kennington Tandoori *(SE11)*
Kishmish *(SW6)**
Kricket *(SW9)*
Lahore Karahi *(SW17)**
Lahore Kebab House *(SW16)**
Ma Goa *(SW15)**
Mirch Masala *(SW17)**
Radha Krishna Bhaven *(SW17)*
Sree Krishna *(SW17)**
Tandoori Nights *(SE22)**

East

Café Spice Namaste *(E1)**
Cinnamon Kitchen *(EC2)**
Dishoom *(E2)**
Lahore Kebab House *(E1)**
Mint Leaf *(EC2)*
Needoo *(E1)**
Tayyabs *(E1)**

INDIAN, SOUTHERN

Central

Hoppers *(W1)*
India Club *(WC2)*
Malabar Junction *(WC1)*
Quilon *(SW1)**
Ragam *(W1)**
Rasa *(W1)**
Rasa Maricham *(WC1)**
Sagar *(W1, WC2)**
Woodlands *(SW1, W1)*

West

Sagar *(W6)**
Shilpa *(W6)**

North

Chutneys *(NW1)*
Rani *(N3)*
Rasa Travancore *(N16)**
Vijay *(NW6)*
Woodlands *(NW3)*

South

Ganapati *(SE15)**
Sree Krishna *(SW17)**

JAPANESE

Central

Abeno *(WC1, WC2)*
aqua kyoto *(W1)*
The Araki *(W1)**
Atari-Ya *(W1)**
Bone Daddies *(W1)**
Chisou *(W1)**
Chotto Matte *(W1)**
Defune *(W1)**
Dinings *(W1)**
Eat Tokyo *(WC1, WC2)**
Engawa *(W1)*
Flesh and Buns *(WC2)*
Ippudo London *(WC2)*
Kanada-Ya *(SW1, WC2)**
Kiku *(W1)**
Kikuchi *(W1)**
Kintan *(WC1)**
Koya-Bar *(W1)**
Kulu Kulu *(W1, WC2)*
Kurobuta Harvey Nics *(SW1)**
Matsuri *(SW1)*
Murakami *(WC2)*
Nobu *(W1)*
Nobu Berkeley *(W1)*
Oka *(W1)**
Roka *(W1, WC2)**
Sakana-tei *(W1)**
Sake No Hana *(SW1)*
Salmontini *(SW1)*
Shackfuyu *(W1)**
Shoryu Ramen *(SW1, W1)**
Sticks'n'Sushi *(WC2)*
Sumosan *(W1)**
Taro *(W1)**
Tokyo Diner *(WC2)*
Tonkotsu *(W1)**
Tsunami *(W1)**
Umu *(W1)*
The Woodstock *(W1)*
Yoshino *(W1)**

West

Atari-Ya *(W3, W5)**
Bone Daddies *(W8)**
Chisou *(SW3)**
Eat Tokyo *(W6, W8)**
Flat Three *(W11)*
Hare & Tortoise *(W4)*
Inaho *(W2)**
Kiraku *(W5)**
Kulu Kulu *(SW7)*
Kurobuta *(SW3, W2)**
Maguro *(W9)*
Tokyo Sukiyaji-Tei & Bar *(SW3)*
Tosa *(W6)*
Yashin *(W8)**
Yashin Ocean House *(SW7)*
Yoshi Sushi *(W6)*
Zuma *(SW7)**

North

Asakusa *(NW1)**
Atari-Ya *(N12, NW4, NW6)**
Dotori *(N4)**
Eat Tokyo *(NW11)**
Jin Kichi *(NW3)**
Sushi-Say *(NW2)**

South

Hashi *(SW20)**
Matsuba *(TW9)**
Sticks'n'Sushi *(SE10, SW19)*
Tonkotsu Bankside *(SE1)**
Tsunami *(SW4)**
Yama Momo *(SE22)**
Zaibatsu *(SE10)**

East

Beer and Buns *(EC2)*
Bone Daddies *(EC1)**
City Miyama *(EC4)*
Ippudo London *(E14)*
K10, Appold Street *(EC2, EC3)*
Pham Sushi *(EC1)**
Roka *(E14)**
Shoryu Ramen *(EC2)**
Sosharu *(EC1)*
Sticks'n'Sushi *(E14)*
Sushisamba *(EC2)*
Sushi Tetsu *(EC1)**
Tajima Tei *(EC1)**
Tonkotsu East *(E8)**
Yum Bun *(EC1)**

KOREAN

Central

Bibimbap Soho *(W1)*
Bó Drake *(W1)*
Jinjuu *(W1)*
Kimchee *(WC1)*
Kintan *(WC1)**
Koba *(W1)*
On The Bab *(WC2)**
On The Bab Express *(W1)**

West

Yoshi Sushi *(W6)*

North

Dotori *(N4)**
The Petite Coree *(NW6)**

South

Cah-Chi *(SW18, SW20)*
Matsuba *(TW9)**

East

Bibimbap *(EC3)*
On The Bab *(EC1)**

MALAYSIAN

Central

C&R Café *(W1)**

West

C&R Café *(W2)**
Satay House *(W2)*

North

Roti King *(NW1)**
Singapore Garden *(NW6)**

South

Champor-Champor *(SE1)*

PAKISTANI

Central

Salloos *(SW1)**

West

Nayaab *(SW6)**

South

Lahore Karahi *(SW17)**
Lahore Kebab House *(SW16)**
Mirch Masala *(SW17)**

East
Lahore Kebab House *(E1)**
Needoo *(E1)**
Tayyabs *(E1)**

PAN-ASIAN
Central
Banana Tree Canteen *(W1)*
Buddha-Bar London *(SW1)*
Cocochan *(W1)*
Hare & Tortoise *(WC1)*
Inamo *(SW1, W1)*
Novikov (Asian restaurant) *(W1)*
West
Banana Tree Canteen *(W2, W9)*
E&O *(W11)*
Eight Over Eight *(SW3)*
Hare & Tortoise *(W14, W5)*
North
The Banana Tree Canteen *(NW6)*
Gilgamesh *(NW1)*
XO *(NW3)*
South
The Banana Tree Canteen *(SW11)*
Hare & Tortoise *(SW15)*
East
Banana Tree Canteen *(EC1)*
Hare & Tortoise *(EC4)*

THAI
Central
Crazy Bear *(W1)*
Patara Fitzrovia *(W1)*
Rosa's Soho *(W1)**
Smoking Goat *(WC2)**
West
Addie's *Thai* Café *(SW5)**
Bangkok *(SW7)*
Café 209 *(SW6)*
Churchill Arms *(W8)*
Esarn Kheaw *(W12)**
The Heron *(W2)**
101 *Thai* Kitchen *(W6)**
Patara South Kensington *(SW3)*
Rosa's Fulham *(SW10)**
Sukho Fine *Thai* Cuisine *(SW6)**
Suksan *(SW10)**
North
Isarn *(N1)**
Yum Yum *(N16)*
South
Awesome *Thai* *(SW13)*
The Begging Bowl *(SE15)*
Blue Elephant *(SW6)*
Kaosarn *(SW11, SW9)*
The Pepper Tree *(SW4)*
Suk Saran *(SW19)*
Talad *Thai* *(SW15)**
East
Rosa's *(E1)**
Rosa's Soho *(E15)**
Som Saa *(E8)**

VIETNAMESE
Central
Cây Tre *(W1)*
House of Ho *(W1)*
West
Saigon Saigon *(W6)*
Tem Tép *(W8)*
North
Salvation In Noodles *(N1, N4)*
South
Café East *(SE16)**
Mien Tay *(SW11)*
East
Cây Tre *(EC1)*
City Càphê *(EC2)**
Mien Tay *(E2)*
Sông Quê *(E2)*
Viet Grill *(E2)**

TAIWANESE
Central
Bao *(W1)**
Leong's Legends *(W1)**
West
Taiwan Village *(SW6)**

LONDON AREA OVERVIEWS

CENTRAL

Soho, Covent Garden & Bloomsbury (Parts of W1, all WC2 and WC1)

Price	Restaurant	Cuisine	Rating
£100+	Smith & Wollensky	*Steak & grills*	
£90+	L'Atelier de Joel Robuchon	*French*	333
£80+	Spring	*British, Modern*	332
	Savoy Grill	*British, Traditional*	233
	Asia de Cuba	*Fusion*	222
	MASH Steakhouse	*Steaks & grills*	221
	Engawa	*Japanese*	343
	Roka	"	433
£70+	Christopher's	*American*	223
	Social Eating House	*British, Modern*	443
	Rules	*British, Traditional*	325
	Simpsons-in-the-Strand	"	111
	Kaspar's Seafood and Grill	*Fish & seafood*	333
	J Sheekey	"	444
	J Sheekey Oyster Bar	"	445
	The Salon	*Fusion*	– – –
	Massimo	*Mediterranean*	243
	Nopi	"	322
	STK Steakhouse	*Steaks & grills*	112
	Yauatcha	*Chinese*	523
	aqua kyoto	*Japanese*	223
£60+	Balthazar	*British, Modern*	223
	Bob Bob Ricard	"	345
	Hix	"	222
	Hush	"	233
	Indigo	"	243
	The Ivy	"	– – –
	Tom's Kitchen	"	121
	Holborn Dining Room	*British, Traditional*	234
	Antidote	*French*	433
	Clos Maggiore	"	455
	L'Escargot	"	333
	Gauthier Soho	"	554
	Otto's	"	454
	Kopapa	*Fusion*	222
	aqua nueva	*Spanish*	334
	Hawksmoor	*Steaks & grills*	333
	Lima Floral	*Peruvian*	332
	Shanghai Blues	*Chinese*	333
	Moti Mahal	*Indian*	332
	Red Fort	"	222

£50+	Big Easy	*American*	223
	Hubbard & Bell	”	334
	Joe Allen	”	124
	Arbutus	*British, Modern*	332
	Aurora	”	345
	Coopers	”	223
	Dean Street Townhouse	”	234
	Ducksoup	”	344
	Ham Yard Restaurant	”	114
	The Ivy Market Grill	”	223
	Kettners	”	---
	The Portrait	”	234
	Quo Vadis	”	354
	Tredwell's	”	121
	The Lady Ottoline	*British, Traditional*	333
	The National Dining Rms	”	113
	Strand Dining Rooms	”	---
	The Delaunay	*Mittel-European*	345
	Randall & Aubin	*Fish & seafood*	444
	Wright Brothers	”	443
	Cigalon	*French*	332
	Compagnie des Vins S.	”	334
	Les Deux Salons	”	---
	Mon Plaisir	”	224
	Gay Hussar	*Hungarian*	225
	The 10 Cases	*International*	243
	Bocca Di Lupo	*Italian*	544
	Café Murano	”	444
	Dehesa	”	334
	Luce e Limoni	”	444
	Mele e Pere	”	333
	Orso	”	222
	San Carlo Cicchetti	”	333
	Vasco & Piero's Pavilion	”	343
	Vico	”	---
	Cigala	*Spanish*	222
	Sophie's Steakhouse	*Steaks & grills*	222
	Rainforest Café	*Burgers, etc*	123
	La Bodega Negra	*Mexican/TexMex*	224
	Cantina Laredo	”	444
	Barshu	*Chinese*	412
	The Duck & Rice	”	235
	Plum Valley	”	323
	Chotto Matte	*Japanese*	434
	Flesh and Buns	”	333
	Patara Soho	*Thai*	333
	House of Ho	*Vietnamese*	322
£40+	Bodean's	*American*	223
	Jackson & Rye	”	123

Jamie's Diner	"	2 2 2
Mishkin's	"	1 2 3
Spuntino	"	3 3 4
Belgo Soho	*Belgian*	2 2 2
Andrew Edmunds	*British, Modern*	4 4 5
Jar Kitchen	"	3 3 3
Morden & Lea	"	– – –
The Norfolk Arms	"	4 3 3
Old Tom & English	"	– – –
Polpo at Ape & Bird	"	2 2 3
Shampers	"	2 4 5
10 Greek Street	"	5 4 3
Vinoteca	"	2 3 4
VQ	"	2 4 3
Great Queen Street	*British, Traditional*	2 2 3
Brasserie Zédel	*French*	2 4 5
Café Bohème	"	2 4 4
Chez Antoinette	"	– – –
Le Garrick	"	2 3 3
Terroirs	"	3 3 4
Balans	*International*	2 3 3
Cork & Bottle	"	2 3 5
Ember Yard	"	3 3 3
Rocket Holborn	"	3 3 3
Ciao Bella	*Italian*	2 4 4
Da Mario	"	3 4 4
Obicà	"	3 3 2
Polpetto	"	3 3 3
Polpo	"	2 2 3
Rex & Mariano	"	5 4 3
Barrafina Drury Lane	*Spanish*	5 5 5
Opera Tavern	"	4 4 4
Tapas Brindisa Soho	"	3 3 3
Mildreds	*Vegetarian*	3 3 2
Burger & Lobster	*Burgers, etc*	3 2 3
Wolfe's	"	3 2 2
Bianco43	*Pizza*	3 2 2
Fire & Stone	"	2 2 2
Lupita	*Mexican/TexMex*	3 3 2
Ceviche Soho	*Peruvian*	3 4 4
Señor Ceviche	"	3 3 4
The Palomar	*Israeli*	4 4 4
New Mayflower	*Chinese*	3 2 2
Yming	"	3 5 4
Cinnamon Soho	*Indian*	4 2 2
Dishoom	"	4 3 4
Imli Street	"	3 2 2
Malabar Junction	"	3 4 3
Abeno	*Japanese*	3 4 1
Kintan	"	4 3 3

Price	Restaurant	Cuisine	Ratings
	Murakami	"	– – –
	Oka	"	4 3 3
	Shoryu Ramen	"	4 2 2
	Sticks'n'Sushi	"	3 3 3
	Bó Drake	*Korean*	2 2 3
	Jinjuu	"	3 3 3
	Kimchee	"	3 2 2
	Inamo	*Pan-Asian*	2 2 2
£35+	Blacklock	*British, Modern*	4 4 3
	Pennethorne's Cafe Bar	"	– – –
	Blanchette	*French*	3 4 5
	Prix Fixe	"	3 2 3
	Le Restaurant de Paul	"	4 4 3
	Savoir Faire	"	3 3 2
	Bar Termini	*Italian*	4 4 4
	Caffé Vergnano	"	2 2 3
	Princi	"	3 2 4
	Amico Bio	*Vegetarian*	2 3 2
	Balls & Company	*Burgers, etc*	– – –
	North Sea Fish	*Fish & chips*	3 3 2
	Rossopomodoro	*Pizza*	2 2 2
	Bea's Of Bloomsbury	*Sandwiches, cakes, etc*	4 3 3
	Caffé Vergnano	"	2 2 3
	Yalla Yalla	*Lebanese*	3 3 4
	Harbour City	*Chinese*	2 1 1
	Joy King Lau	"	3 2 2
	New World	"	3 2 3
	Dumplings' Legend	*Chinese, Dim sum*	4 2 3
	Carom at Meza	*Indian*	2 3 3
	Sagar	"	4 4 3
	Salaam Namaste	"	3 2 2
	Rasa Maricham	*Indian, Southern*	4 3 3
	Ippudo London	*Japanese*	2 3 2
	Taro	"	4 3 3
	On The Bab	*Korean*	4 3 2
	C&R Café	*Malaysian*	4 2 2
	Banana Tree Canteen	*Pan-Asian*	2 2 2
	Rosa's Soho	*Thai*	4 3 2
	Smoking Goat	"	5 2 3
	Cây Tre	*Vietnamese*	3 2 3
	Leong's Legends	*Taiwanese*	4 2 2
£30+	Seven Stars	*British, Modern*	3 2 3
	Café in the Crypt	*International*	2 2 3
	Gordon's Wine Bar	"	2 3 5
	La Porchetta Pizzeria	*Italian*	2 3 3
	MEATmarket	*Burgers, etc*	4 2 2
	Pizza Pilgrims	*Pizza*	3 3 4
	Fernandez & Wells	*Sandwiches, cakes, etc*	2 2 4

Price	Restaurant	Cuisine	Rating
	Chicken Shop	*Chicken*	344
	Clockjack Oven	"	333
	Chilli Cool	*Chinese*	311
	The Four Seasons	"	411
	Golden Dragon	"	322
	Wong Kei	"	222
	Punjab	*Indian*	333
	Bone Daddies	*Japanese*	444
	Koya-Bar	"	444
	Kulu Kulu	"	312
	Shackfuyu	"	544
	Tonkotsu	"	443
	Hare & Tortoise	*Pan-Asian*	323
£25+	Pitt Cue Co	*American*	533
	Bistro 1	*Mediterranean*	232
	Bar Italia	*Sandwiches, cakes, etc*	345
	Gaby's	*Israeli*	333
	India Club	*Indian*	321
	Bibimbap Soho	*Korean*	322
	Bao	*Taiwanese*	542
£20+	Flat Iron Henrietta Street	*Steaks & grills*	444
	Dub Jam	*Burgers, etc*	443
	Shake Shack	"	322
	Morelli's Gelato	*Ice cream*	– – –
	Homeslice	*Pizza*	544
	Konditor & Cook	*Sandwiches, cakes, etc*	332
	Sesame	*Middle Eastern*	222
	Baozi Inn	*Chinese*	432
	Eat Tokyo	*Japanese*	422
	Tokyo Diner	"	343
£15+	Nordic Bakery	*Scandinavian*	333
	Maison Bertaux	*Afternoon tea*	423
	The Melt Room	*Sandwiches, cakes, etc*	– – –
	Chilango	*Mexican/TexMex*	332
	Kanada-Ya	*Japanese*	532
£10+	Five Guys	*Burgers, etc*	222
	Bageriet	*Sandwiches, cakes, etc*	444
	Monmouth Coffee Co	"	554
	Jamaica Patty Co.	*Afro-Caribbean*	332
	Bunnychow	*South African*	322
£5+	Gelupo	*Ice cream*	433
	Crosstown Doughnuts	*Sandwiches, cakes, etc*	342

Mayfair & St James's (Parts of W1 and SW1)

Price	Restaurant	Cuisine	Ratings
£360+	The Araki	*Japanese*	544
£140+	Fera at Claridge's	*British, Modern*	344
£130+	Le Gavroche	*French*	554
	The Greenhouse	"	344
	Sketch (Lecture Rm)	"	335
£120+	Alain Ducasse	*French*	222
	Hélène Darroze	"	233
	Hibiscus	"	443
	The Ritz Restaurant	"	245
	The Square	"	422
	Umu	*Japanese*	222
£110+	Novikov (Italian restaurant)	*Italian*	222
	Cut	*Steaks & grills*	222
£100+	Dorchester Grill	*British, Modern*	232
	Galvin at Windows	*French*	224
	Assunta Madre	*Italian*	332
	C London	"	123
	Novikov (Asian restaurant)	*Pan-Asian*	112
£90+	Pollen Street Social	*British, Modern*	222
	Seven Park Place	"	334
	Corrigan's Mayfair	*British, Traditional*	344
	Wiltons	"	334
	Murano	*Italian*	333
	Quattro Passi	"	232
	Theo Randall	"	321
	Kai Mayfair	*Chinese*	322
	Benares	*Indian*	322
	Nobu, Park Ln	*Japanese*	332
	Nobu, Berkeley St	"	322
£80+	Alyn Williams	*British, Modern*	453
	Bentley's	*Fish & seafood*	443
	Bouillabaisse	"	– – –
	Scott's	"	444
	maze	*French*	222
	La Petite Maison	"	434
	Sketch (Gallery)	"	224
	Rextail	*International*	333
	Babbo	*Italian*	333
	Hakkasan Mayfair	*Chinese*	434
	Matsuri	*Japanese*	331
	Roka	"	433

Price	Restaurant	Cuisine	Rating
£70+	The Berners Tavern	*British, Modern*	224
	Le Caprice	"	344
	Little Social	"	333
	Wild Honey	"	222
	Browns (Albemarle)	*British, Traditional*	222
	Green's	"	333
	Boulestin	*French*	232
	Brasserie Chavot	"	344
	Cecconi's	*Italian*	335
	Franco's	"	343
	Ristorante Frescobaldi	"	344
	The Guinea Grill	*Steaks & grills*	233
	maze Grill	"	222
	34	"	333
	Peyote	*Mexican/TexMex*	223
	Coya	*Peruvian*	323
	China Tang	*Chinese*	213
	Tamarind	*Indian*	332
	Veeraswamy	"	333
	Sake No Hana	*Japanese*	312
	Sumosan	"	432
£60+	Athenaeum	*British, Modern*	333
	Bellamy's	"	344
	Bonhams Restaurant	"	433
	Hush	"	233
	Kitty Fisher's	"	444
	Langan's Brasserie	"	224
	Mews of Mayfair	"	234
	The Only Running Footman	"	333
	Quaglino's	"	223
	Sotheby's Café	"	332
	The Wolseley	"	345
	The Keeper's House	*British, Traditional*	222
	Sexy Fish	*Fish & seafood*	– – –
	La Genova	*Italian*	333
	Sartoria	"	– – –
	Barbecoa Piccadilly	*Steaks & grills*	121
	Goodman	"	443
	Hawksmoor	"	333
	Rowley's	"	222
	Sackville's	"	– – –
	Diamond Jub' Salon	*Afternoon tea*	333
	Ritz (Palm Court)	"	245
	Momo North	*African*	223
	Chor Bizarre	*Indian*	323
	Gymkhana	"	544
£50+	The Avenue	*American*	233
	Hard Rock Café	"	224

	Heddon Street Kitchen	*British, Modern*	233
	1707	"	223
	Fishworks	*Fish & seafood*	322
	Pescatori	"	322
	The Balcon	*French*	232
	Boudin Blanc	"	224
	28-50	"	334
	Colony Grill Room	*International*	322
	Café Murano	*Italian*	444
	Princess Garden	*Chinese*	333
	Chutney Mary	*Indian*	444
	Mint Leaf	"	332
	Chisou	*Japanese*	442
	Kiku	"	432
	Patara Mayfair	*Thai*	333
£40+	The Punchbowl	*British, Modern*	334
	The Windmill	*British, Traditional*	323
	L'Artiste Musclé	*French*	224
	Al Duca	*Italian*	332
	Il Vicolo	"	344
	Burger & Lobster	*Burgers, etc*	323
	Delfino	*Pizza*	322
	Mayfair Pizza Company	"	334
	Royal Academy	*Sandwiches, cakes, etc*	222
	Sakana-tei	*Japanese*	521
	Shoryu Ramen	"	422
	Yoshino	"	432
	Inamo	*Pan-Asian*	222
£35+	El Pirata	*Spanish*	344
	tibits	*Vegetarian*	323
	Woodlands	*Indian*	322
	Rasa	*Indian, Southern*	433
£30+	Stock Pot	*International*	222
	The Woodstock	*Japanese*	– – –

Fitzrovia & Marylebone (Part of W1)

£110+	Pied à Terre	*French*	553
	Beast	*Steaks & grills*	222
£100+	Roux at the Landau	*British, Modern*	234
	Bubbledogs (Kitchen Table)	*Fusion*	444
£90+	Texture	*Scandinavian*	442
£80+	The Chiltern Firehouse	*American*	124
	L'Autre Pied	*French*	443

Price	Restaurant	Cuisine	Ratings
	Orrery	"	343
	Dabbous	Fusion	332
	Hakkasan	Chinese	434
	Roka	Japanese	433
£70+	The Cavendish	*British, Modern*	344
	The Providores	*Fusion*	332
	Locanda Locatelli	*Italian*	333
	Royal China Club	*Chinese*	432
£60+	Galvin Bistrot de Luxe	*French*	444
	Il Baretto	*Italian*	322
	Caffè Caldesi	"	343
	Lima	*Peruvian*	332
	La Porte des Indes	*Indian*	334
	Trishna	"	543
	Defune	*Japanese*	432
	Crazy Bear	*Thai*	334
£50+	The Lockhart	*American*	222
	The Grazing Goat	*British, Modern*	333
	Percy & Founders	"	333
	Portland	"	553
	Fischer's	*Mittel-European*	344
	Bonnie Gull	*Fish & seafood*	443
	Fishworks	"	322
	Pescatori	"	322
	Elena's L'Etoile	*French*	111
	Piquet	"	– – –
	28-50	"	334
	Villandry	"	112
	The Wallace	"	225
	Carousel	*Fusion*	433
	Providores (Tapa Room)	"	333
	Twist At Crawford	"	444
	Latium	*Italian*	453
	Sardo	"	322
	Riding House Café	*Mediterranean*	224
	Lurra	*Spanish*	– – –
	Zoilo	*Argentinian*	433
	Pachamama	*Peruvian*	332
	Reubens	*Kosher*	332
	Maroush	*Lebanese*	322
	The Bright Courtyard	*Chinese*	434
	Gaylord	*Indian*	333
	Dinings	*Japanese*	541
	Kikuchi	"	532
	Cocochan	*Pan-Asian*	333
	Patara Fitzrovia	*Thai*	333
	House of Ho	*Vietnamese*	322

£40+	Barnyard	*British, Modern*	2 2 2
	Daylesford Organic	"	2 1 3
	Hardy's Brasserie	"	2 3 3
	The Newman Arms	"	– – –
	Newman Street Tavern	"	3 3 4
	Picture	"	3 4 3
	Vinoteca Seymour Place	"	2 3 4
	Boopshis	*Mittel-European*	3 3 3
	Opso	*Greek*	2 2 4
	Briciole	*Italian*	3 4 3
	Made in Italy	"	3 3 3
	Obicà	"	3 3 2
	2 Veneti	"	3 4 3
	Barrica	*Spanish*	3 3 3
	Donostia	"	5 4 4
	Drakes Tabanco	"	3 2 3
	Ibérica	"	3 3 4
	Salt Yard	"	3 2 3
	Social Wine & Tapas	"	– – –
	Le Relais de Venise	*Steaks & grills*	3 2 2
	Bobo Social	*Burgers, etc*	4 4 3
	Burger & Lobster	"	3 2 3
	Daylesford Organic	*Sandwiches, cakes, etc*	2 1 3
	Workshop Coffee Fitzrovia	"	3 4 4
	Fairuz	*Lebanese*	3 4 3
	Honey & Co	*Middle Eastern*	5 4 2
	Ishtar	*Turkish*	3 3 2
	Royal China	*Chinese*	4 1 2
	Roti Chai	*Indian*	4 4 3
	Zayna	"	4 3 2
	Tsunami	*Japanese*	5 3 3
	Koba	*Korean*	3 3 3
£35+	Lantana Café	*Australian*	3 3 3
	Ethos	*Vegetarian*	4 2 3
	MEATLiquor	*Burgers, etc*	3 2 4
	La Fromagerie Café	*Sandwiches, cakes, etc*	3 2 3
	Yalla Yalla	*Lebanese*	3 3 4
	Babaji Pide	*Turkish*	3 4 3
	Chettinad	*Indian*	4 3 3
	Sagar	"	4 4 3
	Woodlands	"	3 2 2
	On The Bab Express	*Korean*	4 3 2
£30+	Bubbledogs	*American*	1 2 3
	Stock Pot	*International*	2 2 2
	Vapiano	*Italian*	3 2 2
	DF Mexico	*Mexican/TexMex*	4 3 3
	Atari-Ya	*Japanese*	5 3 2
	Tonkotsu	"	4 4 3

£25+	The Joint Marylebone	*American*	532
	Golden Hind	*Fish & chips*	443
	Ragam	*Indian*	542
	Bibimbap Soho	*Korean*	322
£20+	Patty and Bun	*Burgers, etc*	433
	Tommi's Burger Joint	*"*	444
	Homeslice	*Pizza*	544
	Patogh	*Middle Eastern*	444
£15+	Delancey & Co.	*American*	433
	Nordic Bakery	*Scandinavian*	333
£10+	Scandinavian	*Kitchen Scandinavian*	353
	Kaffeine	*Sandwiches, cakes, etc*	455

Belgravia, Pimlico, Victoria & Westminster (SW1, except St James's)

£110+	Marcus	*French*	232
£100+	Dinner	*British, Traditional*	333
	One-O-One	*Fish & seafood*	521
	Pétrus	*French*	343
	Rib Room	*Steaks & grills*	342
£80+	The Goring Hotel	*British, Modern*	355
	The Northall	*"*	344
	Roux at Parliament Square	*"*	553
	Koffmann's	*French*	553
	Zafferano	*Italian*	222
	Ametsa	*Spanish*	442
	Mr Chow	*Chinese*	333
£70+	Adam Handling at Caxton	*British, Modern*	332
	Salmontini	*Fish & seafood*	– – –
	Bar Boulud	*French*	333
	Canvas	*International*	– – –
	Santini	*Italian*	222
	Mari Vanna	*Russian*	234
	M Restaurant Victoria Street	*Steaks & grills*	433
	Hunan	*Chinese*	521
	Amaya	*Indian*	534
	The Cinnamon Club	*"*	334
	Quilon	*Indian, Southern*	442
£60+	Bank Westminster	*British, Modern*	222
	The Botanist	*"*	223
	The Fifth Floor Restaurant	*"*	333

	The Thomas Cubitt	"	344
	Olivomare	*Fish & seafood*	432
	Les Gourmets des Ternes	*French*	223
	La Poule au Pot	"	335
	Motcombs	*International*	233
	Olivocarne	*Italian*	442
	Quirinale	"	332
	Sale e Pepe	"	343
	Signor Sassi	"	334
	Boisdale	*Scottish*	223
	Oliveto	*Pizza*	422
	The Grand Imperial	*Chinese*	332
	Ken Lo's Memories	"	342
	Buddha-Bar London	*Pan-Asian*	333
£50+	Ebury Rest' & Wine Bar	*British, Modern*	233
	The Orange	"	334
	The Pantechnicon	"	334
	Tate Britain (Rex Whistler)	"	235
	Shepherd's	*British, Traditional*	343
	Colbert	*French*	123
	Villandry St James's	"	112
	Caraffini	*Italian*	354
	Il Convivio	"	333
	Olivo	"	342
	Ottolenghi	"	422
	Tinello	"	444
	About Thyme	*Mediterranean*	344
	Bilbao Berria	*Spanish*	223
	Kurobuta Harvey Nics	*Japanese*	423
	Salloos	*Pakistani*	443
£40+	Daylesford Organic	*British, Modern*	213
	The Queens Arms	"	344
	Grumbles	*International*	233
	Como Lario	*Italian*	244
	Gustoso	"	353
	Tozi	"	333
	Goya	*Spanish*	333
	Ibérica	"	334
	Kateh Knightsbridge	*Persian*	542
	Kazan (Café)	*Turkish*	342
£35+	The Vincent Rooms	*British, Modern*	333
	Seafresh	*Fish & chips*	432
	A Wong	*Chinese*	543
£15+	Kanada-Ya	*Japanese*	532

WEST

Chelsea, South Kensington, Kensington, Earl's Court & Fulham (SW3, SW5, SW6, SW7, SW10 & W8)

Price	Restaurant	Cuisine	Rating
£120+	Gordon Ramsay	*French*	343
£90+	Rasoi	*Indian*	423
£80+	Outlaw's Seafood and Grill	Fish & seafood	442
	Toto's	*Italian*	233
	Yashin Ocean House	Japanese	222
	Zuma	"	534
£70+	Babylon	*British, Modern*	234
	The Five Fields	"	555
	Launceston Place	"	454
	maze Grill	"	222
	Medlar	"	443
	Poissonnerie de l'Av.	*Fish & seafood*	333
	Bibendum	*French*	233
	Cheyne Walk Bras'	"	333
	L'Etranger	"	342
	Rivea	*International*	242
	Daphne's	*Italian*	232
	Scalini	"	333
	Min Jiang	*Chinese*	435
	Yashin	*Japanese*	532
£60+	The Abingdon	*British, Modern*	344
	Bluebird	"	123
	Clarke's	"	443
	Harwood Arms	"	533
	Kensington Place	"	333
	Kitchen W8	"	543
	The Terrace	"	344
	Tom's Kitchen	"	121
	Belvedere	*French*	224
	Le Colombier	"	334
	Mazi	*Greek*	334
	Margaux	*International*	323
	Lucio	*Italian*	333
	Manicomio	"	223
	Locanda Ottomezzo	*Mediterranean*	343
	Cambio de Tercio	*Spanish*	333
	Hawksmoor Knightsbridge	*Steaks & grills*	333
	Zaika	*Indian*	333
£50+	Big Easy	*American*	223

	Brinkley's	*British, Modern*	224
	The Enterprise	"	233
	The Ivy Chelsea Garden	"	225
	The Sands End	"	344
	The Admiral Codrington	*British, Traditional*	224
	Bumpkin	"	222
	Ffiona's	"	344
	Maggie Jones's	"	235
	Bibendum Oyster Bar	*Fish & seafood*	242
	Wright Brothers	"	443
	La Brasserie	*French*	224
	Chez Patrick	"	353
	Garnier	"	441
	Eelbrook	*International*	343
	Gallery Mess	"	223
	The Kensington Wine Rms	"	223
	La Famiglia	*Italian*	222
	Frantoio	"	233
	Ottolenghi	"	422
	Pellicanino	"	343
	Il Portico	"	354
	Tartufo	"	442
	Terra Vergine	"	433
	Ziani's	"	333
	The Cross Keys	*Mediterranean*	334
	Polish Club	*Polish*	334
	Tendido Cero	*Spanish*	333
	MacellaioRC	*Steaks & grills*	534
	PJ's Bar and Grill	"	344
	Sophie's Steakhouse	"	222
	Geales Chelsea Green	*Fish & chips*	233
	Maroush	*Lebanese*	322
	Good Earth	*Chinese*	332
	Bombay Brasserie	*Indian*	333
	Masala Grill	"	444
	The Painted Heron	"	443
	Star of India	"	323
	Chisou	*Japanese*	442
	Kurobuta	"	423
	Eight Over Eight	*Pan-Asian*	324
	Patara South Kensington	*Thai*	333
	Sukho Fine Thai Cuisine	"	543
£40+	Bodean's	*American*	223
	The Builders Arms	*British, Modern*	234
	The Butcher's Hook	"	343
	Joe's Brasserie	"	233
	Megan's Delicatessen	"	224
	The Phoenix	"	233
	Rabbit	"	444

	The Shed	"	333
	VQ	"	243
	The Brown Cow	*British, Traditional*	333
	Brasserie Gustave	*French*	453
	Balans	*International*	233
	The Scarsdale	"	234
	Troubadour	"	234
	Aglio e Olio	*Italian*	332
	Buona Sera	"	333
	Da Mario	"	233
	Iddu	"	212
	Made in Italy	"	333
	Nuovi Sapori	"	343
	Obicà	"	332
	Polpo	"	223
	Riccardo's	"	233
	The Atlas	*Mediterranean*	444
	Daquise	*Polish*	222
	Capote Y Toros	*Spanish*	344
	Casa Brindisa	"	232
	Tendido Cuatro	"	232
	La Delizia Limbara	*Pizza*	323
	Royal China	*Chinese*	412
	Malabar	*Indian*	442
	Noor Jahan	"	433
	Thali	"	444
	Tokyo Sukiyaji-Tei & Bar	*Japanese*	— — —
	Bangkok	*Thai*	332
	Suksan	"	443
	Tem Tép	*Vietnamese*	333
£35+	Haché	*Steaks & grills*	334
	Rocca Di Papa	*Pizza*	234
	Rossopomodoro	"	222
	Best Mangal	*Turkish*	432
	Nayaab	*Indian*	432
	Churchill Arms	*Thai*	345
	Rosa's Fulham	"	432
£30+	Kensington Square Kitchen	*British, Modern*	343
	Stock Pot	*International*	222
	Pappa Ciccia	*Italian*	444
	The Greedy Buddha	*Indian*	322
	Bone Daddies	*Japanese*	444
	Kulu Kulu	"	312
	Addie's Thai Café	*Thai*	442
	Taiwan Village	*Taiwanese*	453

£25+	Mona Lisa	*International*	332
	Café 209	*Thai*	233
£20+	Tommi's Burger Joint	*Burgers, etc*	444
	Eat Tokyo	*Japanese*	422

Notting Hill, Holland Park, Bayswater, North Kensington & Maida Vale (W2,W9,W10,W11)

£130+	The Ledbury	*British, Modern*	555
£120+	Marianne	*British, Modern*	454
£70+	Angelus	*French*	353
	Flat Three	*Japanese*	233
£60+	Beach Blanket Babylon	*British, Modern*	113
	The Dock Kitchen	*"*	345
	Julie's	*"*	– – –
	Les Gourmets des Ternes	*French*	223
	Edera	*Italian*	353
	Essenza	*"*	323
	Mediterraneo	*"*	334
	Wormwood	*Mediterranean*	443
	West Thirty Six	*Steaks & grills*	– – –
	E&O	*Pan-Asian*	334
£50+	The Frontline Club	*British, Modern*	333
	The Ladbroke Arms	*"*	434
	The Magazine Restaurant	*"*	345
	Paradise, Kensal Green	*"*	225
	The Truscott Arms	*"*	434
	The Waterway	*"*	234
	Bumpkin	*British, Traditional*	222
	The Summerhouse	*Fish & seafood*	225
	Bel Canto	*French*	244
	The Cow	*Irish*	444
	The Oak	*Italian*	424
	Osteria Basilico	*"*	324
	Ottolenghi	*"*	422
	Portobello Ristorante	*"*	333
	Casa Malevo	*Argentinian*	323
	Maroush Gardens	*Lebanese*	322
	Chakra	*Indian*	312
	Kurobuta	*Japanese*	423
£40+	Pizza Metro	*"*	432
	Electric Diner	*American*	244
	Granger & Co	*Australian*	324

	Daylesford Organic	*British, Modern*	213
	Salt & Honey	*"*	– – –
	Hereford Road	*British, Traditional*	423
	Snaps & Rye	*Danish*	434
	Polpo	*Italian*	223
	Raoul's Café & Deli	*Mediterranean*	223
	John Doe	*Steaks & grills*	433
	Pizza East Portobello	*Pizza*	434
	The Red Pepper	*"*	322
	Casa Cruz South	*American*	– – –
	Kateh	*Persian*	542
	Mandarin Kitchen	*Chinese*	422
	Pearl Liang	*"*	432
	Royal China	*"*	412
	Bombay Palace	*Indian*	542
	Noor Jahan	*"*	433
	Inaho	*Japanese*	515

£35+	Lucky Seven	*American*	333
	Taqueria	*Mexican/TexMex*	433
	Maguro	*Japanese*	343
	C&R Café	*Malaysian*	422
	Satay House	*"*	322
	Banana Tree Canteen	*Pan-Asian*	222

£30+	Alounak	*Persian*	323
	Mandalay	*Burmese*	221
	The Four Seasons	*Chinese*	411
	Gold Mine	*"*	521
	The Heron	*Thai*	521

£25+	Fez Mangal	*Turkish*	543

£20+	Boom Burger	*Burgers, etc*	332
	Khan's	*Indian*	332

£10+	Lisboa Pâtisserie	*Sandwiches, cakes, etc*	335

Hammersmith, Shepherd's Bush, Olympia, Chiswick, Brentford & Ealing (W4,W5,W6,W12,W13,W14,TW8)

£100+	Hedone	*British, Modern*	433
	The River Café	*Italian*	323

£70+	La Trompette	*French*	444

£60+	Le Vacherin	*French*	322
	Villa Di Geggiano	*Italian*	222

Price	Restaurant	Cuisine	Rating
£50+	The Anglesea Arms	*British, Modern*	334
	The Brackenbury	"	343
	Charlotte'sW5	"	344
	High Road Brasserie	"	113
	The Hampshire Hog	*British, Traditional*	223
	Charlotte's Place	*French*	343
	Charlotte'sW4	"	344
	Michael Nadra	"	432
	Cibo	*Italian*	454
	The Oak W12	"	424
£40+	Jackson & Rye Chiswick	*American*	123
	Bush Dining Hall	*British, Modern*	222
	The Carpenter's Arms	"	333
	City Barge	"	333
	The Dartmouth Castle	"	344
	The Dove	"	225
	Duke of Sussex	"	334
	Ealing Park Tavern	"	334
	The Havelock Tavern	"	324
	The Pear Tree	"	334
	Princess Victoria	"	333
	Vinoteca	"	234
	The Andover Arms	*International*	344
	Annie's	"	235
	Balans	"	233
	L'Amorosa	*Italian*	543
	Pentolina	"	454
	Cumberland Arms	*Mediterranean*	443
	The Swan	"	455
	Popeseye	*Steaks & grills*	342
	Smokehouse Chiswick	"	333
	The Gate	*Vegetarian*	423
	Bird in Hand	*Pizza*	333
	Fire & Stone	"	222
	Quantus South	*American*	454
	Azou	*North African*	333
	North China	*Chinese*	432
	Indian Zing	*Indian*	532
	Karma	"	432
	Potli	"	433
£35+	Albertine	*French*	234
	Canta Napoli	*Italian*	332
	Patio	*Polish*	355
	Habanera	*Mexican/TexMex*	323
	Chez Abir	*Lebanese*	432
	Best Mangal	*Turkish*	432
	Shikumen	*Chinese*	522
	Anarkali	*Indian*	342

	Brilliant	"	443
	Madhu's	"	433
	Sagar	"	443
	Kiraku	*Japanese*	532
	Tosa	"	332
	Yoshi Sushi	"	342
	Saigon Saigon	*Vietnamese*	344
	30+ The Italian Job	*Italian*	224
	Santa Maria	*Pizza*	533
	Adams Café	*Moroccan*	353
	Alounak	*Persian*	323
	Shilpa	*Indian, Southern*	542
	Atari-Ya	*Japanese*	532
	Hare & Tortoise	*Pan-Asian*	323
	Esarn Kheaw	*Thai*	441
	101 Thai Kitchen	"	421
£25+	Faanoos	*Persian*	223
£20+	Kerbisher & Malt	*Fish & chips*	332
	Abu Zaad	*Syrian*	332
	Gifto's	*Indian*	432
	Eat Tokyo	*Japanese*	422

NORTH

Hampstead, West Hampstead, St John's Wood, Regent's Park, Kilburn & Camden Town (NW postcodes)

£70+	Landmark (Winter Gdn)	*British, Modern*	234
£60+	The Booking Office	*British, Modern*	224
	Odette's	*"*	333
	Bull & Last	*British, Traditional*	433
	Gilbert Scott	*"*	223
	L'Aventure	*French*	455
	Oslo Court	*"*	354
	Kaifeng	*Chinese*	323
	Gilgamesh	*Pan-Asian*	223
£50+	One Sixty Smokehouse	*American*	443
	Bradley's	*British, Modern*	332
	Crocker's Folly	*"*	223
	Market	*"*	332
	St Pancras Grand	*"*	123
	Michael Nadra	*French*	432
	Mill Lane Bistro	*"*	232
	La Collina	*Italian*	322
	Villa Bianca	*"*	232
	York & Albany	*"*	223
	Manna	*Vegetarian*	332
	Greenberry Café	*Sandwiches, cakes, etc*	223
	Good Earth	*Chinese*	332
	Phoenix Palace	*"*	322
£40+	Belgo Noord	*Belgian*	222
	The Horseshoe	*British, Modern*	323
	The Junction Tavern	*"*	333
	Made In Camden	*"*	222
	Megan's	*"*	224
	The North London Tavern	*"*	333
	Parlour	*"*	444
	The Refinery	*"*	233
	Rising Sun	*"*	343
	Shoe Shop	*"*	542
	The Wells	*"*	224
	The Wet Fish Café	*"*	333
	The Bull & Gate	*British, Traditional*	323
	Lure	*Fish & seafood*	433
	L'Absinthe	*French*	233
	La Cage Imaginaire	*"*	344
	Patron	*"*	334
	Lemonia	*Greek*	245
	Anima e Cuore	*Italian*	432

	Artigiano	"	333
	Ostuni	"	334
	The Salt House	"	333
	Sarracino	"	422
	Harry Morgan's	*Burgers, etc*	221
	Nautilus	*Fish & chips*	441
	The Sea Shell	"	322
	Pizza East	*Pizza*	434
	Zest	*Kosher*	323
	Yasmeen	*Middle Eastern*	– – –
	Gung-Ho	*Chinese*	232
	Jun Ming Xuan	*Chinese, Dim sum*	442
	Namaaste Kitchen	*Indian*	442
	Jin Kichi	*Japanese*	543
	Sushi-Say	"	542
	Singapore Garden	*Malaysian*	433
	XO	*Pan-Asian*	222
£35+	Lantana Cafe	*Australian*	333
	The Truscott Cellar	*British, Traditional*	– – –
	Carob Tree	*Greek*	454
	Giacomo's	*Italian*	453
	El Parador	*Spanish*	454
	Haché	*Steaks & grills*	334
	L' Antica Pizzeria	*Pizza*	433
	Rossopomodoro	"	222
	Sacro Cuore	"	433
	Green Cottage	*Chinese*	322
	Great Nepalese	*Indian*	332
	Woodlands	"	322
	Asakusa	*Japanese*	532
	The Petite Coree	*Korean*	542
	The Banana Tree Canteen	*Pan-Asian*	222
£30+	L'Artista	*Italian*	244
	La Porchetta Pizzeria	"	233
	Skipjacks	*Fish & chips*	443
	Kenwood (Brew House)	*Sandwiches, cakes, etc*	224
	Chicken Shop	*Chicken*	344
	Ariana II	*Afghani*	432
	Chutneys	*Indian*	222
	Guglee	"	333
	Paradise Hampstead	"	454
	Ravi Shankar	"	322
	Vijay	"	341
	Atari-Ya	*Japanese*	532
£25+	The Little Bay	*Mediterranean*	235
	Poppies Camden	*Fish & chips*	434
	Diwana B-P House	*Indian*	321

£20+	Ali Baba	*Egyptian*	323
	Kadiri's	*Indian*	432
	Eat Tokyo	*Japanese*	422
	Roti King	*Malaysian*	511
£15+	Ginger & White	*Sandwiches, cakes, etc*	333
£10+	Dirty Burger	*Burgers, etc*	322

Hoxton, Islington, Highgate, Crouch End, Stoke Newington, Finsbury Park, Muswell Hill & Finchley (N postcodes)

£60+	Frederick's	*British, Modern*	224
	Plum + Spilt Milk	*"*	233
	The Almeida	*French*	222
	Fifteen Restaurant	*Italian*	122
£50+	The Drapers Arms	*British, Modern*	223
	Grain Store	*"*	223
	The Haven	*"*	222
	Pig & Butcher	*"*	444
	Rotunda Bar & Restaurant	*"*	223
	Bistro Aix	*French*	442
	The Greek Larder	*Greek*	332
	Ottolenghi	*Italian*	422
	Trullo	*"*	443
	Foxlow	*Steaks & grills*	333
	The Smokehouse Islington	*"*	333
	Duke's Brew & Que	*"*	323
£40+	Red Dog Saloon	*American*	323
	Granger & Co	*Australian*	324
	Sunday	*"*	433
	The Albion	*British, Modern*	213
	Bald Faced Stag	*"*	333
	The Bull	*"*	234
	Caravan King's Cross	*"*	323
	Heirloom	*"*	343
	Oldroyd	*"*	– – –
	Season Kitchen	*"*	333
	White Rabbit	*"*	434
	St Johns	*British, Traditional*	435
	Kipferl	*Mittel-European*	333
	Prawn On The Lawn	*Fish & seafood*	443
	Banners	*International*	345
	8 Hoxton Square	*"*	443
	The Orange Tree	*"*	223
	Primeur	*"*	433
	500	*Italian*	342

	Osteria Tufo	"	453
	Pizzeria Oregano	"	443
	San Daniele	"	343
	Vinoteca	*Mediterranean*	234
	Café del Parc	*Spanish*	543
	Camino	"	333
	Trangallan	"	544
	Popeseye	*Steaks & grills*	342
	Toff's	*Fish & chips*	432
	Two Brothers	"	332
	Vintage Salt	"	443
	Sweet Thursday	*Pizza*	333
	Le Coq	*Chicken*	232
	Yipin China	*Chinese*	221
	Dishoom	*Indian*	434
	Roots at N1	"	553
	Zaffrani	"	322
	Isarn	*Thai*	432
	Yum Yum	"	344
£35+	Le Sacré-Coeur	*French*	334
	Vrisaki	*Greek*	332
	Pizzeria Pappagone	*Italian*	344
	Rugoletta	"	333
	Bar Esteban	*Spanish*	534
	La Bota	"	334
	MEATLiquor Islington	*Burgers, etc*	324
	Il Bacio	*Pizza*	333
	Fabrizio	"	242
	Rossopomodoro	"	222
	Bird Islington	*Chicken*	332
	Gallipoli	*Turkish*	343
	Mangal II	"	432
	Little Georgia Café	*Georgian*	334
	Delhi Grill	*Indian*	443
	Indian Rasoi	"	433
	Rasa Travancore	*Indian, Southern*	433
£30+	Le Mercury	*French*	234
	La Porchetta Pizzeria	*Italian*	233
	Meat Mission	*Burgers, etc*	334
	Olympus Fish	*Fish & chips*	452
	Durum Ocakbasi	*Turkish*	322
	Gem	"	444
	Gökyüzü	"	433
	Izgara	"	322
	Jashan	*Indian*	542
	Atari-Ya	*Japanese*	532
	Salvation In Noodles	*Vietnamese*	322

£25+	Chriskitch	*British, Modern*	442
	Afghan Kitchen	*Afghani*	421
	Abi Ruchi	*Indian*	442
	Rani	*"*	322
	Dotori	*Korean*	432
£20+	Max's Sandwich Shop	*Sandwiches, cakes, etc*	422
£15+	Friends of Ours	*Australian*	442
	Piebury Corner	*British, Traditional*	433
	Chilango	*Mexican/TexMex*	332
£10+	Five Guys Islington	*Burgers, etc*	222
	Indian Veg	*Indian*	433

SOUTH

South Bank (SE1)

£100+	Story	British, Modern	543
£80+	Oblix	American	224
	Aqua Shard	British, Modern	114
	Oxo Tower (Rest')	"	111
	Le Pont de la Tour	"	224
	Ting	International	224
	Hutong	Chinese	224
£70+	Skylon	British, Modern	122
	Roast	British, Traditional	222
	La Barca	Italian	232
	Oxo Tower (Brass')	Mediterranean	112
£60+	Sea Containers	British, Modern	233
	Skylon Grill	"	113
	The Swan at the Globe	"	212
	Tentazioni	Italian	223
£50+	Albion	British, Modern	122
	Elliot's Café	"	223
	The Garrison	"	333
	House Restaurant	"	232
	Magdalen	"	443
	Menier Chocolate Factory	"	123
	RSJ	"	332
	Tate Modern (Level 7)	"	214
	Union Street Café	"	222
	Waterloo Bar & Kitchen	"	222
	The Anchor & Hope	British, Traditional	433
	Butlers W'f Chop-house	"	233
	fish!	Fish & seafood	322
	Wright Brothers	"	443
	Champor-Champor	Fusion	334
	Village East	"	333
	Brigade	International	233
	Rabot 1745	"	223
	Vivat Bacchus	"	222
	Zucca	Italian	443
	Baltic	Polish	333
	Pizarro	Spanish	344
	Archduke Wine Bar	Steaks & grills	222
£40+	Blueprint Café	British, Modern	235
	Edwins	"	333
	40 Maltby Street	"	434

	The Green Room	"	222
	Canteen	*British, Traditional*	221
	Applebee's Café	*Fish & seafood*	443
	Boro Bistro	*French*	333
	Casse-Croute	"	444
	The Rooftop Café	*International*	335
	Antico	*Italian*	343
	Camino	*Spanish*	333
	José	"	555
	Meson don Felipe	"	223
	Tapas Brindisa	"	333
	Arabica Bar and Kitchen	*Lebanese*	323
	Tas Pide	*Turkish*	233
	Bengal Clipper	*Indian*	322
£35+	The Table	*British, Modern*	333
	Pulia	*Italian*	– – –
	Ceru	*Mediterranean*	333
	Gourmet Pizza Co.	*Pizza*	333
	Caffé Vergnano	*Sandwiches, cakes, etc*	223
£30+	Vapiano	*Italian*	322
	Mar I Terra	*Spanish*	232
	El Vergel South	*American*	444
	Tonkotsu Bankside	*Japanese*	443
£25+	Masters Super Fish	*Fish & chips*	422
	Kitchen	*Sandwiches, cakes, etc*	222
£20+	Konditor & Cook	*Sandwiches, cakes, etc*	332
£10+	Monmouth Coffee Co	*Sandwiches, cakes, etc*	554

Greenwich, Lewisham, Dulwich & Blackheath
(All SE postcodes, except SE1)

£60+	Craft London	*British, Modern*	224
	Lobster Pot	*Fish & seafood*	433
£50+	The Camberwell Arms	*British, Modern*	433
	Chapters	"	332
	Franklins	"	434
	The Palmerston	"	433
	Rivington Grill	"	333
	Buenos Aires Café	*Argentinian*	343
	Babur	*Indian*	554
	Yama Momo	*Japanese*	433
£40+	The Crooked Well	*British, Modern*	344

	Inside	"	441
	The Lido Café	"	334
	Peckham Refreshment Rms	"	323
	Brasserie Toulouse-Lautrec	*French*	333
	Toasted	"	233
	Joanna's	*International*	334
	Tulse Hill Hotel	"	333
	The Yellow House	"	332
	Artusi	*Italian*	432
	Lorenzo	"	223
	Peckham Bazaar	*Mediterranean*	444
	Angels & Gypsies	*Spanish*	333
	Cau	*Steaks & grills*	433
	Bianco43	*Pizza*	322
	Ganapati	*Indian*	544
	Kennington Tandoori	"	333
	Sticks'n'Sushi	*Japanese*	333
£35+	The Lord Northbrook	*British, Traditional*	444
	Pedler	*Fusion*	324
	Le Querce	*Italian*	443
	The Sea Cow	*Fish & chips*	332
	Rocca Di Papa	*Pizza*	234
	Yalla Yalla	*Lebanese*	334
	Dragon Castle	*Chinese*	332
	Everest Inn	*Indian*	453
	Tandoori Nights	"	433
	The Begging Bowl	*Thai*	333
£30+	The Gowlett	*Pizza*	434
	Zaibatsu	*Japanese*	442
£25+	Rox Burger	*Burgers, etc*	433
	Mamma Dough	*Pizza*	333
	FM Mangal	*Turkish*	322
£20+	Silk Road	*Chinese*	522
	Café East	*Vietnamese*	422
£10+	Monmouth Coffee Company	*Sandwiches, cakes, etc*	554
£5+	Kappacasein	*Sandwiches, cakes, etc*	532

Battersea, Brixton, Clapham, Wandsworth
Barnes, Putney & Wimbledon
(All SW postcodes south of the river)

£60+	Hotel du Vin	*British, Modern*	233
	Chez Bruce	"	554

	Trinity	"	554
	The White Onion	*French*	443
	London House	*International*	332
	Enoteca Turi	*Italian*	443
	Riva	"	442
£50+	Abbeville Kitchen	*British, Modern*	333
	The Brown Dog	"	334
	Claude's Kitchen	"	444
	Lamberts	"	554
	The Lucky Pig Fulham	"	– – –
	The Manor	"	543
	Olympic Café	"	224
	Sonny's Kitchen	"	222
	Source	"	224
	The Tommy Tucker	"	334
	The Victoria	"	344
	Fox & Grapes	*British, Traditional*	222
	Soif	*French*	333
	The Light House	*International*	222
	The Ship	"	334
	Bibo	*Italian*	443
	Numero Uno	"	444
	Alquimia	*Spanish*	342
	Cornish Tiger	*Steaks & grills*	333
	Fulham Wine Rooms	*Sandwiches, cakes, etc*	334
	Good Earth	*Chinese*	332
	Kishmish	*Indian*	443
	Blue Elephant	*Thai*	223
	Suk Saran	"	332
£40+	Bodean's	*American*	223
	Red Dog South	"	323
	Bistro Union	*British, Modern*	343
	Brunswick House Café	"	225
	Counter	"	222
	The Dairy	"	543
	The Depot	"	225
	Earl Spencer	"	423
	Emile's	"	342
	Hood	"	442
	Manuka Kitchen	"	444
	The Prince Of Wales	"	434
	The Tree House	"	333
	Wimsey's	"	333
	Canton Arms	*British, Traditional*	324
	Jolly Gardners	"	433
	Augustine Kitchen	*French*	341
	Bellevue Rendez-Vous	"	333
	Bistrò by Shot	*Fusion*	343

	Queenswood	"	223
	Annie's	*International*	235
	The Plough	"	344
	Buona Sera	*Italian*	333
	Donna Margherita	"	433
	Ost.Antica Bologna	"	433
	Pizza Metro	"	432
	Sapori Sardi	"	442
	The Bobbin	*Mediterranean*	343
	The Fox & Hounds	"	444
	Brindisa Food Rooms	*Spanish*	333
	Gremio de Brixton	"	324
	Lola Rojo	"	434
	Butcher & Grill	*Steaks & grills*	223
	Cau	"	433
	Naughty Piglets	"	452
	Popeseye	"	342
	Fish Club	*Fish & chips*	422
	Indian Zilla	*Indian*	332
	Kricket	"	– – –
	Ma Goa	"	442
	Sticks'n'Sushi	*Japanese*	333
	Tsunami	"	533
£35+	Gazette	*French*	244
	MOMMI	*Fusion*	– – –
	Brew	*International*	223
	Fish in a Tie	*Mediterranean*	243
	Haché	*Burgers, etc*	334
	Eco	*Pizza*	224
	Rossopomodoro	"	222
	Dalchini	*Chinese*	342
	Indian Moment	*Indian*	343
	Hashi	*Japanese*	443
	Cah-Chi	*Korean*	332
	The Banana Tree Canteen	*Pan-Asian*	222
£30+	Fields	*British, Modern*	– – –
	Boqueria	*Spanish*	344
	Brady's	*Fish & chips*	333
	Al Forno	*Pizza*	244
	Chicken & Egg Shop	*Chicken*	344
	Meza Trinity Road	*Lebanese*	532
	Indian Ocean	*Indian*	453
	Hare & Tortoise	*Pan-Asian*	323
	The Pepper Tree	*Thai*	333
	Talad Thai	"	431
	Mien Tay	*Vietnamese*	311

£25+	The Joint	*American*	532
	Dip & Flip	*Burgers, etc*	422
	Mamma Dough	*Pizza*	333
	Orange Pekoe	*Sandwiches, cakes, etc*	344
	Faanoos	*Persian*	223
	Radha Krishna Bhaven	*Indian*	332
	Sree Krishna	"	432
	Mirch Masala SW17	*Pakistani*	521
	Awesome Thai	*Thai*	342
	Kaosarn	"	343
£20+	Boom Burger	*Burgers, etc*	332
	Kerbisher & Malt	*Fish & chips*	332
	Apollo Banana Leaf	*Indian*	421
	Hot Stuff	"	442
	Lahore Karahi	*Pakistani*	412
	Lahore Kebab House	"	412
£15+	Grind Coffee Bar	*Sandwiches, cakes, etc*	424
	Jaffna House	*Indian*	542
£10+	Flotsam and Jetsam	*Australian*	434
	Dirty Burger	*Burgers, etc*	322
	Milk	*Sandwiches, cakes, etc*	444

Outer western suburbs
Kew, Richmond,Twickenham,Teddington

£70+	The Glasshouse	*British, Modern*	443
	Petersham Nurseries	"	224
£60+	The Bingham	*British, Modern*	324
	The Dysart Petersham	"	443
	Petersham Hotel	"	345
	Al Boccon di'vino	*Italian*	445
£50+	Linnea	*British, Modern*	443
	A Cena	*Italian*	444
£40+	Jackson & Rye Richmond	*American*	123
	La Buvette	*French*	334
	Ma Cuisine	"	222
	Le Salon Privé	"	345
	Bacco	*Italian*	343
	Pizzeria Rustica	*Pizza*	443
	Matsuba	*Japanese*	443
£35+	Canta Napoli	*Italian*	332

EAST

Smithfield & Farringdon (EC1)

Price	Restaurant	Cuisine	Rating
£90+	The Clove Club	*British, Modern*	433
£70+	Club Gascon	*French*	333
	Smiths (Top Floor)	*Steaks & grills*	334
£60+	Bird of Smithfield	*British, Modern*	223
	Chiswell Street Dining Rms	"	222
	The Jugged Hare	"	323
	St John	*British, Traditional*	543
	Bleeding Heart Restaurant	*French*	335
	Moro	*Spanish*	543
£50+	The Modern Pantry	*British, Modern*	334
	Tonic & Remedy	"	– – –
	Bonnie Gull Seafood Bar	*Fish & seafood*	332
	Café du Marché	*French*	334
	Fabrizio	*Italian*	442
	Foxlow	*Steaks & grills*	333
	Hix	"	333
	Smiths (Dining Rm)	"	222
	Sushi Tetsu	*Japanese*	553
£40+	Bodean's	*American*	223
	Granger & Co	*Australian*	324
	Blackfoot	*British, Modern*	333
	Caravan	"	323
	Vinoteca	"	234
	The Fox and Anchor	*British, Traditional*	334
	The Quality Chop House	"	353
	Café Pistou	*French*	323
	Comptoir Gascon	"	333
	Enoteca Rabezzana	*Italian*	223
	Polpo	"	223
	Santore	"	433
	Ibérica	*Spanish*	334
	The Gate	*Vegetarian*	423
	Burger & Lobster	*Burgers, etc*	323
	Workshop Coffee Holborn	*Sandwiches, cakes, etc*	344
	Ceviche Old St	*Peruvian*	344
£35+	Lantana Café	*Australian*	333
	Apulia	*Italian*	332
	Morito	*Spanish*	432
	Amico Bio	*Vegetarian*	232
	Pham Sushi	*Japanese*	531
	Tajima Tei	"	433

	On The Bab	*Korean*	432
	Banana Tree Canteen	*Pan-Asian*	222
	Cây Tre	*Vietnamese*	323
£30+	Smiths (Ground Floor)	*British, Modern*	223
	Fish Central	*Fish & seafood*	332
	Cellar Gascon	*French*	333
	Kolossi Grill	*Greek*	343
	La Porchetta Pizzeria	*Italian*	233
	The Eagle	*Mediterranean*	435
	Bone Daddies	*Japanese*	444
£25+	The Little Bay	*Mediterranean*	235
£20+	Kerbisher & Malt	*Fish & chips*	332
£15+	Department of Coffee	*Sandwiches, cakes, etc*	445
	Daddy Donkey	*Mexican/TexMex*	432
	Yum Bun	*Japanese*	52 –
£10+	Nusa Kitchen	*Sandwiches, cakes, etc*	443
	Prufrock Coffee	"	344
	Chifafa	*Turkish*	433

The City (EC2, EC3, EC4)

£70+	City Social	*British, Modern*	335
	Angler	*Fish & seafood*	444
	M Raw Threadneedle Street	"	433
	Sweetings	"	223
	Coq d'Argent	*French*	233
	Lutyens	"	222
	Sauterelle	"	333
	L'Anima	*Italian*	333
	M Grill Threadneedle Street	*Steaks & grills*	433
	HKK	*Chinese*	543
	Yauatcha City	"	523
	Sushisamba	*Japanese*	335
£60+	The Botanist	*British, Modern*	223
	Bread Street Kitchen	"	111
	The Chancery	"	443
	Darwin Brasserie	"	223
	The Don	"	333
	Duck & Waffle	"	225
	High Timber	"	223
	The Mercer	"	222
	I Lombard Street	"	233
	3 South Place	"	323

	The White Swan	"	343
	Chamberlain's	*Fish & seafood*	343
	Caravaggio	*Italian*	332
	Gatti's City Point	"	343
	Manicomio	"	223
	Boisdale of Bishopsgate	*Scottish*	222
	Eyre Brothers	*Spanish*	533
	Barbecoa	*Steaks & grills*	121
	Goodman City	"	443
	Hawksmoor	"	333
	Vanilla Black	*Vegetarian*	432
	Chinese Cricket Club	*Chinese*	431
£50+	The Hoxton Grill	*American*	234
	Gin Joint	*British, Modern*	233
	Merchants Tavern	"	334
	Modern Pantry	"	334
	Northbank	"	344
	Princess of Shoreditch	"	344
	Rivington Grill	"	333
	The Sign of The Don	"	244
	Paternoster Chop House	*British, Traditional*	332
	The Royal Exchange	*French*	224
	28-50	"	334
	Vivat Bacchus	*International*	222
	Taberna Etrusca	*Italian*	244
	José Pizarro	*Spanish*	443
	The Jones Family Project	*Steaks & grills*	243
	New Street Grill	"	233
	The Tramshed	"	223
	Cinnamon Kitchen	*Indian*	422
	Mint Leaf	"	332
	City Miyama	*Japanese*	342
£40+	Bodean's	*American*	223
	The Anthologist	*British, Modern*	223
	Bad Egg	"	433
	Café Below	"	334
	The Trading House	"	– – –
	George & Vulture	*British, Traditional*	225
	Fish Market	*Fish & seafood*	333
	Orpheus	"	431
	L'Anima Café	*Italian*	444
	Rucoletta	"	432
	Rocket Bishopgate	*Mediterranean*	333
	Camino Blackfriars	*Spanish*	333
	Relais de Venise L'Entrecôte	*Steaks & grills*	322
	Burger & Lobster	*Burgers, etc*	323
	Vintage Salt	*Fish & chips*	443
	Shoryu Ramen	*Japanese*	422

£35+	Simpson's Tavern	*British, Traditional*	245
	Restaurant de Paul	*French*	443
	Haché	*Burgers, etc*	334
	Caffé Vergnano	*Sandwiches, cakes, etc*	223
	Haz	*Turkish*	232
	Beer and Buns	*Japanese*	– – –
	K10, Appold Street	"	332
£30+	The Wine Library	*International*	144
	Hare & Tortoise	*Pan-Asian*	323
£25+	Hilliard	*British, Modern*	443
	Bibimbap	*Korean*	322
£20+	Patty and Bun	*Burgers, etc*	433
	Konditor & Cook	*Sandwiches, cakes, etc*	332
£15+	Street Kitchen (van)	*British, Modern*	33 –
	Chilango	*Mexican/TexMex*	332
	City Càphê	*Vietnamese*	522
£10+	Coco Di Mama	*Italian*	342
	Nusa Kitchen	*Middle Eastern*	443
£5+	Pilpel	*Middle Eastern*	442

East End & Docklands (All E postcodes)

£80+	Galvin La Chapelle	*French*	445
	Typing Room	*International*	543
	Roka	*Japanese*	433
£70+	Plateau	*French*	233
£60+	Beach Blanket Babylon	*British, Modern*	113
	The Boundary	"	335
	Lyle's	"	553
	Tom's Kitchen	"	121
	Boisdale of Canary Wharf	*Scottish*	333
	Goodman	*Steaks & grills*	443
	Hawksmoor	"	333
£50+	Big Easy	*American*	223
	One Sixty Smokehouse	"	443
	The Gun	*British, Modern*	324
	Hoi Polloi	"	234
	Jones & Sons	"	444
	The Morgan Arms	"	433
	The Narrow	"	113

	Restaurant	Cuisine	Ratings
	One Canada Square	"	2 2 2
	The Richmond	"	4 3 3
	Rochelle Canteen	"	4 3 3
	Smith's Of Ongar	"	3 3 4
	Albion	British, Traditional	1 2 2
	Bumpkin	"	2 2 2
	The Marksman	"	– – –
	St John Bread & Wine	"	5 3 3
	Wright Brothers	Fish & seafood	4 4 3
	Brawn	French	5 4 4
	Blixen	International	3 2 3
	Mission	"	2 3 4
	Il Bordello	Italian	3 5 4
	Buen Ayre	Argentinian	5 3 3
	Ottolenghi	Israeli	4 2 2
	Café Spice Namaste	Indian	4 4 3

	Restaurant	Cuisine	Ratings
£40+	Balans	British, Modern	2 3 3
	Beagle	"	4 3 3
	Cafe Football	"	2 3 3
	The Culpepper	"	4 3 4
	The Empress	"	4 4 4
	Paradise Garage	"	– – –
	Resident Of Paradise Row	"	– – –
	Canteen	British, Traditional	2 2 1
	The Grapes	Fish & seafood	2 3 5
	Jago	Fusion	3 2 3
	Hungry Donkey	Greek	– – –
	Verden	International	4 4 4
	Lardo & Lardo Bebè	Italian	3 3 4
	Obicà	"	3 3 2
	Rotorino	"	3 3 3
	Verdi's	"	4 4 3
	Rocket Canary Wharf	Mediterranean	3 3 3
	Corner Room	Portuguese	3 4 4
	Taberna Do Mercado	"	4 3 3
	Bravas	Spanish	3 3 3
	Ibérica	"	3 3 4
	Cau	Steaks & grills	4 3 3
	Hill & Szrok	"	5 4 4
	Relais de Venise L'Entrecôte	"	3 2 2
	Ark Fish	Fish & chips	4 4 2
	Pizza East	Pizza	4 3 4
	Berber & Q	Middle Eastern	4 3 4
	Royal China	Chinese	4 1 2
	Sichuan Folk	"	4 4 2
	Yi-Ban	"	4 3 2
	Dishoom	Indian	4 3 4
	Sticks'n'Sushi	Japanese	3 3 3
	Viet Grill	Vietnamese	4 3 3

Price	Restaurant	Cuisine	Rating
£35+	Eat 17	*British, Modern*	342
	Sager & Wilde	*"*	344
	Provender	*French*	443
	Amaru	*Fusion*	– – –
	Eat 17	*International*	342
	Copita Del Mercado	*Spanish*	432
	Bird	*Chicken*	332
	Andina	*Peruvian*	344
	Haz	*Turkish*	232
	Shanghai	*Chinese*	323
	Little Georgia Café	*Georgian*	334
	Ippudo London	*Japanese*	232
	Rosa's Soho	*Thai*	432
	Som Saa	*"*	533
£30+	Luppolo	*Italian*	– – –
	Caboose	*Burgers, etc*	– – –
	Chick 'n' Sours	*Chicken*	424
	Chicken Shop & Dirty Burger	*"*	344
	DF Mexico	*Mexican/TexMex*	433
	Mangal 1	*Turkish*	544
	Tonkotsu East	*Japanese*	443
	Tayyabs	*Pakistani*	423
	Mien Tay	*Vietnamese*	311
	Sông Quê	*"*	212
£25+	Poppies	*Fish & chips*	434
	Gourmet San	*Chinese*	421
	Needoo	*Pakistani*	422
£20+	Shake Shack	*Burgers, etc*	322
	Lahore Kebab House	*Pakistani*	412
£15+	E Pellicci	*Italian*	345
	Bleecker Street Burger	*Burgers, etc*	432
	Chilango	*Mexican/TexMex*	332
£10+	Dirty Burger Shoreditch	*Burgers, etc*	322
	The Rib Man	*"*	53–
£5+	Brick Lane Beigel Bake	*Sandwiches, cakes, etc*	421
	Pilpel	*Middle Eastern*	442

Le Gavroche

Rules

LONDON MAPS

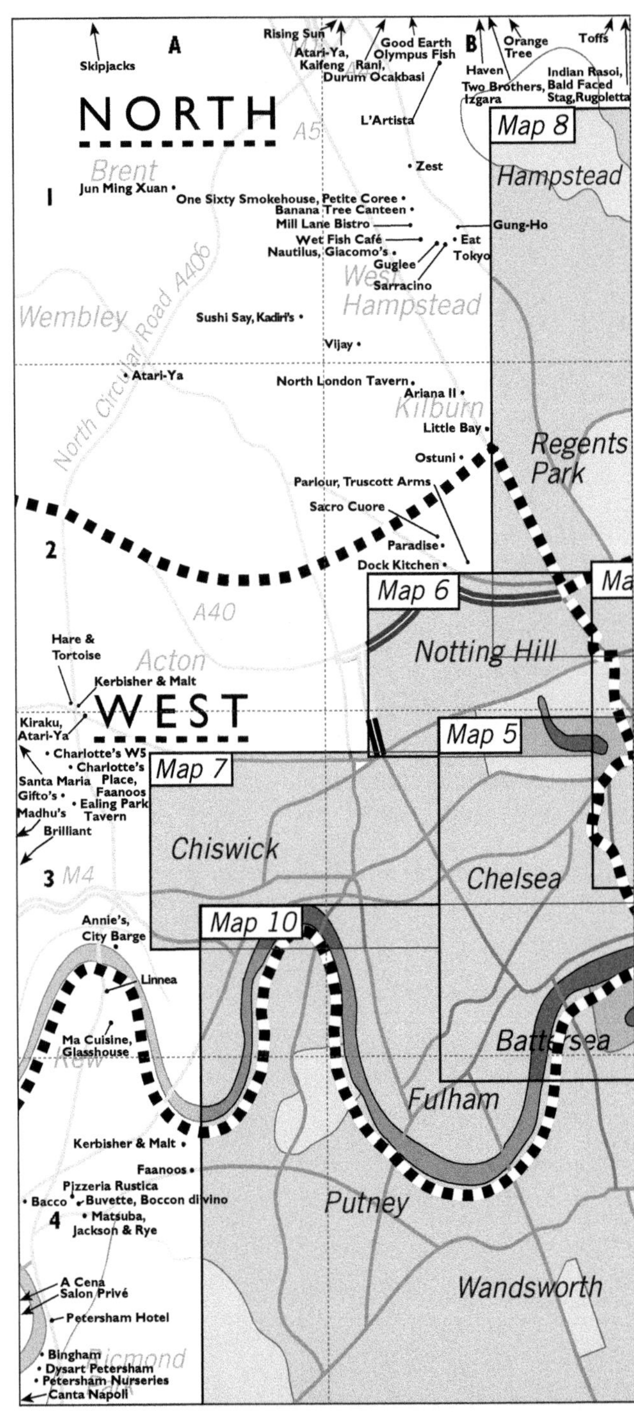
A
B
Skipjacks
Rising Sun
Atari-Ya,
Kaifeng
Rani,
Durum Ocakbasi
Good Earth
Olympus Fish
Haven
Two Brothers,
Izgara
Orange
Tree
Toffs
Indian Rasoi,
Bald Faced
Stag,Rugoletta
NORTH
A5
L'Artista
Map 8
Hampstead
Zest
Brent
1
Jun Ming Xuan
One Sixty Smokehouse, Petite Coree
Banana Tree Canteen
Mill Lane Bistro
Gung-Ho
Wet Fish Café
Eat
Tokyo
Nautilus, Giacomo's
Guglee
Sarracino
West
Hampstead
Wembley
North Circular Road A406
Sushi Say, Kadiri's
Vijay
Atari-Ya
North London Tavern
Ariana II
Kilburn
Little Bay
Regents
Park
Ostuni
Parlour, Truscott Arms
Sacro Cuore
2
Paradise
Dock Kitchen
Map 6
A40
Notting Hill
Hare &
Tortoise
Acton
Kerbisher & Malt
WEST
Kiraku,
Atari-Ya
Map 5
Charlotte's W5
Charlotte's
Place,
Faanoos
Santa Maria
Gifto's
Madhu's
Ealing Park
Tavern
Brilliant
Map 7
Chiswick
3
M4
Chelsea
Annie's,
City Barge
Map 10
Linnea
Ma Cuisine,
Glasshouse
Kew
Battersea
Fulham
Kerbisher & Malt
Faanoos
Pizzeria Rustica
Bacco
Buvette, Boccon di vino
4
Matsuba,
Jackson & Rye
Putney
Wandsworth
A Cena
Salon Privé
Petersham Hotel
Bingham
Dysart Petersham
Petersham Nurseries
Canta Napoli
Ricmond

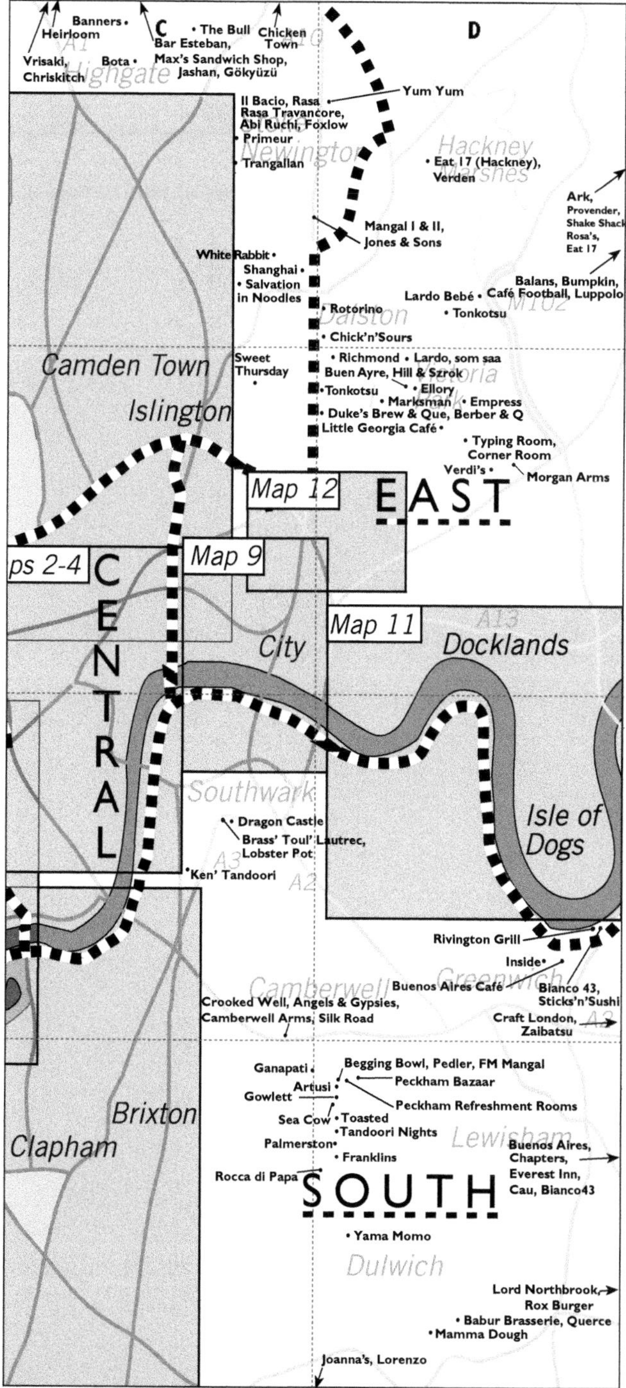
C
D
Banners
Heirloom
Vrisaki, Chriskitch
Bota
The Bull
Bar Esteban, Max's Sandwich Shop, Jashan, Gökyüzü
Chicken Town
Highgate
Yum Yum
Il Bacio, Rasa Rasa Travancore, Abi Ruchi, Foxlow
Primeur
Trangallan
Newington
Hackney Marshes
Eat 17 (Hackney), Verden
Ark, Provender, Shake Shack Rosa's, Eat 17
Mangal I & II, Jones & Sons
White Rabbit
Shanghai
Salvation in Noodles
Balans, Bumpkin, Café Football, Luppolo
Lardo Bebé
Rotorino
Dalston
Tonkotsu
Chick'n'Sours
Camden Town
Sweet Thursday
Richmond
Lardo, som saa
Buen Ayre, Hill & Szrok
Victoria Park
Tonkotsu
Ellory
Marksman
Empress
Duke's Brew & Que, Berber & Q
Little Georgia Café
Islington
Typing Room, Corner Room
Verdi's
Morgan Arms
Map 12
EAST
ps 2-4
Map 9
CENTRAL
Map 11
City
Docklands
Southwark
Dragon Castle
Brass' Toul' Lautrec, Lobster Pot
Isle of Dogs
Ken' Tandoori
Rivington Grill
Inside
Buenos Aires Café
Greenwich
Bianco 43, Sticks'n'Sushi
Camberwell
Crooked Well, Angels & Gypsies, Camberwell Arms, Silk Road
Craft London, Zaibatsu
Ganapati
Begging Bowl, Pedler, FM Mangal
Artusi
Peckham Bazaar
Gowlett
Peckham Refreshment Rooms
Brixton
Sea Cow
Toasted
Tandoori Nights
Lewisham
Clapham
Palmerston
Franklins
Buenos Aires, Chapters, Everest Inn, Cau, Bianco43
Rocca di Papa
SOUTH
Yama Momo
Dulwich
Lord Northbrook, Rox Burger
Babur Brasserie, Querce
Mamma Dough
Joanna's, Lorenzo

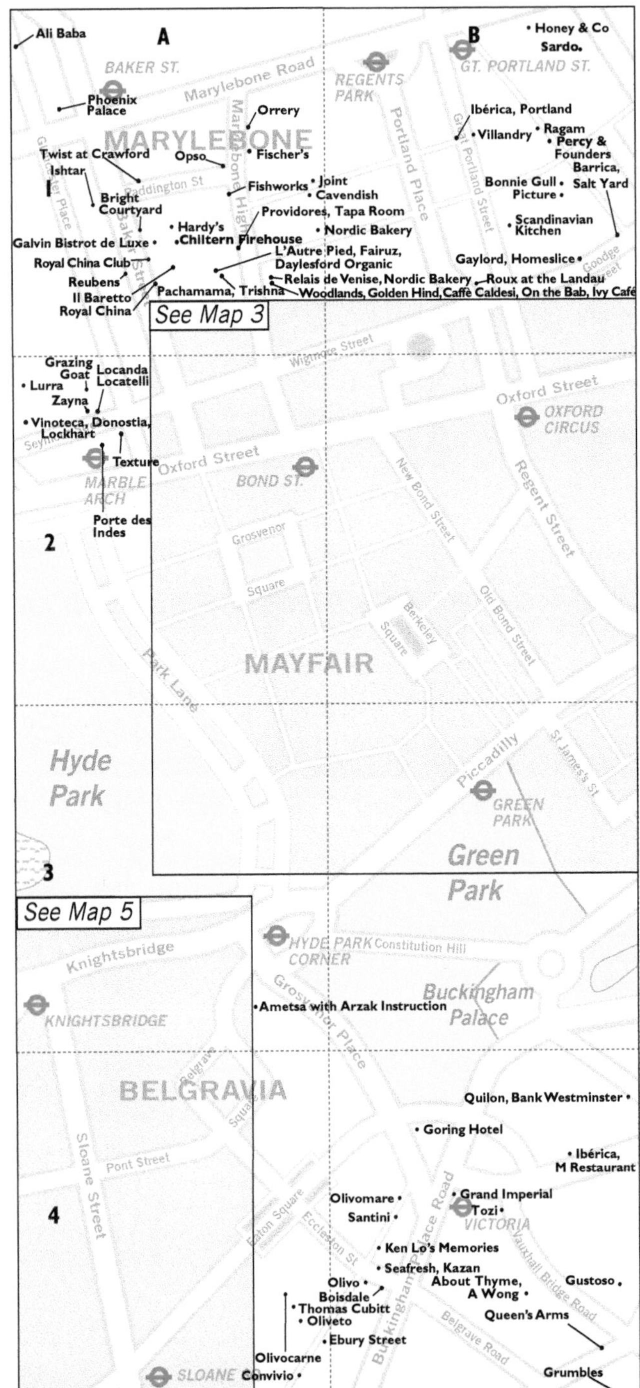

A
B
1
2
3
4
Ali Baba
BAKER ST.
Marylebone Road
Phoenix Palace
MARYLEBONE
Orrery
Opso
Fischer's
Twist at Crawford
Ishtar
Bright Courtyard
Paddington St
Fishworks
Joint
Cavendish
Providores, Tapa Room
Nordic Bakery
Hardy's
Chiltern Firehouse
Galvin Bistrot de Luxe
L'Autre Pied, Fairuz, Daylesford Organic
Royal China Club
Reubens
Il Baretto
Royal China
Pachamama, Trishna
Relais de Venise, Nordic Bakery
Woodlands, Golden Hind, Caffè Caldesi, On the Bab, Ivy Café
Roux at the Landau
Gaylord, Homeslice
REGENTS PARK
Portland Place
GT. PORTLAND ST.
Great Portland Street
Honey & Co
Sardo.
Ibérica, Portland
Villandry
Ragam
Percy & Founders
Barrica, Salt Yard
Bonnie Gull
Picture
Scandinavian Kitchen
Goodge Street
See Map 3
Wigmore Street
Oxford Street
OXFORD CIRCUS
Grazing Goat
Lurra
Locanda Locatelli
Zayna
Vinoteca, Donostia, Lockhart
Texture
MARBLE ARCH
Porte des Indes
BOND ST.
Grosvenor Square
New Bond Street
Regent Street
Old Bond Street
Berkeley Square
MAYFAIR
Park Lane
Hyde Park
Piccadilly
St James's St
GREEN PARK
Green Park
See Map 5
HYDE PARK CORNER
Constitution Hill
Knightsbridge
KNIGHTSBRIDGE
Ametsa with Arzak Instruction
Grosvenor Place
Buckingham Palace
BELGRAVIA
Belgrave Square
Quilon, Bank Westminster
Goring Hotel
Ibérica, M Restaurant
Sloane Street
Pont Street
Olivomare
Santini
Grand Imperial
Tozi
VICTORIA
Eaton Square
Eccleston St
Buckingham Palace Road
Ken Lo's Memories
Seafresh, Kazan
Vauxhall Bridge Road
Olivo
Boisdale
About Thyme, A Wong
Gustoso
Thomas Cubitt
Oliveto
Queen's Arms
Belgrave Road
Ebury Street
Olivocarne
SLOANE
Convivio
Grumbles

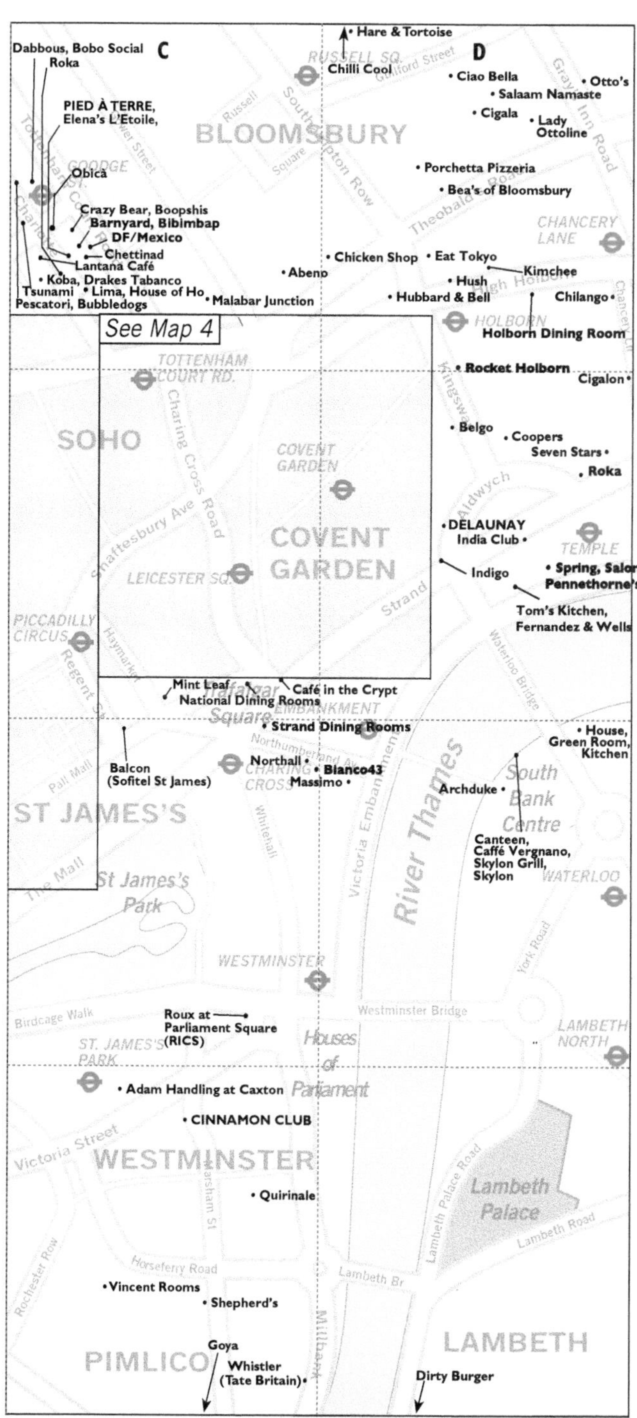
C
D
Dabbous, Bobo Social
Roka
PIED À TERRE,
Elena's L'Etoile,
Obica
Crazy Bear, Boopshis
Barnyard, Bibimbap
DF/Mexico
Chettinad
Lantana Café
Koba, Drakes Tabanco
Tsunami
Lima, House of Ho
Pescatori, Bubbledogs
Malabar Junction
Hare & Tortoise
Chilli Cool
Ciao Bella
Otto's
Salaam Namaste
Cigala
Lady Ottoline
Porchetta Pizzeria
Bea's of Bloomsbury
Chicken Shop
Eat Tokyo
Abeno
Kimchee
Hush
Hubbard & Bell
Chilango
Holborn Dining Room
Rocket Holborn
Cigalon
Belgo
Coopers
Seven Stars
Roka
DELAUNAY
India Club
Indigo
Spring, Salon
Pennethorne's
Tom's Kitchen,
Fernandez & Wells
Mint Leaf
Café in the Crypt
National Dining Rooms
Strand Dining Rooms
House,
Green Room,
Kitchen
Balcon
(Sofitel St James)
Northall
Blanco43
Massimo
Archduke
Canteen,
Caffé Vergnano,
Skylon Grill,
Skylon
Roux at
Parliament Square
(RICS)
Adam Handling at Caxton
CINNAMON CLUB
Quirinale
Vincent Rooms
Shepherd's
Goya
Whistler
(Tate Britain)
Dirty Burger
See Map 4
RUSSELL SQ.
Guilford Street
BLOOMSBURY
Russell
Southampton Row
Gray's Inn Road
Theobald's Road
GOODGE
Tottenham Court Rd
CHANCERY LANE
High Holborn
HOLBORN
Chancery Ln
TOTTENHAM COURT RD.
Kingsway
SOHO
Charing Cross Road
COVENT GARDEN
Aldwych
Shaftesbury Ave
COVENT GARDEN
TEMPLE
LEICESTER SQ.
Strand
PICCADILLY CIRCUS
Regent St
Haymarket
Waterloo Bridge
Trafalgar Square
EMBANKMENT
Northumberland Av
CHARING CROSS
River Thames
South Bank Centre
Pall Mall
ST JAMES'S
Whitehall
Victoria Embankment
The Mall
St James's Park
WATERLOO
York Road
WESTMINSTER
Westminster Bridge
Birdcage Walk
ST. JAMES'S PARK
LAMBETH NORTH
Houses of Parliament
Victoria Street
WESTMINSTER
Lambeth Palace Road
Lambeth Palace
Lambeth Road
Marsham St
Horseferry Road
Lambeth Br
Rochester Row
Millbank
PIMLICO
LAMBETH

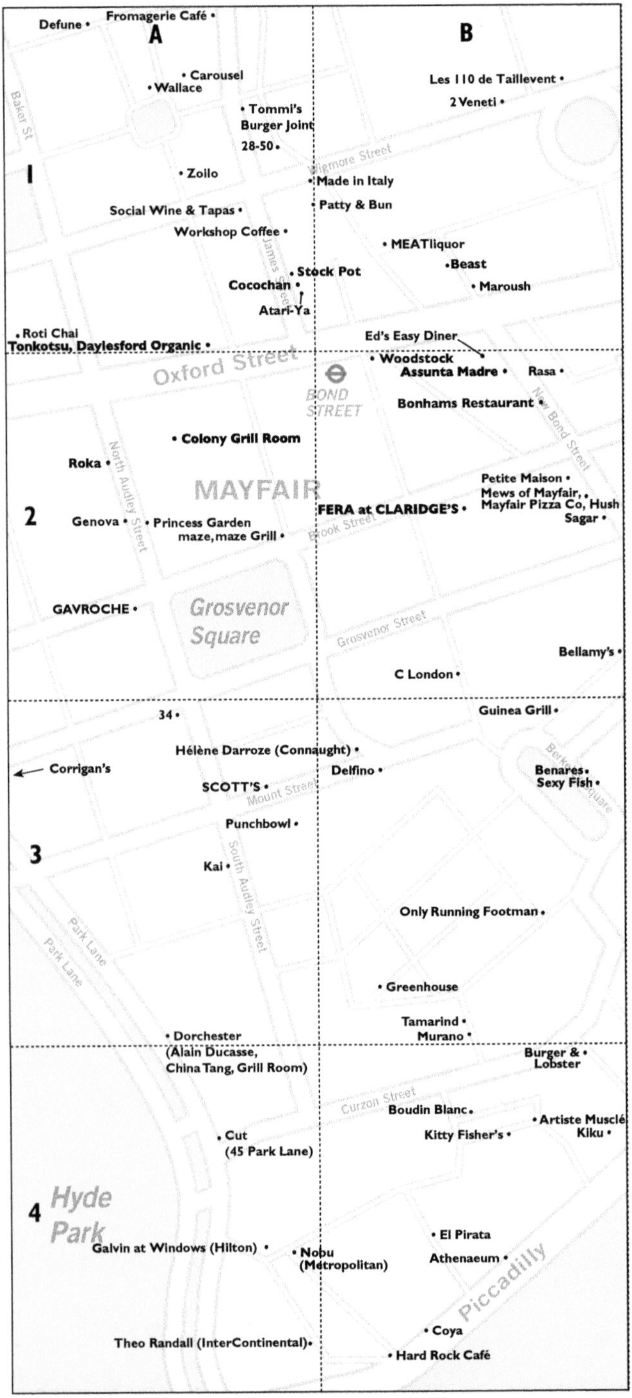

A

B

1

Defune •
Fromagerie Café •
• Carousel
• Wallace
Baker St
• Tommi's Burger Joint
28-50 •
• Zoilo
Social Wine & Tapas •
Workshop Coffee •
James Street
• Stock Pot
Cocochan •
Atari-Ya
• Roti Chai
Tonkotsu, Daylesford Organic •
Les 110 de Taillevent •
2 Veneti •
Wigmore Street
• Made in Italy
• Patty & Bun
• MEATliquor
• Beast
• Maroush
Ed's Easy Diner

2

Oxford Street
BOND STREET
• Woodstock
Assunta Madre •
Rasa •
Bonhams Restaurant •
New Bond Street
• Colony Grill Room
Roka •
North Audley Street
MAYFAIR
Genova •
• Princess Garden
maze, maze Grill •
GAVROCHE •
Grosvenor Square
Petite Maison •
Mews of Mayfair, Mayfair Pizza Co, Hush •
Sagar •
FERA at CLARIDGE'S •
Brook Street
Grosvenor Street
Bellamy's •
C London •

3

34 •
Hélène Darroze (Connaught) •
← Corrigan's
SCOTT'S •
Mount Street
Punchbowl •
Kai •
South Audley Street
Park Lane
Park Lane
Guinea Grill •
Delfino •
Berkeley Square
Benares •
Sexy Fish •
Only Running Footman •
• Greenhouse
Tamarind •
Murano •

4

• Dorchester (Alain Ducasse, China Tang, Grill Room)
Burger & Lobster •
Curzon Street
Boudin Blanc •
• Artiste Musclé
Kiku •
Kitty Fisher's •
• Cut (45 Park Lane)
Hyde Park
Galvin at Windows (Hilton) •
• Nobu (Metropolitan)
• El Pirata
Athenaeum •
Piccadilly
• Coya
Theo Randall (InterContinental) •
• Hard Rock Café

Kaffeine
C
Riding House Café
D
Delancey & Co
Regent Street
Piquet
Newman Street Tavern
Kaffeine
Patara
Latium
Berners Tavern
Burger & Lobster
Vapiano
Yalla Yalla
Ethos
Oxford Street
Old Tom & English
Fernandez & Wells
OXFORD CIRCUS
Ember Yard
Obicà
Pizza Pilgrims
Wardour Street
Dean Street
Imli
Vasco & Piero's
Melt Room
Chisou
Inamo
Bodean's
Blanchette
Gt Marlborough Street
SOHO
aqua nueva, aqua kyoto
Princi
Bunnychow
Social Eating House
Crosstown Doughnuts
Carom at Meza
POLLEN STREET SOCIAL
Little Social
Yauatcha
Bao
Banana Tree
Patara
Pitt Cue Co
Duck & Rice
Hibiscus
Sakana-tei
Aurora
Jackson & Rye
Goodman
Mildred's
Andrew Edmunds
Antidote
Polpetto
28-50
Tapas Brindisa
Fernandez & Wells
Sketch (Lecture room & Gallery)
Dehesa
Fernandez & Wells
Bone Daddies
Maddox Street
Shotgun
Pizza Pilgrims, Oka, Señor Ceviche
Randall & Aubin
Rosa's
Ristorante Frescobaldi
Shoryu Ramen
Vinoteca
Yalla Yalla
Windmill
Bouillabaisse
Cinnamon Soho
Wright Brothers
Dishoom, Jinjuu
Polpo
Wild Honey
Shampers
Flat Iron
Bob Bob Ricard
Spuntino
Sotheby's Café
Conduit Street
Blacklock
Araki
BOCCA DI LUPO
Brasserie Chavot
Nopi
Mele e Pere
Alyn Williams (Westbury)
Sartoria
Gelupo
Nordic Bakery
Rainforest Café
Umu
Hix
Mash
Ham Yard, Engawa
tibits
Brewer Street
Momo
Kulu Kulu
SQUARE
Heddon St Kitchen
BRASSERIE ZEDEL
Taro
Hakkasan
Shoryu Ramen
Clockjack Oven
Old Bond Street
Jamie's Diner
Peyote
PICCADILLY CIRCUS
Veeraswamy
Sumosan
Hawksmoor
Fishworks
Sackville's
Bentley's
Yoshino
Regent
Chor Bizarre
San Carlo Cicchetti
Rextail
Inamo
Cecconi's
Barbecoa
Hix at Albemarle
Rowley's
Keeper's House
Quattro Passi
Shoryu Ramen
Royal Academy
Berkeley Street
Nobu Berkeley
Babbo
Bilbao Berria, Villandry St James's
Piccadilly
GYMKHANA
45 Jermyn St, 1707, Diamond Jubilee Tea Salon
Al Duca
Jermyn Street
Pescatori
Francos
Novikov
Wiltons
Green's
WOLSELEY
Langan's Brasserie
Quaglino's
Café Murano
Matsuri
Ritz, Palm Court
Sake No Hana
St James's Street
CAPRICE
GREEN PARK
Seven Park Place
Vicolo
Pall Mall
Avenue
Boulestin
Chutney Mary
Green Park
ST JAMES'S
The Mall

MAP 4 – EAST SOHO, CHINATOWN & COVENT GARDEN

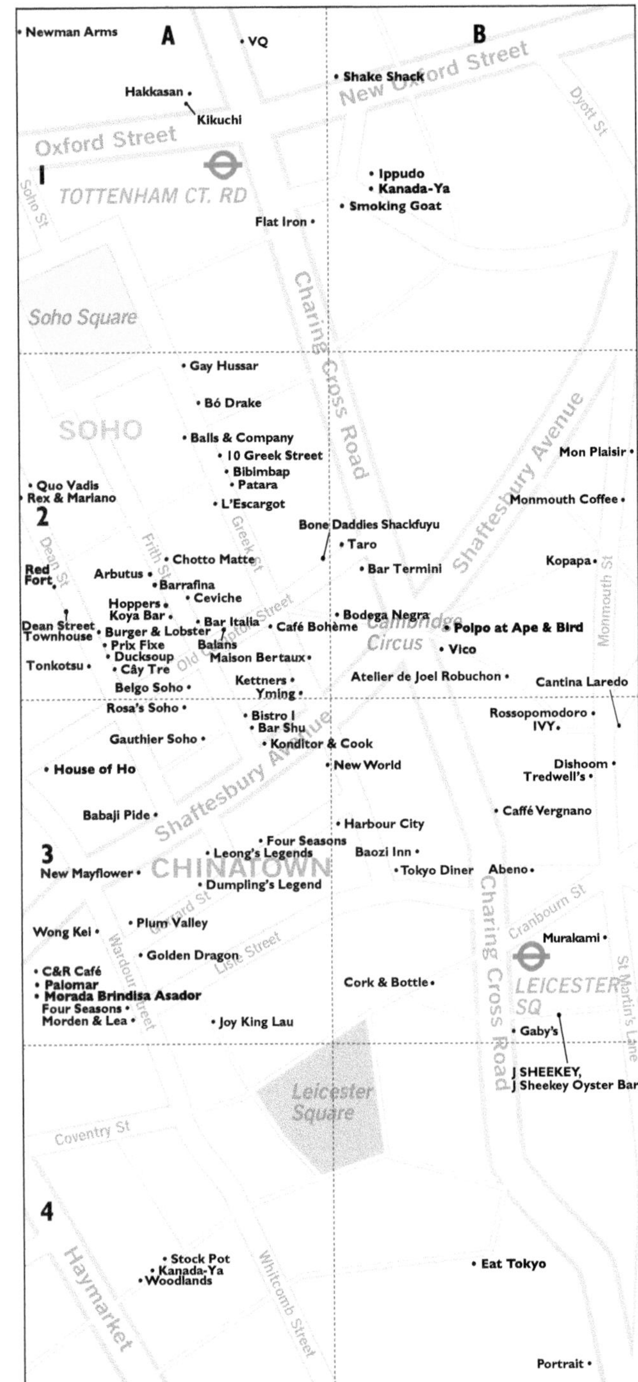

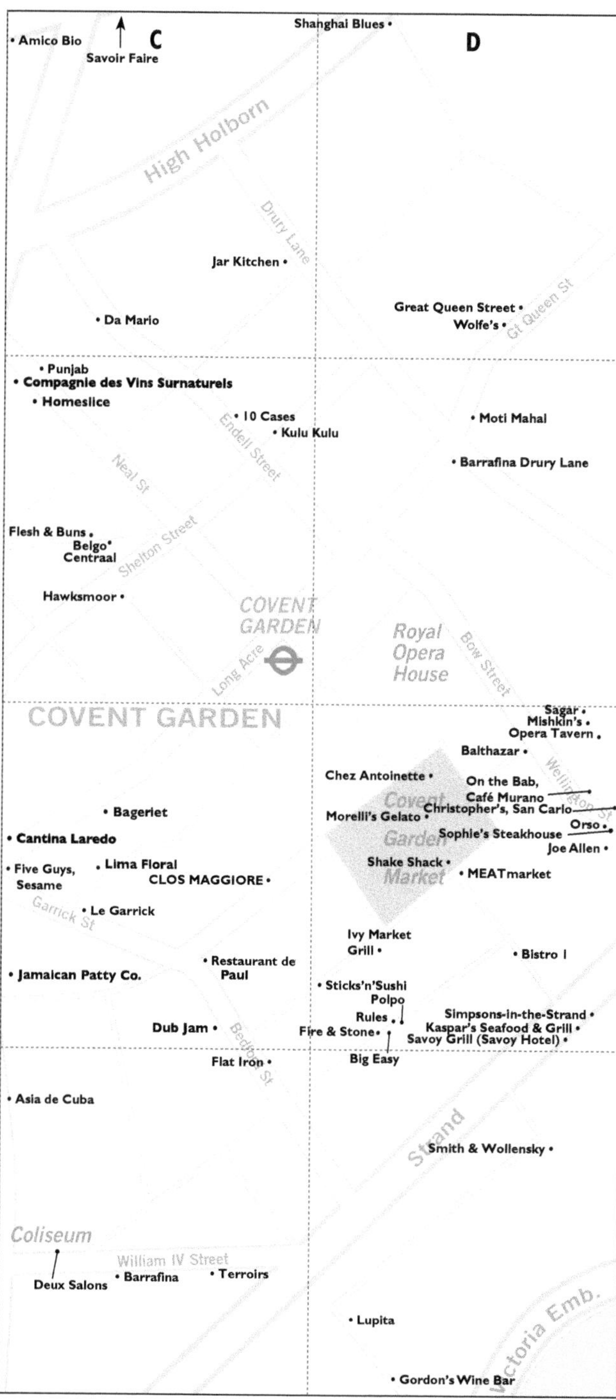

C
D
Amico Bio
Savoir Faire
Shanghai Blues
High Holborn
Drury Lane
Jar Kitchen
Da Mario
Great Queen Street
Wolfe's
Gt Queen St
Punjab
Compagnie des Vins Surnaturels
Homeslice
10 Cases
Kulu Kulu
Endell Street
Neal St
Moti Mahal
Barrafina Drury Lane
Flesh & Buns
Belgo Centraal
Shelton Street
Hawksmoor
COVENT GARDEN
Long Acre
Royal Opera House
Bow Street
COVENT GARDEN
Sagar
Mishkin's
Opera Tavern
Balthazar
Chez Antoinette
On the Bab, Café Murano
Covent Garden Market
Morelli's Gelato
Christopher's, San Carlo
Wellington St
Orso
Sophie's Steakhouse
Joe Allen
Bageriet
Cantina Laredo
Five Guys, Sesame
Lima Floral
CLOS MAGGIORE
Shake Shack
MEATmarket
Garrick St
Le Garrick
Ivy Market Grill
Bistro 1
Restaurant de Paul
Jamaican Patty Co.
Sticks'n'Sushi
Polpo
Rules
Simpsons-in-the-Strand
Kaspar's Seafood & Grill
Savoy Grill (Savoy Hotel)
Dub Jam
Bedford St
Fire & Stone
Big Easy
Flat Iron
Asia de Cuba
Strand
Smith & Wollensky
Coliseum
William IV Street
Deux Salons
Barrafina
Terroirs
Victoria Emb.
Lupita
Gordon's Wine Bar

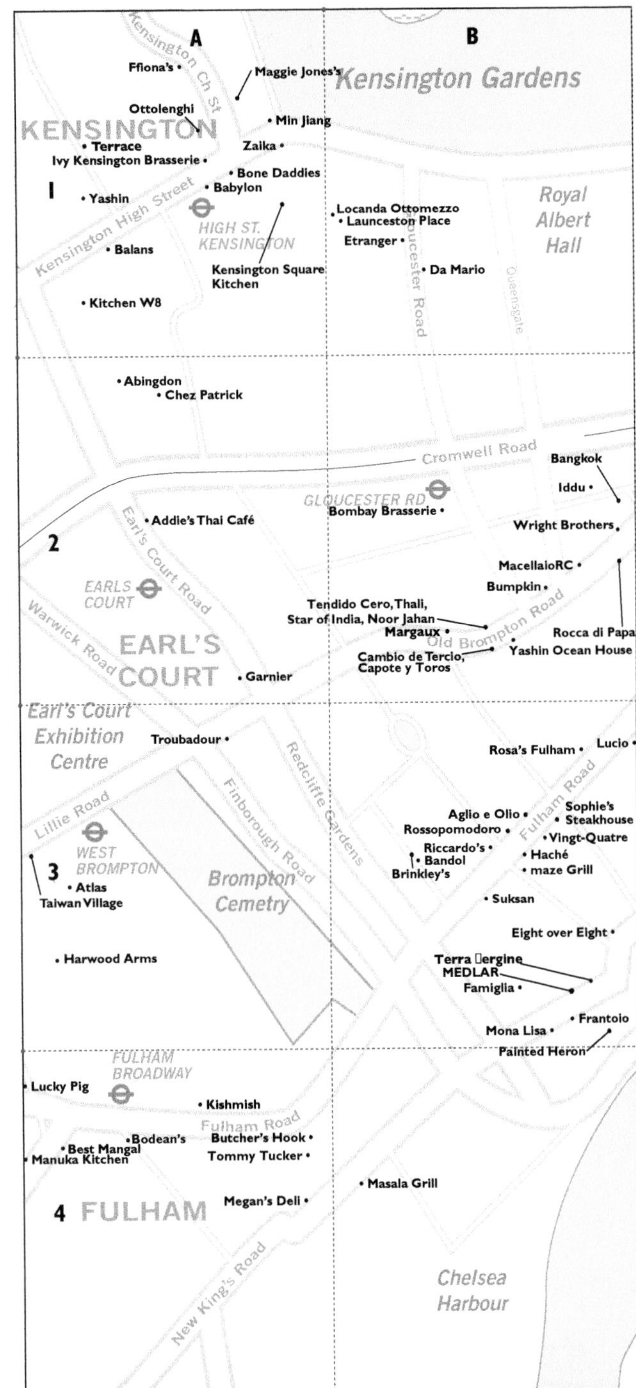
A
B
1
2
3
4
Kensington Gardens
KENSINGTON
Kensington Ch St
Kensington High Street
HIGH ST. KENSINGTON
Royal Albert Hall
Gloucester Road
Queensgate
Cromwell Road
GLOUCESTER RD
EARLS COURT
Earl's Court Road
Warwick Road
EARL'S COURT
Old Brompton Road
Earl's Court Exhibition Centre
Redcliffe Gardens
Finborough Road
Lillie Road
WEST BROMPTON
Brompton Cemetery
Fulham Road
FULHAM BROADWAY
FULHAM
New King's Road
Chelsea Harbour
Ffiona's
Maggie Jones's
Ottolenghi
Min Jiang
Terrace
Zaika
Ivy Kensington Brasserie
Bone Daddies
Babylon
Yashin
Locanda Ottomezzo
Launceston Place
Etranger
Balans
Kensington Square Kitchen
Da Mario
Kitchen W8
Abingdon
Chez Patrick
Bangkok
Iddu
Bombay Brasserie
Addie's Thai Café
Wright Brothers
MacellaioRC
Bumpkin
Tendido Cero, Thali, Star of India, Noor Jahan
Margaux
Rocca di Papa
Cambio de Tercio, Capote y Toros
Yashin Ocean House
Garnier
Troubadour
Rosa's Fulham
Lucio
Aglio e Olio
Sophie's Steakhouse
Rossopomodoro
Vingt-Quatre
Riccardo's
Bandol
Brinkley's
Haché
maze Grill
Atlas
Taiwan Village
Suksan
Eight over Eight
Harwood Arms
Terra ▯ergine
MEDLAR
Famiglia
Frantoio
Mona Lisa
Painted Heron
Lucky Pig
Kishmish
Bodean's
Butcher's Hook
Best Mangal
Manuka Kitchen
Tommy Tucker
Masala Grill
Megan's Deli

MAP 5 – KNIGHTSBRIDGE, CHELSEA & SOUTH KENSINGTON

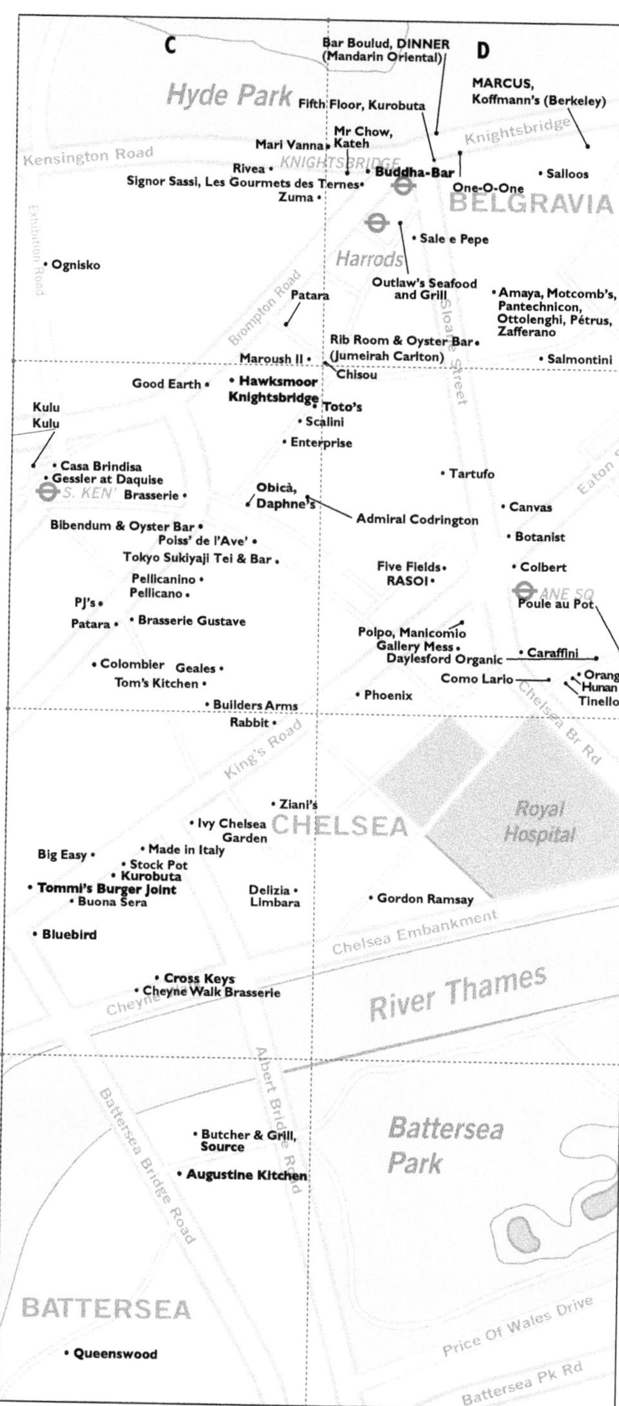

MAP 6 – NOTTING HILL & BAYSWATER

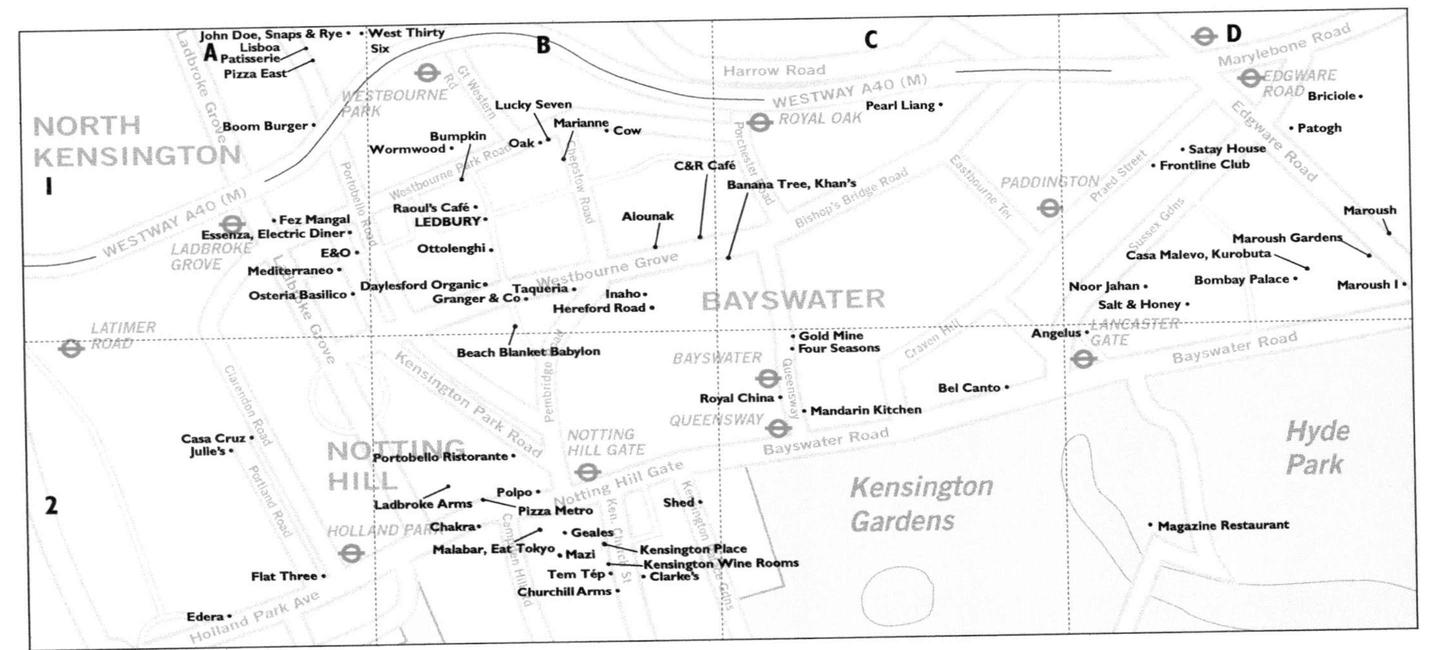

MAP 7 – HAMMERSMITH & CHISWICK

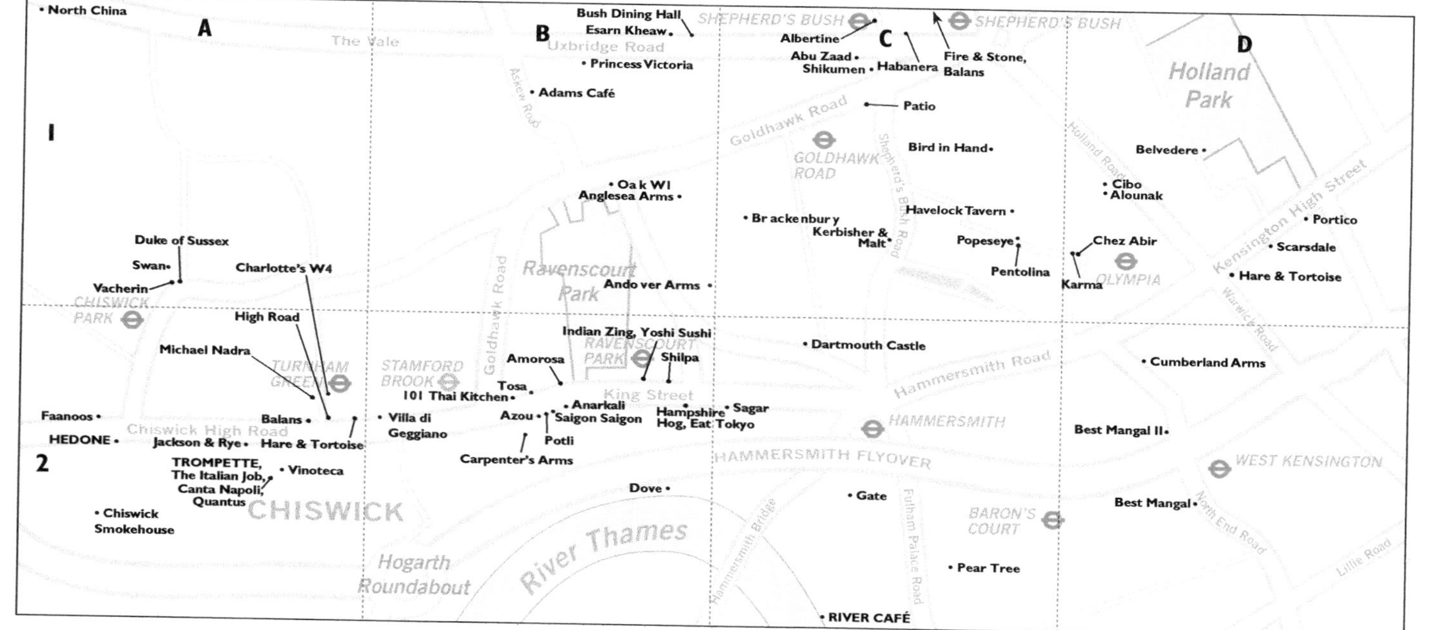

MAP 8 – HAMPSTEAD, CAMDEN TOWN & ISLINGTON

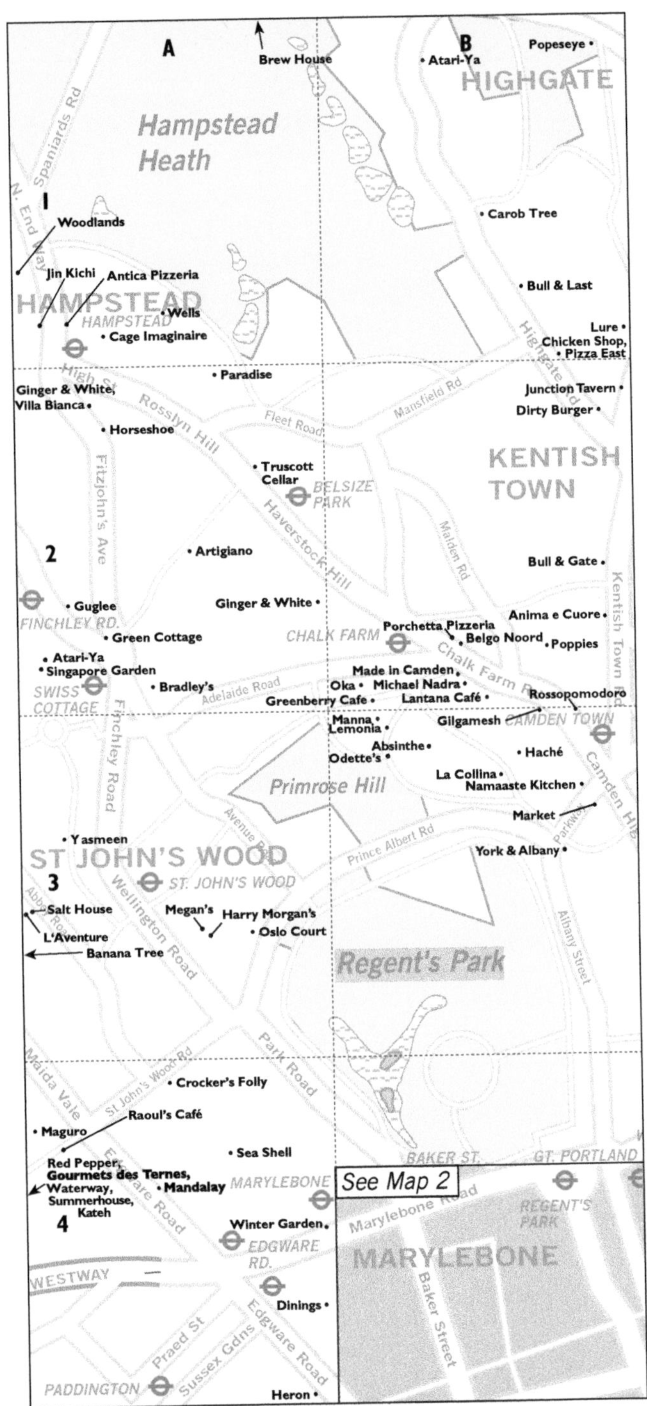

MAP 8 – HAMPSTEAD, CAMDEN TOWN & ISLINGTON

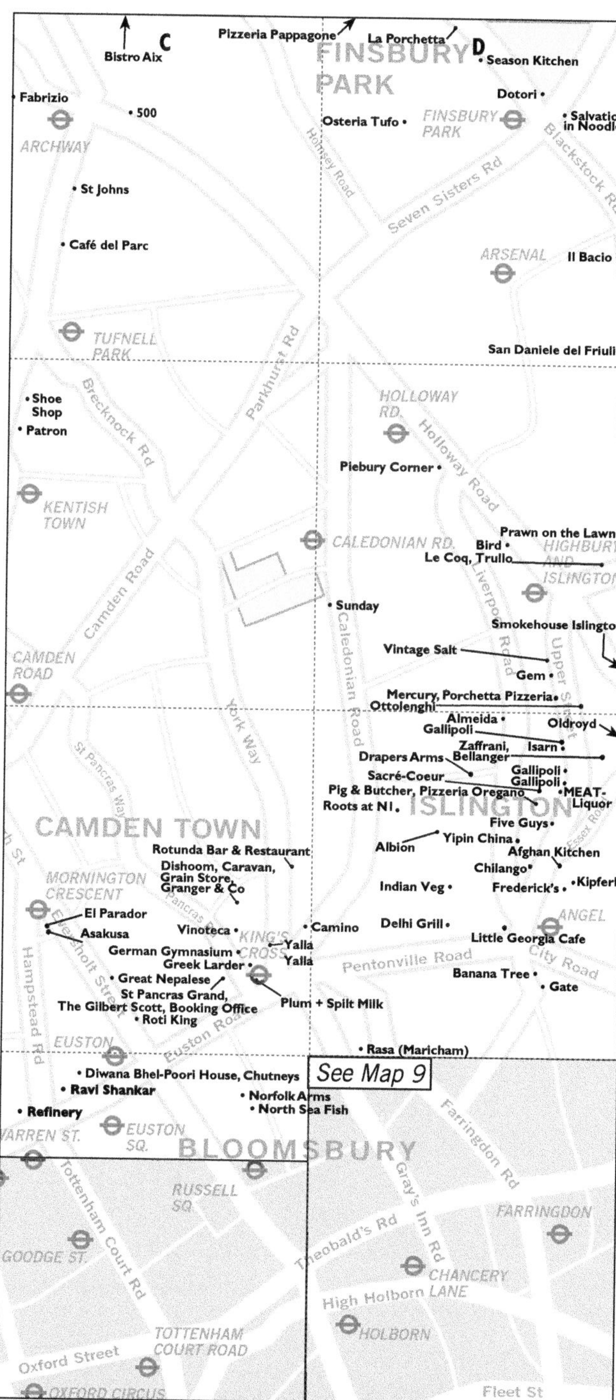

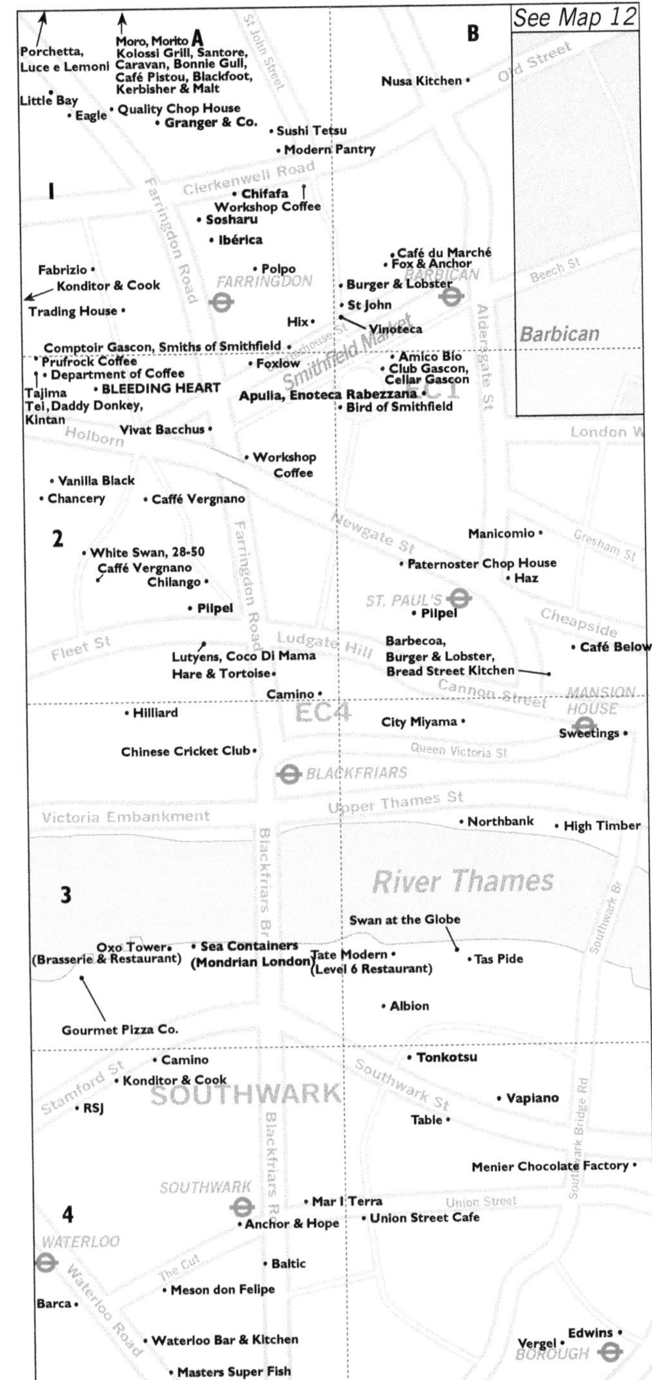
See Map 12
A
B
1
2
3
4
Porchetta,
Luce e Lemoni
Moro, Morito
Kolossi Grill, Santore,
Caravan, Bonnie Gull,
Café Pistou, Blackfoot,
Kerbisher & Malt
St John Street
Nusa Kitchen
Old Street
Little Bay
Eagle
Quality Chop House
Granger & Co.
Sushi Tetsu
Modern Pantry
Clerkenwell Road
Chifafa
Workshop Coffee
Sosharu
Ibérica
Farringdon Road
Café du Marché
Fox & Anchor
BARBICAN
Beech St
Fabrizio
Konditor & Cook
Polpo
FARRINGDON
Burger & Lobster
Trading House
St John
Hix
Vinoteca
Smithfield Market
Aldersgate St
Barbican
Comptoir Gascon, Smiths of Smithfield
Prufrock Coffee
Department of Coffee
Foxlow
Amico Bio
Club Gascon,
Cellar Gascon
Tajima
Tei, Daddy Donkey,
Kintan
BLEEDING HEART
Apulia, Enoteca Rabezzana
Bird of Smithfield
EC1
Holborn
Vivat Bacchus
London W
Workshop
Coffee
Vanilla Black
Chancery
Caffé Vergnano
Newgate St
Manicomio
Gresham St
White Swan, 28-50
Caffé Vergnano
Chilango
Farringdon Road
Paternoster Chop House
Haz
ST. PAUL'S
Pilpel
Pilpel
Cheapside
Fleet St
Ludgate Hill
Barbecoa,
Burger & Lobster,
Bread Street Kitchen
Café Below
Lutyens, Coco Di Mama
Hare & Tortoise
Camino
Cannon Street
MANSION
HOUSE
Hilliard
EC4
City Miyama
Sweetings
Chinese Cricket Club
Queen Victoria St
BLACKFRIARS
Upper Thames St
Victoria Embankment
Northbank
High Timber
Blackfriars Br
River Thames
Southwark Br
Swan at the Globe
Oxo Tower
(Brasserie & Restaurant)
Sea Containers
(Mondrian London)
Tate Modern
(Level 6 Restaurant)
Tas Pide
Albion
Gourmet Pizza Co.
Camino
Tonkotsu
Konditor & Cook
Stamford St
SOUTHWARK
Southwark St
Vapiano
RSJ
Table
Blackfriars Rd
Southwark Bridge Rd
Menier Chocolate Factory
SOUTHWARK
Mar I Terra
Union Street
Anchor & Hope
Union Street Cafe
WATERLOO
Baltic
The Cut
Waterloo Road
Meson don Felipe
Barca
Waterloo Bar & Kitchen
Edwins
Vergel
BOROUGH
Masters Super Fish

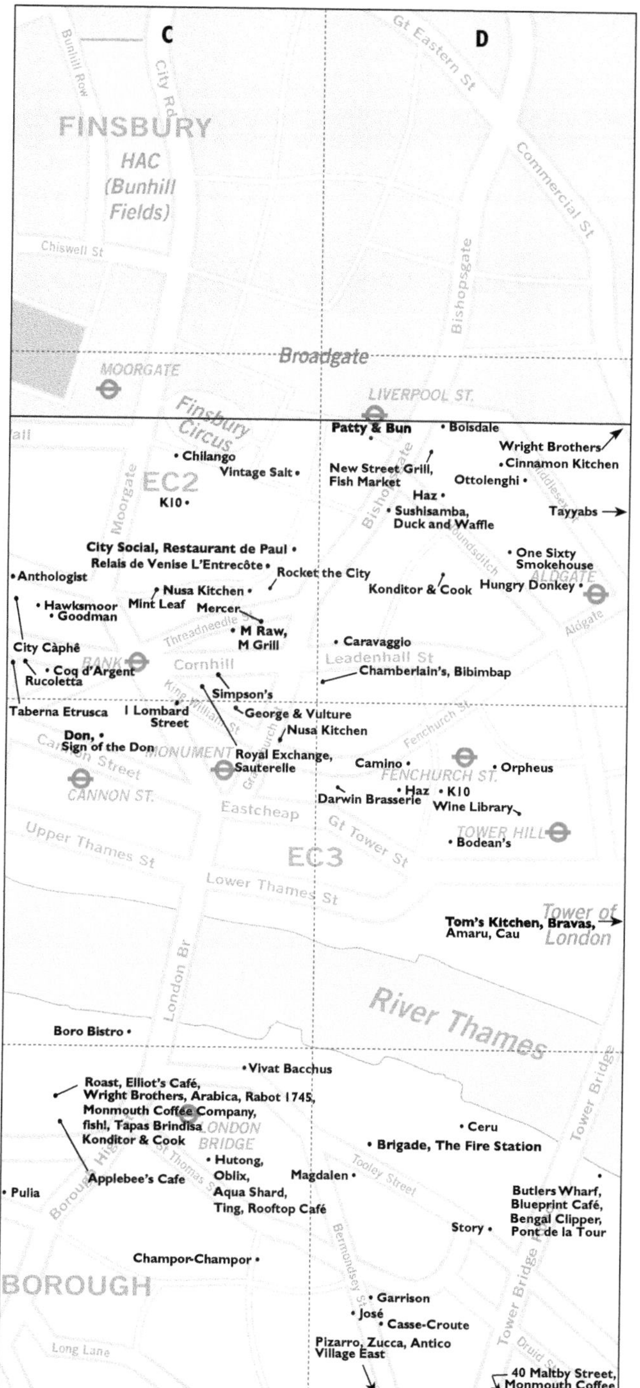
C
D
Bunhill Row
City Rd
Gt Eastern St
FINSBURY
HAC
(Bunhill
Fields)
Commercial St
Chiswell St
Bishopsgate
Broadgate
MOORGATE
LIVERPOOL ST.
Finsbury
Circus
Patty & Bun
• Boisdale
Wright Brothers
• Cinnamon Kitchen
• Chilango
Vintage Salt •
New Street Grill,
Fish Market
Ottolenghi •
EC2
Moorgate
Haz •
K10 •
• Sushisamba,
Duck and Waffle
Tayyabs
City Social, Restaurant de Paul •
Relais de Venise L'Entrecôte •
• One Sixty
Smokehouse
Houndsditch
• Anthologist
Rocket the City
Hungry Donkey •
ALDGATE
Nusa Kitchen •
Konditor & Cook
• Hawksmoor
• Goodman
Mint Leaf
Mercer
Threadneedle St
Aldgate
• M Raw,
M Grill
City Càphê
• Caravaggio
BANK
Cornhill
Leadenhall St
• Coq d'Argent
Rucoletta
Chamberlain's, Bibimbap
Simpson's
Taberna Etrusca
1 Lombard
Street
King William St
George & Vulture
Nusa Kitchen
Fenchurch St
Don, •
Sign of the Don
MONUMENT
Royal Exchange,
Sauterelle
Cannon Street
Camino •
• Orpheus
FENCHURCH ST.
CANNON ST.
• Haz
• K10
Darwin Brasserie
Wine Library
Eastcheap
Upper Thames St
Gt Tower St
TOWER HILL
• Bodean's
EC3
Lower Thames St
Tom's Kitchen, Bravas,
Amaru, Cau
Tower of
London
London Br
River Thames
Boro Bistro •
• Vivat Bacchus
Roast, Elliot's Café,
Wright Brothers, Arabica, Rabot 1745,
Monmouth Coffee Company,
fish!, Tapas Brindisa
Konditor & Cook
LONDON
BRIDGE
Tower Bridge
• Ceru
• Brigade, The Fire Station
• Hutong,
Oblix,
Aqua Shard,
Ting, Rooftop Café
Magdalen •
Tooley Street
Applebee's Cafe
St Thomas St
• Pulia
Borough High St
Butlers Wharf,
Blueprint Café,
Bengal Clipper,
Pont de la Tour
Story •
Champor-Champor •
Bermondsey St
Tower Bridge Rd
BOROUGH
• Garrison
• José
• Casse-Croute
Pizarro, Zucca, Antico
Village East
Druid St
Long Lane
40 Maltby Street,
Monmouth Coffee

MAP 10 – SOUTH LONDON (& FULHAM)

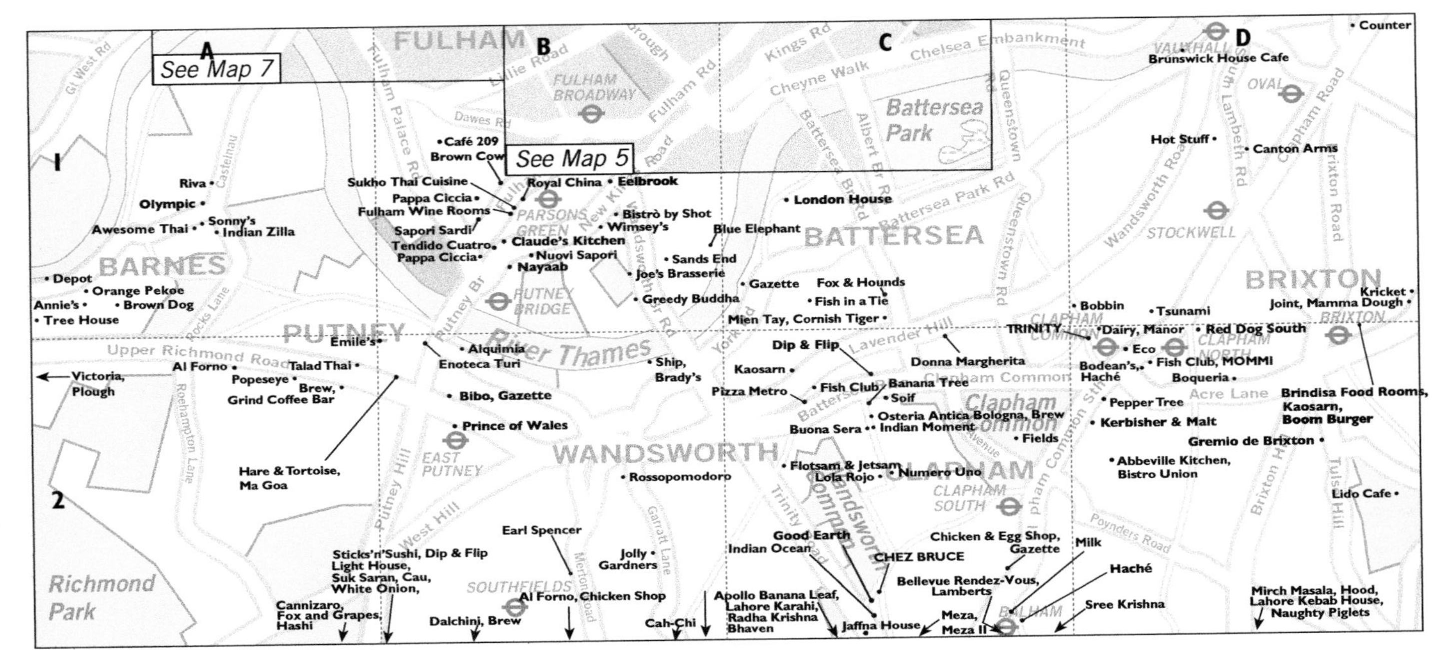

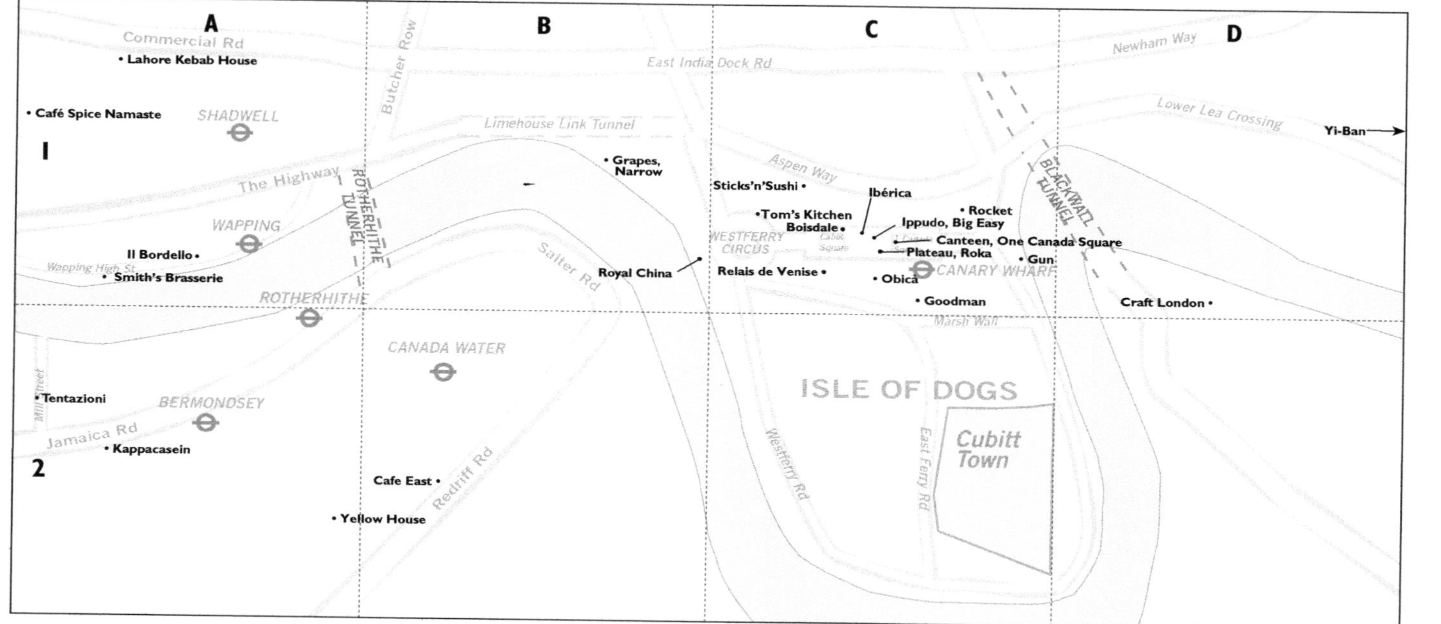

MAP 11 – EAST END & DOCKLANDS

MAP 12 – SHOREDITCH & BETHNAL GREEN

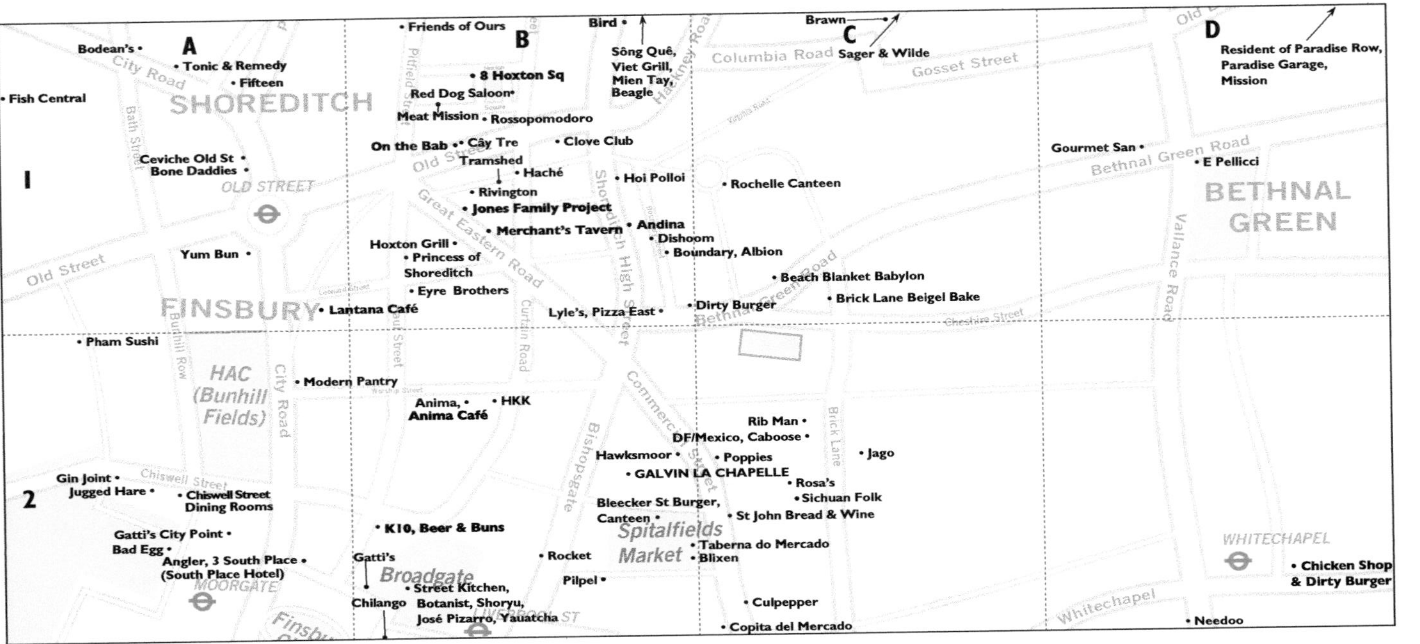

UK SURVEY RESULTS & TOP SCORERS

PLACES PEOPLE TALK ABOUT

These are the restaurants outside London that were mentioned most frequently by reporters (last year's position is shown in brackets). For a list of London's most mentioned restaurants, see page 16.

1 Manoir aux Quat' Saisons (1)
Great Milton, Oxon

2 Waterside Inn (2)
Bray, Berks

3 L'Enclume (3)
Cartmel, Cumbria

4 Hand & Flowers (5)
Marlow, Buckss

5 Sportsman (6)
Whitstable, Kent

Manoir aux Quat' Saisons

6 Midsummer House (13=)
Cambridge, Cambs

7 Northcote (9)
Langho, Lancs

8 Artichoke (12)
Amershams

9 Seafood Restaurant (11)
Padstow, Cornwall

10 Gidleigh Park (10)
Chagford, Devon

Northcote

11 Great House (15=)
Lavenham, Suffolk

12 Fat Duck (4)
Bray, Berks

13 Chapter One (9)
Locksbottom, Kent

14 Hind's Head (8)
Bray, Berks

15 Restaurant Sat Bains (17=)
Nottingham, Notts

Great House

16= Restaurant Nathan Outlaw (13=)
Rock, Cornwall

16= Champignon Sauvage (-)
Cheltenham, Gloucestershire

18= Hambleton Hall (-)
Hambleton, Rutland

18= Mr Cooper's (-)
Manchester, Greater Manchester

20 Magpie (19=)
Whitby, N Yorks

Magpie

All restaurants whose food rating is 5 plus restaurants whose prices is £50+ with a food rating of 4

£270	The Fat Duck *(Bray)*	454
£220	Waterside Inn *(Bray)*	555
£190	Le Manoir aux Quat' Saisons *(Great Milton)*	554
£150	Gidleigh Park *(Chagford)*	554
	L'Enclume *(Cartmel)*	554
£140	Restaurant Nathan Outlaw *(Port Isaac)*	554
£130	Midsummer House *(Cambridge)*	544
	Andrew Fairlie *(Auchterarder)*	444
	The Latymer *(Bagshot)*	443
£120	Restaurant Sat Bains *(Nottingham)*	543
£100	Martin Wishart *(Loch Lomond)*	554
	Mr Underhill's *(Ludlow)*	554
	Fraiche *(Oxton)*	544
	Restaurant Coworth Park *(Ascot)*	455
	Bybrook Restaurant *(Castle Combe)*	444
	Winteringham Fields *(Winteringham)*	444
	Llangoed Hall *(Llyswen)*	424
	Lucknam Park *(Colerne)*	443
	Purnells *(Birmingham)*	433
	Simon Radley *(Chester)*	433
£90	Hambleton Hall *(Hambleton)*	545
	Northcote *(Langho)*	554
	Restaurant Martin Wishart *(Edinburgh)*	554
	Kinloch Lodge *(Sleat)*	544
	Number One *(Edinburgh)*	544
	Yorke Arms *(Ramsgill-in-Nidderdale)*	534
	Amberley Castle *(Amberley)*	435
	André Garrett At Cliveden *(Taplow)*	435
	21212 *(Edinburgh)*	444
	Fischers at Baslow Hall *(Baslow)*	444
	L'Ortolan *(Shinfield)*	444
	Manchester House *(Manchester)*	444
	The Man Behind The Curtain *(Leeds)*	453

	The Kitchin *(Edinburgh)*	4 3 3
	The Pass Restaurant *(Horsham)*	4 4 2
£80	Gilpin Hotel *(Windermere)*	5 3 5
	Ocean Restaurant *(Jersey)*	5 5 4
	Black Swan *(Oldstead)*	5 4 4
	Bohemia *(Jersey)*	5 4 4
	Lake Road Kitchen *(Ambleside)*	5 4 4
	Raby Hunt *(Summerhouse)*	5 4 4
	Drakes *(Ripley)*	5 4 3
	Harry's Place *(Great Gonerby)*	5 5 2
	Cotto *(Cambridge)*	5 4 2
	Seafood Restaurant *(St Andrews)*	4 3 5
	Read's *(Faversham)*	4 4 4
	The Peat Inn *(Cupar)*	4 4 4
	Le Champignon Sauvage *(Cheltenham)*	4 3 4
	Lumière *(Cheltenham)*	4 4 3
	Paul Ainsworth at Number 6 *(Padstow)*	4 4 3
	Hand & Flowers *(Marlow)*	4 3 3
	Turners *(Birmingham)*	4 2 3
£70	The Box Tree *(Ilkley)*	5 5 4
	The Harrow at Little Bedwyn *(Marlborough)*	5 5 4
	Adam's *(Birmingham)*	5 4 4
	Artichoke *(Amersham)*	5 4 4
	Monachyle Mhor *(Balquhidder)*	5 4 4
	The Old Inn *(Drewsteignton)*	5 4 4
	The Neptune *(Old Hunstanton)*	5 5 3
	Carters of Moseley *(Birmingham)*	5 4 3
	Little Fish Market *(Brighton)*	5 4 3
	The Cottage In The Wood *(Keswick)*	5 4 3
	Menu Gordon Jones *(Bath)*	5 5 2
	Driftwood Hotel *(Rosevine)*	4 4 5
	Le Talbooth *(Dedham)*	4 4 5
	Rampsbeck Hotel *(Watermillock)*	4 4 5
	Samuel's *(Masham)*	4 4 5
	Summer Lodge *(Evershot)*	4 4 5
	The Three Chimneys *(Dunvegan)*	4 4 5
	Hipping Hall *(Kirkby Lonsdale)*	4 4 4
	Kinloch House *(Blairgowrie)*	4 4 4
	The Alderley *(Alderley Edge)*	4 4 4
	The Horn of Plenty *(Gulworthy)*	4 4 4
	Tyddyn Llan *(Llandrillo)*	4 4 4
	Dining Room *(Aylesbury)*	4 3 4

	The Cross *(Kingussie)*	434
	Terravina *(Woodlands)*	453
	Caldesi in Campagna *(Bray)*	443
	Edmunds *(Birmingham)*	443
	Fallowfields *(Kingston Bagpuize)*	443
	Longueville Manor *(Jersey)*	443
	Restaurant Mark Greenaway *(Edinburgh)*	443
	Airds Hotel *(Port Appin)*	433
	Thackeray's *(Tunbridge Wells)*	442
	Van Zeller *(Harrogate)*	442
	Restaurant James Sommerin *(Penarth)*	432
£60	Braidwoods *(Dalry)*	554
	Checkers *(Montgomery)*	554
	Freemasons at Wiswell *(Wiswell)*	554
	Little Barwick House *(Barwick)*	554
	Chapter One *(Locksbottom)*	544
	Roger Hickman's *(Norwich)*	544
	Sosban And The Old Butchers *(Menai Bridge)*	544
	The Seahorse *(Dartmouth)*	544
	Woodspeen *(Newbury)*	544
	Fairyhill *(Reynoldston)*	553
	Grenache *(Worsley)*	553
	Lickfold Inn *(Lickfold)*	543
	Restaurant 27 *(Portsmouth)*	543
	Restaurant Tristan *(Horsham)*	543
	The Chef's Dozen *(Chipping Campden)*	543
	The Vanilla Pod *(Marlow)*	543
	The Walnut Tree *(Llandewi Skirrid)*	543
	The Mason's Arms *(Knowstone)*	533
	Verveine Fishmarket Restaurant *(Milford-on-Sea)*	532
	Mallory Court *(Bishops Tachbrook)*	455
	Timberyard *(Edinburgh)*	455
	Plas Bodegroes *(Pwllheli)*	445
	The Feathered Nest Inn *(Nether Westcote)*	445
	The George Hotel *(Stamford)*	445
	Crab & Lobster *(Asenby)*	435
	Silver Darling *(Aberdeen)*	435
	The Crazy Bear *(Stadhampton)*	435
	Killiecrankie House Hotel *(Killiecrankie)*	454
	Stock Hill House *(Gillingham)*	454
	The Albannach *(Lochinver)*	454
	The Pheasant Hotel *(Harome)*	454
	Barley Bree *(Muthill)*	444

	Brockencote Hall *(Chaddesley Corbett)*	4 4 4
	Northcote Manor *(Burrington)*	4 4 4
	Ondine *(Edinburgh)*	4 4 4
	Restaurant 23 *(Leamington Spa)*	4 4 4
	The Hind's Head *(Bray)*	4 4 4
	Black Swan *(Helmsley)*	4 3 4
	Michael Caines *(Chester)*	4 3 4
	Shaun Dickens at The Boathouse *(Henley-on-Thames)*	4 3 4
	The Estate Grill *(Egham)*	4 3 4
	The Nut Tree Inn *(Murcott)*	4 3 4
	Whitstable Oyster Fishery Co. *(Whitstable)*	4 3 4
	Hart's *(Nottingham)*	4 5 3
	The Restaurant at Drakes *(Brighton)*	4 5 3
	Gamba *(Glasgow)*	4 4 3
	La Rock *(Nottingham)*	4 4 3
	Outlaw's *(Rock)*	4 4 3
	The Butcher's Arms *(Eldersfield)*	4 4 3
	The Cross at Kenilworth *(Kenilworth)*	4 4 3
	5 North Street *(Winchcombe)*	4 3 3
	Alec's *(Brentwood)*	4 3 3
	The Marquis *(Alkham)*	4 3 3
	The Old Passage Inn *(Arlingham)*	4 3 3
	The Olive Tree *(Bath)*	4 3 3
	The Star Inn *(Harome)*	4 3 3
	Wilks *(Bristol)*	4 4 2
	Dining Room *(Rock)*	4 3 2
	Lavender House *(Brundall)*	4 3 2
	Michael Caines Cafe Bar & Grill *(Exeter)*	4 3 2
	Orwells *(Shiplake)*	4 3 2
£50	Fat Olives *(Emsworth)*	5 5 4
	Great House *(Lavenham)*	5 5 4
	Les Mirabelles *(Nomansland)*	5 5 4
	Red Lion *(East Chisenbury)*	5 5 4
	The Pipe & Glass Inn *(Beverley)*	5 5 4
	The Plough at Bolnhurst *(Bolnhurst)*	5 5 4
	The Sportsman *(Whitstable)*	5 5 4
	Yalbury Cottage *(Lower Bockhampton)*	5 5 4
	Bilash *(Wolverhampton)*	5 4 4
	Carpenter's Arms *(Sunninghill)*	5 4 4
	Crabshakk *(Glasgow)*	5 4 4
	Elephant Restaurant & Brasserie *(Torquay)*	5 4 4
	Kentish Hare *(Bidborough)*	5 4 4
	Pea Porridge *(Bury St Edmunds)*	5 4 4

	Riverside *(Bridport)*	544
	Stagg Inn *(Titley)*	544
	The Samuel Fox Country Inn *(Bradwell)*	544
	Stravaigin *(Glasgow)*	534
	The Pot Kiln *(Frilsham)*	534
	Gingerman *(Brighton)*	553
	Lanterna *(Scarborough)*	553
	Bandera *(Manchester)*	543
	Bosquet *(Kenilworth)*	543
	Chez Vous *(Warlingham)*	543
	James Martin *(Manchester)*	543
	Kilberry Inn *(Argyll)*	543
	No 7 Fish Bistro *(Torquay)*	543
	Rick Stein *(Winchester)*	543
	Tailors *(Warwick)*	543
	The Boat House *(Bangor)*	543
	The West House *(Biddenden)*	543
	Wedgwood *(Edinburgh)*	552
	Haywards Restaurant *(Epping)*	542
	Terre à Terre *(Brighton)*	542
	Le Langhe *(York)*	512
£40	Wheelers Oyster Bar *(Whitstable)*	555
	The Oyster Shack *(Bigbury-on-Sea)*	545
	Iberico *(Nottingham)*	554
	Orchid *(Harrogate)*	554
	Sukhothai *(Leeds)*	554
	Food by Breda Murphy *(Whalley)*	544
	Hare Inn *(Scawton)*	544
	Indian Summer *(Brighton)*	544
	Indian Zest *(Sunbury on Thames)*	544
	Lavenham Greyhound *(Lavenham)*	544
	Loch Leven Seafood Café *(Onich)*	544
	Mourne Seafood Bar *(Belfast)*	544
	Prithvi *(Cheltenham)*	544
	The Cove Restaurant & Bar *(Falmouth)*	544
	The Old Boat House *(Amble)*	544
	The Parkers Arms *(Newton-in-Bowland)*	544
	The Pendleton *(Redhill)*	544
	Wallfish Bistro *(Bristol)*	544
	White Swan at Fence *(Fence)*	544
	Yu And You *(Copster Green)*	544
	Maliks *(Cookham)*	534
	Austells *(St Austell)*	553

TOP SCORERS

	Bia Bistrot *(Edinburgh)*	553
	Etsu *(Liverpool)*	553
	Rose Garden *(Manchester)*	553
	The Wild Mushroom *(Westfield)*	553
	Ben's Cornish Kitchen *(Marazion)*	543
	Café Fish *(Tobermory)*	543
	Crab Shack *(Teignmouth)*	543
	Hooked *(Windermere)*	543
	Prashad *(Leeds)*	543
	Raval *(Gateshead)*	543
	The Chilli Pickle *(Brighton)*	543
	The Gannet *(Glasgow)*	543
	Tolcarne Inn *(Penzance)*	543
	Trenchers *(Whitby)*	543
	Black Bull *(Moulton)*	533
	My Sichuan *(Oxford)*	533
	Riverford Field Kitchen *(Buckfastleigh)*	533
	Acorn Vegetarian Kitchen *(Bath)*	542
	Sojo *(Oxford)*	542
	The Feathers Inn *(Hedley On The Hill)*	542
	Yang Sing *(Manchester)*	522
£30	Levanter *(Ramsbottom)*	545
	Porthmeor Beach Cafe *(St Ives)*	545
	Green Café *(Ludlow)*	554
	JoJo *(Whitstable)*	554
	Mezzet *(East Molesey)*	554
	Oli's Thai *(Oxford)*	554
	Doi Intanon *(Ambleside)*	544
	Wheelhouse *(Falmouth)*	544
	King And Thai *(Broseley)*	534
	The Company Shed *(West Mersea)*	524
	The Cumin *(Nottingham)*	553
	Bosco Pizzeria *(Bristol)*	543
	Flavours By Kumar *(Ramsgate)*	543
	No I *(Cromer)*	543
	Norse *(Harrogate)*	543
	Tharavadu *(Leeds)*	543
	Hansa's *(Leeds)*	542
	Magpie Café *(Whitby)*	542
	Xian *(Orpington)*	542
	Yammo *(Bath)*	542
	Yuzu *(Manchester)*	542
	Butley Orford Oysterage *(Orford)*	532

	Ebi Sushi *(Derby)*	5 3 2
	Sky Apple Cafe *(Newcastle upon Tyne)*	5 3 2
	Shanghai Shanghai *(Nottingham)*	5 2 2
	Zheng *(Oxford)*	5 3 1
£25	Anstruther Fish Bar *(Anstruther)*	5 4 3
	Sole Bay Fish Company *(Southwold)*	5 3 3
	Al Frash *(Birmingham)*	5 3 2
	Cods Scallops *(Wollaton)*	5 3 2
	Fuji Hiro *(Leeds)*	5 3 2
	McDermotts Fish & Chips *(Croydon)*	5 3 2
£20	Karachi *(Bradford)*	5 2 2
£10	This & That *(Manchester)*	5 2 1

Bel & The Dragon, Cookham

Bohemia, Jersey

Daylesford Cafe, Kingham

UK DIRECTORY

ABERAERON, CEREDIGION 4–3C

Harbourmaster £44 333

2 Quay Pde SA46 0BT (01545) 570755

*This harbourside hotel sits a few metres from the sea wall and provides both this main restaurant, and a bar/bistro ("less special but reasonable value"). Service is "prompt and polite" and the cooking "excellent, using fresh local ingredients". / **Details:** www.harbour-master.com; 9 pm; no Amex. **Accommodation:** 13 rooms, from £110*

ABERDEEN, ABERDEENSHIRE 9–2D

Moonfish Cafe £49 443

9 Correction Wynd AB10 1HP (01224) 644166

*Chef "Brian McLeish was runner-up in MasterChef" and now he's onto another winner with this "intimate" year-old Merchant Quarter restaurant. It serves up some "exceptional local produce", with "outstanding" presentation too. / **Details:** www.moonfishcafe.co.uk; 9 pm; closed Sun.*

Silver Darling £63 435

Pocra Quay, North Pier AB11 5DQ (01224) 576229

*There's "still great food, mainly fish" to be had at this modern glass venue – a former harbour control building with "breathtaking views" of the water; OK, it's "expensive, but it works!" / **Details:** www.thesilverdarling.co.uk; 9.30 pm; closed Sat L & Sun; children: +16 after 8 pm.*

ABERDOUR, FIFE 9–4C

Room With A View £46 345

Hawkcraig Point KY3 0TZ (01383) 860 402

*The name doesn't lie – this little, seaside seafood spot (part of a hotel) enjoys "spectacular views over the Forth estuary to Edinburgh". "A small but varied menu is expertly prepared by the chef/owner Tim, and professionally served by co-owner Hannah." / **Details:** www.roomwithaviewrestaurant.co.uk; 9 pm; closed Mon, Tue & Sun D.*

ABERGAVENNY, MONMOUTHSHIRE 2–1A

The Angel Hotel £51 223

15 Cross St NP7 5EN (01873) 857121

*"A great place – one-third pub, two-thirds smart country hotel", with a "cosy" bar and "comfy sofas" in the dining room; the food is "always a little more than serviceable" but can "suffer a bit from the town centre location" – it gets "seriously busy". / **Details:** www.angelabergavenny.com; 10 pm. **Accommodation:** 35 rooms, from £101*

The Hardwick £58 323

Old Raglan Rd NP7 9AA (01873) 854220

*Stephen Terry's illustrious pedigree only partially shines through at his "informal and comfortable" rural gastropub with rooms. The food is often "fabulous" but its ratings are under-cut by niggles that "success is going to its head a bit". / **Details:** www.thehardwick.co.uk; 10 pm, Sun 9 pm; no Amex. **Accommodation:** 8 rooms, from £150*

ABERYSTWYTH, POWYS 4–3C

Gwesty Cymru £46 322

19 Marine Ter SY23 2AZ (01970) 612252

*It's "one of the better venues in the area", but despite solid ratings this boutique-y seafront hotel inspired the odd disappointment this year, not helped by sometimes "perfunctory" service; still, most reports are of "excellent" dishes from local produce. "If the weather permits, get into the garden". / **Details:** www.gwestycymru.com; 9 pm; closed Tue L; no Amex; children: 5+. **Accommodation:** 8 rooms, from £85*

Ultracomida £33 442

31 Pier St SY23 2LN (01970) 630686

*"What a find" – "at the back of a very good Spanish delicatessen", a "cheerful" and "very relaxed" tapas joint, serving "excellent" food and "brilliant" wines; it's a "bit cramped and so can feel crowded", but "their olives are worth the trip alone!" / **Details:** www.ultracomida.com; 9 pm; Mon-Thu & Sat L only, Fri open L & D, closed Sun.*

ACHILTIBUIE, ROSSSHIRE 9–1B

Summer Isles Hotel £78 333

IV26 2YG (01854) 622282

*"Right on the coast looking over the water to the Summer Isles", this reputed, "comfortable" hotel with a "delightful" dining room "takes a bit of getting to". It doesn't attract the volume of feedback it once did – such as there is says it's "worth that effort" for "good locally sourced food and beautiful tasting menus with well-matched wine". / **Details:** www.summerisleshotel.com; 25m N of Ullapool on A835; 8 pm; Closed from 1st Nov - 1st Apr; no Amex; no jeans; children: 8+. **Accommodation:** 13 rooms, from £155*

ALBOURNE, WEST SUSSEX 3–4B

The Ginger Fox £49 343

Muddleswood Road BN6 9EA (01273) 857 888

*"Consistent top-notch pub food" with "subtle flavour combinations" as well as "enthusiastic and personable service" make the Gingerman Group's rural outpost a hit with all who comment on it. / **Details:** www.gingermanrestaurants.com; 10 pm, Sun 9 pm.*

ALDEBURGH, SUFFOLK 3–1D

Aldeburgh Fish And Chips £15 322

226 High St IP15 5DB (01728) 452250
"A 'must do' when in Aldeburgh" – this famous chippy serves "fish 'n' chips that's well worth queueing for". "The meal is best eaten fighting off the gulls on the beach, or with a pint of Adnams in the pub courtyard next door." / **Details:** *www.aldeburghfishandchips.co.uk; 8 pm, Fri 9 pm; closed Mon, Tue D, Wed D & Sun D; no credit cards.*

The Lighthouse £43 343

77 High St IP15 5AU (01728) 453377
"Very cheerful and bubbly" – this linchpin of the High Street has long been reporters' favourite destination in town. Primarily "it wins on atmosphere and service-with-a-smile", but the fish-centric cooking is "simple, but well-cooked, hearty and good value". / **Details:** *www.lighthouserestaurant.co.uk; 10 pm.*

Regatta £43 333

171-173 High St IP15 5AN (01728) 452011
"Jolly" and "well-priced" stalwart that "remains ever-popular", and is particularly "strong on fish". / **Details:** *www.regattaaldeburgh.com; 10 pm.*

ALDERLEY EDGE, CHESHIRE 5–2B

The Alderley Alderley Edge Hotel £75 444

Macclesfield Rd SK9 7BJ (01625) 583033
In the heart of Cheshire WAG-land, Chris Holland's superior venture is uniformly recommended for "fine dining in lovely surroundings"; it's "not cheap", though – presumably not a problem for all those footballers' wives... / **Details:** *www.alderleyedgehotel.com; 9.45 pm; closed Sun.*

ALDFORD, CHESHIRE 5–3A

The Grosvenor Arms £40 344

Chester Rd CH3 6HJ (01244) 620228
"Another Brunning & Price gastropub that gets the formula right" – the formula being "consistent" grub, a "great range of guest ales", and a "friendly village atmosphere"; thankfully the spacious and attractive inn, part of the Duke of Westminster's estate, has "retained its old charm" too. / **Details:** *www.grosvenorarms-aldford.co.uk; 6m S of Chester on B5130; 10 pm, Sun 9 pm.*

ALKHAM, KENT 3–3D

The Marquis £61 433

Alkham Valley Rd CT15 7DF (01304) 873410
"Keeps me coming back time and time again" – a "smart former pub in a delightful valley" offering "very good food, much of it locally sourced" and "served with great attention to detail". / **Details:** *www.themarquisatalkham.co.uk; 9.30 pm, Sun 8.30 pm; children: 8+ at D.* **Accommodation:** *10 rooms, from £95*

ALLOSTOCK, CHESHIRE 4–2B

Three Greyhounds £41 334

Holmes Chapel Rd WA16 9JY (01565) 723455
This Georgian pub, relaunched in 2012 by the owners of the Cholmondeley Arms near Bunbury, features a "great interior with small rooms and open fires"; on most (if not quite all accounts) the food is "good value" too. / **Details:** *www.thethreegreyhoundsinn.co.uk; 9.15 pm, Fri & Sat 9.45 pm, Sun 8.45 pm.*

ALLTAMI, FLINTSHIRE 5–2A

The Tavern Bar and Restaurant £41 343

Mold Rd CH7 6LG (01244) 550485
"A fun style and an original menu" boost the appeal of this "cosy" pub-conversion – "a particularly useful find in this slightly staid town". "Young and friendly staff" provide polished staples (from their 'pub classic' menu) alongside some (slightly) more exotic 'chef's choice' dishes. / **Details:** *www.thetavernmold.co.uk; 8+; pre-order.*

ALNWICK, NORTHUMBERLAND 8–1B

Treehouse Alnwick Castle £44 335

Denwick Ln NE66 1YU (01665) 511350
This "brilliant, quirky restaurant in a treehouse", set by the castle's new gardens, is "really fun and away from the norm"; unsurprisingly, the "amazing setting can overshadow the food a bit, but it's still a great choice in the area". / **Details:** *www.alnwickgarden.com; 9.15 pm; closed Mon D, Tue D & Wed D.*

ALRESFORD, HAMPSHIRE 2–3D

Caracoli £17 443

15 Broad St SO24 9AR (01962) 738730
"An experience not to be missed when shopping"; this "classy deli" attached to a cookware shop (with branches locally) makes "a perfect pitstop in the centre of town", with "great coffee and snacks", including "wholesome cakes and muffins". / **Details:** *www.caracoli.co.uk; 2.30 pm; L only; no Amex; no booking.*

Pulpo Negro **£38** 4 4 4
28 Broad St SO24 9AQ (01962) 732262
The "new venture from the people (Andres & Marie-Lou Alemany) behind the Purefoy Arms" up the road is "not well known yet, but it will be" thanks to its "fabulous", "authentically Spanish" tapas and elegant décor. / **Details:** *www.pulponegro.co.uk; 10.30 pm; closed Mon & Sun.*

ALSTONEFIELD, DERBYSHIRE 5–3C

The George **£47** 4 4 3
DE6 2FX (01335) 310205
"An atmospheric Peak District pub" in a beautiful Lakeland setting, with "tasty food" and "enthusiastic service" – the kind of place to enjoy "a top burger" or "delicious steak and Stilton pie". / **Details:** *www.thegeorgeatalstonefield.com; 11 pm, Sun 9.30 pm.*

ALVESTON, WARWICKSHIRE 2–1C

Baraset Barn **£46** 3 4 4
1 Pimlico Lane CV37 7RJ (01789) 295510
A "great local"; it's the buzzing atmosphere and opulent décor of this contemporary boozer that attract the most acclaim, but there has also been support for its "first-class food" of late. / **Details:** *www.lovelypubs.co.uk/baraset-barn; 10 pm; closed Sun D; no Amex.*

AMBERLEY, WEST SUSSEX 3–4A

Amberley Castle **£91** 4 3 5
BN18 9LT (01798) 831992
"Like a magic castle!" – the "very special" setting is "so romantic" at this "wonderful medieval fortress" (complete with working portcullis!); ex-Gidleigh chef, Robby Jenks is really starting to make a major impression here with "to-die-for" cuisine (which is "reasonably priced" too). / **Details:** *www.amberleycastle.co.uk; N of Arundel on B2139; 9 pm; no jeans or trainers; booking: max 6; children: 12+.* **Accommodation:** *19 rooms, from £265*

AMBLE, NORTHUMBERLAND 8–1B

The Old Boat House **£47** 5 4 4
Leazes St NE65 0AA (01665) 711 232
"A tremendous find"; OK, so there's "nothing fussy or frilly" about the décor, but this "rustic" two-year-old, on the harbour, serves "as fresh a fish as you will find" and there's "a wonderful buzz on Friday night". / **Details:** *www.boathousefoodgroup.co.uk/theoldboathouse-amble; 9 pm, Fri & Sat 9.30 pm.*

AMBLESIDE, CUMBRIA 7–3D

Doi Intanon **£32** 5 4 4
Market Place LA22 9BU (01539) 432119
"Top quality", "fantastic!", "highly recommended" – a sample of the glowing feedback on this stylish Thai ten-year-old; evidently the "Thai/English couple who run it know exactly what they are doing"! / **Details:** *ambleside-thai-restaurant.com/about-us/; Mon-Thu 10 pm, Fri-Sat 10.30 pm, Sun 10 pm; D only.*

Drunken Duck **£57** 3 3 4
Barngates LA22 0NG (01539) 436347
"An institution in the Lakes" – this "quintessential" country pub and microbrewery enjoys a "terrific location" with great views, and makes "a handy pitstop after a long walk", where you can enjoy "delicious locally sourced food", "washed down with a pint of excellent homebrewed ale". / **Details:** *www.drunkenduckinn.co.uk; 3m from Ambleside, towards Hawkshead; 9 pm; no Amex; booking: max 10 (D only).* **Accommodation:** *17 rooms, from £105*

Fellini's **£40** 4 2 4
Church St LA22 0BT (01539) 432487
"This is the vegetarian restaurant to persuade carnivores that a great dining experience is possible without meat!" – a "sophisticated" ("for Ambleside"!) operation with a "delightful" Med-influenced menu; "packages for their adjacent cinema are a brilliant idea". / **Details:** *www.fellinisambleside.com; 10 pm; D only; no Amex.*

Lake Road Kitchen **£86** 5 4 4
Lake Rd LA22 0AD (01539) 422 012
Expect a "dining experience of the highest order", at this ambitious "Scandi-inspired" yearling, from chef-owner James Cross, ex-of Noma; like the latter, this no-frills spot's "emphasis on foraging" leads to some "absolutely fantastic" dishes from its tasting menus. / **Details:** *www.lakeroadkitchen.co.uk/; 9.30 pm; closed Mon & Tue.*

Old Stamp House **£56** 4 4 3
Church St LA22 0BU (015394) 32775
"Culinary perfection"... "really up there with the greats" – the verdict on young chef Ryan Blackburn's "outstanding" new basement venture. The décor's rather "Spartan", but given how restaurants round here "become quite starchy quickly", it strikes some as being "refreshingly unslick". / **Details:** *www.oldstamphouse.com; closed Mon & Sun.*

Zeffirelli's **£34** 3 3 4
Compston Rd LA22 9AD (01539) 433845
"An old favourite" with a "happy atmosphere" offering "consistently good vegetarian food" (although you "forget it's just vegetarian"), particularly pizza. It's longer-established, but its appeal is still very "competitive with" Fellini's (the

*site's chicer, newer veggie). Combi-tickets to the attached jazz bar or cinema are "especially good value". / **Details:** www.zeffirellis.com; 10 pm; no Amex.*

AMERSHAM, BUCKINGHAMSHIRE 3–2A

Artichoke £75 544

9 Market Sq HP7 0DF (01494) 726611

*Michelin's brazen lack of recognition for this "superlative" venture, in the heart of Old Amersham is beyond comprehension – in fact the debate should not be whether or not it should have a star, but whether or not it should have two. The setting is perhaps "stark" but also "calming" and "romantic"; staff "are on a mission to make your meal enjoyable"; and "wow-factor is the norm" for the food from Laurie Gear's "technically refined and creative" kitchen, which "displays more than just talent, but also innovation without losing sight of the basics". / **Details:** www.theartichokerestaurant.co.uk; 9.15 pm, Fri & Sat 9.30 pm; closed Mon & Sun; no shorts.*

Gilbey's £50 343

1 Market Sq HP7 0DF (01494) 727242

*"Genuinely friendly", "thoughtful" staff add to the charm of this wine bar (named for the gin dynasty which owns it, and with wines from their own vineyards). The setting is a little "squashed-in", but it wins uniform praise for its "surprisingly good" (if "not entirely consistent") cooking. / **Details:** www.gilbeygroup.com; 9.30 pm, Sat 9.45 pm, Sun 8.45 pm.*

ANSTRUTHER, FIFE 9–4D

Anstruther Fish Bar £25 543

42-44 Shore St KY10 3AQ (01333) 310518

*The "BEST fish and chips ever... EVER!" is the main draw at this "popular" venue, with a "good location on the harbour"; this being so, there's "no pretence to excel in terms of ambience, which is a bit in the style of a 1950s American diner". / **Details:** www.anstrutherfishbar.co.uk; 9.30 pm; no Amex; no booking.*

APPLECROSS, HIGHLAND 9–2B

Applecross Inn £41 444

Shore St IV54 8LT (01520) 744262

*"A B&B and great family pub in a beautiful part of the world" – a remote peninsula in the Highlands. "The atmosphere of the place is amazing", and for fish and seafood, it's "tremendous" ("you'll meet the langoustine fisherman at the bar!") / **Details:** www.applecross.uk.com/inn/; off A896, S of Shieldaig; 9 pm; no Amex; need 6+ to book. **Accommodation:** 7 rooms, from £90*

APPLEDORE, DEVON 1–2C

The Coffee Cabin £15 444

22 The Quay EX39 1QS (01237) 475843

*"Best Victoria sponge I've ever tasted!", "best crab sandwich I've EVER had!" – a sample of the superlatives directed at this "brilliant" year-old café, which also offers "inspiring décor" and estuary views. / **Details:** L only.*

ARGYLL, ARGYLL AND BUTE 9–3B

Kilberry Inn £54 543

Nr Tarbert PA29 6YD (01880) 770223

*It "feels like it's in the middle of nowhere" (and it is) but this small, red-roofed restaurant-with-rooms is "worth the journey" (down a "beautiful if difficult" single track) thanks to its "achingly good" food and "reasonably priced" wines. / **Details:** www.kilberryinn.com; 9 pm; closed Mon, Tue L & Wed L; no Amex; booking: max 10. **Accommodation:** 5 rooms, from £210*

ARLINGHAM, GLOUCESTERSHIRE 2–2B

The Old Passage Inn £67 433

Passage Rd GL2 7JR (01452) 740547

*"On the banks of the Severn", a "happy, friendly" restaurant-with-rooms that's particularly of note for its "exceptionally good" fish and seafood; "go there for lunch on a summer's day". / **Details:** www.theoldpassage.com; 9 pm; closed Mon & Sun D. **Accommodation:** 2 rooms, from £80*

ARUNDEL, WEST SUSSEX 3–4A

The Town House £47 433

65 High St BN18 9AJ (01903) 883847

*"A jewel in a charming town"; "everything is fresh and they cook it brilliantly" at this "fantastic-value" restaurant-with-rooms, overlooking the castle. / **Details:** www.thetownhouse.co.uk; 9.30 pm; closed Mon & Sun. **Accommodation:** 4 + family room rooms, from £95*

ASCOT, BERKSHIRE 3–3A

Restaurant Coworth Park Coworth Park £105 455

Blacknest Rd SL5 7SE (01344) 876 600

*"Beautiful dining room, delicious food, wonderful experience"... despite going through chefs at a rate of knots since John Campbell's 2011 departure, the Dorchester Collection's country house hotel – now under Simon Whitley (ex-Simpson's in The Strand) – remains "superb"; "the bill can be high" though! / **Details:** www.coworthpark.com; 9.30 pm; closed Mon & Sun D. **Accommodation:** 17 rooms, from £*

ASENBY, NORTH YORKSHIRE 8–4C

Crab & Lobster £65 435

Dishforth Rd YO7 3QL (01845) 577286

"Bonkers décor" (with bric-à-brac everywhere) is "always a topic of conversation" while visiting this "quirky", very well-known inn. It's not a substitute for good cooking however – the food is "always memorable" and "justifies the (not cheap) price". / **Details:** *www.crabandlobster.co.uk; at junction of Asenby Rd & Topcliffe Rd; 9 pm, Sat 9.30 pm.* **Accommodation:** *17 rooms, from £160*

ASTON TIRROLD, OXFORDSHIRE 2–2D

The Sweet Olive £56 432

Baker St OX11 9DD (01235) 851272

An "excellent" spot offering "lovely French food in the Oxfordshire countryside"; "you have to listen carefully to the longish list of specials recited by Stephane Brun, but it's just so reliable". / **Details:** *www.sweet-olive.com; half a mile off the A417 between Streatley & Wantage; 9 pm; closed 2 weeks in February, and 3 weeks in July.*

AUCHTERARDER, PERTH AND KINROSS 9–3C

Andrew Fairlie Gleneagles Hotel £130 444

PH3 1NF (01764) 694267

"Nothing disappoints at this bastion of excellence in Scotland". Perhaps "it's a shame it's located in a windowless ground floor room", but all-in-all the setting is "magnificent", the service is "impeccable", the cuisine – "firmly rooted in the French classical tradition" – "outstanding", and the wine "superb". Top Menu Tip – "surely the finest lobster dish on the planet". / **Details:** *www.andrewfairlie.co.uk; 10 pm; L only, closed Sun; children: 12+.*

Jon & Fernanda's £49 342

34 High St PH3 1DB (01764) 662442

A handy (and more affordable) alternative to Gleneagles, run by two refugees from the hotel; he turns out "delicious" locally sourced food in the kitchen, while she offers "extremely patient and helpful" service out front. / **Details:** *www.jonandfernandas.co.uk; 9 pm; D only, closed Mon & Sun; no Amex; children: 10+.*

Strathearn Restaurant Gleneagles Hotel £84 333

PH3 1NF (01764) 662231

This "beautiful, old-fashioned dining room" is particularly acclaimed for its "fabulous" buffet ("such an indulgence, such a fantastic display"); for the odd critic, though, the cuisine more generally is a tad "over-ambitious" – and "perhaps designed to please the overseas tourist". / **Details:** *www.gleneagles.com; 10 pm; D only, ex Sun open L & D.* **Accommodation:** *232 rooms, from £*

AXMINSTER, DEVON 2–4A

River Cottage Canteen £41 333

Trinity Sq EX13 5AN (01297) 630 300

TV-chef, Hugh Fearnley-Whittingstall "needs to pull his socks up" with the operation of this "well-converted, beautiful building", or "it will lose all its magic". At its best (often reported at brunch) this "communal dining space with a difference" provides "innovative, small, healthy plates" but on the downside some results are "no better than your average pub". / **Details:** *www.rivercottage.net; 8.30 pm; closed Mon D & Sun D.*

AYLESBURY, BUCKINGHAMSHIRE 3–2A

Dining Room Hartwell House £70 434

Oxford Rd HP17 8NR (01296) 747444

In "magnificent" surroundings, this "splendid" hotel dining room provides "imaginative" food, including "stupendous" afternoon teas served "in the lounges that in their day received Louis XVIII". / **Details:** *www.hartwell-house.com/wine-and-dine/; 2m W of Aylesbury on A418; 9.45 pm; no jeans or trainers; children: 4+.* **Accommodation:** *50 rooms, from £290*

AYLESFORD, KENT 3–3C

Hengist £54 444

7-9 High St ME20 7AX (01622) 885800

Relaunched in 2014 after a glossy makeover by the new owners, this once-illustrious village inn appears to be gathering momentum again; its "consistently good" food and ambience make it "great for a romantic meal". / **Details:** *www.hengistrestaurant.co.uk; 9 pm, Fri-Sat 9.30 pm; closed Sun D; no Amex.*

BAGSHOT, SURREY 3–3A

The Latymer Pennyhill Park Hotel £130 443

London Rd GU19 5EU (01276) 471774

"A focused and exquisite marriage of adventurous tastes" is beautifully presented by Michael Wignall's "fine and complex" 7- and 10-course tasting menus, at this luxurious and highly fêted country house hotel dining room. There are quibbles though – prices are almost as "spectacular" as the food, service can be "uneven", and what is a "gorgeous", "olde worlde" wood-panelled room to some, is to others a little overblown and "old-fashioned". Stop press – Michael Wignall leaves the Latymer to take over Michael Caines's role at Gidleigh Park in

January 2016. / **Details:** www.pennyhillpark.co.uk; 9.15 pm, Fri & Sat 9.30 pm; closed Mon, Tue L, Sat L & Sun; booking: max 8; children: 12+. **Accommodation:** 123 rooms, from £315

BAKEWELL, DERBYSHIRE 5–2C

Piedaniels £49 343

Bath St DE45 1BX (01629) 812687

*"Great-value French cuisine, particularly midweek and lunch" (and with "one or two imaginative touches") is the secret behind the success of this "smart" venture. "Friendly welcome from the enthusiastic owners" too. / **Details:** www.piedaniels-restaurant.com; 10.30 pm, open on Sun only 2 weekends per month; closed Mon & Sun D.*

BALQUHIDDER, PERTH AND KINROSS 9–3C

Monachyle Mhor £79 544

FK19 8PQ (01877) 384622

*"Just a sublime getaway"; this hotel and restaurant in the Trossachs National Park is a "real find at the end of a rough road (although there is a seaplane option!)" and the food is particularly "superlative". / **Details:** www.mhor.net; take the Kings House turning off the A84; 9 pm. **Accommodation:** 14 rooms, from £195*

BANGOR, COUNTY DOWN 10–1D

The Boat House £50 543

1a, Seacliff Rd BT20 5HA (028) 9146 9253

*"It has to the best restaurant in Northern Ireland by a long stretch!"; this "old harbourmaster's building at the marina" – "owned and run by two Dutch brothers" – has been sensitively restored, and wins the highest esteem for its "understated" and "professional" approach, and its "eclectic" cuisine "taking a serious approach to the use of organic local produce"; "interesting wine at really good prices" too and a well-stocked gin bar. Top Tip – "great-value tasting menu". / **Details:** www.theboathouseni.co.uk; 10 pm; closed Mon & Tue.*

BARNET, HERTFORDSHIRE 3–2B

Savoro £45 443

206 High St EN5 5SZ (020) 8449 9888

*"A real hidden treasure in a sea of suburban mediocrity"; with its "lovely table settings" and "fantastic looking, beautifully tasting" food, this hotel dining room strikes more than one reporter as being "unexpectedly good" – and, given "the work and effort that can be seen on the plate", it's also "amazing value for money". / **Details:** www.savoro.co.uk; 10 pm; closed Sun D. **Accommodation:** 9 rooms, from £75*

BARNSLEY, GLOUCESTERSHIRE 2–2C

Barnsley House £58 344

GL7 5EE (01285) 740000

*The "lovely" restaurant of this posh boutique hotel – sibling to The Village Pub just over the road – is "worth a visit even if you are not a resident", thanks to its "exceptionally light" and "flavoursome" cuisine; "a tour round the famous garden adds to the experience" too. / **Details:** www.barnsleyhouse.com; 9 pm, Sat & Sun 9.30 pm; children: 14+ after 7.30 pm. **Accommodation:** 18 rooms, from £290*

The Village Pub £47 343

GL7 5EF (01285) 740421

*A "splendid local" that's "a cut above the average gastroboozer without being pretentious"; it offers "decent food and willing service" in a "cosy" ambience "with open fires" – and, despite being "very busy" (mostly with overnighters) "you still get a good meal". / **Details:** www.thevillagepub.co.uk; 9.30 pm, Sun 9 pm. **Accommodation:** 6 rooms, from £130*

BARRASFORD, NORTHUMBERLAND 8–2A

Barrasford Arms £42 342

NE48 4AA (01434) 681237

*It's a "real treat" to dine at this "slightly faded" pub-with-rooms, overlooking Northumberland National Park; it serves "consistently good food", and chef Tony Binks is "now growing his own salads and vegetables" too! / **Details:** www.barrasfordarms.co.uk; 9 pm; closed Mon & Sun D; no Amex; children: 18 + in bar after 9.30pm. **Accommodation:** 7 rooms, from £85*

BARTON-ON-SEA, HAMPSHIRE 2–4C

Pebble Beach £55 434

Marine Drive BH25 7DZ (01425) 627777

*Pierre Chevillard's "beautifully located cliff top restaurant enjoys lovely views over Bournemouth and Poole Bay, the Isle of Wight and the Needles" ("especially from the garden terrace"), and it serves "sublime local seafood with typically Gallic flair!" ("Lovely accommodation also".) / **Details:** www.pebblebeach-uk.com; 9 pm, Fri & Sat 9.30 pm. **Accommodation:** 4 rooms, from £99.95*

BARWICK, SOMERSET 2–3B

Little Barwick House £69 554

BA22 9TD (01935) 423902

*There's a "superb experience" to be had at Tim & Emma Ford's "lovely" restaurant-with-rooms; it combines "fantastic food without the hype of Michelin stars" and an "excellent wine list with some interesting rarities". / **Details:** www.littlebarwick.co.uk; take the A37 Yeovil to Dorchester road, turn left at* *the brown sign for Little Barwick House; 9 pm; closed Mon, Tue L & Sun; children: 5+ .* ***Accommodation:*** *6 rooms, from £69 pp*

BASLOW, DERBYSHIRE 5–2C

Fischers at Baslow Hall £98 444
Calver Rd DE45 1RR (01246) 583259
"In gorgeous surroundings" (and with "beautiful gardens"), this "romantic" country house hotel sits near the Chatsworth estate (and provides "comfy welcoming rooms for overnight stays"). It's Derbyshire's greatest claim to culinary fame, delivering "exceptional cuisine that's worth every penny". / ***Details:*** *www.fischers-baslowhall.co.uk; on the A623; 8.30 pm; no jeans or trainers.* ***Accommodation:*** *11 rooms, from £180*

Rowley's £53 343
Church Ln DE45 1RY (01246) 583880
"From the team that also run Fischers of Baslow Hall", this "excellent bar-bistro", on the fringe of the Chatsworth Estate, is "back to its best"; it's "hard to find fault" with the "really well thought-out food" – and it's "nigh on half the price" of the owners' other venture! / ***Details:*** *www.rowleysrestaurant.co.uk; 9 pm, Sat 9.30 pm; closed Mon & Sun D; no Amex.*

BASSENTHWAITE, CUMBRIA 7–3C

Bistro At The Distillery £48 223
Setmurthy CA13 9SJ (01768) 788857
"New to the foodie scene this year", an "airy" bistro in a lavishly revamped Victorian cattle parlour; the food (overseen by Northern luminary Terry Laybourne) is "certainly trying hard", but with mixed results so far, and pricing "needs to be seriously looked at" too. / ***Details****: www.bistroatthedistillery.com/; 9 pm.*

BATH, SOMERSET 2–2B

Acorn Vegetarian Kitchen £46 542
2 North Parade Pas BA1 1NX (01225) 446059
"Much improved from (old tenants) Demouths" – this "cramped" spot in a cute alley in the city centre serves "brilliantly tasty dishes with not a morsel of any creature in sight". "On a recent visit, the diners at three other tables were visiting Bath mainly to eat here, and some weren't even vegetarian"! / ***Details****: www.acornvegetariankitchen.co.uk; 9.30 pm, Sat 10 pm.*

Allium Brasserie Abbey Hotel £52 333
1 North Pde BA1 1LF (01225) 809469
"One to watch" – Chris Staines (ex-the Mandarin Oriental, Knightsbridge) can seem "to be trying too hard", but is capable of producing some "stunning" dishes at this newish venture, in a longtime Best Western hotel, now under independent ownership. It wins most acclaim as a good choice for business – "the ambience is great, especially by the window overlooking the square". / ***Details:*** *www.abbeyhotelbath.co.uk/allium/; 9 pm, Fri & Sat 10 pm.*

Bath Priory Hotel £109 233
Weston Rd BA1 2XT (01225) 331922
Amidst "beautiful grounds", this "very smart" property (a Brownsword Hotel) at best offers "precise" cooking, and "impeccable" service in "a lovely and formal" setting. Prices remain "eye-watering" though, and its ratings slipped a notch this year. / ***Details:*** *www.thebathpriory.co.uk; 9.30 pm; no jeans or trainers; children: 5+ L, 12+ D.* ***Accommodation:*** *33 rooms, from £205*

Casanis £52 443
4 Saville Row BA1 2QP (01225) 780055
"The tables are quite close together", but that's the only gripe about this "delightful" and highly popular bistro – "why go anywhere else, when you can enjoy proper French cooking, rather than a copy of it?" / ***Details:*** *www.casanis.co.uk; 10 pm; closed Mon & Sun; no Amex.*

The Circus £45 343
34 Brock St BA1 2LN (01225) 466020
"Enthusiastic and well-informed staff" contribute to the high popularity of this family-owned bistro, near the Royal Crescent. The "reliable" seasonal cooking seldom disappoints, and the setting is "relaxed" (with lunch on the pavement a possibility in summer). / ***Details:*** *www.thecircuscafeandrestaurant.co.uk; 10 pm; closed Sun; no Amex; children: 7+ at D.*

Clayton's Kitchen £55 433
15A, George St BA1 2EN (01225) 585 100
"A great place to come for top-notch cooking" in the city centre – the verdict on Rob Clayton's "relaxing" yet "buzzy" operation; there's a "good bar upstairs too for pre-dinner drinks". / ***Details:*** *www.theporter.co.uk/claytons-kitchen; 10 pm, Fri & Sat 10.30 pm, Sun 9 pm.*

Colonna & Smalls £15 444
6 Chapel Row BA1 1HN (07766) 808067
"The best coffee in Bath, made and served by experts" – the unanimous verdict on this attractively minimal café, by Queen Square, which also does great cakes. / ***Details:*** *www.colonnaandsmalls.co.uk; 5.30 pm, Sun 4 pm; no Amex; booking: max 6.*

Cowshed **£51** 4 5 4
5 The Paragon BA1 5LS (0117) 973 3550
*In a "beautifully restored" Georgian house, this city-centre yearling boasts "fabulous views of the Bath hills"; like the Bristol original, it wins raves for simple things done well (think "great meat from Bristol's Ruby & White" and "excellent hot-stone steak"). / **Details:** www.cowshedrestaurants.com/; 10 pm, Sat 10.30 pm, Sun 3.15 pm.*

The Eastern Eye **£41** 3 4 5
8a Quiet St BA1 2JS (01225) 422323
*A "Georgian Indian", unlikely as it sounds, set in a "unique and grandiose 1800s ballroom, with three massive vaulted glass ceiling domes"; happily, "the extravagance of the venue extends to the food!" / **Details:** www.easterneye.co.uk; 11.30 pm.*

Gascoyne Place **£46** 3 3 2
1 Sawclose BA1 1EY (01225) 445854
*Whilst "unprepossessing from the outside", this Georgian inn is worth a try for its "consistent" and "reasonably priced" food. / **Details:** www.gascoyneplace.com; 10 pm; no Amex.*

Hare & Hounds **£46** 3 2 3
Lansdown Rd BA1 5TJ (01225) 482682
*"Good food and service" are the order of the day at this "pleasantly renovated pub just outside the city centre"; "stunning views" from the garden too. / **Details:** www.hareandhoundsbath.com; 9.30 pm, sun 9 pm; no Amex.*

Menu Gordon Jones **£73** 5 5 2
2 Wellsway BA2 3AQ (01225) 480871
*"Off-beat, irreverent, and exciting!" – the "experimental" cuisine is "really surprising" at this "progressive" but "no-frills" and "cramped" gourmet experience to the south of the city centre. When it comes to the tasting menu, "it's so much fun, as you don't know what you're going to get", but "the flavours are always firing on all cylinders", and there's "a very original wine flight accompaniment". / **Details:** www.menugordonjones.co.uk; 9 pm; closed Mon & Sun; no Amex.*

The Mint Room **£37** 4 3 3
Longmead Gospel Hall, Lower Bristol Rd BA2 3EB (01225) 446656
*"The location is not the usual pretty setting in Bath", but don't be put off – this lavish city-fringes venue is a top destination for "slightly different, upmarket" Indian cuisine "piled high on fancy plates". / **Details:** www.themintroom.co.uk; 11 pm, Fri & Sat 11.30 pm.*

The Olive Tree Queensberry Hotel **£65** 4 3 3
Russell St BA1 2QF (01225) 447928
*"A great element of Bath's restaurant scene" – although this smart (slightly muted) basement hotel dining room is less famous than once it was, chef Chris Cleghorn continues to provide "accomplished, classical dishes with a modern execution". / **Details:** www.olivetreebath.co.uk; 10 pm; Mon-Thu D only, Fri-Sun open L & D. **Accommodation:** 29 rooms, from £125*

The Pump Room **£48** 2 2 5
Stall St BA1 1LZ (01225) 444477
*This "beautiful" and famous Georgian landmark (it's "especially magical with the trio playing") is a "busy" feature of the city centre (as it has been for 200 years); the food can seem a "tad disappointing" in comparison – best play it safe with a "great" breakfast or afternoon tea. / **Details:** www.searcys.co.uk; L only; no booking, Sat & Sun.*

Scallop Shell **£32** 4 2 2
20 Monmouth St BA1 2AY (01225) 420928
*"A modern, new restaurant and fish take-away" (sibling to an older business in Frome) that's "comfy enough, although no bookings are taken". "Quality is all – choose from posh fish 'n' chips, as well as several varieties of grill, plus shellfish dishes". / **Details:** www.thescallopshell.co.uk/fish-chips-bath/; 9.30 pm; closed Sun.*

Sotto Sotto **£45** 4 4 5
10 North Pde BA2 4AL (01225) 330236
*A "very atmospheric" Italian located in old vaults on North Parade, with its "ground level facing out onto an orange grove"; "the food is always deliciously authentic" and the service "superbly professional"... no wonder it's "sometimes difficult to get in"! / **Details:** www.sottosotto.co.uk; 10 pm.*

The Wheatsheaf **£50** 3 4 4
Combe Hay BA2 7EG (01225) 833504
*A "lovely country pub with a warm welcome", just outside the city; reporters were a bit divided on the food this year – evaluations ranged from "just OK" to "excellent". / **Details:** www.wheatsheafcombehay.com; 9.30 pm; closed Mon & Sun D; no Amex. **Accommodation:** 3 rooms, from £120*

Yak Yeti Yak **£34** 3 4 2
12 Pierrepont St BA1 1LA (01225) 442299
*This "original and cosy, if slightly shabby basement", on the fringe of the city centre, is well worth discovering for a "different", "very casual" (and affordable) meal. The food is "a far cry from the usual heavy-handed curry house fare" – "fresh, tasty, with lighter flavours, many grilled dishes, and sauces featuring Sichuan pepper and Himalayan herbs". / **Details:** www.yakyetiyak.co.uk.*

Yammo £37 5 4 2

66 Walcot St BA1 5BD (01225) 938328

A "great-value, friendly, simple, little bistro café", within "spitting distance of all the city's main landmarks". The "basic set-up" is "not elegant, but – with its 'Neapolitan street food formula' – it isn't trying to be". "Stunning pizza" is the highlight you might hope for, alongside other "fresh and really tasty" dishes (such as meatballs) from a "small menu" that "makes passionate use of local ingredients". / **Details:** *www.yammo.co.uk; 10.30 pm, Fri & Sat 11.30 pm, Sun 9 pm.*

BAUGHURST, HAMPSHIRE 2–3D

The Wellington Arms £60 4 4 4

Baughurst Rd RG26 5LP (0118) 982 0110

"A perfect country pub... well, perhaps a perfect country restaurant... oh hang on, and the rooms are nice too!" – Jason King and Simon Page's country inn is consistently praised for its "sublime, but not over-showy cooking" with many items sourced from their garden or restaurant farm. Even fans however, note that it's "not cheap"... / **Details:** *www.thewellingtonarms.com; 9.30 pm; closed Sun D; no Amex.* **Accommodation:** *2 rooms, from £130*

BEACONSFIELD, BUCKINGHAMSHIRE 3–3A

The Cape Grand Cafe & Restaurant £49 3 3 4

6a, Station Rd HP9 1NN (01494) 681137

"Great South African dishes" (and wines) are the hallmark of this "lovely", pleasingly "theatrical" fixture; it makes a "tasty destination for brunch with friends" too. / **Details:** *www.thecapeonline.com; 9.30 pm; closed Mon D, Tue D, Wed D, Thu D & Sun D; no Amex.*

Crazy Bear £65 2 2 5

75 Wycombe End HP9 1LX (01494) 673086

"The sparkling bar... the garden... the crystal-studded leather areas (without mentioning the unique loo set-up)" – this bling-tastic venue is certainly "fantastically different". The Anglo-Thai food? "OK, but not up to what is being charged for it". / **Details:** *www.crazybeargroup.co.uk/beaconsfield; 10 pm; closed Mon & Sun L; children: bar, not after 6pm.* **Accommodation:** *19 rooms, from £220*

The Royal Standard of England £43 2 2 4

Brindle Ln HP9 1XS (01494) 673382

Standards at England's oldest freehouse have seemed a fraction less regal of late. "Certainly it is charming – set off a narrow country lane in woodlands, and with a quaint, olde worlde interior", but food and service can vary. / **Details:** *www.rsoe.co.uk; 10 pm, Sun 9 pm; no Amex.*

Spice Merchant £51 3 3 2

33 London End HP9 2HW (01494) 675474

"Situated in Old Beaconsfield (thus being impossible to park)", this contemporary Indian features a "very varied" menu which includes "some unusual dishes"; "sitting in the conservatory is a pleasant experience". / **Details:** *www.spicemerchantgroup.com; 11 pm, Sun 9.30 pm; no Amex.*

BEAMINSTER, DORSET 2–4B

Brassica £42 4 3 3

4 The Sq DT8 3AS (01308) 538 100

A new venture from Cass Titcombe, ex-of the Canteen chain, to replace MasterChef winner Matt Follas's old restaurant; it's a "pleasing addition" to the local scene, where "the passion for good food shines through by letting local ingredients speak for themselves". / **Details:** *www.brassicarestaurant.co.uk/Site/Home.html; 9 pm, Sun 5 pm; closed Sun D.*

BEARSTED, KENT 3–3C

Fish On The Green £57 4 3 2

Church Ln ME14 4EJ (01622) 738 300

"Very good fish cooked extremely well" is the order of the day at this "fantastic" spot, which fans proclaim as the "only good restaurant" in these parts; caveats? – it's a noisy space and "so very popular" it can feel "rather cramped". / **Details:** *www.fishonthegreen.com; 9.30 pm, Fri & Sat 10 pm; closed Mon & Sun D; no Amex.*

BEAULIEU, HAMPSHIRE 2–4D

The Terrace Montagu Arms Hotel £103 3 4 3

SO42 7ZL (01590) 612324

With its "olde-worlde charm and service", this grand New Forest inn offers the "very best in fine dining but at a cost"; whilst not everyone is wowed, fans claim the food is "utterly superb" – "with the tasting menu being a novel, customisable pick-and-mix, and the cheeseboard finishing the meal off in fine fashion". / **Details:** *www.montaguarmshotel.co.uk; 9.30 pm ; closed Mon & Tue L; no jeans or trainers; children: 11+ D.* **Accommodation:** *22 rooms, from £143*

BEAUMARIS, ISLE OF ANGLESEY 4–1C

The Annex Ye Olde Bull's Head £42 4 2 3

Castle St LL58 8AP (01248) 810329

"In the main street of pretty Beaumaris", a superbly characterful, ancient coaching inn that's "well worth a diversion"; the "light and airy" downstairs

brasserie "tries hard to update pub classics and in the main succeeds" (while upstairs holds an equally pleasing, but much smarter and pricier dining room – 'The Loft' – formula price £67). / **Details:** www.bullsheadinn.co.uk; on the High Street; 9.30 pm; D only, closed Mon & Sun; no jeans; children: 7+ at D. **Accommodation:** 26 rooms, from £105

BEELEY, DERBYSHIRE 5–2C

Devonshire Arms £47 323
Devonshire Sq DE4 2NR (01629) 733259
There's a "cosmopolitan touch" to dishes at this "nice, busy" Chatsworth estate inn ("with a sister restaurant in Pilsey") – "well worth a visit when in the area" according to fans. / **Details:** www.devonshirebeeley.co.uk; 9.30 pm. **Accommodation:** 14 rooms, from £125

BELFAST, COUNTY ANTRIM 10–1D

The Bar & Grill At James Street South £50 443
21 James Street South BT2 7GA
(028) 9560 0700
"Grilled meat is the thing here and other dishes are really sidelines". If that's what's required though this central haunt – where much of the cooking is from a Josper grill – is just the ticket. / **Details:** www.belfastbargrill.co.uk; 10.15 pm; no Amex.

Coppi £40 444
Unit 2 St Anne's Sq BT1 2LR (028) 9031 1959
"Very tasty small dishes and well-balanced mains" win plenty of fans for this Cathedral Quarter Italian; even a reporter who finds it "too dark" ("you can hardly read the menu") concedes that it's "otherwise excellent".

Hadskis £44 443
Commercial Ct BT1 2NB (028) 9032 5444
In the Cathedral Quarter, this small, bare-walled newcomer is proving a very welcome addition to the City, winning consistently high ratings for its contemporary cooking, with many items cooked on a charcoal grill. / **Details:** www.hadskis.co.uk/; midnight.

James Street South £55 233
21 James Street South BT2 7GA
(028) 9043 4310
Opinion remains a little up-and-down on Niall McKenna's fine dining venture; while fans say that it's "consistently good in all respects", others feel the experience was "not what was expected after the refit". / **Details:** www.jamesstreetsouth.co.uk; 10.45 pm; closed Sun.

Mourne Seafood Bar £42 544
34-36 Bank St BT1 1HL (028) 9024 8544
"A charming fish restaurant with a fishmonger at the front", where the cooking is "very inventive and unusual" and "not rapaciously priced" ("wish they'd told me how cheap the lobster was before I ordered something else"!) / **Details:** www.mourneseafood.com; 9.30 pm, Fri & Sat 10.30 pm, Sun 9 pm; no booking at L.

Ox £40 443
1 Oxford St BT1 3LA (028) 9031 4121
It's still early days, but this city-centre two-year-old – from two chefs who met at the iconic L'Arpège in Paris – is already well-recognised for its "marvellous" cooking, "unassuming" service and "funky" wines; in many reporters' view, it's "easily the best restaurant in Belfast".

Il Pirata £38 444
279-281 Upper Newtownards Rd BT4 3JF
(028) 9067 3421
"It's hard to get better value" (especially at lunchtime) than at this trendy but casual Italian in Ballyhackamore Village; "there's a great variety of dishes – you can choose something different every time!" / **Details:** www.ilpiratabelfast.com; 10 pm, Fri & Sat 11 pm; no Amex.

Tedfords Restaurant £53 432
5 Donegall Quay BT1 3EA (028) 90434000
It may not elicit much in the way of commentary, but those who do comment on it are demonstrative in their praise for this airy, seafood-centric venue in a Victorian riverside building near Waterfront Hall. / **Details:** www.tedfordsrestaurant.com; 9.30 pm; closed Mon, Tue L, Sat L & Sun.

Zen £38 434
55-59 Adelaide St BT2 8FE (028) 9023 2244
"Staff are so friendly, and the food is superb (presentation is second to none)", at this stylish and accomplished Japanese – a local fixture of over a decade's standing. / **Details:** www.zenbelfast.co.uk; 11.30 pm, Sun 10.30 pm; closed Sat L.

BEMBRIDGE, ISLE OF WIGHT 2–2D

Fox's Restaurant £41 333
11 High St PO35 5SD (01983) 872626
"Almost unbelievably low prices" are the sweetener at this High Street outfit, with a nice garden; there are "no gimmicks, no fancy décor, just really tasty food beloved by locals" (much of it supplied via the fishmonger next door).

BERKHAMSTED, HERTFORDSHIRE 3–2A

The Gatsby £54 323
97 High St HP4 2DG (01442) 870403
A former cinema foyer with romantic Art Deco décor; recommendations by fans include "good-value" set meals, the "monthly Jazz Brunch" and "top Sunday roasts". / **Details:** *www.thegatsby.net; 10.30 pm, Sun 9.30 pm; no Amex; booking: max 10.*

Porters Restaurant £43 333
Unit 3, 300 High St HP4 1ZZ (01442) 876666
"Just what Berkhamsted needed!", say fans of Richard Bradford's newly relocated newcomer, whose clean, contemporary styling makes a total break from the English heritage theme of its decades in Covent Garden (from which it was driven out by a rent review). Its nowadays "sensibly more limited" brasserie menu still has the pies that used to be its hallmark, but is much more modern in style, and seems a good fit with its local market. / **Details:** *www.porters.uk.com; 10 pm.*

Zaza £42 333
21-23 Lower Kings Rd HP4 2AB
(01442) 767055
A well-regarded branch of this "top-rate small Italian chain" offering the usual staples plus "imaginative" chalkboard specials; it's set in a "really noisy room with le tout Bushey and its environs having a talkative time". / **Details:** *www.zaza.co.uk; 10.30 pm, Sun 10 pm.*

BEVERLEY, EAST YORKSHIRE 6–2A

The Pipe & Glass Inn £57 554
West End HU17 7PN (01430) 810246
"Everything that a gastropub or local ought to be" – James & Kate Mackenzie's "special", "off-the-beaten-track" inn provides "outstanding" cooking and "fabulous Northern hospitality", all in "a very accessible and down-to-earth manner". "Sweet lord, if I lived in this village, none of my children would have an inheritance..." / **Details:** *www.pipeandglass.co.uk; 9.30 pm, Sat 11 pm; closed Mon & Sun D.*

Westwood Bar & Grill £55 433
New Walk HU17 7AE (01482) 881999
"A little gem, run by a lovely lady and her brother" that "keeps getting better and better"; it's praised for an "imaginative use of local produce", "very good-value set menus", and an "upmarket" setting that makes it ideal for a special occasion. / **Details:** *www.thewestwood.co.uk; 9.30 pm; closed Mon & Sun D; no Amex.*

BEXLEY, KENT 3–3B

Miller & Carter Bexley £48 223
Bourne Rd DA5 1PQ (01322) 552748
Mixed feedback this year on this outpost of a small chain, occupying a converted Jacobean barn. Critics feel it's "disappointing all-round", while fans recommend it "for an easygoing meal", with "an interesting range of steaks at reasonable prices". / **Details:** *www.millerandcarter.co.uk/millerandcarerbexley/.*

BIDBOROUGH, KENT 3–3B

Kentish Hare £51 544
95 Bidbourough Ridge TN3 0XB
(01892) 525709
"Just exceptional" – a "recently and tastefully renovated" gastropub "in a beautiful part of the countryside", offering "very skilfully prepared food"; it's a "very popular Sunday rendezvous for families" owing to its "great-value" roasts. "Eat in the attractive outside area if the weather is good." / **Details:** *www.thekentishhare.com/; 9.30 pm, Sun 4pm; closed Mon.*

BIDDENDEN, KENT 3–4C

The Three Chimneys £51 222
Hareplain Rd TN27 8LW (01580) 291472
In picturesque countryside, this 15th-century half-timbered pub has long been well-acclaimed for its food, and fans do praise it for its "consistently high standard". Does it risk complacency though? – there were gripes too this year about toppish prices and an "indifferent attitude". / **Details:** *www.thethreechimneys.co.uk; A262 between Biddenden and Sissinghurst; 9 pm, Fri & Sat 9.30 pm; no Amex; booking: max 20.*

The West House £59 543
28 High St TN27 8AH (01580) 291341
"A lovely old building, in a lovely old village" hosts Graham Garrett's ambitious venture, which serves "stunning" cuisine "with an easy confidence". Service – often "tremendous" – can dip however, and a sceptical minority feel "the price/quality ratio's not great". / **Details:** *www.thewesthouserestaurant.co.uk; Tue-Fri 9 pm, Sat 10 pm; closed Mon, Sat L & Sun D; no Amex.*

BIGBURY-ON-SEA, DEVON 1–4C

Burgh Island Hotel £91 235
TQ7 4BG (01548) 810514
With its "idyllic" setting on a small island, this famous, Agatha Christie-style, 1920s hotel is a "really special" place, especially during one of its regular black-tie dinners. To a minority its

cuisine doesn't match up, but most reports say the "brilliant" cooking makes for an "absolutely fantastic" all-round experience. / **Details:** *www.burghisland.com; 8.30 pm; D only, ex Sun open L & D; no Amex; jacket & tie; children: 12+ at D.* **Accommodation:** *25 rooms, from £400*

The Oyster Shack £49 545
Millburn Orchard Farm, Stakes Hills TQ7 4BE (01548) 810876
"Don't expect creature comforts" at this well-known shack, with its plastic tables and chairs... do expect "great fresh seafood" (including "fantastic lobsters") that's "definitely worth the trek" across mud flats. / **Details:** *www.oystershack.co.uk; 9 pm.*

BILDESTON, SUFFOLK 3–1C

The Bildeston Crown The Crown Hotel £60 433
104 High St IP7 7EB (01449) 740510
Zack Deakins serves up some "wonderful" ("albeit pricey") dishes at this "pleasant" 15th-century coaching inn, with "the main advantage being that it is all local produce and fine dining"; even those who believe it's "not quite there" award it excellent marks. / **Details:** *www.thebildestoncrown.com; from the A14, take the B115 to Bildeston; 9.45 pm, Sun 9 pm.* **Accommodation:** *12 rooms, from £100*

BILLERICAY, ESSEX 3–2C

The Magic Mushroom £51 332
Barleyland Rd CM11 2UD (01268) 289963
With its "reliable" cooking, Darren Bennet's bistro is "probably the best restaurant of its type in the area" (although one reporter who notes that it "continues to benefit from the lack of competition", feels that it "needs to be a little more adventurous"). Top Tip – "good, fixed price midweek menus". / **Details:** *www.magicmushroomrestaurant.co.uk; next to "Barleylands Farm"; midnight; closed Mon & Sun D.*

BIRMINGHAM, WEST MIDLANDS 5–4C

Adam's £73 544
21a Bennetts Hill B2 5QP (01216) 433745
"A new standard of fine dining in Birmingham" – Adam Stokes and wife Natasha's city-centre two-year-old is hailed by fans as Brum's best, with "genuinely seasonal, fresh and inspired" cuisine that "avoids distracting gimmicks to put the focus on the plate" (and there's an "extravaganza" of a 9-course tasting menu). In early 2016 there are plans to re-locate and expand, with the inclusion of a bar, wine room and chef's table. / **Details:** *www.adamsrestaurant.co.uk; 9.30 pm; closed Mon & Sun; children: 8+ at D.*

Al Frash £25 532
186 Ladypool Rd B12 8JS (0121) 753 3120
Probably the Balti Triangle's most famous feature, this brightly-lit, no-frills curry legend provides notably "splendid" baltis to a very "consistent" standard. It's not licensed, but you can BYO.

Asha's Indian Bar and Restaurant £49 332
12-22 Newhall St B3 3LX (0121) 200 2767
"As if (Bollywood legend) Asha Bhosle's name wasn't enough, time after time they keep churning out fine Indian cuisine" at this "excellent" (if rather pricey) city-centre branch of a Gulf States chain; fans NB – the owners launched a glitzy Manchester sibling in September 2015. / **Details:** *www.ashasuk.co.uk; 10.30 pm, Thu-Sun 11 pm; closed Sat L & Sun L.*

Carters of Moseley £70 543
20 Wake Green Rd B13 9EZ (0121) 449 8885
An "unbeatable gastronomic experience in the heart of Moseley"; "Brad Carter produces high quality and imaginative food" at this neighbourhood local and service is "eager to please". / **Details:** *www.cartersofmoseley.co.uk; 9.30 pm; closed Mon & Tue; children: 8+.*

Cielo £56 223
6 Oozells Sq B1 2JB (0121) 632 6882
"Conveniently close to Symphony Hall", this Brindleyplace Italian is a "popular" spot, particularly for a "refined business lunch"; there has been the odd report of "inattentive service" and "disappointing" food of late, however – hopefully just a blip. / **Details:** *www.cielobirmingham.com; 11 pm, Sun 10 pm; no Amex; booking: max 20, Sat & Sun D.*

Edmunds £70 443
6 Central Sq B1 2JB (0121) 633 4944
"Comfortable, spacious tables suit business or romantic occasions", and this Brindleyplace venture pleases all of its small fan club with its "excellent menu" and "impeccable service". / **Details:** *www.edmundsrestaurant.co.uk; 10 pm; closed Mon, Sat L & Sun; no Amex.*

Hotel du Vin et Bistro £50 233
25 Church St B3 2NR (0121) 794 3005
A "pretty consistent" outpost of the attractive hotel-bistro chain that wins most support nowadays as a "good business-lunch venue". / **Details:** *www.hotelduvin.com; 10 pm, Fri & Sat 10.30 pm, Sun 9.30 pm; booking: max 12.* **Accommodation:** *66 rooms, from £160*

Itihaas £47 333
18 Fleet St B3 1JL (0121) 212 3383
Lavish city-centre spot (with a Selfridges spin-off) that continues to elicit high praise indeed for its Mughal-inspired cuisine. / **Details:** *www.itihaas.co.uk; 10 pm; closed Sat L & Sun L.*

Jyoti £23 4 2 1
1045 Stratford Rd B28 8AS (0121) 778 5501
A Formica-topped Indian veggie, in Hall Green, where "you don't miss the meat" (or the atmosphere!) owing to the "fabulous" food on offer, and it's just "so cheap". / **Details:** *www.jyotis.co.uk; 9 pm, Sun 7 pm; no Amex.*

Lasan £58 4 4 2
3-4 Dakota Buildings, James St B3 1SD
(0121) 212 3664
"Deserving much more recognition!" – this modern Jewellery Quarter venture (Brum's best-rated Indian of any ambition) "delivers way ahead of expectations", with its "tremendous", "tingly-fresh" cooking, and "beautiful presentation". Opinions divide on the "white-walled interior with Indian sculptures" – what's an "unpromising space" to sceptics is to most reporters "very inviting". / **Details:** *www.lasan.co.uk; 11 pm; closed Sat L; no trainers.*

Karczma £42 3 3 4
Polish Millennium House, Bordesley Street
B5 5PH (0121) 448 0017
"Close to the city-centre", this offbeat venue (part of Brum's Polish Centre) is decked out like an old Polish country cottage (complete with thatched room and "sheepskins everywhere"). Fans say it's "marvellous", not least the solid Polish fare in "impossibly large portions"..

Opus Restaurant £61 2 3 3
54 Cornwall St B3 2DE (0121) 200 2323
A "large", rather barnlike city-centre outfit offering "consistently good food and service"; it's a versatile spot, tipped for occasions ranging from breakfast to business. / **Details:** *www.opusrestaurant.co.uk; 9.30 pm; closed Sun D; no Amex.*

Purecraft Bar and Kitchen £37 3 2 4
30 Waterloo St B2 5TJ (0121) 237 5666
An "enjoyable new addition to Birmingham's casual eating scene" from Midlands brewery Purity and Simpsons; it offers a predictably "great beer selection" (craft beers plus real ales) but also "good honest cooking". / **Details:** *www.purecraftbars.com/food/; 11 pm, Fri & Sat midnight, Sun 10 pm.*

Purnells £102 4 3 3
55 Cornwall St B3 2DH (0121) 212 9799
Glynn Purnell's city-centre fixture remains many reporters' top choice in Birmingham (although it has some stiff oppo from Adam's nowadays); the setting can seem "slightly clinical", but it delivers a "fabulous" culinary experience, with "well-balanced and striking cuisine". / **Details:** *www.purnellsrestaurant.com; 9.30 pm; closed Mon, Sat L & Sun; children: 6+.*

Rico Libre £32 4 3 3
1 Barn St B5 5QD (01216) 878730
"In what used to be a ratty ex-caff (which was itself an ex-pub)" in Digbeth – complete with "un-ironic mismatched furniture" – a BYO that "makes the stuff you cook at home, but way, way better, and with a convivial front of house". It's open for group bookings Monday and Tuesday, then generally for the rest of the week. / **Details:** *www.rico-libre.co.uk; 10 pm; closed Mon, Tue, Wed L, Thu L, Fri L, Sat L & Sun D.*

San Carlo £51 2 3 4
4 Temple St B2 5BN (0121) 633 0251
A "very busy, buzzy" city-centre outpost of the increasingly well-known Italian chain. The "menus are too long and the tables are too close together", but most – if not quite all – reporters feel "well compensated by the quality of the food". / **Details:** *www.sancarlo.co.uk; 11 pm.*

Simpsons £82 3 3 3
20 Highfield Rd B15 3DU (0121) 454 3434
It's a new era at this Edwardian villa in Edgbaston, which has long offered "the most reliable posh night out in Brum". It reopened in September 2015 after a hefty makeover and a change-up in the kitchen (Nathan Eades replaces longtime head chef Matt Cheal) – the aim is a switch up in gear, but we've left it un-rated till next year's results are in. / **Details:** *www.simpsonsrestaurant.co.uk; 9 pm, Fri & Sat 9.30 pm; closed Sun D.* **Accommodation:** *4 rooms, from £160*

Turners £83 4 2 3
69 High St B17 9NS (0121) 426 4440
"You feel a million miles from the rest of the world" at Richard Turner's recently revamped and "bijou" local; "the bang-on, seasonal cooking has no gimmicks" and on practically all accounts is "excellent", but even fans can find it "expensive" and service can be so-so. / **Details:** *www.turnersrestaurantbirmingham.co.uk; 9.30 pm; closed Mon, Tue L, Wed L, Thu L & Sun; no Amex.*

BISHOP'S STORTFORD, HERTFORDSHIRE 3–2B

Baan Thitiya £36 3 3 2
102 London Rd CM23 3DS (01279) 658575
Located in a 1930s pub with a canalside garden, this suburban Thai serves up some "fantastic" cuisine; there's the odd critic, but the majority of reporters insist it's simply "amazing". / **Details:** *www.baan-thitiya.com; 10 pm, Fri & Sat 10.30 pm, Sun 9.30 pm.*

BISHOPS TACHBROOK, WARWICKSHIRE 5–4C

Mallory Court £68 455
Harbury Ln CV33 9QB (01926) 330214
*It has been "having a bad time of late, having lost many accolades" (including the tyre men's) but this "lovely", Lutyens-style Relais & Châteaux country house hotel seems to be on the up; it won enthusiastic praise this year for its "beautifully presented" food, "excellent" drinks list and "genuinely warm and welcoming staff". / **Details:** www.mallory.co.uk; 2m S of Leamington Spa, off B4087; 8.30 pm; closed Sat L; no trainers. **Accommodation:** 31 rooms, from £159*

BLAIRGOWRIE, PERTH AND KINROSS 9–3C

Kinloch House £78 444
PH10 6SG (01250) 884237
*A "very smart and professional" Relais & Chateaux property offering a "lovely country-house hotel experience"; the food is "not too fussy but everything is done just right" and service "makes every aspect of a stay feel special". / **Details:** www.kinlochhouse.com; past the Cottage Hospital, turn L, procede 3m along A923, (signposted Dunkeld Road); 8.30 pm; no Amex; jacket required; children: 6 for dinner. **Accommodation:** 15 rooms, from £230*

BLAKENEY, NORFOLK 6–3C

The Moorings £43 443
High St NR25 7NA (01263) 740054
*"Still a little gem" – a "busy" bistro that serves "consistently good food" (especially fish) and where the staff are "very willing to go the extra mile". / **Details:** www.blakeney-moorings.co.uk; 10.30 pm; closed Mon & Sun; no Amex.*

BODIAM, EAST SUSSEX 3–4C

The Curlew £56 323
Junction Rd TN32 5UY (01580) 861 394
*This old coaching inn by a busy road in the middle of nowhere is of some renown for its cuisine; as with last year's survey, some reporters found it "a little disappointing" but it undoubtedly retains a good number of fans for whom it's "worth the trip" for its "delicate" cuisine and "lovely atmosphere". / **Details:** www.thecurlewrestaurant.co.uk; 9.30 pm, Sun 9 pm; closed Mon.*

BOLLINGTON, CHESHIRE 5–2B

The Lime Tree £39 233
18-20 High St SK10 5PH (01625) 578182
*An "informal" semi-rural venture that elicits decent feedback, though it's "not up to the high standards" of its legendary Didsbury sibling. (One reporter had a chuckle at their 'Mill Workers' lunch: "I don't think my mill worker ancestors enjoyed such fare!") / **Details:** www.limetreebollington.co.uk; 10 pm, Fri & Sat 11 pm, Sun 6pm; closed Mon; min 9 to book.*

Lord Clyde £45 443
Kerridge SK10 5AH (01625) 562123
*"Fine dining – much better than pub food" in a "small and isolated" inn. Ernst van Zyl's markedly ambitious venture "deserves to be better known because his cooking is top quality". / **Details:** www.thelordclyde.co.uk; 9 pm; closed Mon & Sun D.*

BOLNHURST, BEDFORDSHIRE 3–1A

The Plough at Bolnhurst £50 554
MK44 2EX (01234) 376274
*"Very accomplished" cooking and "delightful" staff win triumphant all-round praise for Martin Lee's "fabulous" gastropub; the extension is a bit soulless, though – "best get in the old part if you can". / **Details:** www.bolnhurst.com; 9.30 pm; closed Mon & Sun D; no Amex.*

BOLTON ABBEY, NORTH YORKSHIRE 5–1B

Burlington The Devonshire Arms £91 333
BD23 6AJ (01756) 718 111
*The Duke of Devonshire's country house hotel certainly offers "delightful surroundings and service"; as ever, there are naysayers who finds the experience "vastly overpriced", but the majority hail its "interesting" food and famously "extensive" wine list. / **Details:** www.thedevonshirearms.co.uk; 9.30 pm, Sat & Sun 10 pm; closed Mon; jacket at D; children: 7+. **Accommodation:** 40 rooms, from £250*

BOUGHTON LEES, KENT 3–3C

The Manor Restaurant Eastwell Manor £70 345
Eastwell Pk TN25 4HR (01233) 213000
*A "lovely" Elizabethan manor house hotel, "overlooking the rolling countryside", that's "always a real treat for a spa break and a gastronomic weekend away". The "very creative" new chef serves up a range of "extremely good-value" menus. / **Details:** www.eastwellmanor.co.uk; 3m N of Ashford on A251; 9.30 pm; no jeans or shorts; booking: max 8. **Accommodation:** 62 rooms, from £180*

BOUGHTON MONCHELSEA, KENT 3–3C

The Mulberry Tree £50 333
Hermitage Ln ME17 4DA (01622) 749082
*"A bit out-of-the-way", but this "lovely" bar-restaurant, set in "pleasant grounds" just outside Maidstone, continues to draw acclaim for its "good selection of dishes in the modern British style". / **Details:** www.themulberrytreekent.co.uk; 9 pm, Fri & Sat 9.30 pm; closed Mon & Sun D; no Amex.*

BOURNEMOUTH, DORSET 2–4C

Chez Fred £28 442
10 Seamoor Rd BH4 9AN (01202) 761023
*Fred Capel's upmarket but "affordable" fixture still offers "the best fish 'n' chips in Bournemouth", with fish as "fresh and tasty as you could wish", and "the chips and mushy peas are up to the mark as well"! "Get there early to avoid the queues (out the door)!" / **Details:** www.chezfred.co.uk; 9.45 pm, Sun 9 pm; closed Sun L; no Amex; no booking.*

WestBeach £51 334
Pier Approach BH2 5AA (01202) 587785
*A "beautiful restaurant right on the seafront by the pier", combining "lovely" sea views and "excellent, well-executed" food (especially the fishy kind). / **Details:** www.west-beach.co.uk; 10 pm.*

BOURTON ON HILL, GLOUCESTERSHIRE 2–1C

Horse & Groom £42 444
GL56 9AQ (01386) 700413
*"Great food, reasonable quantities, unpretentious, not expensive... did I dream it?" – so says a fan of this "upmarket Cotswold pub with a great garden", praised also for its "pleasant and friendly" style. / **Details:** www.horseandgroom.info; 9 pm, Fri & Sat 9.30 pm; closed Sun D; no Amex. **Accommodation:** 5 rooms, from £120*

BOWNESS-ON-WINDERMERE, CUMBRIA 7–3D

Miller Howe Restaurant & Hotel £67 334
Rayrigg Rd LA23 1EY (01539) 442536
*A once-famous Lakeland country house hotel whose setting and "amazing" views (of Lake Windermere) "must be the finest in England". The food can be "variable" but "when it is good, it is very good" (and, as further affirmation, "HM the Queen and Princess Anne ate here in recent times"!) / **Details:** www.millerhowe.com; on A592 between Windermere & Bowness; 8.45 pm; no Amex. **Accommodation:** 15 rooms, from £125*

BRADFORD ON AVON, WILTSHIRE 2–3B

Three Gables £54 444
1 St Margaret's St BA15 1DA (01225) 781666
*Refurbed and relaunched a few years ago, this restaurant in a 17th-century building with leaded windows and the eponymous gables delivers "interesting and imaginative" cuisine from Bath Priory-trained chef Marc Salmon; its small fan club feel it "certainly deserves to succeed". / **Details:** www.thethreegables.com; 10 pm; closed Mon & Sun.*

Timbrells Yard £48 323
49 St Margaret's St BA15 1DE
(01225) 869492
*After a huge investment from Draco Pubs, this old boozer, with its "lovely waterside location" and "suntrap garden", has emerged as an upscale boutique hotel, and garners modest but upbeat feedback. / **Details:** www.timbrellsyard.com; 9.45 pm.*

BRADFORD, WEST YORKSHIRE 5–1C

Akbar's £30 443
1276 Leeds Rd BD3 8LF (01274) 773311
*This "big, noisy Indian", the original outpost of a hit local chain, "is just sooo busy" but despite the "chaos" they "manage to serve good curries at a good price"; it's "popular with the local Asian community, which is a good sign". / **Details:** www.akbars.co.uk; midnight, Sun 11.30 pm; D only.*

Karachi £22 522
15-17 Neal St BD5 0BX (01274) 732015
*This "no-frills Bradford curry house always hits the spot" with "so fresh", "truly authentic" Indian dishes that are "incredible value for money" – just "don't expect smiles or cutlery"! / **Details:** 1 am, Fri & Sat 2 am; no credit cards.*

Mumtaz £28 433
386-410 Great Horton Rd BD7 3HS
(01274) 571861
*"Been going for nearly 30 years and just keeps growing"; OK, so "service standards occasionally slip" nowadays, but the food can still be "brilliant" at this landmark curry house. "It's not BYO – alcohol isn't allowed on the premises". / **Details:** www.mumtaz.com; midnight, Fri & Sat 1 am.*

Zouk £34 433
1312 Leeds Rd BD3 8LF (01274) 258 025
*"My favourite enormo-curry house!" – a big, buzzy outfit where "curries are always of an excellent standard". / **Details:** www.zoukteabar.co.uk; 10.30 pm; no Amex; no shorts.*

BRADWELL, DERBYSHIRE 5–2C

The Samuel Fox Country Inn £50 544

Stretfield Rd S33 9JT (01433) 621 562

*"Nothing like it for miles" – a "fine dining" country inn, where chef/patron James Duckett turns out "very accomplished" food that's "brimming with flavour", both from the "short à la carte" and "very accomplished" tasting menu. "Friends from the smoke are slightly disbelieving that we have such a high standard on our doorstep!" / **Details:** www.samuelfox.co.uk; 9 pm, Sun 8pm.*

BRANCASTER STAITHE, NORFOLK 6–3B

The White Horse £50 323

Main Rd PE31 8BY (01485) 210262

*"A lovely terrace and orangery overlooking the beautiful North Norfolk coast" ("you sit overlooking the wetlands and sea which you can see through large glass windows") is the main draw to this "popular" spot, but "the food is also worth trying" – not least the "large, juicy and succulent" oysters. / **Details:** www.whitehorsebrancaster.co.uk; 9 pm; no Amex. **Accommodation:** 15 rooms, from £94*

BRAY, BERKSHIRE 3–3A

Caldesi in Campagna £71 443

Old Mill Ln SL6 2BG (01628) 788500

*"Holding its own in a village packed with Michelin stars" – Giancario Caldesi's tucked-away, Thames-side Italian "can always be relied-on to provide a splendid experience", with "fine Italian cooking", well-chosen wines and "impeccable" service. And "sitting in the garden on a sunny afternoon enjoying a superb Italian meal is just heaven!" / **Details:** www.caldesi.com; 9.30 pm; closed Mon & Sun D.*

Crown Inn £53 323

High St SL6 2AH (01628) 621936

*With its "low beams, village location, fires in winter" this "quality" boozer has "a real local / community feel", and "does all the traditional dishes well". If you didn't know that this was part of Heston's empire however, you'd never guess. / **Details:** www.crownatbray.com; 9.30 pm, Fri & Sat 10 pm, Sun 8 pm.*

The Fat Duck £276 454

High St SL6 2AQ (01628) 580333

*"The Fat Duck is to food what Cirque du Soleil is to circuses – a wonderful, and unique, experience". And in spite of the terrifying prices, it is striking how satisfied most reporters are with its "pure theatre and pure gastronomic experience". For much of this year, this world-famous converted pub has been closed for a complete overhaul, and in September 2015 it re-opened promising 'a nostalgic trip full of playful memories, filled with curiosity, discovery and adventure' (for which you have to buy your ticket up-front!) We're looking forward to hearing what this means in next year's survey, but – despite the absence of snail porridge and egg-and-bacon ice cream from the new menu, and the addition of a new £150,000, Willy Wonka-esque roving sweet dispenser – our rating is a bet that it will turn out a case of 'plus ça change'. / **Details:** www.thefatduck.co.uk; 9 pm; closed Mon & Sun.*

The Hind's Head £65 444

High St SL6 2AB (01628) 626151

*"Incredibly refined pub food" – "the depth of flavour they give to traditional dishes is amazing" – justifies many-a-trip to Heston's "very relaxed" pub, next door to The Fat Duck. It's not quite as commented-on as The Hand & Flowers nowadays, but reporters say it has the edge on its nearby rival. / **Details:** www.hindsheadbray.com; 9.30 pm; closed Sun D.*

Riverside Brasserie £56 335

Monkey Island Ln, Bray Marina SL6 2EB (01628) 780553

*What's in a name? – in this case, the main attraction of this tucked-away brasserie which, despite offering some "lovely" food, attracts the most acclaim for its "divine" and "romantic" Thames-side setting; "sit outside, and watch the big boats go by..." / **Details:** www.riversidebrasserie.com; 10 pm.*

Waterside Inn £220 555

Ferry Rd SL6 2AT (01628) 620691

*"Perfect in every way!" – Alain Roux's "heavenly" Thames-side legend is at "the very pinnacle of classic French cuisine" ("with a few modern, but unpretentious twists along the way"). Aperitifs on the terrace in summer are a particular highlight, but the "elegant", if "slightly old-school" setting is also "wonderful in winter", and the ambience is enhanced by the impeccably well-judged service led by "masterful maître d' Diego". "Your plastic needs a very high melting point" to cope with the "toe-curling prices", but for the vast majority of reporters "it's a spectacular experience for your bank account to die for". / **Details:** www.waterside-inn.co.uk; off A308 between Windsor & Maidenhead; 9.30 pm; closed Mon & Tue; no jeans or trainers; booking: max 10; children: 9+. **Accommodation:** 11 rooms, from £240*

BREARTON, NORTH YORKSHIRE 8–4B

The Malt Shovel £48 433

HG3 3BX (01423) 862929

*A "busy yet relaxed" rural inn that's "settling down well under the new ownership"; "everything is cooked to a turn". / **Details:** www.themaltshovelbrearton.co.uk; off A61, 6m N of Harrogate; 10 pm, Sun 4 pm; closed Mon & Sun D; no Amex.*

BRECON, POWYS 2–1A

The Felin Fach Griffin **£48** 4 5 4
Felin Fach LD3 0UB (01874) 620111
Profound satisfaction this year with this "wonderful" pub in the Brecon Beacons – one of Wales's more consistent culinary destinations. "Lovely", "relaxed and confident" service earns particular praise, but the "excellent locally sourced food" is highly rated too. / ***Details:*** *www.eatdrinksleep.ltd.uk; 20 mins NW of Abergavenny on A470; 9 pm, Fri & Sat 9.30 pm; no Amex.* ***Accommodation:*** *7 rooms, from £115*

BRENTWOOD, ESSEX 3–2B

Alec's **£65** 4 3 3
Navestock Side CM14 5SD (01277) 375 696
Some may find it "too full of TOWIE types!" – but this "glitzy" dining room, "set in a modern, spacious building", is universally acclaimed as "a surprising and great find in Essex" thanks to its "beautifully cooked seafood". / ***Details:*** *www.alecsrestaurant.co.uk; 10 pm, Sun 4.30 pm; closed Mon, Tue L, Wed L & Sun D; no Amex; children: 12+.*

BRIDPORT, DORSET 2–4B

Hive Beach Cafe **£42** 4 3 3
Beach Rd DT6 4RF (01308) 897070
"Basic, canteen-style service belies the quality of the food" at this "dog and kid-friendly" haunt – "a perfect place to eat al fresco on a sunny day" (but "busy, even on a rainy day" – "be prepared to queue"). On the menu, "the freshest of seafood" – "it's essentially a glorified picnic with five-star fish!" / ***Details:*** *www.hivebeachcafe.co.uk; 8 pm July & August only; L only; no booking.* ***Accommodation:*** *2 rooms, from £95*

Riverside **£52** 5 4 4
West Bay DT6 4EZ (01308) 422011
"With a very picturesque setting, in the middle of the river estuary in West Bay (TV's 'Broadchurch')", Arthur Watson's "informal, timbered restaurant" provides "the most delightful blend of warm and friendly service, with simple ingredients cooked superbly well" – "translucently fresh fish", much of it "caught in the harbour that morning". / ***Details:*** *www.thefishrestaurant-westbay.co.uk; 9 pm; closed Mon & Sun D.*

Watch House Cafe **£35** 3 3 3
West Bay DT6 4EN (01308) 459330
Offering "Hive Beach-quality" (its more famous rival) but "fewer queues", this waterside West Bay café is a top pick for wood-fired pizzas "plus the catch of the day". / ***Details:*** *www.watchhousecafe.co.uk; 8 pm; closed Mon D, Tue D, Wed D, Thu D & Sun D.*

BRIGHTON, EAST SUSSEX 3–4B

Basketmakers Arms **£40** 4 4 4
12 Gloucester Rd BN1 4AD (01273) 689006
"By far Brighton's best pub" – so say fans of this North Laine boozer serving "proper pub food, done superbly well". / ***Details:*** *www.basketmakersarms.co.uk; 9 pm; no booking.*

Bill's at the Depot **£41** 2 2 3
100 North Rd, The Depot BN1 1YE
(01273) 692894
The chain's "buzzing" North Laine outpost still offers "reliable" breakfasts – albeit "nothing to frighten the horses"; now under restaurant mogul Richard Caring, the mini-empire is, say sceptics, "starting to show 'chain'-quality food and service"... "perhaps it's expanding too much"? / ***Details:*** *www.bills-website.co.uk; 10 pm; no Amex.*

Burger Brothers **£13** 4 4 2
97 North Rd BN1 1YE (01273) 706980
It's "pretty much a take-away" (having "about 6 seats") but "bloody hell they make a good burger" at this "must-try" joint, and the add-ons are also "spot-on"; "I've eaten them drunk and sober, and they blow me away each time"!

Casa Don Carlos **£34** 3 3 4
5 Union St BN1 1HA (01273) 327177
"Still the best tapas place in town" – the reason why this no-frills Lanes stalwart remains ever-popular amongst locals; good sherries too. / ***Details:*** *11 pm, Thu 9 pm, Fri-Sun 10 pm; closed Thu L.*

The Chilli Pickle **£45** 5 4 3
17 Jubilee St BN1 1GE (01273) 900 383
"Bright, colourful and buzzing describe both the ambience and the food" at this city-centre destination – what most reporters consider "Brighton's best Indian". "In a country full of curry houses that label themselves 'modern', because they have finally renewed their '70s décor and now use square plates, this is a genuine stand-out", with "magical" food that's "zingy and so moreish". / ***Details:*** *www.thechillipickle.com; 10.30 pm, Sun 10.15 pm; closed Tue.*

La Choza **£23** 4 4 4
36 Gloucester Rd BN1 4AQ (01273) 945 926
"You won't go hungry" after a visit to this North Laine burrito bar. A "bright" space – it may be "cramped and noisy" but it's "full of fun" and its Mexican street food is "wonderful, especially for the bargain price". / ***Details:*** *www.lachoza.co.uk; Mon 10 pm, Tue-Sun 9 pm.*

The Coal Shed **£54** 3 2 3
8 Boyces St BN1 1AN (01273) 322998
"It's not quite Hawksmoor, and not cheap", but this city-centre grillhouse yearling receives a

good rep on the whole from reporters who laud its "wonderful" steaks and burgers. / **Details:** *www.coalshed-restaurant.co.uk; 10 pm, Fri & Sat 10.30 pm.*

Coggings & Co £34 442

87-93 Dyke Rd BN1 3JE (01273) 220220

Just off Seven Dials, a "solid addition to the Brighton burger scene" from Andrew Coggings (ex-Preston Park Tavern); the formula? – "burgers, burgers, more burgers, tasty ones though" (and with a focus on Sussex produce) in a smartish setting. / **Details:** *www.coggingsandco.com; 11 pm, Sun 7pm.*

Curry Leaf Cafe £38 433

60 Ship St BN1 1AE (01273) 207070

"Miles away from your standard anglicised British curry house", this year-old café wins raves for "absolutely bang-on southern Indian cooking" ("a sublime marriage of flavours" that's "very realistically priced") and a "huge range of craft beers too". (It's "about to expand to a second site which is very exciting!") / **Details:** *www.curryleafcafe.com; 10 pm.*

Donatello £32 333

1-3 Brighton Pl BN1 1HJ (01273) 775477

This well-established Lanes Italian remains a "very cheerful" spot offering "exceptional value for money"; "every town should have a family-run local like this!" / **Details:** *www.donatello.co.uk; 11.30 pm.*

The Restaurant at Drakes Drakes Hotel £69 453

44 Marine Pde BN2 1PE (01273) 696934

In the basement of a Kemptown boutique hotel, on the seafront, this small dining room continues to garner very enthusiastic – if oddly limited – feedback, mostly for its exceptional cuisine, and "very knowledgeable and experienced" service. / **Details:** *www.therestaurantatdrakes.co.uk; 9.45 pm.* **Accommodation:** *20 rooms, from £115*

English's £52 323

29-31 East St BN1 1HL (01273) 327980

"Still reigning supreme for fish!" – so say fans of this "historic landmark" (est. 1890s) in The Lanes, which, though slightly "old-fashioned and worn" has "attractive fin de siècle murals" and a "long and illustrious seafood pedigree". "Standards have varied widely" over time, and it is something of "a tourist trap", but on most accounts it's on a roll currently, serving "excellent seafood". / **Details:** *www.englishs.co.uk; 10 pm, Sun 9.30 pm.*

Fishy Fishy £49 333

36 East St BN1 1HL (01273) 723750

"You can be sure that the fish is always freshly caught" at this packed Lanes staple, where "crab is cooked to perfection"; "being by the sea in Brighton you would think they would have loads of competition, but that's not so!" / **Details:** *www.fishyfishy.co.uk; 9.30 pm, Fri & Sat 10 pm.*

Food for Friends £41 323

17-18 Prince Albert St BN1 1HF (01273) 202310

There's some sentiment that this Lanes institution is "not as good as it used to be", with gripes about "stretched" service, "lacklustre", dishes, and a longing for "the old version of this place, before it got 'upmarket'". No doubting though that for most folk, it continues to offer "lovely" meat-free cooking. / **Details:** *www.foodforfriends.com; 10 pm, Fri & Sat 10.30 pm; no booking, S & Sun L.*

Giggling Squid £27 233

129 Church Rd BN3 2AE (01273) 771991

"Not the place for a romantic lingering meal", but "for a tasty, fast and fun" bite to eat it's hard to beat the Thai chain's "lively" (and original) outpost, in Hove. / **Details:** *www.gigglingsquid.com; Mon-Sat 10.45 pm Sun 9.45 pm.*

The Ginger Dog £52 222

12 College Pl BN2 1HN (01273) 620 990

Somewhat mixed opinions on this Gingerman Group gastropub in Kemptown: to fans it's "a useful place" with "more interesting menu options than most places", and "good for a casual meal"; to critics, though, it's "uninspiring" and "doesn't live up to its good reputation". / **Details**: *www.gingermanrestaurants.com; off Eastern Road near Brighton College; 10 pm.*

The Ginger Pig £52 344

3 Hove St BN3 2TR (01273) 736123

"Casual but special!" – that's how legions of locals see this "unfailing" Hove gastropub (part of the local Gingerman empire), which, despite the odd accusation that it's "overpriced", wins a hymn of praise for its "effortless" service and "consistently excellent" cooking. / **Details:** *www.thegingermanrestaurants.com; 10 pm, Sun 9 pm; no trainers.*

Gingerman £55 553

21a Norfolk Sq BN1 2PD (01273) 326688

"The original, and still the best, of the Ginger-collection" – this "small" favourite, "just back from the seafront" has a "new, bare-brick look" nowadays. It's a "cosy, neighbourhood-style" (rather "cramped") place, with a large, loyal clientele, and its "always dependable" cooking ("never cutting edge, and the better for it") maintains it as "Brighton's best restaurant" for many reporters. / **Details:** *www.gingermanrestaurant.com; 9.45 pm; closed Mon.*

Indian Summer £45 544

69 East St BN1 1HQ (01273) 711001

"Some of the best Indian food ever (and I come from near Brum!)" – this "modern Indian" in The

Lanes now incorporates a street food selection into its "very different" selection of "fabulous", "subtly spiced" dishes. "They just moved next door to gain 50% more seating so they won't have to turn away so many disappointed customers!" / **Details:** *www.indian-summer.org.uk; 10.30 pm, Sun 10 pm; closed Mon L.*

Iydea **£20** **4 3 3**
17 Kensington Gdns BN1 4AL (01273) 667 992
A "Brighton gem" whose "simply excellent and well-priced vegetarian food" – "often raw", some of it vegan – make it a "consistently reliable spot despite being both busy and slightly utilitarian"; its Hove sibling on "Western Road opens for dinner, which is a great move". / **Details:** *www.iydea.co.uk; 5 pm; no Amex or Maestro.*

The Lion & Lobster **£34** **4 3 3**
24 Sillwood St BN1 2PS (01273) 327299
It's a "bit of a noisy, rough-looking pub downstairs", but venture on to the upstairs restaurant of this boozer, in a Hove backstreet, and you'll be "pleasantly surprised" by the "excellent" menu on offer (fish and seafood in particular). / **Details:** *www.thelionandlobster.co.uk; 10 pm .*

Little Fish Market **£70** **5 4 3**
10 Upper Market St BN3 1AS (01273) 722213
"Simplicity is the charm" of this "wonderfully intimate little restaurant" located in a former fishmonger's and serving the "highest quality" fish prepared by chef Duncan Ray, ex-of the Fat Duck, It's a "must-try when in Brighton", only don't forget to "book in advance" (and bring cash)! / **Details:** *www.thelittlefishmarket.co.uk; closed Mon, Tue L, Wed L, Thu L, Fri L & Sun.*

Market **£41** **3 3 3**
42 Western Rd BN3 1JD
From the owners of Brighton's Graze (RIP) a new all-day restaurant and bar in the heart of Hove's Brunswick village. It opened in September 2015, too late for our survey.

Plateau **£47** **3 4 3**
1 Bartholomews BN1 1HG (01273) 733085
"A lively bar and restaurant in the heart of The Lanes" that's "very, very French in concept", offering a "good if eccentric" range of sharing plates, a "great natural wine list" and characterful Gallic service ("Madame host was on one knee by our table as we joked cosily..."). / **Details:** *www.plateaubrighton.co.uk; 10 pm.*

The Regency **£31** **3 3 3**
131 Kings Rd BN1 2HH (01273) 325014
"Despite being firmly on the tourist trail", this "old-style chippy, with decent sea views" is "a classic". Perhaps "it's better away from the peak of summer when the charmingly brusque staff aren't run ragged", but the place is "always reliable" for "great chips and well-battered fish, all very fresh, plus a good deal of other dishes". / **Details:** *www.theregencyrestaurant.co.uk; 10 pm.* **Accommodation:** *30 rooms, from £50*

Riddle & Finns **£48** **4 4 4**
12b, Meeting House Ln BN1 1HB
(01273) 323008
"Super crab salad" and other "lovely" seafood dishes inspire nothing but high praise for this popular, communal-eating destination – the candlelit Lanes original of what now has a sister operation (see also its beachside offshoot). / **Details:** *www.riddleandfinns.co.uk; 10 pm, Fri & Sat 11 pm; no booking.*

Riddle & Finns On The Beach **£48** **4 3 4**
139 Kings Road Arches BN3 2FN
(01273) 821218
An "excellent addition for Riddle & Finns on the seafront"; in a "lovely spot under the arches, right by the beach" (that some still remember as Due South, RIP), this new sibling to The Lanes original offers a "great range of oysters" plus "seafood cooked to perfection" and "run to table from kitchen"; upstairs tables are preferred. / **Details:** *www.riddleandfinns.co.uk; 10 pm.*

Salt Room **£54** **4 3 2**
106 Kings Rd BN1 2FU (01273) 929488
"Overlooking the ruins of the West Pier", the Hilton Metropole's sleek new restaurant is an "unexpected gem", offering "really innovative fish dishes"; being a seriously "buzzy" spot, it's perhaps not one for a tête-à-tête. Top Menu Tip – "the dessert called 'Taste of the Pier' is utterly wonderful". / **Details:** *www.saltroom-restaurant.co.uk; 10 pm, Fri & Sat 10.30 pm.*

Set **£48** **4 3 3**
33 Regency Sq BN1 2GG (01273) 324302
This modish pop-up from two Brighton chefs now has a "cool" new home in a Regency Square boutique hotel; it offers a "mix of fine dining and comfort food" with "punchy flavour combinations", and while it may "overreach" at times, reporters "can't fault the ambition". / **Details:** *www.thesetrestaurant.com/; 9.30 pm; closed Mon & Sun.*

Silo **£30** **4 4 4**
39 Upper Gardner St, North Laine BN1 4AN
(01273) 674 259
"This really is just the place for the raging eco-foodie!" – a rugged North Laine spot with a "zero-waste policy and the hipster vibe that goes with it"; "in another restaurant I'd find the jam-jar drinking vessels and plates made from recycled shopping

bags a bit much, but the food is seriously good and I forgive them"! / **Details:** *www.silobrighton.com; 5 pm, Thu-Sat 8.30 pm; closed Mon D, Tue D, Wed D & Sun D.*

64 Degrees £47 332

53 Meeting House Ln BN1 1HB
(01273) 770115

"Exciting small sharing plates" with "superb flavours and combinations" inspire armies of local fans for this Lanes yearling. Results can be "hit-and-miss" though, and even fans can find it "cramped and uncomfortable" (and also "loud" – "I could have done without the Iron Maiden blaring out!") / **Details:** *www.64degrees.co.uk; 9.45 pm.*

Small Batch Coffee £15 444

17 Jubilee St BN1 1GE (01273) 697597

This fast-growing ethical chain "is consistent in the excellence of its coffee", with "decent sandwiches and cakes and buttery yummy pastries" another plus; "staff are usually hipster types, but friendly and know their stuff"! / **Details:** *www.smallbatchcoffee.co.uk; 7 pm, Sun 6 pm.*

Terre à Terre £52 542

71 East St BN1 1HQ (01273) 729051

"The best veggie in the World!" – practically no-one (meat-eaters included) has a bad word to say about this "amazingly inventive" Lanes fixture, whose "slightly bonkers" creations are "always spectacular" – "I'd never heard of most of the ingredients, but all the dishes tasted amazing!" / **Details:** *www.terreaterre.co.uk; 10.30 pm, Sat 11 pm, Sun 10 pm; booking: max 8, Fri & Sat.*

24 St Georges £48 432

24-25 St Georges Rd BN2 1ED
(01273) 626060

There's "some serious cooking to be had" at this Kemptown restaurant (including some "delicious" veggie options) but some reporters feel that "atmosphere's somewhat lacking", or that "it could do with lightening up". / **Details:** *www.24stgeorges.co.uk/; 5.30 pm, Sat 12.30 pm.*

Urchin £38 434

15-17 Belfast St BN3 3YS (01273) 241881

"Hidden down a backstreet" – atop the Brighton Gin distillery – this new venue from the teams behind Small Batch and Velo Café is a "first for Hove": a pub specialising in "craft beers galore" (over 100) and "cracking" seafood. It's a "bold concept" but "very well executed" and "excellent value". / **Details:** *www.facebook.com/urchinpubhove; 11 pm, Fri & Sat midnight.*

Warung Tujuh £37 442

7 Pool Valley BN1 1NJ (01273) 720 784

An "amazing find in the seafront area" (which abounds with "poor value eateries"); they may have "no idea how to pronounce anything on the menu" (or the name of the place) but reporters have no doubts about this "small" venue's "wonderful Indonesian food". / **Details:** *www.warungtujuh.com; 11 pm.*

BRIGHTWELL BALDWIN, OXFORDSHIRE 2–2D

Lord Nelson £47 322

OX49 5NP (01491) 612497

Ancient, antique-laden village inn especially recommended for its "very enjoyable Sunday lunch"; service, while "friendly", can be "hit-and-miss". / **Details:** *www.lordnelson-inn.co.uk; Mon-Sat 10 pm, Sun 9.30 pm; no Amex.*

BRISTOL, CITY OF BRISTOL 2–2B

Bell's Diner And Bar Rooms £49 323

1 York Rd BS6 5QB (0117) 924 0357

Little in the way of survey commentary of late on this Montpellier stalwart, which was reborn in a small plates incarnation in 2013; now under an ex-Rocinantes team, it's serving up modern Med food in the same ramshackle setting with a vinyl-only music policy to go with it... more feedback please! A sister site, Bellita, opened in Bristol's Cotham Hill in October 2015. / **Details:** *www.bellsdiner.com; 10 pm; closed Mon L & Sun.*

Birch £41 453

47 Raleigh Rd BS3 1QS (01179) 028 326

"Simple, understated and excellent value" – the virtues of Sam Leach and Beccy Massey's small, white-walled shop-conversion in Southville, where engaging staff provide "a limited, daily changing menu, using locally grown produce" (much of it from their own allotment). "Everything is to a very high standard, and the best dishes are divine!" / **Details:** *www.birchbristol.co; 10 pm; D only, closed Sun-Tue.*

Bordeaux Quay £54 423

Canons Way BS1 5UH (0117) 943 1200

"A view over boats bobbing on the water" adds to the charms of a visit to this "vast" warehouse conversion, spanning an "airy, attractive" brasserie, formal restaurant, deli and cookery school. The eco-minded food is also judged "inventive and well-presented", but there's been a couple of service blips of late. / **Details:** *www.bordeaux-quay.co.uk; Mon-Sat 10.30 pm, Sun 9.30 pm.*

Bosco Pizzeria £37 5 4 3

96 Whiteladies Rd BS8 2QX
(01179) 737 978

"A new addition to Bristol's burgeoning pizza scene, but what an addition!" – a "stylish" Soho-chic one-year-old where "Neapolitan pizzas are the main attraction", but where "steak, fish and poultry dishes sing with authenticity" too. / **Details:** *www.boscopizzeria.co.uk/#contact; 10 pm.*

Bravas £36 4 4 4

7 Cotham Hill BS6 6LD (01173) 296887

"Bravas has found its feet" in its new post pop-up form, and serves "wondrous" tapas – "more adventurous than the usual staples" with many "new twists on old-favourite dishes". It occupies a "cosy" and "fun" space, which "does an excellent job of making you think you are actually in Spain" (quite a coup in Cotham Hill!) / **Details:** *www.bravas.co.uk; 11 pm, Thu-Sat midnight; closed Mon & Sun.*

Casamia £114

38 High St BS9 3DZ (0117) 959 2884

"If you like clever, technical, pretty cuisine", the Sanchez-Iglesias brothers's "thoughtful and exciting gastronomical experience" – "an event rather than a mere meal" – is based on "a procession of fabulous tasting plates". Closed in summer 2015, it will re-open in January 2016 on this new site (about five miles from its Westbury-on-Trym origins) on the ground floor of the former Bristol General Hospital, overlooking the harbourside. For the time being, we've left it un-rated. Stop Press – in November 2015 Jonray Sánchez-Iglesias lost his fight with skin cancer aged 32 and passed away. Where this leaves plans for the re-launch is unknown. / **Details:** *www.casamiarestaurant.co.uk; 9.30 pm; closed Mon & Sun; no Amex.*

The Cowshed £48 3 3 2

44-46 Whiteladies Rd BS8 2NH
(0117) 973 3550

"If you like meat this is the place to go" – a "spacious, exposed brick" venture with "top steaks"; even fans can find it "a little overpriced" or "too echoey for comfort"... you can always "buy the raw material to take away from their butcher's next door!" / **Details:** *www.cowshedrestaurants.com; 10 pm, Fri & Sat 10.30 pm, Sun 9.15 pm.*

Hotel du Vin et Bistro £55 2 2 3

Sugar Hs, Narrow Lewins Mead BS1 2NU
(0117) 403 2979

More muted feedback of late on this outpost of the hotel-bistro chain; it's most supported as a "romantic" spot, and for "really great wine list" as you'd expect, but some feel the formula generally has a sell-by – "it looked OK in the late '90s, but now?" / **Details:** *www.hotelduvin.com; 10.30 pm; booking: max 10.* **Accommodation:** *40 rooms, from £119*

Lido £52 3 3 5

Oakfield Pl BS8 2BJ (0117) 933 9533

"Eating in a Victorian lido watching people swim is a lovely experience" and seals the "romantic" appeal ("slightly depending on the pool's clientele that day") of this "very unusual" venture. The Mediterranean/North African food from an ex-Moro chef is "reliably very good" too ("and the downstairs café is also a very good option – the tapas selection is first-class"). Top Menu Tip – "gorgeous ice cream". / **Details:** *www.lidobristol.com; 10 pm; closed Sun D; no Amex.*

Maitreya Social £39 4 4 3

89 St Marks Rd BS5 6HY (0117) 951 0100

An Easton institution, opposite Thali Café, that "serves vegetarian food to convert any carnivore"; "don't be put off by the appearance of the neighbourhood – the natives are extremely friendly!" / **Details:** *www.maitreyasocial.co.uk; 9.30 pm; closed Mon, Tue L, Wed L, Thu L & Sun D; no Amex.*

No Man's Grace £36 3 2 2

BS6 6PE (01176) 744077

Mixed feedback on this quite "new kid on the Chandos Road block" (helmed by John Watson, formerly of Casamia); fans do praise its "imaginative and locally sourced small plate combos", but at its worst it seems like "boring little parcels of food served by amateur staff". / **Details:** *www. nomansgrace.com.*

Poco £30 3 4 4

45 Jamaica St BS2 8JP (01179) 232 233

"Cheap 'n' cheerful", but high quality café/bar in Stokes Croft, that's consistently highly rated all-round for its ethically sourced, seasonal tapas (and also with a brunch menu). (In September 2015, it launched a new London sibling in Hackney's trendy Broadway Market). / **Details:** *www.eatpoco.com; Fri D & Sat D no bookings.*

Primrose Café £46 4 4 4

1 Clifton Arcade, 6 Boyces Ave BS8 4AA
(0117) 946 6577

This "friendly, shabby-chic" Clifton Village spot is "not in any way a café" in some people's books – instead, a "rather nice bistro". Whatever the correct nomenclature, it offers "very well-executed" Med-inspired cooking, as well as "unfailingly attractive cakes"; "get a table at the window and watch the world go by". / **Details:** *www.primrosecafe.co.uk; 10 pm; Sun D; no booking at L.*

River Cottage Canteen £45 233
St Johns Ct, Whiteladies Rd BS8 2QY
(0117) 973 2458
*HFW's family-friendly two-year-old, in a converted Victorian church, features a "spacious, attractive dining area" and occasional live music; the food can seem a "little dull and uninspiring given the price", although fans say its new small plates menu is "fantastic-value". / **Details:** www.rivercottage.net/canteens/bristol; 9.30 pm, Sun 9 pm.*

riverstation £49 335
The Grove BS1 4RB (0117) 914 4434
*On a sunny lunchtime, the city has few more "delightful" places to eat than this striking-looking venue – a former river police station, in the historic dockside area. Sceptics say "the location overcomes the average food", but on most accounts it's a "safe" bet, in particular for a "perfect brunch". / **Details:** www.riverstation.co.uk; 10.30 pm, Fri & Sat 11 pm; closed Sun D; no Amex.*

San Carlo £41 335
44 Corn St BS1 1HQ (0117) 922 6586
*This "consistently excellent" and "lively" outpost of the glossy Italian chain is of particular note for its "superb range of fish dishes"; a visit here is "not cheap, but always a joy", for business or pleasure. / **Details:** www.sancarlo.co.uk; 11 pm.*

Souk Kitchen £37 443
277 North St BS3 1JP (01179) 666880
*Opposite the Tobacco Theatre, this "bright and busy" spot "looks like just another small, neighbourhood restaurant", but the "whopping flavours" of its "excellent, authentic cuisine sets it head-and-shoulders above an average Middle Eastern venue". / **Details:** www.soukitchen.co.uk; 10 pm, Sun 9 pm.*

Spiny Lobster £45 232
128-130 Whiteladies Road BS8 2RS (0117) 9737384
*Mitch Tonks's "renamed, slightly refurbed, re-incarnated" fishmonger-cum-restaurant (ex-The Rockfish Grill) offers "beautiful seafood dishes" in a "comfortable" room with a "lovely, airy New England feel"; even fans though can find it "slightly overpriced (especially à la carte)". / **Details:** www.thespinylobster.co.uk; 10 pm, Fri & Sat 10.30 pm; closed Mon & Sun.*

The Thali Café £31 333
12 York Rd BS6 5QE (0117) 942 6687
*This "quirky, low-key" chain serves "genuinely interesting" Indian food with "particularly good" veggie dishes (and "they do cheap tiffin takeaways" too); it's a rare subcontinental that "genuinely welcomes young children" with a kids menu, hence the presence of "many trendy mothers"! / **Details:** www.thethalicafe.co.uk; 10 pm; closed weekday L; no Amex.*

Wallfish Bistro £48 544
112 Princess Victoria St BS8 4DB
(01179) 735435
*On a site once known to foodies as Keith Floyd's first restaurant, a bistro that's especially strong on fish; it's a "romantic" little spot, and one that's well-rated all-round. / **Details:** www.wallfishbistro.co.uk; 10 pm, Sun 9 pm; closed Mon & Tue.*

Wilks £63 442
1 Chandos Rd BS6 6PG (0117) 9737 999
*"James Wilkin's superbly presented food is a delight to behold and enjoy", according to the vast majority of reports on his "lovely and high quality" small haven in a Redland backstreet (still remembered by some as Stephen Markwick's Culinaria, long RIP). Notwithstanding a recent refurb, the ambience is the weakest link, but fans say "it doesn't matter when the food's this good". / **Details:** www.wilksrestaurant.co.uk/; 10 pm, sun 9 pm; closed Mon & Tue; no Amex.*

BROADSTAIRS, KENT 3–3D

Wyatt & Jones £46 434
23-27 Harbour St CT10 1EU (01843) 865126
*A seaside outfit with a "perfect" location under the historic York Gate, and "overlooking Viking Bay"; the food here (served from breakfast onwards) is consistently well-rated. / **Details:** www.wyattandjones.co.uk.*

BROADWAY, WORCESTERSHIRE 2–1C

Russell's £59 332
20 High St WR12 7DT (01386) 853555
*In a tranquil Cotswolds village, this restaurant-with-rooms is "still holding its own" courtesy of some "beautiful" food. Top Tip – the owners' "great" chippy next door elicits even higher praise! / **Details:** www.russellsofbroadway.co.uk; 9.15 pm; closed Sun D. **Accommodation:** 7 rooms, from £110*

BROCKENHURST, HAMPSHIRE 2–4D

The Pig £55 324
Beaulieu Rd SO42 7QL (0845) 077 9494
*This "out-of-the-way" country house in the New Forest expresses a lot of the restaurant 'DNA' of Hotel du Vin founder, Roger Hutson (who established it in 2011). While "the furniture has been rather self-consciously mismatched", the overall effect is "lovely", but slightly outshines the "competent" cuisine, majoring in meaty fare and "piggy bits". / **Details:** www.thepighotel.com; 9.30 pm. **Accommodation:** 26 rooms, from £139*

BROCKHAM, SURREY 3–3A

The Grumpy Mole £44 2 3 3

RH3 7JS (01737) 845 101

An "attractive" bistro-pub in "nice village surroundings" that wins plaudits for its "consistently good" food; the main annoyance? – "you need to book weeks in advance for Sunday lunch". / ***Details:*** *www.thegrumpymole.co.uk; 9.30 pm; no Amex.*

BROMLEY, GREATER LONDON 3–3B

Cinnamon Culture £56 4 4 3

46 Plaistow Ln BR1 3PA (020) 8289 0322

"In a town where independents are nigh on extinct", this "converted pub serving innovative Indian fare in elegant surroundings" makes for a "very pleasant surprise". / ***Details:*** *www.cinnamonculture.com; 10.30 pm, weekends 11 pm; closed Mon.*

BROSELEY, SHROPSHIRE 5–4B

King And Thai £39 5 3 4

Broseley TF12 5DL (01952) 882 004

"It might come as a shock to find some of the best Thai food in England is in a former pub in Shropshire", but that's a visiting Londoner's assessment of this "unfailing" venture. Suree Coates "fuses traditional cuisine with more modern methods" (plus the very best local ingredients) to create "cutting-edge" dishes. / ***Details:*** *www.thekingandthai.co.uk/; 9 pm.*

BROUGHTON GIFFORD, WILTSHIRE 2–2B

Fox £48 4 2 3

The St SN12 8PN (01225) 782949

A "perfect local with a lovely garden" that offers "good" gastro fare with plenty of produce "from their own smallholding"; there's particular acclaim for the "fantastic Sunday lunch". / ***Details:*** *www.thefox-broughtongifford.co.uk; 9.30 pm; closed Mon & Sun D.*

BROUGHTON, NORTH YORKSHIRE 8–4B

Bull at Broughton £42 4 4 4

BD23 3AE (01756) 792065

"A new team and a spruce-up has put this much-improved dining pub firmly back on form". Part of the Ribble Valley Inns chain, it serves "brilliant" locally sourced pub grub, with "a nice range of regional ales" in a "lovely" setting ("you can eat outside when the weather is good"). / ***Details:*** *www.thebullatbroughton.com; 8.30 pm, Fri & Sat 9 pm.*

BRUNDALL, NORFOLK 6–4D

Lavender House £67 4 3 2

39 The St NR13 5AA (01603) 712215

Richard Hughes's "intimate" fixture (plus cookery school) continues to please with its "rich, enjoyable" locally sourced cuisine; alas, the tables are "still too close together", which can make for a somewhat "intrusive" meal. / ***Details:*** *www.thelavenderhouse.co.uk; 9 pm; D only, closed Sun & Mon; no Amex.*

BRUTON, SOMERSET 2–3B

At the Chapel £48 3 2 5

28 High St BA10 0AE (01749) 814070

A "beautiful converted chapel" which is "at once refined and relaxed, grand and informal"; while the pizza is "very good indeed", "the (otherwise "ordinary") food doesn't quite live up the building", and service can be a bit "amateur" on occasion, too. / ***Details:*** *www.atthechapel.co.uk; 9.30 pm, Sun 8 pm.* ***Accommodation:*** *8 rooms, from £100*

Roth Bar & Grill £38 3 3 4

Durslade Farm, Dropping Ln BA10 0NL (01749) 814060

Catherine Butler (of locally loved venue At The Chapel) continues to preside over some "very good" farm-to-table food at this salvage-chic dining room – part of the "interesting" rural outpost of heavyweight gallery Hauser & Wirth. / ***Details:*** *www.hauserwirthsomerset.com.*

BUCKFASTLEIGH, DEVON 1–3D

Riverford Field Kitchen £48 5 3 3

Wash Barn, Buckfast Leigh TQ11 0JU (01803) 762074

"Communal dining it might be", but this purpose-built restaurant on the owners' farm offers a "remarkable" experience, thanks to "imaginative" cooking using the "freshest of ingredients"; "if you arrive early, wander through the surrounding fields accompanied by an audio tour to bring it all to life"! / ***Details:*** *www.riverford.co.uk/restaurant; 8 pm; closed Sun D; no Amex.*

BUNBURY, CHESHIRE 5–3B

The Dysart Arms £43 3 3 4

Bowes Gate Rd CW6 9PH (01829) 260183

"A quintessential Cheshire pub"; part of the Brunning & Price chain, this "longtime favourite" is a real crowd-pleaser which combines a "relaxed and quirky dining room" with "outstanding food and service". / ***Details:*** *www.dysartarms-bunbury.co.uk; 9.30 pm, Sun 9 pm.*

BURNHAM MARKET, NORFOLK 6–3B

Hoste Arms £68 3 2 3
The Grn PE31 8HD (01328) 738777
*Reports on the new regime at this famously hospitable inn continue to be somewhat polarised; while fans "look forward to returning very soon to feast on the excellent locally sourced food", critics continue to find the experience a let down compared with yesteryear. / **Details:** www.thehoste.com; 6m W of Wells; 9.15 pm. **Accommodation:** 62 rooms, from £115*

BURRINGTON, DEVON 1–2C

Northcote Manor £68 4 4 4
EX37 9LZ (01769) 560501
*"Outstanding in every way" – the consensus on Richie Herkes's manor house hotel, in the wooded Devon Hills; "fabulous" cuisine from a 5-course tasting menu in "lovely" surroundings. / **Details:** www.northcotemanor.co.uk; 9 pm; no jeans. **Accommodation:** 11 rooms, from £155*

BURTON BRADSTOCK, DORSET 2–4B

Seaside Boarding House Hotel £53 3 4 5
Cliff Rd DT6 4RB (01308) 897205
*From the people behind London luvvie linchpin, the Groucho Club, a swish new hotel-restaurant "perched high on a cliff" and with "stupendous" views of Dorset's heritage coast. The verdict? – it's "very civilised" with food that's "good but not outstanding", but "getting better all the time". / **Details:** www.theseasideboardinghouse.com; 10 pm.*

BURY ST EDMUNDS, SUFFOLK 3–1C

Benson Blakes £24 4 2 2
88-89 St. Johns St IP33 1SQ (01284) 755188
*"Phenomenal burgers" are the highlight of this funky bar-diner, which has an extensive global menu. / **Details**: www.bensonblakes.co.uk; 9 pm, Fri & Sat 9.30 pm.*

Maison Bleue £55 4 4 4
30-31 Churchgate St IP33 1RG
(01284) 760 623
*"A slice of France in the heart of East Anglia" – Pascal & Karine Canavet's "fabulous" favourite, near the cathedral, "never fails to please" with its all-round combination of "wonderfully cooked fish", "helpful and charming" service and "civilised and elegant" style. / **Details:** www.maisonbleue.co.uk; 9 pm, Sat 9.30 pm; closed Mon & Sun.*

1921 £48 4 3 4
19-21 Angel Hill IP33 1UZ (01284) 704870
*"A really impressive arrival" near the Abbey (RIP Graze) that attracts nothing but the highest praise for its "outstanding cooking" and "clever food combinations" (and at a "great price" too). / **Details:** nineteen-twentyone.co.uk/contact-us/; 9.30 pm; closed Sun.*

Pea Porridge £51 5 4 4
28-29 Cannon St IP33 1JR (01284) 700200
*"Big-flavoured" dishes, featuring 'nose-to-tail' ingredients often feature in the "seriously impressive" dishes emerging from Justin Sharp's "inventive" kitchen, at this "tucked-away, old bakery". The service overseen by his wife, Jurga, is "wonderfully warm" too, and although the interior is "low key", many find the overall effect "romantic". / **Details:** www.peaporridge.co.uk; 10 pm; closed Mon, Tue L & Sun; no Amex.*

Voujon £34 3 3 3
29 Mustow St IP33 1XL (01284) 488122
*This two-year-old (the replacement for Shapla, RIP) is "by far the best Indian in the area" according to fans; it offers "consistently tasty" curries in a contemporary setting. / **Details:** www.voujonburystedmunds.co.uk/; 11.30 pm.*

BUSHEY HEATH, HERTFORDSHIRE 3–2A

The Alpine £50 3 3 3
135 High Rd WD23 1JA (020) 8950 2024
*After "nearly five decades of continuing excellence", this veteran (est. 1969) continues to offer "delicious" Italian food "10 feet outside London" (or at least suburban Harrow); it wins praise for a "wide menu" featuring some "fine" dishes. / **Details:** www.thealpinerestaurant.co.uk; 10.30 pm, Sun 10 pm; closed Mon.*

BUSHEY, HERTFORDSHIRE 3–2A

St James £45 3 3 2
30 High St WD23 3HL (020) 8950 2480
*The "ever-cheerful Italian owner" of this "stalwart of reliability" has "upped the game considerably" in recent times, "whilst still keeping things good value and informal"; it remains "noisy not cosy", but these days "the telling thing is how even mid-week the place is packed". / **Details:** www.stjamesrestaurant.co.uk; opp St James Church; 10 pm; closed Sun D.*

CAERNARFON, GWYNEDD 4–2C

Blas £46 4 4 3
23-25 Hole in the Wall St LL55 1RF
(01286) 677707
"Considering the location, this lovely little place is hitting culinary heights hitherto unseen in the locale" – a typically effusive report on this "very friendly" venue, near the Royal Welch Fusiliers Museum... "if only all small restaurants in small towns were this good!" (NB. The evening menu is much more ambitious than the lunchtime one, the latter incorporating sarnies, burgers and so on). / **Details:** *www.blascaernarfon.co.uk; 9 pm; closed Mon & Sun D.*

CAMBER, EAST SUSSEX 3–4C

The Gallivant £51 3 3 3
New Lydd Rd TN31 7RB (01797) 225 057
In a nautically inspired, rather "unassuming"-looking hotel, this "lovely" seaside spot does take some flak for "ill-judged combinations" and "a cook-by-numbers" approach, but for the most part wins over reporters with its "well-prepared" fish ("and of course Romney Marsh lamb in season"), plus an above-average wine list "with a very narrow mark-up"; "it's worth staying in one of their rooms so you can enjoy an excellent breakfast before a walk on the sands at Camber". / **Details:** *www.thegallivanthotel.com; 9.30 pm; booking: max 10; children: under 12s 8.30.* **Accommodation:** *20 rooms, from £115*

CAMBRIDGE, CAMBRIDGESHIRE 3–1B

Alimentum £75 3 3 2
152-154 Hills Rd CB2 8PB (01223) 413000
Mark Poynton's "innovative, precise and beautiful" cuisine has carved a major reputation for his "stark" foodie temple, not far from the station. It's a case of love-it-or-hate-it though – to fans "always a great experience", to foes with "no wow-factor, and no buzz", and a "customer-is-always-wrong" attitude. / **Details:** *www.restaurantalimentum.co.uk; Mon-Thu 9.30 pm, Sat 10 pm, Sun 9 pm.*

Bill's £42 2 2 3
34-35 Green St CB2 3JX (01223) 329638
A "friendly and lively" branch of the ever-more homogenised chain, featuring the usual "fun" décor ("raffia and chillies hanging from the ceiling"); the highpoint? – "they cover most breakfasts you could imagine". / **Details:** *www.bills-website.co.uk; 11 pm, Sun 10.30 pm.*

The Cambridge Chop House £52 2 2 2
1 Kings Pde CB2 1SJ (01223) 359506
A "good pre-theatre standby", opposite King's; there are those who feel its "traditional" British menu is perhaps "dull-looking" and "a bit inconsistent", but on most accounts this is a place where the cooking (much of it meat-focused) "tries hard", and there's an "interesting value wine list", plus "excellent cask ales". / **Details:** *www.cambscuisine.com/cambridge-chop-house; 10.30 pm, Sat 11 pm, Sun 9.30 pm.*

Cotto £82 5 4 2
183 East Rd CB1 1BG (01223) 302010
"The location leaves much to be desired" (an "out-of-the-way" spot, on a busy road near the Grafton Centre) but all reporters are mightily impressed by Hans Schweitzer's brave and experimental dining room. His "distinctive and imaginative" cuisine is "meticulous in its presentation and the ingredients used", and – "it shows that he's a pâtissier by trade" – his "wonderfully complicated" puddings are "the beautifully presented pièce de résistance". / **Details:** *www.cottocambridge.co.uk; 9.15 pm; D only, Wed-Sat; no Amex.*

d'Arry's £46 2 3 3
2-4 King St CB1 1LN (01223) 505015
Gastropub behind Christ's that's still praised for its "convivial" atmosphere and "good Australian wine list"; to more sceptical types however, the food is merely "OK" nowadays. / **Details:** *www.darrys.co.uk; 9.30 pm, Sun 8.30 pm; no Amex; need 8+ to book.*

Fitzbillies £44 2 1 3
52 Trumpington St CB2 1RG (01223) 352500
"Still an institution" – a "crowded" café "famous for its Chelsea buns and cakes" but where the Full English is also "superb"; on the downside, the atmosphere can seem "noisy and busy" (in a bad way) and service can be "lovely" or it can be "non-existent". / **Details:** *www.fitzbillies.com; 9.30 pm; closed Mon D, Tue D, Wed D & Sun D.*

Hotel du Vin et Bistro £59 2 2 3
15-19 Trumpington St CB2 1QA
(01223) 227330
Admittedly, it's "not scaling culinary heights...", "the food doesn't live on in the memory..." but this outpost of the wine-fuelled hotel-bistro chain is certainly a "pleasant" establishment – and one that's "particularly good for a quick business lunch". / **Details:** *www.hotelduvin.com; 9.45 pm, Fri & Sat 10.30 pm.* **Accommodation:** *41 rooms, from £180*

Midsummer House £138 5 4 4
Midsummer Common CB4 1HA
(01223) 369299
"An ideal location next to the River Cam adjacent to Midsummer Common" provides a glorious setting for this fine Victorian riverside villa, where "Daniel Clifford is pushing on to new levels" – reporters rated it No. 2 in our Top-100 UK Restaurants this year, and some would argue that Michelin should

bestow it that third star. "The level of detail is second-to-none" and the "spectacular and surprising food combinations" create "complex" and "exciting" dishes, delivered by "attentive but un-cloying" staff. Even many fans though feel it's "too expensive". / **Details:** www.midsummerhouse.co.uk; 9.30 pm; closed Mon, Tue L & Sun.

Oak Bistro £46 343
6 Lensfield Rd CB2 1EG (01223) 323361
A "cosy" bistro, handy for the railway and city centre, that's "just about great food without being pretentious", and where the quality is "bang-on for the price"; the "lovely" patio area in particular is "ideal for the summer and very romantic". / **Details:** www.theoakbistro.co.uk; 10 pm; closed Sun.

Pint Shop £43 344
10 Peas Hill CB2 3PN (01223) 352293
"Very cool" gastropub yearling that's proving "a lovely addition to Cambridge", on account of its "superior" cooking (from a "substantial" somewhat "meat-heavy" menu), "the best selection of unusual ales in town", and "huge selection of gins". Top Menu Tip – "the best Scotch eggs around". / **Details:** www.pintshop.co.uk.

Pipasha Restaurant £36 432
529c, Newmarket Rd CB5 8PA
(01223) 577786
Fans of this Bangladeshi on the city outskirts, say "it's in a class of its own" thanks to its very good cooking. / **Details:** www.pipasha-restaurant.co.uk; 11 pm; D only.

Sea Tree £28 432
13 The Broadway CB1 3AH (01223) 414349
"A welcome option amongst the Mill Road eateries" offering "high quality and reliable fish 'n' chips", "great crispy calamari" and "even a wet fish counter"; given all this, it's "worth the price compared to its competitors". / **Details:** www.theseatree.co.uk; 10 pm, Sun 9 pm; closed Mon L & Sun L.

The St John's Chop House £49 332
21-24 Northampton St CB3 0AD
(01223) 353 110
Specialising in classic British fare and real ales, much like its sibling the Cambridge Chophouse; solid all-round ratings suggest it's worth considering. / **Details:** www.cambscuisine.com; 10.30 pm, Sun 9 pm.

Steak & Honour £15 44
various locations CB2 1AA (07766) 568430
"Everything a burger should be" ("great ingredients, no messing about") and "delivered from a very funky van!" – the formula behind this winning outfit. / **Details:** www.steakandhonour.co.uk; 10 pm.

Restaurant 22 £55 434
22 Chesterton Rd CB4 3AX (01223) 351880
"Though not exactly cheap", this "unique" and "really intimate" restaurant, in a riverside villa outside the city centre, offers "sublime" food at times; the prix-fixe gives a "good choice" too... "just as well since it's the only menu available"! / **Details:** www.restaurant22.co.uk; 9 pm; D only, closed Mon & Sun; children: 12+.

Yippee Noodle Bar £30 433
7-9 King St CB1 1LH (01223) 518111
"So much better than the chains"; this "very noisy" city-centre joint is "a great place to catch a bite". / **Details:** www.yippeenoodlebar.co.uk; 10 pm.

CANTERBURY, KENT 3–3D

The Ambrette £47 444
14-15 Beer Cart Ln CT1 2NY
(01227) 200 777
The younger sister of The Ambrette in Margate is "an airy, converted pub", near the Heritage Museum. Dev Biswal's spin-off "combines the best of English ingredients with Indian spicing and heritage" and the cooking here comes "highly recommended". / **Details:** www.theambrette.co.uk; 9.30 pm.

Café des Amis £41 434
95 St Dunstan's St CT2 8AD (01227) 464390
This long-running Mexican, by the Westgate is "full of atmosphere, noise and sizzling food" ("I've been going since it opened 28 years ago and never fail to enjoy it"); the caveat? – service "can be very slow". / **Details:** www.cafedez.com; 10 pm, Fri & Sat 10.30 pm, Sun 9.30 pm; booking: max 6 at certain times.

Cafe du Soleil £42 333
4-5 Pound Lane CT1 2BZ (01227) 479999
A "cosy and warm" sibling to the Café des Amis, "in a lovely setting on the river" and built into the city wall; the "great pizza oven" is the main draw, but there are other "innovative" dishes on offer too. / **Details:** www.cafedusoleil.co.uk; 10 pm.

Cafe Mauresque £39 434
8 Butchery Ln CT1 2JR (01227) 464300
A "lovely Andalucian/North African restaurant" in the city centre; its "intimate, candlelit" basement is especially praised for its "real Moorish atmosphere". / **Details:** www.cafemauresque.com; 10 pm, Fri & Sat 10.30 pm.

Deeson's British Restaurant £51 443
25-27 Sun St CT1 2HX (01227) 767854
Handy for the cathedral and theatre, this "friendly" bistro-style restaurant wins plaudits for its "unfussy British cooking" and "flexible staff"; it's a "real find in a city brimming with mediocre chain restaurants". / **Details:** www.deesonsrestaurant.co.uk; 10 pm; booking: max 12.

Goods Shed £49 [4][4][5]
Station Road West CT2 8AN (01227) 459153
Near Canterbury West station, a "lovely restaurant on a raised platform looking over the permanent farmers' market"; "they serve locally sourced ingredients (mostly from the market itself) well prepared in a convivial setting". / **Details:** *www.thegoodsshed.co.uk; 9.30 pm; closed Mon & Sun D.*

La Trappiste £40 [3][3][3]
1-2 Sun St CT1 2HX (01227) 479111
A quirky "Belgian-themed bar" (and bistro) located in a former gentlemen's outfitters by the cathedral; it offers plenty of locally sourced fare and gluggable Continental beers. / **Details:** *www.latrappiste.com; 10.30 pm; no Amex.*

CARDIFF, CARDIFF 2–2A

Arbennig £44 [4][4][3]
6-10 Romilly Cr CF11 9NR (02920) 341264
John and Ceri Cook run this contemporary (no table cloths) venture in Pontcanna; its name means 'special' in Welsh, which on reporters' ratings is appropriate for its accomplished modern British cuisine, with a strong emphasis on local sourcing. / **Details:** *www.arbennig.co.uk; 9.30 pm, Sat 10 pm; closed Mon & Sun D.*

Casanova £41 [4][3][2]
13 Quay St CF10 1EA (029) 2034 4044
"Trattoria-style Italian" attracting nothing but praise for its "really interesting" food served in "very well-judged portions", and aided and abetted by a "well-chosen wine list". / **Details:** *www.casanovacardiff.com; 10 pm; closed Sun.*

Fish at 85 £50 [3][2][2]
85 Pontcanna St CF11 9HS (02920) 235666
"The tang of fresh fish pervades the air as you sit staring at a row of gaping fish-heads", at this "fishmonger-cum-restaurant". "Choose your fish from the ice and give instructions as to how it's to be cooked, and what with"; "beginners may need a nose peg!" but "don't be put off", as results are "deliciously simple and exquisitely tasty". / **Details:** *www.fishat85.co.uk; Tue & Wed 8.30 pm, Thu-Sat 9 pm; closed Mon & Sun; no Amex.*

Happy Gathering £33 [4][2][3]
233 Cowbridge Road East CF11 9AL
(029) 2039 7531
"Still trucking on after all these years and still the best in South Wales"; this "barn-like" stalwart Cantonese, amusingly located in its namesake Canton, is just "so consistent", although there has been one change of late... "the stairs have got a new carpet (after what feels like 25 years!)" / **Details:** *www.happygatheringcardiff.co.uk; 10.30 pm, Sun 9 pm.*

Mint and Mustard £42 [4][4][3]
134 Whitchurch Rd CF14 3LZ
(02920) 620333
A "first-class" subcontinental that "shines as a beacon among the plethora of taste-alikes with which Cardiff abounds"; its cuisine is "more fusion Indian than regional", and even sceptics of the genre agree that it "takes Asian food up a notch". / **Details:** *www.mintandmustard.com; 11 pm; no shorts.*

Moksh £37 [4][3][3]
Ocean Building, Bute Cr CF10 5AY
(029) 2049 8120
"A bizarre mix of Indian with a pseudo-Heston Blumenthal edge" ("candy floss anyone?") certainly earns extra points for effort for this quayside sub-continental. All agree the results are "very enjoyable" – the odd reporter thought one or two dishes a little "fussy", but the winning view is that they are "unusual and subtle". / **Details:** *www.moksh.co.uk; 10.30 pm, Fri & Sat 11.30 pm; closed Mon.*

The Plan Café £29 [3][2][2]
28-29 Morgan Arc CF10 1AF (02920) 398764
"In one of the city-centre's numerous arcades, this is a Wholefoods sort of place"; "everything is organic" but "despite the labels, the food lives up to its promise – which, in a town of junk food outlets, makes it quite a find!" It's particularly a place for caffeine-addicts, with "excellent brews from local craft roasters". / **Details:** *www.theplancafe.co.uk/; 5 pm, Sun 3.30 pm; L only.*

The Potted Pig £52 [3][2][3]
27 High St CF10 1PU (029) 2022 4817
"A real experience" – this dining room in underground former bank vaults offers some "excellent" food; there has been the odd off-report of late, though, for one reason or another. / **Details:** *www.thepottedpig.com; 9 pm, Fri & Sat 9.30 pm; closed Mon & Sun D.*

Purple Poppadom £46 [4][4][3]
185a, Cowbridge Road East CF11 9AJ
(029) 2022 0026
It's "not the most desirable location" – above a shop in Canton – but this "unassuming" venture wows reporters with its "refined" service and "exceptional" nouvelle Indian cuisine; ratings continue to support claims that it's now the "best Indian restaurant in Cardiff", having surpassed the chef's former haunt Mint and Mustard. / **Details:** *www.purplepoppadom.com; Mon-Sat 11 pm Sun 9 pm.*

Vegetarian Food Studio £21 [4][4][3]
115-117 Penarth Rd CF11 6JU
(029) 2023 8222
"Wow this place still does it for me!" – continued kudos for this much-loved, meat-free Indian fixture, near the Taff, which recently moved

into bigger premises next door. / **Details:** www.vegetarianfoodstudio.co.uk; 9.30 pm, Sun 7 pm; closed Mon; no Amex.

CARLISLE, CUMBRIA 7–2D

Alexandros £43 442

68 Warwick Rd CA1 1DR (01228) 592227

"The food just gets better and better at this well-established local Greek", which offers a "varied" menu (plus "weekly specials such as octopus"); "nothing is too much trouble for the owner Aris, who really cares about the food he serves and that his clients enjoy it!" / **Details:** *www.thegreek.co.uk; 10 pm; closed Mon L & Sun.*

CARTMEL FELL, CUMBRIA 7–4D

The Masons Arms £43 344

Strawberry Bank LA11 6NW (01539) 568486

"Wholesome yet inventive dishes, splendid beers, great warm fires and a friendly atmosphere" – one reporter neatly sums up the charms of this remote Lakeland inn. / **Details:** *www.strawberrybank.com; W from Bowland Bridge, off A5074; 9 pm.* **Accommodation:** *7 rooms, from £75*

CARTMEL, CUMBRIA 7–4D

L'Enclume £150 554

Cavendish St LA11 6PZ (01539) 536362

"At the top of UK gastronomy" (No. 3 in our Top-100 Restaurants this year); Simon Rogan's converted smithy in a "hard-to-find" Lakeland riverside village provides an "exciting and unique" venue, "full of Cumbrian stone, Scandinavian furnishing and eye-catching art". The "exquisite" menu is "ever-changing to reflect the seasons"; presentation is "worthy of a Turner prize"; and "no-one uses way-out ingredients to such eye-opening effect" (although nowadays "a foraging ethos prevails, with no foams to be seen, thank goodness)!". "Genuine" staff led by "star of a maître d'", Sam Ward, "prove the English can do high-end service as well as the French or the Italians" (although the run-down of each dish can risk appearing as something of "a well-practiced spiel"). Stop Press – In July 2015, long-standing chef, Mark Birchall, quit to open his own restaurant. / **Details:** *www.lenclume.co.uk; J36 from M6, down A590 towards Cartmel; 9 pm; closed Mon L & Tue L.* **Accommodation:** *16 rooms, from £119*

Pig & Whistle £37 322

Aynesome Rd LA11 6PL (015395) 36482

A revamped gastroboozer that was, until recently, part of Simon Rogan's empire. The chef (of nearby L'Enclume fame) surrendered the lease in February 2015 and new owners took possession in August, too late for our survey. / **Details:** *www.pigandwhistlecartmel.co.uk.*

Rogan & Co £58 332

Devonshire Sq LA11 6QD (01539) 535917

Is Simon Rogan spending less time in Cartmel? – this previously formidable brasserie spin-off inspired much more criticism this year. Many reports do still acclaim its "lovely", "different" cooking, but there's a strong sense that "it used to be better, and is becoming very expensive for the type of food served". / **Details:** *www.roganandcompany.co.uk; 9 pm; closed Sun; no Amex.*

CASTLE COMBE, WILTSHIRE 2–2B

Bybrook Restaurant Manor House Hotel £102 444

SN14 7HR (01249) 782206

In a "lovely little Cotswold village", a "grand medieval house" with a "great atmosphere of tranquillity"; chef "Richard Davies's inventiveness and technical ability" shines through in the "beautifully presented" food, and everything else is "just as it should be". / **Details:** *www.exclusivehotels.co.uk; 9 pm, Fri & Sat 9.30 pm; closed Mon L & Tue L; no jeans or trainers; children: 11+.* **Accommodation:** *48 rooms, from £205*

CAVENDISH, SUFFOLK 3–1C

The George £45 444

The Green CO10 8BA (01787) 280248

"The type of establishment you hope to find in an English village" – a "brilliant gem" of a 16th-century coaching inn whose set menus in particular are "a real steal". / **Details:** *www.thecavendishgeorge.co.uk; 9.30 pm; closed Sun D.* **Accommodation:** *5 rooms, from £75*

CHADDESLEY CORBETT, WORCESTERSHIRE 5–4B

Brockencote Hall £64 444

DY10 4PY (01562) 777876

"Magical" Victorian country house hotel, now part of the Eden Collection – a "truly amazing place" offering "superb food" that's "worth every penny"; it's an undoubtedly "formal" spot, but "the sincerity of the staff breaks the ice". / **Details:** *www.brockencotehall.com; on A448, outside village; 9 pm; no trainers.* **Accommodation:** *21 rooms, from £135*

CHAGFORD, DEVON 1–3C

Gidleigh Park £154 554

TQ13 8HH (01647) 432367

"I don't think as a package it can be bettered in the UK!" – this "luxurious yet understated" Tudorbethan manor set amidst "wonderful garden

and grounds" in a fairly remote corner of Dartmoor is a culinary Xanadu that's long been a mainstay of the survey's Top-10 UK Restaurants (No. 6 this year). Michael Caines's "sumptuous" cuisine – "traditional yet tweaked with a modern edge" – is a "pure indulgence" ("like a team of magicians have been at work in the kitchen!") and backed up by a particularly impressive cellar. In mid-2015 he announced that he would start stepping gradually back from the kitchen here to open his own hotel in Lympstone in early-2017 – The Latymer's Michael Wignall will succeed him. / **Details:** www.gidleigh.com; from village, right at Lloyds TSB, take right fork to end of lane; no jeans or trainers; children: 8+. **Accommodation:** 24 rooms, from £350

CHANDLER'S CROSS, HERTFORDSHIRE 3–2A

Colette's The Grove £103 233

WD17 3NL (01923) 296015

Russell Bateman's "clever, playful but very approachable" food has won positive reports of late for the main dining room of this luxury country house hotel; as ever though, its toppish prices give some cause for complaint. / **Details:** www.thegrove.co.uk; 9.30 pm; D only, closed Mon & Sun; children: 16+. **Accommodation:** 227 rooms, from £310

The Glasshouse The Grove £74 332

WD3 4TG (01923) 296015

"Wow, what a buffet!" – there's "great choice and quality" of dishes in the "spacious and relaxed" No 2. dining room of this super-swish, country house hotel. / **Details:** www.thegrove.co.uk; 9.30 pm, Sat 10 pm. **Accommodation:** 227 rooms, from £

CHEDDINGTON, BUCKINGHAMSHIRE 3–2A

Old Swan £38 334

58 High St LU7 0RQ (01296) 668171

Under new ownership since January 2015, this picturesque thatched pub, handy for the Grand Union Canal, now "combines warmth, good friendly service and excellent and hearty pub fare". / **Details:** www.theoldswancheddington.co.uk; 9 pm; closed Sun D.

CHELTENHAM, GLOUCESTERSHIRE 2–1C

L'Artisan £49 334

30 Clarence St GL50 3NX (01242) 571257

Yves & Elisabeth Ogrodzki's "typical, old-style" Gallic two-year-old, replete with "absolutely lovely" décor, is a real hit with locals; "the best thing about the service was zee outRAGEous French accents!" / **Details:** www.lartisan-restaurant.com.

Le Champignon Sauvage £83 434

24-28 Suffolk Rd GL50 2AQ (01242) 573449

This wasn't a vintage year for the Everitt-Matthias's foodie legend. To fans, chef David remains "the unsung hero of British cooking", and they report "food that's always breathtaking, ahead of fashion and trends in terms of influence, and yet for a Michelin two-star not over-priced or pretentious". Even many supporters would concede that the ambience of this low-key dining room can seem "flat" however, and what is "excellent and understated" service to fans can also seem "unengaging" to the uninitiated. More concerning, though, were the unusually high number of disappointments in this survey when it came to the cuisine – "nothing to actually complain about, but little character or sparkle to match its lofty ranking." / **Details:** www.lechampignonsauvage.co.uk; 8.30 pm; closed Mon & Sun.

The Curry Corner £46 322

133 Fairview Rd GL52 2EX (01242) 528449

"A really good curry house, with more authenticity than most" – "it's not fine dining but results are quite splendid". / **Details:** www.thecurrycorner.com; 11 pm; closed Mon & Fri L.

The Daffodil £56 344

18-20 Suffolk Pde GL50 2AE (01242) 700055

"A lovely, former Art Deco cinema which has been sympathetically converted into an elegant and popular brasserie"; this "fabulously different" spot offers a "bargain set lunch" and "fantastic afternoon tea"... in fact, it's "always good". / **Details:** www.thedaffodil.com; 10 pm, Sat 10.30 pm; closed Sun.

East India Cafe £49 343

103 Promenade GL50 1NW (01242) 300850

"The British Raj is the theme" at this "small" but "characterful" basement newbie – a "standout addition" to the town; it offers "refreshingly different" dishes and "fabulous libations with historical notes". / **Details:** www.eastindiacafe.com/; 10 pm; closed Mon.

Lumière £82 443

Clarence Pde GL50 3PA (01242) 222200

Jon Howe & Helen Aubry's "relaxed" (if perhaps slightly "austere") venue offers a "first-class experience overall"; "local produce is at the fore of Jon's inventive dishes (from "personalised tasting menus" to "good-value lunches") and Helen makes a very charming front of house". / **Details:** www.lumiere.cc; 8.45 pm; closed Mon, Tue L, Wed L, Thu L & Sun; children: 8+ at D.

No 131 £62 323

131 Promenade GL50 1NW (01242) 822939

In a fabulous White House-esque hotel backed by Superdry's co-founder (he also provides the uniforms) this newish dining room is certainly a "funky" spot, replete with a "great" zinc bar; its *small fan club claims it also offers the "best beef" in town, but the bill can seem "difficult to justify". / **Details:** www.no131.com; 11 pm.*

Prithvi £47 544
37 Bath Rd GL53 7HG (01242) 226229
*"Superb" Indian dishes are "far removed from standard curry house fare" (and with the option of an "amazing tasting menu"), at this popular three-year-old. Excellent service too, if at times "over-attentive" ("I didn't need the staff to become my new best friend!") / **Details:** www.prithvirestaurant.com; 10.30 pm; closed Mon & Tue L; no Amex.*

Purslane £50 443
16 Rodney Rd GL50 1JJ (01242) 321639
*A menu that's "mostly fishy, and executed well" wins some very enthusiastic praise for this "very good" city-centre three-year-old. / **Details:** www.purslane-restaurant.co.uk; 9.30 pm; closed Mon & Sun.*

CHESTER, CHESHIRE 5–2A

Architect £43 233
54 Nicholas St CH1 2NX (01244) 353070
*"Overlooking Chester Racecourse", a "delightful Georgian house" offering the "usual Brunning & Price winning formula when it comes to décor and set-up"; the food's "not bad", but for the majority it "lacks any real flair". / **Details:** www.brunningandprice.co.uk/architect; 10 pm, Sun 9.30 pm; no Amex.*

La Brasserie Chester Grosvenor £67 343
Eastgate CH1 1LT (01244) 324024
*This "handy city-centre venue", in the shadow of the city's famous clock, offers "decent brasserie food" and a "very wide-ranging wine and cocktail list"; not everyone is keen on the refurb of a couple of years ago though, feeling "it was better before with a Parisian feel to the dining area". / **Details:** www.chestergrosvenor.com; 10 pm, Sun 9 pm. **Accommodation:** 80 rooms, from £230*

The Chef's Table £48 442
4 Music Hall Pas CH1 2EU (01244) 403040
*"It's only a small place", but this newcomer – tucked away in a city-centre passage and featuring local art – has "quickly grown in popularity" owing to its "delicious and beautiful" food "using lots of local produce"; add in an "affordable" wine list and it's easy to fathom why "you'll need to book a couple of weeks in advance". / **Details:** www.chefstablechester.co.uk; 9 pm, Fri & Sat 10 pm; closed Mon & Sun.*

1539 £52 324
The Racecourse CH1 2LY (01244) 304 611
*A "wonderful location overlooking Chester racecourse" is the special feature of this attractive operation, but the food is also "interesting and good value". / **Details:** www.restaurant1539.co.uk; Mon-Sat 10pm, Sun 8pm.*

Joseph Benjamin £49 342
140 Northgate St CH1 2HT (01244) 344295
*A relaxed deli-restaurant with a short, uncomplicated menu; the most sceptical report feels its "young MasterChef-style cooking might not cut it in a more demanding market", but even so says it's "definitely a welcome addition in Chester". / **Details:** www.josephbenjamin.co.uk; 9.30 pm; closed Mon, Tue D, Wed D & Sun D.*

Michael Caines ABode Hotels £66 434
Grosvener Rd CH1 2DJ (01244) 347 000
*"Located in a new development near Chester town centre and the racecourse" (a redevelopment of what was once Cheshire Police HQ), and affording "good" views, a hotel-restaurant offering a "smallish" menu. The style-over-substance brigade was again vocal this year, with complaints over "high prices", but the winning view is that the cooking is "excellently prepared and presented". / **Details:** www.abodechester.co.uk/michael-caines-dining/michael-caines-restaurants; 9.45 pm, Sun 9 pm; no jeans or trainers. **Accommodation:** 85 rooms, from £100*

Moules A Go Go £41 332
39 Watergate Row CH1 2LE (01244) 348818
*A "great lunch location" (amid shops on the covered medieval Rows) that serves steak and rotisserie fare alongside the eponymous molluscs; "good value" too. / **Details:** www.moulesagogo.co.uk; 10 pm, Sun 9 pm.*

Simon Radley The Chester Grosvenor £105 433
Eastgate CH1 1LT (01244) 324024
*Few small provincial cities have grander hotels than this "elegant" property (next to the town's landmark Eastgate Clock), which is owned by The Duke of Westminster (whose family seat, Eaton Hall, is a short drive out of town). Its "formal" and rather "old-fashioned" dining room feels as "smart" as its windowless position in the bowels of the building will allow, and is a showcase for Simon Radley's cuisine, which is "the epitome of classic style mixed with modern and creative ideas" and consistently delivers "first class" results. Also vying for attention is the "massive" wine list, which "bamboozles with the sheer choice on offer". / **Details:** www.chestergrosvenor.com/simon-radley-restaurant; 9 pm; D only, closed Mon & Sun; no trainers; children: 12+. **Accommodation:** 80 rooms, from £230*

Sticky Walnut £49 454
11 Charles St CH2 3AZ (01244) 400400
*Garry Usher's "lovely", little Hoole bistro "surpasses all expectations" for a local on the fringes of the city, combining service that's "so helpful and professional" with "reliably original" food and a "lively" atmosphere. He's a whizz at social media promotion too, as demonstrated by his new venture, Burnt Truffle (see Heswall). / **Details:** www.stickywalnut.com; 9 pm, Fri & Sat 10 pm; no Amex.*

Upstairs at the Grill £50 443
70 Watergate St CH1 2LA (01244) 344883
*A "great steakhouse in the heart of Chester" that's one of the best places in town – "prices aren't too extortionate", and the room is "so cosy, warm and friendly" too. / **Details:** www.upstairsatthegrill.co.uk; 10.30 pm, Sun 9.30 pm; closed Mon L, Tue L & Wed L.*

CHESTERFIELD, DERBYSHIRE 5–2C

Nonna's £46 423
131 Chatsworth Rd S40 2AH (01246) 380035
*"Authentic Italian food" ("not all the staff seem to speak English!") is the draw of this venture, also with a Sheffield sibling; "the recent makeover really enhances the atmosphere" too. / **Details:** 11 pm; closed Mon.*

CHEW MAGNA, BRISTOL 2–2B

The Pony & Trap £51 444
Newtown BS40 8TQ (01275) 332 627
*"The backdrop of Somerset's rolling hills is breathtaking", at this "outstanding" gastropub, which provides "the perfect combination of expertly sourced produce skilfully prepared and a warm, relaxed but highly professional approach, with charming and quietly slick staff". / **Details:** www.theponyandtrap.co.uk; 9.30 pm; closed Mon; no Amex.*

CHICHESTER, WEST SUSSEX 3–4A

Amelie And Friends £45 332
31 North St PO19 1LY (01243) 771444
*In a pretty Georgian house with a "lovely terrace", this wine-bar/restaurant is "family owned, and it shows"; the cooking "seems to be modern European, and is usually carefully done". / **Details:** www.amelieandfriends.com; 11 pm, Sun 2.30 pm; closed Sun D.*

Field & Fork £45 322
4 Guildhall St PO19 1NJ (01243) 789915
*After stints at the Pallant House Gallery and Chichester Festival Theatre, Sam & Janet Mahoney moved into this "very pleasant" new conservatory in 2014; "the food is sometimes surprisingly good" and it makes a "great pre-theatre venue". / **Details:** www.fieldandfork.co.uk; 8.45 pm; closed Mon, Tue D, Wed D, Thu D, Fri D, Sat D & Sun D.*

The Kennels £63 344
Goodwood Hs PO18 0PX (01243) 755000
*A "delightful", and beautifully situated contemporary dining room on the Goodwood Estate; the food is not cheap, but fans say that it's "always enjoyable" and you can "take the dog which is a great bonus!" / **Details:** www.goodwood.co.uk/thekennels; Tue-Fri 9.15 pm, Sun 3pm; closed Mon & Sun D.*

Lemongrass £36 442
PO19 7SJ (01243) 533280
*An "authentic" town-centre spot where "the food is a perfect mix of spice and flavour – just what you want from a Thai"; it's "a definite must-visit when in Chichester". / **Details:** www.lgchichester.co.uk; 10.45 pm; no Amex.*

The Richmond Arms £49 443
West Ashling Rd PO18 8EA (01243) 572046
*Next to a large duck pond, a "cheerful" country pub-with-rooms "serving imaginative food including tapas" plus "different" wood-fired pizzas (the latter in a new, stripped-back annex). / **Details:** 9 pm; closed Mon, Tue & Sun D.*

CHIDDINGFOLD, SURREY 3–3A

The Swan Inn £48 322
Petworth Rd GU8 4TY (01428) 684 688
*A "worthy local player"; this "deceptively large" boutique hotel-gastropub from the people behind Swag 'n' Tails (Knightsbridge) offers "beautiful seasonal produce" and "probably the best Sunday lunches in the area"; watch out, though, noise levels can be "painful"! / **Details:** www.theswaninnchiddingfold.com; 10 pm, Sun 9 pm. **Accommodation:** 10 rooms, from £100*

CHINNOR, OXFORDSHIRE 2–2D

The Sir Charles Napier £58 445
Spriggs Alley OX39 4BX (01494) 483011
*"On a beautiful summer evening, it can be heaven to drink a glass of bubbly in the stunning garden" of Julie Griffiths's well-known escape – a "wonderfully cosy" pub-conversion ("more restaurant than pub"), in a hard-to-find, leafy Chilterns location, off the M40. "It's one of the longest-running UK destinations to be consistently running at the top of its game", and its quite "fancy" cuisine "goes from strength to strength". And though far from cheap, and with a few quirks ("I don't like being directed to the bar area to wait ages"), on most accounts its "idiosyncratic" style "all adds to the charm". / **Details:** www.sircharlesnapier.co.uk; Tue-Fri 9.30 pm, Sat 10 pm; closed Mon & Sun D.*

Adam's, Birmigham

Gingerman, Brighton

64 Degrees, Brighton

CHIPPING CAMPDEN, GLOUCESTERSHIRE 2–1C

The Chef's Dozen £60 543
Island Hs, High St GL55 6AL (01386) 840598
*In the centre of this beautiful village, a husband-and-wife operation offering "friendly" service, "good value for money" and food that's "fantastic". / **Details:** www.thechefsdozen.co.uk/; 9 pm; closed Mon, Tue L & Sun.*

The Ebrington Arms £50 344
GL55 6NH (01386) 593 223
*"Hidden in a little village", this sibling to the Killingworth Castle is a "gem of a pub" offering "honest" food "cooked with some flair", and "excellent ales" from the owners' microbrewery. / **Details:** www.theebringtonarms.co.uk; 9 pm.*

CHIPPING NORTON, OXFORDSHIRE 2–1C

Wild Thyme £52 332
10 New St OX7 5LJ (01608) 645060
*This "surprisingly good restaurant might be beginning to feel the strain of its success"; while fans still speak of "top-notch cooking", there's a sense that it's a bit of a "curate's egg"... "some of the mains were a triumph, others a non-event". / **Details:** www.wildthymerestaurant.co.uk; 9 pm, Fri & Sat 9.30 pm; closed Mon & Sun. **Accommodation:** 3 rooms, from £75*

CHIPSTEAD, KENT 3–3B

The George & Dragon £42 333
39 High St TN13 2RW (01732) 779 019
*"A proper English pub in a pretty village", with a good-sized garden, that's consistently praised for its very decent food. / **Details:** www.georgeanddragonchipstead.com; 9.30 pm, Sun 8.30 pm; no Amex.*

CHOBHAM, SURREY 3–3A

Stovell's £59 444
125 Windsor Rd GU24 8QS (01276) 858000
*"We are not blessed with lots of top restaurants in these parts", but Fernando & Kristy Stovell's tastefully updated, "romantic and candlelit", 16th-century farmhouse is "going from strength to strength"; "creativity and flavour" characterise "beautifully presented" contemporary cuisine. / **Details:** www.stovells.com; 9.30 pm; closed Mon, Sat L & Sun D.*

White Heart £46 333
High St GU24 8AA (01276) 857580
*In a village "becoming a bit of a foodie destination", this Brunning & Price pub, has undergone a makeover under its new owners. Fans say it's "improved" serving a "decent range of common-sense dishes", but more critical types say it's "not yet good enough to search out among the local competition". / **Details:** www.brunningandprice.co.uk/whitehartchobham/; 10 pm, Sun 9.30 pm.*

CHOLMONDELEY, CHESHIRE 5–3A

Cholmondeley Arms £42 344
Wrenbury Rd SY14 8HN (01829) 720300
*A "super" gastropub in an "attractive" former Victorian schoolhouse combining a "great selection of real ales and hundreds of different gins" with "very good" cuisine; one reporter worried that "it would lose its charms" after a recent-ish refurb by the new owners, but "not so" – it's "better than ever". / **Details:** www.cholmondeleyarms.co.uk; on A49, 6m N of Whitchurch; 10.30 pm; no Amex. **Accommodation:** 6 rooms, from £80*

CHRISTCHURCH, DORSET 2–4C

The Jetty £55 445
95 Mudeford BH23 3NT (01202) 400950
*"The beautiful view of Christchurch harbour" is the crown jewel feature of Alex Aitken's "thriving" favourite, but most reporters feel "the restaurant lives up to its location", with "fabulous and fresh fish and seafood". The biggest niggles? – "London prices" and "inadequate parking". / **Details:** www.thejetty.co.uk; 9.45 pm, Sun 7.45 pm.*

CHURCHILL, OXFORDSHIRE 2–1C

Chequers £48 324
Church Ln OX7 6NJ (01608) 659393
*It can, on occasion, "feel like a bit of a club for locals" (that'll be the Chippy set) and service can sometimes be "lacklustre", but with its "good food, log fires, papers, and interesting people" this cosy and "atmospheric" pub offers "more satisfactory experiences than disappointments". / **Details:** www.thechequerschurchill.com; 9.30 pm, Fri & Sat 10.30 pm; closed Sun D.*

CIRENCESTER, GLOUCESTERSHIRE 2–2C

Jesses Bistro £60 322
14 Black Jack St GL7 2AA (01285) 641497
*"In a nicely hidden alleyway behind a good butcher's shop", this cosy town-centre bistro is a simple kind of spot specialising in food of the "good, fairly plain" variety. / **Details:** www.jessesbistro.co.uk; 9.15 pm; closed Mon D & Sun.*

Made By Bob £45 4 3 3
The Cornhall 26 Market Pl GL7 2NY
(01285) 641818
A "stylish and lively restaurant/deli in the centre of Cirencester serving excellent food"; the "great buzzing atmosphere" feels "like a big hug" to some, and to others just a "bit frenetic" ("expect to queue"). / ***Details:*** *www.foodmadebybob.com; 9.30 pm; closed Mon D, Tue D, Wed D, Sat D & Sun D.*

Soushi £36 3 3 2
12 Castle St GL7 1QA (01285) 641414
A "small restaurant off the market in Circencester" whose USP locally is an "interesting" Japanese menu. / ***Details:*** *www.soushi.co.uk; 10 pm.*

CLACHAN, ARGYLL AND BUTE 9–3B

Loch Fyne Oyster Bar £52 3 2 3
PA26 8BL (01499) 600264
"Get by the window and enjoy the views, and the so-fresh seafood – the less cooked the better" at this remote but famous lochside deli and restaurant, which inspired (but is only loosely affiliated with) the national chain. / ***Details:*** *www.lochfyne.com; 10m E of Inveraray on A83; 6.30 pm, Fri-Sun 7.30 pm.*

CLAVERING, ESSEX 3–2B

The Cricketers £44 3 3 3
Wicken Rd CB11 4QT (01799) 550442
"Everyone's idea of a country pub"; "notwithstanding its celeb associations" (it's run by Jamie Oliver's folks) this north Essex boozer is a real hit, offering "good to very good gastro fare" (and rooms "of a very high standard" too). / ***Details:*** *www.thecricketers.co.uk; on B1038 between Newport & Buntingford; 9.30 pm; no Amex.* ***Accommodation:*** *14 rooms, from £95*

CLIFTON, CUMBRIA 8–3A

George & Dragon £48 3 4 3
CA10 2ER (01768) 865381
None of the many reports has a bad word to say about this "good all-rounder with an emphasis on local produce", plus a "friendly atmosphere"; "for anyone who stays overnight the breakfast is exceptional" too. / ***Details:*** *www.georgeanddragonclifton.co.uk; on the A6 in the village of Clifton; 9 pm.* ***Accommodation:*** *12 rooms, from £95*

CLIPSHAM, RUTLAND 6–4A

The Olive Branch £52 4 4 4
Main St LE15 7SH (01780) 410355
"Scrumptious food and wine" and "very friendly and knowledgeable staff" maintain the "eternally high standards" of this "lovely" and "relaxed" venture off the A1 – if "not as extra-special as it once was", still one of the UK's more notable gastropubs. / ***Details:*** *www.theolivebranchpub.com; 2m E from A1 on B664; 9.30 pm, Sun 9 pm; no Amex.* ***Accommodation:*** *6 rooms, from £135*

CLITHEROE, LANCASHIRE 5–1B

The Assheton Arms £46 4 4 5
BB7 4BJ (01200) 441227
"Set in a beautiful village, with outside tables overlooking Pendle Hill" this "ancient pub" is "picture postcard stuff", and "as good in summer with its garden, as in winter with its real fires". It lives up to its ownership by The Seafood Pub Company with an "unusual" menu of "stunning fish dishes". / ***Details:*** *www.seafoodubcomany.com; 9 pm.*

Inn at Whitewell £52 3 2 5
Forest of Bowland BB7 3AT (01200) 448222
"Always well worth the journey" – this "archetypal, traditional English inn" is "a stunning and eccentric, former fishing lodge on the Duchy of Lancaster estate, complete with flagged floors, labradors and amazing views". It's become famous over the years: "weekends are a veritable sea of corduroy and brogues, as though you are part of a social event!" and when busy (always) service – though "sensationally welcoming" – can be "erratic". Its food rating continues to slide year-on-year – "since appearing on 'The Trip' the place seems to have gotten a bit ahead of itself – the food is less special, and prices seem to be edging up". / ***Details:*** *www.innatwhitewell.com; 9.30 pm; bar open L & D, restaurant D only; no Amex.* ***Accommodation:*** *23 rooms, from £120*

CLYST HYDON, DEVON 1–3D

The Five Bells Inn £47 4 3 4
EX15 2NT (01884) 277288
"Tucked in a fold of the Kent Downs", this "very pretty", thatched 16th-century inn is "just a lovely experience"; the "tastefully furnished" interior looks "proper posh" and the locally sourced cooking is "delicious". / ***Details:*** *www.fivebells.uk.com; 10 pm.*

CLYTHA, MONMOUTHSHIRE 2–1A

Clytha Arms £49 3 3 2
NP7 9BW (01873) 840206
"Quirky but also good rustic cuisine" (albeit "with influences from all over Europe") are the hallmark of this well-known, rural, family-run inn. / ***Details:*** *www.clytha-arms.com; on Old Abergavenny to Raglan road; 9.30 pm, Mon 9 pm; closed Mon L & Sun D.* ***Accommodation:*** *4 rooms, from £80*

Llansantffraed Court Hotel £58 [2][3][4]

NP7 9BA (01873) 840678

"A fabulous building in a gorgeous spot" just outside Abergavenny. Whilst there's "no doubt it's a very romantic venue", there are repeated fears that they are "over-reaching" themselves in terms of ambition. That said, even a reporter who thought "they have work to do" praised some "very pleasing" dishes and "obliging" staff and thought "it could be a really exceptional place". / **Details:** *www.llch.co.uk; 9 pm; no Amex.*

COBHAM, SURREY 3–3A

La Rive £61

48 High St KT11 3EF (01932) 862 121

This "superior Italian" (known for aeons as Capanna, RIP) in an "attractive" conversion of a 16th-century house was due to re-open in September 2015 after an extensive makeover and rebranding (including a name change) by the existing owners. It's always been one of the areas top destinations – hopefully the relaunch will only enhance that position. / **Details:** *www.facebook.com/pages/La-Rive/1661510910760704.*

COLCHESTER, ESSEX 3–2C

The Lion £42 [3][2][2]

9-11 High St CO6 2PA (01787) 226823

Betwixt Colchester and Sudbury, this traditional country pub is praised for its "excellent twist on ordinary dishes and a very good and reasonable wine list". / **Details:** *www.lionearlscolne.co.uk; 10 pm.*

COLERNE, WILTSHIRE 2–2B

Lucknam Park Luckham Park Hotel £105 [4][4][3]

SN14 8AZ (01225) 742777

This "beautiful" Palladian country house hotel offers a "memorable" experience, from the "really attentive staff" to Hywel Jones's "fantastic, grown-up" food; "both (fine-dining venue) The Park and The Brasserie are top-notch". / **Details:** *www.lucknampark.co.uk; 6m NE of Bath; 10 pm, Sun 2.30 pm; closed Mon, Tue–Sat D only, closed Sun D; jacket and/or tie; children: 5+ D & Sun L* **Accommodation:** *42 rooms, from £360*

COLNE, LANCASHIRE 5–1B

Banny's Restaurant £26 [4][4][2]

1 Vivary Way BB8 9NW (01282) 856220

"Perfect fish 'n' chips, served piping hot straight from the fryer" attract acclaim for this venture, consisting of two "modern, purpose-built restaurants", attached to the Boundary Mill outlet – "you want to return again and again!" / **Details:** *www.bannys.co.uk; 8.45 pm; no Amex.*

CONGLETON, CHESHIRE 5–2B

Pecks £65 [3][3][3]

Newcastle Rd CW12 4SB (01260) 275161

"Theatrical" family-run fixture, which "remains the place in Cheshire for a unique and special" meal, and their "100% consistency year on year" strikes one reporter as simply "remarkable"; the best bit? – rounding things off "with an impressive array of Peck's own desserts". / **Details:** *www.pecksrest.co.uk; off A34; 8 pm; closed Mon & Sun D; practically no walk-ins – you must book.*

COOKHAM, BERKSHIRE 3–3A

Bel & The Dragon £52 [3][2][4]

High St SL6 9SQ (01628) 521263

A large and "stylish" gastroboozer (part of a small chain) primarily of note for its "charming" ambience; the food is generally "tasty and well-prepared" too, although service can be "a bit haphazard". / **Details:** *www.belandthedragon-cookham.co.uk; 10 pm, Sun 9.30 pm.*

Maliks £42 [5][3][4]

High St SL6 9SF (01628) 520085

This snug beamed cottage on the High Street remains a top choice for many miles locally thanks to its "fantastic" Indian cuisine and "an excellent ambience to match". Top Tip – the Sunday buffet is "very good value". / **Details:** *www.maliks.co.uk; from the M4, Junction 7 for A4 for Maidenhead; 11.30 pm, Sun 10.30 pm.*

The White Oak £42 [3][3][3]

The Pound SL6 9QE (01628) 523043

"Clive Dixon cooks rustic-but-refined dishes in this stylish venture", which one fan proclaims as "the best of Cookham's various gastropubs"; the "well-set-up garden" is a further boon. / **Details:** *www.thewhiteoak.co.uk; 9.30 pm, Sun 8.30 pm.*

COPSTER GREEN, LANCASHIRE 5–1B

Yu And You £49 [5][4][4]

500 Longsight Rd BB1 9EU (01254) 247111

Expect "Chinese food light years ahead" of the competition at this "busy" and "fun" Ribble Valley spot – a former 'Ramsay's Best Restaurant' winner; it's "expensive, yes, but so, so worth it". / **Details:** *www.yuandyou.com; off the A59 7 miles towards Clitheroe; 11 pm, Fri & Sat 2 am; D only, closed Mon; no Amex.*

CORSE LAWN, GLOUCESTERSHIRE 2–1B

Corse Lawn Hotel £54 443
GL19 4LZ (01452) 780771
The Hine family's "wonderfully located" country house hotel maintained its high ratings this year; one diehard fan had a bad trip, but for the most part feedback remains very upbeat on the "brilliant", traditional cooking and "charming hosts". / ***Details:*** *www.corselawn.com; 5m SW of Tewkesbury on B4211; 9.30 pm.* ***Accommodation:*** *18 rooms, from £120*

COWBRIDGE, VALE OF GLAMORGAN 1–1D

Bar 44 £36 433
44c High St CF71 7AG (01446) 776488
"Tapas at its best" ("especially the fish") continues to inspire solid feedback for this buzzy café-bar with an open kitchen. / ***Details:*** *www.bar44.co.uk; 9 pm, Fri-Sun 10 pm; closed Mon D; no Amex.*

CRASTER, NORTHUMBERLAND 8–1B

Jolly Fisherman £42 335
Haven Hill NE66 3TR (01665) 576461
"Sensational views" and "unbeatable seafood, straight from the boat" are twin attractions of this seaside inn, which enjoys a "fantastic village setting" (and has "a lovely terrace overlooking the sea"). Top Menu Tip – "the most amazing crab sandwiches money can buy!" / ***Details:*** *www.thejollyfishermancraster.co.uk; near Dunstanburgh Castle; 8.30 pm, Sun 7 pm; no Amex; no booking.*

CRATHORNE, NORTH YORKSHIRE 8–3C

Crathorne Arms £48 444
TS15 0BA (01642) 961402
"Eugene and Barbara McCoy (until lately, of the Cleveland Tontine) are back in the game at this lovely village venue" ("transforming a sleepy pub into something special") and their "loyal army of fans" are "delighted". There's "a menu that will appeal to most" (including a range of tapas-y dishes), plus a "well-stocked bar for the local farmers!" / ***Details:*** *thecrathornearms.co.uk/; 11 pm, Sun 7 pm.*

CRAYKE, NORTH YORKSHIRE 5–1D

Durham Ox £49 433
Westway YO61 4TE (01347) 821506
This "lovely old pub", famous in the region, can get a "bit cramped these days" thanks to its "very reliable" cooking; "rooms are a bonus too". / ***Details:*** *www.thedurhamox.com; 9.30 pm, Sun 8.30 pm.* ***Accommodation:*** *5 + 1 studio suite rooms, from £100*

CREIGIAU, CARDIFF 2–2A

Caesars Arms £49 343
Cardiff Rd CF15 9NN (029) 2089 0486
There's "always a fun atmosphere" at this "festive" pub-restaurant; it's praised for "fantastic fish and chips" and "exotic" local meats – in either case, you pick out your own cut and specify how you'd like it prepared. / ***Details:*** *www.caesarsarms.co.uk; beyond Creigiau, past the golf club; 10 pm; closed Sun D.*

CROMER, NORFOLK 6–3C

No1 £33 543
1 New St NR27 9HP (01263) 512316
"Superb views" add to the lustre of this year-old venture of Galton Blackiston (of Morston Hall fame). Downstairs, the main restaurant, is "a superior chippy, that's very good of its kind" – his newer 'Upstairs at No. 1' has "more finesse and patchier service", serving "mainly fish, but also tapas-style dishes". / ***Details:*** *www.no1cromer.com; 9 pm.*

CROYDON, SURREY 3–3B

Albert's Table £54 433
49c South End CR0 1BF (020) 8680 2010
"Still the best restaurant in Croydon"; despite a "poor" location and décor that's rather "beige", this venture continues to elicit superlatives for its "imaginative, inexpensive" cuisine (not least the "particularly good" bread and "superb" desserts). / ***Details:*** *www.albertstable.co.uk; 10.30 pm; closed Mon & Sun D.*

Karnavar £40 443
62 Southend CR0 1DP (020) 8686 2436
"An excellent newcomer to the Croydon restaurant scene"; this modern Indian may be "rather drab inside", but its "phenomenal" cuisine ("with many inspired vegetarian dishes") makes it a real "gem". / ***Details:*** *Karnavar.com; 11 pm, Sun 10 pm; closed Mon.*

McDermotts Fish & Chips £28 532
5-7 The Forestdale Shopping Centre Featherbed Ln CR0 9AS (020) 8651 1440
Tony McDermott's chippy continues to win raves for "the best fish and chips in the South-East". OK, so it's in a "fairly horrible shopping arcade" in the 'burbs, but "this doesn't put you off an outstanding meal". / ***Details:*** *www.mcdermottsfishandchips.co.uk; 9.30 pm, Sat 9 pm; closed Mon & Sun.*

CRUDWELL, WILTSHIRE 2–2C

The Potting Shed £46 324
The St SN16 9EW (01666) 577833
"After a massive makeover", this "relaxed"

country pub now offers an even more "lovely" ambience, and the food is also "consistently good"; no doubt owing to its popularity however, service is regularly "overwhelmed". / **Details:** *www.thepottingshedpub.com; 9.30 pm, Sun 9 pm; no Amex.* **Accommodation:** *12 rooms, from £95*

CUCKFIELD, WEST SUSSEX 3–4B

Ockenden Manor £88 322

Ockenden Ln RH17 5LD (01444) 416111

The odd long-term fan of this Elizabethan country house hotel feels it "has not sustained its high standards" of late, but it nevertheless remains consistently well-rated, and at its best offers "superb classic cooking". / **Details:** *www.hshotels.co.uk; 8.30 pm; no jeans or trainers.* **Accommodation:** *28 rooms, from £190*

CUPAR, FIFE 9–3D

Ostlers Close £51 444

25 Bonnygate KY15 4BU (01334) 655574

Down a narrow alley in the town centre, this "intimate" stalwart run by chef Jimmy Graham was one of the original standard bearers of locally sourced Scottish cuisine; it remains an "excellent" – and perennially oversubscribed – destination for unfussy fine dining. / **Details:** *www.ostlersclose.co.uk; centrally situated in the Howe of Fife; 9.30 pm; closed Sun & Mon, Tue-Fri D only, Sat L & D; children: 5+.*

The Peat Inn £85 444

KY15 5LH (01334) 840206

"What a splendid establishment!" – Geoffrey & Katherine Smeddles' classic country inn has long been known as a source of "Michelin magic just outside St Andrews", with "excellent, locally sourced ingredients (especially meat) perfectly cooked, appetisingly presented and professionally served"; and "recent renovations mean that it now has less of an olde-worlde feel". / **Details:** *www.thepeatinn.co.uk; at junction of B940 & B941, SW of St Andrews; 9 pm; closed Mon & Sun.* **Accommodation:** *8 rooms, from £180*

DALRY, NORTH AYRSHIRE 9–4B

Braidwoods £68 554

Drumastle Mill Cottage KA24 4LN
(01294) 833544

Keith & Nicola Braidwood's "tiny" converted croft remains "the very best and most welcoming restaurant that anyone could wish for"; "the way they maintain the standard of cooking is really quite astonishing, and Mrs Braidwood is as charming and welcoming as ever". / **Details:** *www.braidwoods.co.uk; 9 pm; closed Mon, Tue L & Sun D (open Sun L Oct-April); children: 12+ at D.*

DANEHILL, EAST SUSSEX 3–4B

Coach And Horses £49 353

School Ln RH17 7JF (01825) 740369

"The model of a great country pub" with a "tip-top food offering", a "cosy" ambience and "now a new terrace" too; it's "well worth a detour" not least for its "excellent wines and beers". / **Details:** *www.coachandhorses.co; off A275; 9 pm, Fri & Sat 9.30 pm, Sun 3 pm; closed Sun D.*

DARSHAM, SUFFOLK 6–4D

Darsham Nurseries £42 442

Main Rd IP17 3PW (01728) 667022

A modish nursery/shop and newly revamped café in a sprawling barn with a vibrant checkerboard floor; young chef Lola DeMille, who has replaced James Dodd (ex-Mark Hix) at the pass, does the small plates thing – including for brunch – "with style". / **Details:** *www.darshamnurseries.co.uk; 9.30 pm; closed Mon D, Tue D, Wed D, Thu D, Sat D & Sun D.*

DARTMOUTH, DEVON 1–4D

RockFish £39 423

8 South Embankment TQ6 9BH
(01803) 832800

Mitch Tonks's "very buzzy" riverside venture, now with a Plymouth sibling, offers "fish 'n' chips to die for" (and at "reasonable" prices too) from a "wonderful selection" of options. / **Details:** *www.rockfishdevon.co.uk/index.php; 9.30 pm.*

The Seahorse £65 544

5 South Embankment TQ6 9BH
(01803) 835147

"Splendid" fish and seafood, "cooked with skill and empathy", generate huge enthusiasm for Mitch Tonk's "small, closely packed dining room, opening directly onto the seafront"; it helps that its style is "lovely and friendly" too. / **Details:** *www.seahorserestaurant.co.uk; 9.30 pm; closed Mon & Sun.*

DATCHWORTH, HERTFORDSHIRE 3–2B

The Tilbury £50 434

Watton Rd SG3 6TB (01438) 815 550

"What a hidden gem"; James & Tom Bainbridge's gastropub "deserves to be called a high-quality restaurant in its own right", owing to its "fantastic" modern British fare "served with real flair", and its "very good choice" of tipples. / **Details:** *www.thetilbury.co.uk; 9 pm, Fri & Sat 9.30 pm; closed Mon & Sun D.*

DEAL, KENT 3–3D

81 Beach Street £45 [3][3][2]
81 Beach St CT14 6JB (01304) 368136
A "good, down-to-earth restaurant on Deal front" that "can always be trusted" thanks to its "fresh and interesting" cooking, and good sea views. / **Details:** *www.81beachstreet.co.uk; 10 pm, Sun 4 pm; closed Sun D.*

Victuals & Company £49 [3][3][3]
02-Mar, St George's Pas CT14 6TA
(01304) 374389
A "cosy and chic" newcomer in pedestrianised St George's Passage; fans say its "imaginative" food makes it the "stand-out best restaurant in town", and even a couple of critics say "the ambition is good" and "the hosts are trying hard". / **Details:** *www.victualsandco.com; 10 pm.*

DEDHAM, ESSEX 3–2C

Milsoms £46 [2][3][4]
Stratford Rd CO7 6HW (01206) 322795
A brasserie serving decent fare that's elevated by its Constable Country location and attachment to a "lovely" hotel; owned by the Milsom family (of nearby Le Talbooth fame). / **Details:** *www.milsomhotels.com; 9.30 pm, Fri & Sat 10 pm; no booking.* **Accommodation:** *15 rooms, from £120*

The Sun Inn £45 [2][2][3]
High St CO7 6DF (01206) 323351
The food at this "refreshingly unpretentious" Constable Country inn "has become better of late" ("inventive, quite simple, seasonal and well-prepared"), however it's the wine list ("curated by Hamish, the exemplary wine guru of the Tate") "where it truly excels". / **Details:** *www.thesuninndedham.com; Fri & Sat 10 pm, 9.30 pm; no Amex.* **Accommodation:** *7 rooms, from £110*

Le Talbooth £74 [4][4][5]
Gun Hill CO7 6HP (01206) 321105
In a "wonderful" riverside setting, this well-known and extremely "lovely" Constable Country landmark offers a "very agreeable experience all round", from the "memorable" cuisine to the "impeccable and unobtrusive" service. / **Details:** *www.milsomhotels.com; 5m N of Colchester on A12, take B1029; 9 pm; closed Sun D; no jeans or trainers.*

DENHAM, BUCKINGHAMSHIRE 3–3A

Swan Inn £46 [3][3][3]
Village Rd UB9 5BH (01895) 832085
"A quality pub in a quality village" that garners nothing but praise for its "interesting" food and "good" wine list; a "great place for Sunday lunch" for refugees from the smoke, who can bomb out on the A40. / **Details:** *www.swaninndenham.co.uk; 9.30 pm, Fri & Sat 10 pm.*

DERBY, DERBYSHIRE 5–3C

Anoki £43 [4][3][3]
First Floor, 129 London Rd DE1 2QN
(01332) 292888
In a former Art Deco cinema, this city-centre Indian wins raves for its "very tasty" and "well-presented" dishes, accompanied by a pleasing "number of freebies"; "altogether a most delightful evening". / **Details:** *www.anokiderby.co.uk; 11.30 pm, Sun 9.30; D only.*

Darleys £56 [4][5][4]
Darley Abbey Mill DE22 1DZ (01332) 364987
"Still the best restaurant in Derby" – this "reliably excellent" staple – part of an old mill – combines a "spacious" room with "enjoyable" food (including a separate vegetarian menu); "now that it has added a terrace where you can enjoy World Heritage river views, the food tastes better too"! / **Details:** *www.darleys.com; 9 pm; closed Sun D; no Amex; children: 10+ Sat eve.*

Ebi Sushi £39 [5][3][2]
59 Abbey St DE22 3SJ (01332) 265656
"You need to book well in advance now" for this surprisingly authentic Japanese (the executives from the local Toyota factory have to eat somewhere!), which serves "fantastically light, but balanced and tasty Japanese fare". / **Details:** *10 pm; D only, closed Mon & Sun; no Amex.*

The Wonky Table £43 [3][3][3]
32 Sadler Gate DE1 3NR (01332) 295000
A thoroughly "decent" café-restaurant, on the city's best independent shopping street, which continues to garner solid feedback for its European cooking; the biggest gripe this year wouldn't bother all diners – "I was overwhelmed by the quantity!" / **Details:** *www.wonkytable.co.uk.*

DINTON, BUCKINGHAMSHIRE 2–3C

La Chouette £59 [4][2][3]
Westlington Grn HP17 8UW (01296) 747422
A venue that's "right in Midsomer Murder territory", and where "you sometimes think the mad Belgian chef is about to commit another" himself. Fortunately Freddie continues to serve up "delicious" food instead, and his passionate approach just "adds to the entertainment!" / **Details:** *www.lachouette.co.uk; off A418 between Aylesbury & Thame; 9 pm; closed Sat L & Sun; no Amex.*

DODDISCOMBSLEIGH, DEVON 1–3D

The NoBody Inn £48 [2][2][3]
EX6 7PS (01647) 252394
A "great pub off the beaten track" near Exeter, where the "extensive" and "interesting" wine list continues to be of particular note; the food? – "reliable rather than outstanding". / **Details:** *www.nobodyinn.co.uk; off A38 at Haldon Hill (signed Dunchidrock); 9 pm, Fri & Sat 9.30 pm; no Amex.* **Accommodation:** *5 rooms, from £60*

DONHEAD ST ANDREW, WILTSHIRE 2–3C

The Forester £43 [3][3][3]
Lower St SP7 9EE (01747) 828038
A village gastroboozer, with beamed dining room, acclaimed for "excellent" cuisine that's "hard to beat" in these parts. / **Details:** *www.theforesterdonheadstandrew.co.uk; off A30; 9 pm; closed Sun D.*

DORCHESTER, DORSET 2–4B

Sienna £66
36 High West St DT1 1UP (01305) 250022
In May 2015, MasterChef-finalist, Marcus Wilcox took over the stoves from Russell & Elena Brown at this tiny, town-centre fixture; it was too late for any survey feedback, but the aim is to maintain its position as one of Dorset's foremost destinations. / **Details:** *www.siennarestaurant.co.uk; 9 pm; closed Mon, Tue L & Sun; no Amex; children: 12+.*

DORKING, SURREY 3–3A

Restaurant Two To Four £57 [3][3][3]
2-4 West St RH4 1BL (01306) 889923
A "lovely", little beamed spot, on the fringe of the town – it's a local favourite on accounts of its "pleasant" staff and ambience and food that's "well-presented and interesting". / **Details:** *www.2to4.co.uk; 10.15 pm; closed Sun.*

DOUGLAS, ISLE OF MAN 7–4B

Tanroagan £52 [4][4][3]
9 Ridgeway St IM1 1EW (01624) 612 355
"The quality continues" say fans of this fishy temple – a perennial contender for the best restaurant on the Isle of Man, which looks less bare-bones since a revamp a couple of years ago. / **Details:** *www.tanroagan.co.uk; 9.30 pm; closed Mon, Sat L & Sun; no Amex.*

DREWSTEIGNTON, DEVON 1–3C

The Old Inn £70 [5][4][4]
EX6 6QR (01647) 281 276
Chef Duncan Walker (ex-22 Mill Street) and Anthea Christmas's "warm, cosy and comfortable" inn combines a "wonderful welcome" with some truly "masterful" cuisine; it's a big hit with all reporters. / **Details:** *www.old-inn.co.uk; 9 pm; closed Sun-Tue, Wed L, Thu L; no Amex; children: 12+.* **Accommodation:** *3 rooms, from £90*

DULVERTON, SOMERSET 1–2D

Tongdam £45 [3][4][3]
26 High St TA22 9DJ (01398) 323397
"What a surprise in the middle of Dulverton" – a Thai restaurant (with rooms) set in a "traditional" building "with flame torches burning at night"; "you can choose between the intimate dining area or vine-covered patio" before enjoying a "real taste of the exotic East presented in a cheerful, happy atmosphere". / **Details:** *www.tongdamthai.co.uk; 10.30 pm; closed Tue.*

DUNBAR, EAST LOTHIAN 9–4D

The Rocks £41 [4][4][2]
Marine Rd EH42 1AR (01368) 862287
Set atop a cliff overlooking the Dunbar coast, this "lovely" restaurant-with-rooms wins plaudits for its "excellent" fish and seafood and "knowledgeable" staff; "only the ambience (think "rundown country hotel") lets this place down a bit". / **Details:** *www.therocksdunbar.co.uk; 9 pm; no Amex.* **Accommodation:** *11 rooms, from £75*

DUNVEGAN, HIGHLAND 9–2A

The Three Chimneys £79 [4][4][5]
Colbost IV55 8ZT (01470) 511258
"Their take on Cullen Skink is well worth the 400-mile drive!" – Eddie and Shirley Spears's famous former crofter's cottage, by Loch Dunvegan, provides some of the UK's best food, as well as some of its most remote; most notably "seafood straight from the sea". For a "great and romantic get-away", it's "simply the best". / **Details:** *www.threechimneys.co.uk; 5m from Dunvegan Castle on B884 to Glendale; 9.45 pm; children: 8+.* **Accommodation:** *6 rooms, from £345*

DURHAM, COUNTY DURHAM 8–3B

The Crown at Mickleton £38 [3][3][3]
Mickleton, Barnard Castle DL12 0JZ (01833) 640 381
A "great country village pub" offering solid food

options and a good range of wines, and where the open kitchen adds a touch of drama. / ***Details:*** *www.thecrownatmickleton.co.uk; 9 pm; closed Mon, Tue & Sun D.*

Finbarr's £49 342

Flass Vale DH1 4BG (0191) 370 9999

"A great addition to the Durham restaurant scene and now thankfully saved from being turned into student accommodation"!; it's a "comfortable, reliable" operation, where the "helpful" staff serve "standard bistro food, but done very well". / ***Details:*** *www.finbarrsrestaurant.co.uk; 9.30 pm, Sun 9 pm.*

DUSTON, NORTHAMPTONSHIRE 2–1D

The Hopping Hare £42 322

18 Hopping Hill Gdns NN5 6PF
(01604) 580090

On the outskirts of the city, a small inn offering "very good food that's well presented", and good ales to boot. / ***Details:*** *www.hoppinghare.com; 9.30 pm, Fri & Sat 10 pm, Sun 8.30 pm.*

DYFED, PEMBROKESHIRE 4–4B

The Grove - Narberth £79 344

Molleston, Narberth SA67 8BX
(01834) 860915

"A real pleasure, and a lovely place to stay" – this country house hotel is a "peaceful haven", whose dining room won strong all-round praise this year for its "really accomplished dishes" and "capable" service. / ***Details:*** *www.thegrove-narberth.co.uk/; 9.30 pm.*

EAST CHILTINGTON, EAST SUSSEX 3–4B

Jolly Sportsman £49 333

Chapel Ln BN7 3BA (01273) 890400

It's "not easy to find" ("a sat nav is useful") but Bruce Wass's "very welcoming" and "properly rural" pub is "well worth the effort" by all accounts; its "interesting and tasty options" make it a "foodie paradise", and there's also a "fantastic outdoor playground" for kids. / ***Details:*** *www.thejollysportsman.com; NW of Lewes; 9.30 pm, Fri & Sat 10 pm; closed Mon & Sun D; no Amex.*

EAST CHISENBURY, WILTSHIRE 2–3C

Red Lion £55 554

SN9 6AQ (01980) 671124

"Exceptional cooking with a local flavour" helps inspire reams of rapturous feedback on this culinarily acclaimed, "peacefully situated" thatched village pub (with rooms), which is "outstanding in every way". / ***Details:*** *www.redlionfreehouse.com; 9 pm, Sun 8 pm; no Amex.* ***Accommodation:*** *5 rooms, from £130*

EAST CLANDON, SURREY 3–3A

Queen's Head £42 333

The Street GU4 7RY (01483) 222332

"A joy of a country gastropub", in the Surrey Hills, offering "London quality" (and, alas, "London prices" too); a "comfortable" sort of spot that's both "very busy" yet also "relaxing". / ***Details:*** *www.queensheadeastclandon.co.uk; Mon-Thu 9 pm, Fri & Sat 9.30 pm, Sun 8 pm.*

EAST GRINSTEAD, WEST SUSSEX 3–4B

Gravetye Manor £96 224

Vowels Ln RH19 4LJ (01342) 810567

"Gorgeous gardens" create a particularly lovely setting for this "magnificent" Elizabethan country house hotel. Under its 'new' regime of recent years reports on its dining room remain up-and-down, and though all agree the cuisine can be "excellent", to sceptics it is merely "acceptable" at the "mind-bending prices". / ***Details:*** *www.gravetyemanor.co.uk; 2m outside Turner's Hill; 9.30 pm, Sun 9 pm; booking: max 8; children: 7+.* ***Accommodation:*** *17 rooms, from £250*

EAST HADDON, NORTHAMPTONSHIRE 5–4D

The Red Lion £47 444

Main St NN6 8BU (01604) 770223

An "excellent stopping place just off the M1"; this gastropub-with-rooms is "all-round tops", combining "scrumptious food, excellent service" and a "buzzing atmosphere"... all you need to do is "get booked in!" / ***Details:*** *www.redlioneasthaddon.co.uk; 9.30 pm; no Amex.* ***Accommodation:*** *5 rooms, from £75*

EAST HENDRED, OXFORDSHIRE 2–2D

The Eyston Arms £48 334

High St OX12 8JY (01235) 833320

In a pretty village, this pub continues to elicit positive, if limited, feedback; it serves a "red Thai curry better than most Thai restaurants" and has a "good, tongue-in-cheek wine list" too ('Typically Vatican Square Paving slab dry and absolutely tasteless' being one recommendation). / ***Details:*** *www.eystons.co.uk; 9 pm, Sun 8 pm.*

EAST MOLESEY, SURREY 3–3A

Mezzet £34 554

43 Bridge Rd KT8 9ER (020) 8979 4088

"Always busy and buzzy" neighbourhood restaurant that's a real hit thanks to its "outstanding" and "very reasonably priced" Lebanese cuisine; service is "very much with a smile". / ***Details:*** *www.mezzet.co.uk; 10 pm, Sun 9 pm.*

EAST WITTON, NORTH YORKSHIRE 8–4B

Blue Lion £49 334
DL8 4SN (01969) 624273
*In a "beautiful location", this grand coaching inn makes a "marvellous place for a break", and on nearly all accounts is "very reliable" food-wise. Top Menu Tip – "exceptional grouse". / **Details:** www.thebluelion.co.uk; between Masham & Leyburn on A6108; 9.15 pm; no Amex. **Accommodation:** 15 rooms, from £94*

EASTBOURNE, EAST SUSSEX 3–4B

The Mirabelle The Grand Hotel £65 343
King Edwards Pde BN21 4EQ (01323) 412345
*"Impeccable service" (including "much to-do with salvers") is the undoubted highlight of a visit to this "admirable, old-school" restaurant in "the grandest of hotels" by the seaside. The food is "traditional and well-executed", but perhaps "lacking the pizzazz" one might expect from the price tag. / **Details:** www.grandeastbourne.com/eastbourne-restaurants; 9.45 pm; closed Mon & Sun; jacket or tie required at D. **Accommodation:** 152 rooms, from £199*

EASTON GREY, WILTSHIRE 2–2C

The Dining Room Whatley Manor £140 323
SN16 0RB (01666) 822888
*"A very special luxury hotel", where Martin Bruge has carved the highest culinary reputation for his indulgent cuisine. The Cotswolds manor house setting is "fantastic", and on all accounts here the food is "lovely" (but even fans can caution that its "unadventurous" style, perhaps, "lacks the wow factor expected in a Michelin two-star"). / **Details:** www.whatleymanor.com; 8 miles from J17 on the M4, follow A429 towards Cirencester to Malmesbury on the B4040; 9.30 pm; D only, closed Mon-Tue; no jeans or trainers; children: 12+. **Accommodation:** 23 rooms, from £305*

EDINBURGH, CITY OF EDINBURGH 9–4C

Angels With Bagpipes £52 334
343 High St, Royal Mile EH1 1PW
(0131) 2201111
*Valvona & Crolla's Royal Mile outpost is a "real favourite" amongst reporters; fans claim that it's "outstanding on all levels", while the worst anyone has to say is that it's "good for a quick gastropub meal". / **Details:** www.angelswithbagpipes.co.uk; 9.45 pm.*

Bell's Diner £30 342
7 St Stephen St EH3 5EN (0131) 225 8116
*"A classic and classy" joint which "has been doing burgers (well) for many years"; "it's cramped or cosy, depending on your view, but always reliable". / **Details:** 10 pm; closed weekday L & Sun L; no Amex.*

Bia Bistrot £40 553
19 Colinton Rd EH10 5DP (0131) 452 8453
*A "consistently great, neighbourhood bistro" in Morningside, where "the best ingredients are treated with respect" to create some "stunning" dishes, served very "professionally". There's an "unbelievably good-value set lunch, but à la carte shows how well they can cook if you want to trade up" (and "it still won't break the bank"). / **Details:** www.biabistrot.co.uk; 10 pm.*

Café Marlayne £44 323
1 Thistle St EH2 1EN (0131) 226 2230
*This "informal, authentic" New Town bistro – with an equally popular Antigua Street outpost – serves "simple", "very well-prepared" food that comes at "reasonable prices too". / **Details:** www.cafemarlayne.com; 10 pm; no Amex.*

Café St-Honoré £49 334
34 NW Thistle Street Ln EH2 1EA
(0131) 226 2211
*Fans "return again and again", to this "jolly", "very busy" Gallic "classic", tucked away in the New Town; critics feel its "very French" menu "promises more than it delivers", but most reporters feel it's of "good quality", with a "sweet" atmosphere that's ideal for romance. / **Details:** www.cafesthonore.com; 10 pm.*

Calistoga Central £43 243
70 Rose St EH2 3DX (01312) 251233
*"Well worth the trip up the dingy back alleys", this is a "place you would go just for the wine", also sold retail in the attached shop; "there's nothing wrong with the food" (and it can be "delicious") "but the gap between it and the quality of the Californian wine list is Conference to Championship"! / **Details:** www.calistoga.co.uk; 10 pm.*

The Castle Terrace £81 332
33-35 Castle Ter EH1 2EL (0131) 229 1222
*"Creative (but not laboratory-style)" cooking "artistically presented" inspires rave reviews from foodie fans of Tom Kitchin's "unstuffy and friendly" dining room, by the castle. Its ratings slipped noticeably this year however, with quite a few reports suggesting it's "OK, but vastly over-rated". / **Details:** www.castleterracerestaurant.com; 10 pm; closed Mon & Sun.*

David Bann £41 323
56-58 St Marys St EH1 1SX (0131) 556 5888
David Bann produces some "unforgettable" dishes at this "well-run" and well-established Old Town veteran,

which "takes vegetarian cooking up a notch";"it is wonderful to find any vegetarian restaurant these days, let alone a truly special one!" / **Details:** www.davidbann.com; 10 pm, Fri & Sat 10.30 pm.

The Dogs £39 334
110 Hanover St EH2 1DR (0131) 220 1208
*A "reliable" city-centre boozer – a "busy, bustling" sort of place, offering "fun and hearty" food (and "at reasonable prices" too). / **Details:** www.thedogsonline.co.uk; 10 pm.*

L'Escargot Blanc £45 322
17 Queensferry St EH2 4QW
(0131) 226 1890
*"Although access is a little difficult with stairs to climb, the meal experience is most satisfactory" at this simple Gallic bistro, in the New Town; also a sister venue down the road. / **Details:** www.lescargotblanc.co.uk; 9 pm, Fri & Sat 10 pm; closed Sun.*

L'Escargot Bleu £46 344
56 Broughton St EH1 3SA (0131) 557 1600
*"Always feels like stepping into France" – an "excellent" and extremely popular New Town bistro combining "outstanding cooking" of "farm-fresh produce" and "pleasant" staff; all at affordable prices too. / **Details:** www.lescargotblanc.co.uk; 10 pm, Fri & Sat 10.30 pm; closed Sun (except Festival); no Amex.*

Favorita £44 343
325 Leith Walk EH6 8SA (0131) 554 2430
*Expect a "wonderful family welcome" at the Crolla family's "friendly" and "busy" Leith Walk venture, part of their citywide empire; it serves "dependable" Italian fare and, with regard to the "excellent" pizzas, the "wood-fired oven makes all the difference". / **Details:** www.la-favorita.com; 11 pm.*

Field £42 442
41 West Nicolson St EH8 9DB
(01316) 677010
*"A tiny, simple two-year-old" in Southside, near the university, with "ambitious" contemporary British food that's "well-balanced", "well-presented" and "reasonably priced". / **Details:** www.fieldrestaurant.co.uk; 9 pm; closed Mon.*

Fishers in the City £53 333
58 Thistle St EH2 1EN (0131) 225 5109
*This "busy and popular" fish bistro near the National Gallery is a well-known "local staple" thanks to its "very reliable fish" – "the usual options, well presented and in generous portions". / **Details:** www.fishersbistros.co.uk; 10.30 pm.*

Galvin Brasserie de Luxe The Caledonian £45 222
Princes St EH1 2AB (0131) 222 8988
*After a couple of years of operation, the Galvin brothers' Parisian-style brasserie, in this famous hotel, continues to put in a middling performance. Sometimes it's a "buzzing and busy" complement to their London empire, but too often there's "not much atmosphere", service can struggle, and the cooking is "underwhelming". / **Details:** www.galvinbrasserie.com; 10 pm; booking: max 8. **Accommodation:** 245 rooms, from £325*

Gardener's Cottage £47 444
1 Royal Terrace Gdns, London Rd EH7 5DX
(0131) 558 1221
*There's a "great social dining experience" to be had at this tiny 19th-century venue, which features communal tables and a "varied" local/seasonal menu; it has made quite a splash since opening in 2012, and some reporters had their best meal of the year here. / **Details:** www.thegardenerscottage.co; 10 pm; closed Tue & Wed.*

La Garrigue £51 343
31 Jeffrey St EH1 1DH (0131) 557 3032
*A "lovely" Old Town staple offering "genuine French cooking", "great service" and a pleasingly "informal" atmosphere; whilst "the focus is on the food", there's also a "superb wine list" full of "rare bottles from the south of France". / **Details:** www.lagarrigue.co.uk; 9.30 pm.*

Grain Store £60 334
30 Victoria St EH1 2JW (0131) 225 7635
*The ambience at this "lovely" and "always buzzing" warehouse in the Old Town is "hard to beat" – and, being "matched by very well-executed food", it's "well recommended as a good all-round package" in the city, particularly for a "romantic" occasion. / **Details:** www.grainstore-restaurant.co.uk; 9.45 pm, Sun 9.30 pm; closed Sun L.*

Hanam's Kurdish & Middle East Restaurant £36 334
3 Johnston Terrace EH1 2PW
(0131) 225 1329
*"On two levels, with a large outside terrace overlooking Grassmarket", this "professional" central venue is an "atmospheric (without being kitsch)" location, serving a Middle Eastern menu of mezze and kebabs; the ability to BYO helps manage costs. / **Details:** www.hanams.com.*

Henderson's £35 342
94 Hanover St EH2 1DR (0131) 225 2131
*Despite being in "a time warp" and arguably "in need of investment", this self-service veggie, in the crypt of a New Town church, is a venerable and highly popular local institution, serving "straightforward" dishes. An offshoot, Henderson's Vegan, opened in July 2015, too late for our survey. / **Details:** www.hendersonsofedinburgh.co.uk; 10 pm, Thu-Sat 11 pm; closed Sun; no Amex.*

The Honours £64 344
58a, North Castle St EH2 3LU
(0131) 220 2513
*Martin Wishart's "top-quality" New Town bistro offers a "relaxed, contemporary vibe backed up by very good cooking and knowledgeable staff"; that said, reports were a little more up-and-down this year – hopefully just a blip. / **Details:** www.thehonours.co.uk; 10 pm; closed Mon & Sun.*

Kanpai £35 443
8-10 Grindlay St EH3 9AS (01312) 281602
*Handy for the Traverse Theatre, this diminutive but sleek Japanese spot (the name means 'Bottoms up!') pairs "wonderful, fresh sushi" (arguably Scotland's best) with a "tiny, appropriate wine list". / **Details:** www.kanpaisushi.co.uk; 10.30 pm; closed Mon.*

Karen's Unicorn £32 432
8b Aberecomby Pl EH3 6LB (01315) 566333
*"Maintaining high standards!"; this "popular and busy" New Town Cantonese is "a cut above the average Chinese"; there's also an outpost in Stockbridge (at St Stephen Street). / **Details:** www.karensunicorn.com; 11 pm; closed Mon.*

The Kitchin £96 433
78 Commercial Quay EH6 6LX
(0131) 555 1755
*Tom & Michaela Kitchin's "luxurious and bustling" Leith warehouse-conversion remains at the forefront of Edinburgh's culinary scene, while maintaining a "relaxed" style with "warm and friendly" service. "Tom knows how to make magic happen on a plate" and provides "stunning dishes with true flavours from Scottish produce". "Maybe now they've extended into next door, it will be easier to get into too..." / **Details:** www.thekitchin.com; Tue-Thu 10 pm, Fri & Sat 10.30 pm; closed Mon & Sun; children: 5+.*

Mother India's Cafe £33 433
3-5 Infirmary St EH1 1LT (0131) 524 9801
*"Why don't all Indian restaurants do tapas like this?" – this "buzzing and vibrant" joint is perpetually "rammed", although the staff cope well given how very "busy" it often becomes. Its "super", "interesting" small dishes "wouldn't be out of place in Benares or Cinnamon Club, but come at around a third of the price" – "get a table, order lots, and marvel at the low bill!"; it has two more basic siblings which are also a "really pleasant surprise"/ **Details:** www.motherindia.co.uk; 10.30 pm, Fri & Sat 11 pm, Sun 10 pm; no Amex.*

Mussel Inn £42 433
61-65 Rose St EH2 2NH (0131) 225 5979
*"In a bright set of rooms close to the Royal Mile", an Old Town stalwart whose "superb seafood" ("fine mussels" of course, plus other fish and meat) ensure it's "always busy". / **Details:** www.mussel-inn.com; 9.50 pm.*

Number One Balmoral Hotel £98 544
1 Princes St EH2 2EQ (0131) 557 6727
*"If only all places could be this good", say fans of Jeff Bland's long-standing fixture – a "wonderful" space in the basement of the city's grandest hotel. His "fantastic", "classical" cuisine – the tasting menu with wine flights attracts particular acclaim – "never fails to reward a visit", but the "attentive" staff ("I even left a note thanking them!") also rate mention. / **Details:** www.roccofortehotels.com/hotels-and-resorts the-balmoral-hotel/restaurants-and-bars/number-one/; 10 pm; D only; no jeans or trainers. **Accommodation:** 188 rooms, from £360*

Ondine £68 444
2 George IV Bridge EH1 1AD (0131) 2261888
*"A superb choice of fish of the highest quality" and "superb" seafood has established this "lovely, light and bright" operation (part of an office block off the Royal Mile) as one of Edinburgh's most popular dining destinations. / **Details:** www.ondinerestaurant.co.uk; 10 pm; closed Sun; booking: max 8.*

The Outsider £43 224
15-16 George IV Bridge EH1 1EE
(0131) 226 3131
*The "modern Scottish" food and service "can both vary" at this "airy" Edinburgh institution "but it always delivers a slab of sexy, modern urban dining and drinking", with "great views over the castle (spectacularly lit-up at night)". / **Details:** www.theoutsiderrestaurant.com; 11 pm; no Amex; booking: max 12.*

The Pompadour by Galvin The Caledonian £85 345
Princes St EH1 2AB (0131) 222 8975
*"Another winner from the Galvin brothers" – their tenancy at this "charming and glamorous" chamber has made it into the landmark destination it long deserved to be, with "clever and perfectly executed" Gallic cuisine paired with "perfect" wines. / **Details:** www.galvinrestaurants.com; 10 pm; D only, closed Sun-Tue.*

Restaurant Mark Greenaway £72 443
67 North Castle St EH2 3LJ (0131) 226 1155
*The TV chef's stylish New Town two-year-old, in an "extensive" Georgian townhouse, continues to win raves for its "exciting and interesting dishes with a twist". / **Details:** markgreenaway.com; 10 pm.*

Restaurant Martin Wishart £94 554
54 The Shore EH6 6RA (0131) 553 3557
"Words cannot describe how good the food is here!" – Martin Wishart's Leith venture inspires a hymn of praise from reporters who again rank it as

Scotland's top gastronomic destination. "Helpful and highly polished" staff deliver "plate after plate of exquisite, precisely executed dishes" that "combine lightness of touch with depth of flavour", while "the wine pairings work wondrously too". / **Details:** www.martin-wishart.co.uk; 9.30 pm; closed Mon & Sun; no trainers.

Scran & Scallie £42 344
1 Comely Bank Rd EH4 1DT
(0131) 332 6281
Despite the odd accusation of "hype", there's no doubting Tom Kitchin has a hit on his hands with his year-old "comfy and stylish" Stockbridge gastropub, serving "proper pub food, with a sprinkling of TK's magic". Top Menu Tip – "excellent steak pie". / **Details:** scranandscallie.com/; 10 pm.

The Stockbridge £54 443
54 St Stephen's St EH3 5AL (0131) 226 6766
A "pleasant" picture-lined basement in the city centre offering "delightful" cuisine (with a slight Scottish accent); according to one reporter of presumably Anglo origins, it's the "perfect place for visiting Englishmen to take out Edinburgh friends!" / **Details:** www.thestockbridgerestaurant.co.uk; 9.30 pm; D only, closed Mon; children: 18+ after 8 pm.

Timberyard £65 455
10 Lady Lawson St EH3 9DS (01312) 211222
"Scandinavia meets Scotland" in this "forgivably pretentious", "hipster" hang-out – "a converted brick warehouse, with outside terrace in an unremarkable street", near the Traverse Theatre. "Sustainable is the watch-word", on the "eclectic" menu – "it's an amazing place to sample local produce", with "great cocktails". / **Details:** www.timberyard.co; 9.30 pm; closed Mon & Sun.

Twenty Princes Street £48 323
20 Princes St EH2 2AN (0131) 652 7370
On this major shopping thoroughfare, a modern booth-style spot that makes a "good venue for a business lunch" – fans praise "beautifully presented" dishes "which taste as good as they look". / **Details:** www.twnetyprincesstreet.co.uk; 11 pm.

21212 £92 444
3 Royal Ter EH7 5AB (0845) 222 1212
"Witty, subversive, delicious, surprising, serious...." – Paul Kitching's cuisine is certainly anything but predictable, and especially "for something different" the open kitchen at his "romantic" Calton Hill townhouse is just the job for an "unusual" culinary experience that fans find nothing short of "sublime". / **Details:** www.21212restaurant.co.uk; 9.30 pm; closed Mon & Sun; children: 5+. **Accommodation:** 4 rooms, from £95

Valvona & Crolla £38 333
19 Elm Row EH7 4AA (0131) 556 6066
At the rear of an 80-year-old deli/wine importer that's one of the city's most revered foodie destinations, this café annex achieves little survey feedback nowadays; such as exists is all positive, but not outstanding. Top Tip – wine from their superb selection at retail plus corkage. / **Details:** www.valvonacrolla.com; 11.30 pm, Sun 6 pm.

Wedgwood £58 552
267 Canongate EH8 8BQ (0131) 558 8737
Paul Wedgwood's "very special" spot, just off the Royal Mile, provides "faultless cuisine, with service to match"; the "only quibble is related to the size of the restaurant (small)" and its basement setting ("slightly sterile"). Top Tip – "the incredibly low-price lunch menu is Edinburgh's special treat". / **Details:** www.wedgwoodtherestaurant.co.uk; 10 pm; 8+ take a deposit.

The Witchery by the Castle £72 235
Castlehill, The Royal Mile EH1 2NF
(0131) 225 5613
There's no denying the bewitchingly "romantic" appeal of this "very atmospheric" Gothic landmark near the castle ("equally lovely in the wood-panelled room, or the beautiful garden room"), and its "stupendous" wine list is equally intoxicating. The food, though, can seem "staggeringly average and eyewateringly expensive". / **Details:** www.thewitchery.com; 11.30 pm. **Accommodation:** 8 rooms, from £325

EGHAM, SURREY 3–3A

The Estate Grill Great Fosters Hotel £62 434
Stroude Rd TW20 9UR (01784) 433822
Reopened in April 2015, the "lovely" oak-beamed dining room of this "glorious" Elizabethan hotel (with "stunning" garden) offers "top-quality" classics, alongside the property's more casual grill; it's a "bit on the expensive side, but it cannot be bettered for a romantic overnight break". / **Details:** www.greatfosters.co.uk; no jeans or trainers; booking: max 12. **Accommodation:** 43 rooms, from £155

ELDERSFIELD, GLOUCESTERSHIRE 2–1B

The Butcher's Arms £66 443
Lime St GL19 4NX (01452) 840 381
James & Elizabeth Winter's "superb, old-style village pub" is proof that "brilliant cooking doesn't have to be in London nor in a swanky restaurant". Whilst it's the sort of spot where "locals are welcome in the bar", there's no mistaking the "Michelin star-worthy food". / **Details:** www.thebutchersarms.net; 9 pm; closed Mon, Tue L, Wed L, Thu L & Sun D; children: 10+.

ELLAND, WEST YORKSHIRE 5–1C

La Cachette £50 444

31 Huddersfield Rd HX5 9AH
(01422) 378833
"The best in the area"; Jonathan Nichols's "very French" fixture combines "consistently good food" with an "excellent wine list". **/ Details:** *www.lacachette-elland.com; 9.30 pm, Fri & Sat 10 pm; closed Sun; no Amex.*

ELLEL, LANCASHIRE 5–1A

The Bay Horse £45 423

Bay Horse Ln LA2 0HR (01524) 791204
"A minor refurb has done a remarkable world of good to the Wilkinson family's pub, handy for the M6", making it "better suited to the excellent and precise food from son-of-the-family Craig Wilkinson". It can be "a bit inconsistent" though. **/ Details:** *www.bayhorseinn.com; 9 pm, Sun 8 pm; closed Mon; no Amex.*

ELLON, ABERDEENSHIRE 9–2D

Eat on the Green £66 343

Udny Grn AB41 7RS (01651) 842337
"'The Kilted Chef' wins every time!"; in a former inn, tartan-loving Chris Wilkinson's well-established venue offers a "continually changing menu that reflects the seasons". **/ Details:** *www.eatonthegreen.co.uk; 9 pm, Sun 8 pm; closed Mon & Tue.*

ELSLACK, NORTH YORKSHIRE 5–1B

The Tempest Arms £42 334

Elsack Ln BD23 3AY (01282) 842 450
"A real surprise"; expect "proper Yorkshire portions and hospitality" at this "really warm and welcoming" inn. **/ Details:** *www.tempestarms.co.uk; 9 pm, Sun 7.30 pm.* **Accommodation:** *21 rooms, from £89.95*

ELY, CAMBRIDGESHIRE 3–1B

Old Fire Engine House £45 343

25 St Mary's St CB7 4ER (01353) 662582
The "best in town, it never disappoints!" – so say loyal fans of this city-centre institution (est. 1968) and art gallery in a pretty Georgian house. **/ Details:** *www.theoldfireenginehouse.co.uk; 9 pm; closed Sun D; no Amex.*

EMSWORTH, HAMPSHIRE 2–4D

36 on the Quay £81 324

47 South St PO10 7EG (01243) 375592
A "wonderful setting that cannot fail to set your heart aflutter and food to match" win raves for Ramon Farthing's "small, unpretentious" venue, right on the harbour; despite its long-standing culinary reputation, however, not everyone is quite convinced. **/ Details:** *www.36onthequay.co.uk; off A27 between Portsmouth & Chichester; 9 pm; closed Mon & Sun; no Amex.* **Accommodation:** *5 (plus cottage) rooms, from £100*

Fat Olives £50 554

30 South St PO10 7EH (01243) 377914
"Close to the water" a short walk up the hill from the harbour, Lawrence and Julia Murphy's "small and friendly" venue (in an old terraced house) is an all-round winner. The food from a "limited" menu is "nothing fancy", but "little tweaks here and there keep it at the top of its game". **/ Details:** *www.fatolives.co.uk; 9.15 pm; closed Mon & Sun; no Amex; children: 8+, except Sat L*

EPPING, ESSEX 3–2B

Haywards Restaurant £56 542

111 Bell Common CM16 4DZ
(01992) 577350
This "adventurous" yearling is "as close as you will get to fine dining" in this part of the world – "it's the equal of a good West End restaurant". **/ Details:** *www.haywardsrestaurant.co.uk.*

EPSOM, SURREY 3–3B

Le Raj £37 433

211 Fir Tree Rd KT17 3LB (01737) 371371
"The only Indian I will eat in outside of India!" – this well-established suburban subcontinental is acclaimed locally for its "high standard of cooking" that's "a bit different from the norm". **/ Details:** *www.lerajrestaurant.co.uk; 11 pm; no jeans or trainers.*

ESHER, SURREY 3–3A

Good Earth £56 433

14-18 High St KT10 9RT (01372) 462489
The "best Chinese for miles around"; this fine dining stalwart – the "equally good sister of the Knightsbridge branch" – combines "exemplary" food with "the chance for some celeb spotting". **/ Details:** *www.goodearthgroup.co.uk; 11.15 pm, Sun 10.45 pm; booking: max 12, Fri & Sat.*

ETON, BERKSHIRE 3–3A

Gilbey's £47 334

82-83 High St SL4 6AF (01753) 854921
On the High Street, an attractive and "reasonably priced" stalwart fixture, with a front-room bar, and "spacious" dining conservatory hidden at the rear; it's all "most pleasant". (There's also accommodation – the top-floor studio suite offers prime Windsor

*Castle views). / **Details:** www.gilbeygroup.com; 5 min walk from Windsor Castle; 9.45 pm, Fri & Sat 10 pm.*

EVERSHOT, DORSET 2–4B

Summer Lodge **£75** 4 4 5
DT2 0JR (01935) 482000
*At the heart of a picturesque village, this five-star, Georgian, country house hotel (a Relais & Chateaux property) is "full of old-school charm", and its dining conservatory "is lovely in summer, overlooking the beautiful gardens". Chef Steven Titman creates some "memorable" cuisine, and there's a "quite outstanding wine list, overseen by an outstanding sommelier" (plus a "great choice of whiskies" too). / **Details:** www.summerlodgehotel.co.uk; 12m NW of Dorchester on A37; 9.30 pm; no jeans or trainers. **Accommodation:** 24 rooms, from £235*

EXETER, DEVON 1–3D

Michael Caines Cafe Bar & Grill ABode Hotel Exeter **£68** 4 3 2
Cathedral Yd EX1 1DZ (01392) 319 955
*"Overlooking the cathedral", the celeb chef's city-centre venue wins consistent praise for its "lovely" food, even if some reporters consider the interior to be "ambience-free". Top Tip – "amazing-value set lunch". / **Details:** www.abodeexeter.co.uk/michael caines-dining/michael-caines-restaurants; 9.30 pm, Frki & Sat 10 pm, Sun 9 pm. **Accommodation:** 53 rooms, from £79*

Rendezvous **£43** 2 2 3
38-40 Southernhay East EX1 1PE
(01392) 270 222
*This Southernhay basement wine-bar is a "useful option in the city scene"; alongside top tipples, it's praised for its food too – a combination "seemingly popular with the area's professional class". / **Details:** www.winebar10.co.uk; 10 pm; closed Sun.*

EXTON, HAMPSHIRE 2–3D

Shoe Inn **£42** 4 3 2
Shoe Ln SO32 3NT (01489) 877526
*An "old-fashioned pub" in the Meon Valley that's "worth seeking out" for its "clear and gutsy" food. "The only complaint – they need to stop serving kids' meals on fancy boards"! / **Details:** www.theshoeexton.co.uk/; 11 pm.*

FALMOUTH, CORNWALL 1–4B

The Cove Restaurant & Bar **£48** 5 4 4
Maenporth Beach TR11 5HN (01326) 251136
*"Straightforward food that excites and wows" plus "great views" of Maenporth Beach – the winning assets of this sleek terraced restaurant, whose many fans "always want to keep going back for more". / **Details:** www.thecovemaenporth.co.uk; 9.30 pm; closed Sun D.*

Rick Stein's Fish & Chips **£40** 4 3 3
Discovery Quay TR11 3XA (01841) 532700
*"Fabulous fish from a wide range of sometimes unusual choices", plus "cheery, professional service" – the winning formula at the TV chef's posh chippy, with a "great location" near the Maritime Museum. / **Details:** www.rickstein.com; 9 pm; no Amex; no booking.*

Wheelhouse **£38** 5 4 4
Upton Slip TR11 3DQ (01326) 318050
*Hidden down a small side street, this "tiny", "fun" outfit, with open kitchen, serves "the freshest seafood you could imagine" and offers "remarkable value" too; limited opening hours. / **Details:** no web; 9 pm; D only, closed Sun-Tue; no credit cards.*

FARNBOROUGH, HAMPSHIRE 3–3A

Aviator **£55** 3 2 4
55 Farnborough Rd GU14 6EL
(01252) 555890
*A slick hotel which is "aping London food standards" with its "delicious" dishes (although the service can be "below par"); "the sky bar is well worth a visit" beforehand. / **Details:** www.aviatorbytag.com; 10 pm, Fri & Sat 10.30 pm, Sun 9.30 pm.*

FAVERSHAM, KENT 3–3C

Read's **£82** 4 4 4
Macknade Manor, Canterbury Rd ME13 8XE
(01795) 535344
*"Beautifully laid tables" and "excellent, old-fashioned service" – "too polite for this century", but very "un-snooty" – characterise the old-school approach of David and Rona Pitchford's long-established, "high-class" Kent favourite. "Take your mother-in-law, and any wounds will be healed..." / **Details:** www.reads.com; 9.30 pm; closed Mon & Sun. **Accommodation:** 6 rooms, from £165*

Yard **£14** 3 3 3
10 Jacob Yd, Preston St ME13 8NY
(01795) 538265
*A "cosy" new foodie hideaway in an historic mews which has already proved "very popular" – be it for "amazing" Kentish breakfasts which are "too good to miss out on", or "interesting" salads, sarnies and soups. / **Details:** 5 pm; L only, closed Sun.*

FENCE, LANCASHIRE 5–1B

White Swan at Fence £40 544

300 Wheatley Lane Rd BB12 9QA
(01282) 611773
"The only Timothy Taylor's tied house west of the Pennines" – this pretty, "humble" rural inn is also distinguished by its "brilliant, ever-changing" 2-course and 3-course menus which offer "unbeatable value". Chef Tom Parker's "ex-Northcote pedigree shines through" in the "confident and skilled" cooking "quality ingredients", while staff "go the extra mile". / **Details:** *www.whiteswanatfence.co.uk; 8.30 pm, Fri & Sat 9 pm, Sun 7 pm; closed Mon.*

FERRENSBY, NORTH YORKSHIRE 8–4B

General Tarleton £50 443

Boroughbridge Rd HG5 0PZ (01423) 340284
Just off the A1, John Topham's "very upmarket" inn has been "a consistent performer over many years" and still "stands out as the best gastropub in an area of intense competition"; the "extremely varied" menu comes at "keen prices" and rooms are "excellent" too. / **Details:** *www.generaltarleton.co.uk; 2m from A1, J48 towards Knaresborough; 9.15 pm.* **Accommodation:** *14 rooms, from £129*

FLAUNDEN, HERTFORDSHIRE 3–2A

The Bricklayers Arms £52 344

Hogpits Bottom HP3 0PH (01442) 833322
"If you want a drive out to the country" this "charming hostelry" is "definitely worth a visit", owing its "phenomenal success" to "a menu that makes you want to choose everything", "always reliable" service and a "traditional", "pubby" atmosphere. / **Details:** *www.bricklayersarms.com; J18 off the M25, past Chorleywood; 9.30 pm, Sun 8.30 pm.*

FLETCHING, EAST SUSSEX 3–4B

The Griffin Inn £48 323

TN22 3SS (01825) 722890
"So often when one ventures into the shires one is disappointed on F, S and/or A" – but "not so this time!"; "set in a picturesque country village", this venue with an "amazing" garden, great food and an "owner into his wines" can seem like the "perfect pub", and to the extent that there are grumbles they seem fairly minor league. / **Details:** *www.thegriffininn.co.uk; off A272; 9.30 pm, Sun 9 pm.* **Accommodation:** *13 rooms, from £85*

FOLKESTONE, KENT 3–4D

Rocksalt £48 334

4-5 Fishmarket CT19 6AA (01303) 212 070
"Unsurpassable harbour views" are the highlight at Mark Sargeant's "contemporary-style" three-year-old, which is best enjoyed from the "fantastic, sunny-day terrace" (especially as the interior can be "incredibly noisy"). Food-wise, "local fish is prepared with a sure touch", but it's "expensive". / **Details:** *www.rocksaltfolkestone.co.uk; 10 pm; closed Sun D; no Amex.* **Accommodation:** *4 rooms, from £85*

FONTHILL GIFFORD, WILTSHIRE 2–3C

Beckford Arms £44 344

SP3 6PX (01747) 870 385
"Everything a country pub should be" – "a lovely choice for a meal in beautiful countryside". There's "a splendid menu incorporating both traditional choices and some more interesting dishes, and all are cooked superbly." / **Details:** *www.thebeckfordarms.co.uk; 9.30 pm, Sun 9 pm; no Amex.* **Accommodation:** *10 rooms, from £95*

FORDHAM, CAMBRIDGESHIRE 3–1B

White Pheasant £53 433

21 Market St CB7 5LQ (01638) 720414
This smart 17th-century gastropub (a favourite of the Newmarket set) is "growing in reputation" for young chef/owner Calvin Holland's cuisine – "far above the standard expected of a local, county restaurant". / **Details:** *www.whitepheasant.com; 9.30 pm, Sun 2.30 pm; closed Mon.*

FORMBY, MERSEYSIDE 5–2A

The Sparrowhawk £42 333

Southport Old Rd L37 0AB (01704) 882 350
In a "pleasant and comfortable" country house, amid five acres of woods, this Brunning & Price outpost is "trying to be a cut above average" (and succeeding on some accounts). / **Details:** *www.brunningandprice.co.uk/sparrowhawk/; 10 pm, Sun 9.30 pm.*

FORT WILLIAM, HIGHLAND 9–3B

Crannog £54 423

Town Centre Pier PH33 6DB (01397) 705589
On a pier over the water at the top of Loch Linnhe (they run cruises too) this well-known destination is a "lovely place to eat on a sunny day"; its MO is "solid seafood, cooked well". / **Details:** *www.crannog.net; 9 pm; no Amex.*

21212, Edinburgh

Timberyard, Edinburgh

Gamba, Glasgow

FRESSINGFIELD, SUFFOLK 3–1D

The Fox & Goose £49 334

Church Rd IP21 5PB (01379) 586247

*A "comfortable" and spacious country inn run by the same couple for over a decade. The style of cuisine is fairly ambitious and "elaborate" and on all accounts "reliable and excellent value". Top Tip – the fixed-price lunch "must be one of the best-value meals in East Anglia". / **Details:** www.foxandgoose.net; off A143; 8.30 pm, Sun 8.15 pm; closed Mon; no Amex; children: 9+ at D.*

FRILSHAM, BERKSHIRE 2–2D

The Pot Kiln £52 534

RG18 0XX (01635) 201366

*This "remote", "quiet" pub, "beautifully located in lovely countryside" fully repays the time taken in finding it. Its relationship to Fulham's famous Harwood Arms is evident in the "fabulous" locally shot game served by its "professional, but not over-trained" staff in its agreeably straightforward dining room. You can eat in the huge garden too (although just from the bar menu). / **Details:** www.potkiln.org; between J12 and J13 of the M4; 9 pm, Sun 8 pm.*

FRITHSDEN, HERTFORDSHIRE 3–2A

The Alford Arms £48 344

HP1 3DD (01442) 864480

*"There's a high standard of food, and always a very warm welcome" at this "sophisticated pub in a lovely rural setting". If there's a downside it's that it's immensely popular, and at peak times it's "rammed". / **Details:** www.alfordarmsfrithsden.co.uk; near Ashridge College and vineyard; 9.30 pm, Fri & Sat 10 pm, Sun 9 pm; booking: max 12.*

FROXFIELD, WILTSHIRE 2–2C

The Palm £37 443

Bath Rd SN8 3HT (01672) 871 818

*"Quite a find on the A4"; despite being "in the middle of nowhere", this "swanky" South Indian, with "large windows looking out over the countryside", is "always full and buzzing"; the reason? – it serves "the best curry ever!". / **Details:** www.thepalmindian.com; 11.30 pm.*

FYFIELD, OXFORDSHIRE 2–3C

White Hart £48 434

OX13 5LW (01865) 390585

*A "simply brilliant" gastropub in a fascinating 15th-century building with a vaulted dining room and minstrels' gallery; the "sensational" food features "a lot of homegrown and locally sourced products". Top Tip – "very good lunch offer". / **Details:** www.whitehart-fyfield.com; off A420; 9.30 pm, Sun 3 pm; closed Sun D.*

GATESHEAD, TYNE AND WEAR 8–2B

Eslington Villa Hotel £44 344

8 Station Rd NE9 6DR (0191) 487 6017

*With its "discreet", "country house"-style surroundings and "courteous" staff, this "small" Victorian hotel is a "good place away from the Newcastle bustle"; the cooking could be a tad "more attentive" at times, but it still makes a "top pick for a special occasion". / **Details:** www.eslingtonvilla.co.uk; A1 exit for Team Valley Trading Estate, then left off Eastern Avenue; 9.30 pm; closed Sat L & Sun D. **Accommodation:** 18 rooms, from £89.50*

Raval £47 543

Church St, Gateshead Quays NE8 2AT (0191) 4771700

*"A lovely surprise!" – a "luxurious restaurant with an open kitchen" that serves a "standard of Indian cuisine that's hard to beat" (and "plenty of it" too); a real hit with all who comment on it. / **Details:** www.ravalrestaurant.com; 11 pm; D only, closed Sun; no shorts.*

GERRARDS CROSS, BUCKINGHAMSHIRE 3–3A

Maliks £43 322

14 Oak End Way SL9 8BR (01753) 880888

*The Cookham tandoori's spin-off doesn't quite inspire the same level of dedication as its famous sibling; the food is mostly "very good" – "a couple of notches above standard curry house fare" – the atmosphere "pleasant but nothing to go out of your way for". / **Details:** www.maliks.co.uk; 10.45 pm.*

Three Oaks £48 434

Austenwood Ln SL9 8NL (01753) 899 016

*This country gastropub continues to please reporters with its "consistently good, tasty food" and "attentive" service; it's the sort of place which "always sets a reasonable standard and sometimes excels". / **Details:** www.thethreeoaksgx.co.uk; 9.15 pm.*

GILLINGHAM, DORSET 2–3B

Stock Hill House £61 454

SP8 5NR (01747) 823626

*From the "old-style service", to the "old-school Austrian cooking prepared with real love", Peter Hauser's "elegant" country house hotel provides a "lovely and peaceful retreat" that some who report on it have enjoyed for decades – "we drive nearly 200 miles to visit, so it must be good"! / **Details:** www.stockhillhouse.co.uk; 8.30 pm; closed Mon L;*

no Amex; no jeans; children: 8+ at D in dining room. **Accommodation:** *10 rooms, from £260 incl dinner*

GLASGOW, CITY OF GLASGOW 9–4C

Babu £26 4 3 2
186 W Regent St G2 4RU (0141) 204 4042
A "tiny" (only three tables) two-year-old, all-day café and take-away in the city centre, offering "exciting and delicious" Indian street food "with a Scottish twist"; fans say it "deserves recognition for being tasty, different... and good!" / **Details:** *www.babu-kitchen.com/; 9 pm, Mon 4 pm; closed Mon D & Sun.*

Café Cossachok £36 3 3 3
10 King St G1 5QP (0141) 553 0733
"Quirky little Russian restaurant" in the Merchant City – fans applaud its "interesting food, and great value".

Café Gandolfi £44 3 4 4
64 Albion St G1 1NY (0141) 552 6813
The very characterful, "slightly Bohemian" setting is the winning feature of this Merchant City institution (which has spawned a number of spin-offs nearby). "Straightforward Scottish food is very competently cooked"; "if your heart warms to neeps and tatties, haggis, and black pudding, you can't do better than this". / **Details:** *www.cafegandolfi.com; 11 pm; no booking, Sat.*

Cail Bruich £54 4 4 3
725 Great Western Rd G12 8QX
(01413) 346265
Chris Charalambous' ambitious West End venue continues to attract nothing but upbeat feedback. There is an à la carte, but the focus is on the "excellent" and "excellent value" tasting menus with "interesting wine pairings". / **Details:** *www.cailbruichreatruants.co.uk; 9 pm; closed Mon.*

Crabshakk £50 5 4 4
Finnestone G3 8TD (0141) 334 6127
"Hugely popular" and "exuberantly cheerful" West End spot universal praised for its "soul-restoring" seafood; OK, so it's "not THAT cheap", but "the quality of the ingredients would preclude that" – and "it's so tiny that you feel quite triumphant getting a table!" / **Details:** *www.crabshakk.com; 10 pm; closed Mon; no Amex; booking: max 12.*

The Fish People Cafe £47 4 3 2
350 Scotland St G5 8QF (0141) 429 8787
Reports continue to extol the many virtues of this "lively, welcoming" café ("nothing failed to set our taste buds exploding with joy", says one, and "even the coffee was ace"); the only downside? – a rather "odd site" by Shields Road subway station. / **Details:** *www.thefishpeoplecafe.co.uk/; 9 pm, Fri & Sat 10 pm, Sun 8.45 pm; closed Mon.*

Gamba £65 4 4 3
225a West George St G2 2ND
(0141) 572 0899
This city-centre basement continues to maintain its reputation for the "best fish and seafood in Glasgow"; the latter comes "cooked simply or not at all (sashimi)" and "they also do good cocktails" ("the Yuzu Margarita is not to be missed"!) / **Details:** *www.gamba.co.uk; 10 pm; closed Sun L.*

Gandolfi Fish £46 4 3 3
84-86 Albion St G1 1NY (0141) 552 6813
"The fishy companion to the ever-wonderful Café Gandolfi"; it's "perhaps a little expensive as it is in the trendy Merchant City, but no more so than its competitors, and on balance it's one of the very best"! / **Details:** *www.cafegandolfi.com; 11.30 pm.*

The Gannet £47 5 4 3
1155 Argyle St G3 8TB (0141) 2042081
"Creative and innovative" but slightly "stark" Finnestoun yearling, run by refugees from the hallowed ABode hotel, which wows reporters with its "exciting" small plates (featuring "excellent Scottish produce", particularly "unusual and sometimes foraged ingredients"); "I don't expect Ed Miliband will be back but we will"! / **Details:** *www.thegannetgla.com; 9.30 pm, Sun 7.30 pm.*

Hanoi Bike Shop £29 3 2 1
8 Ruthven Ln G12 9BG (01413) 347165
"Tastes explode in the mouth", at this "quirky" West End café specialising in Vietnamese street food – a two-floor site that some will remember as Stravaigin 2 (RIP). To some critics, the cooking is "hot, but lacks depth", but on most accounts the dishes here are of "solid" quality, and overall results are "authentic and good value". / **Details:** *www.hanoibikeshop.co.uk; 11 pm.*

Mother India £37 4 2 3
28 Westminster Ter G3 7RU (0141) 221 1663
A West End fixture that's invariably "always crowded" owing to its "interesting" and "deliciously tasty" tapas-style dishes – just avoid the "very noisy" basement; it has two less formal siblings on nearby Argyll St which are also a "really pleasant surprise". / **Details:** *www.motherindia.co.uk; 10.30 pm, Fri & Sat 11 pm, Sun 10 pm; Mon-Thu D only, Fri-Sun open L & D.*

Ox and Finch £40 4 4 3
920 Sauchiehall St G3 7TF (0141) 339 8627
A "converted pub with a Scottish take on tapas" from Jon MacDonald (ex-chef for the McLaren F1 team); it wins praise for its "outstanding" results and "fabulous" service, and more than holds its own "in an area with loads of top-class choice". / **Details:** *www.oxandfinch.com/; 10 pm; 9+ must book.*

La Parmigiana £56 443

447 Great Western Rd G12 8HH
(0141) 334 0686
"Consistently brilliant"... "consistently exceptional" – the concepts of reliability and excellence feature in all reports on this tiny, traditional Italian favourite, on the borders between the West End and city centre. / **Details:** *www.laparmigiana.co.uk; 10.30 pm, Sun 6 pm.*

Rogano £64 345

11 Exchange Pl G1 3AN (0141) 248 4055
It's hard not to just "love the history" (reflected in the elegant interior by the people who did the Queen Mary) of this famous Art Deco landmark, in the city centre. There's the odd gripe that it "lives on its past reputation", but for the most part there's praise for its "spot on" fish and seafood. A good choice for business entertaining. / **Details:** *www.roganoglasgow.com; 10.30 pm.*

Shish Mahal £39 443

66-68 Park Rd G4 9JF (0141) 334 7899
"You can't possibly go wrong" at this establishment, near Kelvinbridge subway; "since the times of Mr Ali and his invention of chicken tikka masala (nearly 50 years ago now) it has been a Glasgow legend"; "their businessmen's lunches are fantastic value" too. / **Details:** *www.shishmahal.co.uk; 11 pm; closed Sun L.*

Stravaigin £52 534

28 Gibson St G12 8NX (0141) 334 2665
Colin Clydesdale's unique venue symbolises "genuine Glasgow" and although – with its bar and basement restaurant (for which you can book) – it "feels akin to a gastropub" the "décor is something else" and the "inventive and classy" cooking "so far ahead of the usual pub fare it's not true". "The quality and choice is equally good upstairs or down, and in the bar you're surrounded by an eclectic West End mix of people". / **Details:** *www.stravaigin.co.uk; 11 pm; no Amex.*

Two Fat Ladies at The Buttery £60 445

652 Argyle St G3 8UF (0141) 221 8188
A "great institution that remains consistent"; near the SECC, this "traditional" (read plush) outpost of the small local seafood chain occupies very characterful Victorian premises, and wins praise for its "quiet booths" and very "consistent" cooking. / **Details:** *www.twofatladiesrestaurant.com; 10 pm, Sun 9 pm.*

Ubiquitous Chip £59 334

12 Ashton Ln G12 8SJ (0141) 334 5007
"Though it's been going for decades", this famous West End institution (est. 1971) with its "very pretty conservatory" and idiosyncratic lay-out is "still lovely", combining "quite pricey but good" modern Scottish cooking with "one of the best wine lists you'll find anywhere". / **Details:** *www.ubiquitouschip.co.uk; 11 pm.*

GODALMING, SURREY 3–3A

La Luna £45 353

10-14 Wharf St GU7 1NN (01483) 414155
"Not your average Italian!"; this "cosy neighbourhood restaurant of class" provides an "all-round excellent dining experience", ranging from the "really interesting" cooking to the "great wine list" and "personable and engaging" host. / **Details:** *www.lalunarestaurant.co.uk; 10 pm; no Amex.*

GOLDSBOROUGH, N YORKS 8–3D

The Fox And Hounds Inn £60 453

YO21 3RX (01947) 893372
A "tiny and family-run" country inn; Jason Davies's remote venture continues to garner impressive ratings, especially for its "fantastic" food. / **Details:** *www.foxandhoundsgoldsborough.co.uk; 8.30 pm; D only, closed Sun-Tue; no Amex.*

GORING-ON-THAMES, BERKSHIRE 2–2D

Leatherne Bottel (Rossini at) £62 235

Bridleway RG8 0HS (01491) 872667
Mixed opinions on this riverside stalwart which reopened after a revamp in August 2014. Its "delightful" location – "within a few feet of the lovely peaceful River Thames" – makes for "outstanding alfresco dining when the weather is kind", but whereas for some reporters its Italian cuisine is an equal attraction, more than one critic feels it's "not a patch on the old Leatherne Bottel". / **Details:** *www.leathernebottel.co.uk; 9 pm; closed Sun D; children: 10+ for D.*

GRASMERE, CUMBRIA 7–3D

The Jumble Room £47 334

Langdale Rd LA22 9SU (01539) 435188
"Quirky menu, quirky service, quirky ambience"... whilst "such a combination can often mean disaster", in this case it "all seems to work" – resulting in a "vibrant, chatty dining room that makes for a fun night out". / **Details:** *www.thejumbleroom.co.uk; 9.30 pm; closed Tue.* **Accommodation:** *3 rooms, from £180*

GREAT GONERBY, LINCOLNSHIRE 5–3D

Harry's Place £82 552

17 High St NG31 8JS (01476) 561780

*"Everyone should book and make a detour when heading past on the A1, for this total delight from start to finish". Harry & Caroline Hallam's "cosy" front room provides the venue for this unique 10-seat venture which delivers "ravishing yet simple haute cuisine from a tiny hand-written menu" (with Harry buying "whatever is available and good on the day"). Caroline's service "couldn't be more friendly and welcoming" – if there's a concern it's that it can "feel slightly awkward if you're the only table there" (but even that strikes some reporters as "romantic"). / **Details:** on B1174 1m N of Grantham; 8.30 pm; closed Mon & Sun; no Amex; booking essential; children: 5+.*

GREAT LIMBER, LINCOLNSHIRE 6–2A

The New Inn £45 333

2 High St DN37 8JL (01469) 569998

*A "great addition to the rather sparse Lincolnshire foodie scene"; the former village pub has been converted into a "tasteful" boutique hotel where chef Ian Matfin (ex-Gordon Ramsay and Michael Caines) produces "great cuisine based on local ingredients" from the Brocklesby Estate. / **Details:** www.thenewinngreatlimber.co.uk/; 9.30 pm.*

GREAT MILTON, OXFORDSHIRE 2–2D

Le Manoir aux Quat' Saisons £190 554

Church Rd OX44 7PD (01844) 278881

*"A wander around the magnificent gardens" is the overture to a "blissful" all-round experience (especially if you are staying the night) at Légion d'Honneur winner, Raymond Blanc's "immaculate" Elizabethan manor house, which has few rivals in the UK as the choice "for a very special occasion". "Exquisite" modern French cuisine – with much produce from the grounds – is delivered by "sensitive" staff in a "light and airy" conservatory. On the downside "you need a second mortgage", but most reporters feel "it's an investment worth making". / **Details:** www.belmond.com/le-manoir-aux quat-saisons-oxfordshire/www.belmond.com/le-manoir aux-quat-saisons-oxfordshire/; from M40, J7 take A329 towards Wallingford; 9.15 pm; booking: max 12. **Accommodation:** 32 rooms, from £555*

GREETHAM, RUTLAND 5–3D

The Wheatsheaf £42 433

Stretton Rd LE15 7NP (01572) 812325

*A village gastropub where "the stars of the show are Scott and Carol – him as wine host, and her at the stove"; "the quality of cooking and ingredients is high", the menu always provides a "new inventive twist", and there's "good drinking across the board". / **Details:** www.wheatsheaf-greetham.co.uk; 9 pm; closed Mon & Sun D.*

GRESFORD, WREXHAM 5–3A

Pant-yr-Ochain £46 345

Old Wrexham Rd LL12 8TY (01978) 853525

*This rambling and club-like venue (a small manor house, complete with a little lake) is nowadays part of the well-established Brunning & Price empire. It makes a particularly comfortable and atmospheric destination for some enjoyable food (and there's an "excellent selection" of beers too). / **Details:** www.brunningandprice.co.uk/pantyrochain; 1m N of Wrexham; 9.30 pm, Sun 9 pm.*

GRINDLETON, LANCASHIRE 5–1B

The Duke Of York Inn £46 343

Clitheroe BB7 4QR (01200) 441266

*This Ribble Valley stalwart has achieved a "consistently high standard" over the years; it offers "delicious pub food in a true pub" setting (i.e. it's "not just a gastropub where locals can't drink"). / **Details:** www.dukeofyorkgrindleton.com; 9 pm, Sun 7.30 pm; closed Mon & Tue; no Amex.*

GUERNSEY, CHANNEL ISLANDS –

Da Nello £47 443

46 Lower Pollet St GY1 1WF (01481) 721552

*"Our continuing favourite restaurant in Guernsey over the last 15 years"; this surprisingly capacious St Peter Port trattoria continues to please reporters, despite strong competition from Le Petit Bistro nearby. / **Details:** www.danello.gg; 10 pm.*

Le Petit Bistro £52 444

56 Le Pollet GY1 1WF (01481) 725055

*You "can't beat a cosy little corner table for two" at this "buzzy" Gallic venture "overlooking the harbour" in St Peter Port – the food just keeps getting "delicious-er and delicious-er (as Alice might have said...)" / **Details:** www.petitbistro.co.uk; 10 pm, 10.30 pm Fri & Sat; closed Sun.*

Red £55 434
61 The Pollet, St Peter Port GY1 1WL
(01481) 700299
*Jovial St Peter Port spot that's "great for lunch or dinner, as long as you like steak!"; besides its "outstanding" meat options, there are also some "excellent" wines and cocktails. / **Details:** www.red.gg; 9.45 pm; closed Sun.*

GUILDFORD, SURREY 3–3A

Britten's £49 343
1C, Sydenham Rd GU1 3RT (01483) 302888
*MasterChef competitor Dan Britten's two-year-old is "just what Guildford has lacked" – a restaurant offering "stylish and individual cooking" and "bright service" too; the place is "even better since a subtle refurb". / **Details:** www.brittensrestaurant.com; 9.15 pm; closed Mon & Sun.*

Cau £46 232
274 High St GU1 3JL (01483) 459777
*"For a chain, the main event (meat!) is good" at this "trendy" Argentinian steakhouse; downsides? – it's "a bit on the pricey side". / **Details:** www.caurestaurants.com; 11 pm, Sun 10.30 pm.*

Rumwong £41 343
18-20 London Rd GU1 2AF (01483) 536092
*A "superb" Thai veteran (est. 1978) offering "rich and decadent cooking allied with fabulously slick and professional service"... no wonder it's so "busy". / **Details:** www.rumwong.co.uk; 10.30 pm; closed Mon; no Amex.*

The Thai Terrace £41 344
Castle Car Pk, Sydenham Rd GU1 3RW
(01483) 503350
*The "wonderful roof-top setting", with "fantastic panoramic views over the town", can come as a surprise at this "big and buzzing" ("loud") venue, given its "inauspicious location in a concrete, multi-storey car park". So can the quality of the Thai cooking, which on practically all accounts is "excellent" too (though its ratings dipped a little compared with last year). / **Details:** www.thaiterrace.co.uk; 10.30 pm; closed Sun; no Amex.*

GULLANE, EAST LOTHIAN 9–4D

Chez Roux Greywalls Hotel £59 344
EH31 2EG (01620) 842144
*A "wonderful" outpost of the Roux empire in a classy Lutyens-designed house; it's an ideal spot for a "perfect weekend lunch", bookended by "drinks in the library" and "coffee in the beautiful garden". / **Details:** www.greywalls.co.uk; 10 pm; jacket at D. **Accommodation:** 23 rooms, from £260*

La Potinière £53 443
Main St EH31 2AA (01620) 843214
*Keith Marley & Mary Runciman's petite venue has a long history, but garners only limited feedback nowadays. Such as there is however, suggests it continues to offer "superb precision cooking from locally sourced ingredients" and that service is "very welcoming" too. / **Details:** www.lapotiniere.co.uk; 20m SE of Edinburgh, off A198; 8.30 pm; closed Mon, Tue & Sun D; no Amex; no jeans or trainers.*

GULWORTHY, DEVON 1–3C

The Horn of Plenty Country House Hotel & Restaurant £72 444
PL19 8JD (01822) 832528
*This once-celebrated restaurant, in a "peaceful location with good views" of the Tamar Valley, seems to be on the up once more. Feedback is still limited, but it seems "very much better than our last visit 10 years ago!", and perhaps even worthy of regaining recognition by the tyre men. / **Details:** www.thehornofplenty.co.uk; 3m W of Tavistock on A390; 9 pm; no jeans or trainers. **Accommodation:** 10 rooms, from £95*

GWITHIAN TOWANS, CORNWALL 1–4A

Godrevy Beach Cafe £26 323
TR27 5ED (01736) 757999
*"A definite improvement on the usual beachside café"; this award-winning modern building serves "fresh and tasty" sandwiches, "excellent" coffee and cakes, and platters for "over-excited children to pick at"; the best spot? – "a table on the sunny deck". / **Details:** www.godrevycafe.co.uk.*

HALE, CHESHIRE 5–2B

Earle £49 343
4 Cecil Rd WA15 9PA (0161) 929 8869
*"A super bistro-style option"; fans say it's a "warm" and "friendly" operation, with "surprisingly great" food, and even its least enthusiastic reviewer says the food's "not fantastic, but good", and that the "fun" style of the place helps make it "a useful local". / **Details:** www.earlebysimonrimmer.com; 9.30 pm, Sun 8 pm; closed Mon L.*

HALIFAX, WEST YORKSHIRE 5–1C

Cafe Thai £26 433
35 Stainland Rd HX4 8AD (01422) 310804
"This Thai café-restaurant is a new addition to the Halifax area but it's run by the same folk as a popular take-away"; it's already "very lively" – "you

need to book, even at 6.30 pm midweek!" / **Details:** www.cafethaiwest.co.uk/; 11 pm, Sun 10 pm; closed Mon.

Ricci's Place **£35** 4 4 3

4 Crossley Hs, Crossley St HX1 1UG (01422) 646422

Thin feedback this year on this modish tapas bar, in a listed building, although it continues to attain high marks; the venue was refurbished in June 2015, and now boasts a Dean Clough sibling (Ricci's Tapas & Cicchetti) that's "as good if not better than the original" according to one eary report. / **Details:** www.riccisplace.co.uk; 9 pm; closed Sun; no Amex.

HAMBLETON, RUTLAND 5–4D

Finch's Arms **£44** 2 2 4

Oakham Rd LE15 8TL (01572) 756575

"Always a great place to visit for the interior, the views, and the overall location!" This characterful pub, in a super-cute village overlooking Rutland Water has many charms, but doesn't fully achieve its potential – "the food is a curate's egg of some good, some slipshod; service can come adrift; and I take exception to some of the prices... but I still go back". / **Details**: www.finchsarms.co.uk; 9.30 pm, Sun 8 pm. **Accommodation:** 10 rooms, from £100

Hambleton Hall **£90** 5 4 5

LE15 8TH (01572) 756991

"Classically traditional in every way, and none the worse for that!" – Tim Hart's "grand" and luxurious mansion enjoys "an idyllic setting with views over Rutland Water" (although, in fact, the house was built before the lake!) The "consistency of excellent standards here is extraordinary" over many years – not least Aaron Patterson's classic cuisine that's "perfectly balanced and packed with taste"; "superb wine" too. / **Details:** www.hambletonhall.com; near Rutland Water; 9.30 pm; children: 5+. **Accommodation:** 17 rooms, from £265

HARDWICK, CAMBRIDGESHIRE 3–1B

The Blue Lion **£46** 3 4 2

74 Main St CB23 7QU (01954) 210328

A "lovely" olde-worlde gastroboozer "in easy reach of Cambridge" whose charms include "great, tasty pub grub", a "fab garden" and a "good choice for veggies". / **Details:** www.bluelionhardwick.co.uk; 9 pm, Fri & Sat 9.30, Sun 8 pm; no Amex.

HAROME, NORTH YORKSHIRE 8–4C

The Pheasant Hotel **£62** 4 5 4

YO62 5JG (01439) 771241

"Log fires, comfortable sofas, a relaxed atmosphere and excellent food and service... what else do you need?" – one reporter captures the charms of the "sophisticated and serene" sibling to the famous Star Inn nearby (which fans say is "better than its stablemate".) / **Details:** www.thepheasanthotel.com; 9 pm; no Amex. **Accommodation:** 15 rooms, from £155

The Star Inn **£68** 4 3 3

YO62 5JE (01439) 770397

That it's "back on form", and has "deservedly reclaimed its Michelin star" is a regular refrain in reports on Andrew Pern's "beautiful and atmospheric" pub, in the North York Moors, acclaimed for its "tremendous local food, with the accent on game and foraged ingredients". There continues to be a sizeable undercurrent of more negative themes, however – many reporters "expected more given the price", or felt its performance is "not at all up to the hype". / **Details:** www.thestaratharome.co.uk; 3m SE of Helmsley off A170; 9.30 pm, Sun 6 pm; closed Mon L & Sun D; no Amex. **Accommodation:** 8 rooms, from £150

HARROGATE, NORTH YORKSHIRE 5–1C

Bettys **£43** 3 4 5

1 Parliament St HG1 2QU (01423) 814070

For a "leisurely afternoon tea, elegantly served", few institutions deliver such a "lovely, traditional experience" as these renowned, "stately" tea-rooms – "even though there are long queues to enter, once inside you are in an unhurried world where time stands still". "It's always a magical visit; a treat for my mum, shared history with my sister, and introducing my daughter to its delights; the raclette, the fish 'n' chips, the citron pressé, the cake trolley... need I go on?" / **Details:** www.bettysandtaylors.co.uk; 9 pm; no Amex; no booking.

Drum & Monkey **£45** 4 3 3

5 Montpellier Gdns HG1 2TF (01423) 502650

"Long may it continue!" – a "lovely, old fish restaurant in the centre of town" that's long been a local institution. "Very civilised" in style, the whole operation "has had its ups and downs over the years", but all reports agree its seafood-based cuisine is "currently excellent". / **Details:** www.drumandmonkey.co.uk; 9 pm; closed Sun; no Amex; booking: max 10.

Graveley's Fish & Chip Restaurant **£44** 3 3 2

8-12 Cheltenham Pde HG1 1DB (01423) 507093

"Really fresh fish" ('n' chips) served in "lovely decent portions" is the winning formula at this long-standing family favourite; better still, "the service is old-fashioned Yorkshire – no-one will be asking you to 'have a nice day'!" / **Details:** www.graveleysofharrogate.com; 9 pm, Fri & Sat 10 pm, Sun 8-9 pm.

Norse £32 543
22 Oxford St HG1 1PU (01423) 202363
A "well-loved local café" that, by night, is "taken over by a pop-up serving a tasting menu based on modern Nordic cuisine". "Following the example of Noma", the cooking offers "plenty of surprises using seasonal ingredients (and the likes of goat, snails, etc)" and results here can be "really exceptional". "They also make a big selection of very tasty, flavoured schnapps, so don't even think of driving..." / **Details:** *www.baltzersens.co.uk; 5 pm, Sun 4 pm.*

Orchid £42 554
28 Swan Rd HG1 2SE (01423) 560425
"A stand-out for all-round quality in the crowded Harrogate restaurant scene!" – this "very fine" Pan-Asian favourite "always hits the mark". Service is "slick" and there's "no dumbing down on the chilli heat" when it comes to the cooking – a "superb choice" of "wonderfully tasty" dishes. Top Tip – the Sunday buffet brunch is quite a local event. / **Details:** *www.orchidrestaurant.co.uk; 10 pm; closed Sat L* **Accommodation:** *28 rooms, from £115*

Quantro £46 343
3 Royal Pde HG1 2SZ (01423) 503034
A "splendidly consistent" Harrogate stalwart, in the town centre. Top Tip – "outstanding" set lunches, representing "an amazing deal for bargain hunters as well as foodies". / **Details:** *www.quantro.co.uk; 10 pm; closed Sun; children: 4+ at D.*

Sasso £46 343
8-10 Princes Sq HG1 1LX (01423) 508 838
A "normal Italian", but one where the offering "goes beyond the usual pasta style of food"; it can split opinion, but of late reporters have all left "highly satisfied". / **Details:** *www.sassorestaurant.co.uk; 10 pm, Fri & Sat 10.30 pm; closed Sun.*

Van Zeller £72 442
8 Montpellier St HG1 2TQ (01423) 508762
Tom Van Zeller's "undoubted skill" results in some "simply superb" cuisine (not least an "innovative and delicious tasting menu") at this Montpellier Quarter venture; "the dining room lacks character but that is the only downside". / **Details:** *www.vanzellerrestaurants.co.uk; 9.30 pm; closed Mon & Sun.*

HARROW, GREATER LONDON 3–3A

Incanto The Old Post Office £52 343
41 High St, Harrow On The Hill HA1 3HT
(020) 8426 6767
"A great neighbourhood restaurant" – this "inventive modern Italian" in Harrow is well-located on the Hill, and fans hail the food as "amazing". However, there is a school of thought that while "in central London the prices could be justified by its first class service and very good, if elaborate, food, in the 'burbs it feels overpriced." / **Details:** *www.incanto.co.uk; 10.30 pm; closed Mon & Sun D.*

HARTSHEAD, WEST YORKSHIRE 5–1C

The Gray Ox Inn £43 323
15 Hartshead Ln WF15 8AL (01274) 872845
"While beers are local, diners take precedence over drinkers" at this "very pleasant" country pub. There's the odd gripe that it's too "crowded", but most reports focus on the "lovely" food. / **Details:** *www.grayoxinn.co.uk; Mon-Fri 8.45 pm, Sat 9.15 pm, Sun 6.45 pm; closed Sun D.*

HARWICH, ESSEX 3–2D

The Pier at Harwich £58 322
The Quay CO12 3HH (01255) 241212
There's a casual ground-floor bistro and "rather posher" upstairs restaurant at the Milsom family's boutique hotel; the most critical report this year suggests that, "as they have an ideal location, they seem to think they don't need to try", but still acclaims the "good fish". / **Details:** *www.milsomhotels.com; 9.30 pm, Sat 10 pm; closed Mon & Tue; no jeans.* **Accommodation:** *14 rooms, from £117*

HASSOP, DERBYSHIRE 5–2C

Hassop Hall £60 454
DE45 1NS (01629) 640488
The Chapman family's country house hotel "can't be anything other than romantic" given its "beautiful parkland setting"; OK, "maybe the menu needs updating", but "it's worth it for the whole ambience" and some "truly wonderful" food. / **Details:** *www.hassophall.co.uk; on the B6001 Bakewell - Hathersage Road, Junction 29 of M1; 9 pm; closed Mon L, Sat L & Sun D.* **Accommodation:** *13 rooms, from £100*

HASTINGS, EAST SUSSEX 3–4C

Maggie's £24 443
TN34 3DW (01424) 430 205
"A trip to the seaside isn't complete without a visit to Maggie's" – a modest café atop the fishmarket (and handy for the beach) which serves "excellent" fish 'n' chips (and in "huge" portions too). / **Details:** *2 pm, Fri & Sat later; closed Mon D, Tue D, Wed D, Thu D & Sun; no credit cards.*

The Pelican Diner £15 344
East Parade TN34 3AL (01424) 421555
"Quirky, cute, seafront building" whose American

owner helps create "food based on the classic US diner menu, but produced with a modern, fresh twist".

Webbe's Rock-a-Nore £48 334
TN34 3DW (01424) 721650
"Fab fish" and "excellent" seafood are the reasons to truffle out this consistently highly rated branch of Paul Webbe's local chain. / ***Details:*** *www.webbesrestaurants.co.uk; 9.30 pm.*

HATFIELD PEVEREL, ESSEX 3–2C

The Blue Strawberry £46 344
The St CM3 2DW (01245) 381333
"Still one of the best-value restaurants in the centre of Essex"; in an area "desperately short of quality eating places", this "very reliable" village fixture stands out – and, being the kind of place where "they look after you well", it's particularly good for a celebration. / ***Details:*** *www.bluestrawberrybistro.co.uk; 3m E of Chelmsford; 10 pm; closed Sun D.*

HAUGHTON MOSS, CHESHIRE 5–3B

The Nag's Head £42 323
Long Ln CW6 9RN (01829) 260265
A "great addition to the Ribble Valley Inns portfolio" that "stills feels welcoming and pub-like" after chain-ification, with the added boon of an "interesting" menu too. / ***Details:*** *www.nagsheadhaughton.co.uk; 9 pm .*

HAWKHURST, KENT 3–4C

The Great House £46 333
Gills Grn TN18 5EJ (01580) 753119
A characterful 16th-century inn at the heart of the Kentish weald with exposed beams, log fires and an orangery; for what it aims to do, it's a very consistent performer, with reliable fare and "very good beers"; nice garden. / ***Details:*** *www.elitepubs.com/the_greathouse; 9.30 pm; no Amex.*

HAYWARDS HEATH, WEST SUSSEX 3–4B

Jeremy's at Borde Hill £54 444
Balcombe Rd RH16 1XP (01444) 441102
"Eat outside in warm weather, otherwise ask for a window table overlooking the terrace and walled garden", if you dine at Jeremy Ashpool's "very romantic", "friendly and professional" favourite, which is "perfect for a special occasion (and sometimes the occasion is that we're eating at Jeremy's!)" Most reports remain of "exquisite" cooking too (although there were a few former fans this year who said it fell short – "hopefully a blip not a trend"). / ***Details:*** *www.jeremysrestaurant.com; Exit 10A from the A23; 10 pm; closed Mon & Sun D.*

HEDLEY ON THE HILL, NORTHUMBERLAND 8–2B

The Feathers Inn £43 542
NE43 7SW (01661) 843607
That it's "rather squashed" is the only drawback of this "rustic" pub, whose huge fan club is at odds with its "out-of-the-way" location. Staff are "straightforward and friendly", and the "fairly traditional fare" ("using local meats and lots of game") "close to perfection". / ***Details:*** *www.thefeathers.net; 8.30 pm; closed Mon & Sun D; no Amex.*

HELMSLEY, NORTH YORKSHIRE 8–4C

Black Swan £66 434
Market Pl YO62 5BJ (01439) 770466
A "lovely" boutique hotel dining room, where chef Paul Peters turns out "trendy" cuisine (including daring tasting menus) that's "up to the best standards"; service "can slightly let it down", but most reporters left impressed. / ***Details:*** *www.blackswan-helmsley.co.uk; 9.30 pm.* ***Accommodation:*** *45 rooms, from £130*

HEMINGFORD GREY, CAMBRIDGESHIRE 3–1B

The Cock £49 343
47 High St PE28 9BJ (01480) 463609
A "busy, friendly" gastroboozer in a "big, well-decorated room" offering "just the best pub food" and a "good-value" Sunday lunch; added boon? – "all is supported by decent beers and an excellent wine list centred on Languedoc and the South of France". / ***Details:*** *www.thecockhemingford.co.uk; off the A14; follow signs to the river; 9 pm, Fri & Sat 9.30 pm, Sun 8.30 pm; children: 5+ at D.*

HENLEY IN ARDEN, WARWICKSHIRE 5–4C

Cheal's of Henley £71
64 High St B95 5BX
Matt Cheal, formerly head chef of Simpson's in Edgbaston, opened in October 2015 at this new venture. Early press and online reports are encouraging.

HENLEY, WEST SUSSEX 3–4A

The Duke Of Cumberland £51 435
GU27 3HQ (01428) 652280
"Is this the PERFECT country pub?" – so say fans of this "airy, modern" spot, with its "log fires, flagstone floors and beautiful period interior"; its "excellent, hearty country food" is one reason to think so, but it's the "wonderful" garden with "fantastic" South

*Downs views "which makes it so special". / **Details:** www.thedukeofcumberland.com; 10 pm.*

HENLEY-ON-THAMES, OXFORDSHIRE 3–3A

Giggling Squid £27 4 3 3
40 Hart St RG9 2AU (01491) 411044
*A very popular branch of the south-eastern chain of Thai restaurants; fans say it's "brilliant value", with "surprisingly good food", "quick and efficient" service and a "great location". / **Details:** www.gigglingsquid.com; 10 pm.*

Luscombes at the Golden Ball £55 3 4 3
Lower Assendon RG9 6AH (01491) 574157
*A bar-restaurant in a beautiful rustic setting. Even its worst critic – who feels the cooking is "no better than good" – says it's "much improved" of late, and more upbeat fans say "think Hand & Flowers without the six-month wait and big bill". / **Details:** www.luscombes.co.uk; 10 pm; no Amex.*

Shaun Dickens at The Boathouse £65 4 3 4
Station Rd RG9 1AZ (01491) 577937
*"A lovely Thames-side position" with a terrace for use in summer creates a "memorable" location for this contemporary-style three-year-old. There's the odd gripe that "service is almost over-attentive", but most feedback focuses on its "very well-executed" fare. / **Details:** www.shaundickens.co.uk; 9.30 pm; closed Mon & Tue.*

Spice Merchant £41 4 3 3
25 Thameside RG9 2LJ (01491) 636118
*In an area well-supplied with good Indians, "it's the quality of the food that makes the difference" at this "lovely" riverside venue; it's "not cheap, but you get what you pay for" – it "always impresses visitors". / **Details:** www.spicemerchantgroup.com; 11 pm, Sun 10 pm; no Amex.*

The Three Tuns £46 3 3 4
5 Market Pl RG9 2AA (01491) 410 138
*It may be "small", but this town-centre pub "just gets better and better" and a visit is now "a real treat"; "the meat is the star of the show here, travelling a short distance from the award-winning butcher next door". / **Details:** www.threetunshenley.co.uk; 11 pm, Sat midnight, Sun 10 pm.*

Villa Marina £43 3 4 3
18 Thameside RG9 1BH (01491) 575262
*Sibling to the Villa d'Este in Marlow that's "been around for some while" and remains a "really reliable" choice for "good Italian fare"; "great ambience close by the river" too. / **Details:** www.villamarina-henley.com; opp Angel pub, nr Bridge; 10.30 pm, Sun 9 pm.*

HEREFORD, HEREFORDSHIRE 2–1B

Castle House Restaurant Castle House Hotel £53 3 4 4
Castle St HR1 2NW (01432) 356321
*"A short walk from the cathedral in an attractive location", there's a "wonderful experience" to be had at this central, townhouse-hotel dining room, "well patronised by local residents" thanks to its consistent all-round standards. / **Details:** www.castlehse.co.uk; 9.30 pm, Sun 9 pm. **Accommodation:** 24 rooms, from £150*

HERNE BAY, KENT 3–3D

Le Petit Poisson £41 4 2 3
Pier Approach, Central Parade CT6 5JN
(01227) 361199
*"Great fish and half the price of Whitstable" – the winning formula behind this "delightful" and "quietly charming" venue "right on the seafront", which fans acclaim as the "best restaurant in Herne Bay". / **Details:** www.lepetitpoisson.co.uk; 9.30 pm, Sun 15.30 pm; closed Mon & Sun D; no Amex.*

HESWALL, MERSEYSIDE 5–2A

Burnt Truffle £47
104-106 Telegraph Rd CH60 0AQ
(0151) 342 1111
*Gary Usher, owner of Chester's majorly popular 'Sticky Walnut' (see also) set up his new Wirral venture crowd-funded by seed capital website, Kickstarter. It opened in July 2015 – too late for survey feedback – but we hear good things about its affordable, accomplished food and light, contemporary interior. / **Details:** www.burnttruffle.net/; Wed & Thu 9 pm, Fri & Sat 10 pm.*

HETHE, OXFORDSHIRE 2–1D

The Muddy Duck £52 3 4 4
Main St OX27 8ES (01869) 278099
*A newish gastropub "in the middle of nowhere" in quiet countryside a short drive from Bicester, whose tasteful styling both inside and outside in the large and attractive garden (with funky carvings) is "top notch". It's "well worth the effort" to find on account of its "generous portions of locally sourced food" – "perhaps a shade expensive, but one does get what one pays for..." / **Details:** www.themuddyduckpub.co.uk; 9 pm, Sun 4 pm; closed Sun D.*

HETTON, NORTH YORKSHIRE 5–1B

The Angel Inn £48 434

BD23 6LT (01756) 730263

*This "charming Dales gastropub" with its "wonderful village location" and "lovely rooms" has been a beacon of "robust country cooking" for many decades now, although it's still at heart "a local, with great beer". Once one of the most commented-on destinations in the country, it no longer generates the volume of feedback it once did, but it's still "always busy and welcoming". / **Details:** www.angelhetton.co.uk; 5m N of Skipton off B6265 at Rylstone; 9 pm; D only, ex Sun open L only. **Accommodation:** 9 rooms, from £150*

HEXHAM, NORTHUMBERLAND 8–2A

Bouchon Bistrot £45 332

4-6 Gilesgate NE46 3NJ (01434) 609943

*In a "far northern town", a bistro that's "back to its best" serving "solid" Gallic cuisine – "you could be in France!" / **Details:** www.bouchonbistrot.co.uk; 9 pm; closed Sun; no Amex.*

The Rat Inn £40 434

Anick NE46 4LN (014) 3460 2814

*In an "out-of-the-way" rural location, a "delightful country pub with a small but enticing garden, a roaring fire, and great ale"; it serves "robust, at times rustic, food prepared with care from good ingredients" (including "superb local beef") and served "with no rush at all"; "simple and delicious!" / **Details:** www.theratinn.com; closed Sun D.*

HINTLESHAM, SUFFOLK 3–1D

Hintlesham Hall £69 224

Duke St IP8 3NS (01473) 652334

*"With such a historical reputation and attractive surroundings", this country house hotel should have everything going for it; of late, though, the majority of reporters cite the "mundane food" ("like the food served up at wedding receptions") as proof that "things have really slipped since the old days of Robert Carrier!" / **Details**: www.hintleshamhall.com; 4m W of Ipswich on A1071; 9.30 pm; jacket required at D; children: 12+. **Accommodation**: 33 rooms, from £99*

HINTON ST GEORGE, SOMERSET 2–3A

Lord Poulett Arms £46 323

TA17 8SE (01460) 73149

*A "lovely old" village gastropub-with-rooms featuring "real fires, mismatched furniture and good quality local and seasonal food"; its highlight remains the especially "atmospheric setting" – "like dining in a private house" (although it struck the wrong note with a couple of reporters this year). / **Details:** www.lordpoulettarms.com; 9 pm; no Amex. **Accommodation:** 4 rooms, from £85*

HOLKHAM, NORFOLK 6–3C

The Victoria at Holkham £48 324

Park Rd NR23 1RG (01328) 711008

*"It has been through its phases but currently The Vic is on a high"; whilst it may strike cynics as a bit of a "rip-off joint", the Holkham Estate's coastal hotel has a "lovely" atmosphere, and "the kitchen has been a little better of late" ("almost to the extent that it half-justifies the London prices!") / **Details:** www.holkham.co.uk; on the main coast road, between Wells-next-the Sea and Burnham Overy Staithe; 9 pm; no Amex. **Accommodation:** 10 rooms, from £140*

HOLT, NORFOLK 6–3C

The Pigs £44 343

Norwich Rd NR24 2RL (01263) 587634

*This rural boozer is "always a great place to eat and stay" ("as a bonus their cookbook is one of my most used", says a loyal fan); "excellent" children's playground too. / **Details:** www.thepigs.org.uk; 9 pm. **Accommodation:** 10 rooms, from £145*

Wiveton Hall Cafe £44 434

1 Marsh Ln NR25 7TE (01263) 740525

*"Yum yum... what a find!" – an "absolutely wonderful" fruit farm café (you can Pick-Your-Own) that wins rave reviews for its "idiosyncratic" tapas (from home grown or very locally sourced ingredients) and wood-fired pizza, delivered in a "superb" setting (outside tables have views over the marshes to the sea). / **Details:** www.wivetonhall.co.uk/thecafe; Fri & Sat 8.30 pm; closed Mon D, Tue D, Wed D, Thu D & Sun D.*

HONITON, DEVON 2–4A

The Pig Combe House £62 223

Gittisham EX14 3AD (0345) 225 9494

*A "stately house in rolling Devon countryside using all local produce, some of which may be seen roaming the fields nearby"! Even a reporter who said the food has "dipped a little" of late thinks "it's still very good" (if perhaps "a bit overpriced"?), but the wine list has become more "selective" and "limited" in recent times. / **Details**: www.thepighotel.com/at-combe/; on the outskirts of Honiton; not far from the A30, A375, 303; 9.30 pm; no Amex. **Accommodation:** 15, cottage for 2 ppl, thatched house for 8 ppl rooms, from £215*

The Holt £43 [3][3][2]
178 High St EX14 1LA (01404) 47707
A "very consistent" boozer owned by Otter Brewery; with its "innovative and frequently changing menu", it "cleverly combines being a real pub with gastropub food". / ***Details:*** *www.theholt-honiton.com; 11 pm; closed Mon & Sun.*

HORDLE, HAMPSHIRE 2–4C

The Mill at Gordleton £47 [4][3][5]
Silver St SO41 6DJ (01590) 682219
"What a treat" – a "really comfortable" spot combining "wonderful, homely but well-presented food" and "excellent beer". It is best to "dine on the veranda if possible" to profit from the "perfect backdrop" ("beautiful gardens and interesting statues"). / ***Details:*** *www.themillatgordleton.co.uk; on the A337, off the M27; 9.15 pm, Sun 8.15 pm; no Amex.* ***Accommodation:*** *8 rooms, from £150*

HORNDON ON THE HILL, ESSEX 3–3C

The Bell Inn £49 [4][3][4]
High Rd SS17 8LD (01375) 642463
Even after 40 years, John & Christine Vereker's "very full and very friendly" inn remains "brilliant all round" – offering, as it does, an "excellent" menu, "great" rooms and a "bustling" atmosphere; it's "terrific value" too! / ***Details:*** *www.bell-inn.co.uk; signposted off B1007, off A13; 9.45 pm; booking: max 12.* ***Accommodation:*** *15 rooms, from £50*

HORSHAM, WEST SUSSEX 3–4A

Camellia Restaurant South Lodge Hotel £70
Brighton Rd RH13 6PS (01403) 891711
Mixed feedback on the dining room of this country house hotel, where mid-survey MasterChef-winner, Steven Edwards, quit the stoves. What was, to fans, an accomplished venue with "obliging staff" was, to critics, "distinctly average", not helped by "very amateur service". Given that it's a time of change, we've left it un-rated. / ***Details:*** *www.southlodgehotel.co.uk; 9.30 pm.* ***Accommodation:*** *85 rooms, from £195*

The Pass Restaurant South Lodge Hotel £92 [4][4][2]
Brighton Rd RH13 6PS (01403) 892235
"It's fascinating to watch the chefs calmly preparing exquisite dishes", at this "wonderful concept, where the kitchen and dining room are one space, and the chefs bring your meals to the table, so you can discuss the ingredients and preparation". Best of all, the resulting dishes are "consistently tremendous". Not everyone likes the "stark" setting though, and "the raised seats which help you view the cooking are not comfortable". / ***Details:*** *www.southlodgehotel.co.uk; 8.30 pm; closed Mon & Tue; children: 12+.* ***Accommodation:*** *89 rooms, from £235*

Restaurant Tristan £65 [5][4][3]
3 Stans Way, East St RH12 1HU
(01403) 255688
"The crème de la crème of Horsham!" – in a handsome 16th-century building in the town centre, Tristan Mason turns out some "exceptional and clever" cuisine, and there's an "excellent level of service" too. / ***Details:*** *www.restauranttristan.co.uk; 9.30 pm; closed Mon & Sun.*

HORSTED KEYNES, WEST SUSSEX 3–4B

The Crown Inn £45 [4][4][3]
The Green RH17 7AW (01825) 791609
"The chef-patron has an excellent CV (Gravetye Manor) and it shows in the style and quality of the meals" at this "warm" gastropub yearling, hailed by all reporters for its "outstanding dishes". / ***Details:*** *www.thecrown-horstedkeynes.co.uk; 9 pm; closed Mon & Sun.*

HOUGH ON THE HILL, LINCOLNSHIRE 6–3A

Brownlow Arms £50 [3][3][2]
NG32 2AZ (01400) 250234
In a scenic village setting, this "very busy" gastropub elicits solid feedback for its "good meat and fish" and "high quality wines". / ***Details:*** *www.thebrownlowarms.com/; on the Grantham Road; 9.15 pm; closed Mon, Tue–Sat D only, closed Sun D; no Amex; children: 10+.* ***Accommodation:*** *5 rooms, from £98*

HOYLAKE, MERSEYSIDE 5–2A

Lino's £38 [4][4][4]
122 Market St CH47 3BH (0151) 632 1408
An "old reliable" that's "back on top form" and now offers "considerably improved" food and "friendly" service; the return of The Open to the local links has undoubtedly inspired more competition, but "the fact that they are still here" is "testament to the continuing values maintained by Enrico and his staff". / ***Details:*** *www.linosrestaurant.co.uk; 3m from M53, J2; 10 pm; D only, closed Mon & Sun; no Amex.*

HUDDERSFIELD, WEST YORKSHIRE 5–1C

Eric's £54 [4][3][3]
73-75 Lidget St HD3 3JP (01484) 646416
"Where else can you eat well in Huddersfield?" – Eric Paxman's Lindley fixture provides "original and adventurous" quality dining in a "stylish setting";

gripes? – the occasional service blip. / **Details:** www.ericsrestaurant.co.uk; 10 pm; closed Mon, Sat L & Sun D; no Amex.

Med One £41 3 3 3
10-12 West Gate HD1 1NN (01484) 511100
"The mains are big and the prices are small" at this "wonderful" town-centre Lebanese; "I've dined alongside Sir Patrick Stewart, so who knows who you'll see there?" / **Details:** www.med-one.co.uk; 10 pm.

HULL, EAST YORKSHIRE 6–2A

1884 Dock Street Kitchen £59 4 4 4
Humber Dock Street, Marina HU1 1TB (01482) 222260
"A really great addition to the Hull dining scene" – a "metropolitan" two-year-old "in a well-restored dock-side building with lovely views over the Hull Marina and River Humber"; despite being early days, it "has already caught on" locally, owing to its "amazing" food and "outstanding" service. / **Details:** www.1884dockstreetkitchen.co.uk/events.html; 9.30 pm; closed Mon & Sun D.

HUNSDON, HERTFORDSHIRE 3–2B

The Fox And Hounds £42 3 5 4
2 High St SG12 8NH (01279) 843999
Locally sourced meat and game is much-featured on the menu of this "lovely and buzzy" pub, which particularly "stands out in an area with limited gastronomic offerings", aided by its "excellent" service. The worst comment this year? – "they seem a bit overly proud of their Josper oven!" / **Details:** www.foxandhounds-hunsdon.co.uk; off the A414, 10 min from Hertford; 9.30 pm; no Amex.

HUNTINGDON, CAMBRIDGESHIRE 3–1B

The Abbot's Elm £44 3 4 3
Abbot's Ripton PE28 2PA (01487) 773773
From the "chatty hosts" to the "excellent" food and "short-but-varied wine list", reporters find little not to like at this "refreshingly good" thatched inn; "it already says in the guide that service is impeccable – it is indeed!" / **Details:** www.theabbotselm.co.uk; 10 pm; closed Mon & Sun D.

Old Bridge Hotel £50 3 3 3
1 High St PE29 3TQ (01480) 424300
"As everyone knows, the wine is the star" at this "noisy" ivy-covered townhouse hotel dining room, with an attached wine shop (owned by Master of Wine, John Hoskins). Despite this, the food is never less than "reliable" (and sometimes even "excellent"), and "very comfortable" rooms are another plus. / **Details:** www.huntsbridge.com; off A1, off A14; 10 pm. **Accommodation:** 24 rooms, from £160

HURWORTH, COUNTY DURHAM 8–3B

The Bay Horse £50 4 3 3
45 The Grn DL2 2AA (01325) 720 663
"Delightful" period gastropub serving "simple, traditional" British classics – "excellent fresh produce" is used to create "fantastic" results. / **Details:** www.thebayhorsehurworth.com; 9.30 pm, Sun 8 pm.

HUTTON MAGNA, NORTH YORKSHIRE 8–

The Oak Tree Inn £45 4 4 3
DL11 7HH (01833) 627371
It may be a "tiny restaurant in a tiny pub", but the "consistent quality" of the food at this Yorkshire village spot pleases all who comment on it – and, what an "interesting wine list for such a small place"! / **Details:** www.theoaktreehutton.co.uk; Tue-Sat 11pm Sun 10.30pm; closed Mon.

HYTHE, KENT 3–4D

Hythe Bay £45 3 3 3
Marine Pde CT21 6AW (01303) 233844
"If you hanker for fish come here!" – a "consistently good" operation offering "first-class" fare in a "stunning position on Hythe seafront"; there are "great views from most tables although it's best to book at busy times" to secure a premium spot. / **Details:** www.thehythebay.co.uk; 9.30 pm.

The Hythe Brasserie £43 4 3 3
Douglas Ave CT21 5JT (01303) 267912
An "excellent" husband-and-wife outfit offering a "small but interesting" menu which "changes with the seasons" (and "never disappoints"); "to be sure to get a reservation book well in advance!" / **Details:** www.hythebrasserie.com; 9 pm.

Saltwood On The Green £48 3 3 3
The Grn CT21 4PS (01303) 237 800
"Chef Jeff Kipp, having worked in several of the best kitchens (Duck & Waffle, Gordon Ramsay SW3)" has launched his own venture, set "in a former general store which retains tasteful period features"; he's "knocking out some brilliant dishes without pontification" – and "so good is breakfast and brunch that several local B&Bs farm out their guests here"! / **Details:** www.saltwoodrestaurant.co.uk; 11 pm; closed Mon, Tue & Sun D.

ILKLEY, WEST YORKSHIRE 5–1C

Bettys £46 455
32-34 The Grove LS29 9EE (01943) 608029
This branch of the "fabulous tea rooms" continues to prosper "with its good range of specialist coffees" and "well-cooked" lunches, as well of course (above all) its "classic afternoon teas". / **Details:** *www.bettys.co.uk/tea-rooms/locations/ilkley; 5.30 pm; no Amex; no booking.*

Bistro Saigon £40 432
1A, Railway Rd LS29 8DE (01943) 817999
"Very popular" town-centre bistro, handy for the railway, that's "upped its game significantly" of late, and now offers "wonderfully fresh-tasting" Vietnamese fare; "be warned you will have to book... and once you have eaten there you will understand why!" / **Details:** *www.bistrosaigon.co.uk; 10 pm, Sun 8.30 pm; closed Mon.*

The Box Tree £77 554
35-37 Church St LS29 9DR (01943) 608484
"A must-visit institution that's well worth its place amongst the country's finest establishments". Under Simon and Rena Gueller's 10-year tenure this traditional icon (established in 1962) has "gone from strength to strength", not least as regards head chef Laurence Yates's "very accomplished" cuisine. / **Details:** *www.theboxtree.co.uk; on A65 near town centre; 9.30 pm; closed Mon, Tue L, Wed L, Thu L & Sun D; no jeans or trainers; children: 10+.*

Quinta £44 334
10 Wells Rd LS29 9JD (01943) 602670
"What a find"; "tucked away up Wells Road", this "promising newcomer" ("run by the former head of Martha & Vincents") wins praise for its "well-presented and well-cooked" Mediterranean food. / **Details:** *www.quintabarandgrill.com; 9.30 pm, Fri 10 pm, Sat 10.30 pm, Sun 8 pm.*

INVERNESS, HIGHLAND 9–2C

The Mustard Seed £44 323
16 Fraser St IV1 1DW (01463) 220220
A "fine find in Inverness" – this "former Georgian church with views over the river" serves some "decent-value" food. / **Details:** *www.themustardseedrestaurant.co.uk; 10 pm.*

IPSWICH, SUFFOLK 3–1D

Aqua Eight £44 432
8 Lion St IP1 1DB (01473) 218989
"If you want to taste what pan-Asian cuisine is really about", head to this "warm and friendly" (sometimes "noisy") local, offering "traditional Chinese dishes with a twist" – its "authentic" and "evocative" flavours are excellent value. / **Details:** *www.aquaeight.com; 11, Sun 10 pm.*

Mariners at Il Punto £47 435
Neptune Quay IP4 1AX (01473) 289748
The Crépy family's "unconventional" venue combines a "perfect" waterside setting aboard a newly revamped Belgian gunboat with some truly "superb" Gallic food. / **Details:** *www.marinersipswich.co.uk; 9.30 pm; closed Mon & Sun; no Amex.*

Trongs £33 453
23 St Nicholas St IP1 1TW (01473) 256833
"The best Chinese in the area by far"; even after all these years "Trongs never fails to deliver", offering "top-class" cuisine "with a slight Vietnamese twist"; it's "not a very large restaurant and always busy so you must book to get a table". / **Details:** *www.trongs.co.uk; 10.30 pm; closed Sun.*

The Waterfront Bar & Bistro £42 323
15 Regatta Quay IP4 1FH (01473) 226 082
An "excellent bistro on the waterfront" combining a "buzzy atmosphere" with "very good and quite quirky food"; "ask for a table upstairs" to capitalise on the views. / **Details:** *www.waterfrontbistroipswich.co.uk; 9.30 pm, Sun 7.30 pm.*

IRBY, MERSEYSIDE 5–2A

Da Piero £50 432
5-7 Mill Hill Rd CH61 4UB (0151) 648 7373
"Getting to be one of our favourites"; despite its "unfortunate (rather anonymous) location", this "small, friendly" Italian serves some "VERY flavoursome" Sicilian food. / **Details:** *www.dapiero.co.uk; 9 pm; D only, closed Mon & Sun; no Amex.*

JERSEY, CHANNEL ISLANDS

Bohemia The Club Hotel & Spa £83 544
Green St, St Helier JE2 4UH (01534) 880588
"A warmer, more intimate look is a big improvement", at this famous St Helier dining room (which used to suffer from a rather "funereal" ambience). Given Stephen Smith's "sensational", much accoladed cuisine, fans say "the new décor is the final missing link in the push to make Bohemia seem stand-out special". / **Details:** *www.bohemiajersey.com; 10 pm; no trainers.* **Accommodation:** *46 rooms, from £185*

Chateau La Chaire £55 444
La Vallee de Rozel JE3 6AJ (01534) 863354
"Difficult to find but so worth it" – an upscale lodge, in St Martin, which offers "excellent food" and "very

correct service"; "the outside terrace is so romantic – like a secret garden in the hills!" / **Details:** chateau-la-chaire.co.uk; 9 pm .

Longueville Manor £77 443
Longueville Rd, St Saviour JE2 7WF (01534) 725501
*A "fab" and "luxurious" country house hotel, on the edge of St Helier, whose "delightful" dining room offers "thoroughly consistent" food. The "service and setting are old-style", but absolutely none the worse for it. / **Details:** www.longuevillemanor.com; head from St. Helier on the A3 towards Gorey; less than 1 mile from St. Helier; 10 pm; no jeans or trainers.* **Accommodation:** *31 rooms, from £170*

Mark Jordan at the Beach £50 443
La Plage, La Route de la Haule, St Peter JE3 7YD (01534) 780180
*A "relaxed" St Aubin's Bay spot whose "lovely" seaside views are "matched with very good seasonal food" (and in "wonderful Jersey-sized portions" too); "superb" fish in particular. / **Details:** www.markjordanatthebeach.com; 9.30 pm; closed Mon.*

Ocean Restaurant Atlantic Hotel £82 554
Le Mont de la Pulente, St Brelade JE3 8HE (01534) 744101
*"Mark Jordan at his best"; this "very comfortable" dining room "with a colonial feel" and scenic views of the bay wins raves for "impeccable" cuisine and "smooth service" in a "family-run (i.e. non-corporate) environment" – "go!" / **Details:** www.theatlantichotel.com/dining/ocean-restaurant; 10 pm; no jeans or trainers.* **Accommodation:** *50 rooms, from £150 - 250*

Ormer £76 322
7-11 Don St, St Helier JE2 4TQ (015) 3472 5100
*"Shaun Rankin (ex-Bohemia) may be a TV star, but to be tops means to be consistent"; fans, especially those on business, do hail his St Helier two-year-old for "brilliant" cuisine and the cocktails are roundly judged "superb" too, but critics say the food's "muted to blandness" and that service can be "disinterested". / **Details:** www.ormerjersey.com; 10 pm; closed Sun.*

The Oyster Box £58 323
St Brelade's Bay JE3 8EF (01534) 850888
*In a "great location overlooking St Brelade's Bay", this New England-style bistro is a "buzzy" spot offering "fantastic fresh fish"; it pleases all reporters – though even fans concede that it's "a bit on the pricey side", and that "slow service always lets it down". / **Details:** www.oysterbox.co.uk; 9 pm; closed Mon L & Sun D; no Amex.*

Suma's £56 334
Gorey Hill, Gorey JE3 6ET (01534) 853291
*A "pleasant, small restaurant overlooking Gorey harbour" with a "new extended outdoor seating area"; its food is "relatively simple but of a high standard". / **Details:** www.sumasrestaurant.com; underneath castle in Gorey Harbour; 9.30 pm, Sun 3.30 pm; closed Sun D; booking: max 12.*

KENILWORTH, WARWICKSHIRE 5–4C

Bosquet £55 543
97a Warwick Rd CV8 1HP (01926) 852463
*A visit to Bernard and Mary Lignier's "longtime family favourite" is "like going to a good-quality rural restaurant in France"; the "superb" SW French cuisine is "full of interesting surprises and temptations", and this combined with "top-notch, personal service" makes it an "always immensely impressive" experience. / **Details:** www.restaurantbosquet.co.uk; 9.15 pm; closed Mon, Sat L & Sun; closed 2 weeks in Aug.*

The Cross at Kenilworth £67 443
16 New St CV8 2EZ (01926) 853840
*Andreas Antona's (of gingermanSimpson's Birmingham) "delightful" year-old former pub comprises two dining areas, a bar and "tranquil garden". In the kitchen, 'Great British Chef' Adam Bennett "has lived up to his early great promise" with "superb" cooking from a variety of menus (including a tasting option). / **Details:** www.thecrossatkenilworth.co.uk; 10 pm; closed Sun L*

KESTON, KENT 3–3B

Herbert's £46 443
6 Commonside BR2 6BP (01689) 855501
*"We stumbled by chance on this delightful new(ish) restaurant and loved everything about it" – a typically glowing review of Angela Herbert-Bell's follow-up to Lujon, overlooking the pretty village common. / **Details:** www.thisisherberts.co.uk/; midnight, Sun 6 pm.*

KESWICK, CUMBRIA 7–3D

The Cottage In The Wood £72 543
Whinlatter Forest CA12 5TW (01768) 778409
*"A cosy, tucked away" restaurant in a boutique hotel with "great views of the Whinlatter Forest and mountains" from the window seats; it "stands out" thanks to the "adventurous and interesting" tasting menu and the "eclectic choice of wines". / **Details:** www.thecottageinthewood.co.uk; 9 pm; closed Mon & Sun; no Amex.* **Accommodation:** *10 rooms, from £96*

Lyzzick Hall Country House Hotel £52 443

Underskiddaw CA12 4PY (017687) 72277
"This family-run hotel near Keswick ticks all the right boxes", from food that "seems to get better and better" to a "magnificent range of Spanish and Portuguese wines";"the expansion of a few years ago hasn't taken away any of the qualities that make this a Spanish retreat in the Lakes". / **Details:** *www.lyzzickhall.co.uk; 9 pm; no Amex.* **Accommodation:** *30 rooms, from £148*

KETTLESHULME, CHESHIRE 5–2B

The Swan Inn £45 433

Macclesfield Rd SK23 7QU (01663) 732943
"Fabulous fresh fish brought in daily from Scotland make this isolated pub out in the hills one to visit" (particularly pre- or post-walk) and of late the "new Josper oven in the refurbished kitchen has taken things to a higher level". / **Details:** *www.verynicepubs.co.uk/swankettleshulme/; 8.30 pm, Thu-Fri 7 pm, Sat 9 pm, Sun 4 pm; closed Mon; no Amex.*

KEYSTON, CAMBRIDGESHIRE 3–1A

The Pheasant at Keyston £51 333

Loop Rd PE28 0RE (01832) 710241
It's the "reliable quality" of the gastro fare on offer, rather than any huge finesse, which wins praise for this "quintessential English thatched pub" (the sibling to the better-known Old Bridge in Huntingdon). / **Details:** *www.thepheasant-keyston.co.uk; 1m S of A14 between Huntingdon & Kettering, J15; 9.30 pm; closed Mon & Sun D; no Amex.*

KIBWORTH BEAUCHAMP, LEICESTERSHIRE 5–4D

The Lighthouse £47 433

9 Station St LE8 0LN (0116) 279 6260
The Bobolis's "lovely, informal" venue (the British successor to their more ambitious hit Italian Firenze) garners particular praise for its "great fish and seafood" and "really nice-value wines". Service can lag but is "genuinely friendly". / **Details:** *www.lighthousekibworth.co.uk; 9.30 pm; D only, closed Mon & Sun; no Amex.*

KILLIECRANKIE, PERTH AND KINROSS 9–3C

Killiecrankie House Hotel £62 454

PH16 5LG (01796) 473220
"A little gem in the most beautiful part of Scotland" – a "peaceful, comfortable" spot, combining "marvellous service by Henrietta and her team" and "great local produce wonderfully executed";"I'd like to have my last meal on Earth here!" / **Details:** *www.killiecrankiehotel.co.uk; 8.30 pm; no Amex; no shorts.* **Accommodation:** *10 rooms, from £150*

KINGHAM, GLOUCESTERSHIRE 2–1C

Daylesford Café £44 334

GL56 0YG (01608) 731700
With its modish "accent on fresh, organic food", this strenuously chi-chi farmshop and café is "buzzing at lunchtime on every day of the week"; no gripes this year about the service, praised for its "professional" and "caring" attitude. / **Details:** *www.daylesfordorganic.com; Mon-Wed 5 pm, Thu-Sat 6 pm, Sun 4pm; L only.*

KINGHAM, OXFORDSHIRE 2–1C

The Kingham Plough £59 434

The Green OX7 6YD (01608) 658327
Blumenthal protégé, Emily Watkins's "interesting approach to food" has won a certain amount of renown for this "lovely" Cotswolds village pub. "Irresistible people watching" too "if you want to see the local landed gentry and their Barbour-clad children in full cry". / **Details:** *www.thekinghamplough.co.uk; 9 pm; closed Sun D; no Amex.* **Accommodation:** *7 rooms, from £95*

The Wild Rabbit £60 334

Church St OX7 6YA (01608) 658 389
JCB bride Lady Bamford's "flashy" Daylesford-style venture wins praise for its "atmospheric" décor – though you'll "pay through the nose for snob value!"; the food has historically been just "OK"... perhaps ex-Launceston Place chef Tim Allen, who joined in October 2015, can pep it up? / **Details:** *www.thewildrabbit.co.uk; 10 pm; closed Sun.*

KINGSTON BAGPUIZE, OXFORDSHIRE 2–2C

Fallowfields £78 443

Faringdon Rd OX13 5BH (01865) 820416
Acclaimed chef Matt Weedon left this attractive country house hotel dining room in late-2014, in order to set up his own country pub; by all accounts, his former sous chef is doing a fine job as his replacement, with fans praising his "consistently good performance". / **Details:** *www.fallowfields.com; just off A420 at junction with A415; 9.30 pm; children: 8+.* **Accommodation:** *10 rooms, from £123*

KINGSTON UPON THAMES, SURREY 3–3A

The Canbury Arms £43 333
49 Canbury Park Rd KT2 6LQ
(020) 8255 9129
"A great local" with "imaginative", "well-priced" fare – "a 'true' gastropub, rather than that just being a fancy title". / ***Details:*** *www.thecanburyarms.com; 10 pm, Sun 9 pm.*

fish! Kitchen £46 321
56-58 Coombe Rd KT2 7AF (020) 8546 2886
It's "more like an eat-in fish 'n' chip shop than a restaurant", but this bare dining room continues to attract solid marks for its fresh fish and "good" wines. / ***Details:*** *www.fishkitchen.com; 10 pm; closed Mon & Sun.*

Jin Go Gae £45 443
272 Burlington Rd KT3 4NL (020) 8949 2506
"Always a favourite" down Kingston way (especially amongst the local Korean community) – an "authentic" Korean fixture, which specialises in "fantastic" BBQ dishes. / ***Details:*** *www.jingogae.co.uk; 10 pm.*

Roz ana £45 422
4-8 Kingston Hill KT2 7NH (020) 8546 6388
Fans suspect that this "lovely" Norbiton Indian "would be getting rave reviews if in the West End or City"; its food is "fully seasoned and light" and "not made up of the usual suspects". / ***Details:*** *www.roz-ana.com; 10.30 pm, Fri & Sat 11 pm, Sun 10 pm; no Amex.*

KINGUSSIE, HIGHLAND 9–2C

The Cross £77 434
Tweed Mill Brae, Ardbroilach Rd PH21 1LB
(01540) 661166
With a scenic location amid the Cairngorms National Park, this 1800s inn is "an absolute gem" food-wise; "rooms are wonderful too". / ***Details:*** *www.thecross.co.uk; 8.30 pm; children: 9+.* ***Accommodation:*** *8 rooms, from £100*

KIRKBY LONSDALE, CUMBRIA 7–4D

Hipping Hall £77 444
Cowan Bridge LA6 2JJ (01524) 271187
From the "superb" cuisine, to the "outstanding" service and "extensive biodynamic wine list", reporters "could fault nothing" about this "peaceful and idyllic" hotel with a 15th-century hall; "an overnight stay in the excellent bedrooms is well worth it" too. / ***Details:*** *www.hippinghall.com; 9.30 pm; closed weekday L; no Amex; no trainers; children: 12+.* ***Accommodation:*** *10 rooms, from £239*

KNOWSTONE, DEVON 1–2D

The Mason's Arms £65 533
EX36 4RY (01398) 341231
A "wonderful" gastropub "hidden away in the Devon countryside" where chef Mark Dodson (erstwhile head chef of the Waterside Inn) turns out some "spectacular, sophisticated and delicious" cuisine. "We travelled across the county on a wild winter evening, and were well pleased". / ***Details:*** *www.masonsarmsdevon.co.uk; 9 pm; closed Mon & Sun D; children: 5+ after 6pm.*

KNUTSFORD, CHESHIRE 5–2B

Belle Époque £53 234
60 King St WA16 6DT (01565) 633060
"Still the class act in Knutsford" – a town-centre landmark occupying a "stylish" (Art Nouveau) building. It's "not cheap" however, and the odd critic feels that the "grand surroundings are not matched by the food quality these days". / ***Details:*** *www.thebelleepoque.com; 1.5m from M6, J19; 9.30 pm; closed Sun D.* ***Accommodation:*** *7 rooms, from £110*

KYLESKU, HIGHLAND 9–1B

Kylesku Hotel £43 444
IV27 4HW (01971) 502231
"Fantastic seafood" (sometimes served "theatrically on a hanging skewer") and "great" views win plenty of praise for this very remote, loch-side dining room; the "airy" new extension "makes dining and staying even better". / ***Details:*** *www.kyleskuhotel.co.uk; on A894, S of Scourie, N of loch inver; 8.30 pm; no Amex.* ***Accommodation:*** *8 rooms, from £55*

LANGAR, NOTTINGHAMSHIRE 5–3D

Langar Hall £49 455
Church Ln NG13 9HG (01949) 860559
Imogen Skirving (whose family have owned the hall since 1868) imbues "a spirit of generous hospitality" into this "significantly charming", "slightly old-fashioned" and "romantic" country house hotel. "Staff waft-in and waft-out un-noticed" delivering "dependable, unfussy" cooking that's "first class". / ***Details:*** *www.langarhall.com; off A52 between Nottingham & Grantham; 9.30 pm; no Amex; no trainers.* ***Accommodation:*** *12 rooms, from £100*

LANGHO, LANCASHIRE 5–1B

Northcote £96 554
Northcote Rd BB6 8BE (01254) 240555
A "love-it-or-hate-it" refurb a couple of years ago (most reporters love it), complete with "numerous alterations and extensions" (and the installation

of a "flashy bar") has zhooshed up the North West's most prominent country house hotel. Nigel Haworth's and Lisa Allen's "effortlessly delicious" seasonal cuisine ("so intense it makes you drool!") is matched with a "tremendous" and "constantly evolving" wine list, and served "without undue formality" by staff who "couldn't be more helpful". Top Menu Tip – "the table d'hote lunch is simply stunning value". / **Details:** *www.northcote.com; M6, J31 then A59; 10 pm, Sun 9 pm; no trainers.* **Accommodation:** *26 rooms, from £260*

LAVENHAM, SUFFOLK 3–1C

Great House £55 554
Market Pl CO10 9QZ (01787) 247431
"Where would you want to have your last meal? Mine would be here!" – the Crépy family's "wonderful, timbered building" enjoys "a lovely and quiet location" in arguably "East Anglia's most beautiful village", and provides "a unique and delightful marriage of France and Olde Englande". All-in-all "it's hard to find fault" – the classic cuisine "never disappoints", wines are "superb", the cheese selection "unrivalled", and staff are "charming, discreet and efficient". / **Details:** *www.greathouse.co.uk; follow directions to Guildhall; 9.30 pm; closed Mon & Sun D; closed Jan; no Amex.* **Accommodation:** *5 rooms, from £95*

Lavenham Greyhound £42 544
97 High St CO10 9PZ (01787) 249553
Under the new regime (the people behind the Swan in Melford) what used to be a "very ordinary local boozer" has become "something special"; it serves "pub grub with a difference" and a "superb" makeover has resulted in a "lovely, modern interior". / **Details:** *www.lavenhamgreyhound.com; 10 pm.*

Number Ten £38 434
10 Lady St CO10 9RA (01787) 249438
Reporters "just adore this newish venture of a wine bar in an old village and a very authentic old house"; besides "great" bottles from the owner's SA vineyard, it wins on "outstanding service and delicious food". / **Details:** *www.ten-lavenham.co.uk; 9 pm.*

Swan Hotel £60 225
High St CO10 9QA (01787) 247477
There's no doubt that "the setting of this restaurant, in a 15th-century inn, is magnificent" – the "crown jewel" of this pretty town; while fans say that the food is also "superb", critics argue that it's too "unexciting". / **Details**: *www.theswanatlavenham.co.uk; 9 pm; no jeans or trainers; children: 12+ at D.* **Accommodation**: *45 rooms, from £195*

LEAMINGTON SPA, WARWICKSHIRE 5–4C

La Coppola £49 442
86 Regent St CV32 4NS (01926) 888 873
"Still extremely popular", this upmarket operation "can always be relied upon for a splendid Italian meal" ("especially the fish and shellfish"). / **Details:** *www.lacoppola.co.uk; 10 pm, Sun 9 pm; no Amex.*

Oscars French Bistro £46 444
39 Chandos St CV32 4RL (01926) 452807
"Small, unassuming" French bistro "deserving an accolade for providing what most diners need – simple food, presented well and attention to detail, without the hefty price tag"; despite the "busy, buzzy" ambience, service is "spot on" too. / **Details:** *www.oscarsfrenchbistro.co.uk; 9.30 pm; closed Mon & Sun.*

Restaurant 23 £64 444
34 Hamilton Ter CV32 4LY (01926) 422422
An "inventive" restaurant which relocated to its current premises – an elegant, high-ceilinged Victorian house – in 2012, gaining a sleek cocktail bar in the process; on limited feedback, there's praise for the "lovely" food. / **Details:** *www.restaurant23.com; 9.30 pm; closed Mon & Sun; children: 12+.*

LECHLADE, GLOUCESTERSHIRE 2–2C

The Five Alls £49 333
Filkins GL7 3JQ (01367) 860875
Sebastian Snow's "traditional" village gastroboozer is mostly praised for its "restaurant-quality" cuisine and "charming" staff. There's a dissatisfied undercurrent of opinion though, who feel "it thinks it's better than it is", and who accuse service of "letting it down". / **Details:** *www.thefiveallsfilkins.co.uk; 9.30 pm, Fri & Sat 10 pm; closed Sun D; no Amex.*

LEEDS, WEST YORKSHIRE 5–1C

Aagrah £35 423
Aberford Rd LS25 2HF (0113) 2455 667
This city-centre outpost of the well-known northern chain is, true to form, "a consistent performer", offering "really good" Kashmiri cuisine and "great value for money" too. / **Details:** *www.aagrah.com; from A1 take A642 Aberford Rd to Garforth; midnight, Sun 10.30 pm; D only.*

Akbar's £33 323
16 Greek St LS1 5RU (0113) 242 5426
A "bustling" branch of the growing South Asian chain, specialising in "excellent" curries and baltis; it attracted limited feedback this year, but of a largely positive variety. / **Details:** *www.akbars.co.uk; midnight; D only.*

Art's
£42 3 2 2

42 Call Ln LS1 6DT (0113) 243 8243

*Near the Corn Exchange, this cool arts café and bar – a pioneer for the city when it launched back in 1994 – is "still a good place to hang out" by all accounts. / **Details:** www.artscafebar.com; 11 pm.*

The Bird And Beast
£35 3 3 3

Central Rd LS1 6DX (0113) 245 3348

*From the man behind Gato Negro in Rippon, a new city-centre rotisserie that "focuses very heavily on locally sourced chicken – like an upmarket and more ethical Nando's"; the results are positive, although "it can get a bit noisy in the evenings". / **Details:** thebirdandbeast.co.uk/; 10 pm, Sun 7 pm.*

Chaophraya
£48 3 4 4

20a, Blayds Ct LS1 4AG (0113) 244 9339

*"Wonderful Thai food, exemplary service and a smart non-tacky environment" ensure that this shopping-centre outpost of a small Northern chain is "always packed". / **Details:** www.chaophraya.co.uk; in Swinegate; 10.30 pm, Sun 10 pm.*

Flying Pizza
£37 3 2 3

60 Street Ln LS8 2DQ (0113) 266 6501

*A "very good 'trat' of the old school" that has long been a Headingley hotspot; "the take-over by San Carlo has added a layer of finesse to the café-like ambience", making it decidedly "glamorous" of late. / **Details:** www.theflyingpizza.co.uk; 11 pm, Sun 10 pm; no shorts.*

Fourth Floor Café Harvey Nichols
£46 3 4 3

107-111 Briggate LS1 6AZ (0113) 204 8000

*"For a restaurant in a store", this "bright" dining room is a "perfectly pleasant place to eat" – particularly "in a city without many strong options". It's usually full of "ladies who lunch and early-retirees on (secret?) dates!" / **Details:** www.harveynichols.com; 10 pm; L only, ex Thu-Sat open L & D.*

Fuji Hiro
£25 5 3 2

45 Wade Ln LS2 8NJ (0113) 243 9184

*"Never fails to please" – a "no frills, Formica-tabled" ramen bar in the city centre, where the "food is great and portions are massive"; "you can forgive any shortcomings for the best noodles ever!" / **Details:** 10 pm, Fri & Sat 11 pm; need 5+ to book.*

Hansa's
£31 5 4 2

72-74 North St LS2 7PN (0113) 244 4408

*"Avoiding the 'brown sludge' of many veggies with aplomb" – Mrs Hansa Dabhi's renowned Gujarati is a stalwart of the city centre and "serves lovely food with alacrity". "It's the only vegetarian restaurant my meat-loving husband actually WANTS to visit!" / **Details:** www.hansasrestaurant.com; 10 pm, Sat 11 pm; D only, ex Sun L only.*

Kendells Bistro
£44 3 4 4

St Peters square LS9 8AH (0113) 243 6553

*This "sound and fairly priced" French bistro, with "dark candlelit tables" and a "romantic ambience", is a real hit; "fresh-faced and intelligent service by Leeds U students". / **Details:** www.kendellsbistro.co.uk; 9 pm, Fri & Sat 10 pm; D only, closed Mon & Sun; no Amex.*

The Man Behind The Curtain
£95 4 5 3

68-78 Vicar Ln LS1 7JH (0113) 2432376

*"Unique, esoteric, a bit mad, but ultimately one of the UK's most interesting restaurants!" – Michael Hare's "thrilling" city-centre venue – a rooftop space over a men's clothes store – leaves most reporters "blown away". "It's a bit weird entering through a shop", but the "airy, light and barn-like space", while a tad "strange", is "not unpleasant". A meal comprises "a never-ending set of startlingly presented dishes", and though "some of them sound outrageous" the food that arrives is "exquisitely composed and brilliant", and "with remarkably little gimmickry or striving for effect". It is robbed of our highest marks by one or two refuseniks who found the performance too "bizarre, and very expensive for what you get". / **Details:** www.themanbehindthecurtain.co.uk; 8.30 pm; closed Mon, Tue & Sun.*

MEATliquor
£36 4 3 2

Bank St LS1 5AT (01138) 346 090

*"The undisputed heavyweight champion of the burger world (in Leeds anyway)". "These guys don't mess about, and the sides (especially deep-fried pickles) are also superb", as are the "cracking cocktails". / **Details:** meatliquor.com/leeds; midnight, Fri & Sat 1 am, Sun 11 pm.*

Prashad
£41 5 4 3

137 Whitehall Rd BD11 1AT (0113) 285 2037

*An "outstanding and consistent" Gujarati fixture that continues not only to produce "excellent vegetarian dishes" but also in many reporters' experiences "better subcontinental food than experienced just about anywhere else"; it can be "pricey" though – "are they trying to cover the new (Drighlington) premises?!" / **Details:** www.prashad.co.uk; 11 pm; closed Mon, Tue L, Wed L & Thu L; no Amex.*

Red Chilli
£40 3 3 3

6 Great George St LS1 3DW (01132) 429688

*A city-centre basement where the Sichuanese dishes are generally preferred to the more standard Cantonese fare; not for the first time, it's hailed as "probably the best in Leeds", with the caveat that this "doesn't say much"! / **Details:** www.redchillirestaurant.co.uk; 10.30 pm, Fri & Sat 11.30 pm; closed Mon.*

Reds True Barbecue £41 4 3 4

Cloth Hall St LS1 2HD (0113) 834 5834

*This "buzzing, edgy-yet-friendly" US-style venue is "full of atmosphere, life and scents" from its "great BBQ'd meat" – a good range from "way-out offerings like Donut burgers, through to traditional-but-hard-to-find options like ox cheek with marrow bone", plus "fantastic ribs and very good burgers"; "get there early at the weekends". / **Details:** www.trucebarbecue.com; 11 pm, Fri & Sat midnight, Sun 10 pm.*

The Reliance £38 3 4 4

76-78 North St LS2 7PN (0113) 295 6060

*"Leeds is lucky to have this place" – a "tucked away" boozer that's always "packed" thanks its "super artisanal charcuterie" and "unusual beers and ciders"; "some of its experiments can go a bit wonky" but it's "always worth a visit" ("particularly if you play it safe"!) / **Details:** www.the-reliance.co.uk; 10 pm, Thu-Sat 10.30 pm, Sun 9.30 pm; no booking.*

Salvo's £47 4 4 4

111-115 Otley Rd LS6 3PX (0113) 275 5017

*It's "nearly 40 years old now", but this Headingley stalwart still offers a "consistently great experience" revolving around "surprisingly authentic and bountiful Sicilian cuisine – in Leeds of all places"!; Top Tip – "the owners' café/deli next door is a great place for lunch". / **Details:** www.salvos.co.uk; 10 pm, Fri & Sat 10.30 pm, Sun 9 pm; no booking at D.*

Sous le Nez en Ville £45 3 4 3

Quebec Hs, Quebec St LS1 2HA (0113) 244 0108

*"You can settle in for a long lunch" at this "really good, long-standing Leeds business restaurant", occupying a "busy, often noisy" cellar "in the heart of the city centre". Service can become a little "ragged", but the "staple French food" is better than "passable", and there's excellent wine. Top Tip – "very good value, evening, early bird menu". / **Details:** www.souslenez.com; 9.45 pm, Sat 10.30 pm; closed Sun.*

Sukhothai £41 5 5 4

8 Regent St LS7 4PE (0113) 237 0141

*"Top Thai cooking in the North of England"; the Chapel Allerton HQ of this four-strong chain "still has the magic", combining "gorgeous" and "consistent" dishes with notably "helpful" service. / **Details:** www.sukhothai.co.uk; 11 pm; Mon-Thu D only, Fri-Sun open L & D; no Amex.*

Tharavadu £37 5 4 3

7 Mill Hill LS1 5DQ (0113) 244 0500

*"Conveniently located near the station", this "friendly and professional" yearling has become "very popular" thanks to its "superbly spiced and flavourful" dishes from an "interesting" Keralan menu. / **Details:** www.tharavadurestaurants.com; 10 pm; closed Sun.*

LEICESTER, LEICESTERSHIRE 5–4D

Bobby's £24 4 2 2

154-156 Belgrave Rd LE4 5AT (0116) 266 0106

*"A star in Leicester" – this decrepit sweet shop and canteen has been a linchpin of the city's 'Golden Mile' since 1976. Critics dismiss its performance nowadays as "awful", but to fans it's still an authentic subcontinental experience – "no flock wallpaper in sight" – with "genuine" Gujarati cuisine at bargain prices. / **Details:** www.eatatbobbys.com; 10 pm; no Amex.*

Hotel Maiyango £50 4 4 4

13-21 St Nicholas Pl LE1 4LD (0116) 251 8898

*Since the arrival of head chef Nick Wilson (ex-Jean-Christophe Novelli) in 2013, this town-centre boutique hotel-restaurant seems to be "maintaining an excellent standard of food and wine"; more feedback please! / **Details:** www.maiyango.com; 9.30 pm, Sun 9 pm; closed Mon L & Sun L. **Accommodation:** 14 rooms, from £90*

Kayal £35 4 3 2

153 Granby St LE1 6FE (0116) 255 4667

*"Still the best curry in Leicester" – "you experience the lovely tastes of Keralan cooking in this busy restaurant", near the railway station, which on all accounts is "superb" and "great value for money". / **Details:** www.kayalrestaurant.com; 11 pm, Sun 10 pm.*

White Peacock £46 3 4 3

16 King St LE1 6RJ (01162) 547663

*"Phillip Sharpe, who put Hotel Maiyango on the map, now runs his own excellent restaurant" in a "very attractive Regency house" on the city's famous New Walk; the "varied tasting menus are particularly special". / **Details:** www.the-white-peacock.co.uk; 9.45 pm; closed Mon & Sun D.*

LEIGHTON BUZZARD, BEDFORDSHIRE 3–2A

The Kings Head £58 4 3 3

Ivinghoe LU7 9EB (01296) 668388

*The owner of this ancient inn trained at the mythical Tour d'Argent in Paris, and his pedigree continues to show through in a "superb" menu that includes the "best duck ever" ("genuine Aylesbury"); in keeping with the old-school vibe, it's also "one of the few restaurants still serving Melba toast"! / **Details:** www.kingsheadivinghoe.co.uk; 3m N of Tring on B489 to Dunstable; 9.15 pm; closed Sun D; jacket & tie required at D.*

LEINTWARDINE, SHROPSHIRE 5–4A

Jolly Frog £49 [4][3][2]
The Todden SY7 0LX (01547) 540298
*"A super neighbourhood restaurant", near Ludlow Castle, with a "slightly offbeat, French bistro-style atmosphere"; it's a "great place to go for a fun evening out with delicious food" – "particularly fish, in which they specialise". / **Details:** www.thejollyfrog.co.uk; 9 pm; closed Mon; no Amex.*

LEWES, EAST SUSSEX 3–4B

Bill's Produce Store £41 [3][4][4]
56 Cliffe High St BN7 2AN (01273) 476918
*"The first Bill's retains a more authentic feel" than its spin-offs, and this "efficient and fun" operation has a particularly "delightful" setting on the pedestrianised High Street of this picturesque town; add in "very friendly" staff and "good-value" food – with breakfasts the big highlight – and it's "always a treat". / **Details:** www.bills-website.co.uk; 10.30 pm, Fri-Sat 11.30 pm; no Amex.*

Pelham House £42 [3][2][3]
BN7 1UW (01273) 488600
*"A relatively sophisticated option for Lewes" – a hotel-restaurant with a "panelled interior" that's "especially nice on a summer's day", thanks to its terrace with "180-degree views of the South Downs". The food is "tasty" and "the price is good too" (especially if you stick to the bar menu). / **Details:** www.pelhamhouse.com; off the High Street in Lewes; 9 pm, Sun 8.30 pm. **Accommodation:** 31 rooms, from £130*

LICKFOLD, WEST SUSSEX 3–4A

Lickfold Inn £62 [5][4][3]
Highstead Ln GU28 9EY (01789) 532535
*"What was always the most delightful inn is now back with a new team", since the November 2014 take-over by Tom Sellers of Bermondsey's Story fame, and nowadays delivers "a stunning foodie experience" with "unbeatably accommodating service and the most incredible cooking". Even ardent fans, though, can feel it's perhaps "too expensive in its current guise". / **Details:** www.thelickfoldinn.co.uk; 3m N of A272 between Midhurst & Petworth; 9.30 pm, Sun 4 pm; closed Mon & Sun D; no Amex.*

LINCOLN, LINCOLNSHIRE 6–3A

Browns Pie Shop £45 [2][2][3]
33 Steep Hill LN2 1LU (01522) 527330
*Somewhat muted praise for this local institution, located in an ancient vaulted cellar; everyone agrees it's "OK for a cheapish evening", but "not as special as its longevity and reputation suggest". / **Details:** www.brownspieshop.co.uk; 9.30 pm, Sun 8 pm; no Amex.*

Jew's House Restaurant £55 [4][4][3]
15 The Strait LN2 1JD (01522) 524851
*Located in an "exceptional" 12th-century building "with exposed stone walls" and "higgledy-piggledy rooms", this "always enjoyable" establishment wins praise for "imaginative" food that "avoids gimmickry for its own sake". / **Details:** www.jewshouserestaurant.co.uk; 9.30 pm; closed Mon, Tue L & Sun; no Amex.*

The Old Bakery £56 [3][3][4]
26-28 Burton Rd LN1 3LB (01522) 576057
*A "delightful", olde worlde restaurant-with-rooms with an "ever-changing menu" (mostly Anglo-Italian) from chef Ivan de Serio; the odd disappointment is reported, but for the most part it's hailed as "a fantastic local". / **Details:** www.theold-bakery.co.uk; 9 pm; closed Mon; no jeans. **Accommodation:** 4 rooms, from £65*

LISS, HAMPSHIRE 2–3D

Madhubon £31 [4][4][3]
94 Station Rd GU33 7AQ (01730) 893363
*"This is just a great quality Indian with absolutely no pretensions" – the consensus on this classy village tandoori, which pleases all reporters. / **Details:** www.madhubanrestaurant.co.uk; 10 pm; closed Fri L.*

LITTLE ECCLESTON, LANCASHIRE 5–1A

The Cartford Inn £42 [4][3][2]
Cartford Ln PR3 0YP (01995) 670 166
*"In an attractive village, and with panoramic windows, overlooking the River Wyre", this "quirkily decorated and spacious" Gallic-run restaurant-with-rooms "stands out from others locally". It offers "the welcoming ambience of a rural pub, with seriously good cooking focusing on seasonal and local produce." / **Details:** www.thecartfordinn.co.uk; 9 pm, Fri & Sat 10 pm, Sun 8.30 pm; closed Mon L.*

LITTLE WILBRAHAM, CAMBRIDGESHIRE 3–1B

The Hole In The Wall £48 [3][4][3]
2 High St CB21 5JY (01223) 812282
*MasterChef winner "Alex Rushmer's inn continues to provide really good, interesting food in a lovely environment"; it also continues to split opinion somewhat, though, with one dissenter claiming that it's "too concerned with selling the celebrity chef experience..." / **Details:** www.holeinthewallcambridge.com; 9 pm; closed Mon & Sun D; no Amex.*

LITTLEHAMPTON, WEST SUSSEX 3–4A

East Beach Cafe £43 334

Sea Rd, The Promenade BN17 5GB
(01903) 731903
*"A real gem right by the seaside"; this "cramped" spot, "in an architecturally unusual 'pebble'", offers "surprisingly" good fish dishes, and there's "nothing better than having a tasty lunch looking out to the English Channel". / **Details:** www.eastbeachcafe.co.uk; 8.30 pm; closed Mon D, Tue D, Wed D & Sun D.*

LIVERPOOL, MERSEYSIDE 5–2A

The Art School £49 354

Sugnall St L7 7DX (0151) 230 8600
*Paul Askew, formerly of the Hope Street Hotel and London Carriage Works, has opened a "gorgeous" new fine dining venture in a Victorian ex-children's home; it's certainly a "bold" venture, and while fans proclaim the experience "superb", sceptics cite "variable" food as proof that he's "not quite pulling it off so far". / **Details:** www.theartschoolrestaurant.co.uk/; 9 pm; closed Mon & Sun.*

Etsu £42 553

25 The Strand L2 0XJ (0151) 236 7530
*The "best Japanese" in the city occupies a "modern office complex, off the business centre"; "beautifully presented food is prepared using the freshest of ingredients", notably the "seriously good sashimi". / **Details:** www.etsu-restaurant.co.uk; off Brunswick street; 10 pm; closed Mon, Wed L & Sat L.*

Fazenda £50 333

Unit B, Horton Hs L2 3YL (0151) 227 2733
*Fans are "blown away" by this fixed-price Brazilian steakhouse where, owing to the "fab" selection of meat, salads and vegetables, "there is going to be something that everyone likes"; the "ambience allows plenty of time to catch up on business" too. / **Details:** www.fazenda.co.uk/liverpool; 9.30 pm, Sun 8.30 pm.*

Fonseca's £42 333

12 Stanley St L1 6AF (0151) 255 0808
*A "deli that does meals"; it's a "comfortable" spot offering "good, imaginative cooking"... "what's not to like about the place?" / **Details:** www.delifonseca.co.uk; 9 pm, Fri & Sat 10 pm; closed Mon & Sun.*

Hanover Street Social £38 344

16-20 Hanover St L1 4AA (0151) 709 8764
*A "fun", rustic-chic spot, near the docks, offering brasserie fare that's "a little more interesting than most". "Try the Liverpool gin here"! / **Details:** www.hanoverstreetsocial.com; 6 pm, Sat 5 pm.*

Host £39 332

31 Hope St L1 9XH (0151) 708 5831
*Near the Phil, a "consistent" and "vibrant" 60 Hope Street spin-off serving "well-thought-out" Asian fusion fare; "as an independent, it's rather more interesting (not to say better) than the likes of Wagamama". / **Details:** www.ho-st.co.uk; 11 pm, Sun 10 pm.*

The Italian Club Fish £44 332

128 Bold St L1 4JA (0151) 707 2110
*This "lovely" and "buzzy" Italian bistro, near Central Station, is "a reliably good place for fish", and the oysters are "excellent value" too. / **Details:** www.theitalianclubfish.co.uk; 10 pm, Sun 9 pm; no Amex.*

The London Carriage Works Hope Street Hotel £54 233

40 Hope St L1 9DA (0151) 705 2222
*The dining room of the city's original design hotel wins fans for its "high standard" of cooking (including Liverpool FC, "who stay here before a home match"). Overall however, its ratings have been rather middling across the board in recent times. / **Details:** www.thelondoncarriageworks.co.uk; 10 pm, Sun 9 pm; no shorts. **Accommodation:** 89 rooms, from £150*

Lunya £44 433

18-20 College Ln L1 3DS (0151) 706 9770
*"Catalonia comes to The 'Pool", at this inspired yearling, which defies its "sterile location, in the middle of a shopping mall" to produce "Spanish cooking with real heart" ("you won't find tapas to beat this outside of Spain, and in fact it's better than much of that you find IN Spain"). Top Tip – check out its "fascinating adjoining deli". / **Details:** www.lunya.co.uk; 11 pm, Sun 10 pm.*

Maray £42 333

91 Bold St L1 4HF (0151) 709 5825
*A "good newcomer on the Bold St scene" serving "Middle Eastern-inspired food and cocktails"; the formula is "mostly small plates, some big ones and lots of imagination" and, whilst they "try a bit too hard", "most dishes are really good". / **Details:** www.maray.co.uk/#home; 10 pm, Fri & Sat 11 pm, Sun 9 pm.*

Mowgli £30 334

69 Bold St L1 4EZ (0151) 708 9356
*A "fresh, modern and authentic" newcomer on increasingly foodie Bold Street from self-proclaimed curry evangelist Nisha Katona. It serves "an excellent choice" of Indian tapas, in tiffin boxes and on tin plates, that's "a bit different" to the norm – ditto the décor, with its birdcage lights and railway sleeper bar. / **Details:** www.mowglistreetfood.com/; 9.30 pm, Thu-Sat 10.30 pm.*

Panoramic Beetham West Tower £61 224
Brook St L3 9PJ (0151) 236 5534
No doubting the "terrific views" on offer at this "fabulous" 34th-floor dining room; the food, by comparison, can feel like a "great disappointment", and service – previously a strength – has been somewhat up and down of late too. / ***Details:*** *www.panoramicliverpool.com; 9.30 pm, Sun 8 pm; closed Mon; no Amex; no trainers.*

Pen Factory £36 433
13 Hope St L1 9BQ (01517) 097887
"Paddy Byrne has triumphed with this re-incarnation of the Everyman Bistro", located "next door to and in competition with the Everyman's own refurbished premises". The setting is an "interesting '30s factory" and to eat there's "all manner of lovely stuff"; there's even a small garden. / ***Details:*** *www.pen-factory.co.uk; midnight; closed Mon & Sun.*

Puschka £51 433
16 Rodney St L1 2TE (0151) 708 8698
A "small and intimate" Georgian quarter restaurant – "the menu always has something new" and it "never fails" to deliver "fresh and mouth-watering" dishes. / ***Details:*** *www.puschka.co.uk; 10 pm, Sun 9 pm; D only.*

Salt House £36 343
Hanover Sq L1 3DW (0151) 706 0092
"Are there more tapas restaurants in this small area of Liverpool than anywhere else in the UK?" – at any rate "this one is very good" thanks to its "traditional" yet "very imaginative" food; it "can get very noisy though"! / ***Details:*** *www.salthousetapas.co.uk; 10.30 pm.*

Salt House Bacaro £35 323
47 Castle St L2 9UB (0151) 665 0047
In the business district, "a newcomer opened by the Salt House Tapas people"; it serves "very good Italian tapas/cicchetti", and "standards are nearly as high as at its sister restaurant". / ***Details:*** *www.salthousebacaro.co.uk/; 10.30 pm.*

San Carlo £46 234
41 Castle St L2 9SH (0151) 236 0073
This "fun and bustling" and "very plush" outpost of the national chain is "great for WAG-watching", and offers "good" (if "eye-watering"-ly expensive) food. The "over-the-top bling style" and "sometimes overly charming" staff are "not to everyone's taste", but it's a "successful formula" nonetheless. / ***Details:*** *www.sancarlo.co.uk; 11 pm.*

60 Hope Street £58 443
60 Hope St L1 9BZ (0151) 707 6060
"London quality food at Liverpool prices", say fans of this "lovely" townhouse restaurant, near the Anglican Cathedral – the first modern British restaurant of any renown in the city, and "still one of the best". / ***Details:*** *www.60hopestreet.com; 10.30 pm, Sun 8 pm.*

Spire £47 432
1 Church Rd L15 9EA (0151) 734 5040
"Consistently wonderful dishes and the most fantastic value for money" ensure that this smart Wavertree restaurant, near Penny Lane, remains a highly rated favourite for many reporters. / ***Details:*** *www.spirerestaurant.co.uk; Mon-Thu 9 pm, Fri & Sat 9.30 pm; closed Mon L, Sat L & Sun.*

Yukti £40 443
393 Prescot Rd L13 3BS (0151) 228 2225
"Fabulous" service and Indian-fusion cuisine (the latter from one of Raymond Blanc's protégés) win acclaim (but still only from a small fan club) for this two-year-old, in a modern building in Old Swan. / ***Details:*** *www.yukti.co.uk; 10.30 pm, Sun 9.30 pm; D only, ex Sun open L & D.*

LLANARMON DC, DENBIGHSHIRE 5–3A

The West Arms Hotel £47 323
LL20 7LD (01691) 600665
"A hidden gem" in an underserved area; this "lovely" if "dated" hotel wins warm praise for its "delicious" food, "roaring fires" and "dog-friendly" stance. / ***Details:*** *www.thewestarms.co.uk; 9 pm; no Amex.* ***Accommodation:*** *15 rooms, from £65*

LLANARTHNE, CARMARTHENSHIRE 4–4C

Wrights Food Emporium £35 443
Golden Grove Arms SA32 8JU
(01558) 668929
Ex-AA chief inspector Simon Wright (who also runs Y Polyn) owns this "wonderfully relaxed", new café/deli, "which is spread over three rooms" of a former pub. There's a versatile selection of "mouthwatering" dishes from the blackboard menu – it's most often recommended as a lunch stop, but also good for breakfast or "just coffee and amazing cakes" (and they also do dinner on Friday and Saturday). / ***Details:*** *www.wrightsfood.co.uk; 11 pm; closed Mon D, Tue D, Wed D, Thu D & Sun D.*

LLANDENNY, MONMOUTHSHIRE 2–2A

Raglan Arms £51 432
NP15 1DL (01291) 690800
This country gastropub has recently changed hands and the kitchen is now run by Matthew Long; according to one early report, "the food is at least as good as it was" (with a focus on seafood, as befits a Cornish chef), but the décor has become "more functional". / ***Details:*** *www.raglanarms.com; 9 pm; closed Mon & Sun D.*

LLANDEWI SKIRRID, MONMOUTHSHIRE 2–1A

The Walnut Tree **£64** 5 4 3

Llanddewi Skirrid NP7 8AW (01873) 852797

"We drove 2 1/2 hours each way and it was well worth it!" – Shaun Hill's modest rural inn (made famous in the '70s under Franco and Ann Taruschio) has re-established itself under his ownership as one of Wales's top destinations. It may be "very crowded" and with "challenging acoustics", but the "perfectly pitched" cooking – "eschewing the ostentatious novelty of many top chefs" – is "tremendously honest, with great sensitivity to tastes and flavours." / **Details:** *www.thewalnuttreeinn.com; 3m NE of Abergavenny on B4521; 9.30 pm; closed Mon & Sun.* **Accommodation:** *5 rooms, from £300 (2 bed cottage)*

LLANDRILLO, DENBIGHSHIRE 4–2D

Tyddyn Llan **£78** 4 4 4

LL21 0ST (01490) 440264

"For a special treat" (particularly a romantic one), Bryan & Susan Webb's country house hotel – regularly one of Wales's highest-rated destinations in the survey – remains "on top form". The cuisine is "superb", "the cellar is a match to anywhere", service is "unobtrusive", and the "cosy" ambience "fabulous". Top Menu Tip – "beautifully prepared Welsh lamb". / **Details:** *www.tyddynllan.co.uk; on B4401 between Corwen and Bala; 9 pm; (Mon-Thu L by prior arrangement only).* **Accommodation:** *12 rooms, from £180*

LLANDUDNO, CONWY 4–1D

Dining Room Bodysgallen Hall **£71** 3 4 5

The Royal Welsh Way LL30 1RS
(01492) 584466

This "old-fashioned" National Trust-owned Elizabethan manor house hotel with a spa, sits just outside the town amidst 200 acres of gardens; more feedback wouldn't go amiss, but all reports applaud its silver service charms, and it's consistently well-rated. / **Details:** *www.bodysgallen.com; 2m off A55 on A470; 9.15 pm, Fri & Sat 9.30 pm; closed Mon; no sportswear; children: 6+.* **Accommodation:** *31 rooms, from £179*

Jaya **£38** 4 3 3

36 Church Walks LL30 2HN (01492) 818 198

The well-presented Indian cuisine at Sunita Katoch's contemporary-style restaurant-with-rooms away from the sea often comes with an East African twist – quite 'outré' for this bit of N Wales! / **Details:** *www.jayarestaurant.co.uk; 9.15 pm; closed Mon, Tue, Wed L, Thu L, Fri L, Sat L & Sun L; no Amex.*

Terrace Restaurant St Tudno Hotel **£49** 3 2 2

Promenade LL30 2LP (01492) 874411

This traditional hotel on the front has won a solid reputation in the area for its cuisine (including Welsh afternoon teas); feedback is limited, but all basically enthusiastic. / **Details:** *www.stgeorgewales.co.uk/terrace-restaurant/; 9.30 pm; no shorts; children: 6+ after 6.30 pm.* **Accommodation:** *18 rooms, from £100*

LLANGYBI, MONMOUTHSHIRE 2–2A

The White Hart Village Inn **£39** 3 3 3

Old Usk Rd NP15 1NP (01633) 450258

Rather limited feedback of late on this relaxed village pub; fans, though, say its "great-quality" dishes (running the whole gamut from snacks to tasting menus) make it a "lovely place to go". / **Details:** *www.thewhitehartvillageinn.com; 9 pm, Sun 2.45 pm; closed Mon & Sun D.*

LLANWRTYD WELLS, POWYS 4–4D

Carlton Riverside **£52** 4 3 3

Irfon Cr LD5 4SP (01591) 610248

"Still a blessing in an otherwise trying area"; Alan Gilchrist always ensures "delightfully relaxed evenings" at this "determinedly consistent" mid-Wales inn, which has "a lovely riverside situation in a small town". "Mary Ann's expeditions into TV seem to have re-invigorated the menu" too. / **Details:** *www.carltonriverside.com; 8.30 pm; closed Mon L & Sun; no Amex.* **Accommodation:** *4 rooms, from £60*

LLYSWEN, POWYS 2–1A

Llangoed Hall **£105** 4 2 4

Llyswen LD3 0YP (01874) 754525

Nick Brodie's "exceptional" cuisine won the highest ratings in Wales this year for this "lovely" and "romantic" country house hotel, with its "marvellous" setting in the Wye Valley. A niggle? – service strikes some reporters as "Dickensian in attitude" (ie "a bit intimidating"), but perhaps the spring 2015 arrival of new manager Bruno Asselin will improve matters? / **Details:** *www.llangoedhall.com; 11m NW of Brecon on A470; 8.45 pm; no Amex; jacket required at D.* **Accommodation:** *23 rooms, from £210*

LOCH LOMOND, DUNBARTONSHIRE 9–4B

Martin Wishart Cameron House **£100** 5 5 4

G83 8QZ (01389) 722504

Martin Wishart's "small and intimate" country house hotel dining room is "still hitting the high spots", from its "stunning" food ("especially the tasting menus"), to its "friendly but discreet staff" and Loch Lomond views; by all accounts it's "well worth even a very long detour!" / ***Details:*** *www.mwlochlomond.co.uk; over Erskine Bridge to A82, follow signs to Loch Lomond; 9.45 pm; Mon, Tues.* ***Accommodation:*** *134 rooms, from £215*

LOCHINVER, HIGHLAND 9–1B

The Albannach £67 4 5 4

IV27 4LP (01571) 844407

A "remote" but "magical" restaurant-with-rooms "perched above Lochinver harbour with Suilven visible from the dining room"; it combines the "warmest of welcomes", food that "delights the palate and heart" and wine "with a clear French bias". / ***Details:*** *www.thealbannach.co.uk; closed Mon, Tue, Wed L, Thu L, Fri L, Sat L & Sun L; no Amex; children: 12+.* ***Accommodation:*** *5 rooms, from £295*

LOCKSBOTTOM, KENT 3–3B

Chapter One £60 5 4 4

Farnborough Common BR6 8NF
(01689) 854848

"A real gem on the borders of London" – this rural village restaurant just outside 'the smoke' was "harshly stripped of its Michelin star" in the eyes of most reporters to whom, by-and-large, it's "as brilliant as ever", serving "tempting" cuisine with "aplomb" and "with an unrivalled rapport prix/ qualité for a fine dining restaurant". Top Tip – "the lunchtime special is exceptionally good value". / ***Details:*** *www.chaptersrestaurants.com; Mon-Thu 9.30 pm, Fri & Sat 10.30 pm; no trainers; booking: max 12.*

LONG CRENDON, BUCKINGHAMSHIRE 2–2D

The Angel £50 3 2 2

47 Bicester Rd HP18 9EE (01844) 208268

A restaurant-with-rooms in a "pleasant country setting" with a "well thought-out" menu; even regulars who "do not think the cooking is as good as it used to be" say "you never have a bad meal here". / ***Details:*** *www.angelrestaurant.co.uk; 2m NW of Thames, off B4011; 9.30 pm; closed Sun D.* ***Accommodation:*** *4 rooms, from £110*

The Mole & Chicken £51 3 4 4

Easington HP18 9EY (01844) 208387

A "very friendly" pub-with-rooms where the food is "better than you might expect"; if the weather's fine, sit outside on the "wonderful" terrace, and admire the "lovely" views. / ***Details:*** *www.themoleandchicken.co.uk; follow signs from B4011 at Long Crendon; 9.30 pm, Sun 9 pm.* ***Accommodation:*** *5 rooms, from £110*

LONG MELFORD, SUFFOLK 3–1C

Melford Valley Tandoori £30 4 5 4

Hall St CO10 9JT (01787) 311 518

"Excellent" Indian cuisine to be had at this smart and "busy" subcontinental – "it would blossom, even in Southall!" / ***Details:*** *www.melfordvalley.com; 11.30 pm.*

Swan £52 3 4 3

Hall St CO10 9JQ (01787) 464545

The Macmillan's fine-dining venture – "the first, and still the best, of a local mini-empire" – elicits plenty of survey feedback, all of it enthusiastic. The "new kitchen has allowed them to create a great selection of dishes", and as further incentive, "they've just opened four fabulous boutique rooms". / ***Details:*** *www.longmelfordswan.co.uk; Mon-Thu 9 pm, Fri-Sat 10 pm; closed Sun D.*

LONG WHITTENHAM, OXFORDSHIRE 2–2D

The Vine and Spice £43 4 3 3

High St OX14 4QH (01865) 409 900

A "nice old pub" with a winning line in "interesting" Indian food; "if you're looking for a standard curry, this isn't it" – dishes are unusual and "the focus is on flavour rather than heat". / ***Details:*** *www.thevineandspice.co.uk; 10.30 pm.*

LOUGHBOROUGH, LEICESTERSHIRE 5–3D

The Hammer & Pincers £49 3 3 3

5 East Rd LE12 6ST (01509) 880735

This "delightful", beamed village restaurant "has always been a popular place to eat, but is now one of the best for miles around"; its charms include increasingly "interesting" cuisine plus an "extensive gin menu". / ***Details:*** *www.hammerandpincers.co.uk; 9.30 pm; closed Mon & Sun D; no Amex.*

LOWER BOCKHAMPTON, DORSET 2–4B

Yalbury Cottage £54 5 5 4

DT2 8PZ (01305) 262382

"The food will blow your taste buds" at Ariane & Jamie Jones's "beautiful, homely and intimate cottage restaurant" (with rooms); it continues to inspire nothing but the highest of praise, and it's "in a beautiful area too". / ***Details:*** *www.yalburycottage.com; 9 pm; Tues to Sat L - booking only; no Amex.* ***Accommodation:*** *8 rooms, from £120*

LOWER FROYLE, HAMPSHIRE 2–3D

The Anchor Inn £49 3 2 4

GU34 4NA (01420) 23261

In a "convivial countryside setting", this comely

*pub serves food that's "a hefty cut above the rest". / **Details:** www.anchorinnatlowerfroyle.co.uk; 9.30 pm, Sun 9 pm.* ***Accommodation:*** *5 rooms, from £120*

LOWER ODDINGTON, GLOUCESTERSHIRE 2–1C

The Fox Inn £47 3 2 4

GL56 0UR (01451) 870555

*This "quintessential English pub" has a small but enthusiastic fan club who say it's "improved in recent times" (under newish owners), with cooking that's "less interesting, but better value!" / **Details:** www.foxinn.net; on A436 near Stow-on-the-Wold; 9.30 pm, Sun 9.30 pm; no Amex.* ***Accommodation:*** *3 rooms, from £85*

LOWER SLAUGHTER, GLOUCESTERSHIRE 2–1C

Lower Slaughter Manor Von Essen £90 3 3 2

GL54 2HP (01451) 820456

*Part of the same empire as Gidleigh Park, this Cotswolds country house hotel provides some "imaginative and beautifully presented" cuisine. Top Tip – "superb set lunch". / **Details:** www.lowerslaughter.co.uk; 2m from Burton-on-the-Water on A429; 9 pm; no jeans or trainers.* ***Accommodation:*** *19 rooms, from £310*

LUDLOW, SHROPSHIRE 5–4A

The Charlton Arms Charlton Arms Hotel £46 3 2 3

Ludford Bridge SY8 1PJ (01584) 872813

*A gastroboozer-with-rooms with a "fab setting right on the river", where the food is "now excellent after new owners (Cedric Bosi, brother of Claude of Hibiscus fame) took it over"; reports are still few, but fans say it's "well worth a visit". / **Details:** www.thecharltonarms.co.uk; 9.30 pm, Sun 6 pm.*

The Clive Restaurant With Rooms £53 3 2 3

Bromfield SY8 2JR (01584) 856565

*"All dishes are executed professionally but with the minimum of fussy pretension and served in pleasant modern surroundings" at this restaurant-with-rooms, in an 18th-century farmhouse that's handy for the A49 and castle. / **Details:** www.theclive.co.uk; 2m N of Ludlow on A49 to Shrewsbury; 9.30 pm.* ***Accommodation:*** *15 rooms, from £70*

The Fish House £29 4 4 3

51 Bullring SY8 1AB (01584) 879790

*A "brill fishmonger" with a handful of tables "serving cold fishy lunches", including seafood platters; the food is "always delicious" and there's also a "very jolly atmosphere". / **Details:** www.thefishhouseludlow.co.uk; 5 pm, Sat 4 pm; closed Mon, Tue, Wed D, Thu D, Fri D, Sat D & Sun; Sat no booking.*

The French Pantry £40 4 3 3

15 Tower St SY8 1RL (01584) 879133

*"One of Ludlow's finds"; this ever-consistent French bistro continues to attract nothing but praise for its "tasty" cuisine – in part because there are "few covers, so attention to food is paramount". / **Details:** www.thefrenchpantry.co.uk/; 8.30 pm; closed Sun.*

Green Café Ludlow Mill On The Green £35 5 5 4

Dinham Millennium Grn SY8 1EG (01584) 879872

*"It's only a café", but this uncomplicated spot delivers "gorgeous food, in a gorgeous riverside setting". Chef Clive Davis has the culinary equivalent of "perfect pitch", and his "simple" fare from a "short, spot-on menu" is "cooked and seasoned to a tee". A catch? – "on a busy day (every day nowadays!) you may feel a bit cheek-by-jowl". / **Details:** www.ludlowmillonthegreen.co.uk/tearooms.aspx; 4 pm; closed Mon, L only Tue-Sun; no Amex.*

Mortimers £84 3 3 3

17 Corve St SY8 1DA (01584) 872 325

Once the site of La Bécasse (RIP) – part of the vainglorious (now defunct) '10-in-8' empire – this one-time destination restaurant opened under new ownership in November 2015, after Alan Murchison abandoned plans to take over the lease. Wayne Smith heads up the kitchen.

Mr Underhill's £100 5 5 4

Dinham Weir SY8 1EH (01584) 874431

*"Christopher and Judy Bradley have hit upon a hard-to-beat formula", at their "idyllically located", very "professional" restaurant-with-rooms – a "peaceful", "couples' place", where in summer a meal kicks off with aperitifs in the riverside gardens. Chris consistently produces "stunning", "honest" cooking, while Judy presides extremely knowledgeably over a "formidable" wine list and cheese selection. Stop Press – at the end of 2015 the restaurant is to close while the Bradleys take stock to consider how to develop the business further. / **Details:** www.mr-underhills.co.uk; 8.15 pm; D only, closed Mon & Tue; no Amex; children: 8+.* ***Accommodation:*** *6 rooms, from £140*

Smoke House Deli And Cicchetti £32 4 4 3

10 Broad St SY8 1NG (07890) 412873

A "small and very individual" new joint based on a Venetion bàcaro; it serves "wonderful" coffee and "very lovely" cicchetti to eat in or take-away, but "owing to its uniqueness it justifiably gets very busy". / **Details:** *www.ludlowcicchettibar.wordpress.com/about-us/; 5 pm; L only.*

LUPTON, CUMBRIA 7–4D

The Plough Inn £44 3 2 3
Cow Brow LA6 1PJ (01539) 567 700
An updated pub-with-rooms, just off the M6, that seems to be on an even keel though it's "no longer associated with the (much-vaunted) Punch Bowl at Crossthwaite"; fans praise its "beautifully presented and blooming tasty" food. / **Details:** *www.theploughatlupton.co.uk; 9 pm.* **Accommodation:** *6 rooms, from £115*

LUTON, BEDFORDSHIRE 3–2A

Luton Hoo
Luton Hoo Hotel £51 3 4 4
LU1 3TQ (01582) 734437
A "lovely" country house hotel whose "beautiful dining room" features airy garden views, plenty of marble and "faultless" staff. Even if the menu doesn't always hit the mark, fans say it's "(usually) excellent". / **Details:** *www.lutonhoo.co.uk; 4.45 pm; L only.*

LYDFORD, DEVON 1–3C

The Dartmoor Inn £50 3 3 3
Moorside EX20 4AY (01822) 820221
"Philip Burgess and his team provide consistently good local fare at this old coaching inn", located within the National Park (and thus ideal pre- or post-walk) – by all accounts a "deservedly popular" spot. / **Details:** *www.dartmoorinn.com; on the A386 Tavistock to Okehampton road; 9.30 pm; closed Mon L & Sun D.* **Accommodation:** *3 rooms, from £95*

LYME REGIS, DORSET 2–4A

Hix Oyster & Fish House £54 4 3 5
Cobb Rd DT7 3JP (01297) 446910
"The most awesome views" over Lyme Bay reward a trip to Mark Hix's "beautifully located" cliff-top venture. "It's not the cheapest", but while to a few critics the fish and seafood is "a bit low on wow-factor", to most who have made the pilgrimage it's as "stunning" as the "beautiful location". / **Details:** *www.restaurantsetcltd.co.uk; 10 pm.*

Tierra £46 4 3 3
1a Coombe St DT7 3PY (01297) 445189
"The tastiest of tasty vegetarian food" is the order of the day at this rustic two-year-old with a stream-side terrace – the brainchild of Mark Evans, behind Bristol hit Café Maitreya; feedback is still limited, but fans say the menu features "the most imaginative ever" veggie dishes, and that a visit is "a real privilege". / **Details:** *www.tierrakitchen.co.uk; 9.15 pm; closed Mon, Tue & Sun.*

LYMINGTON, HAMPSHIRE 2–4C

Egan's £49 4 3 2
24 Gosport St SO41 9BE (01590) 676165
The recent departure of longtime owners John & Debbie Egan doesn't seem to have dented feedback on this "really relaxed yet special" bistro; fans say that it's still a "real treat", combining "wonderful cooking, beautiful presentation, and the warmest of welcomes". / **Details:** *www.eganslymington.co.uk; 10 pm; closed Mon & Sun; no Amex.*

Elderflower £56 4 4 4
Quay St SO41 3AS (0159) 676908
Andrew Scott DuBourg (ex-Chewton Glen Hotel and Club Gascon) "leaves your taste buds in awe" at this newcomer, on a cobbled street opposite the Pier; reporters are in unison – the food is "to die for", and a "room upstairs makes it perfect for a weekender". / **Details:** *elderflowerrestaurant.co.uk/index.php/our-story/; Wed & Thu 9.30 pm, Fri & Sat 10 pm.*

LYMM, CHESHIRE 5–2B

La Boheme £42 3 3 3
3 Mill Ln WA13 9SD (01925) 753657
A "very busy" dining room which "consistently surprises" by offering "quite complex French-style" food at "ridiculously low prices"; the main problem? – "it's so popular, it can be difficult getting a booking at a sensible time!" / **Details:** *laboheme.co.uk; Mon-Sat 10 pm; Sun 9 pm; closed Mon L & Sat L.*

LYNDHURST, HAMPSHIRE 2–4C

Hartnett Holder & Co Lime Wood Hotel £67 3 3 4
Beaulieu Rd SO43 7FZ (02380) 287177
At its best, Angela Hartnett's "incredibly luxurious" country house two-year-old, in the New Forest, produces "an amazing experience" founded on "high quality" cooking. The best reports are often from those who went on some kind of deal however, and too many other reports are a tad grudging ("enjoyable enough"... "not bad but rather average"... "OK, but wouldn't cut it in London"). / **Details:** *www.limewoodhotel.co.uk; 11 pm.*

LYTH VALLEY, CUMBRIA 7–4D

The Punch Bowl £50 4 5 5
LA8 8HR (01539) 568237
It may inhabit a tiny village in "a hidden corner of the Lakes", but this "warm, welcoming and

stylish" pub/hotel is "well worth seeking out". "The level of hospitality is exceptional", the "short but interesting menu" is "consistently excellent and keenly priced" and they serve "remarkable real ales". / **Details:** www.the-punchbowl.co.uk; off A5074 towards Bowness, turn right after Lyth Hotel; 8.45 pm. **Accommodation:** 9 rooms, from £105

MADINGLEY, CAMBRIDGESHIRE 3–1B

Three Horseshoes £49 324

High St CB23 8AB (01954) 210221

"Still on good form", a longtime haunt of undergrads and their parents, just outside Cambridge, which benefits from a "delightful conservatory"; on most accounts the food is "lovely" too, but there's the odd gripe that its "over ambitious" menu "does not deliver on its promise". / **Details:** www.threehorseshoesmadingley.co.uk; 2m W of Cambridge, off A14 or M11; 9.30 pm, Sun 8.30 pm.

MAIDENHEAD, BERKSHIRE 3–3A

Boulters Riverside Brasserie £50 224

Boulters Lock Island SL6 8PE (01628) 621291

A venue whose main attraction is "one of the nicest riverside locations in the area" (the building is built out right over the Thames); if the "food was better, it would be an amazing restaurant", but as it is, it's merely "good". / **Details**: www.boultersrestaurant.co.uk; 9.30 pm; closed Sun D.

The Royal Oak £64 234

Paley St SL6 3JN (01628) 620541

Mixed feedback of late for Parkie's "lovely" gastropub in "beautiful surroundings in the country"; while fans still praise the "very consistent" food, there's a sense that it's become rather more "routine" since longtime Head Chef Dominic Chapman's recent-ish departure. / **Details**: www.theroyaloakpaleystreet.com; 9.30 pm, Fri & Sat 10 pm; closed Sun D; children: 3+ .

MAIDSTONE, KENT 3–3C

Frederic Bistro £41 344

Market Buildings, Earl St ME14 1HP (01622) 297414

A "jolly, bustling, side-street bistro" with a "Gallic flavour", serving "traditional, freshly made dishes at very good prices", including "a generous selection of cheeses". There's also "an impressive range of (mostly French) wine", with "helpful advice from owner Ulric". / **Details:** www.fredericbistro.com; 10 pm.

Gem Of Kent £33 343

62 High St ME14 1SR (01622) 675000

A "bustling" new Turkish bar/restaurant which inspires limited but enthusiastic feedback – the "shish is juicy and tender and the lamb cutlets, cooked fresh over charcoal, melt in the mouth". / **Details:** www.gemofkent.co.uk; 10.30 pm; closed Sun.

MALMESBURY, WILTSHIRE 2–2C

The Old Bell Hotel £54 323

Abbey Row SN16 0BW (01666) 822344

"What a fantastic surprise" – an ancient inn near the Abbey that continues to impress guests with its "lovely" restaurant featuring "lots of quiet corners"; the menu may have "sounded pretty standard" to one reporter, "yet the food was anything but!" / **Details:** www.oldbellhotel.com; 9 pm, Fri & Sat 9.30 pm. **Accommodation:** 33 rooms, from £115

MALVERN, WORCESTERSHIRE 2–1B

The Fig Tree £39 332

99b, Church St WR14 2AE (01684) 569909

A "sweet little place" that's "ideally located for pre-theatre" meals; "the (Mediterranean) menu is not extensive but appetising" nonetheless. / **Details:** www.figtreemalvern.co.uk; 2 pm.

MANCHESTER, GREATER MANCHESTER 5–2B

Akbar's £33 423

73-83 Liverpool Rd M3 4NQ (0161) 834 8444

"As authentic as you will get in the North West"; this "fabulous" and "buzzing" Pakistani venture is "still knocking out great-value curries" and "the giant naan breads are legendary" too; minor quibble? – "service could be improved". / **Details:** www.akbars.co.uk; 11 pm, Fri & Sat 11.30 pm; D only; need 10+ to book.

Albert's Worsley £45 232

East Lancashire Rd M27 0AA (0161) 794 1234

This "always reliable" Swinton venture, a "noisy" offshoot of Albert's Shed, wins particular praise for its "excellent lunch menu" ("which runs until 6pm!") / **Details:** www.albertsworsley.com; 10 pm.

Almost Famous £29 323

100-102 High St M4 1HP () no tel

"Manchester's best version of the 'Dirty Burger'... and my god are they good!" The Northern Quarter original of what's now a mini-chain still wins praise for its "lip-smacking" grub, even if it's perhaps "a little less hipster now that it's mid-roll-out, rather than in its early days". / **Details:** www.almostfamousburgers.com; 11 pm.

Australasia **£60** 3 3 5
1 The Avenue Spinningfields M3 3AP
(0161) 831 0288
"Australian, Indonesian, European with a little Japanese thrown in sums up the culinary influences" of this "superbly designed", "swanky" and "romantic" basement, just off Deansgate – a "very trendy and upbeat place" that mostly "lives up to the hype", despite its "elevated prices". / ***Details:*** *www.australasia.uk.com; 10.45 pm.*

Bandera **£50** 5 4 3
2 Ridgefield M2 6EQ (0161) 833 9019
"Setting new standards for Iberian cuisine"; despite only opening in late-2014, this "achingly modern" (think yellow banquettes) new spot, off Deansgate, already "enjoys celebrity status" for its "wonderful, fresh and interesting" tapas from a chef "with a real sense of flavour" (Basque maestro Josetxo Arrieta). / ***Details:*** *www.labandera.co.uk/; midnight.*

Bar San Juan **£31** 3 3 4
56 Beech Rd M21 9EG (0161) 881 9259
In Chorlton, a "tiny, authentic tapas bar run by the super efficient Juan"; it's "always packed and bustling" thanks to its "delicious" dishes. / ***Details:*** *barsanjuan.com; 11 pm, Fri & Sat midnight.*

Chaophraya, **£47** 3 3 3
Chapel Walks M2 1HN (0161) 832 8342
Set in "a wonderful series of rooms, with beautiful décor and an excellent atmosphere", a popular operation offering "brilliant Thai food served efficiently". / ***Details:*** *www.chaophraya.co.uk; 10.30 pm, Sun 10 pm.*

Croma **£35** 3 4 4
1-3 Clarence St M2 4DE (0161) 237 9799
"PizzaExpress plus" is the concept at this "very efficient" venue, near the Town Hall – "it's just great for a casual day out, and always 100% consistent". / ***Details:*** *www.cromapizza.co.uk; 10 pm, Fri & Sat 11 pm.*

Evuna **£43** 3 4 4
Deansgate M3 4EW (0161) 819 2752
"For a fun night out with friends", it's hard to beat the formula of this brick-walled, city-centre bar, with its "gorgeous tapas", washed down with some "fantastic" wines, "cheerful service" and enjoyable "buzz". The worst report? – "it's not stellar but solid". / ***Details:*** *www.evuna.com; 11 pm, Sun 9 pm.*

The French Restaurant Midland Hotel **£96** 3 5 3
Peter St M60 2DS (0161) 236 3333
"The only choice is how many courses you want" (you can have either 6 or 10), when you a secure table in Manchester's grandest dining space, nowadays part of the empire of Simon Rogan of L'Enclume fame. Despite the lack of options, chef Adam Reid's "innovative and amazingly flavourful" parade of dishes are "exceptional", if fully priced; the space itself can appear a tad "corporate". / ***Details:*** *www.the-french.co.uk; 8.45 pm; closed Mon, Tue L & Sun; no jeans or trainers; children: 9+.* **Accommodation:** *312 rooms, from £145*

El Gato Negro **£46**
52 King St M2 4LY () awaiting tel
Simon Shaw is relocating his "splendid" Hispanic venture to Manchester, opening in February 2016. Our review when it was in Ripponden said it was in "the last location you would expect" – hopefully it will repeat its success and more so in this new home.

Glamorous **£39** 4 2 3
Wing Yip Bus' Centre, Oldham Rd M4 5HU
(0161) 839 3312
"HK in Manchester!"; this venue, located atop the Ancoats branch of supermarket chain Wing Yip, is "great for Sunday dim-sum" – just remember to "get there early!" / ***Details:*** *www.glamorous-restaurant.co.uk; 11.30 pm, Fri & Sat midnight, Sun 11 pm.*

Great Kathmandu **£36** 4 3 3
140 Burton Rd M20 1JQ (0161) 445 2145
Fans claim that this West Didsbury spot, which has expanded in recent years, still offers the "best curry in the North". Perhaps that's over-egging it, but even those who say it's "grossly over-rated" or "not as good as it was", still rate it between "consistent" and "very good"! / ***Details:*** *www.greatkathmandu.com; midnight.*

Green's **£43** 3 4 3
43 Lapwing Ln M20 2NT (0161) 434 4259
"Great vegetarian food" is the hallmark of this bustling West Didsbury spot – the kind of place where even "ardent meat eaters have left singing its praises!" / ***Details:*** *www.greensdidsbury.co.uk; 9.30 pm, Thu-Sat 10 pm; closed Mon L; no Amex.*

Grill on the Alley **£54** 3 3 3
5 Ridgefield M2 6EG (0161) 833 3465
It may be "rather loud and brash" but this city-centre spot is "becoming a Manchester institution" thanks to its "great steaks and speedy service". / ***Details:*** *www.blackhouse.uk.com; 11 pm.*

Habesha **£22** 3 3 2
29-31 Sackville St M1 3LZ (0161) 228 7396
"Find out where the Manchester Ethiopian community hangs out!" – near Canal Street, "it's a bizarre location": "sort-of part of a kebab shop", "up a set of spiral staircases". Once you've winkled it out, the reward is "tasty curries and sour pancake-style bread". (It doesn't have the highest hygiene rating though...) / ***Details:*** *www.habesharestaurant.co.uk*

Hawksmoor £60 454
184-186 Deansgate M3 3WB (01618) 366980
"Standards have been maintained in the move to Manchester", and this outpost of the legendary London steakhouse chain "is a fine addition to the city's improving dining scene". In fact enthusiasm here is just as it was in the early days of the brand's original debut in the capital, with adulation for its "confident" menu, "fabulous" steaks, and "engaging and knowledgeable" service. / **Details:** *www.thehawksmoor.com.*

Ibérica Spinningfields £46 434
14-15 The Ave M3 3HF (01613) 581 350
"Yet another high-profile opening for Manchester" – a northern outpost of the London-based modern tapas chain. It can seem "hyped", but most agree that the food is "very good, if pricey", and "helpful" service wins praise too (although "asking for a manzanilla in a Spanish restaurant should not be met with 'yer what?'!") / **Details:** *www.ibericarestaurants.com; 11.30 pm, Sun 11 pm.*

James Martin £53 543
2 Watson St M3 4LP (0161) 828 0345
"A real gem in the centre of Manchester" with a "pleasant", if unlikely sounding, setting in a converted warehouse over a casino; reporters all acclaim the TV chef's "amazing" cuisine ("at an affordable price") and staff who "can't do enough". / **Details:** *www.jamesmartinmanchester.co.uk; 10 pm, Sat 11 pm, Sun 5 pm.*

Katsouris Deli £14 432
113 Deansgate M3 2BQ (0161) 819 1260
"Still one of the best cheap eats in Manchester"; this city-centre fixture wins very consistent recommendations for its "delicious" mezze. / **Details:** *www.katsourisdeli.co.uk; L only; no Amex.*

The Lime Tree £49 454
8 Lapwing Ln M20 2WS (0161) 445 1217
"A favourite of pretty much everybody that's ever been!" – this formidable Didsbury brasserie "never lets you down", not least the "consistently great" service. "You could eat here every week – there's nothing too fancy or clever, and the menu would suit your maiden aunt as well as your new lover." / **Details:** *www.thelimetreerestaurant.co.uk; 10 pm; closed Mon L & Sat L.*

Manchester House £90 444
18-22 Bridge St M3 3BZ (0161) 835 2557
"Don't let its slightly gimmicky reputation put you off!" This year-old, "blingy" office block venture – with "trendy 12th-floor cocktail lounge (limited views)" and "glam industrial-chic" 2nd-floor restaurant (complete with open kitchen) – is "very professional", "very classy", and Aiden Byrnes's "ornate" cuisine is seriously "accomplished". That all said, it can still seem a bit "forced", not helped by the punishing "London prices". / **Details:** *www.manchesterhouse.uk.com; 9.30 pm; closed Mon.*

Michael Caines ABode Hotel £68 343
107 Piccadilly M1 2DB (0161) 247 7744
Despite its "strange setting in a basement", this well-established venue, by Piccadilly Station, wins lots of praise for its "sublime" food ("even the cheapie 3-course option was top-notch") and "professional but friendly service", which "combine to make a memorable occasion". Its ratings are capped though by minority reports of an "off-night". / **Details:** *www.abodemanchester.co.uk/michael-caines-dining michael-caines-restaurantswww.abodemanchester.co.uk michael-caines-dining/michael-caines-restaurants; 10 pm; closed Mon & Sun; no shorts or football colours.* **Accommodation:** *61 rooms, from £79*

Mr Cooper's House & Garden The Midland Hotel £50 333
Peter St M60 2DS (0161) 236 3333
Simon Rogan's more accessible brasserie – "perhaps the airiest restaurant in town, with massively high ceilings, a light cool interior, that all-important bar to achieve success in Manchester" (and even complete with its own tree!) – put in a more mixed performance this year. To most reporters it's "another triumph for Mr R" – a "fantastic space" with "world-class" cooking. There were more critics though for whom "high hopes were somewhat dashed", with gripes about "minute portions", and "restaurant-in-a-hotel-syndrome". / **Details:** *www.mrcoopershouseandgarden.co.uk; 10 pm, Sun 8 pm.*

Mughli £30 432
30 Wilmslow Rd M14 5TQ (01612) 480900
An upmarket Indian "offering something a little different, with a menu of street food alongside more normal stuff"; fans say it's "a world away from the usual Curry Mile fare" right down to the "special gin list". / **Details:** *www.mughli.com.*

Piccolino £49 333
8 Clarence St M2 4DW (0161) 835 9860
A "stylish", "light and airy" Italian brasserie, close to the Town Hall, which offers "consistently good food and drink"; it still "manages to be individual" despite being part of a chain. / **Details:** *www.individualrestaurants.com; 11 pm, Sun 10 pm.*

Red Chilli £39 422
70-72 Portland St M1 4GU (0161) 236 2888
"Still probably the the best cheap lunch in Chinatown"; "get there early enough for the Beijing dumplings!" / **Details:** *www.redchillirestaurant.co.uk; 11 pm, Fri & Sat midnight; closed Mon; need 6+ to book.*

Rose Garden £44 553
218 Burton Rd M20 2LW (0161) 478 0747
*William Mills's "white, minimalist" restaurant "goes from strength to strength" with its "consistently exquisite" and "always inventive" dishes. "The pricing is very fair for the reward of eating so well, with good wines sourced from the local independent wine merchant". / **Details:** www.therosegardendidsbury.com; 9 pm, Fri & Sat 10 pm, Sun 8.30 pm; no Amex.*

Rosso £67 324
43 Spring Gdns M2 2BG (0161) 8321400
*A "lovely historic setting" (a former bank at the top of a popular shopping street) is the highlight of a visit to Rio Ferdinand's "relaxed", rather glitzy, Italian. It can seem overpriced and disappointing, but wins consistent praise from those who opt for the "very good-value" set lunch. / **Details:** www.rossorestaurants.com; 10 pm; closed Sun.*

Sam's Chop House £45 223
Back Pool Fold, Chapel Walks M2 1HN
(0161) 834 3210
*"Ideal if you want filling up on a cold winter's day or night"; this "lovely, atmospheric" room "does British classics well and feels like a proper Victorian chop house"... "I would say the corned beef hash is to die for, but given the number of calories, perhaps it literally is!" / **Details:** www.samschophouse.com; 9.30 pm, Sat 10.30 pm, Sun 8 pm.*

San Carlo £42 324
40 King Street West M3 2WY
(0161) 834 6226
*"Blingy, glitzy, big and brash" – this "glam", "c'lebby" footballer haunt remains "one of Manchester's hotspots" and is "always busy and vibrant". OK, it's arguably "overpriced", and "at its rare worst, service can be uncomprehending and unresponsive", but other staff are "super", "it feels special", and the "large Italian menu" is realised "without messing about with the finest ingredients". / **Details:** www.sancarlo.co.uk; 11 pm.*

San Carlo Cicchetti £48 334
42 King Street West M3 2QG
(0161) 839 2233
*There's an "exciting buzz about this San Carlo small-plates operation", oddly located on the ground floor of House of Fraser. "Seafood is a real strength" but it also does "outstanding breakfasts" – just "go early", as it's "always full to capacity by one o'clock"! / **Details:** www.sancarlocicchetti.co.uk; 11 pm, Sun 10 pm.*

Siam Smiles £28 421
48a George St M1 4HF (0161) 237 1555
*A new basement Chinatown Thai that's "effectively part of an Asian supermarket", but where the ex-solicitor owner's "sensational" food comes "pretty close to sitting in a Bangkok roadside caff!"; "watch out", though, "the Thais like it hot, and it is VERY hot"! / **Details:** www.facebook.com/SiamSmilesCafe; 7.30 pm, Fri & Sat 9.30 pm.*

63 Degrees £70 333
20 Church St M4 1PN (0161) 832 5438
*"They take their ingredients and cooking very seriously" at the Moreau family's Northern Quarter Gallic restaurant, and the results from the "nicely judged tasting menus" can be "simply fabulous"; the "fascinating" French wine list also attracts praise. / **Details:** www.63degrees.co.uk; 10.30 pm, Fri 11 pm; closed Mon & Sun.*

Solita £41 333
37 Turner St M4 1DW (0161) 839 2200
*"Known for, but not limited to their burgers" (there's also "amazing fried chicken" for instance) – "there's some solid culinary expertise behind the hipsterish-ness" of this "friendly" Northern Quarter hang-out. Boosted by its "incessant social media presence", there are also now branches in Didsbury, and Prestwich. / **Details:** www.solita.co.uk; 10 pm, Fri-Sat 11 pm, Sun 9 pm.*

Tai Pan £35 432
81-97 Upper Brook St M13 9TX
(0161) 273 2798
*"Always full-to-bursting with local Chinese families", the atmosphere is "busy and loud" at this "huge warehouse-like building" in Longsight. "Food and flavours are the dominant attraction" – particularly the "excellent" dim sum; service is "efficient" but "without fuss". / **Details:** 10.30 pm, Sun 9.30 pm.*

Tampopo £32 333
16 Albert Sq M2 5PF (0161) 819 1966
*"Still the best for quick and tasty Asian street food" – the "always impressive" HQ of a local mini-empire that "easily outdoes the larger chains" with its "canteen-style" eating and "interesting" SE Asian beers. / **Details:** www.tampopo.co.uk; 11 pm, Sun 10 pm; need 7+ to book.*

Thaikhun £38 434
Unit 17, 3 Hardmen St M3 3HF
(0161) 819 2065
*A "fantastic" new Spinningfields Thai (the flagship of an already four-strong UK chain) with a "fabulous" street-market-style setting; the food – "delicious soups, stir fries and curries" – "isn't half bad either!"; just "don't expect peace and quiet!" / **Details:** thaikhun.co.uk/; 10 pm.*

This & That £12 521
3 Soap St M4 1EW (0161) 832 4971
*"Down a slightly dodgy Northern Quarter sidestreet", it's "well worth seeking out" the "best Indian greasy spoon around!"; when it comes to curry, its flavours could "sink a ship", and the "cost is ridiculously cheap". Top Menu Tip – go for the 'Rice and Three'. / **Details:** www.thisandthatcafe.co.uk; 4 pm, Fri & Sat 8 pm; closed Mon D, Tue D, Wed D, Thu D & Sun D; no credit cards.*

Whitworth Art Gallery £22 425
The University of Manchester, Oxford Rd M15 6ER (01612) 757497
*"An airy, glass-walled café floating above the park" provides "a gorgeous space (especially when bathed in sunlight)" for the new dining room of the recently reopened Whitworth Gallery. Fans also hail its "delicious, fresh salads, soup, etc", and though there are some niggles in early feedback, it appears "worth a visit". / **Details:** www.whitworth.manchester.ac.uk/visit/foodanddrink/; 5 pm, Thu-Sat 9.30 pm, Sun 7 pm; closed Mon D, Tue D & Wed D; book D only.*

Wing's £50 455
1 Lincoln Sq M2 5LN (0161) 834 9000
*This "always brilliant" city-centre spot is "still the best Chinese dining experience in Manchester" for its large fan club, for whom it's "overtaken The Yang Sing"; there are "lots of interesting people to see", too (if you like rubbernecking Man U footballers and their WAGS)! / **Details:** www.wingsrestaurant.co.uk; 11.30 pm, Sun 10.30 pm; closed Sat L; children: 11+ after 8 pm Mon-Fri.*

Yang Sing £42 522
34 Princess St M1 4JY (0161) 236 2200
*"Still the best in Manchester (and very probably further afield)" – the Yeung family's vast Chinatown beacon (est. 1977) remains one of the UK's top Chinese destinations, and its "joyous" dim sum is particularly notable for its "gorgeous delicacy and refinement of flavour". Even one long-term observer who feels this "not amazing-looking, but comfortable place" is "currently on one of its recurring downswings" still thinks it nothing short of "brilliant". Top Tip – "the banquets are especially good – tell the staff what you do/don't like and let them take care of the order..." / **Details:** www.yang-sing.com; 11.30 pm, Fri 11.45 pm, Sat 12.15 am, Sun 10.30 pm.*

Yuzu £39 542
39 Faulkner St M1 4EE (0161) 236 4159
*"Several notches above your average Japanese" – this "simple" and "very approachable" year-old diner in Chinatown (decked out with a "wooden interior") is proving a "very happy" addition to Manchester. "By not serving sushi, they achieve a Zen-like focus on doing other things well, and boy do they succeed", with "spectacularly good tempura" and other dishes (such as noodles and dumplings). "It's worth going just to see how good rice can be!" / **Details:** www.yuzumanchester.co.uk; 9.30 pm; closed Mon & Sun.*

MANNINGTREE, ESSEX 3–2C

Lucca Enoteca £38 443
39-43 High St CO11 1AH (01206) 390044
*Pizzas with a "really distinctive herby flavour" are the highlight at this "outstanding" Italian, from the owners of the Mistley Thorn nearby; locals say it's "increasingly difficult to get a good table" – perhaps because Londonites now know it's "well worth the train ride for lunch". / **Details:** www.luccafoods.co.uk; 9.30 pm, Fri & Sat 10 pm; no Amex.*

MARAZION, CORNWALL 1–4A

Ben's Cornish Kitchen £48 543
West End TR17 0EL (01736) 719200
*No let-up in the raves for this "brilliant little" seaside bistro with "fabulous views"; chef Ben Prior uses local produce to "deliver dishes with flair, invention and great flavours", and wins especial praise for "his incredible skill with fish". / **Details:** www.benscornishkitchen.com; 8.15 pm; closed Mon & Sun.*

MARGATE, KENT 3–3D

The Ambrette £46 433
44 King St CT9 1QE (01843) 231 504
*With its "clever spicing not chilli spicing", the "stunning fusion of western and Indian tastes" continues to wow most who report on Dev Biswal's original venture – "a real surprise" given how "unassuming-looking" its exterior is. "Perhaps it's slipped a fraction since he opened his third place in Canterbury, but it's still very good". / **Details:** www.theambrette.co.uk; 9.30 pm, Fri & Sat 10 pm.*

GB Pizza £30 443
14a Marine Drive CT9 1DH (01843) 297 700
*"The best pizza in Kent" – "proper Italian not Yankee-style with yummy thin crisp-baked base and original toppings" – wins love for this basic, seafront spot (which enjoys fine views). / **Details:** www.greatbritishpizzacompany.wordpress.com; 9.30 pm; closed Sun D.*

The Greedy Cow £14 443
3 Market Pl CT9 1ER (01843) 447557
*In the quaint Old Town, this "shabby chic" café is a "cheap 'n' cheerful" sort of place that's particularly rated for its "great burgers" and good breakfasts. / **Details:** www.thegreedycow.com/; 4 pm, Sat 5 pm; closed Mon, Tue D, Wed D, Thu D, Fri D, Sat D & Sun D.*

Turl Street Kitchen, Oxford

The French Restaurant, Manchester

The Vaults and Garden Cafe, Oxford

Yama's Thai Eaterie £28 432
121 High St CT9 1JT (01843) 229899
A "tiny BYO café" on the High Street with a "busy, fun atmosphere"; its rather unusual mix of "Thai home-cooking in the evening and English home-cooking in the daytime" is a real winner – "we were surprised to find such amazing Asian food on our doorstep!" / **Details:** *www.yamasthaieaterie.co.uk; 10 pm.*

MARLBOROUGH, WILTSHIRE 2–2C

The Harrow at Little Bedwyn £78 554
Little Bedwyn SN8 3JP (01672) 870871
"I'm not sure how it is possible to pop so much flavour into every dish but Roger Jones does it every time!" at his and wife Sue's "warmly welcoming foodie paradise in the middle of nowhere". A rival attraction to the fine cuisine is the "amazing wine list, with fabulous bins from the New World in particular". / **Details:** *www.theharrowatlittlebedwyn.co.uk; 9 pm; closed Mon, Tue & Sun; no trainers.*

MARLOW, BUCKINGHAMSHIRE 3–3A

The Coach £42 444
3 West St SL7 2LS awaiting tel
"Thanks Tom Kerridge" – his new gastropub may offer "uncomplicated" cooking, but the realisation is "spot on" and on practically all accounts its proving "a brilliant new addition to the local food scene". "They don't take bookings, so get there early!" / **Details:** *www.thecoachmarlow.co.uk; 10.30 pm, Sun 9 pm.*

Hand & Flowers £80 433
West St SL7 2BP (01628) 482277
"Tom Kerridge never fails to deliver", according to the armies of fans of his famous, Thames-valley phenomenon (which – notwithstanding its "relaxed", "cosy" and "buzzy" vibe – is sufficiently ambitious it's "hardly a pub" nowadays). But while his "fine-dining-comfort-food" is undoubtedly "spectacular", the place still strikes some folk as "unjustifiably hyped" due to Michelin's "bemusing" award of not one but two stars. Whatever the correct level of guide-book-esteem, shortage of custom is not a problem – "it's a nightmare to book", and "even the extension does little to reduce the over-crowding!" / **Details:** *www.thehandandflowers.co.uk; 9.30 pm; closed Sun D.* **Accommodation:** *4 rooms, from £140*

Marlow Bar & Grill £52 333
92-94 High St SL7 1AQ (01628) 488544
An "excellent-value" town-centre spot combining "good food and a buzzy atmosphere". Even the harshest reporter – who feels "there's so much more competition in town, it needs to do something a bit different" – says it's "still a favourite". / **Details:** *www.therestaurantbarandgrill.co.uk; towards the river end of the High Street; 11 pm, Sun 10.30 pm.*

The Royal Oak £67 323
Frieth Rd, Bovingdon Grn SL7 2JF
(01628) 488611
A "convivial" pub with a garden offering "lovingly presented" food that "supports local butchers etc."; service can be "variable", though, and more than one reporter is "kept at bay" by "near fine dining" prices. / **Details:** *www.royaloakmarlow.co.uk; 9.30 pm, Fri & Sat 10 pm.*

Sindhu Macdonald Compleat Angler Hotel £63 332
Marlow Bridge Ln SL7 1RG (01628) 405 405
Atul Kochar's new régime at this very traditional Thames Valley landmark (with "lovely views over the river") is yet another sign of Indian cuisine's emergence as a 'fine dining' option. However his team's initial performance here is something of a "Curate's Egg". What is a "great venue" to fans is too "sterile" and "quiet" to doubters, service varies from "properly professional" to "shambolic", and food that to critics seems "truly dreadful and expensive", to fans is utterly "inspired" ("a veritable riot of colours and spicy palate-provoking flavours, embellished with telling textures and all masterfully executed!!") / **Details:** *www.sindhurestaurant.co.uk; 10 pm, Sun 3 pm.*

The Vanilla Pod £66 543
31 West St SL7 2LS (01628) 898101
It is "so small", but – on most accounts – Michael Macdonald's well-established venture is "perfectly formed", with a "lovely" atmosphere. The big deal though, is his "wonderful, seasonal cooking" – it's "the epitome of consistent quality", and "every course is a delight". / **Details:** *www.thevanillapod.co.uk; 10 pm; closed Mon & Sun.*

MASHAM, NORTH YORKSHIRE 8–4B

Black Sheep Brewery Bistro £36 343
Wellgarth HG4 4EN (01765) 680101
An "atmospheric and bustling" café "in the famous brewery where you can also have a tour!"; its fans say "you cannot go wrong with a simple menu focusing on what it does best – hearty fare based around beer..." / **Details:** *www.blacksheepbrewery.com; 9 pm; Sun-Wed L only, Thu-Sat L & D; no Amex.*

Samuel's Swinton Park Hotel & Spa £78 445
HG4 4JH (01765) 680900
A "wonderful dining room in a lovely country house hotel", where chef Stephen Bulmer's menu is

"always interesting" and his cooking never less than "good". / **Details:** www.swintonpark.com; 9.30 pm; closed weekday L; no jeans or trainers; booking: max 8; children: 8+ at D. **Accommodation:** 31 rooms, from £185

MELBOURNE, DERBYSHIRE 5–3C

Bay Tree £50 333

4 Potter St DE73 8HW (01332) 863358

This family-run veteran was "always good" but now, under a new regime, it's "superb", say fans; it offers an "imaginative, varied" menu at a "wonderful set price", with the champagne breakfasts, as ever, a highlight. / **Details:** www.baytreerestaurant.co.uk; 9.30 pm; closed Mon, Tue & Sun D.

MELLS, SOMERSET 2–3B

The Talbot Inn £45 334

Selwood St BA11 3PN (01373) 812254

TV chef James Martin's "lovely village inn" combines a "well-run country restaurant" with a grill house occupying a "large and splendid converted barn". The food "can vary" on occasion, but is "unusually good" overall, and staff seem to "care about the business" too. / **Details:** www.talbotinn.com; 9.30 pm.

MENAI BRIDGE, GWYNEDD 4–1C

Dylan's Restaurant £43 333

St George's Rd LL59 5EY (01248) 716 714

"Best in Menai Bridge" is perhaps a slightly double-edged compliment, but "pizza is only part of the excellent menu" at this casual all-day operation, with "fabulous views" over the Menai Straits. / **Details:** www.dylansrestaurant.co.uk; 11 pm.

Sosban And The Old Butchers £62 544

1 High St, Menai Bridge LL59 5EE
(01248) 208131

"In an old butcher's shop with charming antique tiles on the walls", a husband-and-wife-run venture where "chef decides what you eat", resulting in something of a "culinary magical mystery tour"; its tiny fan club hails "exquisite" results, and just "can't believe it isn't getting rave reviews everywhere"! / **Details:** www.sosbanandtheoldbutchers.com/; Thu-Sat midnight.

MILFORD-ON-SEA, HAMPSHIRE 2–4C

La Perle £47 433

Lymington SO41 0QD (01590) 643 557

In this pretty seaside village, a "small" but "attractive" bistro where head chef Lionel Sené turns out "very good French food". / **Details:** www.laperlemilford.co.uk; 9 pm; closed Mon L & Sun.

Verveine Fishmarket Restaurant £60 532

98 High St SO41 0QE (01590) 642 176

Overlooked by many guides, Chef/patron David Wykes deserves much greater recognition for his "stand out" (if "loud and crowded") five-year-old venture, behind a fishmonger. The menu can sound "funny and Wonka-inspired", but "wow!" – "a huge range of fish" is "perfectly prepared" and "exquisitely presented" as part of "imaginative" dishes showing "real innovation and skill". / **Details:** www.verveine.co.uk; 9.30 pm; closed Mon & Sun; no Amex.

MILTON KEYNES, BUCKINGHAMSHIRE 3–2A

Jaipur £36 433

599 Grafton Gate East MK9 1AT
(01908) 669796

This vast, purpose-built landmark near the railway station has had its ups-and-downs this year (having been re-purchased by an original owner from the liquidators in January 2015). It doesn't seem to have affected the grub though, which was consistently highly rated this year. / **Details:** www.jaipur.co.uk; 11.30 pm, Sun 10.30 pm; no shorts.

MINSTER, KENT 3–3D

Corner House £48 432

42 Station Rd CT12 4BZ (01843) 823000

"One to watch" – a "relatively new enterprise" (est 2013) in this historic village helmed by Kentish chef Matt Sworder, who worked under Gordon Ramsay; its menu of British sharing plates contains "a few gems" with the "use of fresh local produce being noticeable". / **Details:** www.thecornerhouseminster.co.uk/; 9.30 pm; closed Sun D.

MISTLEY, ESSEX 3–2D

The Mistley Thorn Hotel £49 443

High St CO11 1HE (01206) 392 821

Built on a site associated with the grisly deeds of Matthew Hopkins, the Witchfinder General, this is now a "very popular" gastropub-with-rooms, where Sherri Singleton produces "excellent" and "good-value" dishes, particularly fish. / **Details:** www.mistleythorn.com; 9.30 pm; no Amex. **Accommodation:** 11 rooms, from £100

MITTON, LANCASHIRE 5–1B

Aspinall Arms £44 333

Mitton Rd BB7 9PQ (01254) 826555

"With a river running by", a "lovely" country pub with "views of the Ribble Valley", which has

"kept its individuality" since acquisition by the Brunning & Price chain in 2014 (and has also benefited from a makeover). "You get plenty of choice on the menu front and in summer they also do BBQs in the garden". / ***Details:*** *www.brunningandprice.co.uk/aspinallarms/; 10 pm, Sun 9.30 pm.*

MOLD, FLINTSHIRE 5–2A

Glasfryn **£44** 2 2 3
Raikes Ln CH7 6LR (01352) 750500
This "large" Brunning & Price gastropub, with panoramic town views, puts in the very solid performance that's typical of the group's characterful venues, and serves a good variety of food; handy for Theatr Clywd too.
/ ***Details***: *www.brunningandprice.co.uk/glasfryn/; 9.30 pm, Sun 9 pm.*

MONTGOMERY, POWYS 5–4A

Checkers **£64** 5 5 4
Broad St, Powys SY15 6PN (01686) 669 822
"Sublime" food and "lovely accommodation in a picture-postcard setting" make Stéphane Borie & Sarah Francis's "faultless" restaurant-with-rooms a "wonderful place for a weekend away". Top Menu Tip – "probably the best soufflés in the UK!" / ***Details:*** *www.thecheckersmontgomery.co.uk; 9 pm; closed Mon, Tue L, Wed L, Thu L & Sun; no Amex; children: 8+ at D.*
Accommodation: *5 rooms, from £125*

MORECAMBE, LANCASHIRE 5–1A

Midland Hotel English Lakes hotels and venues **£52** 4 4 4
Marine Road west LA4 4BU (01524) 424000
A setting "overlooking Morecambe Bay with the lakes in the background takes some beating" at this "lovely" Art Deco hotel-restaurant. The cooking has traditionally played something of a supporting role, but some reporters are "surprised how good it is". / ***Details:*** *www.englishlakes.co.uk; 9.30 pm.*
Accommodation: *44 rooms, from £94*

MORETON-IN-MARSH, GLOUCESTERSHIRE 2–1C

Horse & Groom **£52** 4 4 4
Upper Oddington GL56 0XH (01451) 830584
A "rustic" venue offering "well-cooked" food, "excellent wines" and "a rare atmosphere of happiness"; "only thing is, it's so popular that parking can be a problem". / ***Details:*** *www.horseandgroom.uk.com; 9 pm; no Amex.*
Accommodation: *7 rooms, from £89*

MORSTON, NORFOLK 6–3C

Morston Hall **£94** 3 3 4
Main Coast Rd NR25 7AA (01263) 741041
"A meal is always a special occasion", say fans of the "spacious and pleasant dining conservatory" of Galton Blackiston's country house hotel, near the coast, lauding the "fantastic tasting menu and gorgeous setting". Not everyone is keen on the one-sitting approach however, and sceptics find the cuisine "too ambitious for its own good".
/ ***Details:*** *www.morstonhall.com; between Blakeney & Wells on A149; 8 pm; D only, ex Sun open L & D.*
Accommodation: *13 rooms, from £330*

MOULSFORD, OXFORDSHIRE 2–2D

The Beetle & Wedge Boathouse **£51** 2 3 4
Ferry Ln OX10 9JF (01491) 651381
This rather "romantic" ex-boathouse-turned-rôtisserie has a "beautiful setting on the Thames" (the inspiration for Wind in the Willows no less); it serves some "lovely" dishes, which – if perhaps "slightly overpriced" – come in "hefty" portions.
/ ***Details:*** *www.beetleandwedge.co.uk; on A329 between Streatley & Wallingford, take Ferry Lane at crossroads; 8.45 pm.* ***Accommodation:*** *3 rooms, from £90*

MOULTON, CAMBRIDGESHIRE 3–1C

The Packhorse Inn **£50** 2 2 4
Bridge St CB8 8SP (01638) 751818
A "very smart" gastropub-with-rooms in a "delightful unspoilt village"; the food garners many plaudits too, but there are quite a few accusations too of a "touch of style over substance".
/ ***Details***: *www.packhorseinn.com; 10 pm.*

MOULTON, NORTH YORKSHIRE 8–3B

Black Bull **£48** 5 3 3
DL10 6QJ (01325) 377289
Thanks to an "imaginative redevelopment" by new owners the Provenance Group, this famous pub ("in a peaceful country setting" handy for the A1) has (after a long period of closure) been revivified as "a great blend of traditional pub and contemporary restaurant"; it offers "dishes to suit all tastes" and they're "very competent". / ***Details:*** *www.blackbullmoulton.com; 1m S of Scotch Corner; 9.30 pm, Sun 8.30 pm.*

MOUSEHOLE, CORNWALL 1–4A

Old Coastguard Hotel £44 324

TR19 6PR (01736) 731222

"A great place to unwind"; now under the management of the Gurnards Head team, this "very relaxed" hotel dining room, with fantastic sea views, continues to please with its "great" fish-centric menu; "the dinner, bed and breakfast deals are especially good value". / ***Details:*** *www.oldcoastguardhotel.co.uk; 9.30 pm.* ***Accommodation:*** *20 rooms, from £170*

MUCH WENLOCK, SHROPSHIRE 5–4B

The Raven Hotel & Restaurant £59 453

Barrow St TF13 6EN (01952) 727251

"A great find"; just off the M3, this "relaxed and cosy" ivy-covered inn offers a "really good" welcome and "very innovative" five- or seven-course tasting menus which, being "served without a menu", come as a "delicious surprise". / ***Details:*** *www.ravenhotel.com; 9 pm, Sun 8.30 pm.* ***Accommodation:*** *14 rooms, from £110*

MURCOTT, OXFORDSHIRE 2–1D

The Nut Tree Inn £65 434

Main St OX5 2RE (01865) 331253

Michael North and Imogen Young's "very handsome" thatched country pub has a "pleasant rural location" and "oozes intimacy", and makes a "stylish but totally unpretentious" destination for some "brilliant", "high quality" cooking. / ***Details:*** *www.nuttreeinn.co.uk; 9 pm, Sun 3 pm.*

MUTHILL, PERTH AND KINROSS 9–3C

Barley Bree £62 444

6 Willoughby St PH5 2AB (01764) 681451

"Well worth a visit if you're in the vicinity" (about 10 minutes from Gleneagles) – this "charming hotel/restaurant" has a "cosy and intimate dining room (with a snug for pre-dinner drinks)". Chef/patron, Fabrice Bouteloup, provides "adventurous" cuisine, with many dishes featuring "an explosion of different flavours". / ***Details:*** *www.barleybree.com; 9 pm Wed-Sat, 7.30pm Sun; closed Mon & Tue; no Amex.* ***Accommodation:*** *6 rooms, from £110*

NAILSWORTH, GLOUCESTERSHIRE 2–2B

Wild Garlic £51 443

3 Cossacks Sq GL6 0DB (01453) 832615

A diminutive restaurant-with-rooms that's "trying very hard" and mostly succeeding, owing to Matthew Beardshall's "good ideas and ingredients" (including the eponymous one); they're "now doing tapas too". / ***Details:*** *www.wild-garlic.co.uk; 9.30 pm, Sun 2.30 pm; closed Mon, Tue & Sun D; no Amex.* ***Accommodation:*** *3 rooms, from £90*

NANT-Y-DERRY, MONMOUTHSHIRE 2–2A

The Foxhunter £43

NP7 9DN (01873) 881101

TV-chef Matt Tebbutt has moved on from this remote village restaurant-with-rooms, which was re-opened in February 2015 by Sue and Alan Long, plus chef John who worked with Matt for 12 years. Not many reports yet on the new regime, hence we've left it un-rated. / ***Details:*** *www.foxhunterinn.com; 9.30 pm; closed Mon & Sun D.* ***Accommodation:*** *2 cottages rooms, from £155*

NANTGAREDIG, CARMARTHENSHIRE 4–4C

Y Polyn £45 444

Capel Dewi SA32 7LH (01267) 290000

"A unique venture in an old toll house in vaguely rural Wales" (and close to the National Botanic Garden); the atmosphere is "comforting", "they pay loads of attention to cooking extremely good local meat and fish" and "service is unfailingly cheerful". / ***Details:*** *www.ypolyn.co.uk; 9 pm; closed Mon & Sun D.*

NETHER BURROW, CUMBRIA 7–4D

The Highwayman £44 334

LA6 2RJ (01524) 273338

"Great food at sensible prices" maintains the "consistently high standards" of this Ribble Valley Inn, which receives an all-round thumbs-up from (nearly) all reporters. / ***Details:*** *www.highwaymaninn.co.uk; 8.30 pm, Fri & Sat 9 pm, Sun 8 pm.*

NETHER WESTCOTE, OXFORDSHIRE 2–1C

The Feathered Nest Inn £67 445

OX7 6SD (01993) 833 030

"The setting and views are fabulous", at this Cotswolds gastropub, especially if you are lucky with the weather and sit outside. The "wonderful", "restaurant-standard" cooking and great wine list contribute to an all-round "first-class experience" (although "fussy" service can occasionally grate). / ***Details:*** *www.thefeatherednestinn.co.uk; 9.15 pm; closed Mon & Sun D.* ***Accommodation:*** *4 rooms, from £150*

NEW MILTON, HAMPSHIRE 2–4C

Vetiver Chewton Glen £88 333

Chewton Glen Rd BH23 5QL (01425) 275341

Few venues equal the grandeur of this "magnificent country house hotel", set in "well-manicured g rounds" on the edge of the New Forest. The themes in feedback on its dining room have been very consistent over the years – what is "an excellent experience in every respect" for fans (most notably the "spectacular wine list") is – to sceptics – "far too expensive". / **Details:** www.chewtonglen.com; on A337 between New Milton & Highcliffe; 10 pm. **Accommodation:** 70 rooms, from £310

NEWARK, NOTTINGHAMSHIRE 5–3D

Farndon Boathouse £43 234
5 N End NG24 3SX (01636) 676578
*A "fun and lively" restaurant, "overlooking the River Trent", where there's some "lovely" food to be had; an added boon is free live music every Sunday night. / **Details:** www.farndonboathouse.co.uk; 9.30 pm, Sun 8 pm.*

Koinonia £34 443
19 St Marks Ln NG24 1XS (01636) 706230
*"If you like authentic Keralan food make a beeline for Koinonia" – "the best place to eat in Newark by a country mile". The "multi-layered flavours and textures" of dishes (ranging "from the mild to the incendiary") and "warmly welcoming service", "more than compensate for the out-of-the-way location", and veggies are unusually well catered for. / **Details:** www.koinoniarestaurant.com; 11 pm, Sat 11.30 pm, Sun 7.30 pm.*

NEWBURY, BERKSHIRE 2–2D

The Crab & Boar £56 312
Wantage Rd RG20 8UE (01635) 247550
*In a "lovely" setting, this "seafood gastropub" wins applause for its "excellent, fresh fish, imaginatively presented". Not for the first time however, some reporters found "the experience a let down" on account of "chaotic" and "uncaring" service. / **Details:** www.crabandboar.com; M4 J13 to B4494 – 0.5 mile on right; 9.30 pm. **Accommodation:** 14 rooms, from £90*

Woodspeen £60 544
Lambourn Rd RG20 8BM (01635) 265070
*"Brilliant, brilliant, brilliant!"; in a "glorious renovated barn", John Campbell's "really interesting", "Scandi-ish" yearling (and adjoining cookery school) wins raves for its "superb" food and "very special wine list"; it's clearly "aiming for fine dining accolades" and more than one fan is "sure it won't be long". / **Details:** www.thewoodspeen.com/; 9.30 pm, Sun 4 pm; closed Mon.*

NEWCASTLE UPON TYNE, TYNE AND WEAR 8–2B

Artisan The Biscuit Factory £51 432
Stoddard St NE2 1AN (0191) 260 5411
*Despite its location in The Biscuit Gallery, David Kennedy's recently rechristened venture "doesn't feel like a café attached to an art gallery, but more like a 'proper' restaurant"; it attracts nothing but praise for its "well-cooked, inventive food" and reporters are "big fans of the 'Fish Friday' set menu", too. / **Details:** www.artisannewcastle.com; 9 pm, Fri & Sat 9.30 pm; closed Sun D.*

Blackfriars Restaurant £49 325
Friars St NE1 4XN (0191) 261 5945
*"A tranquil setting in the heart of the city" (a cloistered, atmospheric ancient building dating from 1239) is the special feature of this "romantic" venue – "a champion of local produce and local ales". / **Details:** www.blackfriarsrestaurant.co.uk; 10 pm; closed Sun D.*

Broad Chare £42 345
25 Broad Chare NE1 3DQ (019) 1211 2144
*Terry Laybourne has scored another home run with his Quayside venture – "everything a pub should be". There's a "fantastic atmosphere", staff are "very professional", there's a "magnificent beer list", and the kitchen delivers "a superb take on classic British dishes". / **Details:** www.thebroadchare.co.uk; 10 pm; closed Sun D; no Amex.*

Café 21 £50 454
Trinity Gdns NE1 2HH (0191) 222 0755
*That it "can be very noisy at peak times" is testament to the "consistently excellent" standards of Terry Laybourne's "Newcastle benchmark" – the city's most popular eaterie for well over a decade. It offers a "classic brasserie menu", whose "great execution lifts it beyond expectations". / **Details:** www.cafetwentyone.co.uk; 10.30 pm, Sun 8 pm.*

Café Royal £45 333
8 Nelson St NE1 5AW (0191) 231 3000
*"On track again after the revamp", this "very crowded" grand café, by Grainger Market, attracts particular praise for its "tasty breakfasts" – a "cut above the usual café fare" – and as a pitstop for coffee, plus a "lovely" selection of cakes. / **Details:** www.sjf.co.uk/our-pubs/cafe-royal/; 6 pm, Sun 4 pm; L only; no booking, Sat.*

Caffé Vivo £40 332
29 Broad Chare NE1 3DQ (0191) 232 1331
*The food at Terry Laybourne's "small and cramped" restaurant has taken a "real jump in quality" under the new chef, "particularly now the emphasis is more on Italian food". / **Details:** www.caffevivo.co.uk; 10 pm; closed Sun.*

Dabbawal £36 434
69-75 High Bridge NE1 6BX (0191) 232 5133
A menu of "different", street-style food has helped make this "unusual", contemporary subcontinental, near the Theatre Royal, the city's most popular Indian recommendation – "it's always busy". Limited but highly enthusiastic feedback on its Jesmond sibling too. / **Details:** *www.dabbawal.com; 10.30 pm; closed Sun.*

Francesca's £35 344
Manor House Rd NE2 2NE (0191) 281 6586
An "always reliable" Jesmond institution that makes a handy "cheap 'n' cheerful" pitstop, including for pizza. / **Details:** *9.30 pm; closed Sun; no Amex; no booking.*

House of Tides £69 333
28-30 The Close NE1 3RF (0191) 2303720
Mixed feedback this year on Kenny Atkinson's ambitious yearling, well-located "in an old building on the Quayside". Many reports applaud its "innovative tasting menus" (not always available) and "top quality cooking", but quite a number were "disappointed" generally, including by "overworked" cuisine. / **Details:** *www.houseoftides.co.uk; Tue-Thu 9.30 pm, Fri & Sat 10 pm; closed Mon, Tue L & Sun.*

Jesmond Dene House £74 234
Jesmond Dene Rd NE2 2EY (0191) 212 6066
Unusually mixed feedback of late for Terry Laybourne's boutique hotel venture in a wooded gorge ("a great escape within a city"). Whilst it's still a "tasteful venue for a special occasion" (if you ignore the occasional visit of the "brassy Geordie lassie" set), more than one reporter found the food "outrageously disappointing" – hopefully just a blip. / **Details:** *www.jesmonddenehouse.co.uk; 9.30 pm.* **Accommodation:** *40 rooms, from £120*

Lezzes £32 333
Front St, Four Lane End NE7 7XF
(01912) 66 2777
It may look unprepossessing from the outside, but this Turkish restaurant has won a small but dedicated fan base with its "extensive" and "good value" menu including "excellent" mezze; an extension was in the offing in late 2015. / **Details:** *www.lezzetrestaurant.co.uk; 11 pm.*

Osaka £27 433
69 Grey St NE1 6EF (0191) 2615300
"What a delight" – this "surprisingly good Japanese" serves an "excellent range of dishes" with "some very good and very varied sushi options"; it's "opposite the Theatre Royal, so good for a pre-show dinner". / **Details:** *www.osakanewcastle.co.uk; 10 pm, Fri & Sat 10.15 pm.*

Pani's £31 354
61-65 High Bridge NE1 6BX (0191) 232 4366
"So much better than other Italian Johnny (Giovanni?)-come-latelies" – this "always fun" institution of 20+ years's standing continues to combine "incredibly good-value" Sardinian fare with particularly "lovely" service and an "always lively (if rather loud)" style. / **Details:** *www.paniscafe.co.uk; 10 pm; closed Sun; no Amex; no booking at L.*

Paradiso £41 244
1 Market Ln NE1 6QQ (0191) 221 1240
"Like a local restaurant in Italy where you are always remembered and welcomed, but in the heart of the city!" – and one with an "amazingly friendly reception for kids". "Reliable" food (with pizza a recent menu addition) adds to the "enjoyable" all-round experience. "Fab balcony out back." / **Details:** *www.paradiso.co.uk; 10.30 pm, Fri & Sat 10.45 pm; closed Sun.*

Peace & Loaf £56 434
217 Jesmond Rd NE2 1LA (0191) 281 5222
"Very clever food" that's "expertly cooked" (if in "small portions") has established this "innovative" and "lively" three-year-old – which occupies quite a funky-looking split-level space – as one of the city's most interesting culinary arrivals of recent years. / **Details:** *www.peaceandloaf.co.uk; 9.30 pm; closed Sun D.*

Rasa £39 343
27 Queen St NE1 3UG (0191) 232 7799
"Distinctively different" South Indian food with "delicate spices" continues to win renown for this northern outpost of a London-based group of Keralan restaurants; the "décor is a bit quirky" ("very pink"!) but an "enjoyable part of the experience" nonetheless. / **Details:** *www.rasarestaurants.com; 11 pm; closed Sun L.*

Sachins £38 443
Forth Banks NE1 3SG (0191) 261 9035
Near Central Station, "one of the oldest and most well-respected Indians in the region"; "largely due to its popularity, it can get very busy, cramped and noisy". / **Details:** *www.sachins.co.uk; 11.15 pm, Sun 9.30 pm; closed Sun L.*

Six
Baltic Centre for Contemporary Arts £62 324
Gateshead Quays, South Shore Rd NE8 3BA
(0191) 440 4948
On the 6th floor of this Gateshead arts centre, "the most impressive dining room" in town offers "lovely views (especially from the ladies!)"; "prices are not too inflated" either, and "the food, though fairly conventional, is better than it needs to be in this spot". / **Details:** *www.sixbaltic.com; 9.30 pm, Fri & Sat 10 pm; closed Sun D.*

Sky Apple Cafe **£30** 5|3|2
182 Heaton Rd NE6 5HP (01912) 092571
"Taking vegetarian food to a new level" – a "café by day and a bistro by night", whose "tastes, textures, presentation and inventiveness make for a gourmet experience in a very unpretentious setting"; "the only problem is deciding what to choose!" / **Details:** *www.skyapple.co.uk; 10 pm, Sun-Tue 4.30 pm; closed Mon D, Tue D & Sun D; no credit cards.*

Swan With Two Necks **£46** 3|4|4
Nantwich Rd ST5 5EH (01782) 680343
A "real scoop in a culinary wasteland!" – this "true gastropub" is a rather swish, contemporary venue, in open countryside, which offers "top-notch, innovative dining" and service that's "second to none". / **Details:** *www.theswanwithtwonecks.co.uk; 10 pm.*

Taste of Persia **£31** 4|4|3
14 Marlborough Cr NE1 4EE (0191) 221 0088
"Something different" – an "authentic" Iranian, on the outskirts of the city centre, which offers "really enjoyable" food; prices are "still very reasonable" too. / **Details:** *www.atasteofpersia.com; 11 pm; closed Sun.*

Tyneside Coffee Rooms
Tyneside Cinema **£30** 3|5|4
10 Pilgrim St NE1 6QG (0191) 227 5520
"A Tyneside institution beloved by all ages" that's recommended as a "very cosy place to meet before a film"; it offers "straightforward, comfort food (and some adventurous stuff)" in the Art Deco surrounds of a Grade II, 1930s cinema (apparently the last remaining Newsreel theatre to be in full-time operation in the UK). / **Details:** *www.tynesidecinema.co.uk; 9 pm; closed Sun D; no Amex.*

NEWPORT, PEMBROKESHIRE 4–4B

Llys Meddyg **£50** 4|4|4
East St SA42 0SY (01239) 820008
The food and service at this "atmospheric" restaurant-with-rooms have been "a cut above" of late, and "would put many serious London restaurants to shame". Top Tip – "go on one of the owner's foraging trips along the coast" and "eat what you have found that evening"! / **Details:** *www.llysmeddyg.com; 9 pm; D only, closed Sun; no Amex.* **Accommodation:** *8 rooms, from £100*

NEWTON-IN-BOWLAND, LANCASHIRE 5–1B

The Parkers Arms **£43** 5|4|4
Hall Gate Hill BB7 3DY (01200) 446236
"In a beautiful village in the deepest wilds of Bowland", this "idiosyncratic" and "joyous" destination – "a proper, big, slightly ramshackle country pub" – serves "exciting" fare that's "truly exceptional" and "well worth a (long) detour". "Stosie's classical cooking is influenced by cuisines from all over the world, with a real focus on local ingredients (wild produce, game, etc)" to create "something not too fancy and full of terroir". "Hospitality like hers, AJ's and Kathy's is a rare thing", and though service "can come under pressure when it's busy" the overall effect is "engagingly wonderful". And "my god, they feed you!" – "you'll have to undo all trouser buttons and not eat for another 24 hours afterwards!". Top Menu Tips – "the best game pie ever" and "anything that sounds Middle Eastern". / **Details:** *www.parkersarms.co.uk; 8.30 pm, Sun 6.30 pm; closed Mon.* **Accommodation:** *4 rooms, from £77*

NOMANSLAND, WILTSHIRE 2–3C

Les Mirabelles **£53** 5|5|4
Forest Edge Rd SP5 2BN (01794) 390205
"A beautiful outlook over the New Forest" (and the village cricket ground) sets the scene at Claude Laage's "little piece of France in Wiltshire". It's "superb on every level", combining "terrific" Gallic cuisine, with the proprietor's "wonderful" wine selection, and service that's "charming and flexible, informal and efficient". / **Details:** *www.lesmirabelles.co.uk; off A36 between Southampton & Salisbury; 9.30 pm; closed Mon & Sun; no Amex.*

NORDEN, LANCASHIRE 5–1B

Nutter's **£51** 3|3|3
Edenfield Rd OL12 7TT (01706) 650167
Local celebrity chef Andrew Nutter continues to win solid ratings for his manor house hotel venture, in an "impressive conservatory", despite the odd 'off' report; as ever, it's the puddings that are "second to none". / **Details:** *www.nuttersrestaurant.com; between Edenfield & Norden on A680; 9 pm, Fri & Sat 9.30 pm; closed Mon.*

NORTH SHIELDS, TYNE AND WEAR 8–2B

Irvins Brasserie **£44** 4|3|3
Irvin Building, The Fish Quay NE30 1JH
(0191) 296 3238
A "very pleasant brasserie on North Shields Fish Quay" that "uses the daily local catch as the mainstay of its menus"; "the owner deserves a medal for consistently turning out great food at a great price". / **Details:** *www.irvinsbrasserie.co.uk; 10 pm, Fri & Sat 11 pm, Sun 7 pm; closed Mon & Tue.*

Staith House **£45** 4|4|3
57 Low Lights NE30 1JA (0191) 270 8441
MasterChef finalist John Calton "cooks up a storm" at this "outstanding" pub-restaurant yearling, on the fish quay; it specialises in "same-day fresh" fish and "excellent" local meat (and at "very fair prices") and the "monthly tasting menu nights are fantastic" too. / **Details:** *www.thestaithhouse.co.uk; 11.30 pm.*

NORTHALLERTON, NORTH YORKSHIRE 8–4B

The Cleveland Tontine £45 3 2 3
Staddlebridge DL6 3JB (01609) 882 671
The relatively new owners seem to be making a decent go of this popular local (FKA 'McCoy's at the Tontine'). Even an old-time fan who senses it has "lost the magic atmosphere it had" (and who feels the once-superior wine list is now "average") applauds "the very good chef". / ***Details:*** *www.theclevelandtontine.co.uk; near junction of A19 & A172; 9 pm, Fri & Sat 9.30 pm; no Maestro.* ***Accommodation:*** *7 rooms, from £130*

NORTHLEACH, GLOUCESTERSHIRE 2–1C

Wheatsheaf Inn £49 4 4 5
GL54 3EZ (01451) 860244
The "star" of the growing Lucky Onion empire is a "lovely" village gastropub-with-rooms whose "quality is unsurpassed for miles"; it offers "delicious" food that's "still fairly reasonably priced" and an "incredible wine list for a pub" overseen by a "knowledgeable sommelier". / ***Details:*** *www.cotswoldswheatsheaf.com; 9 pm, Sat & Sun 10 pm.* ***Accommodation:*** *14 rooms, from £140*

NORTHWICH, CHESHIRE 5–3B

The Fishpool Inn £45 3 2 3
Fishpool Rd CW8 2HP (01606) 883277
In a "lovely countryside location", a glammed-up gastropub, with a menu spanning "British pub standbys and well-cooked and presented restaurant-style dishes"; "the interior is a bit barn-like so choose a table in the corner". / ***Details:*** *thefishpoolinn.co.uk; 9 pm, Fri & Sun 10 pm, Sun 9 pm.*

NORTON, WILTSHIRE 2–2B

The Vine Tree £46 4 2 3
Foxley Rd SN16 0JP (01666) 837654
This cosy country boozer, handily placed for travellers on the A4, continues to inspire fierce loyalty from a small fan club, for whom it's "exceptional". / ***Details:*** *www.thevinetree.co.uk; 9.30 pm, Fri & Sat 10 pm; closed Sun D.*

NORWICH, NORFOLK 6–4C

The Gunton Arms £48 4 4 5
Cromer Rd, Thorpe Mkt NR11 8TZ
(01263) 832010
"An out-of-the-way location, surrounded by a deer park where you can see your supper walking around", sets the scene at this "quirky but special" country pub. One or two reporters consider it "hyped", but on most accounts the "steaks cooked on the open fire in the dining room are a dream". / ***Details:*** *www.theguntonarms.co.uk; 8.30 pm.* ***Accommodation:*** *8 rooms, from £95*

Last Wine Bar £46 3 3 4
70-76 St Georges St NR3 1AB
(01603) 626626
"Deservedly a Norwich institution" – this "relaxed and informal", 25-year-old bistro and wine bar (in a former shoe factory) is a "fun" and "extremely popular" operation, most notable for its "excellent choice of wines, many by the 250ml carafe", but also serving "flavoursome" food. / ***Details:*** *www.thelastwinebar.co.uk; 10.30 pm; closed Sun.*

Roger Hickman's £68 5 4 4
79 Upper St. Giles St NR2 1AB
(01603) 633522
"The go-to restaurant for Norwich and the southern half of Norfolk" – Roger Hickman's "unpretentious" oasis of gastronomy provides a "comfortable and laid back" setting that's "been hugely improved this year with a fresh and contemporary look (which finally saw the back of the old, tired Adlard's décor)" and installation of a bar. His very "inventive" cooking is "precise, with clear-cut and harmonious flavours". / ***Details:*** *www.rogerhickmansrestaurant.com; 10 pm; closed Mon & Sun.*

NOSS MAYO, DEVON 1–4C

The Ship Inn £43 3 3 4
PL8 1EW (01752) 872387
"Well worth the approach along narrow lanes" – a pub that continues to attract highly positive reports for its "lovely food in a lovely waterside location" (including "really fresh and well-prepared fish"). / ***Details:*** *www.nossmayo.com; 9.30 pm, Sun 9 pm.*

NOTTINGHAM, NOTTINGHAMSHIRE 5–3D

Annie's Burger Shack £16 3 3 3
5 Broadway NG1 1PR (07463 033255)
"There are more options to choose from than you could possibly want to eat in your life", at New Englander, Annie's "buzzing" 'Burger Shack & Freehouse'. On all accounts from its loyal and locally based fan club, it's "a must-try", with "the best-ever burgers". / ***Details:*** *www.anniesburgershack.com.*

Cafe Roya £39 4 4 2
130 Wollaton Rd NG9 2PE (0115) 922 1902
"Even the most fervent carnivore will not miss the meat" at this "outstanding" veggie; it features an "unusual layout" ("several rooms spread over two floors") and a "civilised" ambience "which lends itself to romance" too. / ***Details:*** *11 pm.*

Cast **£33** 2 3 3
The Playhouse, Wellington Circus NG1 5AN
(0115) 852 3898
"Part of the Nottingham Playhouse" ("things go much quieter once the theatre is in action") this is "a wonderful place to have an alfresco cocktail and nibbles in front of Anish Kapoor's Sky Mirror", or in the "slightly more formal" restaurant inside; "the fixed-price menu and wine list embody excellent value". / **Details:** *www.nottinghamplayhouse.co.uk; 10 pm; closed Sun; no Amex.*

Chino Latino
Park Plaza Hotel **£58** 4 2 2
41 Maid Marian Way NG1 6GD
(0115) 947 7444
This trendy Pan-Asian – with a vaguely bizarre location off the foyer of a boring business hotel – remains capable of providing "surprising" dishes that can be "pretty stunning" (though it's a case of "more hits than misses"); service, though, is on the "perfunctory" side. / **Details:** *www.chinolatino.co.uk; 10.30 pm; closed Sun.*

The Cumin **£39** 5 5 3
62-64 Maid Marian Way NG1 6BQ
(0115) 941 9941
Popular family-run fixture in the city centre "serving Indian cuisine at its best, using fresh ingredients and home techniques to bring the true flavours of the Punjab"! Staff are "most attentive", too, with diners "treated as special guests". / **Details:** *www.thecumin.co.uk; 11 pm, Fri & Sat 11.30 pm; D only, closed Sun.*

4550 Miles From Delhi **£35** 3 4 3
Maid Marian Way NG1 6HE (0115) 947 5111
City-centre Indian providing "modern, inspired dishes every time" – the "wide-ranging menu" means there's always "something for every palate". / **Details:** *www.milesfromdelhi.com; Mon-Thu 10 pm, Fri & Sat 11 pm, Sun 10.30 pm; no Amex.*

Fox Café **£28** 3 3 2
9 Pelham St NG1 2EH
On the former site of Nottingham stalwart Atlas (RIP), a new café serving a good selection of gluten-free and veggie options, alongside the usual fare; it opened too late for our survey but early buzz from local bloggers has been very positive, especially about the artisan coffee.

French Living **£42** 3 3 3
27 King St NG1 2AY (0115) 958 5885
This "rustic, authentic" stalwart "keeps on doing what a good French bistro does well, whether in Nottingham or Nantes" – namely "tasty food at very reasonable prices". Top Tip – an especially "excellent-value pre-theatre menu". / **Details:** *www.frenchliving.co.uk; 10 pm; closed Mon & Sun; no Amex.*

Hart's **£68** 4 5 3
Standard Ct, Park Row NG1 6GN
(0115) 988 1900
Tim Hart's "confident" '90s brasserie near the castle is an unusually "discreet and efficient" modern brasserie, serving "totally reliable" modern cuisine in a "light and airy" (slightly "corporate") setting. "For a business meal in particular, it's pitched just right". / **Details:** *www.hartsnottingham.co.uk; 10 pm, Sun 9 pm.* **Accommodation:** *32 rooms, from £125*

Iberico **£42** 5 5 4
The Shire Hall, High Pavement NG1 1HN
(01159) 410410
The extensive vaults of "an historic building in the Lace Market" house this "lovely" and lively haunt. "Nothing is too much effort for the staff", who provide "clever" tapas dishes, many of them "exceptional", all at very "reasonable prices"; "excellent" cocktails and wines too. / **Details:** *www.ibericotapas.com; 10 pm; closed Sun; no Amex; children: 12+ D.*

Kayal **£36** 4 3 3
8 Broad St NG1 3AL (0115) 941 4733
"If you like masala dosas (plus other "fabulous" Keralan dishes, especially veggie) this is the place" – a "well-priced" outlet of a small Midlands chain that's "handy for Nottingham shopping and next door to the Broadway cinema". / **Details:** *www.kayalrestaurant.com; 11 pm, Sun 10 pm.*

Kiosk **£29** 3 4 3
1 Winchester St NG5 4AH (07514 625697)
"Housed in a shipping container in the Sherwood area", this "quirky" and "tiny" café/restaurant "has become a local institution". The "ever-changing" menu is "largely Middle Eastern-inflected with much for the vegetarian (but with some excellent, free-range-meat dishes)", and its "simple, and always imaginative" fare is particularly popular for brunch, but also tipped for mezze evenings, or just coffee and a cake. / **Details:** *www.kiosksherwood.co.uk; 6 pm, Thu 9 pm, Fri & Sat 11 pm; closed Mon D, Tue D, Wed D & Sun D.*

The Larder on
Goosegate **£47** 4 4 4
1st Floor, 16 -22 Goosegate NG1 1FE
(01159) 500 111
A restaurant "above the original Boots shop, with large windows overlooking the busy Hockley nightlife" that's "going from strength to strength each year"; "the food is seasonal, often fairly local, and never disappointing", while service is "just on the right side of relaxed". / **Details:** *www.thelarderongoosegate.co.uk; 10 pm; closed Mon & Sun.*

MemSaab
£41 443

12-14 Maid Marian Way NG1 6HS
(0115) 957 0009

*"There's no shortage of good Indians in Nottingham, but MemSaab has nailed it!" – this central stalwart remains the city's most popular curry house on account of its "tremendous, hearty and refined" cooking (some of it "very unusual") and service that's "always very attentive". / **Details:** www.mem-saab.co.uk; near Castle, opposite Park Plaza Hotel; 10.30 pm, Fri & Sat 11 pm, Sun 10 pm; D only; no shorts.*

Restaurant Sat Bains
£125 543

Lenton Lane NG7 2SA (0115) 986 6566

*"You have to add this to your bucket list!" – Sat Bains's famous restaurant-with-rooms won the No. 1 slot this year in our listing ofTop-100 UK Restaurants. It certainly doesn't win its accolades for its location – on the edge of a city-fringe industrial estate, surrounded by fly-overs and pylons (once memorably described by the chef himself as 'like finding a diamond in a piece of turd'). But in culinary terms, "it's an experience from start to finish", delivering "out-of-this-world, quirky and offbeat" dishes, with "amazing flavours". A seat at the chef's table provides a particularly good trip, and – for those in search of something even more 'experiential' – in June 2015 Sat Bains opened Nucleus, a 'restaurant within-a-restaurant' with just 6 seats and its own dedicated kitchen. / **Details:** www.restaurantsatbains.com; 8.30 pm, Fri & Sat 9.45 pm; closed Mon & Sun; children: 8+. **Accommodation:** 8 rooms, from £129*

La Rock
£65 443

4 Bridge St NG10 5QT (01519) 399833

*"The best in the Nottingham area after Sat Bains" – a "small restaurant tucked away in a side street" where the food is "cooked creatively with a deal of originality" and staff are "friendly and knowledgeable". Even sceptics are impressed – "they are trying to provide a really top class dining experience and nearly pull it off – high prices, but a brave attempt". / **Details:** www.larockrestaurant.co.uk; 9 pm; closed Mon, Tue & Wed L.*

Shanghai Shanghai
£31 522

15 Goose Gate NG1 1FE (0115) 958 4688

*"The real deal" – a "so different" venture serving "truly first-rate Sichuanese cooking that makes no concession to the British palate" (and as such is "packed to the rafters with Chinese students"); as for the "workaday" décor, well, "nobody is there for the stylish surroundings"! / **Details:** www.shanghai-shanghai.co.uk.*

200 Degrees
£12 334

Heston Hs, Meadow Lane NG2 3HE
(0115) 837 3150

*"A lovely antidote to the profusion of coffee shop chains" – a new city-centre indie that "roasts its own beans", and provides "good brunch and lunch options". / **Details:** www.200degs.com; 8pm, Sat 7pm, Sun 6 pm.*

Victoria Hotel
£36 343

Dovecote Ln NG9 1JG (0115) 925 4049

*Near Beeston station, a real ale pub "with a consistently huge menu – there's something for everyone here"; it's "excellent for a Sunday lunch" (taken in the appealing garden come summer). / **Details:** www.victoriabeeston.co.uk; 9.30 pm, Sun-Tue 8.45 pm; closed Mon for food; no Amex; children: 18+ after 8 pm.*

The Wollaton
£42 333

Lambourne Drive NG8 1GR (0115) 9288610

*"They are getting better and better at seasonality and dishes are more imaginative than previously" at this "family-friendly" gastropub, by Wollaton Park; "I wouldn't say it's always top-notch, but they rarely disappoint". / **Details:** www.molefacepubcompany.co.uk; 9 pm, Sun 5 pm; closed Sun D.*

World Service
£55 233

Newdigate Hs, Castlegate NG1 6AF
(0115) 847 5587

*"The outside tables are so pleasant" at this quirky venue, near the castle – a stylish haunt that's long been one of the city's most popular. Its adventurous cuisine inspires mixed feelings though – what is "always a delight" to fans, is to sceptics "overrated" – "it looks enticing, but lacks the level of flavour you'd expect!" / **Details:** www.worldservicerestaurant.com; 10 pm; closed Sun D, except bank holidays; children: 10+ at D.*

OARE, KENT
3–3C

The Three Mariners
£41 223

2 Church Rd ME13 0QA (01795) 533633

*This village gastropub usually "serves food of a high standard" and "being near the sea, the menu has a good range of fish dishes"; it can seem like "a victim of its own popularity though" with a couple of experiences that were "at best good". / **Details:** www.thethreemarinersoare.co.uk; Mon-Thu 9 pm, Fri-Sat 9.30 pm, Sun 9 pm; no Amex.*

OBAN, ARGYLL AND BUTE 9–3B

Ee-Usk (Seafood Restaurant) £50 434

North Pier PA34 5QD (01631) 565666

"The Scottish coastline should be packed with places like Ee-Usk" – a restaurant combining "a beautiful tranquil view of Oban bay" with an "amazing" array of "perfect", simply cooked fish. / **Details:** *www.eeusk.com; 9-9.30 pm; no Amex; children: 12+ at D .*

Seafood Temple £46 323

Dungallan Pk, Gallanach Rd PA34 4LS (01631) 566000

"Spankingly fresh seafood and awesome views" (over the water to the island of Kerrera) are the winning attributes of this tiny family-run restaurant, with an unusual location in a former park pavilion. / **Details:** *www.obanseafood.com; D only.*

OCKHAM, SURREY 3–3A

The Black Swan £49 344

Old Ln KT11 1NG (01932) 862364

"Fab, fab, fab!" – a "classy country pub" whose "fantastic" kids' playground helps make it a "wonderful spot for leisurely dining on a summer's day"; "consistent standards" generally too. / **Details:** *www.blackswanockham.com; 9.30 pm, Fri & Sat 10 pm, Sun 8 pm.*

OCKLEY, SURREY 3–4A

Bryce's at the Old School House £50 332

Stane St RH5 5TH (01306) 627430

A "surprisingly good" landlocked fish restaurant where "they certainly know how to source, cook and serve" the best catch "from a long, long way away"!; not everyone likes the setting – but then again it is located in a former schoolhouse! / **Details:** *www.bryces.co.uk; 8m S of Dorking on A29; 9.30 pm; no Amex.*

OLD HUNSTANTON, NORFOLK 6–3B

The Neptune £79 553

85 Old Hunstanton Rd PE36 6HZ (01485) 532122

"Chef-owner Kevin Mangeolles and his wife run a very efficient ship" (and an extremely "charming" one too) at this "marvellous" 18th-century coaching inn, which offers "unexpectedly fine dining" (with "lots of local produce") in "lovely", remote surroundings. If you wish to stray beyond the more standard set menus, there is a 9-course tasting option. / **Details:** *www.theneptune.co.uk; 9 pm; closed Mon, Tue-Sat D only, Sun open L & D; children: 10+.* **Accommodation:** *6 rooms, from £120*

OLD WOKING, SURREY 3–3A

London House £50 332

134 High St GU22 9JN (01483) 750610

Feedback on MasterChef semi-finalist Ben Piette's local remains upbeat. One critic found cooking that was "nice but unexciting", but for others its "reasonable prices" help make it a local favourite. / **Details:** *www.londonhouseoldwoking.co.uk; 10 pm.*

OLDSTEAD, NORTH YORKSHIRE 5–1D

Black Swan £81 544

YO61 4BL (01347) 868 387

"On the up, and ever-more exciting!" – chef Tommy Banks's "immaculate" cuisine won some of the UK's highest ratings this year for this "quaint" and "tucked-away" converted pub, near Byland Abbey; the highpoint is "a superb 9-course tasting menu, all from local sources", served in a "simple yet beautiful dining room (with lots of copper and china)". / **Details:** *www.blackswanoldstead.co.uk; 9 pm; closed weekday L; no Amex.* **Accommodation:** *4 rooms, from £270 (includes dinner)*

ONGAR, ESSEX 3–2B

Smith's Brasserie £57 453

Fyfield Rd CM5 0AL (01277) 365578

"Very Essex, and very good!" – this "high-end" operation "possesses all the good aspects a restaurant needs" – "consistently brilliant", "very fresh" fare (in particular "outstanding fish"), "exceptional" service, and a "friendly and relaxed" style. / **Details:** *www.smithsbrasserie.com; left off A414 towards Fyfield; Mon-Fri 10 pm, Sat 10.30 pm, Sun 10 pm; closed Mon L; children: 12+.*

ONICH, HIGHLAND 9–3B

Loch Leven Seafood Café £47 544

PH33 6SA (01855) 821048

Reporters are united in their praise for this "simple and pleasant" waterside café's "glorious views" and "stunning" dishes, featuring "the freshest seafood, straight off the boat from the loch just outside". It's "worth travelling to in itself, rather than just being a useful stop-off en route to Fort William". / **Details:** *www.lochlevenseafoodcafe.co.uk; 9 pm; no Amex.*

ORFORD, SUFFOLK 3–1D

Butley Orford Oysterage £38 532
Market Hill IP12 2LH (01394) 450277
"Simple, unadulterated, and so fresh!" – the seafood at this basic, quaint fixture of 50 years' standing. "They know what they do well, they stick to it religiously, and it's completely reliable and excellent every time". Top Menu Tip – "amazing oysters and smoked fish" (from their own smokehouse). / **Details:** *www.pinneysoforford.co.uk; on the B1078, off the A12 from Ipswich; 9 pm; no Amex.*

The Crown & Castle £56 333
IP12 2LJ (01394) 450205
Celebrity co-owner Ruth Watson's gastropub-with-rooms continues to earn solid survey marks for its locally sourced cooking. / **Details:** *www.crownandcastle.co.uk; on main road to Orford, near Woodbridge; 8 pm, Fri & Sat 9 pm; no Amex; booking: max 10; children: 8+ at D.* **Accommodation:** *21 rooms, from £135*

ORPINGTON, KENT 3–3B

Xian £37 542
324 High St BR6 0NG (01689) 871881
"Continuing to nail it time after time"; this "cramped, but efficient and still-wonderful" Chinese "remains the benchmark" for many, many miles around – "we're so lucky to have it on our High Street, it's so much better than anything in Chinatown!" / **Details:** *11 pm; closed Mon & Sun L.*

OSWESTRY, SHROPSHIRE 5–3A

Sebastian's £59 443
45 Willow St SY11 1AQ (01691) 655444
A recently revamped restaurant-with-rooms where the Gallic food is "always of a high standard" and service is "so pleasant and professional"; "if the sweets here are supplied to the Orient Express, then they must be doing something right"! / **Details:** *www.sebastians-hotel.co.uk; 9.30 pm; D only, closed Mon & Sun; no Amex.* **Accommodation:** *5 rooms, from £75*

Townhouse £54 433
35 Willow St SY11 1AQ (01691) 59499
"A welcome, upmarket addition to Oswestry" – a "very stylish" bar-restaurant in a Georgian building which reopened after a major revamp in late-2014, and now offers "beautifully presented food with maximum flavour"; "Michael Caines is involved in the venture, thus the similarity to his menus at Abode". / **Details:** *www.townhouseoswestry.com; 11.30 pm, Fri & Sat 2 am, Sun 7 pm; closed Mon & Sun D.*

OXFORD, OXFORDSHIRE 2–2D

Al-Shami £28 443
25 Walton Cr OX1 2JG (01865) 310066
"Chatty and accommodating staff" add to the appeal of this "unfailingly good" Lebanese, which is "always very lively, despite its out-of-the-way location, in Jericho". Prices are "very reasonable" and although "the mezze are probably the best bet", the more substantial fare is "tender and delicious". / **Details:** *www.al-shami.co.uk; midnight; no Amex.* **Accommodation:** *12 rooms, from £60*

Ashmolean Dining Room £52 234
Beaumont St OX1 2PH (01865) 553 823
"Location, location and location!" An "obviously superb" setting – a "bright and airy" venue with a rooftop terrace "overlooking the Oxford spires" – is the big draw to this "charming" venue. That said, the "good, if unexceptional" food is "much improved" in recent times and "mostly good". / **Details:** *www.ashmoleandiningroom.com; 10 pm; closed Mon, Tue D, Thu D & Sun D.*

Atomic Burger £29 443
92 Cowley Rd OX4 1JE (01865) 790 855
A "very popular" if "oddly funky" venue ("decorated with toys from decades gone by"); the "cheery" staff are "still serving up massive, delicious, pick-and-mix style burgers and sides" from a "huge" and "well-priced" menu. / **Details:** *www.atomicburger.co.uk; 10.30 pm; no Amex.*

Branca £42 333
111 Walton St OX2 6AJ (01865) 556111
"You know what to expect and the standard is fairly uniform" at this "spacious" Jericho staple, where there's "no sign of Italy except for the food". The "airy area at the back is a nice improvement", while the owners' next door deli is "very good too". / **Details:** *www.branca.co.uk; 11 pm; no Amex.*

Brasserie Blanc £51 223
71-72 Walton St OX2 6AG (01865) 510999
The 'Manoir' chef's "recently refurbed" and "uplifted" city-centre brasserie "still has a nice buzzy atmosphere". The food isn't awful, but no great shakes – odd given both its proximity to Monsieur B, and the fact that it was the original. / **Details:** *www.brasserieblanc.com; 10 pm, Sat 10.30 pm, Sun 9.30 pm.*

Cherwell Boathouse £46 335
Bardwell Rd OX2 6ST (01865) 552746
"The location by the Cherwell helps" – it adds to the "lovely" ambience (especially on a warm day) of this well-known riverside venue, where "you can watch the punters trying to control their boats!" It

is known in foodie circles for its formidable wine list, but these days the "light and elegant" cuisine is less of a total sideshow as once was the case. / **Details:** *www.cherwellboathouse.co.uk; 9 pm, Fri & Sat 9.30 pm.*

Chiang Mai £44 443

Kemp Hall Passage OX1 4DH (01865) 202233

"Still going strong" and "still serving some of the best Thai food in the UK" outside of London – this atmospheric haunt occupies a quirky, medieval building, hidden away just off the High Street, and its "Tudor setting and Thai accoutrements blend seamlessly for a great overall ambience". / **Details:** *www.chiangmaikitchen.co.uk; 10.30 pm, Sun 10 pm.*

Edamame £32 442

15 Holywell St OX1 3SA (01865) 246916

"A welcome break from the chain-dominated Oxford food scene" – this "tiny but much-loved independent" offers "quick, tasty and authentic" Japanese food, "served at communal tables". "It's definitely worth queueing for". / **Details:** *www.edamame.co.uk; 8.30 pm; L only, ex Thu-Sat open L & D, closed Mon & Tue; no Amex; no booking.*

The Fishes £44 334

North Hinksey OX2 0NA (01865) 249796

Encouraging feedback of late for this "very attractive" waterside pub with a "lovely" garden; fans say its food is now "really good", and service seems to be much improved too. / **Details:** *www.fishesoxford.co.uk; 9.45 pm.*

The Folly £49 324

1 Folly Bridge OX1 4JU (01865) 201293

A "beautifully located" spot by the eponymous bridge "looking out at boaters on the river" whose food, while sometimes "very good", tends to play second fiddle to the setting. / **Details:** *www.no1-folly-bridge.co.uk/; 11 pm.*

Gee's £53 334

61 Banbury Rd OX2 6PE (01865) 553540

The "unusual and stunning" Victorian glasshouse setting is the stand-out feature of this "chic-casual" north Oxford spot. As ever there's the odd quibble that it's below par and too pricey, but fans – who find it a good all-rounder – were more in evidence this year. / **Details:** *www.gees-restaurant.co.uk; 10 pm, Fri & Sat 10.30 pm.*

The Magdalen Arms £44 423

243 Iffley Rd OX4 1SJ (01865) 243 159

"Characterful" sibling to London's Hope & Anchor acclaimed for "ripping-good pub food in a very dark and proper (read noisy) pub"; "the prices aren't silly", and the "robustly flavoured" food "isn't fancy, but it is delicious". / **Details:** *www.magdalenarms.com; 10 pm, Sun 9.30 pm; closed Mon L; no Amex.*

My Sichuan £41 533

The Old School, Gloucester Grn OX1 2DA (01865) 236 899

"For taste, wow... just wow!" – "amazing" dishes "with lots of exotic items like frogs' legs and ducks' tongues" are all part of the "unabashedly in-yer-face" culinary style ("some stuff you'll need to pluck up courage for") of this centrally located, former school house, next to the bus station. "It's not a good option if you don't appreciate chilli heat", but "it's the closest thing to Chinese food, outside of China" and "the clientele are nearly always over 50% Chinese". Top Menu Tip – "the cumin ribs are really, really good". / **Details:** *www.mysichuan.co.uk; 11 pm.*

Oli's Thai £30 554

38 Magdalen Rd OX4 1RB (01865) 790223

"This is proper Thai food – the very best you could eat"; it may be "tiny", but this "basic" café "has achieved cult status" locally owing to its "incredibly flavoursome" food; "you have to be very organised to get a table", though... "the waiting time is 6-8 weeks"! / **Details:** *www.olisthai.com; 10 pm; closed Mon, Tue L & Sun.*

The Oxford Kitchen £53 332

215 Banbury Rd OX2 7HQ (01865) 511149

"Very promising" newcomer, on the main drag in Summertown, winning plaudits for its "innovative" and "very chef-y" fine dining fare ("think lovage foam, lime foam, and lots of smears"). To be sure it's a "refreshing change from much on offer" round here, but some reporters feel that food-wise "its clear ambitions have yet to be fully realised". / **Details:** *www.theoxfordkitchen.co.uk; 7 pm.*

Pierre Victoire £42 343

Little Clarendon St OX1 2HP (01865) 316616

"Exceptional value for money" (pre-theatre and lunch menus are a particular bargain) underpins the huge popularity of this "buzzing and well-organised" survivor of what was once a national chain – "everything a French bistro should be, with recognisably Gallic dishes and efficient service". / **Details:** *www.pierrevictoire.co.uk; 11 pm, Sun 10 pm; no Amex.*

The Punter £34 334

7 South St OX2 0BE (01865) 248832

An Osney Island pub with a "great" riverside location; the European/North African food is a little "variable" at times, but generally attracts positive reports (if not quite as many as we'd like). / **Details:** *www.thepunteroxford.co.uk; 10 pm, Sun 9 pm.*

Quod
Old Bank Hotel £45 223

92-94 High St OX1 4BJ (01865) 202505

A "big and buzzy" city-centre "brasserie" that continues to be a well-patronised "haunt of would-be alumni and parents"; the food is "unadventurous", but results are generally "tasty". / **Details:** www.oldbank-hotel.co.uk; 11 pm, Sun 10.30 pm; no booking at D. **Accommodation:** 42 rooms, from £140

Sojo £41 542
6-9 Hythe Bridge St OX1 2EW (01865) 202888
*In contention as the venue for "the best Chinese food in Oxford" – this "busy, buzzy, authentic" spot serves some "awesome" dishes and is "spot on with the heat"; it "can be hard to get a table and it's rather noisy, but those are almost the only drawbacks". / **Details:** www.sojooxford.co.uk; 11 pm, Sun 10 pm.*

Turl Street Kitchen £39 323
16 Turl St OX1 3DH (01865) 264 171
*"Whatever your cool credentials (or lack thereof) you can feel hip and trendy dining at this not-for-profit, classy-yet-casual place in central Oxford"; the food is "seasonal, organic and local", and while there's "not a massive menu", there's "always a good (tough, even) choice". / **Details:** www.turlstreetkitchen.co.uk; 10 pm, Fri & Sat 10.30 pm, Sun 10 pm.*

The Vaults and Garden Cafe £20 434
University Church of St Mary the Virgin, Radcliffe Sq OX1 4AH (01865) 279112
*"In the old chapter house of a 14th-century university church" with outside tables on Radcliffe Square, this "idyllic" self-service spot offers "delicious and inexpensive" food ("especially vegetarian");"don't go on a Saturday if you're in a hurry, as queues are long". / **Details:** www.thevaultsandgarden.com; 6 pm; L only.*

Zheng £36 531
82 Walton St OX2 6EA (01865) 51 11 88
*"A pan-Asian menu might send you running for the hills, but here is executed to just-about perfection!" – this "relative newcomer" is "always deservedly packed" thanks to its "extraordinarily good Malaysian, Singaporean, Sichuan and Cantonese dishes", as well as "conventional" (and less noteworthy) dim sum. / **Details:** www.zhengoxford.co.uk; 10.45 pm, Sun 10.15 pm; closed Tue L.*

OXTED, SURREY 3–3B

The Gurkha Kitchen £32 333
111 Station Road East RH8 0AX
(01883) 722621
*Family-run Nepalese, by the station; fans claim that it "never fails to be fantastic", and even a reporter who thought it "perhaps not quite so good as in the past" rates it "very good". / **Details:** www.gurkhakitchen.co.uk; 11 pm, Sun 10 pm; closed Mon L; no Amex.*

Thai Pad £30 334
5-6 Hoskins Walk RH8 9HR (01883) 717190
*"Just what is needed for Oxted" – a "fabulous" new Thai tapas bar and restaurant, near the station, which has already "attracted huge interest"; "very busy, so book!" / **Details:** www.thaipadoxted.co.uk; 10.30 pm, Fri & Sat 11 pm.*

OXTON, CHESHIRE 5–2A

Fraiche £109 544
11 Rose Mount CH43 5SG (0151) 652 2914
*"It's impossible to book" nowadays at Marc Wilkinson's "one-of-a-kind" (and fairly small) Wirral dining room (perhaps something to do with his success last year, when he topped our Top-100 UK Restaurants?) "You should keep trying though as you won't be disappointed" – "brilliant dish follows brilliant dish" from "an amazing menu full of surprises". / **Details:** www.restaurantfraiche.com; 8.30 pm, Sun 7 pm; closed Mon, Tue, Wed L, Thu L, Fri L & Sat L; no Amex.*

PADSTOW, CORNWALL 1–3B

Paul Ainsworth at Number 6 £83 443
6 Middle St PL28 8AP (01841) 532093
*"A jewel in Padstow's crown" – Paul Ainsworth's "sparse", café-style venture, in a "tiny" townhouse, out-guns its more famous neighbour with "top notch" cuisine, "whose freshness takes a lot of beating", and "informal and friendly" service. It helps that the man himself is much in evidence and "totally unpretentious". Top Menu Tip – "it's easy to see why the Trip-To-The-Fairground pudding won on The Great British Menu!" / **Details:** www.number6inpadstow.co.uk; 10 pm; closed Mon & Sun; no Amex; children: 4+.*

Rick Stein's Café £41 434
10 Middle St PL28 8AP (01841) 532700
*"More relaxed and joyous than its glossier stablemate" – the Stein empire's "crowded and bustling" No. 2 place provides a "happy-making experience", combining "different" seafood options from a "limited but interesting" and "reasonably priced" menu, and a "fun atmosphere". / **Details:** www.rickstein.com; 9.30 pm; closed Mon & Tue; no Amex; no booking at L. **Accommodation:** 3 rooms, from £100*

Rojanos £48 333
9 Mill Sq PL28 8AE (01841) 532796
*Paul Ainsworth's "noisy, bustling Italian" continues to impress with its "quality ingredients" and "perfectly cooked" dishes ("best pizza I've tasted this year!"). / **Details:** www.rojanos.co.uk; 10 pm; no Amex.*

St Petroc's Hotel & Bistro £54 3 3 3

4 New St PL28 8EA (01841) 532700

At its best, this Stein-empire property can deliver "a memorable experience"..."a Cornish treat" featuring "excellent" fish and seafood. Its performance is perennially uneven though, and this year's crop of reports also included gripes about "uninspiring food and wayward service". / **Details:** *www.rickstein.com; 10 pm; no Amex.* **Accommodation:** *10 rooms, from £150*

Seafood Restaurant £83 3 3 3

Riverside PL28 8BY (01841) 532700

For fans of TV-megastar Rick Stein's original HQ (run in large part in recent years, like the rest of his UK empire, by ex-wife Jill), this famous harbourside venue is "still perfection, despite its popularity", for when you want to enjoy "top notch" fish and seafood (of which it serves a "mind-bogglingly long menu" that nowadays incorporates numerous ethnic choices and curry). But even fans can find it "very highly priced, even by London standards", especially for somewhere that is "crammed in", and (some feel) "very commercial" nowadays. / **Details:** *www.rickstein.com; 9.45 pm; ; no Amex; booking: max 14; children: 3+.* **Accommodation:** *16 rooms, from £150*

Stein's Fish & Chips £33 4 4 3

South Quay PL28 8BL (01841) 532700

"This good-value yet tiny fish and chip shop from Cornwall's celebrity chef" continues its upward turn; "you have to queue outside for a bit", but it's worth it for "great" food (including "brilliant" gluten-free chips). / **Details:** *www.rickstein.com; 9 pm; no Amex.*

PARKGATE, CHESHIRE 5–2A

The Boathouse £42 2 2 2

1 The Pde CH64 6RN (0151) 336 4187

This "friendly" fixture boasts a "winning location" – marshside, with "beautiful views" of the Dee; "well-prepared and filling" food too. / **Details**: *www.theboathouseparkgate.co.uk/; 10 pm.*

PENALLT, MONMOUTHSHIRE 2–2B

Inn at Penallt £49 4 3 2

NP25 4SE (01600) 772765

In "scenic" countryside near Monmouth, a "very friendly" pub that's "worth the detour" by all accounts; the traditional cooking is a "wonderful surprise", especially given that the "very yellow" dining room "bespeaks a gastropub rather than haute cuisine"! / **Details:** *www.theinnatpenallt.co.uk; 9 pm; closed Mon, Tue L & Sun D; no Amex.* **Accommodation:** *4 rooms, from £75*

PENARTH, VALE OF GLAMORGAN 1–1D

Restaurant James Sommerin £78 4 3 2

The Esplanade CF64 3AU (07722) 216 727

The former Crown at Whitebrook chef's new waterside restaurant-with-rooms continues to attract acclaim for its "refined cooking and excellent ingredients"; "the room is not quite right", though – "the sea view is wasted" and the décor errs on the side of "naff". / **Details:** *www.jamessommerinrestaurant.co.uk/#welcome; 10 pm.*

PENRITH, CUMBRIA 7–3D

Four & Twenty £46 3 3 2

42 King St CA11 7AY (01768) 210231

A new rustic eatery with an open kitchen located on the site of an old bank, hailed by some (if not quite all) reporters as "easily the best foodie option in town". / **Details:** *www.fourandtwentypenrith.co.uk; 9 pm.*

PENSFORD, SOMERSET 2–2B

The Pig Hunstrete House £44 4 4 5

BS39 4NS (01761) 490490

"A great outpost of The Pig family in a beautiful setting in rural Somerset"; this country house hotel boasts the "lovely" shabby chic atmosphere that's the hallmark of the brand, and is a perfect spot for piggish appetites too – "fantastic" locally sourced food (and "opulent breakfasts!") / **Details:** *www.thepighotel.com; 9.30 pm.*

PENZANCE, CORNWALL 1–4A

Tolcarne Inn £40 5 4 3

Tolcarne Pl TR18 5PR (01736) 363074

"The fish market in Newlyn is just 200m away so you can imagine how fresh the fish is!" – what's more Ben Tunnicliffe "does full justice to the ingredients" at his "low key and friendly" old harbourside inn (which he took over three years ago), delivering "gourmet cooking at pub prices". / **Details:** *www.tolcarneinn.co.uk; 10 pm.*

PERRANUTHNOE, CORNWALL 1–4A

Victoria Inn £46 4 4 4

TR20 9NP (01736) 710309

Since a new owner and chef arrived, this "friendly village restaurant" is, say fans, "one to watch": "local ingredients, cooked in a highly attractive way – sauces, flavours, fusions, all worth driving miles for!" / **Details:** *www.victoriainn-penzance.co.uk; 9 pm, Sun 4 pm; closed Sun D.*

PERTH, PERTH AND KINROSS 9–3C

Cafe Tabou **£49** 3 4 2
4 St John's Pl PH1 5SZ (01738) 446698
"A cheerful bonjour as you enter" adds to the "bustling and fun" vibe of this "little bit of Paris" that's actually owned by a Polish family (a "weird but wonderful mix of cultures"). It offers "perfect French classics" and "very good" wines delivered by "smiling staff". / **Details:** *www.cafetabou.com; 9.30 pm, Fri & Sat 10 pm; closed Mon D & Sun; no Amex.*

Pig'Halle **£48** 3 4 3
38 South St PH2 8PG (01738) 248784
A "really enjoyable" Gallic-owned, Breton bistro, where the food is "always genuine" (and "good value" 'en plus')! / **Details:** *www.pighalle.co.uk; 9.30 pm, Thu-Sat 10 pm, Sun & Mon 9 pm.*

63 Tay Street **£60** 3 3 2
63 Tay St PH2 8NN (01738) 441451
Graham Pallister's town-centre venture has "kept the standards high" over many years; even critics of the "imbalance" in portions ("savoury being smaller than sweet") concede "they clearly have a talented chef". / **Details:** *www.63taystreet.com; on city side of River Tay, 1m from Dundee Rd; 9 pm; D only, closed Mon & Sun; no Amex.*

PETERSFIELD, HAMPSHIRE 2–3D

JSW **£74** 3 2 2
20 Dragon St GU31 4JJ (01730) 262030
Jake Saul Watkin's former coaching inn provoked mixed responses from reporters this year. There's still much appreciation for his "precise and not over-complicated" cuisine (from both "excellent tasting menus" and a "well-conceived à la carte"), but quite a number of reports suggest "standards have slipped" with "un-confident, new staff", and too many Groupon deals. / **Details:** *www.jswrestaurant.com; on the old A3; 8 min walk from the railway station; 9 pm; closed Mon, Tue & Sun D; children: 5+ D.* **Accommodation:** *4 rooms, from £95*

PETTS WOOD, KENT 3–3B

Indian Essence **£48** 3 3 3
176-178 Petts Wood Rd BR5 1LG
(01689) 838 700
"It still seems quite bizarre that the great Atul Kochar has his name in Petts Wood!", and many locals give a massive "thank you, thank you, thank you" to have such "exquisite" Indian cuisine brought to this "culinary desert". Ratings slipped across the board this year though, on reports of "disappointing" meals and "very high prices". / **Details:** *www.indianessence.co.uk; 10.45 pm, fri & sat 11 pm, sun 10.30 pm; closed Mon L.*

PETWORTH, WEST SUSSEX 3–4A

The Leconfield **£66** 2 3 3
New St GU28 0AS (01798) 345111
In this well-heeled town, a classy bar-restaurant with "friendly and helpful" service; on most accounts it offers "well-cooked seasonal food", but for sceptics is "nothing spectacular for the price". / **Details:** *www.theleconfield.co.uk; Tue-Sat 11 pm, Sun 4 pm.*

Meghdoots **£35** 3 4 3
East St GU28 0AB (01798) 343217
"A really good and authentic Indian in the heart of Petworth"; "go with their recommendations – they are always great!" / **Details:** *www.meghdoots.com/aboutus.html; 10 pm.*

The Noahs Ark Inn **£46** 4 3 5
Lurgashall GU28 9ET (01428) 707346
"As perfect an English pub as you can find", with "good-value" food and appealing dining options – "eat outside facing the village green" or enjoy the "relaxing atmosphere" within. / **Details:** *www.noahsarkinn.co.uk; 9.30 pm, Sun 3 pm; closed Sun D.*

PICKERING, NORTH YORKSHIRE 8–4C

The White Swan **£51** 3 3 4
Market Pl YO18 7AA (01751) 472288
This old coaching inn combines a "fine" restaurant and small bar with food that's "well above average"; there has been a recent extension out back – "the hope is that the place doesn't become too big!" / **Details:** *www.white-swan.co.uk; 9 pm.*
Accommodation: *21 rooms, from £150*

PINNER, GREATER LONDON 3–3A

Friends **£55** 4 5 4
11 High St HA5 5PJ (020) 8866 0286
The "lovely and intimate" timbered building housing Terry Farr's popular stalwart is nearly 500 years old, and "the folk of Pinner are lucky to have it on their High Street". "Management and staff go out of their way to make guests feel special", and even metropolitan sophisticates are impressed – "I had no positive expectations about this deeply suburban 'local' but the food was surprisingly well-executed, service was charming and efficient, and the wine list very acceptable." / **Details:** *www.friendsrestaurant.co.uk; 9.30 pm; closed Mon & Sun D.*

PLAXTOL, KENT 3–3B

The Papermaker's Arms **£42** 3 3 2
The Street TN15 0QJ (01732) 810407
Still going strong under the newish management, this "hospitable" village pub serves dependable food in

"sizeable portions"; "the garden is very pleasant in good weather". / **Details:** papermakersarms.com/; 9.30 pm.

PLEASINGTON, LANCASHIRE 5–1B

Clog & Billycock £45 3 3 3

Billinge End Rd BB2 6QB (01254) 201163
*"An updated, good old-fashioned pub" (recently refurbished) that's a very solid member of the Ribble Valley Inns chain, providing "above-average pub food" and "a friendly welcome". / **Details:** www.theclogandbillycock.com/; 8.30 pm Mon-Thu, Fri & Sat 9 pm, Sun 8 pm.*

PLUMTREE, NOTTINGHAMSHIRE 5–3D

Perkins £50 3 3 2

Old Railway Station NG12 5NA
(0115) 937 3695
*"The good quality standard has not changed" at this "very popular family restaurant", located in a restored Victorian railway station. / **Details:** www.perkinsrestaurant.co.uk; off A606 between Nottingham & Melton Mowbray; 9.30 pm; closed Sun D.*

PLYMOUTH, DEVON 1–3C

Chloe's Gill Akaster House £58 3 3 4

27 Princess St PL1 2EX (01752) 201523
*"A small but attractive French bistro in the city centre" that is "still a firm favourite" of reporters; it's "ideally situated for pre- and post-theatre dining", and seemingly an apt venue for romance too ("I actually saw someone go down on one knee!") / **Details:** www.chloesrestaurant.co.uk; 9 pm; closed Sun.*

The Dolphin House Brazzerie £46 4 5 5

Sutton Harbour, The Barbican PL4 0DW
(01752) 254879
*"This is one of the hidden gems of Plymouth"; "located on Sutton Harbour, just round the corner from the busy Barbican", this "small indie" serves food "with great style and verve"; it attracts nothing but praise for its "great attention to detail". / **Details:** www.dolphinhousebrazzerie.co.uk; Wed-Sat 10 pm, Sun 5 pm.*

River Cottage Canteen £45 3 2 3

Royal William Yd PL1 3QQ (01752) 252702
*In a "fantastic" location – a warehouse in an ex-navy yard – Hugh Fearnley Whittingstall's canteen has real "buzz" (it's an "echoey room!"); the cuisine strikes most (if not quite all) reporters as "lovely", too. / **Details:** www.rivercottage.net; 9.30 pm.*

Rock Salt £46 3 2 3

31 Stonehouse St PL1 3PE (01752) 225522
*"Fresh fish dishes" plus a "well-varied menu" continue to attract solid feedback for this smart café "in a former red-light area". / **Details:** www.rocksaltcafe.co.uk; 9.30 pm.*

RockFish Sutton Harbour £32 4 4 2

3 Rope Walk PL4 0LB (01752) 255974
"A small Korean restaurant" in the city centre; "attentive and helpful service, provides useful recommendations to navigate the cuisine", and the food – much of it barbecued – is "very interesting and delicious, and exceptionally good value".

POLKERRIS, CORNWALL 1–3B

Sams on the Beach £45 3 3 5

PL24 2TL (01726) 812255
*In a "wonderful location" – an old lifeboat station in "a tiny fishing village" – this "great family restaurant" wins plaudits for its "brilliant pizzas and excellent fish almost served on the beach... what else do you need?" / **Details:** www.samsfowey.co.uk; 9 pm; no Amex.*

POOLE, DORSET 7–3D

Branksome Beach £51 3 3 4

Pinecliff Rd BH13 6LP (01202) 767235
*"Looking onto the wide sandy beaches of Poole", a "glass box" of a restaurant filled with "wonderful" light; by all accounts the food is also "really very good" and it's "THE place for Sunday breakfast". / **Details:** www.branksomebeach.co.uk; 5 pm; L only.*

Guildhall Tavern £53 4 4 4

15 Market St BH15 1NB (01202) 671717
*"A little gem tucked away from the grotty quayside joints" that elicits raves for its "individual, lovely" French food (especially fish) and "friendly" ambience; "prices have increased recently and they do tend to pack 'em in, but it's still always a treat to visit". / **Details:** www.guildhalltavern.co.uk; 9 pm, Fri & Sat 10 pm; closed Mon & Sun; no Amex.*

South Deep £33 3 4 5

Parkstone Bay Marina, Turks Ln BH14 8EW
(01202) 733155
*"A fun, casual eating experience in a marina on the edge of Poole Harbour, that's especially pleasant when sitting out on the decking in summer". "Well-executed" light bites are on offer, and their regular tapas evenings are "very enjoyable and good value". / **Details:** www.parkstonebay.com/cafe/; 9 pm, Fri & Sat 9.30 pm; closed Mon D, Tue D & Sun D.*

Storm £51 322
16 High St BH15 1BP (01202) 674970
*Pete & Frances Miles's fish-centric venture garners solid feedback for its "freshly caught", "good value" fish and seafood; the odd critic, though, "expected more", especially "given the TV hype", but still gave it a good food-rating. / **Details**: www.stormfish.co.uk; 9.30 pm, Fri & Sat 10 pm; closed Mon L, Tue L & Sun L.*

PORT APPIN, ARGYLL AND BUTE 9–3B

Airds Hotel £79 433
PA38 4DF (01631) 730236
*"Airds are right back on song"; glowing reports on the new chef's "superb tasting menu" at this Relais & Châteaux dining room, in a former ferry inn, with "fabulous" West Highland views. / **Details**: www.airds-hotel.com; 20m N of Oban; 9.30 pm; no jeans or trainers; children: 8+ at D. **Accommodation**: 11 rooms, from £290*

Pierhouse Hotel £59 444
PA38 4DE (01631) 730302
*"Standards are maintained at this wonderful spot by the passenger ferry to Lismore", benefitting from "really amazing views" of Loch Lyne. It offers the "freshest fishy ingredients" ("straight from the water's edge") "simply and beautifully cooked", and "lovely rooms to retire to" after dinner. / **Details:** www.pierhousehotel.co.uk; just off A828, follow signs for Port Appin & Lismore Ferry; 9.30 pm. **Accommodation:** 12 rooms, from £100*

PORT ISAAC, CORNWALL 1–3B

Outlaw's Fish Kitchen £35 455
1 Middle St PL29 3RH (01208) 881138
*This "tiny" harbourside spin-off pre-dates Nathan Outlaw moving his main operation to this picturesque village. It's a much more "humble" operation, but "thoroughly special" in its way, with "the best of the local catch" presented in "superb seafood small plates" by "the most considerate staff ever". / **Details:** www.outlaws.co.ukfishkitchen; 9 pm; closed Mon & Sun.*

Restaurant Nathan Outlaw £144 554
6 New Rd PL29 3SB (01208) 880 896
*"Another chapter in the epic tale of this master chef's rise to greatness!" – the move to a "light and airy" new location (formerly The Edge, RIP) in a super-cute fishing village ("with fantastic views over the Cornish coast") has taken Nathan Outlaw's flagship venture to a new level. Service is "the most considerate ever", and the "magical" food features "subtle, visually beautiful ensembles with stunning sauces, imaginative use of the freshest of ingredients, starring perfect fish and seafood, with supporting casts of local and seasonal produce". / **Details:** www.nathan-outlaw.com.*

PORTHGAIN, PEMBROKESHIRE 4–4B

The Shed £41 333
SA62 5BN (01348) 831518
*A "quaint" and "intimate, 'fish 'n' chip bistro' on the quayside, where you sit facing the water"; "stick with plain grilled fish caught fresh" – "straight out of the sea", and "beautifully cooked" – and "let the magic of a balmy Pembroke evening wash over you". / **Details:** www.theshedporthgain.co.uk; 9 pm; no Amex.*

PORTHLEVEN, CORNWALL 1–4A

Kota £50 433
Harbour Head TR13 9JA (01326) 562407
*An attractive spot in the "most beautiful" harbourfront location serving "fantastic" Asian fusion-style food; the owners also have a relaxed, family-friendly sibling (Kota Kai at Celtic House, Harbour Head). / **Details:** www.kotarestaurant.co.uk; 9 pm; D only, closed Sun-Tue; no Amex. **Accommodation:** 2 rooms, from £70*

PORTMAHOMACK , HIGHLAND 9–2C

The Oystercatcher £55 422
Main St IV20 1YB (01862) 871560
*"What a find"; in this small coastal village, a "casual bistro-style restaurant" offering fresh seafood and a simply "exceptional" wine list which (presumably to its credit) "reads like a telephone directory". / **Details:** www.the-oystercatcher.co.uk; 10 pm; closed Mon, Tue, Wed, Thu L & Sun D. **Accommodation:** 3 rooms, from £82*

PORTMEIRION, GWYNEDD 4–2C

Portmeirion Hotel £61 335
LL48 6ET (01766) 772440
*"A long-standing favourite in this fantasy village"; this hotel dining room in Sir Clough Williams-Ellis's fantastical homage to Portofino is still a "real treat", especially for romance, largely due to the "jaw-dropping" development itself, along with lovely estuary views – but the food "isn't bad either", and can be "excellent". / **Details:** www.portmeirion-village.com; off A487 at Minffordd; 9 pm. **Accommodation:** 14 rooms, from £185*

PORTSMOUTH, HAMPSHIRE 2–4D

abarbistro £41 333
58 White Hart Rd PO1 2JA (02392) 811585
Together with (its upstairs bottle shop and tasting venue) Camber Wines, this "cramped and noisy"

Old Portsmouth bistro "offers a constantly changing wine list that helps to ensure that a visit never disappoints". / ***Details:*** *www.abarbistro.co.uk; 11 pm.*

Loch Fyne **£45** **344**
Unit 2 Vulcan Buildings PO1 3TY
(023) 9277 8060
An "atmospheric" outpost of the national fish chain offering "excellent" fish; whilst it does have a "recognisable brand feel", this extends to its "reliable" culinary standards, and service is very "friendly and welcoming". / ***Details:*** *www.lochfyne-restaurants.com; 10.30 pm.*

Restaurant 27 **£62** **543**
27a, Southsea Pde PO5 2JF (023) 9287 6272
An understated Southsea local that provides the "best dining experience in Portsmouth by far", according to fans; it doesn't elicit a huge amount of commentary, but what there is focuses on the tasting menus, which are deemed "outstanding" by all. / ***Details:*** *www.restaurant27.com; 9.30 pm; closed Mon, Tue, Wed L, Thu L, Fri L, Sat L & Sun D.*

Rosie's Vineyard **£43** **334**
87 Elm Grove PO5 1JF (02392) 755944
"The food has never been a disappointment in the 16 years I've been going" – this "lovely" bar/restaurant "just keeps on producing really good food". And with its regular jazz, you can enjoy "some of the best music on the South Coast" too. / ***Details:*** *www.rosies-vineyard.co.uk; S from M275 towards Southsea. At roundabout turn left into King's Rd, leading to Elm Grv; 11 pm; D only, ex Sun open L & D.*

PRESTBURY, CHESHIRE 5–2B

Bacchus **£52** **433**
The Village SK10 4DG (01625) 820009
"Never disappoints for an enjoyable good-value meal" – the tenor of feedback on this venture from the survivors of Manchester's once-hallowed Moss Nook (RIP). / ***Details:*** *www.bacchusprestbury.co.uk; 9.30 pm, Fri & Sat 10 pm; closed Mon & Sun D.*

PRESTON BAGOT, WARWICKSHIRE 5–4C

The Crabmill **£45** **334**
B95 5EE (01926) 843342
"A winner every time"; this "all-round comfortable and welcoming" gastroboozer, with an "extensive (if "not exotic") menu" and "excellent beer", makes for an especially "good lunch stop off the M40". / ***Details:*** *www.lovelypubs.co.uk/the-crabmill-pub; on main road between Warwick & Henley-in-Arden; 9.30 pm; closed Sun D; no Amex.*

PRESTON CANDOVER, HAMPSHIRE 2–3D

The Purefoy Arms **£46** **433**
RG25 2EJ (01256) 389 777
This highly popular "Spanish twist on a gastroboozer", offers the kind of "exciting cooking so rarely actually found in pubs", plus an "outstanding collection of well-priced Spanish wines". / ***Details:*** *www.thepurefoyarms.co.uk; 10 pm; closed Mon & Sun D.*

PRESTON, LANCASHIRE 5–1A

Bukhara **£34** **443**
154 Preston New Rd PR5 0UP
(01772) 877710
"Still the best Indian in central Lancashire" – a venue whose booze-free policy is offset by "great lime soda", "excellent, freshly squeezed juices" and "a large choice of unusual dishes"; "booking is essential as it's smaller than it looks". / ***Details:*** *www.bukharasamlesbury.co.uk; 11 pm; closed weekday L; no Maestro.*

PWLLHELI, GWYNEDD 4–2C

Plas Bodegroes **£68** **445**
Nefyn Rd LL53 5TH (01758) 612363
The Chowns' "elegant" restaurant-with-rooms is "set in beautiful grounds" with a "lovely veranda", and – with its "delicious" food and "unobtrusive" service – has offered a "dining experience to remember" for nearly 30 years now. Stop Press – in September 2015 they put the business up for sale, so the future of one of Wales's best destinations is currently uncertain. / ***Details:*** *www.bodegroes.co.uk; on A497 1m W of Pwllheli; 9.00 pm; closed Mon, Tue-Sat D only, closed Sun D; no Amex; children: 12+ at D.* ***Accommodation:*** *10 rooms, from £130*

QUEENSBURY, MIDDLESEX 3–3A

Regency Club **£36** **423**
19-21 Queensbury Station Pde HA8 5NR
(020) 8952 6300
"A welcome antidote to the growing pretentiousness in Indian cooking"; the "fantastic East-African/Indian food" at this Edgware fixture – part pub, part curry house, and "always with big sporting events on the big screen" – comes "at cheap prices but packs real flavour". / ***Details:*** *www.regencyclub.co.uk; 10.30 pm, Fri & Sat 11 pm, Sun 10 pm; closed Mon L; children: 18+.*

RAMSBOTTOM, GREATER MANCHESTER 5–1B

Levanter £35 545
10 Square St BL0 9BE (01706) 55 1530
What "started as a market stall selling excellent, artisanal Spanish charcuterie" has now morphed into "the sort of backstreet tapas bar you'd feel pleased to find in Spain". A tiny former barber's shop, "it may be cramped, crowded, and not offer bookings, but the tapas is worth any amount of queuing!" / **Details:** *www.levanterfinefoods.co.uk; 11 pm, Sun 8 pm; closed Mon & Tue.*

RAMSGATE, KENT 3–3D

Albion House £48 324
Albion Place CT11 8HQ (01843) 606630
With its line in "high-end comfort food", the restaurant at this "stunning" new Regency-era boutique hotel, on the East Cliff, makes a "lovely addition to local dining". / **Details:** *www.albionhouseramsgate.co.uk/; 9.30 pm.*

Flavours By Kumar £35 543
2 Effingham St CT11 9AT (01843) 852631
"Located in a very unglamorous former pub, up an equally unglamorous side-street, in unglamorous Ramsgate, is what must be one of the best new Indian restaurants of the year"; chef "Anir Kumar has an impressive CV" (Ambrette in Margate) and it shows in "stunning" food that's also "ludicrously cheap". / **Details:** *flavoursbykumar.co.uk/; 10.30 pm.*

RAMSGILL-IN-NIDDERDALE, NORTH YORKSHIRE 8–4B

Yorke Arms £92 534
HG3 5RL (01423) 755243
"A marvellous setting, in the middle of Nidderdale" provides a "lovely" backdrop to this rural but "classy" old inn, in a "beautiful Dales village". Frances Atkins is one of the country's most renowned female chefs, and "local game is often to the fore" in her "unfailingly impressive", "incredibly intensely flavoured cooking", which ranks in the UK top-20 this year. / **Details:** *www.yorke-arms.co.uk; 4m W of Pateley Bridge; 8.45 pm; closed Mon & Sun.* **Accommodation:** *16 rooms, from £200*

RAVENGLASS, CUMBRIA 7–3C

Inn At Ravenglass £36 443
Main St, Ravenglass Cumbria CA18 1SQ
(01229) 717230
In the Lake District National Park, with the "brooding presence of Sellafield up the road", a newly relaunched coastal inn (ex-Holly House) "refurbished with the assistance of EU money intended to support local fisheries"; unsurprisingly, it "majors in ("very fresh") seafood" but is "also the village chippy and pizza takeaway"! / **Details:** *theinnatravenglass.co.uk/; 11 pm, Sun 5 pm; closed Sun.*

READING, BERKSHIRE 2–2D

London Street Brasserie £56 343
2-4 London St RG1 4PN (0118) 950 5036
"A Reading stalwart that can always be relied on" – this "deservedly popular fixture" is "a light-filled space, with a lovely location on the Thames", providing a long and "enticing" menu and "good buzz". Even reporters who say the cooking is "hit 'n' miss" say "this is far and away the best eating option in town!" Top Tip – "great value daytime menu". / **Details:** *www.londonstbrasserie.co.uk; 10.30 pm, Fri & Sat 11 pm.*

REDHILL, SURREY 3–3B

The Pendleton £49 544
26 Pendleton RH1 6QF (01737) 760212
"John (kitchen) & Cynthia (front of house) Coomb maintain their excellent standards" at this "cracking" gastropub – their follow-up to the Westerley in Reigate; it offers some "imaginative" dishes ("Sauternes custard with rhubarb anyone?") that fans acclaim as "the best nosh in the area". / **Details:** *www.thependleton.co.uk.*

REIGATE, SURREY 3–3B

La Barbe £52 223
71 Bell St RH2 7AN (01737) 241966
A "real French restaurant with a great atmosphere"; while some insist that it has "upped its game over the year", offering "more innovative" food, others claim it's "not as good as it used to be" and "needs to sparkle a little more". / **Details:** *www.labarbe.co.uk; 9.30 pm; closed Sat L & Sun D.*

REYNOLDSTON, SWANSEA 1–1C

Fairyhill £66 553
SA3 1BS (01792) 390139
"In the peace and quiet of the beautiful Gower Peninsular", a "welcoming", well-known country house hotel "situated in lovely grounds where diners can stroll between courses"; by all accounts the food remains "top notch", with "lots of excellent very locally sourced meat" the highlight. / **Details:** *www.fairyhill.net; 20 mins from M4, J47 off B4295; 9 pm; no Amex; children: 8+ at D.* **Accommodation:** *8 rooms, from £180*

RIPLEY, SURREY 3–3A

Anchor £52 433
High St GU23 6AE (01483) 211866
"What was a tired and grotty boozer" has been transformed into an "outstanding" gastropub "with the emphasis on the gastro" by new owners Drakes; reporters are "not sure you'd want to pop in for a pint", but for "great" steaks and "inventive" salads it's just the ticket. / **Details:** *www.ripleyanchor.co.uk; 11 pm, Sun 9 pm; closed Mon.*

Drakes £84 543
The Clock Hs, High St GU23 6AQ
(01483) 224777
"If you look up culinary excellence in a dictionary, it would say 'See Drakes'!" – chef/patron Steve Drake's "adventurous" tasting menus "show a talent for extracting the purest of flavours and marrying them with unusual pairings", and maintains his village restaurant in the UK's premier culinary league. "You sometimes have no idea of what is to come from the sparse menu descriptions, but you will always be pleasantly surprised." / **Details:** *www.drakesrestaurant.co.uk; 9.30 pm; closed Mon, Tue L & Sun; no Amex; booking: max 12.*

ROADE, NORTHAMPTONSHIRE 3–1A

Roade House £47 443
16 High St NN7 2NW (01604) 863372
"Still the only place really worth eating in what is a barren part of the world" – a "long-standing favourite" where the food is never less than "very dependable". / **Details:** *www.roadehousehotel.co.uk; 9.30 pm; closed Mon L, Sat L & Sun D; no shorts.* **Accommodation:** *10 rooms, from £82*

ROCK, CORNWALL 1–3B

Dining Room £61 432
Pavilion Buildings, Rock Rd PL27 6JS
(01208) 862622
Husband-and-wife team Fred & Donna Beedle "make for a formidable fine dining experience" at this small and "friendly" venue, located in a modern parade of shops; "Fred's commitment to his food is unsurpassed", while Donna keeps the place "running with ease". / **Details:** *www.thediningroomrock.co.uk; 9 pm; closed Mon, Tue, Wed L, Thu L, Fri L, Sat L & Sun L; no Amex; children: 10+.*

Outlaw's The St Enodoc Hotel £65 443
Rock Road PL27 6LA (01208) 862737
Now that Nathan Outlaw has moved his main HQ to Port Isaac, this hotel dining retaining his brand attracts much less attention and now offers a more "everyday" formula. Feedback is a little more mixed – "some dishes are better than others" – but overall, the location continues to win praise for its "fine estuary views", "relaxed service" and "beautifully presented and delicately flavoured" fish dishes. / **Details:** *www.nathan-outlaw.com; 9 pm; closed Mon & Sun; no Amex; no shorts; children: 12+ D.* **Accommodation:** *20 rooms, from £130*

ROCKBEARE, DEVON 1–3D

Jack in the Green Inn £48 443
London Rd EX5 2EE (01404) 822240
"The quality of food and its presentation is of the highest standard" at this impressive gastroboozer, "and this is complemented by service from properly trained and helpful staff"; "couldn't fault it!" / **Details:** *www.jackinthegreen.uk.com; On the old A30, 3 miles east of junction 29 of M5; 9.30 pm, Sun 9 pm; no Amex.*

ROMALDKIRK, COUNTY DURHAM 8–3B

The Rose & Crown £46 333
DL12 9EB (01833) 650213
A "lovely, traditional inn with good local produce"; one reporter was "a bit underwhelmed", but not sure why... perhaps it's because, as another suggests, what was once "County Durham's answer to a proper gastropub" is now "trying too hard". / **Details:** *www.rose-and-crown.co.uk; 6m NW of Barnard Castle on B6277; 9 pm; D only, ex Sun open L & D; children: 7+ in restaurant.* **Accommodation:** *14 rooms, from £150*

ROSEVINE, CORNWALL 1–4B

Driftwood Hotel £75 445
TR2 5EW (01872) 580644
"Chris Eden and his team never fail to please", say fans of the dining room of this trendy cliff-top hotel, and all agree that with its "stunning views", "you cannot ask for a more romantic setting". The odd critic feels "it's let down by pricey food that tries too hard", but on most accounts it's "divine". / **Details:** *www.driftwoodhotel.co.uk; off the A30 to Truro, towards St Mawes; 9.30 pm; D only; booking: max 6; children: 10+.* **Accommodation:** *15 rooms, from £170*

ROWSLEY, DERBYSHIRE 5–2C

The Peacock at Rowsley £72 333
Bakewell Rd DE4 2EB (01629) 733518
A Peak District country house hotel with a "welcoming fire in the bar" and "delicious food" in the restaurant; it can strike some as "overly formal" ("white gloves to serve the food?") and "expensive" too, but as a "special treat place", it's "worth it" by most accounts. / **Details:**

www.thepeacockatrowsley.com; 9 pm, Sun 8.30 pm; children: 10+ at D. **Accommodation:** *15 rooms, from £160*

RYE, EAST SUSSEX 3–4C

The Ambrette at Rye £49 434
6 High St TN31 7JE (01797) 222 043
Dev Biswal has parted company with the hotel that originally housed his innovative Indian, and moved to another nearby premises on the High Street. On most accounts it's "an improvement", and made no difference to its "exceptional fusion cuisine" (with the tasting menu particularly recommended). / **Details:** *www.theambrette.co.uk; 9.30 pm, Fri & Sat 10 pm; closed Mon L.*

Landgate Bistro £44 453
5-6 Landgate TN31 7LH (01797) 222829
A "small bistro with one chef, one waitress" that's still "strongly recommended" after a quarter of a century; the "really excellent cooking of fine local ingredients", is complemented by "very competent and well-trained staff". / **Details:** *www.landgatebistro.co.uk; 9 pm; closed Mon, Tue, Wed L, Thu L, Fri L & Sun D; no Amex.*

Standard Inn £39 444
33 The Mint TN31 7EN (01797) 225231
In the heart of the Citadel, one of Rye's most beloved pubs has reopened as a restaurant-with-rooms that's already "very popular" amongst locals; besides offering "interesting" locally sourced food, it's "one of those rare places where you come out feeling better than when you went in". / **Details:** *www.thestandardinnrye.co.uk; 10 pm; min 8 to book.*

Webbe's at The Fish Cafe £44 432
17 Tower St TN31 7AT (01797) 222226
Paul Webbe's "unpretentious" venture in a town-centre warehouse conversion can seem a little "short on atmosphere", especially the downstairs café. No gripes about the "extensive and expertly prepared" array of "beautiful" fish and seafood though, which "rarely fails to hit the spot". / **Details:** *www.thefishcafe.com; 9.30 pm.*

SALFORD, GREATER MANCHESTER 5–2B

Damson £57 454
Orange Building, Media City UK M50 2HF
(0161) 751 7020
"At last Media City has a restaurant worthy of it!" – this "hidden gem" is a "delightful place in Salford Quays" whose "special" cooking stands "head and shoulders above anywhere in the vicinity". "Lovely terrace when the sun is out" too. / **Details:** *www.damsonrestaurant.co.uk; Mon-Thu 9.30 pm Fri & Sat 10 pm; closed Sun D.*

SALISBURY, WILTSHIRE 2–3C

Anokaa £42 422
60 Fisherton St SP2 7RB (01722) 414142
With its "tasty, delicately flavoured" food, this "interesting" nouvelle Indian is, for fans, "probably still Salisbury's best restaurant"; there's a slight sense that it "has got expensive" of late, however, and service can range from "inattentive" to "pushy" at times. / **Details:** *www.anokaa.com; 10.30 pm; no shorts.*

SALTAIRE, WEST YORKSHIRE 5–1C

Salts Diner £34 233
Salts Mill, Victoria Rd BD18 3LA
(01274) 531163
"One of the many attractions at the (UNESCO-listed) Salt's Mill" – a gallery café offering "good, fresh", if occasionally "bland", cuisine; it's a very "buzzy" spot, certainly "not for the hard of hearing". / **Details:** *www.saltsmill.org.uk; 2m from Bradford on A650; L & afternoon tea only; no Amex.*

SALTHOUSE, NORFOLK 6–3C

Dun Cow £38 334
Purdy St NR25 7XA (01263) 740467
In a "great location looking out over the marshes", this wood-beamed country boozer has "improved beyond recognition under the new management"; it's "now a wonderful food pub", offering "superbly done" local fare. "There's a great garden at the back (and also lots of space facing the sea at the front)." / **Details:** *salthouseduncow.com; 11 pm.*

SANDSEND, NORTH YORKSHIRE 8–3D

Estbek House £60 454
East Row YO21 3SU (01947) 893424
"If you love fish and want a restaurant for a special occasion, this is the one to choose" – a seafront restaurant-with-rooms combining "stunning views" and seafood that's "out of this world"; admittedly, it's "not cheap", but the consensus is that it's "worth saving up for". / **Details:** *www.estbekhouse.co.uk; 9 pm; D only; no Amex.* **Accommodation:** *5 rooms, from £125*

SAPPERTON, GLOUCESTERSHIRE 2–2C

The Bell at Sapperton £48 234
GL7 6LE (01285) 760298
"A delightful Cotswold pub situated in a very pretty village" where "you can tether the horses at the door"! The food can seem "overpriced", but even some who say it's "not gangbusters", say it "helps justify the trip" and there's a decent range of beers

on tap too. / **Details:** *www.bellsapperton.co.uk; from Cirencester take the A419 towards Stroud, turn right to Sapperton; 9.30 pm, Sun 9 pm; no Amex.*

SAUNDERSFOOT, PEMBROKESHIRE 4–4B

Coast £61 335
Coppet Hall Beach SA69 9AJ (01834) 810800
"An absolute knockout"; Will Holland's venture combines "brilliant cooking" of local fish, with a "vibrant" setting in a purpose-built building, with a "perfect" beachside location; okay, so it's "extremely expensive", but "with this view, who wouldn't feel good?" / **Details:** *www.coastsaundersfoot.co.uk; 9 pm; closed Mon & Tue.*

SAWLEY, LANCASHIRE 5–1B

The Spread Eagle £48 223
BB7 4NH (01200) 441202
"A traditional pub" offering "a mix of traditional dishes" in a "beautiful setting opposite the ruined abbey and next to the River Ribble"; "for a cosy atmosphere, try the bar area with its welcoming fire". / **Details:** *www.spreadeaglesawley.co.uk; 9.15 pm, Sun 7.15 pm.* **Accommodation:** *7 rooms, from £80*

SCARBOROUGH, NORTH YORKSHIRE 8–4D

Lanterna £54 553
33 Queen St YO11 1HQ (01723) 363616
A "reliably superb", if rather "old-fashioned" Italian that invariably pleases reporters with its "excellent fish and seafood dishes"; even loyal fans concede that it's "quite pricey though (particularly the specials)". / **Details:** *www.lanterna-ristorante.co.uk; 9.30 pm; D only, closed Sun; no Amex.*

SCAWTON, NORTH YORKSHIRE 8–4C

Hare Inn £48 544
YO7 2HG (01845) 597769
An historic pub in a village on the edge of the moors which has "really upped the game" with its "indulgent" cooking, producing some simply "stunning" locally sourced fare, with game "a particular strong point". "We visited on a snowy night, but it deserves to be heaving, even in a blizzard!" / **Details:** *www.thehare-inn.com; off A170; 9 pm; closed Mon, Tue & Sun D.*

SCHOLES, WEST YORKSHIRE 5–1C

The House Restaurant £42
1 Scholes Ln BD19 6PA
The owners of the Deisgn House restaurant in Halifax (RIP) move to a new site in Scholes village, bringing with them their tasting menu and early bird set dinner deals.

SEER GREEN, BUCKINGHAMSHIRE 3–3A

The Jolly Cricketers £50 332
24 Chalfont Rd HP9 2YG (01494) 676308
"What was a standard pub" now offers a "memorable experience" for foodies too; whilst it's "still a little cramped", that's "worth putting up with" for some "very good-value" fare in a "nice informal atmosphere". / **Details:** *www.thejollycricketers.co.uk; 11.15 pm, Fri & Sat 11.30, Sun 10.30.*

SEVENOAKS, KENT 3–3B

Little Garden £43 444
1-2 Well Court, Bank Street TN13 1UN
(01732) 469397
"A new and very welcome addition to gastronomically impaired Sevenoaks"; it combines some "wonderful" dishes (many barbecued in the modish Josper oven) with a "pub-worthy selection of ciders and beers", and the "magically lit" courtyard is another boon. / **Details:** *www.littlegardensevenoaks.com/#!menu/c24tf; 11 pm, Fri & Sat midnight, Sun 9 pm.*

SHALDON, DEVON 1–3D

Ode £59 443
Fore St TQ14 0DE (01626) 873977
"An intimate restaurant located in a beautiful village" combining "unfussy" service and a "high standard of cooking with an emphasis on local, sustainable produce"; it has a café sibling (with sea views) too. / **Details:** *www.odetruefood.com; 9.30 pm; D only, closed Sun-Tue; no Amex; children: 8+ after 8pm.*

SHEFFIELD, SOUTH YORKSHIRE 5–2C

Mediterranean £47 442
271 - 273 Sharrow Vale Rd S11 8ZF
(01142) 661069
This Sharrow Vale tapas and fish stalwart is on all accounts "just brilliant on all levels". / **Details:** *www.mediterraneansheffield.co.uk; 10.30 pm; closed Sun.*

The Milestone £46 333
84 Green Lane At Ball St S3 8SE
(0114) 272 8327
"An old favourite", located in an industrial stretch near the canals, which is deemed a "good place for special occasions" and brunch. "Midweek the ambience is not so good, but that's not a problem at the weekend!" / **Details:** *www.the-milestone.co.uk; Mon-Sat 10.30 pm, Sun 9.30 pm; no Amex.*

Nonna's £47 3 3 2
535-541 Ecclesball Rd S11 8PR
(0114) 268 6166
"Still bustling, still very Italian-sounding and very Italian-tasting"; as befits the name, the food at this Eccleshall venue is "more like nonna makes than the superb offerings of the Italian gastronomes" but "you get hefty helpings and all of it's good". / **Details:** *www.nonnas.co.uk; 9.30 pm, Sat & Sun 9.45 pm; no Amex.*

The Old Vicarage £102 3 2 2
Ridgeway Moor, Ridgeway Village S12 3XW
(0114) 247 5814
"The only thing that spoils this place is the enthusiastic up-selling!" – it sometimes seems this highly regarded stalwart venue snatches defeat from the jaws of victory. Without exception, reporters have some esteem for the cuisine here, but the high pricing and a certain stuffiness at times lead to numerous accusations over "laurel-resting" and over-pricing. And "nowadays there's much more competition in town offering better value for money". / **Details:** *www.theoldvicarage.co.uk; 9.30 pm; closed Mon, Sat L & Sun; no Amex; children: call in advance.*

Rafters £60 4 4 4
220 Oakbrook Rd, Nether Grn S11 7ED
(0114) 230 4819
This "romantic" Ranmoor fixture "goes from strength to strength" since it changed hands a couple of years ago; chef-patron Tom Lawson is a "skilful" whizz at the stoves, while front-of-house Alistair Myers "knows his wine" and "maintains an interesting, varied list". / **Details:** *www.raftersrestaurant.co.uk; Wed & Thu 8.30 pm, Fri & Sat 9 pm; D only, closed Tue & Sun.*

Silversmiths £37 3 3 2
111 Arundel St S1 2NT (0114) 270 6160
"A little jewel five minutes' walk from the busy West Street area" which offers "good food, with pretensions to better" – results are "more hit than miss" and "given the realistic prices, who's complaining?" / **Details:** *www.silversmiths-restaurant.com; 11.30 pm, Fri & Sat midnight; D only, closed Mon & Sun; no Amex.*

Street Food Chef £7 4 3 3
90 Arundel St S1 4RE (01142) 752390
"If you want a burrito in Sheffield this is the place to go" – an "ace", "always-bustling" Mexican whose "cheap 'n' cheerful" grub is "perfect for a grab-and-go lunch or speedy dinner". / **Details:** *www.streetfoodchef.co.uk/; 10 pm.*

Vero Gusto £58 4 4 4
12 Norfolk Row S1 2PA (0114) 276 0004
"They strive to be different, and they do darn well at it", say fans of this "crowded" but "endlessly charming" Italian; the food is of a reliably "high standard" and there's a "huge" (but "pricey") wine list to go with it too. / **Details:** *www.verogusto.com; 10 pm; closed Mon & Sun.*

SHEFFORD, BEDFORDSHIRE 3–1A

Black Horse at Ireland £52 3 3 3
SG17 5QL (01462) 811398
This "smooth" country pub-with-rooms – a traditional spot in a small, tranquil hamlet – garners plaudits for its "excellent array of wines expertly paired with food". / **Details:** *www.blackhorseireland.com; 9.30 pm, Fri & Sat 10 pm; closed Sun D.* **Accommodation:** *2 rooms, from £55*

SHELLEY, WEST YORKSHIRE 5–2C

Three Acres £58 3 4 4
Roydhouse HD8 8LR (01484) 602606
In a remote spot near the Emley TV transmitter, a "long-standing moor-top favourite" renowned for its "quirky and cool" interior and its "classic English fayre" in "hearty Yorkshire portions". On most accounts it still lives up with many "superb" reports, but quite a few sceptics find it "totally overpriced" nowadays – "the car park tells a tale of people with too much money, and a place resting on its laurels". / **Details:** *www.3acres.com; 9.30 pm; no Amex.* **Accommodation:** *16 rooms, from £125*

SHENLEY, HERTFORDSHIRE 3–2B

White Horse £47 3 2 3
37 London Rd WD7 9ER (01923) 853054
A "cosy" local (especially "by the log fires") that offers "good honest pub food" from a "wide" menu that's "generally done well". / **Details:** *www.whitehorseradlett.co.uk; 10 pm, Sat 10.30 pm.*

SHERBORNE, DORSET 2–3B

Eastbury Hotel £54 4 3 3
Long St DT9 3BY (01935) 813131
This "small but very comfortable hotel" is particularly rated for its "excellent tasting menu with accompanying wines" – "and if you also stay over, the rooms are lovely and the breakfast buffet wonderful". / **Details:** *www.theeastburyhotel.co.uk.*

The Green £51 3 3 3
3 The Grn DT9 3HY (01935) 813821
A handily central spot that "never fails to please" with its menu of "interesting local food" and "particularly good" lunchtime deals. / **Details:** *www.greenrestaurant.co.uk; 9.30 pm; closed Mon & Sun.*

SHERE, SURREY 3–3A

Kinghams £54 444

Gomshall Ln GU5 9HE (01483) 202168

*"Superb food, first-class service"; this "lovely independent" in a 17th-century building with exposed beams is an "outstanding" sort of spot "which embodies the very best of a country restaurant". / **Details:** www.kinghams-restaurant.co.uk; off A25 between Dorking & Guildford; 9 pm; closed Mon & Sun D.*

The William Bray £51 434

Shere Ln GU5 9HS (01483) 202 044

*A "traditional English country pub in a charming Surrey village" that's "owned by a former Stig from Top Gear"; "the vintage F1 photos are worth the visit alone", but as it happens, the food is great too, and there's a "fun and friendly" vibe to boot. / **Details:** www.thewilliambray.co.uk; 9.45 pm, Sun 7.30 pm.*

SHINFIELD, BERKSHIRE 2–2D

L'Ortolan £97 444

Church Ln RG2 9BY (0118) 988 8500

*"New head chef Tom Clarke is fab-u-lous!" and he's more than carried on where Alan Murchison left off, at this Home Counties foodie bastion, which occupies a very pukka former rectory, and provides "superb" cuisine (including a "cracking 10-course tasting menu"), plus "many thoughtful wine options". / **Details:** www.lortolan.com; 8.30 pm; closed Mon & Sun.*

SHIPBOURNE, KENT 3–3B

The Chaser Inn £43 434

Stumble Hill TN11 9PE (01732) 810360

*This attractive country-style pub – the original outpost of the Whiting & Hammond Group's small south-eastern empire – delivers great, "hearty" food, and is "well worth a visit when in the area". / **Details:** www.thechaser.co.uk; 9.30 pm, Sun 9 pm.*

SHIPLAKE, OXFORDSHIRE 2–2D

Orwells £65 432

Shiplake Row RG9 4DP (0118) 940 3673

*Though it's still "an unexpected find on a walk" for some first-time visitors, this "upmarket gastropub" is becoming increasing well-known as "the best choice in the Reading area". It offers a "genuine welcome", and the "adventurous" food is "superb". / **Details:** www.orwellsatshiplake.co.uk; 9.30 pm; closed Mon, Tue & Sun D.*

SHIPLEY, WEST YORKSHIRE 5–1C

Aagrah £35 443

4 Saltaire Rd BD18 3HN (01274) 530880

*It's "a really special experience" to visit this "buzzing" Kashmiri operation, the HQ of a popular local chain; service is "always so friendly", but the highest praise goes to the "wonderful" upstairs buffet. / **Details:** www.aagrah.com; 11.30 pm, Fri-Sat midnight, Sun 10.30 pm; D only.*

SHIRLEY, DERBYSHIRE 5–3C

The Saracen's Head £40 333

Church Ln DE6 3AS (01335) 360 330

*A "friendly" country pub combining "fantastically creative dishes" (especially meat-based ones), "wonderful beers and wines" and a "great atmosphere"... they've "got it just right!" / **Details:** www.saracens-head-shirley.co.uk; 9 pm; no Amex.*

SHREWSBURY, SHROPSHIRE 5–4A

Number Four £35 344

4 Butcher Row SY1 1UW (01743) 366691

*"A must-visit for lunch when in this lovely medieval town" – this "small", city-centre café has won high local popularity with its brunch-friendly fare, and is also open for a couple of evenings each week; "the fries with béarnaise sauce alone justified the trip". / **Details:** www.number-four.com; 11 pm; closed Mon D, Tue D & Wed D.*

SKENFRITH, MONMOUTHSHIRE 2–1B

The Bell at Skenfrith £52 323

NP7 8UH (01600) 750235

*A "delightful" and remote country inn offering "hearty cooking with a truly rural taste" (not least the "surprisingly successful and stylish" roasts). / **Details:** www.skenfrith.co.uk; on B4521, 10m E of Abergavenny; 9.30 pm, Sun 9 pm; no Amex; children: 8+ at D. **Accommodation:** 11 rooms, from £110*

SLEAT, HIGHLAND 9–2B

Kinloch Lodge £95 544

IV43 8QY (01471) 833333

*There's "no resting on their laurels" for the Macdonald of Macdonalds at this remote and distinctly "grand" old hunting lodge; chef Marcello Tully "continues to impress" and is supported by a "vast" wine list. / **Details:** www.kinloch-lodge.co.uk; 9 pm; no Amex. **Accommodation:** 19 rooms, from £99 winter 180 summer pp*

SNAPE, SUFFOLK 3–1D

The Crown Inn £40 4 2 3
Bridge Rd IP17 1SL (01728) 688324
This 15th-century smugglers' inn is "as good now as it was under previous ownership a few years ago"; it serves "really surprising" food, "with a lot being from their own produce" (not least the in-house goats). / **Details:** *www.snape-crown.co.uk; off A12 towards Aldeburgh; 9.30 pm, Sat 10 pm, Sun 9.30 pm; no Amex.* **Accommodation:** *2 rooms, from £90*

The Plough and Sail £36 3 4 3
Snape Bridge IP17 1SR (01728) 688413
"Under local Suffolk brothers Alex and Oliver Burnside" since 2012, this "jolly" and "clearly popular" pub attracts acclaim for its "creative and locally sourced food"; it's particularly good "as a prelude to a concert at Snape Maltings". / **Details:** *www.theploughandsailsnape.com; 10 pm.*

SNETTISHAM, NORFOLK 6–4B

Rose & Crown £39 3 3 2
Old Church Rd PE31 7LX (01485) 541382
This "lovely", old moorland pub-with-rooms is "very much the centre of the village", offering "fine local produce"; "the older rooms at the front are the places to dine" (tipped over the "barn-like extension"). Garden and playground too. / **Details:** *www.roseandcrownsnettisham.co.uk; 9 pm; no Amex.* **Accommodation:** *16 rooms, from £90*

SONNING-ON-THAMES, BERKSHIRE 2–2D

The French Horn £80 3 4 5
RG4 6TN (0118) 969 2204
"The sort of place one's parents enjoyed in the 70's" – this "romantic" Thames-side venue, known for its "duck roasting on the spit in reception" offers a "lovely, cosy and old-fashioned" experience. "There's no nonsense about the food – it's excellent and plentiful!" ("but boy, those prices...") / **Details:** *www.thefrenchhorn.co.uk; 9.30 pm, Sun 9 pm; booking: max 10.* **Accommodation:** *21 rooms, from £160*

SOUTH FERRIBY, LINCOLNSHIRE 6–2A

Hope And Anchor £45 4 3 3
Sluice Rd DN18 6JQ (01652) 635334
New owner TV chef Colin McGurran has given this pub a major overhaul (including a fancy MaturMeat fridge showcasing the meats) since it was destroyed by floods in 2013; fans say it's a "hidden gem", combining "good" food, a "roaring fire" and "great views (if only of the Humber!)" / **Details:** *www.thehopeandanchorpub.co.uk/; 9 pm, Fri & Sat 10 pm, Sun 6 pm.*

SOUTH SHIELDS, TYNE AND WEAR 8–2B

Colmans £35 4 4 3
182-186 Ocean Rd NE33 2JQ
(0191) 456 1202
This "lovely, modern-looking" establishment (in fact, established way back in 1926) continues to serve "the most reliably excellent fish 'n' chips in the NE" – it's "worth a long drive"! / **Details:** *www.colmansfishandchips.com; L only; no Amex.*

SOUTHAMPTON, HAMPSHIRE 2–3D

Kuti's £36 4 4 3
37-39 Oxford St SO14 3DP (023) 8022 1585
"Very tasty Indian dishes" and "special service from a happy team" mean that it's "always a delight to dine in Kuti's" – not least as "Southampton is such a desert". / **Details:** *www.kutis.co.uk; 11.30 pm.*

Quay Fifteen £53 3 4 3
Bldg Shamrock Quay, William St SO14 5QL
(023) 8033 6615
A "wonderful find"; "despite its unpromising location" by a boat yard, this fine dining one-year-old is – according to its small fan club – "well worth a visit" on account of its "relaxing" interior, "personable service" and superior food. "Great care taken over cocktails" too. / **Details:** *www.quayfifteen.co.uk; 9 pm; closed Mon & Sun.*

SOUTHPORT, MERSEYSIDE 5–1A

Bistrot Vérité £47 3 3 3
7 Liverpool Rd PR8 4AR (01704) 564 199
"The food is always fresh, local and well prepared" at this "cheerful" shop-turned-Gallic-bistro in Birkdale Village; "it's small enough to feel cosy, but big enough to generate a buzz". / **Details:** *www.bistrotverite.co.uk; 10 pm; closed Mon & Sun.*

The Vincent Hotel £47 4 2 3
98 Lord St PR8 1JR (01704) 883800
This "classy" hotel café and sushi bar "specialises in excellent Japanese food" but also has "good soup and sandwich combos at lunchtime"; "it can get quite expensive – lots of new money about, some of it related to football" – but on most accounts it's "good value", and it makes "a great place for people-watching". / **Details:** *www.thevincenthotel.com; 10 pm.* **Accommodation:** *60 rooms, from £93*

SOUTHROP, GLOUCESTERSHIRE 2–2C

The Swan at Southrop £51 2 3 4
GL7 3NU (01367) 850205
A "smart" boozer in a "lovely" Cotswolds village which has been refurbished "to the highest order" and incorporates "a casual dining space, and more

formal dining room"; fans claim "the food rocks", but others feel it's "lost its way a bit". / **Details:** *www.theswanatsouthrop.co.uk; Mon-Thurs 9 pm, Fri-Sat 9.30 pm ; closed Sun D; no Amex.*

SOUTHWOLD, SUFFOLK 3–1D

Coasters £44 [3][3][3]

Queen St IP18 6EQ (01502) 724734

"Taking on the old guard in Southwold – and winning!"; given the "complacent" competition, this "small, friendly" venue strikes its tiny fan club as a "welcome relief"; "the onus is on local and quality food" and, whilst "they could make their menu a bit more complex", in the meantime they "deserve applause". / **Details:** *www.coastersofsouthwold.co.uk; 2 min walk from seafront and Market square; 9 pm; closed Mon & Sun D; no Amex.*

The Crown Adnams Hotel £54 [3][3][4]

90 High St IP18 6DP (01502) 722275

This famous Adnams pub in the heart of the town seems to be on more solid ground of late; it combines a "great" atmosphere, with "quality" gastro fare – and, while you "can hit a bad night if you're unlucky", it remains "better than the average" by all accounts. / **Details:** *www.adnams.co.uk/hotels/the-crown/; 9 pm; no Amex.* **Accommodation:** *14 rooms, from £160*

Sole Bay Fish Company £29 [5][3][3]

22e Blackshore IP18 6ND (01502) 724241

"The opening of their smokehouse, obtaining a wine license and providing toilets (!) has transformed this delightful harbour shack", which provides "spoiling, fresh, cold, smoked seafood platters" and a "buzzy" vibe. "Gone are the days when you could BYO", but it's "still best to BYO salad"! / **Details:** *www.solebayfishco.co.uk; 10 pm; closed Mon.*

The Swan £52 [2][2][3]

The Market Pl IP18 6EG (01502) 722186

Famous Adnams-owned hotel that remains "a favourite to many"; fans say that with its dependable cuisine and "traditional" décor (think "white linen and smartly dressed staff") it's also "a good restaurant in its own right", but it doesn't inspire the volume of praise that once it did. / **Details:** *www.adnams.co.uk/stay-with-us/the-swan; 9 pm; no Amex; no jeans or trainers; children: 5+ at D.* **Accommodation:** *42 rooms, from £185*

SPARKWELL, DEVON 1–3C

Treby Arms £55 [4][3][3]

PL7 5DD (01752) 837363

"Much, much, more than a pub – a destination"; MasterChef winner Anton Piotrowski "serves food prepared and cooked with skill, flare and passion" at this "relaxed and unstuffy" spot, originally built for workers on Brunel's Royal Albert Bridge; one minor downside is that service can be "patchy" at times. / **Details:** *www.thetrebyarms.co.uk; 9 pm; closed Mon.*

SPARSHOLT, HAMPSHIRE 2–3D

The Plough Inn £48 [3][3][3]

SO21 2NW (01962) 776353

A "super" country gastropub that continues to offer "reliably good" food; the worst anyone has to say about it is that it's a "victim of its deserved popularity" (i.e. that service is stretched at times). / **Details:** *www.ploughinnsparsholt.co.uk; 9 pm, Sun & Mon 8.30 pm, Fri & Sat 9.30 pm; no Amex.*

SPELDHURST, KENT 3–4B

George & Dragon £46 [3][2][4]

Speldhurst Hill TN3 0NN (01892) 863125

An attractive 13th-century inn, furnished with oak beams and roaring fires, which has a nice line in dishes of the "local, seasonal" bent. / **Details:** *www.speldhurst.com; 9.30 pm; closed Sun D; no Amex.*

ST ALBANS, HERTFORDSHIRE 3–2A

Barrissimo £12 [4][5][3]

28 St Peters St AL1 3NA (01727) 869999

"The only really outstanding indie café in St Albans", where "everything is always freshly prepared" – be it "good paninis", "very tasty pasta dishes" or "those to-die-for puds"; the "super" service gets a shout-out too. / **Details:** *5.30 pm, Sun 4 pm; L only; no credit cards.*

Cock £38 [3][3][3]

48 St Peters St AL1 3NF (01727) 854 816

"Affordable at the start of the week, sophisticated towards the end, and rocking over the weekend", a "fantastic, traditional" 16th-century inn, well-located between the cathedral and the river, that offers "especially good-value" lunchtime fare. / **Details:** *www.thecockinstalbans.co.uk; 9 pm; no Amex.*

Lussmanns £44 [3][3][3]

Waxhouse Gate, High St AL3 4EW (01727) 851941

"Showing it can be done out in the sticks!" – this "buzzy" and "deservedly popular" local favourite wins significant all-round praise for its "stylish" looks and "reasonably priced" cooking. (Upbeat feedback too on its siblings in Harpenden and Hertford). / **Details:** *www.lussmanns.com; 9.30 pm, Fri & Sat 10 pm, Sun 9 pm.*

Prime Steak & Grill £68 [3][3][3]

83-85 London Rd AL1 1LN (01727) 840309

An "upmarket" new town-centre steakhouse that "deserves to do well" if early feedback is anything to go by; admittedly prices are "Hawksmoor"-esque, but they do "reflect the quality of the produce". / **Details:** *www.primesteakandgrill.com; 11 pm.*

Thompson at Darcy's £70 332
2 Hatfield Rd AL1 3RP (01727) 730777
"Going from strength to strength under the leadership of an ex-Auberge du Lac chef" – Phil Thompson's town-centre venture serves "excellent cooking in the modern British style" and even those who feel "it's not quite up to its full potential" say "it's one of St Albans's better restaurants". / **Details:** *www.thompsonatdarcys.co.uk; 9 pm, Fri & Sat 9.30 pm.*

ST ANDREWS, FIFE 9–3D

Seafood Restaurant £80 435
The Scores, Bruce Embankment KY16 9AB
(01334) 479475
A glass box-style affair on the seaside that pleases all who comment on it thanks to its "very good fish" and "stunning views" ("best to visit on summer evenings"). / **Details:** *www.theseafoodrestaurant.com; 9.30 pm; children: 12+ at D.*

Vine Leaf £47 443
131 South St KY16 9UN (01334) 477497
A perennial favourite with a hard-to-find location down a close off the Main Street; there's a "good range of dishes" to say the least (including seafood and vegetarian menus) and the locally sourced cooking represents "excellent value" for money. / **Details:** *www.vineleafstandrews.co.uk; 9.15 pm; D only, closed Mon & Sun.*

ST AUSTELL, CORNWALL 1–4B

Austells £49 553
10 Beach Rd PL25 3PH (01726) 813888
It may be located in a "most unlikely environment" ("amid a row of '60s-style shops in the suburbs") but make no mistake, Brett Camborne-Paynter's culinarily "interesting" venture is a real "hidden gem", combining "top-notch food" and "lovely service". / **Details:** *www.austells.co.uk; 9 pm; closed Mon.*

ST DAVIDS, PEMBROKESHIRE 4–4A

Cwtch £49 333
22 High St SA62 6SD (01437) 720491
Chef Andy Holcroft's "consistently good" and "well-presented" food continues to win solid feedback for this town-centre bistro. / **Details:** *www.cwtchrestaurant.co.uk; 9.30 pm; D only, ex Sun open L & D.*

ST IVES, CORNWALL 1–4A

Alba Restaurant £48 344
The Old Life Boat Hs, Wharf Rd TR26 1LF
(01736) 797222
A comfortable harbourside spot offering "wonderful fish-based suppers" (with crab linguine a highlight) plus "great views if you can get a window seat upstairs". / **Details:** *www.alba-stives.co.uk; 10 pm.*

Alfresco £52 334
Harbourside Wharf Rd TR26 1LF
(01736) 793737
"A great addition to St Ives"; in a "lovely spot", with "great views of the harbour", this "friendly" outfit is a hit thanks to its "delicious" local produce ("including Cornish wines"). / **Details:** *www.alfresco-stives.co.uk; on harbour front; 9.30 pm; no Amex.*

The Black Rock £46 443
Market Pl TR26 1RZ (01736) 791911
"Far better than external impressions", this town-centre bistro offers a "very enjoyable" experience by all accounts, and its rustic cooking (including plenty of local fish and seafood) "stands out even in St Ives". / **Details:** *www.theblackrockstives.co.uk; 9 pm; D only, closed Sun; no Amex; booking: max 8 in summer.*

Porthgwidden Beach Café £42 333
Porthgwidden Beach TR26 1PL
(01736) 796791
"Classic posh beach shack by the most wonderful child-friendly beach", where the culinary highlight, somewhat unsurprisingly, is fine fish and seafood. / **Details:** *www.porthgwiddencafe.co.uk; 9.30 pm; no Amex; booking: max 10.*

Porthmeor Beach Cafe £39 545
Porthmeor Beach TR26 1JZ (01736) 793366
"If the sun's shining there's no better place in the world to watch the sun set" than at this beachside café near the Tate, which has a "glorious outlook". What's more the food (majoring in fish) "matches the location" – "simple but delicious, and at sensible prices". / **Details:** *www.porthmeor-beach.co.uk; 9 pm; D only. Closed Nov-Mar.; no Amex.*

Porthminster Café £54 345
Porthminster Beach TR26 2EB
(01736) 795352
"What could be better than dining a few yards from the sea?" – all agree that "a beach café doesn't come any better" than this "perfectly located" spot, with its "lovely and helpful" staff. Many reporters would say that goes for the "fun and intriguing" food too, although the odd reporter feels the "ambitious fare doesn't always come off". / **Details:** *www.porthminstercafe.co.uk; 9.30 pm; no Amex.*

Tate Cafe
Tate Gallery £32 224
Porthmeor Beach TR26 1TG (01736) 796226
"Looking out onto St Ives beach and feeling very arty" is perhaps the key feature of this top-floor gallery café, with its lovely, sunny-days terrace. Otherwise its simple fare is no particular draw in itself. / **Details:** *www.tate.org.uk; L only; no Amex.*

ST LEONARDS-ON-SEA, EAST SUSSEX 3–4C

St Clement's £48 442
3 Mercatoria TN38 0EB (01424) 200355
Nick Hales's "fantastic neighbourhood restaurant", hidden in the backstreets of this seaside town, serves "predominantly local fish and shellfish, but meat and veggie options also aren't ignored". / **Details:** *www.stclementsrestaurant.co.uk; 9 pm, Sat 10 pm; closed Mon & Sun D; no Amex.*

ST MAWES, CORNWALL 1–4B

Hotel Tresanton £67 345
27 Lower Castle Rd TR2 5DR (01326) 270055
A view "looking over St Mawes and out to sea is the perfect setting" for Olga Polizzi's upscale bayside hotel, which profits from a glorious terrace in summer; the food, based on "fresh local produce", is somewhat secondary, but fans say it too is "wonderful". / **Details:** *www.tresanton.com; 9.30 pm; booking: max 10; children: 6+ at dinner.* **Accommodation:** *40 rooms, from £250*

ST MERRYN, CORNWALL 1–3B

The Cornish Arms £40 443
Churchtown PL28 8ND (01841) 520288
From the "wholesome Cornish grub" to the "very helpful staff", the Stein-empire's "lovely old village inn" is both "an excellent restaurant, and a busy local"... but watch out – being "really busy", it can "sometimes run out of food!" / **Details:** *www.rickstein.com; 8.30 pm; no Amex.*

ST TUDY, CORNWALL 1–3B

St Tudy Inn £49 443
Bodmin PL30 3NN (01208) 850656
"Emily Scott (late of the Harbour Inn, Port Isaac) is a chef to be watched", say fans of her new venture – a cosy and prettily situated village pub where the "almost exclusively female kitchen" serves up "beautifully executed" food (including "first-class fish"). / **Details:** *www.sttudyinn.com; 9 pm; closed Mon & Sun D.*

STADHAMPTON, OXFORDSHIRE 2–2D

The Crazy Bear £68 435
Bear Ln OX44 7UR (01865) 890714
"Quirky and fun" Anglo-Thai (one dining room each) that's historically been most notable for its funky ambience, and which continues to be "populated by people wanting to see and be seen"; in recent times, however, the cooking seems to be catching up – "especially the Thai, but also anything from the farm shop list". / **Details:** *www.crazybeargroup.co.uk; 10 pm; children: 12+ at Fri & Sat D.* **Accommodation:** *16 rooms, from £169*

STAINES, SURREY 3–3A

Three Horseshoes £42 343
25 Shepperton Rd TW18 1SE (01784) 455014
A "well-refurbished" gastroboozer in a "great location near the River Thames"; its small fan club say that it provides "helpful" service and the "best pub food in the vicinity". / **Details:** *www.3horseshoeslalham.co.uk; 9.45 pm.*

STAMFORD, LINCOLNSHIRE 6–4A

The George Hotel £68 445
71 St Martins PE9 2LB (01780) 750750
"A wonderful place to step back in time" – the "old-school" dining room of this vast and "delightfully old-fashioned", historic coaching inn (on what used to be the A1 before this fine Georgian town was by-passed) "serves the best traditional fare, faultlessly, in impeccable surroundings", backed up by an "a large and well-stocked wine cellar" and is just the place for "an occasion". (If the prices in the "more formal" restaurant are too daunting, there's also the cheaper and more atmospheric 'Garden Room'). / **Details:** *www.georgehotelofstamford.com; 9.30 pm; jacket and/or tie; children: 8+ at D.* **Accommodation:** *47 rooms, from £190*

STANTON, SUFFOLK 3–1C

Leaping Hare Vineyard £50 335
Wyken Vineyards IP31 2DW (01359) 250287
"A stunning 400-year-old barn" creates an "unexpected" and "beautiful" setting for this "smart" vineyard café. Superb wines from the estate (as you might hope for) are complemented by "consistent cooking using great, locally sourced ingredients". / **Details:** *www.wykenvineyards.co.uk; 9m NE of Bury St Edmunds; follow tourist signs off A143; 5.30 pm, Fri & Sat 9 pm; L only, ex Fri & Sat open L & D.*

STATHERN, LEICESTERSHIRE 5–3D

Red Lion Inn £44 344
2 Red Lion St LE14 4HS (01949) 860868
*Hidden away "in a pretty village near Belvoir Castle", this "lovely rural pub" – with its "old-fashioned pub décor" – holds its own with its sibling, The Olive Branch at Clipsham. "It can be crowded" at times (more in the bar than the adjacent dining room), but the cuisine is (notwithstanding a couple of glitches this year) consistently good, and there's a "wide range of interesting beers and wines" to go with it. / **Details:** www.theolivebranchpub.com; 9 pm, Sat 9.30 pm; closed Sun D (and Mondays during Winter); no Amex.*

STOCKBRIDGE, HAMPSHIRE 2–3D

Clos du Marquis £55 333
London Rd SO20 6DE (01264) 810738
*"In the middle of nowhere, this former pub has been transformed into a superb French restaurant" (by a South African). / **Details:** www.closdumarquis.co.uk; 2m E on A30 from Stockbridge; 9 pm; closed Mon & Sun D.*

Greyhound £58 323
31 High St SO20 6EY (01264) 810833
*This 500-year-old pub with rooms, was taken over – and lavishly revamped – by an ex-Peat Spade team in 2013; views are a bit polarised – fans say it's "consistently good", but sceptics say that it "did not live up to expectations" (perhaps raised in recent times by the tyre men, who made it their 'pub of the year' in 2014). / **Details:** www.thegreyhoundonthetest.co.uk; 9 pm, Fri & Sat 9.30 pm, Sun 9 pm; booking: max 12. **Accommodation:** 7 rooms, from £100*

Thyme & Tides £32 332
The High St SO20 6HE (01264) 81 01 01
*This multi-tasking café-deli-fishmonger is "still a local stand-out" by all accounts; "the daily soup and sandwich is always good, and changes enough to keep the menu fresh". / **Details:** thymeandtidesdeli.co.uk/; Tue-Sat 5 pm, Sun 4 pm; closed Mon; no Amex.*

STOCKCROSS, BERKSHIRE 2–2D

The Vineyard at Stockcross £93 332
RG20 8JU (01635) 898454
*"The incredible cellar" ("the best list of Californian wines in the UK") outshines all other elements of Sir Peter Michael's contemporary-style operation. Daniel Galmiche's cuisine can be "excellent" but seems secondary, and the "atmosphere is cool, in temperature and style". / **Details:** www.the-vineyard.co.uk; from M4, J13 take A34 towards Hungerford; 9.30 pm; no jeans or trainers. **Accommodation:** 49 rooms, from £194*

STOCKPORT, CHESHIRE, GREATER MANCHESTER AND LANCASHIRE 5–2B

Brassica Grill £44 434
27 Shaw Rd SK4 4AG (0161) 442 6730
*"A great new addition to Heaton Moor's restaurant scene" from Paul Faulkner (ex-Albert Square Chop House); the "delightful" Mediterranean-style venue offers "fresh, flavourful" dishes "served up with flair". / **Details:** brassicagrill.com/; 10 pm, Sun 7pm; closed Mon.*

Damson £53 444
113 Heaton Moor Rd SK4 4HY
(0161) 4324666
*This "relaxed yet sophisticated" Heaton Moor spot wins plaudits for its "fine seasonal food" and "friendly and unassuming service"; it also has a newer Media City sibling (see also). / **Details:** www.damsonrestaurant.co.uk; 9.30 pm, Sun 7 pm; closed Mon L, Sat L & Sun D.*

The Red Lion £54 332
112 Buxton Rd SK6 8ED (01663) 765 227
*Run by Manchester-based fine dining chain Damson, this "upmarket roadside pub" (with period styling and "spacious" seating) elicits praise for its "innovative twists on pub staples" ("e.g. corned beef hash"). / **Details:** www.redionhighlane.co.uk; 9 pm, Sun 6.30 pm.*

STOKE D'ABERNON, SURREY 3–3A

Grill at the Old Plough £45 333
2 Station Rd KT11 3BN (01932) 862244
*You can "always be sure of good food and wine at reasonable prices" at this "very busy" and "friendly" gastro venture which "still retains a pub atmosphere". / **Details:** www.oldploughcobham.co.uk/; Sun-Thu 9.30 pm, Fri & Sat 10 pm.*

STOKE ROW, OXFORDSHIRE 2–2D

The Crooked Billet £53 445
Newlands Ln RG9 5PU (01491) 681048
*"Tucked out-of-the-way (thankfully otherwise it would be mobbed)" – this "unbeatable" oak-beamed rural favourite is, for fans, "the benchmark for casual relaxed dining", with "a romantic ambience in both rooms" and "always reliable" cooking. / **Details:** www.thecrookedbillet.co.uk; off the A4130; 10 pm, Sat 10.30 pm.*

STOKE-BY-NAYLAND, SUFFOLK 3–2C

The Crown £43 444

Park St CO6 4SE (01206) 262346

A "comfortable and relaxed" village pub and boutique hotel that pleases all who comment on it, owing to its "excellent" Modern European fare and "interesting" wine list. / ***Details:*** *www.crowninn.net; on B1068; 9.30 pm, Fri & Sat 10 pm, Sun 9 pm.* **Accommodation:** *11 rooms, from £130*

STONOR, OXFORDSHIRE 2–2D

Quince Tree £50 434

RG9 6HE (01491) 639039

"A super find in the middle of the countryside" that attracts much glowing feedback; it's a "fabulous" and "romantic" building – combining pub, café and deli – with "well-presented" food, a "good buzz" and "excellent" treats to buy. The end to the least enthusiastic report this year? – "please try it!" / ***Details:*** *www.thequincetree.com; 9.30 pm; closed Sun D.*

STOW ON THE WOLD, GLOUCESTERSHIRE 2–1C

The Old Butchers £45 333

Park St GL54 1AQ (01451) 831700

An "old favourite", whose location is true to its name, praised for its consistently "exemplary" cooking. / ***Details:*** *www.theoldbutchers.com; on the main road heading out of Stow on the Wold towards Oddington; 9.30 pm, Sat 10 pm; closed Mon & Sun; booking: max 12.*

STOWMARKET, SUFFOLK 3–1C

The Shepherd & Dog £46 443

Forward Grn IP14 5HN (01449) 711685

"A real gem in the countryside" – this 'bar/lounge/ eaterie' (er, pub?) has been "much improved" in recent times, and wins very consistent praise for a shortish menu of "superb", straightforward dishes (each with a suggested wine match). / ***Details:*** *www.theshepherdanddog.com; 10 pm.*

STRACHUR, ARGYLL AND BUTE 9–4B

Inver Cottage Restaurant £48 434

Stracthlachlan PA27 8BU (01369) 860537

Taken over by chef Pam Brunton and front-of-house Rob Latimer in March, this "cosy" cottage restaurant is eliciting raves for its "sensational" flavour combinations ("reminiscent of Noma", where they worked); "the view alone would draw me back", says one fan, "but this young chef's skills deserve real recognition". / ***Details:*** *www.invercottage.com; 8.30 pm; closed Mon & Tue; no Amex.*

STRATFORD UPON AVON, WARWICKSHIRE 2–1C

The Fuzzy Duck £48 344

Ilmington Rd CV37 8DD (01608) 682635

A "smart" pub-restaurant-with-rooms, that is "highly recommended" by all reporters, who suggest the food's "surprisingly good"; its virtues include a "gorgeous bar", but "better signs to find it please"! / ***Details:*** *www.fuzzyduckarmscote.com; 9 pm, Fri & Sat 9.30 pm; closed Mon & Sun D.*

Lambs £47 223

12 Sheep St CV37 6EF (01789) 292554

With its "busy, buzzy" atmosphere and "good use of local supplier meats", fans acclaim this "lovely" city-centre stalwart as one of the best pre-theatre dining options in town. / ***Details:*** *www.lambsrestaurant.co.uk; 9 pm; closed Mon L; no Amex.*

Loxleys £49 343

3 Sheep St CV37 6EF (01789) 292128

In the town centre, and handy for the theatre, a "new kid on the block" that "will do a good job in shaking up" the local competition according to early feedback; it occupies the site of a well-known clothes shop, and is of particular note for its "delightful" fish nights. / ***Details:*** *loxleysrestaurant.co.uk/#; 11 pm, Sun 10.30 pm.*

No. 9 £46 433

9 Church St CV37 6HB (01789) 415 522

This "cosy, candlelit" spot remains reporters' default pre-theatre choice thanks to "very good-value" set deals. If there's any criticism it's that some dishes "try a little too hard". / ***Details:*** *no9churchst.com; 9.15 pm; no Amex.*

The Oppo £46 333

13 Sheep St CV37 6EF (01789) 269980

"A great place for a meal before taking on The Bard"; this long-running bistro remains a popular spot owing to its "very good-value" set menus, "tasty food, plus pleasant, efficient service". / ***Details:*** *www.theoppo.co.uk; 9.30 pm, Fri & Sat 11 pm; closed Sun; no Amex; booking: max 12.*

Rooftop Restaurant Royal Shakespeare Theatre £41 334

Waterside CV37 6BB (01789) 403449

"Go for an outside table in the summer with the views across the river!" if you visit this rooftop restaurant, sited in what used to be the gods of the old theatre. The "thoughtfully sourced British food" is "ambitious" and while "it doesn't always quite work", it's usually very "decent". ("We eat here regularly and the RSC should be praised for their

*efforts – they could have outsourced this operation to one of the corporates but, instead, it is all well run in-house"). / **Details:** www.rsc-rooftop-restaurant.co.uk; 9.45 pm; no Amex.*

The Vintner **£48** 2 2 3
4-5 Sheep St CV37 6EF (01789) 297259
*In a "half-timbered", "olde-worlde" building, a town-centre fixture offering an "interesting and varied" menu; it's a "consistent and popular" spot, although the harsh might say that it's "similar to many others close by, neither better nor worse". / **Details:** www.the-vintner.co.uk; 9 pm; no Amex.*

STRETTON, CHESHIRE 5–2B

Hollies **£33** 3 3 3
Northwich Rd WA4 4PG (01925) 730976
*Part of the Cowap family's local mini-empire (butcher shops, forest lodges etc.) this "contemporary" café, adjacent to their farm shop, scores praise for its "excellent homecooked food using locally sourced ingredients". / **Details:** www.theholliesfarmshop.co.uk/farm-shops/farm-shop-lower stretton; 4.30 pm.*

STUCKTON, HAMPSHIRE 2–3C

The Three Lions **£59** 4 4 3
Stuckton Rd SP6 2HF (01425) 652489
*Mike & Jayne Womersley "make this restaurant-with-rooms a special place to stay and eat" – and one that's "run along the theme of a French auberge but slap-bang in the New Forest"; Jayne provides "the friendliest" of welcomes, and there's some "beautiful food, much of it sourced by Mike on foraging trips." / **Details:** www.thethreelionsrestaurant.co.uk; off the A338; 9 pm, Fri & Sat 9.30 pm; closed Mon & Sun D; no Amex. **Accommodation:** 7 rooms, from £105*

STUDLAND, DORSET 2–4C

Pig on the Beach **£52** 3 4 5
Manor Rd BH19 3AU (01929) 450288
*This "fairy tale building, with an idyllic location above Studland Bay" is the latest of Robin Hutson's Pigs, converted from "a formerly very traditional hotel" into a "perfect romantic getaway", complete with "stunning" greenhouse restaurant "in the Pig's trademark shabby-chic style", with views "to die for". "They make a big deal about their kitchen garden" and local sourcing – results are not as spectacular as the setting, but consistently good. / **Details:** www.thepighotel.com/on-the-beach; 9.30 pm.*

Shell Bay **£47** 4 2 5
Ferry Rd BH19 3BA (01929) 450363
*A "stunning location overlooking Sandbanks and Poole Harbour" is the main asset of this minimal venue, but the fish and seafood are "excellent" too. / **Details:** www.shellbay.net; near the Sandbanks to Swanage ferry; 9 pm.*

SUMMERHOUSE, COUNTY DURHAM 8–3B

Raby Hunt **£89** 5 4 4
Summerhouse DL2 3UD (01325) 374237
*"Tucked away in the Durham Dales", James Close's restaurant (with two rooms) revolves around "an ethos of showing off local ingredients to their best effect". "Down-to-earth" staff provide a choice of "clever and delicious" tasting menus, of which the best dishes are "a revelation in simple but confident cooking". / **Details:** www.rabyhuntrestaurant.co.uk/; 9.30 pm; closed Mon, Tue & Sun. **Accommodation:** 2 rooms, from £125*

SUNBURY ON THAMES, SURREY 3–3A

Indian Zest **£43** 5 4 4
21 Thames St TW16 5QF (01932) 765 000
*"If you want your tastebuds well and truly tickled, stroked and kicked into action", Manoj Vasaikar's "large and relaxing", colonial-style villa "never fails to deliver something special" from its nouvelle Indian menu. "Good parking nearby" too! / **Details:** www.indianzest.co.uk; midnight.*

SUNNINGDALE, BERKSHIRE 3–3A

Bluebells **£66** 3 4 3
Shrubs Hill SL5 0LE (01344) 622 722
*"An outstanding local eatery which rarely produces anything other than excellent food and service" – the unvarying verdict on this roadside fixture, which remains hugely popular with all who comment on it. / **Details:** www.bluebells-restaurant.com; 9.45 pm; closed Mon & Sun D.*

SUNNINGHILL, BERKSHIRE 3–3A

Carpenter's Arms **£56** 5 4 4
78 Upper Village Rd SL5 7AQ (01344) 622763
*"Hidden down a quiet road, this apparently normal pub is actually a superb Gallic gem", serving "good-but-simple" cuisine that "never fails to impress". / **Details:** www.lalochepub.com/carpenters; 10 pm.*

SURBITON, SURREY 3–3A

The French Table **£56** 4 5 3
85 Maple Rd KT6 4AW (020) 8399 2365
"One of suburbia's best restaurants!" – on the

London/Surrey borders, "nothing nearby comes close" to this "long-established and deservedly well-regarded" Gallic fixture. Perhaps the interior is a mite "low key", but its "romantic" appeal is enhanced by the "full-hearted and genuine" welcome, and most importantly its eternally "interesting" and "very competent" Gallic cuisine. The biggest problem? – "getting a table!" / **Details:** www.thefrenchtable.co.uk; 10.30 pm; closed Mon & Sun.

Pickled Pantry **£15** **443**
7 Central Pde KT6 4PJ (020) 8399 4694
A "great little coffee (plus brunch and lunch) spot, nestled near the station, with lively, welcoming service"; "Jo's homemade cakes are always to die-for, and George makes a great cup of coffee". / **Details:** *www.pickledpantry.co.uk; 6 pm, Sat 5 pm, Sun 4 pm.*

SUTTON GAULT, CAMBRIDGESHIRE 3–1B

The Anchor **£46** **344**
Bury Ln CB6 2BD (01353) 778537
"It may be in the middle of nowhere", but this Fenland inn is "definitely worth searching out", owing to its "inventive" cooking. / **Details:** *www.anchor-inn-restaurants.co.uk; 7m W of Ely, signposted off B1381 in Sutton; 9 pm, Sat 9.30 pm, Sun 8.30 pm; no Amex.* **Accommodation:** *4 rooms, from £79.5 - 135*

SWANSEA VALLEY, POWYS 4–4D

Pen y Cae Inn **£43** **333**
Brecon Rd SA9 1FA (01639) 730100
This restaurant and gallery (with rooms), in a smartly converted former pub, is a solid all-rounder offering "consistently good" food and "friendly service"; "remember to check out the owners' aviaries (plus meerkats, wallabies etc.) at the back of the pub"! / **Details:** *www.penycaeinn.com; 9 pm; closed Mon; no Amex.*

SWANSEA, SWANSEA 1–1C

Castellamare **£46** **344**
Bracelet Bay, Mumbles Rd SA3 4JT (01792) 369408
A "stunning venue looking out over the sea and the Mumbles lighthouse" which continues to achieve high marks for its Italian fare (served in "gigantic portions"). / **Details:** *www.castellamare.co.uk; 9 pm, Sat & Sun 9.30 pm.*

Didier And Stephanie **£46** **443**
56 Saint Helen's Rd SA1 4BE (01792) 655603
"Delicious French food" that's "great value" too – the invariable theme of all reports on this small city-centre outfit. / **Details:** *9.15 pm; closed Mon & Sun; no Amex.*

Hanson At The Chelsea Restaurant **£48** **433**
17 St Marys St SA1 3LH (01792) 464068
"A great little restaurant" with an "emphasis on local fish"; chef/proprietor Andrew Hanson "trained at The Ritz and it shows". / **Details:** *www.hansonatthechelsea.co.uk; 9.30 pm; no Amex.*

The Kardomah **£17** **233**
11 Portland St SA1 3DH (01792) 652336
Boasting associations with Dylan Thomas – a central coffee-house relic, with splendid, '50s-tastic décor. Well-brewed coffee is its best gastronomic feature, but for a cheap 'n' cheerful fill-up, its very long menu is well-realised, and comes at nostalgic prices.

TAPLOW, BERKSHIRE 3–3A

André Garrett At Cliveden Cliveden House **£99** **435**
Cliveden Rd SL6 0JF (01628) 668561
"Risen from the dead!" – over the past couple of years, André Garrett has transmogrified the cuisine at this impossibly grand Thames-view palazzo, from what used to be perpetually mediocre, to something "exquisite" to match the most "beautiful setting" (with views onto the gardens from the window tables). And by the standards of such indulgent luxury, it's "not beyond the realms of affordability" either. If there is a weak link nowadays, it's sometimes-middling service. / **Details:** *www.clivedenhouse.co.uk; 9.30 pm; no trainers.* **Accommodation:** *38 + cottage rooms, from £252*

TATTENHALL, CHESHIRE 5–3A

The Pheasant Inn **£44** **344**
Higher Burwardsley CH3 9PF (01829) 770434
Handy for the Sandstone Trail, this inn is "much improved" after a recent revamp; it combines enjoyable cuisine with "beautiful views over the Cheshire Plain". / **Details:** *www.thepheasantinn.co.uk; 9.30 pm, Fri & Sat 10 pm, Sun 9 pm.*

TAUNTON, SOMERSET 2–3A

Augustus **£46** **453**
3 The Courtyard, St James St TA1 1JR (01823) 324 354
"A real star"; this bistro from an ex-Castle Hotel team wins raves for its "superb French-inspired food" ("especially seafood") and "interesting wines", with the staff in particular considered to be "first rate". / **Details:** *www.augustustaunton.co.uk; 9.30 pm; closed Mon & Sun; no Amex.*

TEDDINGTON, MIDDLESEX 3–3A

Imperial China £40 [4][1][2]
196-198 Stanley Rd TW11 8UE
(020) 8977 8679
*"Delicious dim sum", "service very variable" – the unchanging verdict on this out-of-the-way gem that's reassuringly "full of Chinese families". / **Details:** www.imperialchinalondon.co.uk; 11 pm, Fri & Sat 11.30 pm, Sun 10 pm.*

Retro £59 [2][4][3]
114-116 High St TW11 8JB (020) 8977 2239
*"Retro is on a roll" – so say fans of this Gallic spot, boosted by "oh-là-là, Vincent, the manager, who charms with his suave, urbane and sexy manner". For some critics, however, it "tries too hard" and, together with the elevated prices, "misses the point of being a bistro". / **Details:** www.retrobistrot.co.uk; Tue-Sat 11 pm; closed Mon & Sun D.*

TEIGNMOUTH, DEVON 1–3D

Crab Shack £41 [5][4][3]
3 Queen St TQ14 9HN (01626) 777956
*"Go hungry" when you visit this family-run beachside shack, which serves "the best seafood for miles around", and has "a fantastic setting on Teignmouth's back beach". "Don't just think about rocking up – it's so difficult to get a table, but worth it if you do!" ("Hopefully the new terrace will end the nightmare of having to book so far in advance.") / **Details:** www.crabshackonthebeach.co.uk/; 9 pm; closed Mon & Tue; no Amex.*

TETBURY, GLOUCESTERSHIRE 2–2B

Calcot Manor £69 [2][2][2]
GL8 8YJ (01666) 890391
*Fans still applaud the conservatory-restaurant of this "family-friendly" country house hotel. It attracted growing criticism this year however, with complaints of service that "lacked finesse" and "over-designed" food. And though the style of the dining room is recommended by locals as ideal for business, to visitors in search of a bucolic idyll it's "out of keeping with the 'country' ambience". / **Details:** www.calcotmanor.co.uk; junction of A46 & A4135; 9.30 pm, Sun 9 pm. **Accommodation:** 35 rooms, from £280*

Gumstool Inn
Calcot Manor £49 [2][2][3]
GL8 8YJ (01666) 890391
*With its "hard-surfaced" interior, this "large brasserie feeling" place attached to a large hotel risks seeming like "an overly polished gastropub". While it's quite "reliable" there's "a few too many Gloucestershire toffs" – "it's full of retired CEOs eating perfectly fine but pricey food". / **Details:** www.calcotmanor.co.uk; crossroads of A46 & A41345; 9.30 pm, Sun 9 pm; no jeans or trainers; children: 12+ at dinner in Conservatory. **Accommodation:** 35 rooms, from £240*

Trouble House Inn £48 [4][3][3]
Cirencester Rd GL8 8SG (01666) 502206
*A "buzzy and popular" gastropub offering "tasty food lovingly made" – the "perfect place to meet someone for an informal lunch" but dinner is "equally nice" too. / **Details:** www.troublehouse.co.uk; 1.5m from Tetbury on A433 towards Cirencester; 5 pm, Fri & Sat 9 pm, Sun 3 pm; closed Mon, Tue D, Wed D, Thu D & Sun D; booking: max 8; children: 14+ in bar.*

THORNBURY, GLOUCESTERSHIRE 2–2B

Ronnie's £47 [3][2][2]
11 St Mary St BS35 2AB (01454) 411137
*Ronnie Faulkner continues to "make great use of local organic ingredients" at this "extremely competitively priced" venture in a 17th-century barn; the downstairs "has now been renamed as a wine/snack bar" and offers "great little nibbles". / **Details:** www.ronnies-restaurant.co.uk; 10 pm; closed Mon & Sun D; no Amex.*

THORNHAM, NORFOLK 6–3B

Eric's Fish & Chips £24 [3][3][3]
Drove Orchard, Thornham Rd PE36 6LS
(01485) 525886
*Glowing feedback for this "fantastic" new chippy from Titchwell Manor chef Eric Snaith; it wins praise for "lovely and chunky" fish plus "more interesting options" amid an industrial-chic interior. / **Details:** www.ericsfishandchips.com; 9 pm.*

The Orange Tree £50 [3][3][4]
High St PE36 6LY (01485) 512 213
*"One of the many old pubs with a trendy facelift" – a "lovely" coastal gastroboozer-with-rooms; fans say it's "fantastic on all levels" with "great and inventive" food, but for the odd sceptic the cooking's "lacking in flavour". / **Details:** www.theorangetreethornham.co.uk; 9.30 pm; no Amex. **Accommodation:** 6 rooms, from £89*

THORNTON HOUGH, MERSEYSIDE 5–2A

The Lawn
Thornton Hall Hotel & Spa £54 [3][2][3]
Neston Rd CH63 1JF (0151) 336 3938
*"A pleasant surprise"; there's some "ambitious cooking" to be had at this hotel dining room, helmed by Matt Worswick (ex-of the Michelin-starred Glenapp Castle). / **Details:** www.thorntonhallhotel.com; 11 pm.*

Red Fox **£47** 224
Liverpool Rd CH64 7TL (01513) 532920
*In a lavishly revamped former country club, this new pub in the Brunning and Price chain has a "definite wow factor"; the food is "good" too, but perhaps "not yet up to speed" – which doesn't stop the place from being "always fully booked". / **Details:** www.brunningandprice.co.uk/redfox/; 10 pm, Sun 9.30 pm; no bookings.*

TILLINGTON, WEST SUSSEX 3–4A

The Horse Guards Inn **£42** 445
Upperton Rd GU28 9AF (01798) 342 332
*A "superb, informal dining pub with good-value rooms and genuinely local sourcing" ("the only place I've met the vintner who made my wine whilst drinking it at the bar!"); an "exceptional, eccentric garden" with "free roaming chickens" is another plus. / **Details:** www.thehorseguardsinn.co.uk; 9 pm, Fri & Sat 9.30 pm; no Amex.*

TITCHWELL, NORFOLK 6–3B

Titchwell Manor **£50** 444
PE31 8BB (01485) 210 221
*Owned by the Snaith family since 1988, a Victorian farmhouse-turned-plush-boutique-hotel on the north Norfolk coast, where "everything is of such a high standard" – not least desserts "beyond belief". / **Details:** www.titchwellmanor.com; 9.30 pm. **Accommodation:** 29 rooms, from £95*

TITLEY, HEREFORDSHIRE 2–1A

Stagg Inn **£51** 544
HR5 3RL (01544) 230221
*To first-timers, this "amiable and welcoming" inn can seem an amazing "find" in a tiny village in rural Herefordshire, although its ongoing success is fully "evidenced by the difficulty in booking somewhere so remote". It combines "gorgeous cooking with stylish ingredients, with an equally delectable and fairly priced wine list". / **Details:** www.thestagg.co.uk; on B4355, NE of Kington; 9 pm; closed Mon & Tue. **Accommodation:** 7 rooms, from £100*

TOBERMORY, ARGYLL AND BUTE 9–3A

Café Fish **£46** 543
The Pier PA75 6NU (01688) 301253
*"You couldn't get fresher than the stunningly good seafood" of this relaxed café-style venue on the harbour, where the main event is typically "caught just a couple of hours before, and then very well cooked". / **Details:** www.thecafefish.com; 10 pm; Closed Nov-Mar; no Amex; children: 14+ after 8 pm.*

TOLLARD ROYAL, WILTSHIRE 2–3C

The King John Inn **£55** 333
SP5 5PS (01725) 516 207
*A "busy local pub", whose charms include "delicious locally sourced food" and an "amazing choice of wines". / **Details:** www.kingjohninn.co.uk; mon-sat 9.30, 9 sun. **Accommodation:** 8 rooms, from £140*

TOPSHAM, DEVON 1–3D

The Galley **£53** 443
41 Fore St, Topsham EX3 0HU
(01392) 876078
*"In a harbourside setting", this well-regarded, relaxed spot offers a "tasty and imaginative" menu making "much use of local produce" – particularly fish – and with well-selected wine. / **Details:** www.galleyrestaurant.co.uk; 9 pm; closed Mon & Sun; booking max: 12; children: 12+.*

TORCROSS, DEVON 1–4D

Start Bay Inn **£34** 433
TQ7 2TQ (01548) 580553
*A beachside pub where the "quality and price is unvarying" even on repeat visits; it's particularly rated for some "outstanding" battered fish. / **Details:** www.startbayinn.co.uk; on beach front (take A379 coastal road to Dartmouth); 9.30 pm; no Amex; no booking.*

TORQUAY, DEVON 1–3D

Elephant Restaurant & Brasserie **£56** 544
3-4 Beacon Ter, Harbourside TQ1 2BH
(01803) 200044
*Simon Hulstone's first-floor restaurant and downstairs brasserie is "going from strength to strength", partly fuelled by produce taken from its new farm. / **Details:** www.elephantrestaurant.co.uk; 9 pm; closed Mon & Sun; children: 14+ at bar.*

No 7 Fish Bistro **£50** 543
7 Beacon Terrace TQ1 2BH (01803) 295055
*A "deservedly popular restaurant" with an "emphasis on fresh seafood, perfectly cooked" – "proof that simplicity can be enticing and delicious"; "I've eaten here for 15+ years and never been disappointed – always book in advance". / **Details:** www.no7-fish.com; 9.45 pm.*

TREBETHERWICK, CORNWALL 1–3B

St Moritz Hotel £62 343

PL27 6SD (01208) 862242

"A pleasant surprise"; in a modernist hotel, a dining room where the food is "very good and slightly unusual" and where, "given the army of chefs on view in the kitchen, there is no expense spared in making sure that every dish has a lot of care and attention"; on sunny days head to the "superior" café by the pool. / **Details:** *www.stmoritzhotel.co.uk; 9.30 pm; D only.*

TREEN, CORNWALL 1–4A

Gurnards Head £45 334

TR26 3DE (01736) 796928

In "deepest Cornwall" – on the coastal path between Land's End and St Ives and with "breathtaking, windswept vistas" – this famous cliff-top venue combines a "lovely, characterful dining room" and a more casual, flagstone-floored bar. By (almost) all accounts, the food is "delicious" and "well priced" too. / **Details:** *www.gurnardshead.co.uk; on coastal road between Land's End & St Ives, near Zennor B3306; 9.15 pm; no Amex.* **Accommodation:** *7 rooms, from £105*

TRING, HERTFORDSHIRE 3–2A

Olive Limes £38 343

60 High St HP23 5AG (01442) 828444

"This is our best local Indian restaurant and the food is consistently good"; by Tring Park, a colonial-style fine dining outfit with an especially elegant upstairs room. / **Details:** *www.olivelimes.co.uk; 11 pm, Fri & Sat 11.30 pm.*

TROON, SOUTH AYRSHIRE 9–4B

MacCallum's Oyster Bar £40 434

The Harbour, Harbour Rd KA10 6DH (01292) 319339

"The freshest and finest seafood anywhere" is the reason for a visit to this local institution (and nearby chippy) which – despite going into administration in June 2015 – remained open when we went to press; here's hoping they can find a new owner! / **Details:** *www.maccallumsoftroon.co.uk; 9.30 pm; closed Sun.*

TRURO, CORNWALL 1–4B

Tabb's £53 333

85 Kenwyn St TR1 3BZ (01872) 262110

"Nigel Tabb's cooking continues to evolve and just gets better and better", say fans of his pastel-coloured fine dining haunt "in quiet surroundings" – "it's a little bit out-of-the-way in the town, but well worth finding". / **Details:** *www.tabbs.co.uk; 9 pm; closed Mon & Sun D; no Amex.*

TUDDENHAM, SUFFOLK 3–1C

Tuddenham Mill Tuddenham Mill Hotel £60 434

High St IP28 6SQ (01638) 713 552

A "friendly" establishment in a "pleasant", rather remote, location in an old mill; "the cooking's better than it was" ("less experimental but more creative"). Top Tip – "magnificent value at lunchtime". / **Details:** *www.tuddenhammill.co.uk; 9.15 pm.* **Accommodation:** *15 rooms, from £205*

TUNBRIDGE WELLS, KENT 3–4B

The Black Pig £43 334

18 Grove Hill Rd TN1 1RZ (01892) 523030

A "ramshackle old building with external eating and car parking to the rear", near the station, well praised for its "interesting blackboard menu" and "superb real ales". / **Details:** *www.theblackpig.net; 9.30 pm, Fri & Sat 10 pm, Sun 9 pm; no Amex.*

Hotel du Vin et Bistro £62 223

Crescent Rd TN1 2LY (01892) 526455

"A classic Hotel du Vin", with a "lovely", "airy" Victorian club-style setting; despite the odd glitch, the food is generally "enjoyable", and it's "a treat to browse the wine list, with lots available by the glass". / **Details:** *www.hotelduvin.com; 10 pm, Fri & Sat 10.30 pm; booking: max 10.* **Accommodation:** *34 rooms, from £120*

Sankey's Champagne & Oyster Bar The Old Fishmarket £48 333

19 The Upper Pantiles TN2 5TN (01892) 511422

Part of a local foodie empire, this "great new restaurant in the Pantiles" occupies a swishly converted historic building, appropriately located in the old fishmarket. The victuals are "top notch" – a fine array of seafood, majoring in oysters, plus a wide selection of fizz. / **Details:** *www.sankeys.co.uk; midnight, Sun & Mon 4 pm; closed Mon D & Sun D.*

Thackeray's £74 442

85 London Rd TN1 1EA (01892) 511921

Richard Phillips's "lovely" and "romantic" Regency villa, near the centre, remains the town's leading culinary light – it's such a consistent destination for "classic, stylish French food". Top Tip – "the set lunch is an absolute bargain for cooking of this calibre". / **Details:** *www.thackerays-restaurant.co.uk; 10.30 pm; closed Mon & Sun D.*

TYTHERLEIGH, DEVON 2–4A

Tytherleigh Arms £44 443

EX13 7BE (01460) 220214

*"In what is really a gourmet desert", this "lovely" old gastropub makes a "perfect rural retreat", with "adventurous, tasty" gastrofare and ales from the local Otter Brewery; locals are "so delighted at its change of fortune... except you now have to book mid-week!" / **Details:** www.tytherleigharms.com; 9 pm, Fri & Sat 9.30 pm, Sun 8.30 pm.*

ULLSWATER, CUMBRIA 7–3D

Sharrow Bay £96 334

CA10 2LZ (01768) 486301

*In its heydey, this "stunning" and "delightfully old-fashioned" venue came to define the country house hotel experience. Nowadays under newish owners, most reports still acclaim its "faultless" cuisine, but its ratings have not quite reclaimed the heights of yesteryear. / **Details:** www.sharrowbay.co.uk; on Pooley Bridge Rd towards Howtown; 9 pm; no jeans or trainers; children: 8+. **Accommodation:** 17 rooms, from £355 (B&B)*

UPPER SLAUGHTER, GLOUCESTERSHIRE 2–1C

Lords of the Manor £92 323

GL54 2JD (01451) 820243

*"Divine grounds" set the scene at this "wonderfully Olde Englishe" hotel, in a 'chocolate box' Cotswolds village. To the odd critic the dining room can seem a tad "bland" by comparison, and service "patchy", but the overall consensus here is of "marvellous" (if "expensive") cuisine and a "romantic" all-round experience. / **Details:** www.lordsofthemanor.com; 4m W of Stow on the Wold; 8.45 pm; D only, ex Sun open L & D; no jeans or trainers; children: 7+ at D in restaurant. **Accommodation:** 26 rooms, from £199*

WADDINGTON, LANCASHIRE 5–1B

The Higher Buck £42 443

The Square BB7 3HZ (01200) 423226

*A "much-renovated" village pub "taken over by Michael Heathcote" (of Duke of York at Grindleton fame); its "modern style of gastronomy" – "small plates, sharing plates" etc. – has already won it a local fan club. / **Details:** www.higherbuck.com; 9 pm, Fri & Sat 9.30 pm, Sun 8 pm.*

WADEBRIDGE, CORNWALL 1–3B

Bridge Bistro £42 332

4 Molesworth St PL27 7DA (01208) 815342

*This "husband-and-wife team's extended bistro goes from strength to strength" – it's "the best place to eat in Wadebridge". / **Details:** www.bridgebistro.co.uk; 9 pm; closed Sun D; no Amex.*

WAKEFIELD, WEST YORKSHIRE 5–1C

Bar Biccari £43 344

2 Highfield Rd WF4 5LU (01924) 263 626

*Still only limited feedback on this "classic Italian", in the attractive village of Horbury. Fans, though, say "the only complaint is remembering to book in good time, as it's seriously busy, and rightly so given the fabulous cooking!" / **Details:** www.barbiccari.co.uk; 10 pm, Sun 9 pm .*

WALBERSWICK, SUFFOLK 3–1D

The Anchor £43 333

Main St IP18 6UA (01502) 722112

*1920s pub, near to a shingle beach, which "gets very busy on sunny weekends as it has a lovely garden"; the food runs the gamut "from posh sandwiches to full meals". / **Details:** www.anchoratwalberswick.com; 9 pm. **Accommodation:** 10 rooms, from £110*

WARLINGHAM, SURREY 3–3B

Chez Vous £54 543

432 Limpsfield Rd CR6 9LA (01883) 620451

*Approaching its fifth year in business, this hotel-restaurant has "improved" with time, and is now judged a "wonderful place to eat and stay"; particular kudos goes to the "superb" tasting menu. / **Details:** www.chezvous.co.uk; 9.30 pm, Fri & Sat 10 pm; closed Mon & Sun D.*

WARWICK, WARWICKSHIRE 5–4C

The Art Kitchen £46 443

7 Swan St CV34 4BJ (01926) 494303

*In a "lovely" town centre setting, a "top-class Thai" with a "great buzz" that's has served "consistently great" food over the years. / **Details:** www.theartkitchen.com; 10 pm.*

Micatto £48 333

62 Market Pl CV34 4SD (01926) 403053

*A "fantastic" town-centre Italian with open kitchen, where there's "always something novel and interesting from the regions" to try from the monthly changing menu; it's a real hit locally "so you need to book". / **Details:** www.micatto.com; 10.30 pm, Sun 9 pm .*

Rose and Crown £47 444
30 Market Pl CV34 4SH (01926) 411117
A "fabulous country pub overlooking Warwick square", praised by a good-sized fan club for its "cheerful and obliging staff", "great vibe" and "super-reliable" grub. / ***Details:*** *www.roseandcrownwarwick.co.uk; 11 pm, Sat midnight.*

Tailors £56 543
22 Market place CV34 4SL (01926) 410590
"Ambitious, competent cooking", "first-rate presentation" and an "excellent wine list" combine to make this "small" venture, in a former tailoring shop in the town centre, the "best Warwick restaurant"; accordingly, "booking is essential". / ***Details:*** *www.tailorsrestaurant.co.uk; 9 pm; closed Mon & Sun; no Amex; children: 12+ for dinner .*

WATERGATE BAY, CORNWALL 1–3B

The Beach Hut Watergate Bay Hotel £45 334
On The Beach TR8 4AA (01637) 860543
"Newquay meets California" at this "reliable" local on the beach, where "dogs, walkers and surf dudes are all welcome"; "what a location" it has – and the food and service live up (well "almost"). / ***Details:*** *www.watergatebay.co.uk; 9 pm; no Amex.* ***Accommodation:*** *69 rooms, from £105*

Fifteen Cornwall Watergate Bay Hotel £82 335
TR8 4AA (01637) 861000
"One of the best sunset-dining locations in the UK" thanks to its "stunning views", helps inspire a raft of rave reviews for Jamie O's beach-side destination. On most accounts its "beautifully prepared, fresh and healthy dishes" (including those for brunch) and "friendly and efficient" service make it an all-round smash hit, but there's a disgruntled minority for whom either "indifferent" service, or "awful" food take the edge off the experience. / ***Details:*** *www.fifteencornwall.co.uk; on the Atlantic coast between Padstow and Newquay; 9.15 pm; children: 4+ at D.*

WATERMILLOCK, CUMBRIA 7–3D

Rampsbeck Hotel £75 445
CA11 0LP (01768) 486442
A "marvellous" country house "gem", with a "lovely setting on the shore of Ullswater", that "epitomises everything good about the Lake District"; the food "has ambition and delivers interest and flavour", while nice rooms make it "a great place for a weekend away with a loved one". / ***Details:*** *www.rampsbeck.co.uk; next to Lake Ullswater, J40 on M6, take A592 to Ullswater; 8.30 pm; no Amex; children: 8+.* ***Accommodation:*** *19 rooms, from £110*

WATERNISH, HIGHLAND 9–2A

Loch Bay £52 345
Stein IV55 8GA (01470) 592235
"It just does not get any better than this! – fresh seafood in a restaurant about 20 yards from the loch". So say fans of this tiny, 7-table venture with fine views (only open in season). / ***Details:*** *www.lochbay-seafood-restaurant.co.uk; 22m from Portree via A87 and B886; 8m from Dunvegan; 8.30 pm; closed Mon, Tue L, Wed L, Thu L, Fri L, Sat & Sun; no Amex; children: 8+ at D.*

WATH-IN-NIDDERDALE, NORTH YORKSHIRE 8–4B

Sportsman's Arms £50 344
HG3 5PP (01423) 711306
"Nestled in beautiful Nidderdale", a "relaxing", "traditional" venue that "must be one of the best country pubs in Yorkshire" given its "very high standards" all round. Top Menu Tip – "the best ever summer pudding". / ***Details:*** *www.sportsmans-arms.co.uk; take Wath Road from Pateley Bridge; 9 pm; closed Sun D; no Amex.* ***Accommodation:*** *11 rooms, from £120*

WELLS NEXT THE SEA, NORFOLK 6–3C

Globe £41 333
The Buttlands NR23 1EU (01328) 710206
On a pretty Georgian square in this bustling seaside town, a "welcoming" pub-with-rooms praised for its hearty fare. / ***Details:*** *www.holkham.co.uk/globe; 9 pm; no Amex.* ***Accommodation:*** *7 rooms, from £100*

WELLS, SOMERSET 2–3B

Goodfellows £55 433
5 Sadler St BA5 2RR (01749) 673866
An "excellent fine dining experience" is to be had at Adam Fellows's "small, intimate" Mediterranean restaurant and adjoining café – and "what a pleasure to find a good seafood restaurant not at the seaside!" / ***Details:*** *www.goodfellowswells.co.uk; 9.30 pm; closed Mon, Tue D & Sun.*

Old Spot £47 234
12 Sadler St BA5 2SE (01749) 689099
Score a table "looking out on Wells Cathedral in the evening sunlight", and this pub can be a "perfect" spot. Even a reporter who thought the cooking "unexciting", says it's "of good quality". / ***Details:*** *www.theoldspot.co.uk; 9.15 pm; closed Mon, Tue L & Sun D.*

WELWYN, HERTFORDSHIRE 3–2B

Auberge du Lac Brocket Hall £88 2 2 3
AL8 7XG (01707) 368888
With its "lovely setting by the lake", this property on the magnificent estate where Margaret Thatcher once wowed world leaders has "so much potential". It's been a rocky year on many levels however (the operator went into administration in April 2015) and reports in this survey were very mixed – many did applaud its "very interesting wines" and "romantic" appeal, but a worrying number focused on "hit-and-miss" cooking at "stratospheric" prices. / ***Details:*** *www.brocket-hall.co.uk; on B653 towards Harpenden; 9.30 pm; closed Mon & Sun L; no jeans or trainers; children: 12+.* ***Accommodation:*** *16 rooms, from £175*

The Wellington £45 2 3 3
1 High St AL6 9LZ (01438) 714036
There are some "interesting specials" to be had at this roomy town-centre inn, but it's the "excellent choice of d'Arenberg wines from South Australia" which stand out. / ***Details:*** *www.wellingtonatwelwyn.co.uk; 10 pm; no Amex.* ***Accommodation:*** *6 rooms, from £100*

WEST BRIDGFORD, NOTTINGHAMSHIRE 5–3D

Larwood And Voce £44 3 3 3
Fox Rd NG2 6AJ (0115) 981 9960
"For general reliability and quality of food and service I've yet to be disappointed" – a typical comment on this consistent boozer, near Trent Bridge cricket ground; prices are "very reasonable" too. / ***Details:*** *www.molefacepubcompany.co.uk; 9 pm, Sun 5 pm; closed Sun D.*

WEST CLANDON, SURREY 3–3A

The Onslow Arms £45 3 3 3
The St GU4 7TE (01483) 222447
An attractive and buzzing village pub with a "fab" garden offering "robust portions at reasonable prices" and especially "great" Sunday roasts. / ***Details:*** *www.onslowarmsclandon.com; 10 pm, Fri & Sat 10.30 pm; children: 18+ after 7.30pm.*

WEST HOATHLY, WEST SUSSEX 3–4B

The Cat Inn £45 3 4 3
Queen's Sq RH19 4PP (01342) 810369
A "traditional" and "cosy" boozer in a "delightful" village which wins plaudits for food that's "well above the average pub fare" – and "with the bonus of nice rooms". / ***Details:*** *www.catinn.co.uk; 9 pm, Fri-Sat 9.30 pm; closed Sun D; no Amex; children: 7+.* ***Accommodation:*** *4 rooms, from £110*

WEST MALLING, KENT 3–3C

The Swan £56 3 3 2
35 Swan St ME19 6JU (01732) 521910
"Great indoors or out" – a "very stylish" vintage-chic brasserie with garden, whose fans praise "consistently excellent" dishes, although it can be a "bit noisy when busy". Top Tip – "superb and good-value set lunch". / ***Details:*** *www.theswanwestmalling.co.uk; 11 pm, Sun 7 pm.*

WEST MEON, HAMPSHIRE 2–3D

The Thomas Lord £44 3 2 3
High St GU32 1LN (01730) 829244
"An excellent gastropub for good, locally sourced food", whose other boons include a "lovely setting" in the South Downs National Park. / ***Details:*** *www.thethomaslord.co.uk; 9 pm, Sat 9.30 pm.*

WEST MERSEA, ESSEX 3–2C

The Company Shed £35 5 2 4
129 Coast Rd CO5 8PA (01206) 382700
"The novelty never wears off", for visitors to this "unique" and "very basic" coastal institution ("it really is a shed – staff wear wellies, and you could find yourself sitting next to a bath full of crab and lobsters"). It sells "the freshest seafood" imaginable, and "although they now are licensed, you can still BYO (and you have to bring your own bread, lemons and salad)." "Arrive early as parking nearby can be a bind", and "take a brolly as you may need to queue for an hour to get in!" / ***Details:*** *www.thecompanyshed.co; 4 pm; L only, closed Mon; no credit cards; no booking.*

West Mersea Oyster Bar £37 4 3 3
Coast Rd CO5 8LT (01206) 381600
"Wonderful fish 'n' chips and oysters" continue to win votes for this no-frills joint, near the famous 'Shed'; there's the odd skeptic (not least "given the location and the hype") but reports are highly positive in the main. / ***Details:*** *www.westmerseaoysterbar.co.uk; 8.30 pm; Sun-Thu closed D; no Amex; no shorts.*

WEST STOUR, DORSET 2–3B

The Ship Inn £43 3 3 2
SP8 5RP (01747) 838 640
This pretty ivy-covered country pub-with-rooms offers "generally good value", and serves "excellent fish". / ***Details:*** *www.shipinn-dorset.com; 9 pm; closed Sun D.*

WEST WITTON, NORTH YORKSHIRE 8–4B

The Wensleydale Heifer £63 2 2 3
Main St DL8 4LS (01969) 622322
For fans it's a "fabulous fish restaurant in the landlocked Yorkshire Dales", but for more sceptical reporters this "vibrant" inn puts in a more average culinary performance. Still it inspires a strong amount of feedback, and has a "lovely" location.
*/ **Details:** www.wensleydaleheifer.co.uk; 9.30 pm.*
***Accommodation:** 13 rooms, from £130*

WESTFIELD, EAST SUSSEX 3–4C

The Wild Mushroom £46 5 5 3
Westfield Ln TN35 4SB (01424) 751137
*Paul Webbe's "magical little restaurant" near Hastings "continues to serve food of excellent quality", with "locally sourced ingredients and interesting mushroom additions" the stand-out; "for this quality, it's a bargain". / **Details:** www.webbesrestaurants.co.uk; 9.30 pm; closed Mon, Tue & Sun D.*

WESTLETON, SUFFOLK 3–1D

The Westleton Crown £45 3 3 2
The St IP17 3AD (01728) 648777
*This "relatively remote" inn is "well worth a visit for the quality locally sourced food"; in peak of summer the bar may be preferable to the glass-roofed dining room, which can become toasty. / **Details:** www.westlecrown.co.uk; 9.30 pm.*

WESTON SUPER MARE, SOMERSET 2–2A

Cove £42 3 3 4
Birnbeck Rd BS23 2BX (01934) 418217
*"Whisper it quietly but WSM is starting to get a small selection of very nice restaurants" – foremost among them being this "relaxed" venture "away from the main hustle and bustle", but still "overlooking the water" from the promenade. Only a few reports, but they say its "high-end" (fish-centric) food represents "exceptional value". / **Details:** www.the-cove.co.uk/; 9 pm, Sun 5 pm ; closed Mon.*

WEYBRIDGE, SURREY 3–3A

Osso Buco £41 3 5 3
23 Church St KT13 8DE (01932) 849949
A "top, top local Italian" where particular praise goes to the "extremely friendly" staff – "if you could put a 6 for service then this place would get it!"
*/ **Details:** www.ossobuco.co.uk; 10.30 pm, Fri & Sat 11 pm; closed Sun.*

WEYMOUTH, DORSET 2–4B

Crab House Café £47 4 4 4
Ferrymans Way, Portland Rd DT4 9YU
(01305) 788867
*"Gloriously fresh fish and seafood" (some of it from the owner's own boat) is what this "no frills" but "welcoming" village gem is all about – "the wonderful crabs, aprons and hammers make for a relaxed if noisy atmosphere", and the result is "real value for money". "Go on a sunny day and sit in the wonderful garden overlooking the oyster beds". / **Details:** www.crabhousecafe.co.uk; overlooking the Fleet Lagoon, on the road to Portland; 8.30 pm, Fri 9 pm, Sat 9.30 pm, Sun 3.30 pm; closed Mon, Tue & Sun D; no Amex; cancellation charge for larger bookings.*

WHALLEY, LANCASHIRE 5–1B

Benedicts of Whalley £34 4 3 3
1 George St BB7 9TH (01254) 824 468
*This "continental-style café-bar in a ("charming") rural village (constantly extended, now with a stand-alone deli") offers a "totally pleasurable experience", from the "bustling" vibe to food that "makes the best of local sourcing". "Baristas abound", and it's just the job for "a stylish and cosmopolitan brunch". / **Details:** www.benedictsofwhalley.co.uk; 7.30 pm, Sun 4 pm.*

Food by Breda Murphy £40 5 4 4
41 Station Rd BB7 9RH (01254) 823446
*This Ribble Valley staple (plus popular deli) continues to elicit odes to its "exquisite" dishes and "oh-so-moreish" puds; still a "pity it's not open more in the evenings, but presumably (Ballymaloe-trained owner) Ms Murphy and co. enjoy a life away from the kitchen!" / **Details:** www.foodbybredamurphy.com; 5.30 pm; closed Mon & Sun, Tue-Sat D; no Amex.*

The Three Fishes £46 4 4 4
Mitton Rd BB7 9PQ (01254) 826888
*"Fantastic, locally sourced pub food" and "helpful" staff win consistently high ratings for this highly popular, "superior-quality gastropub" – the first of the Ribble Valley Inns. "Sit inside or outside if the weather is good". / **Details:** www.thethreefishes.com; 8.30 pm, Fri & Sat 9 pm, Sun 8 pm.*

WHEATHAMPSTEAD, HERTFORDSHIRE 3–2A

L'Olivo £55 3 4 3
135 Marford Rd AL4 8NH (01582) 834 145
A "very popular and buzzy" spot with "all the best elements of what one fondly thinks of as a typical Italian" – namely an "over-the-top owner", "joking waiters", "plenty of noise from people enjoying themselves, and best of all some good food".
*/ **Details:** www.lolivo-restaurant.com; 9.30 pm; D only, closed Mon & Sun.*

WHITBY, NORTH YORKSHIRE 8–3D

Magpie Café £39 542

14 Pier Rd YO21 3PU (01947) 602058
*"Believe the hype!" – The National Dish is "succulently fresh, with marvellous, crispy batter" that's "cooked to perfection", at this "splendid" old-fashioned seaside café, which year-in, year-out is one of the survey's most commented-on destinations, as the UK's most notable chippy. "It's right beside the harbour with views from many windows" and attracts "a lovely mix of ages". "The only downside – there are always massive queues to get in." / **Details:** www.magpiecafe.co.uk; 9 pm; no Amex; no booking at L.*

Trenchers £40 543

New Quay Rd YO21 1DH (01947) 603212
*An "excellent posh fish and chippy" in a town "where competition is strong"; the "sparkling tiled and mirrored décor with separate booths" adds to the experience, while "the lavatories would grace The Ritz... and, if it smells of chips, so what?"! / **Details:** www.trenchersrestaurant.co.uk; 8.30 pm; need 7+ to book.*

WHITE WALTHAM, BUCKINGHAMSHIRE 3–3A

Beehive £53 443

Waltham Rd SL6 3SH (01628) 822877
*Dominic Chapman, ex-of the Michelin-starred Royal Oak nearby, "has had a fantastic first year" at the helm of this red-brick pub, by the village cricket green; it's still "a work in progress" but by all accounts he's already serving up accomplished food at "reasonable prices". / **Details:** thebeehivewhitewaltham.com/; 9 pm, Fri & Sat 10 pm, Sun 4 pm.*

WHITEBROOK, MONMOUTHSHIRE 2–2B

The Crown at Whitebrook £81 332

NP25 4TX (01600) 860254
*This well-known Wye Valley restaurant-with-rooms inspired mixed feedback this year. To fans it's nothing short of "the Noma of Wales" with "tasty, subtle, interesting cuisine that's everything you expect (but don't always get) from a Michelin-starred" venue. Cynics however thought the cooking disappointing (eg "duck too rare for my liking") and insist that "there has to be a limit to foraging!" / **Details:** www.thewhitebrook.co.uk; 2m W of A466, 5m S of Monmouth; 9 pm; closed Mon; children: 12+ for D.* ***Accommodation:*** *8 rooms, from £145*

WHITSTABLE, KENT 3–3C

Crab & Winkle £45 223

South Quay, Whitstable Harbour CT5 1AB
(01227) 779377
*As befits its location "at the lovely Whitstable harbour", this café-like venture serves "a good variety of fish"; it pleases many who comment on it with "excellent" results, but its ratings are undercut by a couple of "very disappointing" reports of "insipid" cooking. / **Details:** www.crabandwinklerestaurant.co.uk; 9.30 pm; closed Mon & Sun D; no Amex.*

East Coast Dining Room £49 433

101 Tankerton Rd CT5 2AJ (01227) 281180
*"In a little row of shops" in Tankerton, this "small but friendly restaurant is very good on all fronts", from the "interesting dishes" to the "pretty fair wine list" and "unbelievable" prices; even those with high expectations "given the owners' antecedents in the area" say that it "did not disappoint". / **Details:** www.eastcoastdiningroom.co.uk; 9 pm, Fri-Sat 9.30 pm; closed Mon, Tue, Wed D & Sun D.*

Elliots @ No. 1 Harbour Street £43 343

1 Harbour St CT5 1AG (01227) 276608
*"Exemplary cooking from a real star"; a "crowded" caff near the beach, offering robust cuisine from Phill MacGregor, formerly of the Dove Inn at Dargate. / **Details:** www.no1harbourstreet.co.uk/; Mon-Wed 4 pm, Thu-Sat 11 pm, Sun 4pm.*

JoJo £36 554

2 Herne Bay Rd CT5 2LQ (01227) 274591
*"A popular relaxed, all-day local star" with "good" cliff-top views, serving "excellent tapas-style food with brilliant specials" – a "desirable draw on any visit to Whitstable". / **Details:** www.jojosrestaurant.co.uk; 9 pm; closed Mon, Tue, Wed L & Sun D; no credit cards.*

Ossies £14 432

205 Tankerton Rd CT5 2AT (01227) 772481
*It may be new, but this no-frills chippy – with two hugely popular siblings locally – is already "the best in town", say fans; there's a sizeable dining area, and if you prefer to take-away, the beach is very close by. / **Details:** no web; 4 pm, Closed Sun.*

Pearson's Arms £50 334

The Horsebridge, Sea Wall CT5 1BT
(01227) 272005
*Richard Phillips's "lovely, casual" pub and fine dining spot, with "wonderful" sea views, continues its "generally excellent" performance. Top Tip – "good-value lunchtime set menus". / **Details:** www.pearsonsarmsbyrichardphillips.co.uk; 9 pm, Fri & Sat 9.30 pm, Sun 8.30 pm; closed Mon D.*

Samphire £46 4 4 3
4 High St CT5 1BQ (01227) 770075
*A "very obliging" spot, just outside the town centre, whose "interesting menu using locally sourced products" wins high praise, albeit on a small amount of feedback. / **Details:** www.samphirerestaurant.co.uk; 10 pm; no Amex.*

The Sportsman £53 5 5 4
Faversham Rd, Seasalter CT5 4BP
(01227) 273370
*"The shabbiness, isolation and beautiful remoteness on the windswept north Kent cost are all part of the charm" of this "phenomenal" coastal pub, whose "unassuming style" (the harsh would say it looks "like a Harvester next to a caravan park") gives no hint that it is one of the UK's most popular gastronomic destinations. Owner, Stephen Harris, takes local produce, and creates "exciting", "pitch-perfect" dishes (most notably on the 12-course tasting menu). "The fine food, the sea air and the scenery all justify the long trip – it's like a day's holiday." Top Menu Tips – "to-die-for slip soles, and lamb cooked to pink perfection". / **Details:** www.thesportsmanseasalter.co.uk; 9 pm, Sun 2.30 pm; closed Mon & Sun D; no Amex; children: 18+ in main bar.*

Wheelers Oyster Bar £46 5 5 5
8 High St CT5 1BQ (01227) 273311
*"You will never experience anything else quite like it!" – this "quirky and pokey" local "institution" (est. 1856) only seats 16 people, and "the freshest local seafood is treated with sympathy and skill" to create "the best ever dishes". "BYO does no harm to the final bill" either. / **Details:** www.wheelersoysterbar.com; 7.30 pm, Sun 7 pm; closed Wed; no credit cards.*

Whitstable Oyster Fishery Co. £61 4 3 4
Royal Native Oyster Stores, Horsebridge CT5 1BU (01227) 276856
*"A holy grail for shellfish lovers" – this impressively popular staple benefits from "lovely surroundings" (a restored warehouse "directly on the beach"), but "it is worth the money" for its "fantastic" oysters and seafood. / **Details:** www.whitstableoystercompany.com; 8.45 pm, Fri 9.15 pm, Sat 9.45 pm, Sun 8.15 pm.*

WILLIAN, HERTFORDSHIRE 3–2B

The Fox £48 3 3 3
SG6 2AE (01462) 480233
*A "popular village pub" with a "lovely, airy feel" which "has been a bit hit-and-miss in the past but seems to have upped its game lately" on the food front, offering "good value and delicious" dishes; service – still sometimes "slow" – won higher ratings too. / **Details:** www.foxatwillian.co.uk; 1 mile from junction 9 off A1M; 9 pm; closed Sun D; no Amex.*

WINCHCOMBE, GLOUCESTERSHIRE 2–1C

5 North Street £66 4 3 3
5 North St GL54 5LH (01242) 604566
*In a modest former tea-room, Marcus & Kate Ashenford's highly esteemed venue continues to win acclaim for its "honest, creative and inspired cooking"; "unpretentious" service too – "without the usual Michelin BS". / **Details:** www.5northstreetrestaurant.co.uk; 9 pm; closed Mon, Tue L & Sun D; no Amex.*

WINCHESTER, HAMPSHIRE 2–3D

Bangkok Brasserie £39 3 4 3
33 Jewry St SO23 8RY (01962) 869 966
*"More spice and flavour than your average Thai" characterises the cooking at this very popular feature – one of the city's most popular eateries, it's "always full". / **Details:** www.bangkokbrasserie.co.uk; 10.30 pm.*

The Bengal Sage £38 4 4 3
72-74 St George's St SO23 8AH
(01962) 862 173
*"Still Winchester's best Indian", say fans of this "jewel box" of a venue, on account of its "superb and unusual", "fresh-tasting and fragrant" dishes. / **Details:** www.thebengalsage.co.uk; 10.30 pm; no Amex.*

The Black Rat £56 3 4 3
88 Chesil St SO23 0HX (01962) 844465
*"Consistently original cooking" – "modern British at its best!" – has carved a big reputation for this former pub, on the fringes of the town centre. Its ratings slipped a notch this year however – it can seem "overpriced", and some meals "were missing their previous highlights". / **Details:** www.theblackrat.co.uk; 9.30 pm; closed weekday L; children: 18+ except weekend L.*

The Chesil Rectory £56 4 3 4
1 Chesil St S023 0HU (01962) 851555
*The "beautiful" ancient building is the star of the show, if you visit this "romantic" central feature. "It's been through many reincarnations over the years, and this is one of the better ones", providing "an all-round, very good experience". / **Details:** www.chesilrectory.co.uk; 9.30 pm, Sat 10 pm, Sun 9 pm; children: 12+ at D .*

Hotel du Vin et Bistro £54 3 2 3
14 Southgate St SO23 9EF (01962) 841414
*The original branch of the '90s boutique hotel chain is "still a bit special"; the "great wine list with some notable good-value vintages" remains the star, but the food is "very good" too, with Sunday brunch "a steal (if tee-total!)" / **Details:** www.hotelduvin.com; 9.45 pm; booking: max 12. **Accommodation:** 24 rooms, from £145*

Kyoto Kitchen £46 443
70 Parchment Street SO23 8AT
(01962) 890895
'Winchester's first authentic Japanese' (so they say) specialises in sushi and sashimi. On practically all accounts it's not just "a pretty good show for this area", but "an amazing find" full stop, with "charming" service and "superb" food that's "great value for money". / **Details:** *www.kyotokitchen.co.uk/; 10.30 pm.*

(The Avenue) Lainston House Hotel £81 222
Woodman Ln SO21 2LT (01962) 776088
Chef Olly Rouse (ex-Coworth Park) serves up some "very competent" (and sometimes "sensational") cuisine at this this "imposing" country house hotel; not all reporters are convinced by the "over-panelled Victorian-style" décor, however, and "somewhat outrageous prices" remain a major sticking point. / **Details:** *www.lainstonhouse.com; 9.30 pm, Fri & Sat 10 pm.* **Accommodation:** *50 rooms, from £245*

The Old Vine £43 333
8 Great Minster St SO23 9HA
(01962) 854616
A "quaint and welcoming" Grade II-listed inn with an "excellent location opposite the cathedral" and "great character and charm"; it wins praise for some "excellent" gastro grub and "it's a GBG pub too", meaning "good beer" is a given! / **Details:** *www.oldvinewinchester.com; 9.30 pm, Sun 9 pm; children: 6+.* **Accommodation:** *5 rooms, from £100*

Rick Stein £53 543
7 High St SO23 9JX (01962) 353535
The Stein empire's first foray beyond Cornwall is proving "a most welcome addition to Winchester's High Street" (on the site of Union Jacks, RIP). As you'd expect, "it doesn't offer the depth of fish and seafood you get in Padstow", but "a more-than-adequate choice is extremely well sourced, cooked and served", service is "very slick" and "though not cheap, it's nevertheless good value." / **Details:** *www.rickstein.com/eat-with-us/rick-stein-winchester/; 10 pm.*

River Cottage Canteen £42 344
Abbey Mill Gdns, The Broadway SO23 9GH
(01962) 457747
"Close to the city centre", this offbeat venue (part of Brum's Polish Centre) is decked out like an old Polish country cottage (complete with thatched room and "sheepskins everywhere"). Fans say it's "marvellous", not least the solid Polish fare in "impossibly large portions".

Wykeham Arms £52 325
75 Kingsgate St SO23 9PE (01962) 853834
In a "lovely location next to cathedral and college", this "old-style" institution has a charming, most "civilised" ambience (and "the candlelit Jameson room is hard to beat"). Some long-term fans say that nowadays the food is "slightly down in standard perhaps", but on most accounts it's nevertheless "enjoyable and fair value". / **Details:** *www.wykemarmswinchester.com; between Cathedral and College; 9.15 pm; children: 14+.* **Accommodation:** *14 rooms, from £139*

WINDERMERE, CUMBRIA 7–3D

First Floor Café Lakeland Limited £33 443
Alexandra Buildings LA23 1BQ
(015394) 47116
"Extremely busy, and with good reason" – a cookware shop café (presided over by ex-Gavroche chef Steven Doherty) where the "short menu of specials delivers innovative dishes" and snacks are "varied and first-rate". / **Details:** *www.lakeland.co.uk; 6 pm, Sat 5 pm, Sun 4 pm; L only; no Amex.*

Gilpin Hotel £86 535
Crook Rd LA23 3NE (01539) 488818
"The décor is stunning, and the views beautiful" at this well-known Lakeland dining room, set in a "lovely" country house hotel. Service "can vary", but no-one has anything other than enthusiastic praise for chef Hrishikesh Desai's "brilliant" cuisine. / **Details:** *www.thegilpin.co.uk; 9.15 pm; no jeans; children: 7+.* **Accommodation:** *20 rooms, from £255*

Holbeck Ghyll £94 223
Holbeck Ln LA23 1LU (01539) 432375
"A magnificent, peaceful situation above Windermere" creates a "marvellous" impression at this luxurious, "slightly old-fashioned" former hunting lodge. Its ratings have waned in recent times however – what is still "a special treat" to many reporters has to some former fans "scored more misses than hits". / **Details:** *www.holbeckghyll.com; 3m N of Windermere, towards Troutbeck; 9.30 pm; no jeans or trainers; children: 7+ at D.* **Accommodation:** *33 rooms, from £190*

Hooked £46 543
Ellerthwaite Sq LA23 1DP (015394) 48443
"For absolutely fresh, beautifully cooked fish", "this is your place" – a "small" and "stylish" venue, "on the fringe of Windermere town", where the "charming" owner "makes everyone feel very special" too. / **Details:** *www.hookedwindermere.co.uk/; 8.30 pm, Fri & Sat 9 pm; D only, closed Mon; no Amex.*

Linthwaite House £77 334
Crook Rd LA23 3JA (015394) 88600
A fine Lakeland location sets the scene at this well-known Edwardian hotel, overlooking Windermere, where the ambitious cuisine is well-rated (if, sometimes, "varying – often extremely well done but occasionally missing its mark").

/ **Details:** *www.linthwaite.com; near Windermere golf club; 9 pm; no jeans or trainers; children: 7+ at D.* **Accommodation:** *30 rooms, from £180*

The Samling **£94** **3 3 4**
Ambleside Rd LA23 1LR (01539) 431922
"In a stunning setting overlooking Windermere", Ian Swainson serves up food with real "panache" (not least the "theatrical 7-course menu gourmand") at this dining room in an "unassuming" country house hotel; it does inspire the odd disappointment, however, and even the odd fan finds it "overpriced". / **Details:** *www.thesamlinghotel.co.uk; take A591 from town; 9.30 pm.* **Accommodation:** *11 rooms, from £300*

WINDSOR, BERKSHIRE 3–3A

Al Fassia **£41** **4 3 2**
27 St Leonards Rd SL4 3BP (01753) 855370
"This has to be one of Windsor's best-kept secrets"; there's "little décor" at this shop conversion, but service is "wonderfully warm and friendly" and the Moroccan cuisine (tagines and so on) is "most authentic", and washed down with "Moroccan beers, and very reasonably priced wine". / **Details:** *www.alfassiarestaurant.com; 10.15 pm, Fri & Sat 10.30 pm, Sun 9.45 pm; closed Mon L.*

WINTERINGHAM, LINCOLNSHIRE 5–1D

Winteringham Fields **£103** **4 4 4**
1 Silver St DN15 9ND (01724) 733096
"Well worth the schlep up the banks of the Humber" – Colin McGurran's "idyllic retreat" is an "amazing destination" for practically all reporters, with "superb" service and "surprising and exciting cuisine". Even fans can feel prices are "daft", but – despite the odd reference to the superiority of the former régime here – it's high time the tyre men gave the place back at least one star. / **Details:** *www.winteringhamfields.co.uk; 4m SW of Humber Bridge; 9 pm; closed Mon & Sun; no Amex.* **Accommodation:** *11 rooms, from £180*

WISWELL, LANCASHIRE 5–1B

Freemasons at Wiswell **£65** **5 5 4**
8 Vicarage Fold Clitheroe BB7 9DF (01254) 822218
"Northcote's only serious competitor in the area!" – Steve Smith's "hard-to-find gastropub, tucked-away in a rural village", gives its grander local rival a good run for its money, with "skilful and complex" local and seasonal cooking that's "full of flair" ("and its pub guise even means there's good ales on draught too"). One or two reporters were "disappointed after all the rave reviews", but they seem like the exception that proves the rule. / **Details:** *www.freemasonswiswell.co.uk; Tue-Thu 9 pm, Fri & Sat 9.30 pm, Sun 8 pm; closed Mon & Tue; no Amex.*

WITHYHAM, EAST SUSSEX 3–4B

Dorset Arms **£47** **3 2 4**
Buckhurst Pk TN7 4BD (01892) 770278
This "lovely old atmospheric pub", briefly run by Harveys, has recently returned to longtime family owners the Sackvilles, who have overseen an "attractive makeover" of late; its menu includes a "good selection of game from the local (Buckhurst) estate". / **Details:** *www.dorset-arms.co.uk; 11 pm, Sun 10.30 pm.*

WIVETON, NORFOLK 6–3C

Wiveton Bell **£45** **3 3 3**
Blakeney Rd NR25 7TL (01263) 740 101
A "dog-friendly pub", by the church, whose boons include a pleasant garden and some "lovely" locally sourced food. / **Details:** *www.wivetonbell.co.uk; 9 pm; no Amex.* **Accommodation:** *4 rooms, from £75*

WOBURN, BUCKINGHAMSHIRE 3–2A

Birch **£48** **3 3 2**
20 Newport Rd MK17 9HX (01525) 290295
A contemporary boozer, on the outskirts of town, that's "popular" in these parts thanks to its line in "simple, understated and extremely good" staples. / **Details:** *www.birchwoburn.com; between Woburn and Woburn Sands on the Newport rd; 9.30 pm; closed Sun D; booking: max 12, Fri & Sat.*

Paris House **£110** **3 3 3**
London Rd MK17 9QP (01525) 290692
With its "individual, relaxed service" and "unique" tasting menus, there's an "amazing experience" to be had at Phil Fanning's well-known dining room – and oh, "what a setting!" (a "fantastic" Tudor building on the deer-strewn Woburn Estate). However for a minority, both food and ambience can on occasion fall short. / **Details:** *www.parishouse.co.uk; on A4012; 8.30 pm, 9 pm Fri-Sat; closed Mon, Tue & Sun D.*

WOLLATON, NOTTINGHAMSHIRE 5–3D

Cods Scallops **£26** **5 3 2**
170 Bramcote Ln NG8 2QP (0115) 985 4107
It may be "set on a nondescript parade of local shops in the suburbs" ("about as far as you can get from the sea!") but this "is no ordinary chippy" – a "heavenly beacon for fish and seafood lovers", serving an "amazing" variety, prepared "battered or baked in lemon, herbs and garlic", plus "an extensive range of classy soft drinks, plus local ales and ciders". Brace yourself though, for a "huge queue". / **Details:** *www.codsscallops.com/; 9 pm, Fri & Sat 9.30 pm; closed Sun.*

WOLVERCOTE, OXFORDSHIRE 2–2D

The Trout Inn £45 225
195 Godstow Rd OX2 8PN (01865) 510930
*"What a wonderful place!" – a "magical" riverside pub-restaurant, made famous as the stomping ground of Inspector Morse, with food that's reliable and "very filling". / **Details:** www.thetroutoxford.co.uk; 2m from junction of A40 & A44; 10 pm, Fri & Sat 10.30 pm, Sun 9 pm.*

WOLVERHAMPTON, WEST MIDLANDS 5–4B

Bilash £51 544
2 Cheapside WV1 1TU (01902) 427762
*"Rivalling the best in Birmingham!" – Sitab Khan's well-established subcontinental may have "décor akin to that of a traditional British curry place", but the "magnificent" cooking – "pushing the range of spicing beyond the norm" – "never fails to impress". / **Details:** www.thebilash.co.uk; 10.30 pm; closed Sun.*

WOODBRIDGE, SUFFOLK 3–1D

The Table £41 333
Quay St IP12 1BX (01394) 382428
*A "reliably good all-rounder", in the town centre, that's "consistent" and therefore always "buzzy" (and which profits from a "nice garden in the summer too"); it's perhaps "not a place to travel to, but really good if you are in the area – especially for lunch with ladies who lunch". / **Details:** www.thetablewoodbridge.co.uk/; 9.30 pm, Sun 3 pm.*

WOODLANDS, HAMPSHIRE 2–4C

Terravina
Hotel Terravina £72 453
174 Woodlands Rd, Netley Marsh, New Forest SO40 7GL (023) 8029 3784
*With renowned wine guru Gerard Basset in charge of the cellar at his (and wife Nina's) eight-year-old venture, "you know it is going to be interesting, informative, eclectic and thoroughly satisfying... and it delivers on every level". All elements of the formula at this New Forest dining room deliver a quality experience however, from the "well-judged" cuisine to the superb, but "relaxed" service. / **Details:** www.hotelterravina.co.uk; 9.30 pm. **Accommodation:** 11 rooms, from £165*

WOOTTON, OXFORDSHIRE 2–1D

The Killingworth Castle £49 443
Glympton Rd OX20 1EJ (01993) 811 401
*In a "sensitively refurbished" 17th-century coaching inn, this three-year-old sibling to the Ebrington Arms is a real hit locally, owing to Andrew Lipp's "interesting" Gallic-inspired cooking and some "excellent home-brewed ales"; it's best experienced "during the week and away from the hordes". / **Details:** www.thekillingworthcastle.com; 9 pm, Fri & Sat 9.30 pm, Sun 8.30 pm.*

WORSLEY, GREATER MANCHESTER 5–2B

Grenache £61 553
15 Bridgewater Rd M28 3JE (0161) 799 8181
*"New management has taken it to another level" – the majority report on this small venue several miles north west of Manchester, which now offers "fantastic" food and "faultless" service. / **Details:** www.grenacherestaurant.co.uk; 5 pm, Sun 4.30 pm; closed Mon, Tue & Sun D; no Amex.*

WORTHING, WEST SUSSEX 3–4A

The Fish Factory £38 432
51-53 Brighton Rd BN11 3EE (01903) 207123
*Most reporters "would certainly come back" to this easy-going seafood restaurant and chippy, which offers "very good value" food; also in Littlehampton. / **Details:** www.protorestaurantgroup.com; 10 pm.*

WRINEHILL, CHESHIRE 5–2B

The Hand & Trumpet £48 233
Main Rd CW3 9BJ (01270) 820048
*"One of the Brunning & Price pubs working to a successful formula", revolving around "interesting surroundings" and "excellent" real ales; the food is "only average", though – and while it's "probably the best" in an under-served area "even this may be slipping". / **Details:** www.brunningandprice.co.uk/hand; 10 pm, Sun 9.30 pm; no Amex.*

WRINGTON, SOMERSET 2–2B

Ethicurean £48 445
Barley Wood Walled Garden, Long Ln BS40 5SA (01934) 863713
*"There is something magical about the Ethicurean"; from "the wonderful, creative and wholesome food", to the setting in a "quaint Victorian walled garden" with valley views, this ethical venture is "a must for those who want to feel connected to what they eat"; "drinks work too!" / **Details:** www.theethicurean.com; 8.30 pm, Sun 5 pm; closed Mon & Sun D.*

WYE, KENT 3–3C

The Wife of Bath £49 323
4 Upper Bridge St TN25 5AF (01233) 812232
A "small" village restaurant-with-rooms which has been revamped by the new management, and is "much better following re-opening" by all accounts.

/ **Details:** www.thewifeofbath.com; off A28 between Ashford & Canterbury; Tue-Thu 9 pm, Fri & Sat 9.30 pm, Sun 3 pm; closed Mon & Sun D; no Amex. **Accommodation:** 5 rooms, from £95

WYMONDHAM, LEICESTERSHIRE 5–3D

The Berkeley Arms £45 443
59 Main St LE14 2AG (01572) 787 587
"Very popular with the County Set (of a certain age) and deservedly so", a "fabulous" inn that "reflects the Hambleton Hall background" of the husband-and-wife owners; "service is brilliant", too, and "they don't forget who they are", namely "a local pub-restaurant". / **Details:** www.theberkeleyarms.co.uk; 9 pm, Fri & Sat 9.30 pm; closed Mon & Sun D; no Amex.

YEADON, WEST YORKSHIRE 5–1C

Murgatroyds £36 432
Harrogate Rd LS19 7BN (0113) 250 0010
A large, bright diner-style venue named after the apparently characterful owner of Moorfield Mill, which used to sit here; its "great fish 'n' chips" mean there's "usually a queue to get in". / **Details:** www.murgatroyds.co.uk; 9 pm.

YORK, NORTH YORKSHIRE 5–1D

Akbars £28 443
6-8 George Hudson Street YO1 6LP
(01904) 679888
"Spot-on" member of the well-known, northern curry house chain, with the best subcontinental cooking in town, serving "excellent Pakistani fare" – "the curries are a sideshow, the grilled meats and breads are the finest". / **Details:** www.akbars.co.uk/york.

Ambiente £26 334
31 Fossgate YO1 9TA (01904) 689784
In Fossgate, the "bigger, newer sister restaurant" to the Goodramgate original is "an inviting social gathering place", offering "a wide selection of delicious tapas" and "a gorgeous Spanish wine list", with sherry flights, or "superb Cava by the glass". / **Details:** www.ambiente-tapas.co.uk/; 9.30 pm.

Bettys £43 344
6-8 St Helen's Sq YO1 8QP (01904) 659142
"A place that's always happy" – these "lovely, classic tearooms" are a "continued delight, with genuine old fashioned charm and excellent service". They're "not cheap", touristy, and "dont expect great fare", but for "a first class breakfast and fabulous afternoon tea" they're still "worth queueing for". / **Details:** www.bettys.co.uk; 9 pm; no Amex; no booking, except Sun.

Cafe No. 8 Bistro £45 443
8 Gillygate YO31 7EQ (01904) 653074
"Cosy and intimate it may be", but the food at this diminutive venue near the Minister is, by all accounts, "first-rate" – "gourmet dining at bistro pricing". (It's "soon set to expand into another outlet at the local art gallery".) / **Details:** www.cafeno8.co.uk; 10 pm; no Amex.

Le Cochon Aveugle £52 444
37 Walmgate YO1 9TX (01904) 640222
Ex-Waterside Inn chef Josh Overington's follow-up to the Blind Swine is a "tiny (seven table) restaurant" serving some of York's best food; the fixed six-course tasting menu, which changes every two weeks, is in fact "not so much a meal as a performance", with "touches of brilliance". / **Details:** www.lecochonaveugleyork.com; 9 pm.

Il Paradiso Del Cibo £36 444
40 Walmgate YO1 9TJ (0190) 461 1444
Run by a "consummate host" ("after a couple of visits you'll be treated like an old friend"), this "warm, welcoming and cosy" Sardinian is "popular with everyone". For a "cheap 'n' cheerful" meal, "the quality cooking knocks the socks off the usual formulaic fare in most High Street chain eateries". / **Details:** www.ilparadisodelciboyork.com; 2.30 pm, Sat & Sun 10 pm; closed Mon D, Tue D, Wed D, Thu D & Fri D; no credit cards.

Le Langhe £50 512
The Old Coach Hs, Peasholme Grn YO1 7PW
(01904) 622584
"Oh my goodness" – "the food is ridiculously good, especially for the price", at this "funnily located" venture ("quirkily entered" by going through a "wonderful deli"). "For grown up Italian fare, albeit from a limited menu it is difficult to imagine something more authentic or better" than its "intensely flavoured dishes and silky pastas", while the "wine list provides blanket coverage of great Italian vintages". There are downsides: the interior is "lacklustre" (in particular, try to avoid the "gloomy" first-floor room), and the "chaotic" service can be "polite", "hostile", "mildly panicked" or "utterly charming". / **Details:** www.lelanghe.co.uk; midnight; closed Mon, Tue, Wed, Thu & Sun; no Amex.

Mannions £26 442
1 Blake St YO1 8QJ (01904) 631030
"Be prepared to wait but its worth it" for a perch in this "wonderful", "hustling-and-bustling" deli/bakery in the city centre; the pay off is "well above-average sandwiches and sharing platters" ("brilliant for brunch"), although "when busy it can feel slightly claustrophobic". / **Details:** www.mannionandco.co.uk; 9, Sun 10 pm; L only.

Melton's **£52** 4 4 3
7 Scarcroft Rd YO23 1ND (01904) 634 341
"Been visiting for years and never disappoints" – this "quietly competent" stalwart, "tucked away on the edge of York" (just outside the city walls), attracts reams of commentary (all hugely positive) for its "sublime" and "imaginative" locally sourced fare. / **Details:** *www.meltonsrestaurant.co.uk; 9 pm; closed Mon & Sun; no Amex.*

Middlethorpe Hall **£71** 3 4 5
Bishopthorpe Rd YO23 2GB (01904) 641241
"Sumptuous lounges" and "a very elegant dining room" all contribute to the "beautiful setting in a National Trust property" of this country house hotel, which boasts 200 acres of gardens on the edge of the city, and makes a "quiet and relaxed" venue recommended both for business or romance on account of its "quality" cooking. / **Details:** *www.middlethorpe.com; 9.30 pm; no shorts; children: 6+.* **Accommodation:** *29 rooms, from £199*

Mumbai Lounge **£33** 3 2 3
47 Fossgate YO1 9TF (01904) 654 155
A "large, bustling" and "trendy" city-centre venue that's still "hailed as the top Indian restaurant in York" by many, owing to its "quirky" menu, which it serves with some "panache". As in previous years, though, the food strikes sceptical reporters as being "very average", and all things considered, the verdict is that "it's not as good as Akbars but worth a try." / **Details:** *www.mumbailoungeyork.co.uk; 11.30 pm, Fri & Sat midnight; closed Fri L*

Oshibi **£32** 4 4 2
9 Franklins Yard, Fossgate YO1 9TN
(01904) 593649
"A small Korean restaurant" in the city-centre; "attentive and helpful service, provide useful recommendations to navigate the cuisine", and the food – much of it barbecued – is "very interesting and delicious, and exceptionally good value".

Star Inn the City **£53** 1 1 3
Lendal Engine Hs, Museum St YO1 7DR
(01904) 619208
It has "a lovely location overlooking the River Ouse", but this "huge" venture – a spin-off from the acclaimed Star at Harome – needs to up its game; service is very "creaky", the locally sourced cooking is "inconsistent" and "uninspired", and bills can be "shocking". / **Details:** *www.starinnthecity.co.uk; 10 pm.*

Walmgate Ale House **£41** 4 3 3
25 Walmgate YO1 9TX (01904) 629222
In a 17th-century building, the Hjort family's venture is "the reincarnation of Meltons Too, which opened recently having had a much needed revamp"; it provides "very reasonably priced and locally sourced" food and "real ales have now been introduced along with interesting bar snacks". / **Details:** *www.walmgateale.co.uk; 10.30 pm, Sun 9.30 pm.*

The Whippet Inn **£40** 3 4 4
15 North St YO1 6JD (01904) 500660
"Tucked out-of-the-way, but nowadays a big player in York" – this "imaginative transformation of an old pub" in the city centre is "top class all round", and its steak "comes particularly recommended". / **Details:** *www.thewhippetinn.co.uk.*

UK MAPS

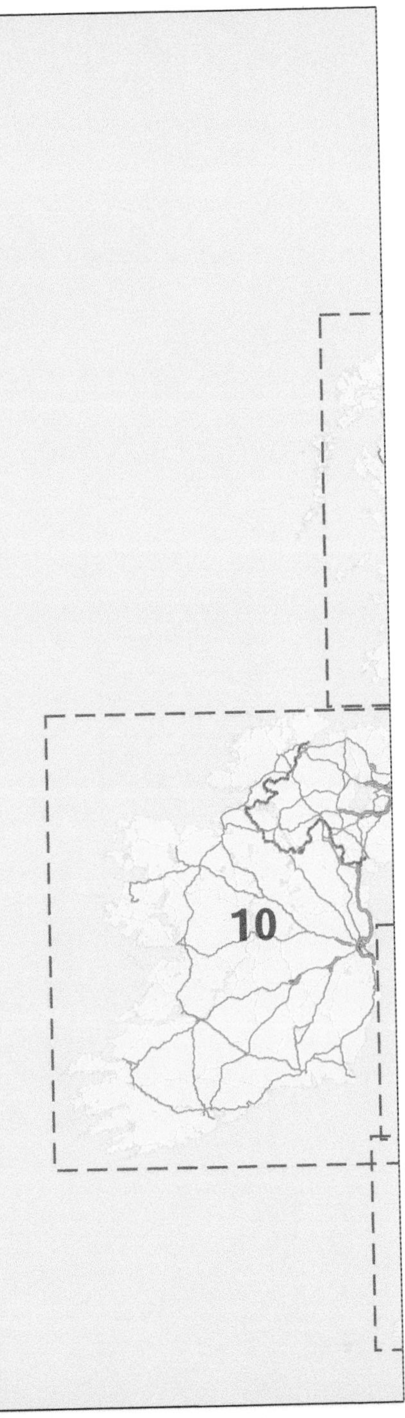
10

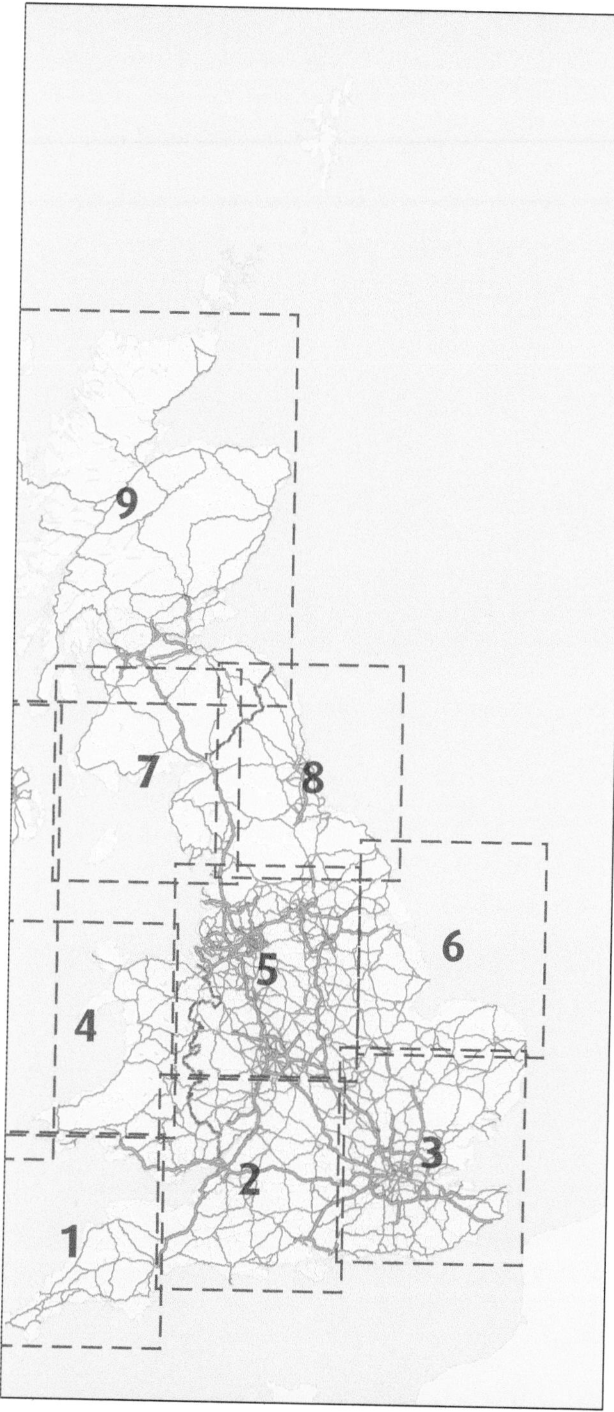
9
7
8
6
5
4
3
2
1

MAP 1

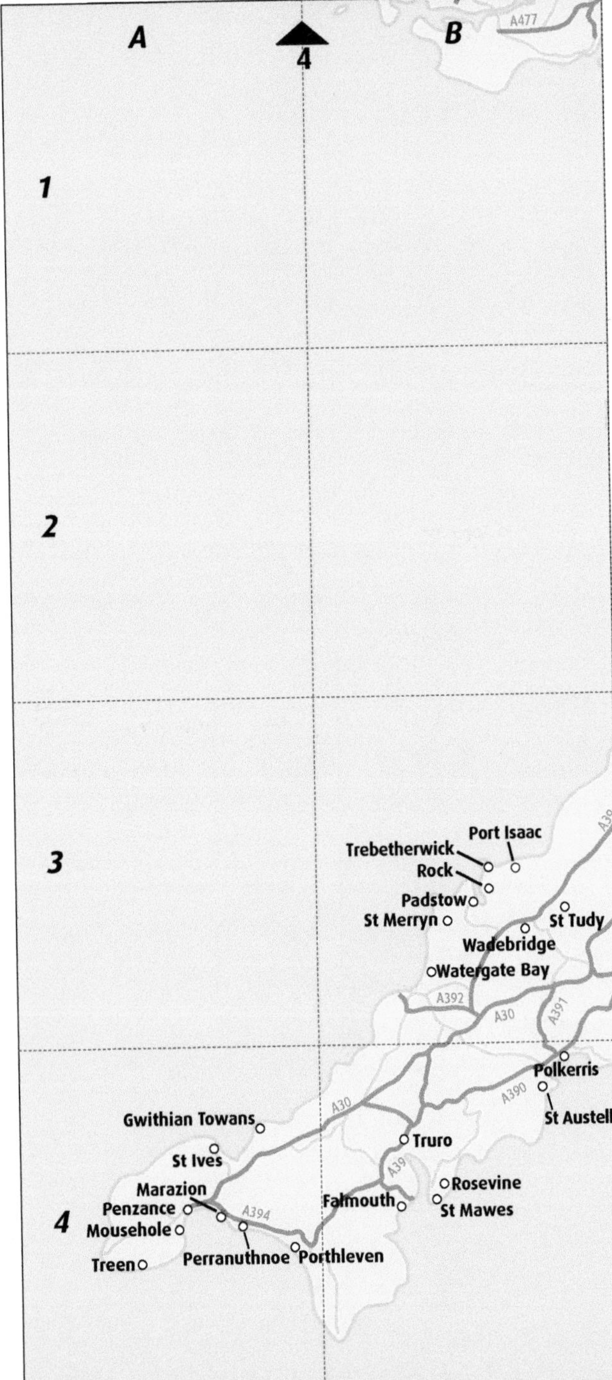

A
4
B
A477
1
2
3
Port Isaac
Trebetherwick
Rock
Padstow
St Merryn
St Tudy
Wadebridge
Watergate Bay
A392
A30
A391
Polkerris
A390
St Austell
A30
Gwithian Towans
Truro
St Ives
A39
Rosevine
Marazion
Penzance
Falmouth
St Mawes
A394
4
Mousehole
Perranuthnoe
Porthleven
Treen

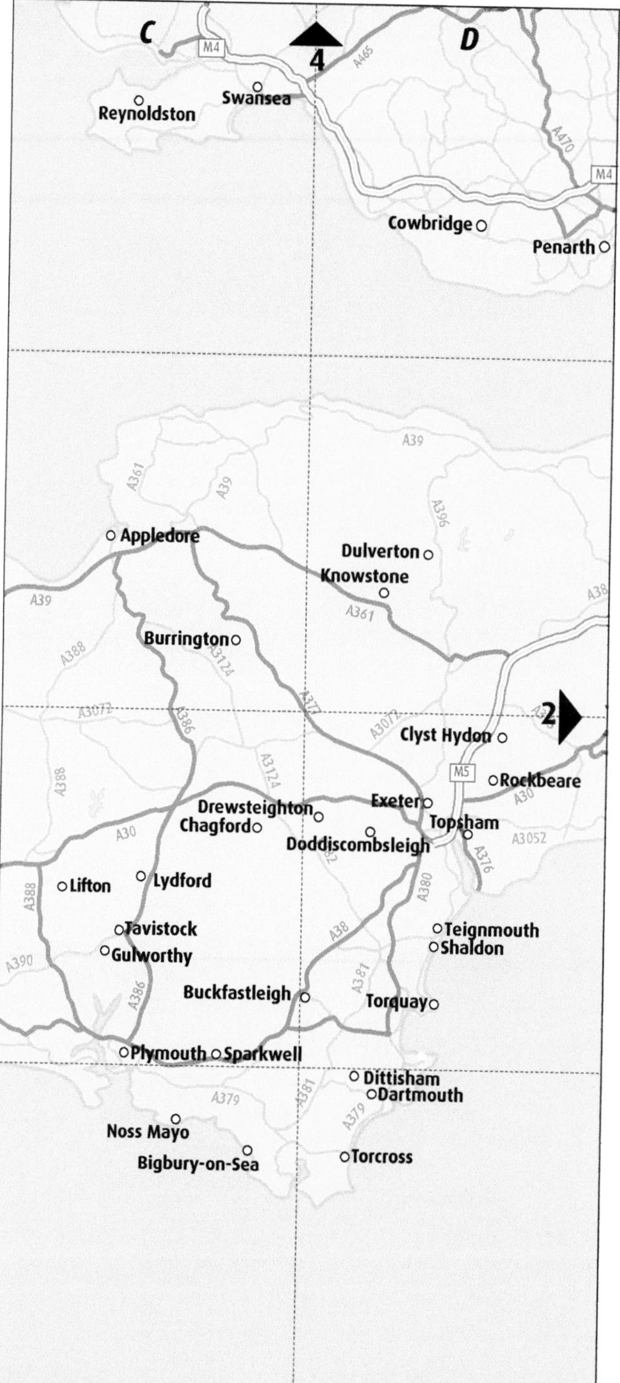

C
D
M4
4
A465
Swansea
Reynoldston
A470
M4
Cowbridge
Penarth
A39
A361
A39
A396
Appledore
Dulverton
Knowstone
A39
A38
A361
Burrington
A388
A3124
A377
A3072
A386
2
A3072
Clyst Hydon
M5
Rockbeare
A388
A3124
Exeter
A30
Drewsteighton
Chagford
Topsham
A30
A3052
Doddiscombsleigh
A376
Lifton
Lydford
A380
A388
Tavistock
Teignmouth
Gulworthy
Shaldon
A38
A390
A381
A386
Buckfastleigh
Torquay
Plymouth
Sparkwell
Dittisham
Dartmouth
A379
A381
A379
Noss Mayo
Bigbury-on-Sea
Torcross

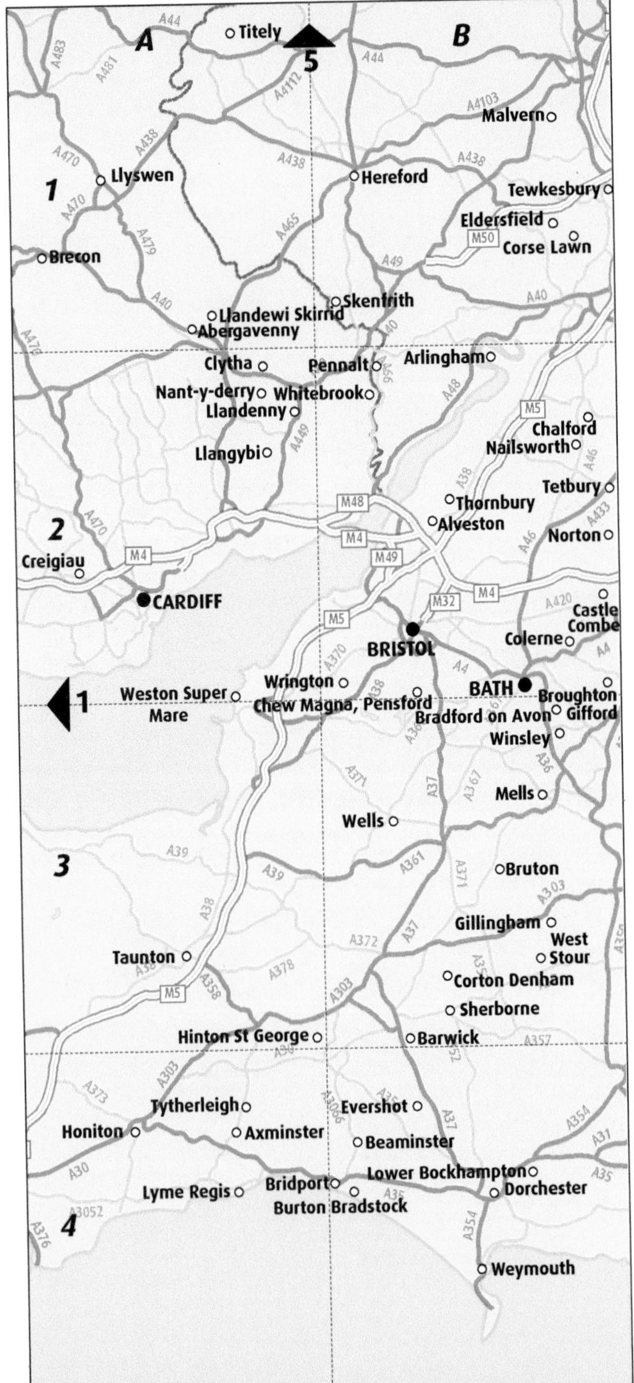
A
B
Titely
5
1
2
3
4
Malvern
Llyswen
Hereford
Tewkesbury
Eldersfield
Corse Lawn
Brecon
Skenfrith
Llandewi Skirrid
Abergavenny
Clytha
Pennalt
Arlingham
Nant-y-derry
Whitebrook
Llandenny
Chalford
Nailsworth
Llangybi
Tetbury
Thornbury
Alveston
Norton
Creigiau
CARDIFF
Castle Combe
BRISTOL
Colerne
Wrington
BATH
Weston Super Mare
Chew Magna, Pensford
Broughton Gifford
Bradford on Avon
Winsley
Mells
Wells
Bruton
Gillingham
West Stour
Taunton
Corton Denham
Sherborne
Hinton St George
Barwick
Tytherleigh
Evershot
Honiton
Axminster
Beaminster
Lower Bockhampton
Lyme Regis
Bridport
Dorchester
Burton Bradstock
Weymouth

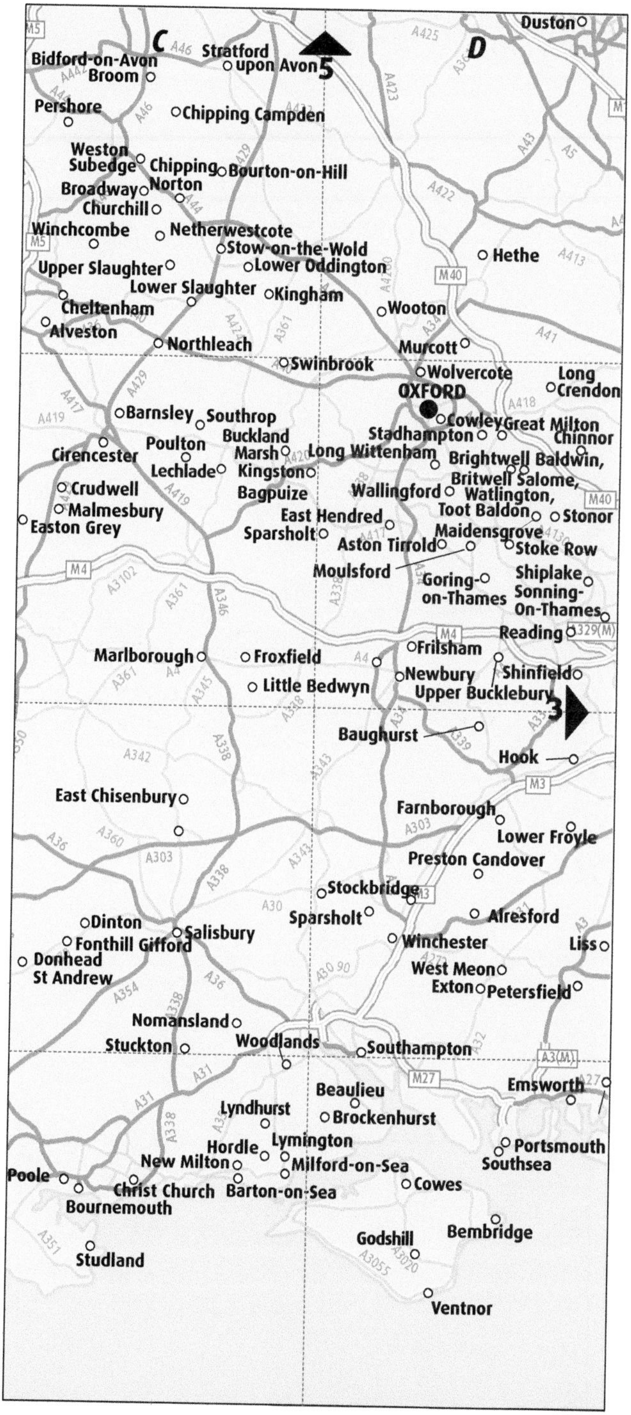

C
D
5

Duston
Bidford-on-Avon
Broom
Stratford upon Avon
Pershore
Chipping Campden
Weston Subedge
Chipping Norton
Bourton-on-Hill
Broadway
Churchill
Winchcombe
Netherwestcote
Stow-on-the-Wold
Hethe
Upper Slaughter
Lower Oddington
Lower Slaughter
Kingham
Cheltenham
Wooton
Alveston
Northleach
Murcott
Swinbrook
Wolvercote
Long Crendon
OXFORD
Barnsley
Southrop
Cowley
Great Milton
Buckland Marsh
Stadhampton
Chinnor
Poulton
Cirencester
Long Wittenham
Brightwell Baldwin,
Lechlade
Kingston Bagpuize
Britwell Salome,
Crudwell
Wallingford
Watlington,
Malmesbury
Toot Baldon
Stonor
Easton Grey
East Hendred
Sparsholt
Maidensgrove
Aston Tirrold
Stoke Row
Moulsford
Goring-on-Thames
Shiplake
Sonning-On-Thames
Reading
Frilsham
Marlborough
Froxfield
Newbury
Shinfield
Little Bedwyn
Upper Bucklebury
3
Baughurst
Hook
East Chisenbury
Farnborough
Lower Froyle
Preston Candover
Stockbridge
Sparsholt
Alresford
Dinton
Salisbury
Fonthill Gifford
Winchester
Liss
Donhead St Andrew
West Meon
Exton
Petersfield
Nomansland
Stuckton
Woodlands
Southampton
Emsworth
Beaulieu
Lyndhurst
Brockenhurst
Lymington
Hordle
New Milton
Milford-on-Sea
Portsmouth
Southsea
Poole
Christ Church
Barton-on-Sea
Cowes
Bournemouth
Bembridge
Godshill
Studland
Ventnor

A
B
6
1
2
3
4
Sutton Gault
Ely
St Ives
Keyston
Huntingdon
Fordham
Hemingford Grey
Madingley
CAMBRIDGE
Bolnhurst
Hardwick
Little Wilbraham
Roade
Shefford
Milton Keynes
Woburn
Willian
Clavering
Stevenage
Leighton Buzzard
Bishop's Stortford
Cheddington
St Ippolyts
Luton
Welwyn
Wheathampstead
Hunsdon
Aylesbury
Tring
Frithsden
Dinton
Berkhamstead
St Albans
Datchworth
Amersham
Flaunden
Epping
Ongar
Bushey
Shenley
Barnet
Brentwood
Bushey Heath
Seer Green
Marlow
Gerrards Cross
Beaconsfield
Denham
Queensbury
Bourne End
Cookham
Harrow
Taplow
Henley-on Thames
Maidenhead
Teddington
Bray
Windsor
White Waltham
Eton
Sunningdale
Kingston upon Thames
Bexley
East Molesley
Petts Wood
Sunninghill
Staines
Orpington
Egham
Surbiton
Ascot
Weybridge
Esher
Croydon
Sunbury on Thames
Cheam
Wallingham
Locksbottom
Bagshot
Redhill
Chobham
Cobham
Epsom
Old Woking
Stoke D'Abernon
Chipstead
Ripley
West Clandon
Plaxtol
Farnborough
Ockham
Shipbourne
Guildford
East Clandon
Westerham
Brockham
Shere
Dorking
Godalming
Bidborough
Ockley
East Grinstead
Speldhurst
Chiddingfold
Horsted Keynes
Tunbridge Wells
West Hoathly
Withyham
Lickfold
Danehill
Horsham
Henley
Cuckfield
Fletching
Tillington
Petworth
Haywards Heath
Strettington
Amberley
Albourne
East Chiltington
Lewes
Chichester
Arundel
BRIGHTON & Hove
Worthing
Littlehampton
Eastbourne
A1(M)
A1
M1
M10
M11
M25
M4
M20
M26
M23
A14
A10
A428
A505
A507
A120
A12
A13
A205
A232
A22
A23
A24
A26
A27
A272
A281
A31
A413
A421
A427
A43
A45
A5
A6
A605
A6116
A509
A1307
A1198
A414
A21
A261

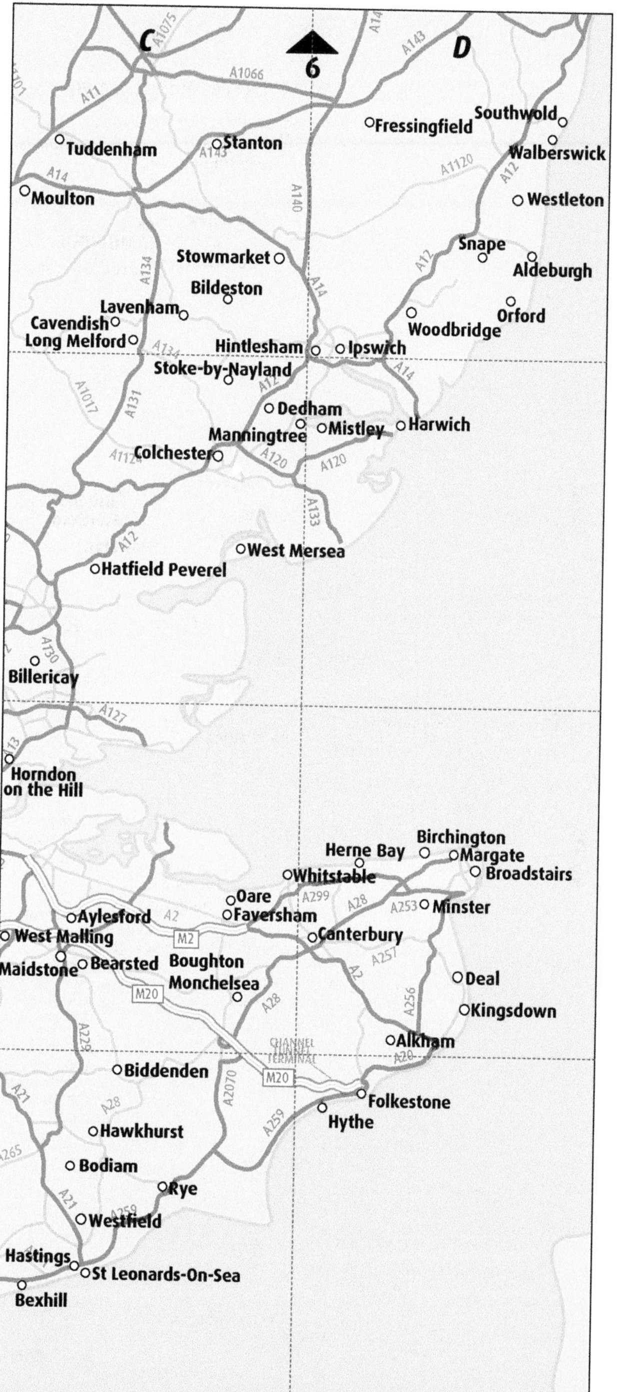
C
D
6
A1075
A1066
A143
A11
A14
Tuddenham
Stanton
Fressingfield
Southwold
Walberswick
Westleton
Moulton
A1120
A12
A140
Stowmarket
Snape
Aldeburgh
A134
Bildeston
Lavenham
Cavendish
Long Melford
Woodbridge
Orford
Hintlesham
Ipswich
Stoke-by-Nayland
A1017
A131
Dedham
Manningtree
Mistley
Harwich
Colchester
A120
A133
West Mersea
Hatfield Peverel
A730
Billericay
A127
A13
Horndon on the Hill
Herne Bay
Birchington
Margate
Whitstable
Broadstairs
Oare
Faversham
A299
A28
A253
Minster
Aylesford
A2
M2
West Malling
Canterbury
Maidstone
Bearsted
Boughton Monchelsea
A257
M20
Deal
A256
Kingsdown
A229
Alkham
A20
Channel Tunnel Terminal
Biddenden
A2070
Folkestone
A21
Hythe
A259
Hawkhurst
A265
Bodiam
Rye
Westfield
Hastings
St Leonards-On-Sea
Bexhill

MAP 4

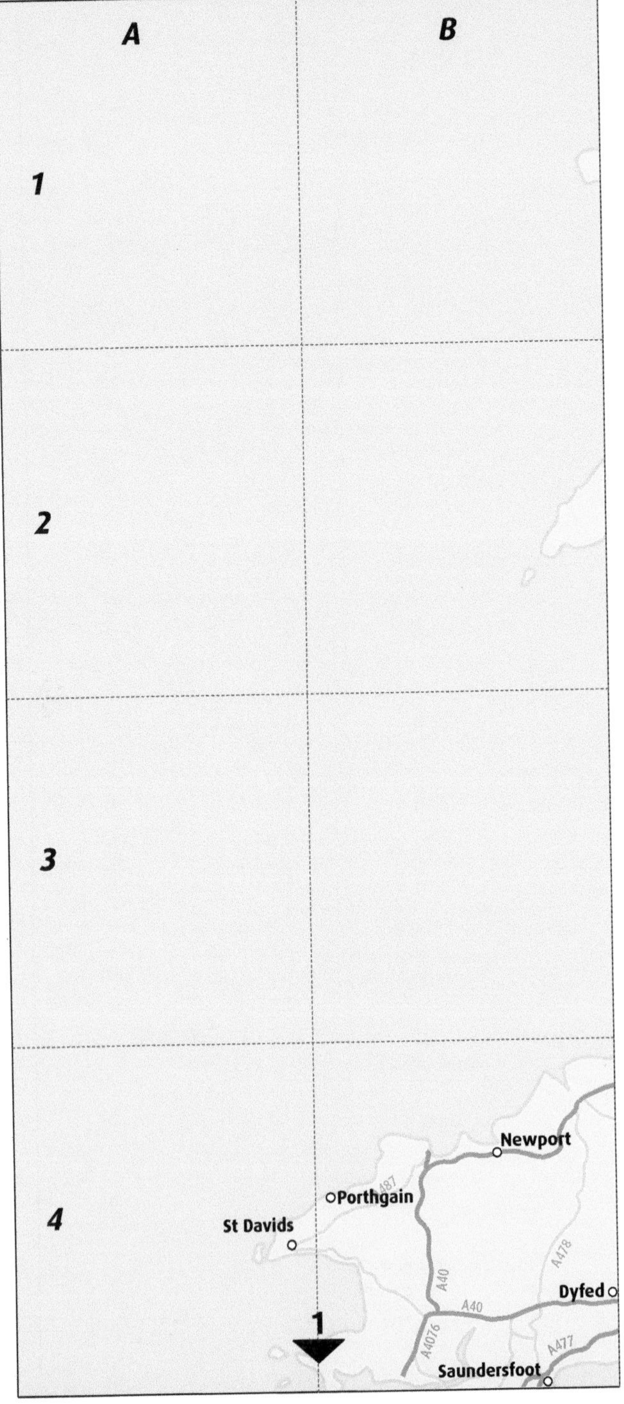

A
B
1
2
3
4
Newport
A487
Porthgain
St Davids
A478
A40
Dyfed
A40
1
A4076
A477
Saundersfoot

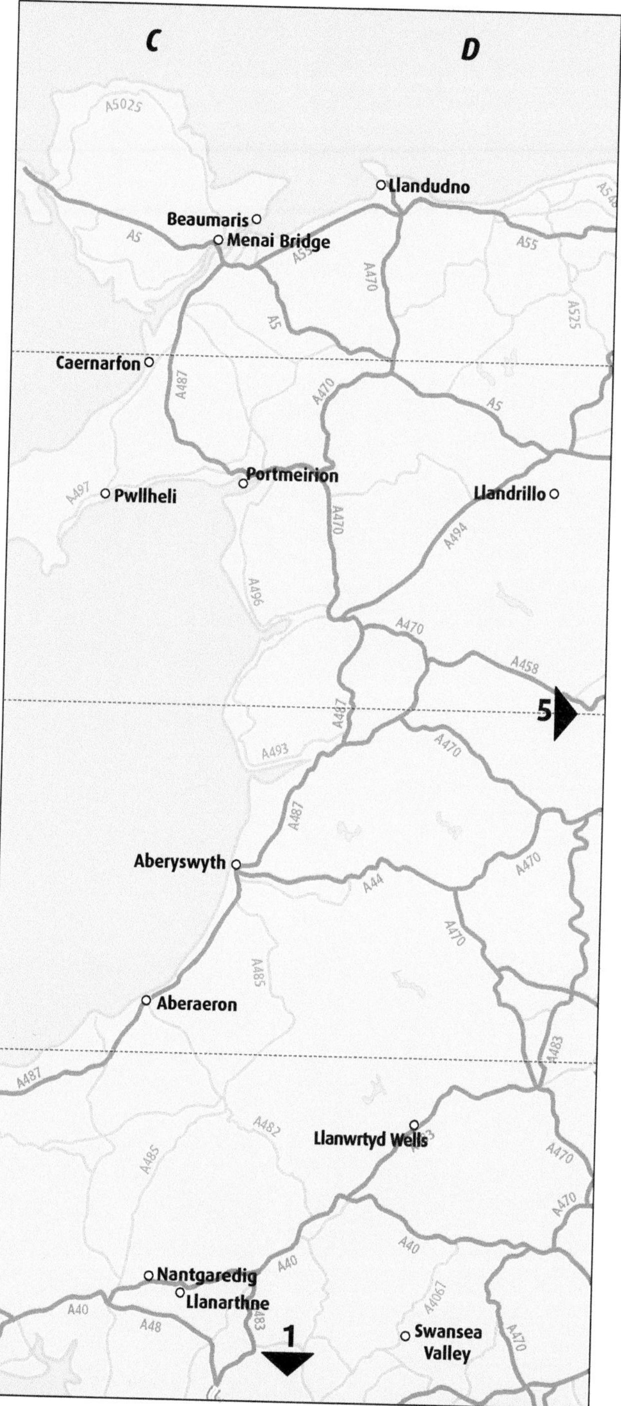
C
D
A5025
Llandudno
Beaumaris
Menai Bridge
A5
A55
A470
A55
A525
A5
Caernarfon
A487
A470
A5
Portmeirion
A497
Pwllheli
Llandrillo
A470
A494
A496
A470
A458
5
A487
A493
A470
A487
Aberyswyth
A44
A470
A470
A485
Aberaeron
A487
A483
A482
Llanwrtyd Wells
A485
A470
A470
A40
Nantgaredig
A40
Llanarthne
A40
A48
A483
1
A4067
Swansea
Valley
A470

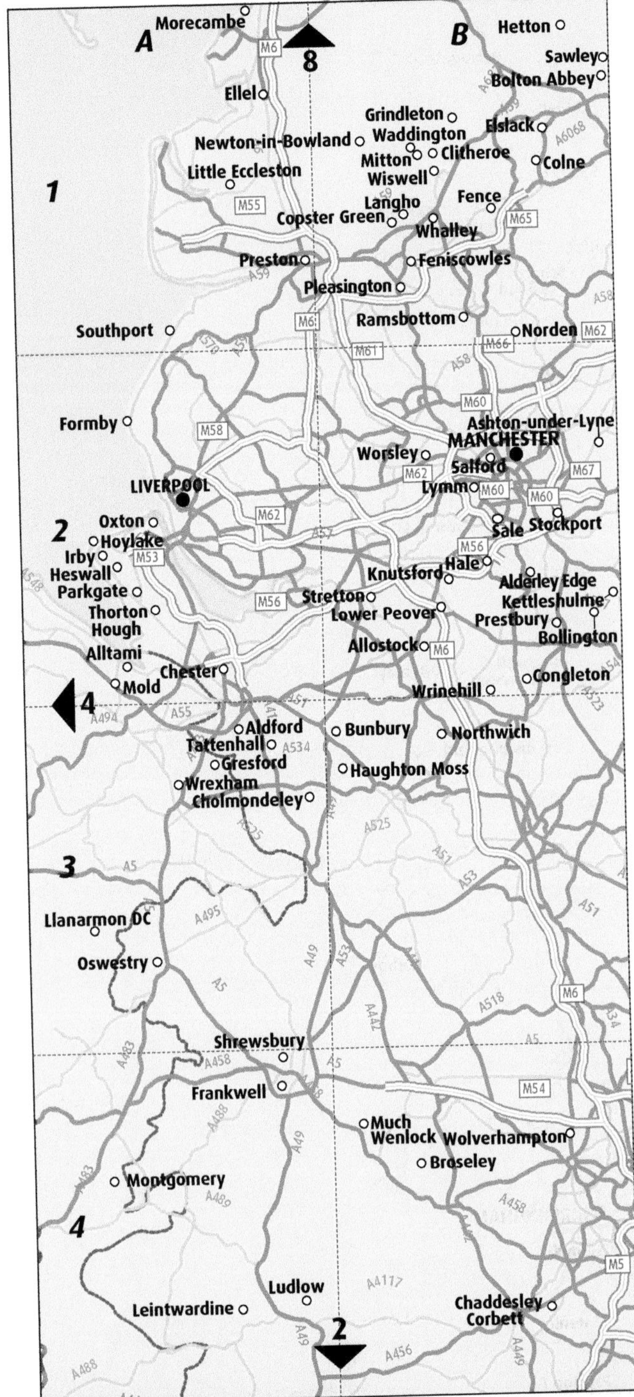
A
B
1
2
3
4
8
2
Morecambe
Hetton
Sawley
Bolton Abbey
Ellel
Grindleton
Waddington
Elslack
Newton-in-Bowland
Mitton
Clitheroe
Colne
Little Eccleston
Wiswell
Fence
Langho
Copster Green
Whalley
Preston
Feniscowles
Pleasington
Ramsbottom
Southport
Norden
Formby
Ashton-under-Lyne
MANCHESTER
Worsley
Salford
LIVERPOOL
Lymm
Oxton
Hoylake
Sale
Stockport
Irby
Heswall
Hale
Knutsford
Alderley Edge
Parkgate
Stretton
Kettleshulme
Lower Peover
Prestbury
Thorton Hough
Bollington
Alltami
Allostock
Chester
Mold
Congleton
Wrinehill
Aldford
Bunbury
Northwich
Tattenhall
Gresford
Haughton Moss
Wrexham
Cholmondeley
Llanarmon DC
Oswestry
Shrewsbury
Frankwell
Much Wenlock
Wolverhampton
Broseley
Montgomery
Ludlow
Leintwardine
Chaddesley Corbett
M6
M55
M65
M62
M66
M61
M60
M58
M67
M53
M56
M54
M5
A59
A6068
A58
A570
A57
A55
A494
A534
A525
A51
A53
A5
A495
A49
A442
A518
A458
A483
A488
A489
A4117
A456
A449
A548
A41
A34
A523
A54

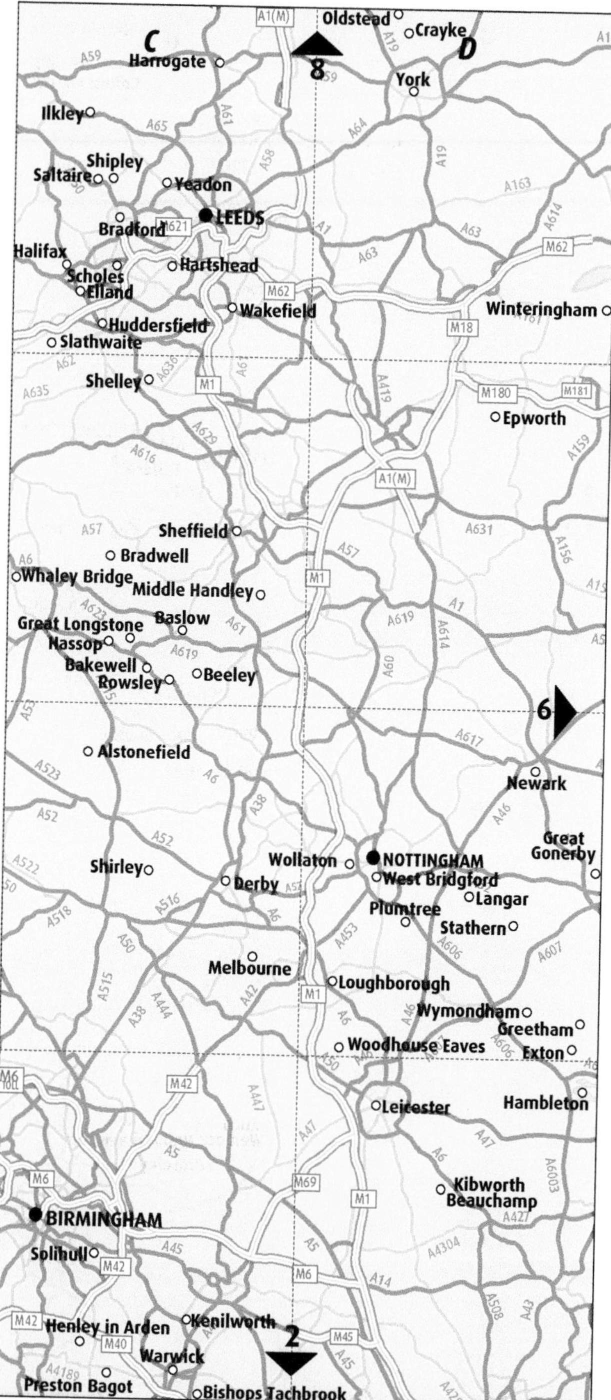
C
D
8
6
2
Oldstead
Crayke
Harrogate
York
Ilkley
Shipley
Saltaire
Yeadon
LEEDS
Bradford
Halifax
Scholes
Hartshead
Elland
Wakefield
Huddersfield
Slathwaite
Winteringham
Shelley
Epworth
Sheffield
Bradwell
Whaley Bridge
Middle Handley
Great Longstone
Baslow
Hassop
Bakewell
Rowsley
Beeley
Alstonefield
Newark
Great Gonerby
Wollaton
NOTTINGHAM
West Bridgford
Langar
Shirley
Derby
Plumtree
Stathern
Melbourne
Loughborough
Wymondham
Greetham
Woodhouse Eaves
Exton
Leicester
Hambleton
Kibworth Beauchamp
BIRMINGHAM
Solihull
Henley in Arden
Kenilworth
Warwick
Preston Bagot
Bishops Tachbrook

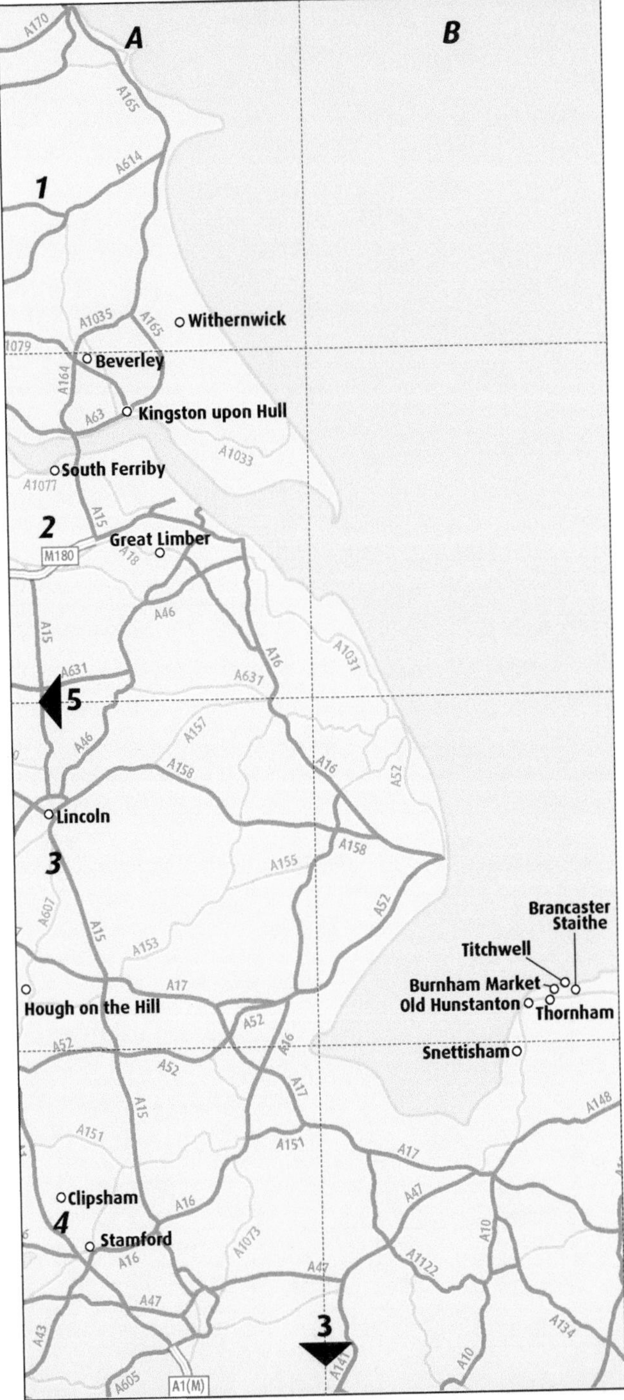

A
B
1
2
3
4
5
3
Withernwick
Beverley
Kingston upon Hull
South Ferriby
Great Limber
Lincoln
Hough on the Hill
Clipsham
Stamford
Brancaster Staithe
Titchwell
Burnham Market
Old Hunstanton
Thornham
Snettisham
A170
A165
A614
A1035
A1079
A164
A63
A1033
A1077
A15
M180
A18
A46
A631
A16
A1031
A157
A158
A52
A155
A607
A153
A17
A151
A148
A47
A10
A1122
A1073
A134
A43
A605
A1(M)
A141

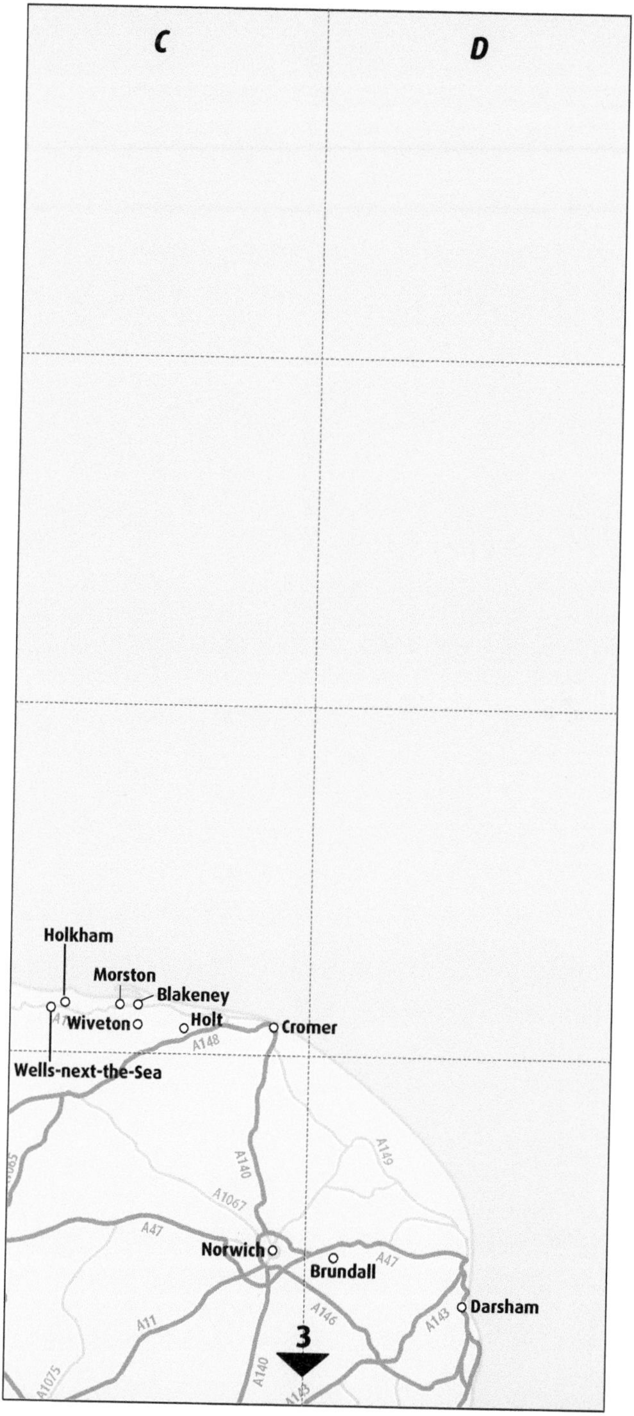

C

D

Holkham

Morston

Blakeney

Wiveton

Holt

Cromer

A148

Wells-next-the-Sea

A140

A149

A1067

A47

Norwich

Brundall

A47

Darsham

A146

A143

A11

3

A140

A1075

A143

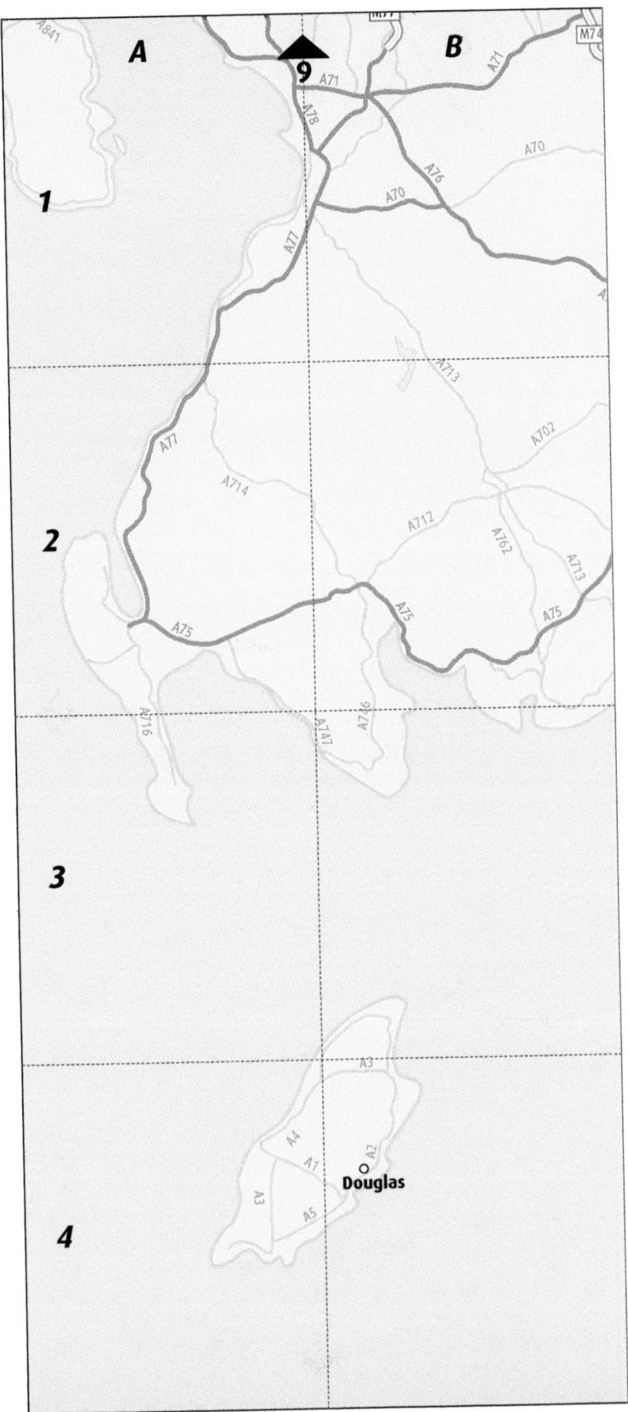

A
B
1
2
3
4
9
M77
M74
A841
A71
A78
A77
A76
A70
A713
A702
A714
A712
A762
A75
A716
A747
A736
A3
A4
A1
A2
A3
A5
Douglas

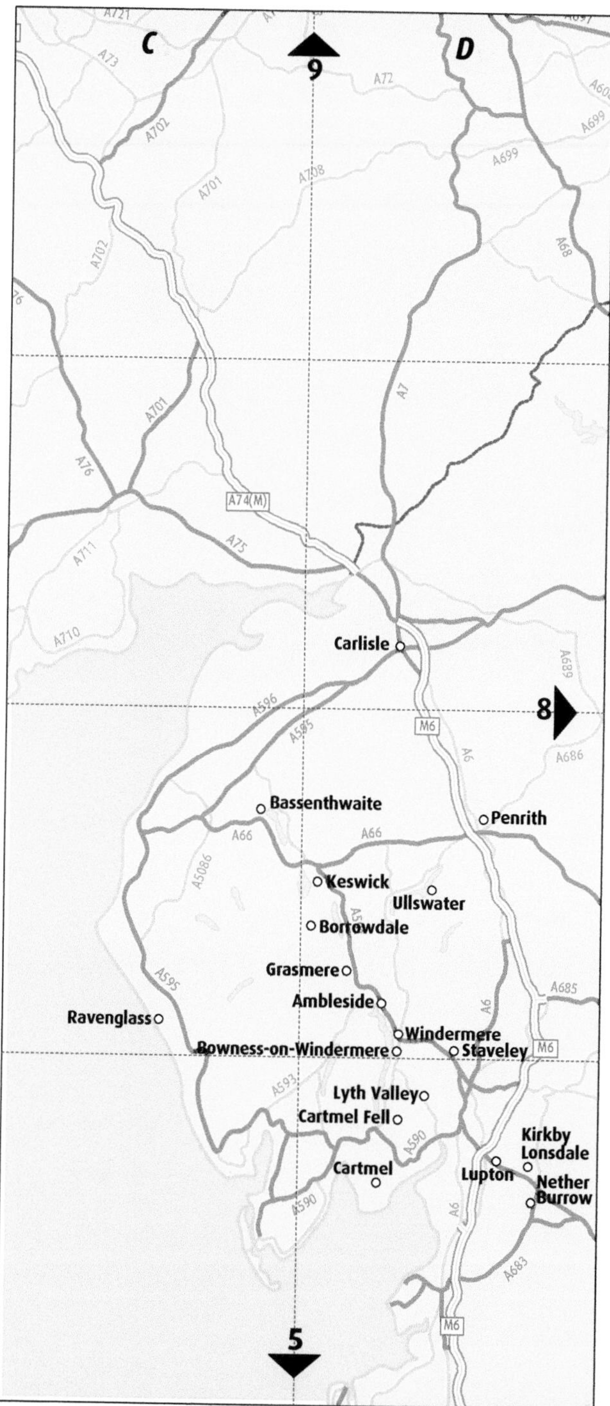
C
D
9
8
5
Carlisle
Bassenthwaite
Penrith
Keswick
Ullswater
Borrowdale
Grasmere
Ambleside
Ravenglass
Windermere
Bowness-on-Windermere
Staveley
Lyth Valley
Cartmel Fell
Kirkby
Lonsdale
Lupton
Cartmel
Nether
Burrow
A74(M)
M6
A75
A7
A6
A66
A596
A595
A590
A685
A683
A686
A689
A699
A68
A702
A701
A708
A72
A76
A711
A710
A5086
A593

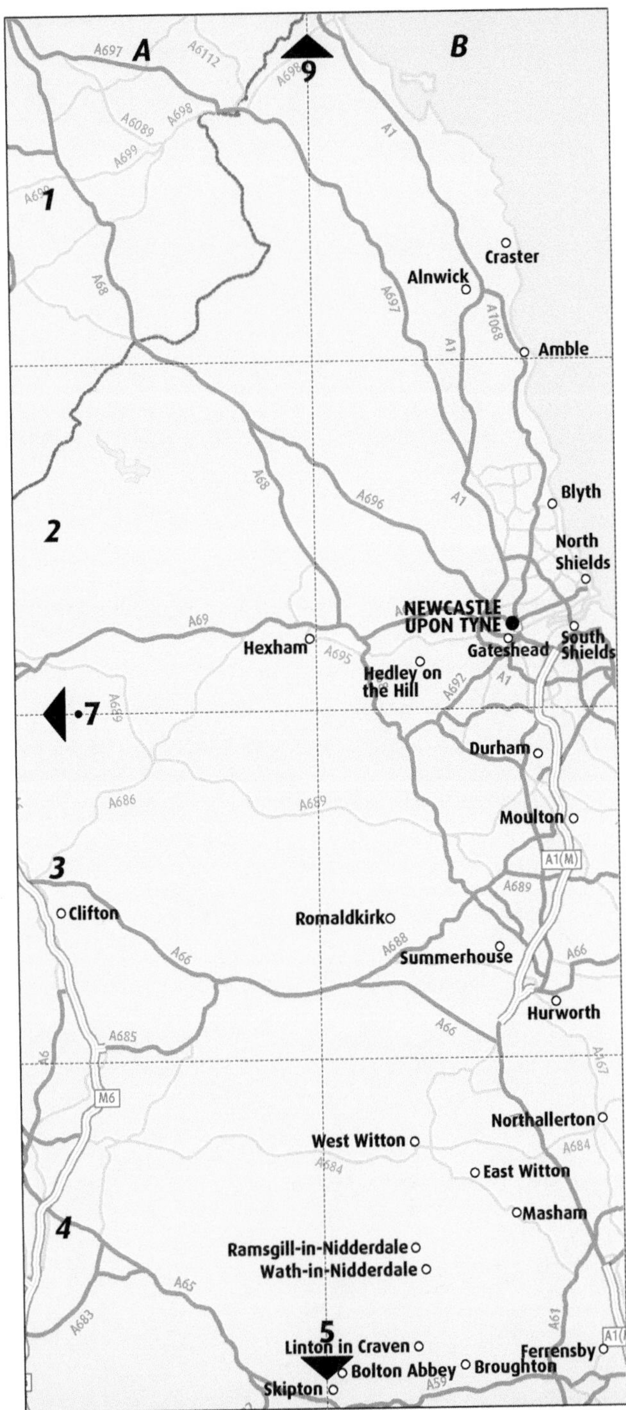
A
B
9
1
2
3
4
5
7
A697
A6112
A698
A6089
A699
A1
A68
A697
A1068
A1
A68
A696
A1
A69
A695
A692
A686
A689
A689
A66
A688
A66
A66
A685
A6
M6
A1(M)
A684
A684
A65
A683
A61
A59
A167
Craster
Alnwick
Amble
Blyth
North Shields
NEWCASTLE UPON TYNE
South Shields
Gateshead
Hexham
Hedley on the Hill
Durham
Moulton
Clifton
Romaldkirk
Summerhouse
Hurworth
Northallerton
West Witton
East Witton
Masham
Ramsgill-in-Nidderdale
Wath-in-Nidderdale
Linton in Craven
Bolton Abbey
Broughton
Ferrensby
Skipton

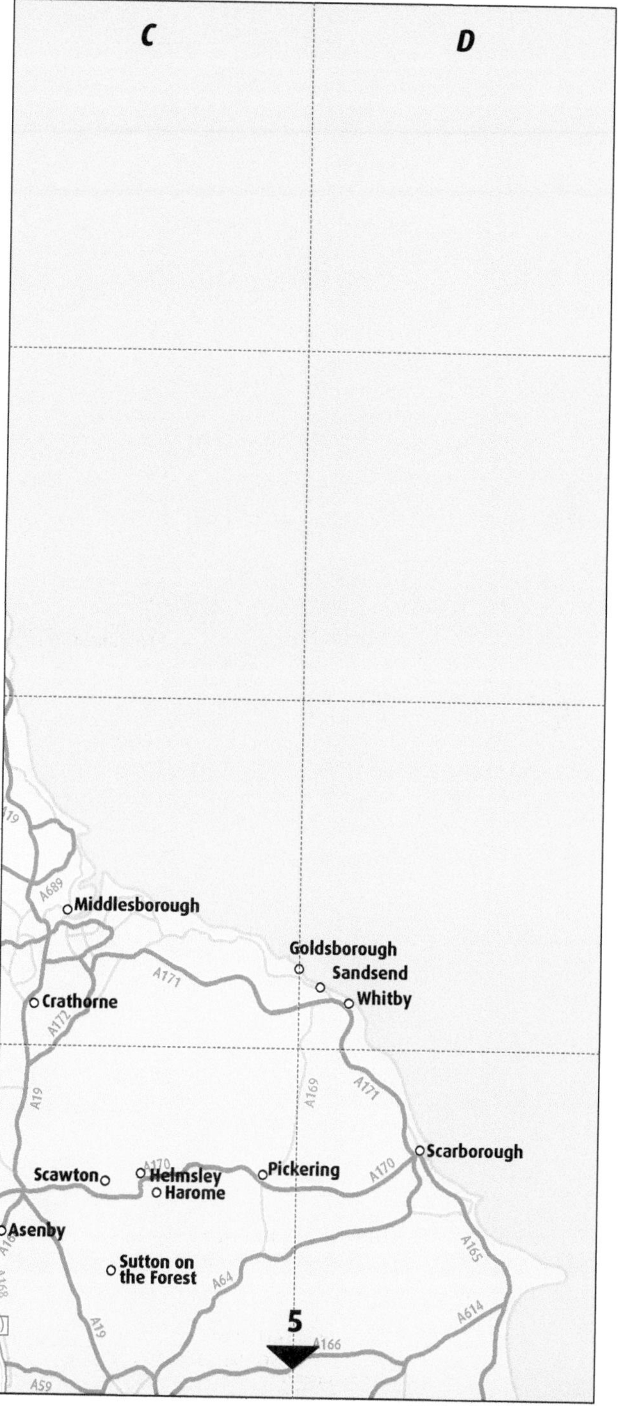

C
D
Middlesborough
Goldsborough
Sandsend
Whitby
Crathorne
Scarborough
Scawton
Helmsley
Harome
Pickering
Asenby
Sutton on the Forest
5
A689
A171
A172
A19
A169
A170
A165
A64
A614
A166
A59
A168

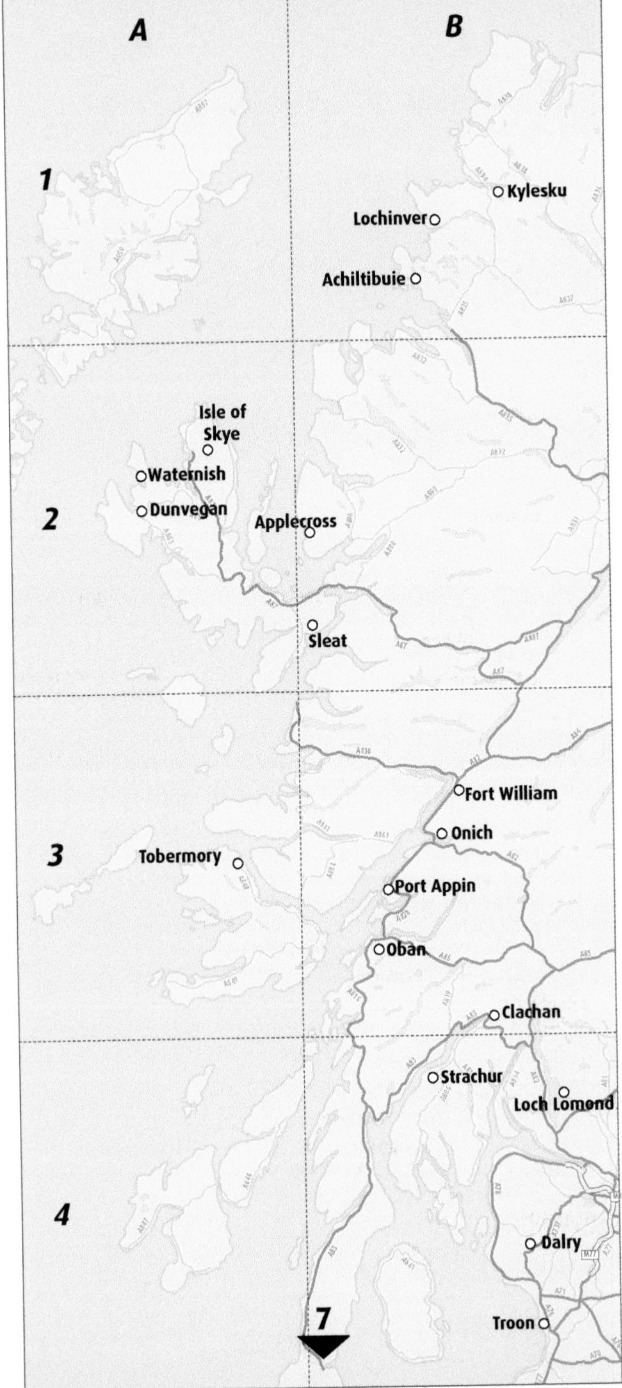
A
B
1
2
3
4
Kylesku
Lochinver
Achiltibuie
Isle of Skye
Waternish
Dunvegan
Applecross
Sleat
Fort William
Onich
Tobermory
Port Appin
Oban
Clachan
Strachur
Loch Lomond
Dalry
Troon
7

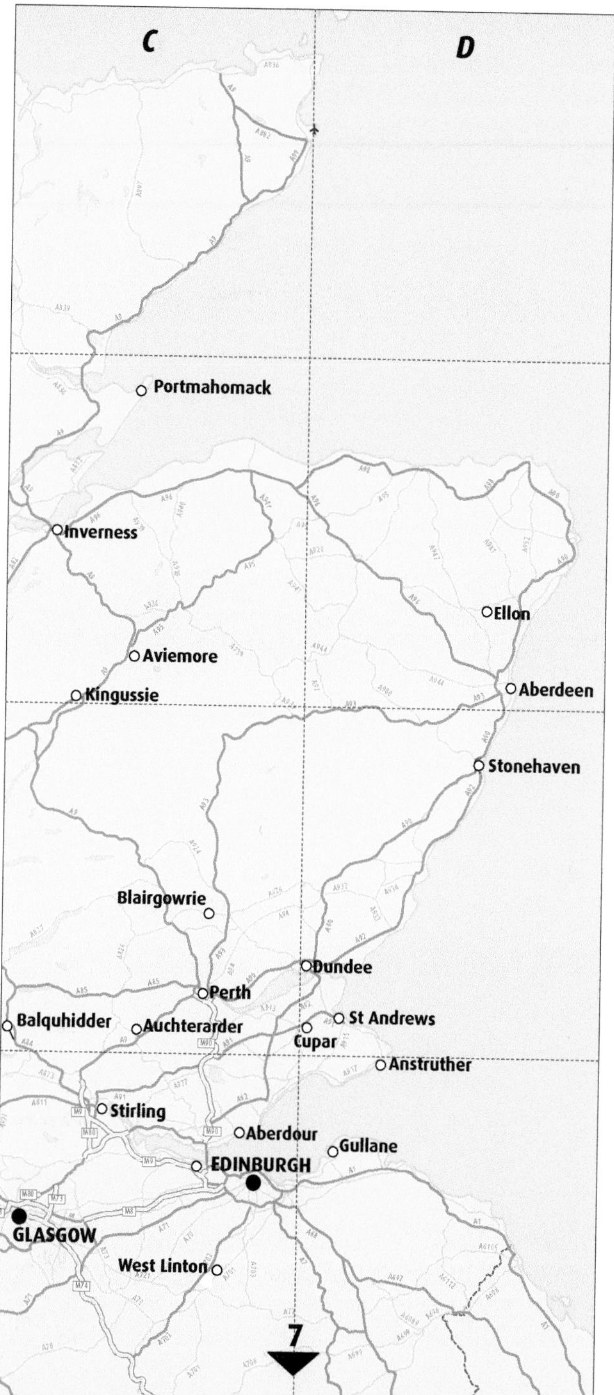
C
D
Portmahomack
Inverness
Ellon
Aviemore
Kingussie
Aberdeen
Stonehaven
Blairgowrie
Dundee
Perth
Balquhidder
Auchterarder
St Andrews
Cupar
Anstruther
Stirling
Aberdour
Gullane
EDINBURGH
GLASGOW
West Linton
7

A
B
1
2
3
4

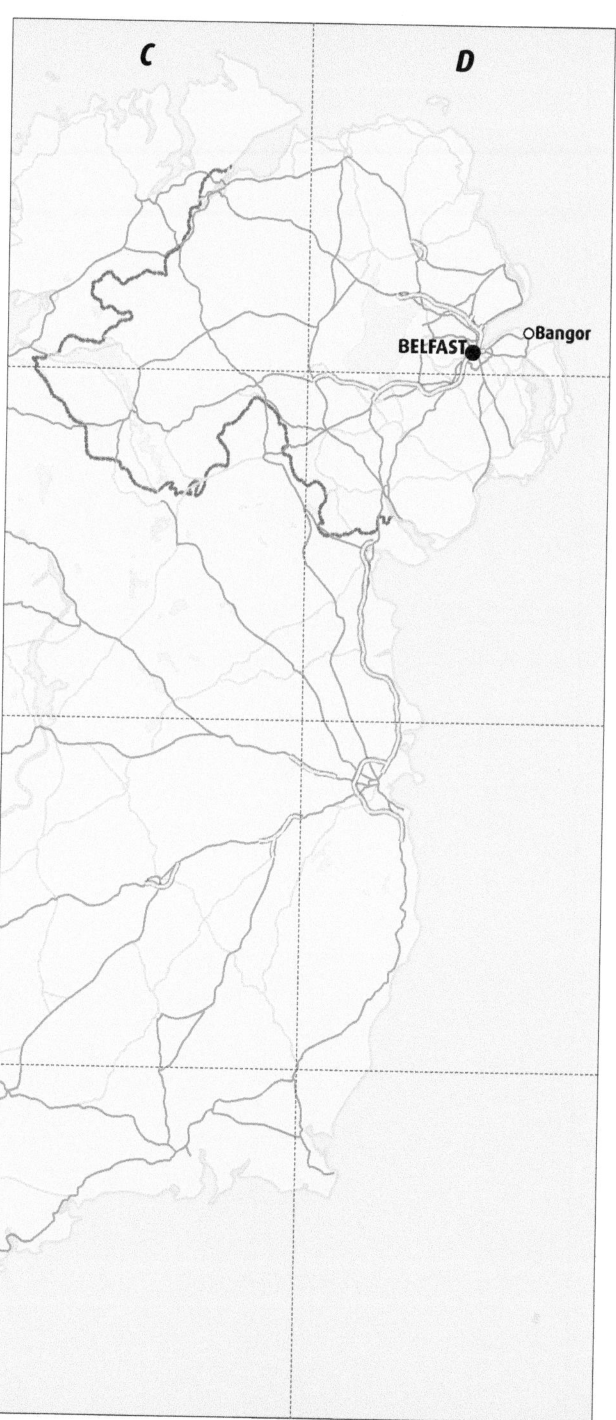
C
D
BELFAST
Bangor

ALPHABETICAL INDEX

ALPHABETICAL INDEX

A Cena *Twickenham* 34
A Wong *London* 34
Aagrah *Leeds* 310
Aagrah *Shipley* 350
abarbistro *Portsmouth* 343
Abbeville Kitchen *London* 34
The Abbot's Elm *Huntingdon* 305
Abeno 34
Abi Ruchi *London* 34
The Abingdon *London* 34
About Thyme *London* 34
L'Absinthe *London* 34
Abu Zaad *London* 34
Acorn Vegetarian Kitchen *Bath* 252
Adam Handling at Caxton *London* 34
Adam's *Birmingham* 257
Adams Café *London* 34
Addie's Thai Café *London* 34
The Admiral Codrington *London* 35
Afghan Kitchen *London* 35
Aglio e Olio *London* 35
Airds Hotel *Port Appin* 343
Akbar's *Manchester* 320
Akbar's *Leeds* 310
Akbar's *Bradford* 260
Akbars *York* 371
Al Duca *London* 35
Al Fassia *Windsor* 369
Al Forno 35
Al Frash *Birmingham* 257
Al-Shami *Oxford* 337
Alain Ducasse at The Dorchester *London* 35
Alba Restaurant *St Ives* 353
The Albannach *Lochinver* 317
Albert's Table *Croydon* 281
Albert's Worsley *Manchester* 320
Albertine *London* 35
The Albion *London* 35
Albion 35
Albion House *Ramsgate* 345
Aldeburgh Fish And Chips *Aldeburgh* 247
The Alderley *Alderley Edge* 247
Alec's *Brentwood* 262
Alexandros *Carlisle* 273
The Alford Arms *Frithsden* 294
Alfresco *St Ives* 353
Ali Baba *London* 35
Alimentum *Cambridge* 270
Allium Brasserie *Bath* 252
The Almeida *London* 35
Almost Famous *Manchester* 320
Alounak 35
The Alpine *Bushey Heath* 269
Alquimia *London* 36
Alyn Williams *London* 36
Amaru *London* 36
Amaya *London* 36
Amberley Castle *Amberley* 248
Ambiente *York* 371
The Ambrette *Canterbury* 271
The Ambrette *Margate* 324
The Ambrette at Rye *Rye* 347
Amelie And Friends *Chichester* 276
Ametsa with Arzak Instruction *London* 36
Amico Bio 36
L'Amorosa *London* 36
Anarkali *London* 36
Anchor *Ripley* 346
The Anchor *Sutton Gault* 358
The Anchor *Walberswick* 362
The Anchor & Hope *London* 36
The Anchor Inn *Lower Froyle* 317
Andina *London* 36
The Andover Arms *London* 37
Andrew Edmunds *London* 37
The Angel Inn *Hetton* 303
The Angel *Long Crendon* 317
The Angel Hotel *Abergavenny* 246
Angels & Gypsies *London* 37
Angels With Bagpipes *Edinburgh* 286
Angelus *London* 37
Angler *London* 37
The Anglesea Arms *London* 37
L'Anima *London* 37
L'Anima Café *London* 37
Anima e Cuore *London* 37
Annie's 37
Annie's Burger Shack *Nottingham* 333
Anokaa *Salisbury* 347
Anoki *Derby* 283
Anstruther Fish Bar *Anstruther* 249
The Anthologist *London* 38
L' Antica Pizzeria *London* 38
Antico *London* 38
Antidote *London* 38
Apollo Banana Leaf *London* 38
Applebee's Café *London* 38
Applecross Inn *Applecross* 249
Apulia *London* 38
Aqua Eight *Ipswich* 306
aqua kyoto *London* 38
aqua nueva *London* 38
Aqua Shard *London* 38
Arabica Bar and Kitchen *London* 38
The Araki *London* 38
Arbennig *Cardiff* 272
Arbutus *London* 39
Archduke Wine Bar *London* 39
Architect *Chester* 275
Ariana II *London* 39
Ark Fish *London* 39
The Art Kitchen *Warwick* 362
The Art School *Liverpool* 314
Art's *Leeds* 311
Artichoke *Amersham* 249
Artigiano *London* 39
L'Artisan *Cheltenham* 274
Artisan *Newcastle upon Tyne* 330
L'Artista *London* 39
L'Artiste Musclé *London* 39
Artusi *London* 39
Asakusa *London* 39
Asha's Indian Bar and Restaurant *Birmingham* 257
Ashmolean Dining Room *Oxford* 337
Asia de Cuba *London* 39
Aspinall Arms *Mitton* 327
The Assheton Arms *Clitheroe* 279
Assunta Madre *London* 39
At the Chapel *Bruton* 268
Atari-Ya 39
L'Atelier de Joel Robuchon *London* 40
Athenaeum *London* 40
The Atlas *London* 40
Atomic Burger *Oxford* 337
Auberge du Lac *Welwyn* 364
Augustine Kitchen *Battersea* 40
Augustus *Taunton* 358
Aurora *London* 40
Austells *St Austell* 353
Australasia *Manchester* 321
L'Autre Pied *London* 40
L'Aventure *London* 40
The Avenue *London* 40
Aviator *Farnborough* 291
Awesome Thai *London* 40
Azou *London* 40
Baan Thitiya *Bishop's Stortford* 258
Babaji Pide *London* 40
Babbo *London* 41
Babu *Glasgow* 295
Babur *London* 41
Babylon *London* 41
Bacchus *Prestbury* 344
Bacco *Richmond* 41
Il Bacio 41
Bad Egg *London* 41
Bageriet *London* 41
Balans 41
The Balcon *London* 41
Bald Faced Stag *London* 41
Balls & Company *London* 42
Balthazar *London* 42
Baltic *London* 42

The Banana Tree Canteen 42
Bandera *Manchester* 321
Bandol *London* 42
Bangkok *London* 42
Bangkok Brasserie *Winchester* 367
Bank Westminster *London* 42
Banners *London* 42
Banny's Restaurant *Colne* 280
Bao *London* 42
Baozi Inn *London* 42
The Bar & Grill At James Street South *Belfast* 255
Bar 44 *Cowbridge* 281
Bar Biccari *Wakefield* 362
Bar Boulud *London* 42
Bar Esteban *London* 43
Bar Italia *London* 43
Bar San Juan *Manchester* 321
Bar Termini *London* 43
Baraset Barn *Alveston* 248
La Barbe *Reigate* 345
Barbecoa 43
La Barca *London* 43
Il Baretto *London* 43
Barrissimo *St Albans* 352
Barley Bree *Muthill* 329
Barnsley House *Barnsley* 251
Barnyard *London* 43
Barrafina 43
Barrasford Arms *Barrasford* 251
Barrica *London* 43
Barshu *London* 43
Basilico 43
Basketmakers Arms *Brighton* 262
Bath Priory Hotel *Bath* 252
The Bay Horse *Ellel* 290
The Bay Horse *Hurworth* 305
Bay Tree *Melbourne* 327
Bea's Of Bloomsbury *London* 44
Beach Blanket Babylon 44
The Beach Hut *Watergate Bay* 363
Beagle *London* 44
Beast *London* 44
Beckford Arms *Fonthill Gifford* 292
Beehive *White Waltham* 366
Beer and Buns *London* 44
The Beetle & Wedge Boathouse *Moulsford* 328
The Begging Bowl *London* 44
Bel & The Dragon *Cookham* 280
Bel Canto *London* 44
Belgo 44
The Bell at Skenfrith *Skenfrith* 350
The Bell at Sapperton *Sapperton* 347
The Bell Inn *Horndon on the Hill* 304
Bell's Diner And Bar Rooms *Bristol* 265
Bell's Diner *Edinburgh* 286
Bellamy's *London* 44
Bellanger *London* 44
Belle Époque *Knutsford* 309
Bellevue Rendez-Vous *London* 45
Belvedere *London* 45
Ben's Cornish Kitchen *Marazion* 324
Benares *London* 45
Benedicts of Whalley *Whalley* 365
Bengal Clipper *London* 45
The Bengal Sage *Winchester* 367
Benson Blakes *Bury St Edmunds* 269
Bentley's *London* 45
Berber & Q *London* 45
The Berkeley Arms *Wymondham* 371
The Berners Tavern *London* 45
Best Mangal *London* 45
Bettys *Harrogate* 299
Bettys *Ilkley* 306
Bettys *York* 371
Bia Bistrot *Edinburgh* 286
Bianco43 45
Bibendum *London* 45
Bibendum Oyster Bar *London* 46
Bibimbap Soho 46
Bibo *London* 46
Big Easy 46
Bilash *Wolverhampton* 370
Bilbao Berria *London* 46
The Bildeston Crown *Bildeston* 257
Bill's 46
Bill's at the Depot *Brighton* 262
Bill's Produce Store *Lewes* 313
Bill's *Cambridge* 270
The Bingham *Richmond* 46
Birch *Bristol* 265
Birch *Woburn* 369
Bird 46
The Bird And Beast *Leeds* 311
Bird in Hand *London* 46
Bird of Smithfield *London* 46
Bistro 1 46
Bistro Aix *London* 46
Bistro At The Distillery *Bassenthwaite* 252
Bistrò by Shot *London* 47
Bistro Saigon *Ilkley* 306
Bistro Union *London* 47
Bistrot Vérité *Southport* 351
Black Bull *Moulton* 328
Black Horse at Ireland *Shefford* 349
The Black Pig *Tunbridge Wells* 361
The Black Rat *Winchester* 367
The Black Rock *St Ives* 353
Black Sheep Brewery Bistro *Masham* 326
Black Swan *Helmsley* 301
The Black Swan *Ockham* 336
Black Swan *Oldstead* 336
Blackfoot Bar & Backroom Dining *London* 47
Blackfriars Restaurant *Newcastle upon Tyne* 330
Blacklock *London* 47
Blanchette *London* 47
Blas *Caernarfon* 270
Bleecker Street Burger *London* 47
Bleeding Heart Restaurant *London* 47
Blixen *London* 47
Blue Elephant *London* 47
Blue Lion *East Witton* 286
The Blue Lion *Hardwick* 299
The Blue Strawberry *Hatfield Peverel* 301
Bluebells *Sunningdale* 357
Bluebird *London* 47
Blueprint Café *London* 47
Bó Drake *London* 48
The Boat House *Bangor* 251
The Boathouse *Parkgate* 340
Bob Bob Ricard *London* 48
The Bobbin *London* 48
Bobby's *Leicester* 312
Bobo Social *London* 48
Bocca Di Lupo *London* 48
Al Boccon di'vino *Richmond* 48
Bodean's 48
La Bodega Negra *London* 48
Dining Room *Llandudno* 316
Bohemia *Jersey* 306
Boisdale *London* 48
Boisdale of Bishopsgate *London* 48
Boisdale of Canary Wharf *London* 49
Bombay Brasserie *London* 49
Bombay Palace *London* 49
Bone Daddies 49
Bonhams Restaurant *London* 49
Bonnie Gull *London* 49
Bonnie Gull Seafood Bar *London* 49
The Booking Office *London* 49
Boom Burger 49
Boopshis *London* 50
Boqueria *London* 50
Bordeaux Quay *Bristol* 265

ALPHABETICAL INDEX

Il Bordello *London* 50
Boro Bistro *London* 50
Bosco Pizzeria *Bristol* 266
Bosquet *Kenilworth* 307
La Bota *London* 50
The Botanist 50
Bouchon Bistrot *Hexham* 303
Boudin Blanc *London* 50
Bouillabaisse *London* 50
Boulestin *London* 50
Boulters Riverside Brasserie *Maidenhead* 320
The Boundary *London* 50
The Box Tree *Ilkley* 306
The Brackenbury *London* 50
Bradley's *London* 50
Brady's *London* 51
Braidwoods *Dalry* 282
Branca *Oxford* 337
Branksome Beach *Poole* 342
La Brasserie *London* 51
La Brasserie *Chester* 275
Brasserie Blanc 51
Brasserie Blanc *Oxford* 337
Brasserie Chavot *London* 51
Brasserie Gustave *London* 51
Brasserie Toulouse-Lautrec *London* 51
Brasserie Zédel *London* 51
Brassica *Beaminster* 254
Brassica Grill *Stockport* 355
Bravas *London* 51
Bravas *Bristol* 266
Brawn *London* 51
Bread Street Kitchen *London* 51
Brew 52
Briciole *London* 52
Brick Lane Beigel Bake *London* 52
The Bricklayers Arms *Flaunden* 292
Bridge Bistro *Wadebridge* 362
Brigade *London* 52
The Bright Courtyard *London* 52
Brilliant *Southall* 52
Brinkley's *London* 52
Britten's *Guildford* 298
Broad Chare *Newcastle upon Tyne* 330
Brockencote Hall *Chaddesley Corbett* 273
The Brown Cow *London* 52
The Brown Dog *London* 52
Hix at Albemarle *London* 52
Brownlow Arms *Hough On The Hill* 304
Browns Pie Shop *Lincoln* 313
Brunswick House Café *London* 52
Bryce's at the Old School House *Ockley* 336
Bubbledogs *London* 53
Kitchen Table *London* 53
Buddha-Bar London *London* 53
Buen Ayre *London* 53
Buenos Aires Cafe 53
The Builders Arms *London* 53
Bukhara *Preston* 344
The Bull *London* 53
The Bull & Gate *London* 53
Bull & Last *London* 53
Bull at Broughton *Broughton* 268
Bumpkin 53
Bunnychow *London* 53
Buona Sera 53
Burger & Lobster 54
Burger Brothers *Brighton* 262
Burgh Island Hotel *Bigbury-on-Sea* 256
Burlington *Bolton Abbey* 259
Burnt Truffle *Heswall* 302
Busaba Eathai 54
Bush Dining Hall *London* 54
Butcher & Grill *London* 54
The Butcher's Arms *Eldersfield* 289
The Butcher's Hook *London* 54
Butlers Wharf Chop House *London* 54
Butley Orford Oysterage *Orford* 337
La Buvette *Richmond* 54
Byron 54
C London *London* 54
C&R Cafe 54
Caboose *London* 54
La Cachette *Elland* 290
Caesars Arms *Creigiau* 281
Café 209 *London* 55
Café 21 *Newcastle upon Tyne* 330
Café Below *London* 55
Café Bohème *London* 55
Café Cossachok *Glasgow* 295
Café del Parc *London* 55
Café des Amis *Canterbury* 271
Café du Marché *London* 55
Cafe du Soleil *Canterbury* 271
Café East *London* 55
Café Fish *Tobermory* 360
Cafe Football *London* 55
Café Gandolfi *Glasgow* 295
Café in the Crypt *London* 55
Café Marlayne *Edinburgh* 286
Cafe Mauresque *Canterbury* 271
Café Murano 55
Cafe No. 8 Bistro *York* 371
Café Pistou *London* 55
Cafe Roya *Nottingham* 333
Café Royal *Newcastle upon Tyne* 330
Café Spice Namaste *London* 55
Café St-Honoré *Edinburgh* 286
Cafe Tabou *Perth* 341
Cafe Thai *Halifax* 298
Caffé Vivo *Newcastle upon Tyne* 330
Caffè Caldesi *London* 55
Caffé Vergnano 56
La Cage Imaginaire *London* 56
Cah-Chi *London* 56
Cail Bruich *Glasgow* 295
Calcot Manor *Tetbury* 359
Caldesi in Campagna *Bray* 261
Calistoga Central *Edinburgh* 286
The Camberwell Arms *London* 56
Cambio de Tercio *London* 56
The Cambridge Chop House *Cambridge* 270
Camellia Restaurant *Horsham* 304
Martin Wishart *Loch Lomond* 316
Camino 56
The Canbury Arms *Kingston upon Thames* 309
Hotel du Vin *London* 56
Canta Napoli 56
Canteen 56
Cantina Laredo *London* 56
Canton Arms *London* 57
Canvas *London* 57
The Cape Grand Cafe & Restaurant *Beaconsfield* 254
Capote Y Toros *London* 57
Le Caprice *London* 57
Caracoli *Alresford* 247
Caraffini *London* 57
Caravaggio *London* 57
Caravan 57
Carlton Riverside *Llanwrtyd Wells* 316
Carob Tree *London* 57
Carom at Meza *London* 57
Carousel *London* 57
The Carpenter's Arms *London* 57
Carpenter's Arms *Sunninghill* 357
Carters of Moseley *Birmingham* 257
The Cartford Inn *Little Eccleston* 313
Casa Brindisa *London* 57
Casa Cruz *London* 58
Casa Don Carlos *Brighton* 262
Casa Malevo *London* 58
Casamia *Bristol* 266
Casanis *Bath* 252
Casanova *Cardiff* 272
Casse-Croute *London* 58

Cast *Nottingham* 334
Castellamare *Swansea* 358
Castle House Restaurant *Hereford* 302
The Castle Terrace *Edinburgh* 286
The Cat Inn *West Hoathly* 364
Cau 58
Cau *Guildford* 298
The Cavendish *London* 58
Cây Tre 58
Cecconi's *London* 58
Cellar Gascon *London* 58
Ceru *London* 58
Ceviche 58
Chakra *London* 58
Chamberlain's *London* 58
Le Champignon Sauvage *Cheltenham* 274
Champor-Champor *London* 59
The Chancery *London* 59
Chaophraya *Leeds* 311
Chaophraya, *Manchester* 321
Chapter One *Locksbottom* 317
Chapters *London* 59
Charlotte's *London* 59
Charlotte's Place *London* 59
The Charlton Arms *Ludlow* 318
The Chaser Inn *Shipbourne* 350
Chateau La Chaire *Jersey* 306
Cheal's of Henley *Henley in Arden* 301
Checkers *Montgomery* 328
The Chef's Dozen *Chipping Campden* 278
The Chef's Table *Chester* 275
Chequers *Churchill* 278
Cherwell Boathouse *Oxford* 337
The Chesil Rectory *Winchester* 367
Chettinad *London* 59
Vetiver *New Milton* 329
Cheyne Walk Brasserie *London* 59
Chez Abir *London* 59
Chez Antoinette *London* 59
Chez Bruce *London* 59
Chez Fred *Bournemouth* 260
Chez Patrick *London* 59
Chez Vous *Warlingham* 362
Chiang Mai *Oxford* 338
Chick 'n' Sours *London* 60
Chicken Shop 60
Chicken Shop & Dirty Burger *London* 60
Chicken Town *London* 60
Chifafa *London* 60
Chilango 60
Chilli Cool *London* 60
The Chilli Pickle *Brighton* 262
The Chiltern Firehouse *London* 60
China Tang *London* 60
Chinese Cricket Club *London* 60
Chino Latino *Nottingham* 334
Chisou 62
Chiswell Street Dining Rooms *London* 62
Chloe's *Plymouth* 342
Cholmondeley Arms *Cholmondeley* 278
Chor Bizarre *London* 62
Chotto Matte *London* 62
La Chouette *Dinton* 283
La Choza *Brighton* 262
Chriskitch *London* 62
Christopher's *London* 62
Churchill Arms *London* 62
Chutney Mary *London* 62
Chutneys *London* 62
Ciao Bella *London* 62
Cibo *London* 62
Cielo *Birmingham* 257
Cigala *London* 63
Cigalon *London* 63
The Cinnamon Club *London* 63
Cinnamon Culture *Bromley* 268
Cinnamon Kitchen *London* 63
Cinnamon Soho *London* 63
The Circus *Bath* 252
City Barge *London* 63
City Càphê *London* 63
City Miyama *London* 63
City Social *London* 63
Clarke's *London* 63
Claude's Kitchen *London* 63
Clayton's Kitchen *Bath* 252
The Cleveland Tontine *Northallerton* 333
The Clive Restaurant With Rooms *Ludlow* 318
André Garrett At Cliveden *Taplow* 358
Clockjack Oven *London* 64
Clog & Billycock *Pleasington* 342
Clos du Marquis *Stockbridge* 355
Clos Maggiore *London* 64
The Clove Club *London* 64
Club Gascon *London* 64
Clytha Arms *Clytha* 280
The Coach *Marlow* 326
Coach And Horses *Danehill* 282
The Coal Shed *Brighton* 262
Coast *Saundersfoot* 348
Coasters *Southwold* 352
Le Cochon Aveugle *York* 371
The Cock *Hemingford Grey* 301
Cock *St Albans* 352
Coco Di Mama *London* 64
Cocochan *London* 64
Cods Scallops *Wollaton* 369
The Coffee Cabin *Appledore* 249
Coggings & Co *Brighton* 263
Colbert *London* 64
Colette's *Chandler's Cross* 274
La Collina *London* 64
Colmans *South Shields* 351
Le Colombier *London* 64
Colonna & Smalls *Bath* 252
Colony Grill Room *London* 64
The Pig *Honiton* 303
Como Lario *London* 64
Compagnie des Vins Surnaturels *London* 64
The Company Shed *West Mersea* 364
Comptoir Gascon *London* 65
Comptoir Libanais 65
Il Convivio *London* 65
Coopers Restaurant & Bar *London* 65
Copita Del Mercado *London* 65
Coppi *Belfast* 255
La Coppola *Leamington Spa* 310
Le Coq *London* 65
Coq d'Argent *London* 65
Cork & Bottle *London* 65
Corner House *Minster* 327
Corner Room *London* 65
The Cornish Arms *St Merryn* 354
Cornish Tiger *London* 65
Corrigan's Mayfair *London* 65
Corse Lawn Hotel *Corse Lawn* 281
Côte 65
The Cottage In The Wood *Keswick* 307
Cotto *Cambridge* 270
Counter *London* 66
Cove *Weston Super Mare* 365
The Cove Restaurant & Bar *Falmouth* 291
The Cow *London* 66
Cowshed *Bath* 253
The Cowshed *Bristol* 266
Coya *London* 66
The Crab & Boar *Newbury* 330
Crab & Lobster *Asenby* 250
Crab & Winkle *Whitstable* 366
Crab House Café *Weymouth* 365
Crab Shack *Teignmouth* 359
The Crabmill *Preston Bagot* 344
Crabshakk *Glasgow* 295
Craft London *London* 66
Crannog *Fort William* 292
Crathorne Arms *Crathorne* 281
Crazy Bear *London* 66
Crazy Bear *Beaconsfield* 254
The Crazy Bear *Stadhampton* 354
The Cricketers *Clavering* 279

Crocker's Folly *London* 66
Croma *Manchester* 321
The Crooked Billet *Stoke Row* 355
The Crooked Well *London* 66
The Cross *Kingussie* 309
The Cross at Kenilworth *Kenilworth* 307
The Cross Keys *London* 66
Crosstown Doughnuts *London* 66
The Crown *Southwold* 352
The Crown *Stoke-by-Nayland* 356
The Crown & Castle *Orford* 337
The Crown at Mickleton *Durham* 284
The Crown at Whitebrook *Whitebrook* 366
Crown Inn *Bray* 261
The Crown Inn *Horsted Keynes* 304
The Crown Inn *Snape* 351
The Culpepper *London* 66
Cumberland Arms *London* 66
The Cumin *Nottingham* 334
The Curlew *Bodiam* 259
The Curry Corner *Cheltenham* 274
Curry Leaf Cafe *Brighton* 263
Cut *London* 67
Cwtch *St Davids* 353
d'Arry's *Cambridge* 270
Da Mario *London* 67
Da Mario *London* 67
Da Nello *Guernsey* 297
Da Piero *Irby* 306
Dabbawal *Newcastle upon Tyne* 331
Dabbous *London* 67
Daddy Donkey *London* 67
The Daffodil *Cheltenham* 274
The Dairy *London* 67
Dalchini *London* 67
Damson *Salford* 347
Damson *Stockport* 355
Daphne's *London* 67
Daquise *London* 67
Darleys *Derby* 283
Darsham Nurseries *Darsham* 282
The Dartmoor Inn *Lydford* 319
The Dartmouth Castle *London* 67
Darwin Brasserie *London* 67
David Bann *Edinburgh* 286
Daylesford Organic 68
Daylesford Café *Kingham* 308
Dean Street Townhouse *London* 68
Deeson's British Restaurant *Canterbury* 271
Defune *London* 68
Dehesa *London* 68
Delancey & Co. *London* 68
The Delaunay *London* 68
Delfino *London* 68
Delhi Grill *London* 68
La Delizia Limbara *London* 68
Department of Coffee *London* 68
The Depot *London* 68
Les Deux Salons *London* 69
Devonshire Arms *Beeley* 255
DF Mexico 69
The Diamond Jubilee Tea Salon *London* 69
Didier And Stephanie *Swansea* 358
Diner 69
The Dining Room *Easton Grey* 286
Dining Room *Rock* 346
Dinings *London* 69
Dinner *London* 69
Dip & Flip 69
Dirty Burger 69
Dishoom 69
Diwana Bhel-Poori House *London* 69
The Dock Kitchen *London* 69
The Dogs *Edinburgh* 287
Doi Intanon *Ambleside* 248
The Dolphin House Brazzerie *Plymouth* 342
The Don *London* 70
Donatello *Brighton* 263
Donna Margherita *London* 70
Donostia *London* 70
Dorchester Grill *London* 70
Dorset Arms *Withyham* 369
Dotori *London* 70
The Dove *London* 70
Dragon Castle *London* 70
The Restaurant at Drakes *Brighton* 263
Drakes *Ripley* 346
Drakes Tabanco *London* 70
The Drapers Arms *London* 70
Driftwood Hotel *Rosevine* 346
Drum & Monkey *Harrogate* 299
Drunken Duck *Ambleside* 248
Dub Jam *London* 70
The Duck & Rice *London* 70
Duck & Waffle *London* 70
Ducksoup *London* 71
The Duke Of Cumberland *Henley* 302
Duke of Sussex *London* 71
The Duke Of York Inn *Grindleton* 297
Duke's Brew & Que *London* 71
Dumplings' Legend *London* 71
Dun Cow *Salthouse* 347
Durham Ox *Crayke* 281
Durum Ocakbasi *London* 71
Dylan's Restaurant *Menai Bridge* 327
The Dysart Petersham *Richmond* 71
The Dysart Arms *Bunbury* 268
E&O *London* 71
The Eagle *London* 71
Ealing Park Tavern *London* 71
Earl Spencer *London* 71
Earle *Hale* 298
East Beach Cafe *Littlehampton* 314
East Coast Dining Room *Whitstable* 366
East India Cafe *Cheltenham* 274
Eastbury Hotel *Sherborne* 349
The Eastern Eye *Bath* 253
The Manor Restaurant *Boughton Lees* 259
Eat 17 71
Eat on the Green *Ellon* 290
Eat Tokyo 71
Ebi Sushi *Derby* 283
The Ebrington Arms *Chipping Campden* 278
Ebury Restaurant & Wine Bar *London* 72
Eco *London* 72
Edamame *Oxford* 338
Edera *London* 72
Edmunds *Birmingham* 257
Edwins *London* 72
Ee-Usk (Seafood Restaurant) *Oban* 336
Eelbrook *London* 72
Egan's *Lymington* 319
8 Hoxton Square *London* 72
Eight Over Eight *London* 72
1884 Dock Street Kitchen *Hull* 305
81 Beach Street *Deal* 283
Elderflower *Lymington* 319
Electric Diner *London* 72
Elena's L'Etoile *London* 72
Elephant Restaurant & Brasserie *Torquay* 360
Elliot's Café *London* 72
Elliots @ No.1 Harbour Street *Whitstable* 366
Ellory *London* 72
Ember Yard *London* 72
Emile's *London* 72
The Empress *London* 73
L'Enclume *Cartmel* 273
Engawa *London* 73
English's *Brighton* 263
Enoteca Rabezzana *London* 73
Enoteca Turi *London* 73

The Enterprise *London* 73
Eric's *Huddersfield* 304
Eric's Fish & Chips *Thornham* 359
Esarn Kheaw *London* 73
L'Escargot *London* 73
L'Escargot Blanc *Edinburgh* 287
L'Escargot Bleu *Edinburgh* 287
Eslington Villa Hotel *Gateshead* 294
Essenza *London* 73
Estbek House *Sandsend* 347
Ethicurean *Wrington* 370
Ethos *London* 73
L'Etranger *London* 73
Etsu *Liverpool* 314
Everest Inn *London* 73
Evuna *Manchester* 321
Eyre Brothers *London* 73
The Eyston Arms *East Hendred* 285
Faanoos *London* 74
Fabrizio *London* 74
Fabrizio *London* 74
Fairuz *London* 74
Fairyhill *Reynoldston* 345
Fallowfields *Kingston Bagpuize* 308
Flavours By Kumar *Ramsgate* 345
La Famiglia *London* 74
Farndon Boathouse *Newark* 330
The Fat Duck *Bray* 261
Fat Olives *Emsworth* 290
Favorita *Edinburgh* 287
Fazenda *Liverpool* 314
The Feathered Nest Inn *Nether Westcote* 329
The Feathers Inn *Hedley On The Hill* 301
The Felin Fach Griffin *Brecon* 262
Fellini's *Ambleside* 248
Fera at Claridge's *London* 74
Fernandez & Wells 74
Fez Mangal *London* 74
Ffiona's *London* 74
Field *Edinburgh* 287
Field & Fork *Chichester* 276
Fields *London* 74
Fifteen *London* 74
Fifteen Cornwall *Watergate Bay* 363
1539 *Chester* 275
The Fifth Floor Restaurant *London* 74
The Fig Tree *Malvern* 320
Finbarr's *Durham* 285
Finch's Arms *Hambleton* 299
Fire & Stone 75
First Floor Café *Windermere* 368
Fischer's *London* 75
Fischers at Baslow Hall *Baslow* 252
Fish at 85 *Cardiff* 272
Fish Central *London* 75
Fish Club 75
The Fish Factory *Worthing* 370
The Fish House *Ludlow* 318
Fish in a Tie *London* 75
Fish Market *London* 75
Fish On The Green *Bearsted* 254
The Fish People Cafe *Glasgow* 295
fish! *London* 75
fish! Kitchen *Kingston upon Thames* 309
Fishers in the City *Edinburgh* 287
The Fishes *Oxford* 338
The Fishpool Inn *Northwich* 333
Fishworks 75
Fishy Fishy *Brighton* 263
Fitzbillies *Cambridge* 270
The Five Alls *Lechlade* 310
The Five Bells Inn *Clyst Hydon* 279
The Five Fields *London* 75
Five Guys 75
500 *London* 75
5 North Street *Winchcombe* 367
Flat Iron 76
Flat Three *London* 76
Flesh and Buns *London* 76
Flotsam and Jetsam *London* 76
Flying Pizza *Leeds* 311
FM Mangal *London* 76
The Folly *Oxford* 338
Fonseca's *Liverpool* 314
Food by Breda Murphy *Whalley* 365
Food for Friends *Brighton* 263
The Forester *Donhead St Andrew* 284
45 Jermyn St *London* 76
40 Maltby Street *London* 76
Four & Twenty *Penrith* 340
The Four Seasons 76
4550 Miles From Delhi *Nottingham* 334
Fourth Floor Café *Leeds* 311
Fox *Broughton Gifford* 268
The Fox *Willian* 367
The Fox & Goose *Fressingfield* 294
Fox & Grapes *London* 77
The Fox & Hounds *London* 77
The Fox and Anchor *London* 77
The Fox And Hounds *Hunsdon* 305
The Fox And Hounds Inn *Goldsborough* 296
Fox Café *Nottingham* 334
The Fox Inn *Lower Oddington* 318
Fox's Restaurant *Bembridge* 255
The Foxhunter *Nant-y-Derry* 329
Foxlow 77
Fraiche *Oxton* 339
Francesca's *Newcastle upon Tyne* 331
Franco Manca 77
Franco's *London* 77
Franklins *London* 77
Frantoio *London* 77
Frederic Bistro *Maidstone* 320
Frederick's *London* 77
Freemasons at Wiswell *Wiswell* 369
The French Horn *Sonning-on-Thames* 351
French Living *Nottingham* 334
The French Pantry *Ludlow* 318
The French Restaurant *Manchester* 321
The French Table *Surbiton* 357
Friends *Pinner* 341
Friends of Ours *London* 77
La Fromagerie Café *London* 77
The Frontline Club *London* 78
Fuji Hiro *Leeds* 311
Fulham Wine Rooms *London* 78
The Fuzzy Duck *Stratford upon Avon* 356
Gaby's *London* 78
Gail's Bread 78
Gallery Mess *London* 78
The Galley *Topsham* 360
Gallipoli 78
The Gallivant *Camber* 270
Galvin at Windows *London* 78
Galvin Bistrot de Luxe *London* 78
Galvin Brasserie de Luxe *Edinburgh* 287
Galvin La Chapelle *London* 78
Gamba *Glasgow* 295
Ganapati *London* 78
Gandolfi Fish *Glasgow* 295
The Gannet *Glasgow* 295
Gardener's Cottage *Edinburgh* 287
Garnier *London* 79
Le Garrick *London* 79
La Garrigue *Edinburgh* 287
The Garrison *London* 79
Gascoyne Place *Bath* 253
The Gate 79
El Gato Negro *Manchester* 321
The Gatsby *Berkhamsted* 256
Gatti's 79
Gaucho 79

Gauthier Soho *London* 79
Le Gavroche *London* 79
Gay Hussar *London* 79
Gaylord *London* 79
Gazette 80
GB Pizza *Margate* 324
Geales 80
Gee's *Oxford* 338
Gelupo *London* 80
Gem *London* 80
Gem Of Kent *Maidstone* 320
General Tarleton *Ferrensby* 292
La Genova *London* 80
The George *Alstonefield* 248
The George *Cavendish* 273
The George & Dragon *Chipstead* 278
George & Dragon *Speldhurst* 352
George & Dragon *Clifton* 279
George & Vulture *London* 80
The George Hotel *Stamford* 354
German Gymnasium *London* 80
Giacomo's *London* 80
Gidleigh Park *Chagford* 273
Gifto's Lahore Karahi *Southall* 80
Giggling Squid *Brighton* 263
Giggling Squid *Henley-on-Thames* 302
Gilbert Scott *London* 80
Gilbey's *Amersham* 249
Gilbey's *Eton* 290
Gilgamesh *London* 80
Gilpin Hotel *Windermere* 368
Gin Joint *London* 80
Ginger & White 81
The Ginger Dog *Brighton* 263
The Ginger Fox *Albourne* 246
The Ginger Pig *Brighton* 263
Gingerman *Brighton* 263
Giraffe 81
Glamorous *Manchester* 321
Glasfryn *Mold* 328
The Glasshouse *Kew* 81
The Glasshouse *Chandler's Cross* 274
Andrew Fairlie *Auchterarder* 250
Globe *Wells Next The Sea* 363
Godrevy Beach Cafe *Gwithian Towans* 298
Gökyüzü *London* 81
Gold Mine *London* 81
Golden Dragon *London* 81
Golden Hind *London* 81
Good Earth 81
Good Earth *Esher* 290
Goodfellows *Wells* 363
Goodman *London* 81
Goods Shed *Canterbury* 272
Gordon Ramsay *London* 81
Gordon's Wine Bar *London* 82
The Goring Hotel *London* 82
Gourmet Burger Kitchen 82
Gourmet Pizza Company *London* 82
Gourmet San *London* 82
Les Gourmets des Ternes 82
The Gowlett *London* 82
Goya *London* 82
Grain Store *London* 82
Grain Store *Edinburgh* 287
The Grand Imperial *London* 82
Granger & Co 82
The Grapes *London* 83
Graveley's Fish & Chip Restaurant *Harrogate* 299
Gravetye Manor *East Grinstead* 285
The Gray Ox Inn *Hartshead* 300
The Grazing Goat *London* 83
The Estate Grill *Egham* 289
The Great House *Hawkhurst* 301
Great House *Lavenham* 310
Great Kathmandu *Manchester* 321
Great Nepalese *London* 83
Great Queen Street *London* 83
The Greedy Buddha *London* 83
The Greedy Cow *Margate* 324
The Greek Larder *London* 83
The Green *Sherborne* 349
Green Café *Ludlow* 318
Green Cottage *London* 83
The Green Room *London* 83
Green's *London* 83
Green's *Manchester* 321
Greenberry Café *London* 83
The Greenhouse *London* 83
Gremio de Brixton *London* 83
Grenache *Worsley* 370
Greyhound *Stockbridge* 355
Chez Roux *Gullane* 298
The Griffin Inn *Fletching* 292
Grill at the Old Plough *Stoke D'Abernon* 355
Grill on the Alley *Manchester* 321
Grind Coffee Bar *London* 84
The Grosvenor Arms *Aldford* 247
The Grove - Narberth *Dyfed* 285
Grumbles *London* 84
The Grumpy Mole *Brockham* 268
Guglee 84
Guildhall Tavern *Poole* 342
The Guinea Grill *London* 84
Gumstool Inn *Tetbury* 359
The Gun *London* 84
Gung-Ho *London* 84
The Gunton Arms *Norwich* 333
The Gurkha Kitchen *Oxted* 339
Gurnards Head *Treen* 361
Gustoso Ristorante & Enoteca *London* 84
Gwesty Cymru *Aberystwyth* 246
Gymkhana *London* 84
Habanera *London* 84
Haché 84
Hadskis *Belfast* 255
Hakkasan 84
Ham Yard Restaurant *London* 85
Hambleton Hall *Hambleton* 299
The Hammer & Pincers *Loughborough* 317
The Hampshire Hog *London* 85
Hanam's Kurdish & Middle East Restaurant *Edinburgh* 287
The Hand & Trumpet *Wrinehill* 370
Hand & Flowers *Marlow* 326
Hanoi Bike Shop *Glasgow* 295
Hanover Street Social *Liverpool* 314
Hansa's *Leeds* 311
Hanson At The Chelsea Restaurant *Swansea* 358
Happy Gathering *Cardiff* 272
Harbour City *London* 85
Harbourmaster *Aberaeron* 246
Hard Rock Café *London* 85
The Hardwick *Abergavenny* 246
Hardy's Brasserie *London* 85
Hare & Hounds *Bath* 253
Hare & Tortoise 85
Hare Inn *Scawton* 348
The Harrow at Little Bedwyn *Marlborough* 326
Harry Morgan's *London* 85
Harry's Place *Great Gonerby* 297
Hart's *Nottingham* 334
Hartnett Holder & Co *Lyndhurst* 319
Dining Room *Aylesbury* 250
Harwood Arms *London* 85
Hashi *London* 85
Hassop Hall *Hassop* 300
The Havelock Tavern *London* 85
The Haven *London* 85
Hawksmoor *London* 85
Hawksmoor *Manchester* 322
Haywards Restaurant *Epping* 290
Haz 86
Heddon Street Kitchen *London* 86
Hedone *London* 86
Heirloom *London* 86
Hélène Darroze *London* 86

Henderson's *Edinburgh* 287
Hengist *Aylesford* 250
Herbert's *Keston* 307
Hereford Road *London* 86
The Heron *London* 86
Hibiscus *London* 86
High Road Brasserie *London* 86
High Timber *London* 86
The Higher Buck *Waddington* 362
The Highwayman *Nether Burrow* 329
Hill & Szrok *London* 86
Hilliard *London* 87
The Hind's Head *Bray* 261
Hintlesham Hall *Hintlesham* 303
Hipping Hall *Kirkby Lonsdale* 309
Hive Beach Cafe *Bridport* 262
Hix *London* 87
Hix Oyster & Chop House *London* 87
Hix Oyster & Fish House *Lyme Regis* 319
HKK *London* 87
Hoi Polloi *London* 87
Holbeck Ghyll *Windermere* 368
Holborn Dining Room *London* 87
The Hole In The Wall *Little Wilbraham* 313
Hollies *Stretton* 357
The Holt *Honiton* 304
Homeslice 87
Honest Burgers 87
Honey & Co *London* 87
The Honours *Edinburgh* 288
Hood *London* 87
Hooked *Windermere* 368
Hope And Anchor *South Ferriby* 351
Hoppers *London* 88
The Hopping Hare *Duston* 285
The Horn of Plenty *Gulworthy* 298
Horse & Groom *Bourton On Hill* 260
Horse & Groom *Moreton-in-Marsh* 328
The Horse Guards Inn *Tillington* 360
The Horseshoe *London* 88
Host *Liverpool* 314
Hoste Arms *Burnham Market* 269
Hot Stuff *London* 88
Hotel du Vin et Bistro *Cambridge* 270
Hotel du Vin et Bistro *Bristol* 266
Hotel du Vin et Bistro *Birmingham* 257
Hotel du Vin et Bistro *Tunbridge Wells* 361
Hotel du Vin et Bistro *Winchester* 367
Hotel Maiyango *Leicester* 312
Hotel Tresanton *St Mawes* 354
House of Ho 88
House of Tides *Newcastle upon Tyne* 331
House Restaurant *London* 88
The House Restaurant *Scholes* 348
The Hoxton Grill *London* 88
Hubbard & Bell *London* 88
Hunan *London* 88
Hungry Donkey *London* 88
Hush 88
Hutong *London* 88
Hythe Bay *Hythe* 305
The Hythe Brasserie *Hythe* 305
Ibérica 89
Ibérica *Manchester* 322
Iberico *Nottingham* 334
Iddu *London* 89
Il Paradiso Del Cibo *York* 371
Imli Street *London* 89
Imperial China *Teddington* 359
Inaho *London* 89
Inamo 89
Incanto *Harrow* 300
India Club *London* 89
Indian Essence *Petts Wood* 341
Indian Moment *London* 89
Indian Ocean *London* 89
Indian Rasoi *London* 89
Indian Summer *Brighton* 263
Indian Veg *London* 89
Indian Zest *Sunbury on Thames* 357
Indian Zilla *London* 89
Indian Zing *London* 89
Indigo *London* 90
Inn at Penallt *Penallt* 340
Inn At Ravenglass *Ravenglass* 345
Inn at Whitewell *Clitheroe* 279
Inside *London* 90
Inver Cottage Restaurant *Strachur* 356
Ippudo London 90
Irvins Brasserie *North Shields* 332
Isarn *London* 90
Ishtar *London* 90
The Italian Club Fish *Liverpool* 314
The Italian Job *London* 90
Itihaas *Birmingham* 257
Itsu 90
The Ivy *London* 90
The Ivy Café *London* 90
The Ivy Chelsea Garden *London* 90
The Ivy Kensington Brasserie *London* 90
The Ivy Market Grill *London* 91
Iydea *Brighton* 264
Izgara *London* 91
Jack in the Green Inn *Rockbeare* 346
Jackson & Rye 91
Jaffna House *London* 91
Jago *London* 91
Jaipur *Milton Keynes* 327
Jamaica Patty Co. *London* 91
James Martin *Manchester* 322
James Street South *Belfast* 255
Jamie's Diner *London* 91
Jamie's Italian 91
Jar Kitchen *London* 91
Jashan *London* 91
Jaya *Llandudno* 316
Jeremy's at Borde Hill *Haywards Heath* 301
Jesmond Dene House *Newcastle upon Tyne* 331
Jesses Bistro *Cirencester* 278
The Jetty *Christchurch* 278
Jew's House Restaurant *Lincoln* 313
Jin Go Gae *Kingston upon Thames* 309
Jin Kichi *London* 91
Jinjuu *London* 91
Joanna's *London* 91
Joe Allen *London* 92
Joe's Brasserie *London* 92
John Doe *London* 92
The Joint 92
JoJo *Whitstable* 366
The Jolly Cricketers *Seer Green* 348
Jolly Fisherman *Craster* 281
Jolly Frog *Leintwardine* 313
Jolly Gardners *London* 92
Jolly Sportsman *East Chiltington* 285
Jon & Fernanda's *Auchterarder* 250
Jones & Sons *London* 92
The Jones Family Project *London* 92
José *London* 92
José Pizarro *London* 92
Joseph Benjamin *Chester* 275
Joy King Lau *London* 92
JSW *Petersfield* 341
The Jugged Hare *London* 92
Julie's *London* 93
The Jumble Room *Grasmere* 296
Jun Ming Xuan *London* 93
The Junction Tavern *London* 93

ALPHABETICAL INDEX

Jyoti *Birmingham* 258
K10 93
Kadiri's *London* 93
Kaffeine 93
Kai Mayfair *London* 93
Kaifeng *London* 93
Kanada-Ya 93
Kanpai *Edinburgh* 288
Kaosarn 93
Kappacasein *London* 93
Karachi *Bradford* 260
The Kardomah *Swansea* 358
Karen's Unicorn *Edinburgh* 288
Karma *London* 93
Karnavar *Croydon* 281
Kaspar's Seafood and Grill *London* 94
Kateh 94
Katsouris Deli *Manchester* 322
Kayal *Leicester* 312
Kayal *Nottingham* 334
Kazan 94
The Keeper's House *London* 94
Ken Lo's Memories *London* 94
Kendells Bistro *Leeds* 311
The Kennels *Chichester* 276
Kennington Tandoori *London* 94
Kensington Place *London* 94
Kensington Square Kitchen *London* 94
The Kensington Wine Rooms *London* 94
Kentish Hare *Bidborough* 256
Brew House *London* 94
Kerbisher & Malt 95
Kettners *London* 95
Khan's *London* 95
Kiku *London* 95
Kikuchi *London* 95
Kilberry Inn *Argyll* 249
Killiecrankie House Hotel *Killiecrankie* 308
The Killingworth Castle *Wootton* 370
Kimchee *London* 95
King And Thai *Broseley* 268
The King John Inn *Tollard Royal* 360
The Kingham Plough *Kingham* 308
Kinghams *Shere* 350
The Kings Head *Leighton Buzzard* 312
Kinloch House *Blairgowrie* 259
Kinloch Lodge *Sleat* 350
Kintan *London* 95
Kiosk *Nottingham* 334
Kipferl *London* 95
Kiraku *London* 95
Kishmish *London* 95
Kitchen *London* 95
Kitchen W8 *London* 96
The Kitchin *Edinburgh* 288
Kitty Fisher's *London* 96
Koba *London* 96
Koffmann's *London* 96
Koinonia *Newark* 330
Kolossi Grill *London* 96
Konditor & Cook 96
Kopapa *London* 96
Kota *Porthleven* 343
Koya-Bar *London* 96
Kricket *London* 96
Kulu Kulu 96
Kurobuta 97
Kuti's *Southampton* 351
Kylesku Hotel *Kylesku* 309
Kyoto Kitchen *Winchester* 368
La Boheme *Lymm* 319
The Ladbroke Arms *London* 97
The Lady Ottoline *London* 97
Lahore Karahi *London* 97
Lahore Kebab House 97
The Avenue *Winchester* 368
Lake Road Kitchen *Ambleside* 248
Lamberts *London* 97
Lambs *Stratford upon Avon* 356
Landgate Bistro *Rye* 347
Winter Garden *London* 97
Langan's Brasserie *London* 97
Langar Hall *Langar* 309
Le Langhe *York* 371
Lantana Cafe 97
Lanterna *Scarborough* 348
The Larder on Goosegate *Nottingham* 334
Lardo 97
Larwood And Voce *West Bridgford* 364
Lasan *Birmingham* 258
Last Wine Bar *Norwich* 333
Latium *London* 98
The Latymer *Bagshot* 250
Launceston Place *London* 98
Lavender House *Brundall* 268
Lavenham Greyhound *Lavenham* 310
The Lawn *Thornton Hough* 359
Leaping Hare Vineyard *Stanton* 354
Leatherne Bottel (Rossini at) *Goring-On-Thames* 296
The Leconfield *Petworth* 341
The Ledbury *London* 98
Lemongrass *Chichester* 276
Lemonia *London* 98
Leon 98
Leong's Legends *London* 98
Levanter *Ramsbottom* 345
Lezzes *Newcastle upon Tyne* 331
Lickfold Inn *Lickfold* 313
Lido *Bristol* 266
The Lido Café *London* 98
The Light House *London* 98
The Lighthouse *Aldeburgh* 247
The Lighthouse *Kibworth Beauchamp* 308
Lima 98
The Lime Tree *Bollington* 259
The Lime Tree *Manchester* 322
Linnea *Kew* 98
Lino's *Hoylake* 304
Linthwaite House *Windermere* 368
The Lion *Colchester* 280
The Lion & Lobster *Brighton* 264
Lisboa Pâtisserie *London* 98
Little Barwick House *Barwick* 251
Little Bay 99
Little Fish Market *Brighton* 264
Little Garden *Sevenoaks* 348
Little Georgia Café 99
Little Social *London* 99
Llangoed Hall *Llyswen* 316
Llansantffraed Court Hotel *Clytha Llanvihangel Gobio* 280
Llys Meddyg *Newport* 332
Lobster Pot *London* 99
Locanda Locatelli *London* 99
Locanda Ottomezzo *London* 99
Loch Bay *Waternish* 363
Loch Fyne 99
Loch Fyne *Portsmouth* 344
Loch Fyne Oyster Bar *Clachan* 279
Loch Leven Seafood Café *Onich* 336
The Lockhart *London* 99
Lola Rojo *London* 99
The London Carriage Works *Liverpool* 314
London House *London* 99
London House *Old Woking* 336
London Street Brasserie *Reading* 345
Longueville Manor *Jersey* 307
Lord Clyde *Bollington* 259
Lord Nelson *Brightwell Baldwin* 265
The Lord Northbrook *London* 99
Lord Poulett Arms *Hinton St George* 303
Lords of the Manor *Upper Slaughter* 362
Lorenzo *London* 99
Loves *Birmingham* 258
Lower Slaughter Manor *Lower Slaughter* 318
Loxleys *Stratford upon Avon* 356

Lucca Enoteca *Manningtree* 324
Luce e Limoni *London* 100
Lucio *London* 100
Lucknam Park *Colerne* 280
The Lucky Pig Fulham *London* 100
Lucky Seven *London* 100
Lumière *Cheltenham* 274
La Luna *Godalming* 296
Lunya *Liverpool* 314
Lupita *London* 100
Luppolo *London* 100
Lure *London* 100
Lurra *London* 100
Luscombes at the Golden Ball *Henley-on-Thames* 302
Lussmanns *St Albans* 352
Luton Hoo *Luton* 319
Lutyens *London* 100
Lyle's *London* 100
Lyzzick Hall Country House Hotel *Keswick* 308
M Restaurants *London* 100
Ma Cuisine *Kew* 100
Ma Goa *London* 101
MacCallum's Oyster Bar *Troon* 361
MacellaioRC *London* 101
Made By Bob *Cirencester* 279
Made In Camden *London* 101
Made in Italy 101
Madhu's *Southall* 101
Madhubon *Liss* 313
The Magazine Restaurant *London* 101
Magdalen *London* 101
The Magdalen Arms *Oxford* 338
Maggie Jones's *London* 101
Maggie's *Hastings* 300
The Magic Mushroom *Billericay* 257
Magpie Café *Whitby* 366
Maguro *London* 101
Maison Bertaux *London* 101
Maison Bleue *Bury St Edmunds* 269
Maitreya Social *Bristol* 266
Malabar *London* 101
Malabar Junction *London* 102
Maliks *Cookham* 280
Maliks *Gerrards Cross* 294
Mallory Court *Bishops Tachbrook* 259
The Malt Shovel *Brearton* 261
Mamma Dough 102
The Man Behind The Curtain *Leeds* 311
Manchester House *Manchester* 322
Mandalay *London* 102
Mandarin Kitchen *London* 102
Mangal I *London* 102
Mangal II *London* 102
Manicomio 102
Manna *London* 102
Mannions *York* 371
Le Manoir aux Quat' Saisons *Great Milton* 297
The Manor *London* 102
Bybrook Restaurant *Castle Combe* 273
Manuka Kitchen *London* 102
Mar I Terra *London* 102
Maray *Liverpool* 314
Marcus *London* 103
Margaux *London* 103
Mari Vanna *London* 103
Marianne *London* 103
Mariners at Il Punto *Ipswich* 306
Mark Jordan at the Beach *Jersey* 307
Market *London* 103
Market *Brighton* 264
The Marksman *London* 103
Marlow Bar & Grill *Marlow* 326
Maroush 103
The Marquis *Alkham* 247
Masala Grill *London* 103
Masala Zone 103
MASH Steakhouse *London* 103
The Mason's Arms *Knowstone* 309
The Masons Arms *Cartmel Fell* 273
Massimo *London* 104
Masters Super Fish *London* 104
Matsuba *Richmond* 104
Matsuri *London* 104
Max's Sandwich Shop *London* 104
Mayfair Pizza Company *London* 104
maze *London* 104
maze Grill *London* 104
maze Grill *London* 104
Mazi *London* 104
McDermotts Fish & Chips *Croydon* 281
Meat Mission *London* 104
MEATLiquor 104
MEATliquor *Leeds* 311
MEATmarket *London* 105
Med One *Huddersfield* 305
Mediterranean *Sheffield* 348
Mediterraneo *London* 105
Medlar *London* 105
Megan's 105
Meghdoots *Petworth* 341
Mele e Pere *London* 105
Melford Valley Tandoori *Long Melford* 317
The Melt Room *London* 105
Melton's *York* 372
MemSaab *Nottingham* 335
Menier Chocolate Factory *London* 105
Menu Gordon Jones *Bath* 253
The Mercer *London* 105
Merchants Tavern *London* 105
Le Mercury *London* 105
Meson don Felipe *London* 105
Mews of Mayfair *London* 106
Meza 106
Mezzet *East Molesey* 285
Micatto *Warwick* 362
Michael Caines *Chester* 275
Michael Caines Cafe Bar & Grill *Exeter* 291
Michael Caines *Manchester* 322
Michael Nadra 106
Middlethorpe Hall *York* 372
Midland Hotel *Morecambe* 328
Midsummer House *Cambridge* 270
Mien Tay 106
Mildreds *London* 106
The Milestone *Sheffield* 348
Milk *London* 106
The Mill at Gordleton *Hordle* 304
Mill Lane Bistro *London* 106
Miller & Carter Bexley *Bexley* 256
Miller Howe Restaurant & Hotel *Bowness-on-Windermere* 260
Milsoms *Dedham* 283
Min Jiang *London* 106
Mint and Mustard *Cardiff* 272
Mint Leaf 106
The Mint Room *Bath* 253
The Mirabelle *Eastbourne* 286
Les Mirabelles *Nomansland* 332
Mirch Masala *London* 106
Mishkin's *London* 106
Mission *London* 106
The Mistley Thorn Hotel *Mistley* 327
The Modern Pantry 107
Moksh *Cardiff* 272
The Mole & Chicken *Long Crendon* 317
MOMMI *London* 107
Momo *London* 107
Mon Plaisir *London* 107
Mona Lisa *London* 107
Monachyle Mhor *Balquhidder* 251
Monmouth Coffee Company 107
Moonfish Cafe *Aberdeen* 246
The Moorings *Blakeney* 259

Morada Brindisa Asador *London* 107
Morden & Lea *London* 107
Morelli's Gelato *London* 107
The Morgan Arms *London* 107
Morito *London* 108
Moro *London* 108
Morston Hall *Morston* 328
Mortimers *Ludlow* 318
Motcombs *London* 108
Mother India *Glasgow* 295
Mother India's Cafe *Edinburgh* 288
Moti Mahal *London* 108
Moules A Go Go *Chester* 275
Mourne Seafood Bar *Belfast* 255
Mowgli *Liverpool* 314
Mr Chow *London* 108
Mr Cooper's House & Garden *Manchester* 322
Mr Underhill's *Ludlow* 318
The Muddy Duck *Hethe* 302
Mughli *Manchester* 322
The Mulberry Tree *Boughton Monchelsea* 260
Mumbai Lounge *York* 372
Mumtaz *Bradford* 260
Murakami *London* 108
Murano *London* 108
Murgatroyds *Yeadon* 371
Mussel Inn *Edinburgh* 288
The Mustard Seed *Inverness* 306
My Sichuan *Oxford* 338
The Nag's Head *Haughton Moss* 301
Namaaste Kitchen *London* 108
The Narrow *London* 108
The National Dining Rooms *London* 108
Naughty Piglets *London* 108
Nautilus *London* 108
Nayaab *London* 109
Needoo *London* 109
The Neptune *Old Hunstanton* 336
The New Inn *Great Limber* 297
New Mayflower *London* 109
New Street Grill *London* 109
New World *London* 109
The Newman Arms *London* 109
Newman Street Tavern *London* 109
1921 *Bury St Edmunds* 269
No 131 *Cheltenham* 274
No 7 Fish Bistro *Torquay* 360
No Man's Grace *Bristol* 266
No. 9 *Stratford upon Avon* 356
No1 *Cromer* 281
The Noahs Ark Inn *Petworth* 341
The NoBody Inn *Doddiscombsleigh* 284
Nobu *London* 109
Nobu Berkeley *London* 109
Nonna's *Chesterfield* 276
Nonna's *Sheffield* 349
Noor Jahan 109
Nopi *London* 109
Nordic Bakery 110
The Norfolk Arms *London* 110
Norse *Harrogate* 300
North China *London* 110
The North London Tavern *London* 110
North Sea Fish *London* 110
The Northall *London* 110
Northbank *London* 110
Northcote *Langho* 309
Northcote Manor *Burrington* 269
Novikov (Asian restaurant) *London* 110
Novikov (Italian restaurant) *London* 110
Number Four *Shrewsbury* 350
Number One *Edinburgh* 288
Number Ten *Lavenham* 310
Numero Uno *London* 110
Nuovi Sapori *London* 110
Nusa Kitchen 110
The Nut Tree Inn *Murcott* 329
Nutter's *Norden* 332
Oak 111
Oak Bistro *Cambridge* 271
The Oak Tree Inn *Hutton Magna* 305
Obicà 111
Oblix *London* 111
Ocean Restaurant *Jersey* 307
Ockenden Manor *Cuckfield* 282
Ode *Shaldon* 348
Odette's *London* 111
Ognisko Restaurant *London* 111
Oka *London* 111
Oka *London* 317
The Old Bakery *Lincoln* 313
The Old Bell Hotel *Malmesbury* 320
The Old Boat House *Amble* 248
Old Bridge Hotel *Huntingdon* 305
The Old Butchers *Stow on the Wold* 356
Old Coastguard Hotel *Mousehole* 329
Old Fire Engine House *Ely* 290
The Old Inn *Drewsteignton* 284
The Old Passage Inn *Arlingham* 249
Old Spot *Wells* 363
Old Stamp House *Ambleside* 248
Old Swan *Cheddington* 274
Old Tom & English *London* 111
The Old Vicarage *Sheffield* 349
The Old Vine *Winchester* 368
The Annex *Beaumaris* 254
Oldroyd *London* 111
Oli's Thai *Oxford* 338
The Olive Branch *Clipsham* 279
Olive Limes *Tring* 361
The Olive Tree *Bath* 253
Oliveto *London* 111
Olivo *London* 111
L'Olivo *Wheathampstead* 365
Olivocarne *London* 111
Olivomare *London* 112
Olympic *Olympic Cinema* 112
Olympus Fish *London* 112
On The Bab 112
Ondine *Edinburgh* 288
One Canada Square *London* 112
101 Thai Kitchen *London* 112
1 Lombard Street *London* 112
One Sixty Smokehouse 112
One-O-One *London* 112
The Only Running Footman *London* 112
Les 110 de Taillevent *London* 113
The Onslow Arms *West Clandon* 364
Opera Tavern *London* 113
The Oppo *Stratford upon Avon* 356
Opso *London* 113
Opus Restaurant *Birmingham* 258
The Orange *London* 113
Orange Pekoe *London* 113
The Orange Tree *London* 113
The Orange Tree *Thornham* 359
Orchid *Harrogate* 300
Ormer *Jersey* 307
Orpheus *London* 113
Orrery *London* 113
Orso *London* 113
L'Ortolan *Shinfield* 350
Orwells *Shiplake* 350
Osaka *Newcastle upon Tyne* 331
Oscars French Bistro *Leamington Spa* 310
Oslo Court *London* 113
Ossies *Whitstable* 366
Osso Buco *Weybridge* 365
Osteria Antica Bologna *London* 113
Osteria Basilico *London* 114
Osteria Tufo *London* 114
Ostlers Close *Cupar* 282
Ostuni *London* 114
Otto's *London* 114
Ottolenghi 114
Outlaw's *Rock* 346

Outlaw's Fish Kitchen *Port Isaac* 343
Outlaw's Seafood and Grill *London* 114
The Outsider *Edinburgh* 288
Ox *Belfast* 255
Ox and Finch *Glasgow* 295
The Oxford Kitchen *Oxford* 338
Restaurant *London* 114
Brasserie *London* 114
The Oyster Box *Jersey* 307
The Oyster Shack *Bigbury-on-Sea* 257
The Oystercatcher *Portmahomack* 343
Pachamama *London* 114
The Packhorse Inn *Moulton* 328
Le Pain Quotidien 114
The Painted Heron *London* 115
The Palm *Froxfield* 294
The Palmerston *London* 115
The Palomar *London* 115
Pani's *Newcastle upon Tyne* 331
Panoramic *Liverpool* 315
Pant-yr-Ochain *Gresford* 297
The Pantechnicon *London* 115
The Papermaker's Arms *Plaxtol* 341
Pappa Ciccia 115
Paradise by Way of Kensal Green *London* 115
Paradise Garage *London* 115
Paradise Hampstead *London* 115
Paradiso *Newcastle upon Tyne* 331
El Parador *London* 115
Paris House *Woburn* 369
The Parkers Arms *Newton-in-Bowland* 332
Parlour *London* 115
La Parmigiana *Glasgow* 296
The Pass Restaurant *Horsham* 304
Patara 116
Paternoster Chop House *London* 116
Patio *London* 116
Pâtisserie Valerie 116
Patogh *London* 116
Patron *London* 116
Patty and Bun 116
Paul Ainsworth at Number 6 *Padstow* 339
Pea Porridge *Bury St Edmunds* 269
Peace & Loaf *Newcastle upon Tyne* 331
The Peacock at Rowsley *Rowsley* 346
The Pear Tree *London* 116
Pearl Liang *London* 116
Pearson's Arms *Whitstable* 366
The Peat Inn *Cupar* 282
Pebble Beach *Barton-on-Sea* 251
Peckham Bazaar *London* 116
Peckham Refreshment Rooms *London* 116
Pecks *Congleton* 280
Pedler *London* 116
Pelham House *Lewes* 313
The Pelican Diner *Hastings* 300
Pellicano 117
E Pellicci *London* 117
Pen Factory *Liverpool* 315
Pen y Cae Inn *Swansea Valley* 358
The Pendleton *Redhill* 345
Pennethorne's Cafe Bar *London* 117
Pentolina *London* 117
The Pepper Tree *London* 117
Percy & Founders *London* 117
Perkins *Plumtree* 342
La Perle *Milford-on-Sea* 327
Pescatori 117
Petersham Hotel *Richmond* 117
Petersham Nurseries *Ham* 117
Le Petit Bistro *Guernsey* 297
Le Petit Poisson *Herne Bay* 302
The Petite Coree *London* 117
La Petite Maison *London* 118
Pétrus *London* 118
Peyote *London* 118
Pham Sushi *London* 118
The Pheasant Inn *Tattenhall* 358
The Pheasant Hotel *Harome* 299
The Pheasant at Keyston *Keyston* 308
Pho 118
The Phoenix *London* 118
Phoenix Palace *London* 118
Piccolino *Manchester* 322
Pickled Pantry *Surbiton* 358
Picture *London* 118
Piebury Corner *London* 118
Pied à Terre *London* 118
Piedaniels *Bakewell* 251
The Pier at Harwich *Harwich* 300
Pierhouse Hotel *Port Appin* 343
Pierre Victoire *Oxford* 338
The Pig *Brockenhurst* 267
The Pig *Pensford* 340
Pig & Butcher *London* 118
Pig & Whistle *Cartmel* 273
Pig on the Beach *Studland* 357
Pig'Halle *Perth* 341
The Pigs *Holt* 303
Pilpel 119
Pint Shop *Cambridge* 271
Pipasha Restaurant *Cambridge* 271
The Pipe & Glass Inn *Beverley* 256
Piquet *London* 119
El Pirata *London* 119
Il Pirata *Belfast* 255
Pitt Cue Co *London* 119
Pizarro *London* 119
Pizza East 119
Pizza Metro 119
Pizza Pilgrims 119
PizzaExpress 119
Pizzeria Oregano *London* 119
Pizzeria Pappagone *London* 119
Pizzeria Rustica *Richmond* 119
PJ's Bar and Grill *London* 120
The Plan Café *Cardiff* 272
Plas Bodegroes *Pwllheli* 344
Plateau *London* 120
Plateau *Brighton* 264
The Plough *London* 120
The Plough and Sail *Snape* 351
The Plough at Bolnhurst *Bolnhurst* 259
The Plough Inn *Lupton* 319
The Plough Inn *Sparsholt* 352
Plum + Spilt Milk *London* 120
Plum Valley *London* 120
Poco *Bristol* 266
Poissonnerie de l'Avenue *London* 120
Pollen Street Social *London* 120
Polpetto *London* 120
Polpo 120
The Pompadour by Galvin *Edinburgh* 288
Le Pont de la Tour *London* 120
The Pony & Trap *Chew Magna* 276
Popeseye 122
Poppies 122
La Porchetta Pizzeria 122
La Porte des Indes *London* 122
Porters Restaurant *Berkhamsted* 256
Porthgwidden Beach Café *St Ives* 353
Porthmeor Beach Cafe *St Ives* 353
Porthminster Café *St Ives* 353
Il Portico *London* 122
Portland *London* 122
Portmeirion Hotel *Portmeirion* 343
Portobello Ristorante *London* 122
The Portrait *London* 122
The Pot Kiln *Frilsham* 294
La Potinière *Gullane* 298
Potli *London* 122
The Potted Pig *Cardiff* 272
The Potting Shed *Crudwell* 281

ALPHABETICAL INDEX

La Poule au Pot *London* 122
Prashad *Leeds* 311
Prawn On The Lawn *London* 123
Prime Steak & Grill *St Albans* 352
Primeur *London* 123
Primrose Café *Bristol* 266
The Prince Of Wales *London* 123
Princess Garden *London* 123
Princess of Shoreditch *London* 123
Princess Victoria *London* 123
Princi *London* 123
Prithvi *Cheltenham* 275
Prix Fixe *London* 123
Provender *London* 123
Tapa Room *London* 123
The Providores *London* 123
Prufrock Coffee *London* 123
Pulia *London* 124
Pulpo Negro *Alresford* 248
The Pump Room *Bath* 253
The Punch Bowl *Lyth Valley* 319
The Punchbowl *London* 124
Punjab *London* 124
The Punter *Oxford* 338
Purecraft Bar and Kitchen *Birmingham* 258
The Purefoy Arms *Preston Candover* 344
Purnells *Birmingham* 258
Purple Poppadom *Cardiff* 272
Purslane *Cheltenham* 275
Puschka *Liverpool* 315
Quaglino's *London* 124
The Quality Chop House *London* 124
Quantro *Harrogate* 300
Quantus *London* 124
Quattro Passi *London* 124
Quay Fifteen *Southampton* 351
Queen's Head *East Clandon* 285
The Queens Arms *London* 124
Queenswood *London* 124
Le Querce *London* 124
Quilon *London* 125
Quince Tree *Stonor* 356
Quinta *Ilkley* 306
Quirinale *London* 125
Quo Vadis *London* 125
Quod *Oxford* 338
Rabbit *London* 125
Rabot 1745 *London* 125
Raby Hunt *Summerhouse* 357
Radha Krishna Bhaven *London* 125
Rafters *Sheffield* 349
Ragam *London* 125
Raglan Arms *Llandenny* 315
Rainforest Café *London* 125
Le Raj *Epsom* 290
Rampsbeck Hotel *Watermillock* 363
Randall & Aubin *London* 125
Rani *London* 125
Raoul's Café 125
Rasa 126
Rasa *Newcastle upon Tyne* 331
Rasoi *London* 126
The Rat Inn *Hexham* 303
Raval *Gateshead* 294
The Raven Hotel & Restaurant *Much Wenlock* 329
Ravi Shankar *London* 126
Read's *Faversham* 291
Red *Guernsey* 298
Red Chilli *Leeds* 311
Red Chilli *Manchester* 322
Red Dog 126
Red Fort *London* 126
Red Fox *Thornton Hough* 360
Red Lion *East Chisenbury* 285
The Red Lion *East Haddon* 285
The Red Lion *Stockport* 355
Red Lion Inn *Stathern* 355
The Red Pepper *London* 126
Reds True Barbecue *Leeds* 312
The Refinery *London* 126
Regatta *Aldeburgh* 247
The Regency *Brighton* 264
Regency Club *Queensbury* 344
Le Relais de Venise L'Entrecôte 126
The Reliance *Leeds* 312
Rendezvous *Exeter* 291
Resident Of Paradise Row *London* 126
Restaurant 23 *Leamington Spa* 310
Restaurant 27 *Portsmouth* 344
Restaurant Coworth Park *Ascot* 249
Le Restaurant de Paul 126
Restaurant James Sommerin *Penarth* 340
Restaurant Mark Greenaway *Edinburgh* 288
Restaurant Martin Wishart *Edinburgh* 288
Restaurant Nathan Outlaw *Port Isaac* 343
Restaurant Sat Bains *Nottingham* 335
Restaurant Tristan *Horsham* 304
Restaurant Two To Four *Dorking* 284
Retro *Teddington* 359
Reubens *London* 127
Rex & Mariano *London* 127
Rextail *London* 127
The Rib Man *London* 127
Rib Room *London* 127
Riccardo's *London* 127
Ricci's Place *Halifax* 299
The Richmond *London* 127
The Richmond Arms *Chichester* 276
Rick Stein *Winchester* 368
Rick Stein's Café *Padstow* 339
Rick Stein's Fish & Chips *Falmouth* 291
Rico Libre *Birmingham* 258
Riddle & Finns *Brighton* 264
Riddle & Finns On The Beach *Brighton* 264
Riding House Café *London* 127
Rising Sun *Harrow* 127
Ristorante Frescobaldi *London* 127
Palm Court *London* 128
The Ritz Restaurant *London* 128
Riva *London* 128
La Rive *Cobham* 280
Rivea *London* 128
The River Café *London* 128
River Cottage Canteen *Axminster* 250
River Cottage Canteen *Bristol* 267
River Cottage Canteen *Plymouth* 342
River Cottage Canteen *Winchester* 368
Riverford Field Kitchen *Buckfastleigh* 268
Riverside *Bridport* 262
Riverside Brasserie *Bray* 261
riverstation *Bristol* 267
Rivington Grill 128
Roade House *Roade* 346
Roast *London* 128
Rocca Di Papa 128
Rochelle Canteen *London* 128
La Rock *Nottingham* 335
Rock Salt *Plymouth* 342
Rocket 128
RockFish *Dartmouth* 282
RockFish *Plymouth* 342
The Rocks *Dunbar* 284
Rocksalt *Folkestone* 292
Rogan & Co *Cartmel* 273
Rogano *Glasgow* 296
Roger Hickman's *Norwich* 333
Rojanos *Padstow* 339
Roka 129
Ronnie's *Thornbury* 359
The Rooftop Café *London* 129
Rooftop Restaurant *Stratford upon Avon* 356
Room With A View *Aberdour* 246

Roots at N1 *London* 129
Rosa's 129
The Rose & Crown *Romaldkirk* 346
Rose & Crown *Snettisham* 351
Rose and Crown *Warwick* 363
Rose Garden *Manchester* 323
Rosie's Vineyard *Portsmouth* 344
Rosso *Manchester* 323
Rossopomodoro 129
Roth Bar & Grill *Bruton* 268
Roti Chai *London* 129
Roti King *London* 129
Rotorino *London* 129
Rotunda Bar & Restaurant *London* 129
Roux at Parliament Square *London* 130
Roux at the Landau *London* 130
Rowley's *London* 130
Rowley's *Baslow* 252
Rox Burger *London* 130
Royal Academy *London* 130
Royal China 130
Royal China Club *London* 130
The Royal Exchange Grand Café *London* 130
The Royal Oak *Maidenhead* 320
The Royal Oak *Marlow* 326
The Royal Standard of England *Beaconsfield* 254
Roz ana *Kingston upon Thames* 309
RSJ *London* 130
Rucoletta *London* 130
Rugoletta 130
Rules *London* 131
Rumwong *Guildford* 298
Russell's *Broadway* 267
Sachins *Newcastle upon Tyne* 331
Sackville's *London* 131
Le Sacré-Coeur *London* 131
Sacro Cuore *London* 131
Sagar 131
Sager & Wilde *London* 131
Saigon Saigon *London* 131
St Clement's *St Leonards-on-Sea* 354
St James *Bushey* 269
St John *London* 131
St John Bread & Wine *London* 131
St Johns *London* 131
St Pancras Grand *London* 131
St Petroc's Hotel & Bistro *Padstow* 340
Terrace Restaurant *Llandudno* 316
Sakana-tei *London* 131
Sake No Hana *London* 132
Salaam Namaste *London* 132
Sale e Pepe *London* 132
Salloos *London* 132
Salmontini *London* 132
The Salon *London* 132
Le Salon Privé *Twickenham* 132
Salt & Honey *London* 132
The Salt House *London* 132
Salt House *Liverpool* 315
Salt House Bacaro *Liverpool* 315
Salt Room *Brighton* 264
Salt Yard *London* 132
Salts Diner *Saltaire* 347
Saltwood On The Green *Hythe* 305
Salvation In Noodles 132
Salvo's *Leeds* 312
Sam's Chop House *Manchester* 323
The Samling *Windermere* 369
Samphire *Whitstable* 367
Sams on the Beach *Polkerris* 342
The Samuel Fox Country Inn *Bradwell* 261
Samuel's *Masham* 326
San Carlo *Birmingham* 258
San Carlo *Bristol* 267
San Carlo *Liverpool* 315
San Carlo *Manchester* 323
San Carlo Cicchetti 132
San Carlo Cicchetti *Manchester* 323
San Daniele del Friuli *London* 132
The Sands End *London* 133
Sankey's Cellar Bar *Tunbridge Wells* 361
Sankey's Champagne & Oyster Bar *Tunbridge Wells* 361
Santa Maria *London* 133
Santini *London* 133
Santore *London* 133
Sapori Sardi *London* 133
The Saracen's Head *Shirley* 350
Sardo *London* 133
Sarracino *London* 133
Sartoria *London* 133
Sasso *Harrogate* 300
Satay House *London* 133
Sauterelle *London* 133
Savoir Faire *London* 133
Savoro *Barnet* 251
Savoy Grill *London* 133
Scalini *London* 133
Scallop Shell *Bath* 253
Scandinavian Kitchen *London* 134
The Scarsdale *London* 134
Scott's *London* 134
Scran & Scallie *Edinburgh* 289
Sea Containers *London* 134
The Sea Cow *London* 134
Sea Tree *Cambridge* 271
Seafood Restaurant *Padstow* 340
Seafood Restaurant *St Andrews* 353
Seafood Temple *Oban* 336
Seafresh *London* 134
The Seahorse *Dartmouth* 282
The Sea Shell *London* 134
Seaside Boarding House Hotel *Burton Bradstock* 269
Season Kitchen *London* 134
Sebastian's *Oswestry* 337
Señor Ceviche *London* 134
Sesame *London* 134
Set *Brighton* 264
Seven Park Place *London* 134
Seven Stars *London* 135
1707 *London* 135
Sexy Fish *London* 135
Shackfuyu *London* 135
Shake Shack 135
Shampers *London* 135
Shanghai *London* 135
Shanghai Blues *London* 135
Shanghai Shanghai *Nottingham* 335
Sharrow Bay *Ullswater* 362
Shaun Dickens at The Boathouse *Henley-on-Thames* 302
The Shed *London* 135
The Shed *Porthgain* 343
J Sheekey *London* 135
J Sheekey Oyster Bar *London* 135
Shell Bay *Studland* 357
The Shepherd & Dog *Stowmarket* 356
Shepherd's *London* 135
Shikumen *London* 136
Shilpa *London* 136
The Ship *London* 136
The Ship Inn *Noss Mayo* 333
The Ship Inn *West Stour* 364
Shish Mahal *Glasgow* 296
Shoe Inn *Exton* 291
Shoe Shop *London* 136
Shoryu Ramen 136
Shotgun *London* 136
Siam Smiles *Manchester* 323
Sichuan Folk *London* 136
Sienna *Dorchester* 284
The Sign of The Don Bar & Bistro *London* 136
Signor Sassi *London* 136
Silk Road *London* 136
Silo *Brighton* 264
Silver Darling *Aberdeen* 246
Silversmiths *Sheffield* 349
Simon Radley *Chester* 275
Simpson's Tavern *London* 136

ALPHABETICAL INDEX

Simpsons *Birmingham* 258
Simpsons-in-the-Strand *London* 137
Sindhu *Marlow* 326
Singapore Garden *London* 137
The Sir Charles Napier *Chinnor* 276
Six *Newcastle upon Tyne* 331
64 Degrees *Brighton* 265
60 Hope Street *Liverpool* 315
63 Degrees *Manchester* 323
63 Tay Street *Perth* 341
Lecture Room *London* 137
Gallery *London* 137
Skipjacks *Harrow* 137
Sky Apple Cafe *Newcastle upon Tyne* 332
Skylon *London* 137
Skylon Grill *London* 137
Small Batch Coffee *Brighton* 265
Smith & Wollensky *London* 137
Smith's Of Ongar *London* 137
Smith's Brasserie *Ongar* 336
Top Floor *London* 137
Dining Room *London* 138
Ground Floor *London* 138
Smoke House Deli And Cicchetti *Ludlow* 318
Smokehouse Chiswick *London* 138
The Smokehouse Islington *London* 138
Smoking Goat *London* 138
Snaps & Rye *London* 138
Social Eating House *London* 138
Social Wine & Tapas *London* 138
Soif *London* 138
Sojo *Oxford* 339
Sole Bay Fish Company *Southwold* 352
Solita *Manchester* 323
Som Saa *London* 138
Sông Quê *London* 139
Sonny's Kitchen *London* 139
Sophie's Steakhouse 139
Sosban And The Old Butchers *Menai Bridge* 327
Sosharu *London* 139
Sotheby's Café *London* 139
Sotto Sotto *Bath* 253
Souk Kitchen *Bristol* 267
Source *London* 139
Sous le Nez en Ville *Leeds* 312
Soushi *Cirencester* 279
South Deep *Poole* 342
The Sparrowhawk *Formby* 292
Spice Merchant *Beaconsfield* 254
Spice Merchant *Henley-on-Thames* 302
Spiny Lobster *Bristol* 267
Spire *Liverpool* 315
The Sportsman *Whitstable* 367
Sportsman's Arms *Wath-in-Nidderdale* 363
The Spread Eagle *Sawley* 348
Spring *London* 139
Spuntino *London* 139
The Square *London* 139
Sree Krishna *London* 139
The St John's Chop House *Cambridge* 271
St Moritz Hotel *Trebetherwick* 361
St Tudy Inn *St Tudy* 354
Stagg Inn *Titley* 360
Staith House *North Shields* 332
Standard Inn *Rye* 347
The Star Inn *Harome* 299
Star Inn the City *York* 372
Star of India *London* 140
Start Bay Inn *Torcross* 360
Steak & Honour *Cambridge* 271
Stein's Fish & Chips *Padstow* 340
Sticks'n'Sushi 140
Sticky Walnut *Chester* 276
STK Steakhouse *London* 140
Stock Hill House *Gillingham* 294
Stock Pot 140
The Stockbridge *Edinburgh* 289
Storm *Poole* 343
Story *London* 140
Stovell's *Chobham* 278
Strand Dining Rooms *London* 140
Strathearn Restaurant *Auchterarder* 250
Stravaigin *Glasgow* 296
Street Food Chef *Sheffield* 349
Street Kitchen (van) *London* 140
Suk Saran *London* 140
Sukho Fine Thai Cuisine *London* 140
Sukhothai *Leeds* 312
Suksan *London* 140
Suma's *Jersey* 307
Summer Isles Hotel *Achiltibuie* 246
Summer Lodge *Evershot* 291
The Summerhouse *London* 140
Sumosan *London* 141
The Sun Inn *Dedham* 283
Sunday *London* 141
Sushisamba *London* 141
Sushi Tetsu *London* 141
Sushi-Say *London* 141
The Swan *London* 141
Swan *Long Melford* 317
The Swan at Southrop *Southrop* 351
The Swan *Southwold* 352
The Swan *West Malling* 364
The Swan at the Globe *London* 141
Swan Hotel *Lavenham* 310
The Swan Inn *Chiddingfold* 276
Swan Inn *Denham* 283
The Swan Inn *Kettleshulme* 308
Swan With Two Necks *Newcastle upon Tyne* 332
The Sweet Olive *Aston Tirrold* 250
Sweet Thursday *London* 141
Sweetings *London* 141
Tabb's *Truro* 361
Taberna Do Mercado *London* 141
Taberna Etrusca *London* 142
The Table *London* 142
The Table *Woodbridge* 370
Tai Pan *Manchester* 323
Tailors *Warwick* 363
Taiwan Village *London* 142
Tajima Tei *London* 142
Talad Thai *London* 142
Le Talbooth *Dedham* 283
The Talbot Inn *Mells* 327
Tamarind *London* 142
Tampopo *Manchester* 323
Tandoori Nights *London* 142
Tanroagan *Douglas* 284
Tapas Brindisa 142
Taqueria *London* 142
Taro 142
Tartufo *London* 142
Tas 142
Tas Pide *London* 143
A Taste of Persia *Newcastle upon Tyne* 332
Whistler Restaurant *London* 143
Tate Cafe *St Ives* 354
Restaurant, Level 6 *London* 143
The Tavern Bar and Restaurant *Alltami* 247
Taylor St Baristas *London* 143
Tayyabs *London* 143
Tedfords Restaurant *Belfast* 255
Tem Tép *London* 143
The Tempest Arms *Elslack* 290
The 10 Cases *London* 143
10 Greek Street *London* 143
Tendido Cero *London* 143
Tendido Cuatro *London* 143
Tentazioni *London* 143
Terra Vergine *London* 143
The Terrace *Beaulieu* 254
The Terrace on Holland Street *London* 144
Terravina *Woodlands* 370
Terre à Terre *Brighton* 265
Terroirs *London* 144

Texture *London* 144
Thackeray's *Tunbridge Wells* 361
Thai Pad *Oxted* 339
The Thai Terrace *Guildford* 298
Thaikhun *Manchester* 323
Thali *London* 144
The Thali Café *Bristol* 267
Tharavadu *Leeds* 312
Theo Randall *London* 144
34 *London* 144
36 on the Quay *Emsworth* 290
This & That *Manchester* 324
The Thomas Cubitt *London* 144
The Thomas Lord *West Meon* 364
Thompson at Darcy's *St Albans* 353
Three Acres *Shelley* 349
The Three Chimneys *Biddenden* 256
The Three Chimneys *Dunvegan* 284
The Three Fishes *Whalley* 365
Three Gables *Bradford On Avon* 260
Three Greyhounds *Allostock* 247
Three Horseshoes *Madingley* 320
Three Horseshoes *Staines* 354
The Three Lions *Stuckton* 357
The Three Mariners *Oare* 335
Three Oaks *Gerrards Cross* 294
3 South Place *London* 144
The Three Tuns *Henley-on-Thames* 302
Thyme & Tides *Stockbridge* 355
tibits *London* 144
Tierra *Lyme Regis* 319
The Tilbury *Datchworth* 282
Timberyard *Edinburgh* 289
Timbrells Yard *Bradford On Avon* 260
Tinello *London* 144
Ting *London* 144
Titchwell Manor *Titchwell* 360
Toasted *London* 145
Toff's *London* 145
Tokyo Diner *London* 145
Tokyo Sukiyaji-Tei & Bar *London* 145
Tolcarne Inn *Penzance* 340
Tom's Kitchen 145
Tommi's Burger Joint 145
The Tommy Tucker *London* 145
Tongdam *Dulverton* 284
Tonic & Remedy *London* 145
Tonkotsu 145
Tortilla 145
Tosa *London* 145
Toto's *London* 146
The Town House *Arundel* 249
Townhouse *Oswestry* 337
Tozi *London* 146
The Trading House *London* 146
The Tramshed *London* 146
Trangallan *London* 146
La Trappiste *Canterbury* 272
Treby Arms *Sparkwell* 352
Tredwell's *London* 146
The Tree House *London* 146
Treehouse *Alnwick* 247
Trenchers *Whitby* 366
Trinity *London* 146
Trishna *London* 146
La Trompette *London* 146
Trongs *Ipswich* 306
Troubadour *London* 146
Trouble House Inn *Tetbury* 359
The Trout Inn *Wolvercote* 370
Trullo *London* 147
The Truscott Arms *London* 147
The Truscott Cellar *London* 147
Tsunami 147
Tuddenham Mill *Tuddenham* 361
Tulse Hill Hotel *London* 147
Turl Street Kitchen *Oxford* 339
Turners *Birmingham* 258
24 St Georges *Brighton* 262
28-50 147
Twenty Princes Street *Edinburgh* 289
Restaurant 22 *Cambridge* 271
Twist At Crawford *London* 147
Two Brothers *London* 147
Two Fat Ladies at The Buttery *Glasgow* 296
200 Degrees *Nottingham* 333
21212 *Edinburgh* 289
2 Veneti *London* 147
Tyddyn Llan *Llandrillo* 316
Tyneside Coffee Rooms *Newcastle upon Tyne* 332
Typing Room *London* 147
Tytherleigh Arms *Tytherleigh* 362
Ubiquitous Chip *Glasgow* 296
Ultracomida *Aberystwyth* 246
Umu *London* 148
Union Street Café *London* 148
Upstairs at the Grill *Chester* 276
Urchin *Brighton* 265
Le Vacherin *London* 148
Valvona & Crolla *Edinburgh* 289
Van Zeller *Harrogate* 300
Vanilla Black *London* 148
The Vanilla Pod *Marlow* 326
Vapiano 148
Vasco & Piero's Pavilion *London* 148
The Vaults And Garden Cafe *Oxford* 339
Veeraswamy *London* 148
Vegetarian Food Studio *Cardiff* 272
Verden *London* 148
Verdi's *London* 148
El Vergel *London* 148
Vero Gusto *Sheffield* 349
Verveine Fishmarket Restaurant *Milford-on-Sea* 327
Vico *London* 148
Il Vicolo *London* 149
The Victoria *London* 149
The Victoria at Holkham *Holkham* 303
Victoria Hotel *Nottingham* 335
Victoria Inn *Perranuthnoe* 340
Victuals & Company *Deal* 283
Viet Grill *London* 149
Vijay *London* 149
Villa Bianca *London* 149
Villa Di Geggiano *London* 149
Villa Marina *Henley-on-Thames* 302
Village East *London* 149
The Village Pub *Barnsley* 251
Villandry 149
The Vincent Hotel *Southport* 351
The Vincent Rooms *London* 149
The Vine and Spice *Long Whittenham* 317
Vine Leaf *St Andrews* 353
The Vine Tree *Norton* 333
The Vineyard at Stockcross *Stockcross* 355
Vinoteca 149
Vintage Salt *London* 149
The Vintner *Stratford upon Avon* 357
Vivat Bacchus 150
Voujon *Bury St Edmunds* 269
VQ 150
Vrisaki *London* 150
Wagamama 150
Wahaca 150
The Wallace *London* 150
Wallfish Bistro *Bristol* 267
Walmgate Ale House *York* 372
The Walnut Tree *Llandewi Skirrid* 316
Warung Tujuh *Brighton* 265
Watch House Cafe *Bridport* 262
The Waterfront Bar & Bistro *Ipswich* 306
Waterloo Bar & Kitchen *London* 150
Waterside Inn *Bray* 261
The Waterway *London* 150
Webbe's at The Fish Cafe *Rye* 347
Webbe's Rock-a-Nore *Hastings* 301

Wedgwood *Edinburgh* 289
The Wellington *Welwyn* 364
The Wellington Arms *Baughurst* 254
The Wells *London* 150
The Wensleydale Heifer *West Witton* 365
The West Arms Hotel *Llanarmon DC* 315
WestBeach *Bournemouth* 260
The West House *Biddenden* 256
West Mersea Oyster Bar *West Mersea* 364
West Thirty Six *London* 150
The Westleton Crown *Westleton* 365
Westwood Bar & Grill *Beverley* 256
The Wet Fish Café *London* 150
The Wheatsheaf *Bath* 253
The Wheatsheaf *Greetham* 297
Wheatsheaf Inn *Northleach* 333
Wheelers Oyster Bar *Whitstable* 367
Wheelhouse *Falmouth* 291
The Whippet Inn *York* 372
White Hart *Fyfield* 294
The White Hart Village Inn *Llangybi* 316
White Heart *Chobham* 278
The White Horse *Brancaster Staithe* 261
White Horse *Shenley* 349
The White Oak *Cookham* 280
The White Onion *London* 150
White Peacock *Leicester* 312
White Pheasant *Fordham* 292
White Rabbit *London* 151
The White Swan *London* 151
The White Swan *Pickering* 341
White Swan at Fence *Fence* 292
Whitstable Oyster Fishery Co. *Whitstable* 367
Whitworth Art Gallery *Manchester* 324
The Wife of Bath *Wye* 370
Wild Garlic *Nailsworth* 329
Wild Honey *London* 151
The Wild Mushroom *Westfield* 365
The Wild Rabbit *Kingham* 308
Wild Thyme *Chipping Norton* 278
Wilks *Bristol* 267
The William Bray *Shere* 350
Wiltons *London* 151
Wimsey's *London* 151
The Windmill *London* 151
The Wine Library *London* 151
Wing's *Manchester* 324
Winteringham Fields *Winteringham* 369
The Witchery by the Castle *Edinburgh* 289
Wiveton Bell *Wiveton* 369
Wiveton Hall Cafe *Holt* 303
Wolfe's *London* 151
The Wollaton *Nottingham* 335
The Wolseley *London* 151
Wong Kei *London* 151
The Wonky Table *Derby* 283
Woodlands 152
Woodspeen *Newbury* 330
The Woodstock *London* 152
Workshop Coffee 152
World Service *Nottingham* 335
Wormwood *London* 152
Wright Brothers 152
Wrights Food Emporium *Llanarthne* 315
Wyatt & Jones *Broadstairs* 267
Wykeham Arms *Winchester* 368
Xian *Orpington* 337
XO *London* 152
Y Polyn *Nantgaredig* 329
Yak Yeti Yak *Bath* 253
Yalbury Cottage *Lower Bockhampton* 317
Yalla Yalla 152
Yama Momo *London* 152
Yama's Thai Eaterie *Margate* 326
Yammo *Bath* 254
Yang Sing *Manchester* 324
Yard *Faversham* 291
Yashin Ocean House *London* 152
Yashin *London* 152
Yasmeen *London* 152
Yauatcha 153
The Yellow House *London* 153
Yi-Ban *London* 153
Yipin China *London* 153
Yippee Noodle Bar *Cambridge* 271
Yming *London* 153
York & Albany *London* 153
Yorke Arms *Ramsgill-in-Nidderdale* 345
Yoshi Sushi *London* 153
Yoshino *London* 153
Yu And You *Copster Green* 280
Yukti *Liverpool* 315
Yum Bun *London* 153
Yum Yum *London* 153
Yuzu *Manchester* 324
Zafferano *London* 153
Zaffrani *London* 153
Zaibatsu *London* 153
Zaika *London* 154
Zayna *London* 154
Zaza *Berkhamsted* 256
Zeffirelli's *Ambleside* 248
Zen *Belfast* 255
Zest *London* 154
Zheng *Oxford* 339
Ziani's *London* 154
Zoilo *London* 154
Zouk *Bradford* 260
Zucca *London* 154
Zuma *London* 154